Essay Exam Writing for the California Bar Exam

Essay Exam Writing for the California Bar Exam

MARY BASICK

TINA SCHINDLER

Published by Wolters Kluwer Law & Business in New York.

Wolters Kluwer Law & Business serves customers worldwide with CCH, Aspen Publishers, and Kluwer Law International products. (www.wolterskluwerlb.com)

To contact Customer Service, e-mail customer.service@wolterskluwer.com, call 1-800-234-1660, fax 1-800-901-9075, or mail correspondence to:

Wolters Kluwer Law & Business
Attn: Order Department
PO Box 990
Frederick, MD 21705

Printed in the United States of America.

7 8 9 0

ISBN 978-0-7355-0993-1

Library of Congress Cataloging-in-Publication Data

Basick, Mary.
Essay exam writing for the California bar exam / Mary Basick, Tina Schindler.
p. cm.
ISBN 978-0-7355-0993-1
1. Bar examinations—California—Examinations, questions, etc. 2. Bar examinations—California—Study guides. 3. Legal composition—Study guides. I. Schindler, Tina. II. Title.
KFC76.B38 2011
349.794076—dc23

2012013608

About Wolters Kluwer Law & Business

Wolters Kluwer Law & Business is a leading global provider of intelligent information and digital solutions for legal and business professionals in key specialty areas, and respected educational resources for professors and law students. Wolters Kluwer Law & Business connects legal and business professionals as well as those in the education market with timely, specialized authoritative content and information-enabled solutions to support success through productivity, accuracy and mobility.

Serving customers worldwide, Wolters Kluwer Law & Business products include those under the Aspen Publishers, CCH, Kluwer Law International, Loislaw, Best Case, ftwilliam.com and MediRegs family of products.

CCH products have been a trusted resource since 1913, and are highly regarded resources for legal, securities, antitrust and trade regulation, government contracting, banking, pension, payroll, employment and labor, and healthcare reimbursement and compliance professionals.

Aspen Publishers products provide essential information to attorneys, business professionals and law students. Written by preeminent authorities, the product line offers analytical and practical information in a range of specialty practice areas from securities law and intellectual property to mergers and acquisitions and pension/benefits. Aspen's trusted legal education resources provide professors and students with high-quality, up-to-date and effective resources for successful instruction and study in all areas of the law.

Kluwer Law International products provide the global business community with reliable international legal information in English. Legal practitioners, corporate counsel and business executives around the world rely on Kluwer Law journals, looseleafs, books, and electronic products for comprehensive information in many areas of international legal practice.

Loislaw is a comprehensive online legal research product providing legal content to law firm practitioners of various specializations. Loislaw provides attorneys with the ability to quickly and efficiently find the necessary legal information they need, when and where they need it, by facilitating access to primary law as well as state-specific law, records, forms and treatises.

Best Case Solutions is the leading bankruptcy software product to the bankruptcy industry. It provides software and workflow tools to flawlessly streamline petition preparation and the electronic filing process, while timely incorporating ever-changing court requirements.

ftwilliam.com offers employee benefits professionals the highest quality plan documents (retirement, welfare and non-qualified) and government forms (5500/PBGC, 1099 and IRS) software at highly competitive prices.

MediRegs products provide integrated health care compliance content and software solutions for professionals in healthcare, higher education and life sciences, including professionals in accounting, law and consulting.

Wolters Kluwer Law & Business, a division of Wolters Kluwer, is headquartered in New York. Wolters Kluwer is a market-leading global information services company focused on professionals.

Summary of Contents

Contents

Preface

Dear Bar Exam Taker,

This book includes everything you need to know to write a passing essay answer for the California bar exam. After much experience working with potential bar takers and extensive analysis of past California bar exams we have created this book to be a condensed, yet thorough, review of all subjects covered on the exam, including instruction in the skill of essay writing.

The introduction covers the skills involved in successfully writing a passing California bar essay. In particular, this section includes valuable information on how to successfully organize and write a passing answer within the allotted time frame.

The substantive law is presented in several ways to assist you in understanding the law and then using it to solve the problem posed by an essay question. Each chapter includes the law in a checklist format for use in issue spotting, a memorization attack sheet to aid in memorizing the rules and their elements, and an efficient rule outline annotated throughout with exam, issue spotting, and memorization tips.

Practice essay questions and sample passing answers are included for each subject and all crossover questions are identified as such. We also include our assessment of each question to point out additional subject specific tips and essay taking strategies. In addition, each question has a corresponding grid identifying the issues, rules, analysis and conclusions that were required of a passing answer to aid you in assessing your own performance.

We wish you the best of luck on the upcoming bar exam!

Mary Basick and Tina Schindler

May 2012

Acknowledgments

We have many people who made this book possible to thank. First, we must thank our wonderful families for their love and support. Tina has the encouragement of Jim, Madilyn, and J.C. Schindler. Mary has the support of Mark, Abby, Tara, and Blake Ribisi, and Zachary Basick. Many of our colleagues have enriched our understanding of the law along the way and we would like to thank Neil Cogan, Andrea Funk, Constance Hood, Jodi Jewell, Deirdre Kelly, Eric Leach, and Paula Manning for their invaluable insights. We are also grateful for the support of Mike Gregory, Lynn Churchill, Dana Wilson, and the rest of the team at Wolters Kluwer.

Essay Exam Writing for the California Bar Exam

INTRODUCTION

THE BASICS OF ESSAY EXAM WRITING

The essay portion of the California bar exam essentially tests two different things simultaneously: (1) a large quantity of substantive material and rules, and (2) essay exam writing skills. Success on the essay portion of the exam requires mastery of both. This introduction condenses into one handy reference section everything you need to know to succeed on the essay portion of the bar exam. As you study for the exam, return to these introductory pages frequently to reinforce your mastery of the most effective essay exam–taking approach and skills. This introduction covers techniques for mastering the substantive material tested on the essay exam, a review of the key exam-taking skills that are also tested on the exam, an approach for successfully combining the substantive mastery with the exam-taking skills, and a section on exam-day strategy.

I. MASTERING THE ESSAY SUBJECTS

There is a vast quantity of substantive material that you are responsible for knowing and potentially tested on for the essay portion of the California bar exam. Depending on how you combine the subjects, there are at least 12 substantive areas of law eligible for testing on the essay portion of the exam. The first step in successfully preparing for the essay exam is creating a study schedule that will allow you to master the material so that you can fully understand and memorize the material. For each substantive area of law, this book contains an *issues checklist* to aid in issue spotting, a *memorization attack sheet* for easy memorization, and a *subject outline* that is tailored to focus on the issues that are essay tested within that subject.

Create a Study Schedule: It is important to map out day by day what you plan to accomplish to successfully prepare for the bar exam. There is a large amount of work to be done, and a schedule is an essential tool for staying on track and ensuring that you are adequately prepared for all of the subjects and skills you will need. If you are not using a commercial bar preparation program that provides a study schedule, you must create your own schedule. Plan to spend two to four days studying each subject eligible for testing, with the time varying depending on the relative depth of the subject and your own facility with the subject. For each subject you will need to study and understand the substantive material, memorize the rules, practice issue-spotting essay exams, and practice writing essay exams under exam-type conditions. It is also important to spend time assessing your progress and reviewing your essays to ensure you successfully spotted all the issues, properly identified and stated the applicable rules, and included all pertinent facts and arguments in the analysis. Of course, your study schedule should also include time dedicated to studying and practicing for the MBE and performance test portions of the exam.

Memorization: Since the essay covers such a large quantity of substantive material, it is important to have a plan for accurately memorizing all of this material. You will notice each subject is presented here in various formats with increasing quantities of details to assist in both your understanding of the subject and to aid memorization. First, each subject is presented in the broad *issue checklist* format, which basically lists the main issues that can arise in that subject. This is followed by the more detailed *memorization attack sheet,* which includes the rule elements. Lastly, there is a detailed *rule outline* for each subject, which explains the rules.

To memorize, take each subject one at a time. Start by reviewing the subject outline. First, be sure to understand the meaning of each rule element. The key to both effective issue spotting and factual analysis is having an understanding of how and when a rule applies. Rote rule memorization without understanding the meaning of the rules will not lead to success. To illustrate, one of the rule elements required for a permanent injunction is "feasibility." Without understanding what it means for a permanent injunction to be "feasible," it is likely the corresponding analysis would be unsatisfactory. Simply memorizing the element "feasible" would not identify what is meant by the term, and thus what facts would make feasibility at issue in an essay question, thus leading to either a missed issue or poor analysis. Make every effort to have an understanding of the meaning of the rules as well as memorizing the rules themselves.

As a general rule, whatever memorization strategies worked in law school should be the main strategies you employ now. However, you may want to try some new ones as well. Start with memorizing individual rules. To memorize rules you can use flashcards, flowcharts, or outlines. You can say the rules aloud, or use a recording device to record your own recitation of the rules and replay them later in the car or at the gym. Go through the issues checklist and try to state or write a rule for each issue listed, which reinforces both the rules and the overall structure of a subject, which impacts how issues arise on an essay. The memorization attack sheets are also a handy way to quiz yourself on the rule elements. Another effective memorization strategy is to practice writing out full rules in sentence format, which gives you an opportunity to practice writing and crafting rule statements that will be used later on the essay exam responses.

Once you have many of the individual rules memorized, move onto reviewing the entire subject. To review an entire subject, try to recreate your entire subject outline (or flowchart) from memory. Start with the big concepts, then add the subtopics, then add the rules that fall under the subtopics, then add the rule elements for each rule, then add the explanations and exceptions for each rule element. Using this method will help you to focus on the rules you know and the rules you don't know so that your studying can be efficient as you focus your energy on understanding and memorizing the rules you don't know well. This study method also assists in issue spotting since the rules in the checklist are presented in the order that they logically arise in an essay question. Reviewing a subject this way also will reinforce how the concepts are interconnected and relate to one another.

Another approach is to try to explain an entire subject, including all issues and how they interrelate, to a willing friend or family member. Challenge yourself to adequately explain the rules in a manner that is logical, correct, and understandable.

Use examples to illustrate the concepts. Have your listener ask questions so you must further explain or rephrase a concept whenever they get confused. This method also ensures that you know the rules well and how they relate to one another.

II. MASTERING THE ESSAY SKILLS

In addition to the vast substantive material covered on the essay exam, the exam also tests essential lawyering skills. The most important of these skills are issue spotting, fact application and analysis, effective time management, and the ability to discern what is more important from what is less important.

Issue Spotting

Issue spotting is an essential skill for any lawyer, and is also essential for success on the essay exam. In this book the substantive material is presented in the order that the issues logically arise in an essay exam to make issue spotting easier. Checklists are great tools to use for issue spotting. A checklist should include the essential issues and be concise so it can be jotted down in less than five minutes. We've provided generic checklists for each subject, but each subject checklist should be personalized to be most effective for you. The purpose of a checklist is to help you spot the issues on an exam, so don't include issues that you would never miss spotting because they're so obvious it simply isn't necessary to take time to write them down. Likewise, do include issues that you have a hard time remembering or have a tendency to miss. It may also be helpful to have mini-checklists for subcategories. For example, on your main constitutional law issues checklist, you might just have First Amendment free speech listed as an issue. If after reading the essay you realize that the majority of the question involves free speech, you should then write out a mini–issues checklist that includes all possible issues that can arise regarding free speech. You should have these checklists memorized for each subject tested on the bar. When doing an essay question, you should jot down your issue-spotting checklist for the corresponding subject as soon as you recognize the subject being tested, unless the call is very specific and tells you exactly what issues they want you to address. As you issue spot the exam, you can consult your checklist to ensure you don't miss any issues because missing issues is fatal on the bar exam. However, be certain to only discuss the issues actually raised by the fact pattern. Discussion of a nonissue is worth no points and wastes valuable time.

The issues checklist also acts as a final check for issue spotting. Remember there are typically no "red herrings" or "homeless" facts on the bar exam. So, if you have facts remaining unused after you have organized the entire question, you should double-check your issues checklist to ensure that the "homeless" facts don't correspond to one of the issues you forgot to address. Although the points on the essay exam are mainly earned in the analysis of an issue, you never get to the analysis if you don't spot the issue in the first place, which is why issue spotting is crucial to your success on the essay exam.

Fact Application and Reasoning

The key to effective analysis is explaining how or why the applicable fact proves or disproves the rule element in question. A good answer will include so many facts that someone can recreate the fact pattern just from reading the answer. Just as you should double-check your issues checklist for any issues corresponding to "homeless" facts, you should also use your issues checklist to ensure that you aren't missing a key argument within your analysis or that the facts don't establish a rule element that you are omitting.

The most important aspect of analysis is being able to explain the importance of the facts rather than just reciting them in the appropriate place. Thus, when comparing your organized or written essay answer to the corresponding sample answer or grid, you should spend ample time comparing which facts were used and how they were used in your answer compared to the sample. Make sure that you are explaining how and why each applicable fact either proves or disproves the rule element that you are analyzing. Use the word "because" or "since" in your analysis because doing so forces you to explain how or why the fact is important. For example, consider the following analytical sentence: "Tom spit on Bob and being spat on would offend a reasonable person's sense of dignity since spitting is generally known in society as a sign of extreme disrespect and thus is offensive." Notice that the key *fact* (Tom spit on Bob) is tied to the *rule element* (offensive) with an explanation of *why* the conduct is offensive (offends a reasonable person's sense of dignity **since** it is a sign of extreme disrespect by societal standards). Compare the analytical sentence above to this one, "On the element of offensive, here the facts state that Tom spit on Bob and spitting offends a reasonable person's sense of dignity, therefore it is offensive." Notice that the key *fact* (Tom spit on Bob) is still tied to the *rule element* (offensive) but there is no explanation of why spitting is offensive. The facts are merely recited and this is followed by the conclusion. This is not proper analysis but instead is a "fact sandwich," since the facts are sandwiched between the rule element and the conclusion with no explanation of why or how the fact (spitting) establishes the rule element (offensive). Always explain how and why the facts prove or disprove the rule or rule element in issue.

To receive the maximum points, an essay must have proper analysis, as indicated above. In addition, sometimes it is necessary to make logical inferences or assumptions from the facts given, which must be identified and then analyzed. This skill arises most often on torts and constitutional law essays, and is discussed in more depth within the introduction to those subjects. Sometimes an example is the best way to make a point and should be included in the analysis. Overall, remember that issue spotting enables you to get to the analysis, but it is the use of the facts in the analysis that results in points being earned on an essay.

Time Management

The skill of time management is a large part of what is being assessed with essay questions. Spend no more than one hour per question, and of the hour spent on a question, plan to spend 15 to 20 minutes organizing your answer and the remaining time writing your answer. Remember that you will have three hours to answer three questions, but you must manage your own time since you receive all three essays at the same time. We recommend that you bring a silent timer or reset your watch to 12:00 when the proctor starts the exam so you can manage your time and know at a glance when you have spent 15 minutes organizing a question, or one hour total on a question.

Some questions are harder than others, but each question is designed to be answered in one hour. Do not spend more than one hour on any single question. You can never do it without shortchanging time on another question, which almost always results in failing the question that got shortchanged. It is never worth the few extra points you may get on the question you take extra time on because you are doing so at the expense of failing another question.

It is imperative that you focus your energy on answering only the question asked. Pay attention to the call of the question. Don't rush through reading the fact pattern and misread what the question is asking; any time spent addressing a nonissue is time wasted. There is no extra credit on the bar exam, so thoroughly answer the question asked, but only the question asked.

Pay careful attention to the facts. For example, if the fact pattern is about a contract dispute but the facts state there is a valid contract, do not waste time discussing contract formation issues except in the briefest of terms.

Discerning What Is Important

This concept is related to time management, but more accurately addresses the concept of deciding the relative importance of all of the issues raised by an essay question and spending your time accordingly. Never lose sight that the goal of the essay answer is to solve the problem presented by the fact pattern. First, focus on the call of the question. Pretend that you are a lawyer and a client walked into your office and told you this story. What issues are raised? What facts pose a problem for the client? Do not shy away from identifying problem areas in the question or identifying areas of ambiguity that need to be resolved. This is what a lawyer would do and that is your task. Your essay answer needs to focus on solving the problem. Spend your time wisely so that you spend the majority of your time on the bigger, more complex issues, and less time on the issues that are less complex.

Generally, you can determine which facts are worth the most points and weighted the most heavily by seeing how many facts are available to use with each issue. The more facts that correspond to a particular issue, the more points it is likely worth. Issues that have colorable arguments on both sides are also worth comparatively more points. Be sure to organize the issues you spot around answering the call of the question. When outlining your answer, once you have matched up the facts to the issues you need only glance at your outline to easily see where most of the points are because it will be the issues with the most facts matched up.

III. PUTTING IT ALL TOGETHER

An Approach to Taking Practice Exams

It is essential to write practice essay exams, and the more the better. When you study a subject, for the first few practice exams you may want to double-check your issue spotting against a sample answer or grid so that you can add any missed issues before writing out the complete answer. Allow yourself 20 minutes to outline the answer, then check your outline against the sample or grid and add any missing issues. Then allow yourself 40 minutes to write out the essay from your outlined notes. With this approach you are still working under timed conditions, but you are allowing yourself some support as you become more familiar with the topic. Another benefit is that you will still get practice writing on all of the issues contained in the essay, even if you didn't spot them all at first. Some students prefer to work under exam conditions from the very first essay: organize their answer and immediately write their essay under timed conditions, and only complete the assessment after they've finished. If this is your preferred approach, it is a good idea to go back and write out the answer to address any missed issues for practice after self-assessing your original essay.

Bar exams are different than the law school exams you are used to. It is essential to practice for the bar exam in replicated bar exam conditions to maximize your effectiveness. You must practice writing the essay exams within the one-hour time limit for two important reasons. First, you need to know exactly what you are capable of completing within one hour so you can properly manage your time during the exam. Second, you want to have already practiced and become comfortable writing on a wide variety of legal issues so during the exam the writing flows quickly and smoothly. For this reason, it is also good to write out more than one essay at a time to simulate real exam conditions. So, if you plan to write two to three essays in a day, do them at the same time just as you would on the real bar exam, rather than one in the morning and another one later in the day. The bar is a marathon and you have to train for it. Work on building your stamina because you are going to need it for the three-day exam.

The goal is to write a passing essay, and the key to writing a good essay is solving the problem presented. Identify all of the issues, use all of the relevant facts, make it easy for the reader to score your essay by using headings, identify any problematic areas or ambiguities for the reader, spend your time wisely, and finish within one hour. Use the following approach:

1. **Read the call of the question first.** This will provide some context as you read the fact pattern. Usually the call of the question will identify the subject, and sometimes a specific call will even identify and limit the legal issues.
2. **Read the fact pattern through once** before you pick up your pen to make notes or start typing. Sit on your hands if you must, but it is important to get a good grasp of the overall story of the fact pattern before you do anything else.
3. **Once you've read the fact pattern, carefully consider the call of the question.** If the call is very specific and, for example, asks, "Can plaintiff get specific performance?" then the bar examiners have issue spotted the exam for you. If the call of the question is more general, write down on your scratch paper your memorized checklist for the subject (or subjects) being tested. Issue spot the exam and use your checklist to assist you in identifying additional issues.
4. **Outline your answer before you begin writing.** You should spend 15 to 20 minutes organizing your answer before you begin writing your answer. A passing essay starts with good organization. Even though you may feel compelled to start writing, it is not possible to write a passing answer if you don't spot all of the issues and use all of the available facts, so it is imperative that you slow down and get it right at the organizational stage. Don't

waste time making your notes look good; they only need to be functional. Liberally use abbreviations, initials, and symbols.

5. **Organize by the call of the question and include all issues, rule elements, and facts.** Note the legal issues you spot for each question call. Identify the rule elements that correspond to each issue. Next, identify the pertinent facts you will use to analyze each rule or element. Be certain to use all of the facts from the fact pattern in your analysis. Either highlight or check off facts as you use them. Do not rely on your memory of the facts; make sure they are accurate by writing them down. Unlike law school exams, there are rarely "red herrings" in bar fact patterns. If there is a "homeless" fact in the fact pattern that you haven't figured out how to use, take a moment while outlining to consider what you can do with it. Go through your issues checklist and see if it raises a new issue you didn't catch. Also, look at the issues you have already identified and see if you can use the fact to add weight to the analysis. Finally, be cognizant of crossover questions as most bar exams test at least one crossover question.
6. **Consider if there are two sides to each issue in the question.** Issues with contrasting arguments are always worth a lot of points, and you don't want to miss these points. Also, it helps to remember that there are always two parties and two sides in a real legal dispute, so always consider what the opposing side would argue when you are arguing one side. There will not always be a colorable argument for the other side, but often there is and students can miss it because they are looking at the issue from only one perspective. Another issue that arises is that students can get personally swept up in the facts. The questions are not about real people. Don't feel sorry for the girl who was kidnapped or the man whose car was stolen to the extent that you automatically write yourself out of points by concluding on their side because you want them to win. Even if the facts are horrible or gruesome, you must follow the law and not your feelings.
7. **Use issue headings for each legal issue to organize your essay answer.** An issue heading is nothing more than the issue—for example, "Specific Performance." The heading doesn't have to be fancy or long but makes it easy for the grader to find the issues and give you points. Each legal issue should have its own heading. You don't want to bury a great issue-spot or key factual analysis where the reader can easily miss it. It's not a hard and fast rule, but generally, if a rule element has its own rule, consider including a heading for the subrule. At a minimum, set off the analysis in its own paragraph.
8. **Decide which issues are major and which are minor and how to apportion your time.** Before you begin to write, look at the outline you've organized and assess where the points are. Issues with a lot of facts to use and those with two-sided arguments are always worth a lot of points, so spend your time accordingly. Put a star next to the major issues on your outline so you can see where the big points are at a glance. Be sure to apportion your writing time appropriately. If an essay has five key issues, you can do more in-depth analysis than if an essay has fifteen key issues to address. Organize your answer first so you know what is being asked of you before you start to write because it is essential that you finish the essay.

What to Include in a Passing Essay Answer

After you've organized your answer, the next step is to actually write the essay answer. A good essay answer should include the following:

Format: The answer should be organized with an issue heading for each legal issue, followed by a rule statement and then the corresponding analysis for that issue. If there are multiple rule elements for the issue, each rule element can be separated and analyzed in its own paragraph. The rule elements should be analyzed in the same order they are presented in the rule. Don't waste time on introductions, random musings, or nonissues.

Issues: Identify each issue raised by the fact pattern.

Rules: Have an accurate and grammatically correct rule statement for each rule. It is most effective to memorize a general statement for each rule, rather than to tailor it to include facts from the fact pattern.

Analysis: An issue is major where it requires (1) a full analysis of a pivotal issue, (2) analysis of an issue where there is an abundance of facts available to use in the analysis, or (3) analysis of any issue where there are facts available to argue both sides of the issue. Though it is important to identify all issues that are raised by the facts, major issues are worth more points than minor issues and are thus worth more time. An issue is minor where it is a "slam dunk" and few students are likely to miss it. For minor issues, you still need to properly address them, but you can typically do so in a more cursory way. Weave the rule and analysis into one sentence where possible. Efficiently identify how the fact establishes the rule or element and move on. If you consider an issue, but aren't sure whether or not to include, err on the side of inclusion, but know that it is likely a minor issue, so spend little time on it.

Conclusion: The conclusion can often go either way. The important thing is to have a conclusion that is consistent with your analysis. Never become so focused on the conclusion that you write yourself out of the question by failing to see alternative issues that may arise if an issue were to conclude the other way.

Self-Assessment

As part of a successful bar preparation strategy, it is essential that you develop the skill of assessing your own performance. You need to be able to assess your own practice essays with a critical eye so you can identify any problem areas in your essay writing or substantive knowledge, and work to correct them. We have provided an Essay Exam Self-Assessment form at the end of the introduction, which you may want to use in your self-assessments. Many students find it is difficult to accurately assess their own written work, and you may need to get some help with this if you are having difficulty.

After writing a practice essay, compare your answer to a sample answer or an answer grid and assess your performance on the following criteria:

Issue Spotting: Issue spotting is key because you can't analyze an issue if you don't spot it first.

Did you spot and identify the same issues?
Did you spot issues that weren't there?

Headings: It is not essential to use the same headings as the sample answer or grid, but the important point is that someone reading your paper should be able to easily find all of the key analysis. Be brief; use a key word, not an entire sentence for the heading. Don't bury important analysis in a place where a grader can't easily locate it.

Did you use the same or similar headings?

Rules: It is important that you accurately state the rules in your essay answer since the rules provide the basis for the analysis that follows.

Is the rule correctly stated, including all essential elements?
Is your rule significantly shorter, or longer, than the one in the sample answer?
Did you use the "buzz words" associated with the rule?
Is the rule in sentence format?

Analysis or Fact Application: The analysis is the most important part of an essay answer, and is also the most difficult part to self-assess. This is because there are many ways to adequately analyze an issue. Consequently, you aren't looking for an exact comparison between your answer and the sample, but more of a general similarity of the analysis and the use of the available facts in the analysis.

Compare your answer to the sample answer (or a grid) issue by issue. Start with the first issue. Locate the first fact used in the analysis of that issue in the sample answer. Now, look for that fact in your analysis of that issue. Highlight your answer where you used the same fact in approximately the same way. If the sample answer used the fact in a more thorough or different way than you did, make a note of it. If the sample answer used a fact that you ignored make a note of it. If you used a fact that the sample answer did not use for that issue, make a note of it. Continue the process looking at all of the facts in the first issue, then move on to the subsequent issues and repeat the process. Now, take a critical look at your analysis:

Did you analyze each legal concept separately?
Did the sample answer use facts from the fact pattern that you ignored?
Did you identify the appropriate facts but leave it to the reader to determine how the existence of that fact established the legal element?
Did you present a one-sided argument when there were two sides to the analysis of that issue or rule element?
Was your analysis of an issue more cursory than the sample answer's?
Was your analysis of an issue deeper than the sample answer's?
Did your answer summarize and condense the facts?

Conclusion: Sometimes the conclusion reached isn't important, and sometimes there is only one logical conclusion or correct answer (especially in Professional Responsibility), but even in that case the points will be missed in the analysis section so the conclusion isn't the focus. The important thing about a conclusion is to have one, and to make sure that it is consistent with your analysis.

Troubleshooting Tips to Improve Exam Performance

Issues: If you missed an issue, or spotted an issue that wasn't there, ask yourself why.

Problem	Solution
Did not know the rule	• Study and memorize the rule • Use a checklist to issue spot • Add the rule to your checklist
Did know the rule, but not well enough to identify how the facts would raise it as an issue	• Understand the meaning of the rule elements, rather than rote memorization • Complete practice issue-spotting exams that raise the issue to identify how facts will be used (see Issues Tested Matrix to locate) • Review fact patterns testing the issue to identify which facts tend to trigger the issue
Saw the issue, but dismissed it as a nonissue	• Any issue that requires thought to dismiss should be included in the answer
The issue seemed too minor to include	• Minor issues should be included, but with truncated analysis
Did not use all the facts in the fact pattern	• Check off facts as they are used to ensure all are used
Addressed a nonissue	• Don't write about issues where there are no facts available from the fact pattern to use

Headings: Were the headings sufficient?

Problem	Solution
Did not use a heading where needed	• Every legal concept should be set off with its own heading so it is easy to locate

Rules: Were the rules accurate and adequate?

Problem	Solution
Did not remember the rule	• Memorize the rules and review all subjects weekly to reinforce
Rule is shorter than sample	• Make sure the rule you memorize includes all essential elements
Rule is longer than sample	• Review the rule to determine if it includes elements that are unnecessary or duplicative and remove them • Carefully craft rule so that it is stated as simply as possible
Rule is missing important "buzz words"	• Craft the rule to include key "buzz words" that are associated with the rule; do not use synonyms
Rule is not in sentence format	• Draft a grammatically correct sentence that includes all rule elements; memorize it

Fact Application: Was the analysis logically organized, sufficient, and thorough?

Problem	Solution
Legal issues are merged together	• Analyze each legal issue separately
Missing key facts in the analysis	• When organizing the answer, cross off each fact as it is used to ensure all are used • Identify a fact to correspond to each rule element
Did not explain how or why a fact established the issue or rule element	• Listing the facts is not enough; the analysis must explain how or why the fact establishes the rule element • Use the words "since" or "because" to force yourself to explain the how or why
One-sided argument instead of two-sided	• Decide if there is a plausible contrary argument for each issue/rule element • Pretend to represent each side of the dispute to see both sides
Analysis is deep when it should be cursory, or analysis is cursory when it should be deep	• At the organization step, decide whether an issue is major or minor and treat each accordingly • For minor issues, practice writing cursory or truncated analysis by weaving the rule and facts together into one sentence • For major issues, be certain to use all available facts to analyze each element • For each issue/rule element, always consider if there is a plausible contrary argument, and if so, argue it
Facts are summarized and less effective	• Use the facts exactly as they appear in the fact pattern, including using quotes, or expand on the facts where appropriate

IV. EXAM DAY STRATEGY

There are exam day strategies pertaining to the essay exam that you should implement to maximize your potential exam score and minimize your stress.

1. **Answer the essay questions in the order presented.** Do not be tempted to even glance at the next question until you are ready to answer it. Some students think it will be helpful to scan the three questions looking for one related to a subject in which they feel particularly confident. However, doing so wastes time and there is no time to waste on the bar exam. Even worse, while a student is answering the chosen question, his mind will keep wandering back to the scary question he skipped. Consequently, he doesn't give his full attention to any of the questions, which is not an effective strategy.
2. **Only spend one hour on each essay question—no matter what.** Some questions are absolutely more difficult than others, but every question is designed to be answered in only one hour. Your essay answers are being

graded in comparison to all of the other bar exam takers who are typically only taking one hour to answer each question. If a question is a real "racehorse"—a question containing many facts and issues to be analyzed—the key to a passing answer is writing an answer that identifies all of the issues and contains very cursory analysis of the non-key issues. If a student takes more than an hour to write a more detailed answer, he will likely not receive much higher than the passing score on that question, which he likely would have received in the first place. However, in the process, he virtually guaranteed failure on the essay question that was shortchanged for time because it is virtually impossible to write a passing answer in less than an hour.

3. **Do not worry about what the people around you are doing**. Bar exam takers will do some unusual things during the exam; ignore them.
4. **Don't panic if you have no idea what to do with an essay question.** There is usually one unusual question on every bar exam. Take a deep breath. The bar exam is graded on a curve. If you have properly studied for the exam, you can be certain that if you are befuddled by the question, so is everyone else in the room. Figure out what the underlying subject is and write down your checklist. Take the fact pattern sentence by sentence and look for issues. Don't take longer than an hour and don't think about it again once the hour is over.
5. **Do not talk about the essay questions** with anyone during the exam. Make a pact not to talk about it with your friends, and use headphones to avoid overhearing what other bar exam takers are saying around the exam site or adjacent hotel. Just like in law school, the people who talk the most and loudest often have the least idea of what they are talking about. No good can come from listening to self-appointed experts theorize about what issues were on the essay questions, and it can actually be harmful if it rattles your confidence or makes you doubt yourself. It is best not to do a post-mortem on this exam; but if you must, wait until the entire exam is over and then only discuss it with someone whose judgment you trust.

ESSAY EXAM SELF-ASSESSMENT

ISSUE SPOTTING

_____ All issues identified

Areas to improve—issue spotting:

_____ Missed major issues
_____ Missed minor issues
_____ Included nonissues

Headings

_____ All necessary headings included

Area to improve—headings:

_____ Include a heading for each legal issue
_____ Heading should be one to two words only

Rules

_____ Accurate and complete rule statements were used

Areas to improve—rules:

_____ Rule included unnecessary elements
_____ Rule failed to include necessary elements
_____ Rules need to be in sentence format
_____ Rule missed important "buzz words"

Fact Application

_____ Analysis was good and explained how and why the facts established the rules

Areas to improve—fact application:

_____ Failed to analyze each legal issue separately
_____ Analysis did not explain "how or why"
_____ Key facts were missing from the analysis
_____ Facts were summarized instead of expanded upon
_____ Analysis was cursory where it should have been deep
_____ Analysis was deep where it should have been cursory
_____ Missed a two-sided argument

PART I BUSINESS ASSOCIATIONS

BUSINESS ASSOCIATIONS TABLE OF CONTENTS

INTRODUCTION TO BUSINESS ASSOCIATIONS

The topic of business associations encompasses the subjects of corporations, agency, and partnership. There are a lot of substantive rules eligible for testing, but the vast majority of essay questions cover the frequently tested topics in corporations: pre-incorporation promoter liability, the duty of care and duty of loyalty, and the federal securities law sections 16(b) and 10b-5. Though the subjects of agency and partnership have only been recently added officially as subjects eligible for testing, the agency issue of authority has arisen frequently in the past, and we predict general partnership issues are the most likely to be tested in partnership.

In business association questions it is important to analyze the conduct of each person presented in the fact pattern separately. There will frequently be a fact pattern that identifies two or more corporate officers or directors, and they will usually take a corporate action leading to liability under 10b-5 or action that breaches a fiduciary duty. Usually, each party is privy to different information and thus won't have equal responsibility. Be certain to analyze the facts pertaining to each party under the rule separately to avoid missing key analysis.

Be certain to thoroughly go through the issues checklist looking for issues pertaining to each party identified in the fact pattern to successfully issue-spot a business associations essay. Business association issues tend to cluster in predictable ways. A party who is in violation of 16(b) is almost always also in violation of 10b-5 (though not necessarily the other way around) and they may have also breached the duty of loyalty. With few exceptions, when the duty of care is at issue, the duty of loyalty is also at issue. The facts that raise issues relating to pre-incorporation liability, piercing the corporate veil, and ultra vires acts also typically raise the issues of duty of care and/or duty of loyalty. The duty of care and duty of loyalty is almost always tested on a business associations questions, so be sure to know those rules very well.

Business association essay questions typically provide a lot of factual detail to analyze, and many of the issues can, and should, be argued both ways to receive maximum points. Business association essays are frequently crossover questions. The business association topics may cross over with each other. For example, an essay may cover corporations and the agency relationship of a corporate promoter or a director who exceeds authority. It is also common to see business associations cross over with professional responsibility where one of the parties is either a lawyer or seeks the advice of a lawyer.

Prior to 2007 the subjects of agency and partnership were not eligible for testing. Consequently, there are few practice essay questions available that cover the agency and partnership topics. In addition, this is why the Issues Tested Matrix has few entries for these subjects prior to 2007, although general agency principles were always eligible for testing as a subtopic of corporations.

ISSUES CHECKLIST

CORPORATIONS

Formation
- De facto and de jure corp.
- Piercing the corp. veil
- Ultra vires acts
- Promoter liability

Corp. Management, Directors & Officers
- Duty of care (BJR)
- Duty of loyalty

Shareholders
- Rights
  - Meetings and elections
  - Voting
  - Inspection
  - Dividend distribution
- Shareholder agreements
- Shareholder derivative suits

Federal Securities Laws
- 16(b)
- 10b-5
  - Fraudulent statements
  - Insider trading
- Sarbanes-Oxley

Fundamental Changes
- Dissolution

AGENCY

Formation
- Principal's duties and remedies
- Agent's duties and remedies
- P's liability for A's k's (authority)
- P's liability for A's torts (scope)

PARTNERSHIP

General partnerships
- Formation
- Partnership assets
- Partner rights & duties
- Relations of partner to 3rd parties
- Partner liability
- Dissociation/Dissolution/Winding up

Limited partnerships
- Formation
- Partner rights & duties
- Partner liability
- Dissociation/dissolution/winding up

LLP (LIMITED LIABILITY PARTNERSHIPS)

- Formation
- Partner rights & duties
- Partner liability
- Dissociation/Dissolution/Winding up

LLC (LIMITED LIABILITY COMPANIES)

- Formation
- Partner rights & duties
- Partner liability
- Dissociation/Dissolution/Winding up

MEMORIZATION ATTACK SHEET

CORPORATION—FORMATION

- ◆ **Formation**
  - De jure corporation—file articles of incorporation:
    - ◆ Authorized shares
    - ◆ Purpose
    - ◆ Agent name/address
    - ◆ Incorporator name/address
    - ◆ Name of corporation
  - De facto corporation
  - Corporation by estoppel
- ◆ **Pierce corporate veil**
  - Alter ego
  - Undercapitalization
  - Fraud
  - Estoppel
- ◆ **Ultra vires**
  - Act outside business purpose
- ◆ **Shares of stock issued**
  - Subscription agreement
  - Types of shares issued
  - Consideration required
  - No preemptive right for existing shareholder
- ◆ **Pre-incorporation liability**
  - Promoter: personal liability
  - Corp: not liable unless
    - ◆ Adopt contract, or
    - ◆ Accept benefit

CORPORATE DIRECTORS & OFFICERS

- ◆ **Meetings**
  - Quorum required
  - No proxy voting
  - No voting agreements
- ◆ **Duty of care**
  - Reasonable prudent person
  - Business judgment rule
    - ◆ Good faith
    - ◆ Corp's best interests
- ◆ **Duty of loyalty—no conflicts of interest**
  - **No self-dealing**
    - ◆ Presumed unfair, but
    - ◆ Conflict can be cured if authorized/approved & fair
  - **No usurp corp. opportunity**
    - ◆ Ok if good faith rejection &
    - ◆ Full disclosure
    - ◆ Remedy: disgorge profits
  - **No unfair competition**
- ◆ **Duty to disclose material info**
- ◆ **Rights of directors & officers**
  - Compensation
  - Indemnification
  - Inspection
- ◆ **Liability of directors & officers**
  - No personal liability generally

CORPORATE SHAREHOLDERS

- ◆ **Rights of shareholders**
  - Meetings
  - Voting
    - ◆ Right to vote by stock type
    - ◆ Voting by proxy allowed
    - ◆ Quorum required
  - Inspection
  - Dividends
- ◆ **Shareholder agreements**
  - Voting trust
  - Voting agreement
  - Management agreement
  - Restrictions on stock transfer
- ◆ **Shareholder suits**
  - Direct suit
  - Derivative suit on corp. behalf
- ◆ **Shareholder duties**
  - General rule: no fiduciary duty
  - Modern trend: controlling shareholders owe a duty care & loyalty

- **Shareholder liability**
  - General rule: no personal liability
  - Except: professional corps.

FEDERAL SECURITIES LAW

- **16(b)—no short-swing profits**
  - Corporation
    - On national exchange, OR
    - 10 million assets &
    - 500 shareholders
  - Corporate insiders
    - Officers & directors
    - 10% shareholders
  - Trading within 6 months
  - Remedy: disgorge profits
- **10b-5—no insider trading**
  - **Misrepresentation requires**
    - Intent
    - Material misrepresentation or omission of insider information
    - Reliance
    - Buy or sell securities
    - Interstate commerce
    - Remedy: disgorge profits
  - **10b-5 insiders—4 ways**
    - Insider direct trading
    - Tipper: giving information
    - Tippee: receiving information
    - Misappropriator
- **Sarbanes-Oxley**
  - **Enhanced corporate reporting requirements**
  - **Increased criminal penalties**

CORPORATE FUNDAMENTAL CHANGES

- **Typical procedure**
  - Board adopts resolution
  - Written notice to shareholders
  - Shareholders approve
- **Types of changes**
  - Merger
  - Stock sale
  - Asset sale
  - Conversion of corporate form
  - Amend bylaws or articles
  - Dissolution & winding up
- **Dissenter appraisal rights**

AGENCY

- **Formation**
  - Agreement
  - Benefit of principal
  - Control of agent
  - All contract formalities not required
- **Principal duties:** as required in the contract
- **Agent duties**
  - **Duty of care**—business judgment rule
  - **Duty of loyalty**—no conflicts
    - No self-dealing
    - No usurp principal opportunity
    - No secret profits
    - No commingling funds
  - **Duty of obedience**
  - **Duty of communicate**
  - **Express contractual duties**
- **Agent is personally liable for third-party contracts only if**
  - Agent acts with no authority
  - Principal's identity unrevealed
  - Principal's existence unrevealed

- **Principal is liable for agent contracts if**
  - **Actual express authority**
  - **Actual implied authority**
    - Can be terminated by:
      - Breach of agent's duty
      - Lapse of stated, or reasonable time
      - Operation law
      - Changed circumstances
      - Happening of specified event
      - Unilateral termination by either party
  - **Apparent authority**
    - Notice to third party required if actual authority terminated
    - Written "lingering" authority
    - Agent exceeds authority
  - **Ratification**
  - **But, if no authority:** agent is personally liable
- **Principal liability for agent torts**
  - **Normal tort:** Liable if tort is within scope of relationship
    - Except frolic or mere detour
  - **Independent contractors:** Not liable (no control of methods)
    - Except:
      - Ultrahazardous activities
      - Nondelegable duties
      - Estoppel (hold out as agent)
  - **Intentional torts:** Not liable
    - Except:
      - Specifically authorized
      - Natural result
      - Motivated by desire to serve

PARTNERSHIP—GENERAL

- **Formation**
  - No formalities required
  - Intent to be co-owners required
  - Agency-like relationship
- **Partnership assets**
  - **Titled property**
    - Titled as partner
    - Partnership funds
  - **Untitled property**
    - Partnership funds
    - Close relationship
    - Listed as an asset in books
- **Partnership rights**
  - Ownership of property
  - Equal control
  - No right to salary (except for winding up)
  - Equal right to profit & losses (unless agreement otherwise)
  - Indemnification
- **Partner duties**
  - **Duty of care** (business judgment rule)
  - **Duty of loyalty**—no conflicts (no self-dealing, usurping opportunity, secret profits, competition)
  - **Duty to disclose** material info
  - **Duty to account**
- **Partner relations w/3rd parties**
  - Personal liability for debts
  - Contract authority
    - Actual authority
    - Apparent authority
    - Estoppel
  - Torts: joint & several liability
- **Partnership liability**
  - Civil liability extends to:
    - Contracts within the scope
    - Tort within the scope
    - Liability is joint & several
  - Incoming partners
  - Outgoing partners
- **Dissociation**—partner leaves
- **Dissolution**—partnership ceases
- **Winding up**
  - Compensation allowed
  - Priority of distribution

- Creditors
- Partner loans
- Capital contributions
- Profits & surplus

PARTNERSHIP—LIMITED

- **Formation:** file certificate
- **Partner rights and duties**
  - General: same as general
  - Limited: no right to act on behalf & owe no duties
- **Partner liabilities**
  - General: same as general
  - Limited: not liable beyond capital contribution
- **Dissolution**—can be prompted by:
  - Time specified in certificate
  - Written consent of all
  - Dissociation of general partner
  - Judicial decree
- **Winding up activities**
  - Priority of distribution
    - Creditors
    - Partners & former partners
    - Capital contributions
    - Partners

LLP

- Formed by filing statement
- LL partners have no personal liability
- Duty of care & loyalty owed
- Dissociation similar to regular partnership

LLC

- Formed by filing articles of organization
- LLCs have no personal liability
- Management interest not freely transferable (limited liquidity)
- Duty of care & loyalty owed

BUSINESS ASSOCIATIONS RULE OUTLINE

I. **CORPORATIONS**

A. **Corporation formation and structure:** A corporation is a legal entity that exists separate from its owners thus shielding the owners and managers from personal liability for the actions of the corporation.

1. **Corporate formation:**

a. A **de jure corporation** meets all of the mandatory statutory requirements including that the incorporators sign and **file an articles of incorporation** with the secretary of state that includes:

1. **Authorized** number of shares (maximum allowed)
2. **Purpose** of corporation (any lawful purpose is allowed)
3. **Agent's** name and address
4. **Incorporator's** name and address
5. **Name** of corporation

> <u>**Memorization tip:**</u> Remember it's "**A PAIN**" to include all of the information required on the **articles of incorporation.**

b. A **de facto corporation** exists where there is **actual use of corporate power** and a good faith, but unsuccessful, **attempt to incorporate** under a valid incorporation statute.

1. **Limited liability:** The law will treat the defectively formed corporation as an actual corporation and the shareholders will not be personally liable for corporate obligations.
2. **Determination:** The state may deny corporate entity status in a quo warranto proceeding, but third parties may not attack the corporate status.

c. **Corporation by estoppel:** A person who deals with a business entity believing it is a corporation, or one who incorrectly holds the business out as a corporation, may be estopped from denying corporation status. This applies on a case-by-case basis and only in contract (reliance on corporate status), not to tort cases.

d. **Piercing the corporate veil:** Generally, a corporate shareholder is not liable for the debts of a corporation, except when the court pierces the corporate veil and disregards the corporate entity, thus holding shareholders personally liable as justice requires.

1. **The veil can be pierced for the following reasons:**

a. **Alter ego:** Where the shareholders fail to treat the corporation as a separate entity, but more like an alter ego where corporate formalities are ignored and/or personal funds are commingled.

b. **Undercapitalization:** Where the shareholders' monetary investment at the time of formation is insufficient to cover foreseeable liabilities.

c. **Fraud:** Where a corporation is formed to commit fraud or as a mechanism for the shareholders to hide *behind to avoid existing obligations.*
d. **Estoppel:** Where a shareholder represents that he will be personally liable for corporate debts.

2. **Effect of piercing the corporate veil:**
   a. **Personal liability:** Active shareholders will have personal joint and several liability.
   b. **Equitable remedy:** It is an equitable remedy and generally only applies in tort cases.

> <u>**Issue-spotting tip:**</u> Where piercing the corporate veil is at issue the facts often will also raise the issue of promoter liability for pre-incorporation contracts.

3. **Deep Rock Doctrine:** When a corporation is insolvent, third-party creditors may be paid off before shareholder creditors, thus subordinating the shareholder claims.

2. **Corporate powers**
   a. **Ultra vires acts:** When a corporation **acts outside its business purpose** it is acting "ultra vires." A corporation usually has a stated purpose, and if not it may conduct any lawful business.
      1. Modernly, ultra vires acts are **generally enforceable.**
      2. However, the issue may still arise when the ultra vires act causes the state to seek dissolution, or the corporation sues an officer, or a shareholder sues to enjoin the proposed act.

> <u>**Issue-spotting tip:**</u> Any time an essay identifies the purpose of the corporation, or places a restriction on corporate activities, consider whether ultra vires is an issue. While ultra vires is modernly not usually an effective defense, on an exam it is important to spot the issue and complete the analysis.

   b. **Acquire debt:** Corporations may borrow funds from outside sources to pursue the corporate purpose. Lenders do not acquire an ownership interest in the corporation. Debts may be secured (a bond) or unsecured (a debenture).
   c. **Issue shares of stock in the corporation**
      1. **Stock subscription agreement** is a contract where a **subscriber** makes a written promise **agreeing to buy a specified number of shares** of stock.
         a. A **post-incorporation subscription** immediately binds both parties.
         b. A **pre-incorporation subscription** is irrevocable for six months and must be accepted by the corporation to be valid.
      2. **Shares of stock** are equity securities that give the shareholder an ownership interest in the corporation.

a. **Quantity of shares available:** The articles of incorporation authorize the number of shares available to be sold. Shares that are sold are issued and outstanding. Shares that have yet to be sold are authorized but unissued.

b. **Types of shares:** The articles of incorporation can provide that different classes of stock shares are available (common or preferred). The rights and limitations of the various classes of stock must be identified before issuance.

c. **Consideration is required** in exchange for stock shares and can include any tangible or intangible property or benefit to the corporation, such as cash, an exchange for services rendered, in cancellation of a debt owed, etc. Consideration in exchange for stock shares may not include the exchange for future services, pre-incorporation services rendered, or an unsecured debt.

i. **Par value** is the stated minimum issuance price and stock may not be sold for less than par value.

ii. **No par** means there is no minimum issuance price for the stock.

iii. **Treasury stock** is stock that was previously issued and had been reacquired by the corporation. It can be re-sold for less than par value and is treated like no par stock.

3. **Preemptive rights** refer to the right of an existing shareholder to maintain her percentage of ownership in a corporation when there is a new issuance of stock for cash. Modernly, unless the articles provide otherwise, a **shareholder does not have preemptive rights.**

3. **Pre-incorporation actions by a promoter:** Promoters are persons acting on behalf of a corporation that is not yet formed. Prior to incorporation it is common for a promoter to raise capital and contract for a location, business materials, equipment, etc.

a. **Liability for promoter contracts:**

1. **Promoters are personally liable** for pre-incorporation contracts until there is clear evidence the parties did not intend for the promoter to be liable or there has been a novation replacing the promoter liability with that of the corporation.

a. **Right of reimbursement:** The promoter may have a right to reimbursement based on quasi contract for the value of the benefit received by the corporation, or on the implied adoption of the contract.

2. A **corporation is not generally liable** for, or bound to, pre-incorporation contracts.

a. **Except** a corporation will be liable where the corporation expressly **adopts the contract** or **accepts the benefits** of the contract.

b. **Promoter duties**: A promoter has a fiduciary relationship with the proposed corporation requiring **good faith.** Promoters cannot make a secret profit on their dealings with the corporation.

Promoter liability (pre-incorporation) fact triggers:
• Rent contract entered into before incorporation
• Equipment contract entered into before incorporation
• De facto company because of failure to properly incorporate
• Piercing the corporate veil

B. **Corporation Management, Directors, and Officers**
  1. **Corporate management structure:**
    a. **Director required:** All corporations must have at least one director, though they may have as many directors as they wish.
    b. **Articles of incorporation** are filed with the state to establish the corporation and any provisions contained in the articles will govern the corporation.
    c. **Bylaws:** Management of the corporation is conducted in accordance with the articles of incorporation and any corporate bylaws adopted by the board, which typically contain management provisions.
    d. **Election of the board of directors:** The initial board is typically identified in the articles of incorporation; when the initial term of service expires the vacancy is filled by a shareholder vote.
    e. **Officers are appointed** by the board of directors to implement the board decisions and carry out operations.
    f. **Officer authority:** Officers have authority to act on behalf of the corporation based on agency law principles. An officer's authority to bind the corporation may be express, inherent or apparent. (See Agency, section II.C.)
    g. **Removal:**
      1. **Director:** Modernly, a director can be removed with or without cause upon a majority shareholder vote.
      2. **Officer:** The board may remove an officer with or without cause.
    h. **Resignation** of an officer or director is allowed at any time with notice.
  2. **Actions of the board of directors**: The directors must **operate as a board to take action**, so actions require that a **majority of directors are present** at a **properly noticed meeting** to be valid.
    a. **Meetings:** The board of directors must hold meetings, which can be regular in accordance with a date and time fixed by the bylaws, or a special meeting requiring proper notice.
      1. **Quorum requirement:** A quorum, which is a majority of the board of directors, must be present for board action to be valid.
        a. **Disinterested directors:** To achieve quorum, the directors must not have an interest in the transaction.
        b. **Withdrawal allowed:** But, unlike shareholders, a director may break quorum by withdrawing from a meeting.

2. **No proxy voting** allowed, though some states allow teleconferencing for board meetings.
3. **No voting agreements allowed.**
4. **Majority requirement:** A majority of those present at the meeting must agree to take the proposed action.
5. **Delegation:** The board may delegate board authority to a committee, or an officer.

b. An **action taken without a meeting** is only valid with unanimous written consent of the directors.

3. **Duties of directors and officers:** A director or officer owes the duty of care, duty of loyalty and duty of disclosure to the corporation.

a. **Duty of care:** A director or officer owes the corporation a duty of care to act as a **reasonably prudent person** would act under similar circumstances.

1. The **business judgment rule (BJR)** applies the standard of care imposed for business judgments and provides the presumption that the directors or officers will manage the corporation in **good faith** and in the **best interests of the corporation** and its shareholders. The BJR is violated when a director or officer's conduct is unreasonable.

Duty of care fact triggers:

- Corporation changes to less profitable line of business
- Large expenditure when a merger is pending
- Officer misrepresents financials to induce contracting
- Subsidiary corp. sells items at cost to corporate owner
- Failure to investigate business opportunity
- Issuing stock as a gift
- Officer makes business decision on personal bias

b. **Duty of loyalty:** A director or officer owes a duty of loyalty to the corporation. A director must put the interests of the corporation above his own interests. The duty of loyalty arises three ways:

1. **Conflict of interest (self-dealing):** A director or officer has a conflict of interest when he (or a corporation he owns or has a relationship with, or his family member) enters into a contract with the corporation or has a beneficial financial interest in a contract.

a. **Self-dealing contracts are presumed unfair** and voidable.
b. **Conflict can be cured** if:
i. **Authorized** by disinterested board members after material disclosure; or
ii. **Approved** by majority of disinterested shareholders after material disclosure; and
iii. The transaction is **fair.**

<u>Duty of loyalty (conflict of interest) fact triggers:</u>
- Directors vote to sell company or give a profitable contract to a director or owner's company or relative
- Directors change business model to benefit corporate owner
- Director or officer buys stock based on insider info
- No proper investigation or inquiry to reveal self-dealing
- Director or relatives benefit from a corp. acquisition
- Any time a director has any personal interest in a transaction

2. **Usurping a corporate opportunity:** A director or officer may not personally act on a business opportunity without first offering it to the corporation where the corporation would expect to be presented the opportunity.
   a. The director or officer may take the opportunity only after **good faith rejection** of the opportunity by the corporation if there was **full disclosure** of all material facts to a disinterested board majority.
   b. **Remedy:** If the director or officer usurps a corporate opportunity, then the corporation may compel the director/officer to turn over the opportunity or **disgorge profits.**

<u>Duty of loyalty (usurp corp. opportunity) fact triggers:</u>
- Officer takes a business opportunity as a side job
- Officer takes opportunity to make a windfall on a deal himself
- Anytime a director learns of a business opportunity

3. **Competition:** A director or officer may not unfairly compete with the corporation.

c. **Duty to disclose:** Directors and officers have a duty to disclose material information relevant to the corporation to board members.

<u>Exam tip:</u> When the duty of care is implicated, the duty of loyalty is usually also in issue. When analyzing the duties owed by a director or officer, always analyze the conduct of each party separately.

4. **Rights of director and officers**
   a. **Compensation:** A director or officer is entitled to fair compensation, the rate of which the board of directors determines.
   b. **Indemnification:** A director or officer is entitled to indemnification for expenses incurred on behalf of the corporation.
   c. **Inspection:** A director or officer has a right to a reasonable inspection of corporate records or facilities.

5. **Liability of director and officers:** A director or officer's personal liability is limited and they aren't personally liable for corporate acts. But, the articles of incorporation may provide that a director or officer is not shielded from liability for intentional wrongful acts or crimes.

C. **Shareholders**

1. **Rights of shareholders**
   a. **Meetings** are typically where shareholders convene and vote on corporate management issues. There are two types of meetings:
      1. **General meetings** or annual meetings occur once a year and are where most shareholder voting occurs.
      2. **Special meetings** can be held upon reasonable notice of the time, place, and business to be discussed.
   b. **Voting:** Shareholders have only indirect corporate power through the right to vote to elect or remove members of the board and approve fundamental changes in the corporate structure, such as mergers, dissolutions, etc.
      1. **Right to vote:** The right to vote attaches to the type of stock held by the shareholder. A corporation can have two types of stock: common and preferred. At least one class of stock (or both) must have voting rights. If the articles do not specify voting rights, both classes of stock may vote. Common stock typically has voting rights.
      2. **Voting by proxy:** A shareholder may vote in person or by proxy. A proxy is a **signed writing authorizing another to cast a vote** on behalf of the shareholder. Small shareholders typically vote by proxy to avoid attending a meeting and to ensure a quorum is obtained.
         a. A **revocable proxy** is an agency relationship between the shareholder and the proxy.
         b. An **irrevocable proxy** occurs when the proxy is coupled with interest. The irrevocable proxy must be so labeled. The interest can relate to an interest in the shares (e.g., creditor or prospective purchaser) or an interest in the corporation (e.g., performance of services or granting credit in exchange for proxy rights).
      3. **Quorum:** For an action to pass there must be a quorum, which is a **majority of outstanding shares represented** (in person or by proxy) at the meeting. Quorum is based on the number of shares, not shareholders.
         a. **Majority vote:** If a quorum is present, a majority of **votes cast** validates the proposed shareholder action.
         b. **Except** votes regarding a **fundamental change** require a **majority vote of all outstanding shares** to validate the proposed action.
      5. **Vote calculation:** Two methods are employed:
         a. **Straight voting:** Each shareholder casts one vote per share held. Therefore, a shareholder with more than 50% of the shares controls the vote.

   b. **Cumulative voting** of directors allows a shareholder to multiply the number of shares held by the number of directors to be elected and then may cast all votes for one or more directors.

  6. **Unanimous written consent:** Shareholders may also take action with unanimous written consent of all shareholders.

c. **Inspection:** A shareholder has a right to inspect the corporate books upon a showing of a proper purpose.

d. **Dividends** are the distribution of cash, property, or stock a shareholder may receive from the corporation.

  1. **Discretionary:** Dividends are given at the board's discretion. But, a distribution is not permitted if it would lead to insolvency or is not allowed in the articles.

  2. **Priority of dividend distribution:**

   a. **Preferred with dividend preference:** Paid first as to preferred stated amount, then remaining amount is paid to common stock.

   b. **Preferred and participating:** Paid first as indicated, then remaining amount is paid to common stock.

   c. **Preferred and cumulative:** Paid first as indicated for number of years not paid in the past, then remaining amount is paid to common stock.

   d. **Common stock:** Paid last and all shares are paid in equal amount.

2. **Shareholder agreements**

a. A **voting trust** occurs when shareholders agree in writing to transfer their shares to a trustee who votes and distributes dividends in accordance with the voting trust. Often seen in closely held corporations.

b. A **voting agreement** is a written agreement where the parties agree to vote their shares as agreed. Often seen in closely held corporations.

c. A **management agreement** occurs where the shareholders agree to manage the corporation in an agreed upon way.

d. **Restrictions on stock transfers** are generally upheld if reasonable—for example a right of first refusal—but absolute restraints are not reasonable. A third party will only be bound if the restriction is conspicuously noted or the third party had knowledge.

3. **Shareholder suits**

a. **Direct suit:** A shareholder may bring a suit for breach of fiduciary duty owed to the shareholder.

b. **Derivative suit:** A shareholder may bring a derivative suit on behalf of the corporation for harm done to the corporation. The corporation receives the recovery, if any, and the shareholder is entitled to reimbursement for the expenses of litigation. The shareholder bringing the suit must:

  1. **Own stock** at time claim arose and throughout litigation

2. **Make a demand** on directors to bring suit or redress the injury and the demand is rejected unless such a demand would be futile.

> **Issue-spotting tip:** When a shareholder derivative suit is at issue also look for the issues of breach of loyalty, breach of care, or disgorging of profits under 16(b).

4. **Shareholder duties**
   a. **General rule: A shareholder owes no fiduciary duty** to the corporation or other shareholders.
   b. **Modern trend: Controlling shareholders owe a fiduciary duty** to the corporation and minority shareholders of the duty of care and duty of loyalty. **A controlling shareholder is one with enough voting strength to have a substantial impact on the corporation.**
      1. **Sale of controlling shares to a looter:** Controlling shareholders cannot sell control of the corporation to a looter if they know, or have reason to know, that the buyer intends to harm the company.
      2. **Sale of controlling shares at a premium** may be allowed where the transaction is made in good faith and is fair. However, a controlling shareholder may not sell her controlling shares and receive a personal benefit for the sale of a corporate asset or corporate office.

> **Issue-spotting tip:** Whenever a controlling shareholder sells shares, consider whether these issues are raised. The analysis is very fact dependent and many facts will be available to use in the analysis. For example, consider how high a premium is paid over trading value for the controlling shares, and if there are any side deals regarding the transaction.

5. **Shareholder liability:** Shareholders are not personally liable for the actions of the corporation.
   a. **Except professional corporations:** Typically, licensed professionals may incorporate but remain personally liable for malpractice (e.g., lawyers, doctors).

D. **Federal Securities Laws**
   1. **Section 16(b) short-swing profits:** Any short-swing trading profits received within a six-month period by a corporate insider must be disgorged to the corporation. Requirements of 16(b):
      a. **Corporation** must be:
         1. **Listed on a national exchange**, or
         2. Have **$10 million** or more in assets **and at least 500** shareholders.

b. **Corporate insiders** are officers, directors, and shareholders that own 10% or more equity stock in the corporation.
   1. **Officers and directors** must be in their position at the time of **either** the purchase or the sale of shares.
   2. **10% shareholders** must be in that position at the time of **both** the purchase and the sale of the shares.
c. **Trading** is making a profitable purchase and sale (or sale and purchase) of company equity stock within a **six-month period.**
d. **Remedy:** The insider must **disgorge the profit** back to the corporation.

> **Issue-spotting tip:** 16(b) may be at issue any time a director, officer, or shareholder buys or sells company stock. Section 10b-5 may also be at issue.

2. **Section 10b-5** disallows **insider trading** and provides liability for any person who employs fraud or deception in connection with the purchase or sale of any security by means of any instrumentality of interstate commerce. In other words, trading securities based on nonpublic corporate information is not permitted.
   a. **Fraud (misrepresentation) prima facie case requirements**
      1. **Intent** to defraud, deceive, or manipulate.
      2. **Material misrepresentation or omission:** Information is material where there is a **substantial likelihood that a reasonable investor would consider it important** in making an investment decision. Omission or failure to disclose only applies if the party has a duty to disclose.
      3. **Reliance:** There must be actual reliance on the misrepresentation or failure to disclose. (Typically a failure to disclose is relied upon anytime one buys or sells securities as a result of a material omission.)
      4. **Purchase or sale** of securities.
      5. **Interstate commerce:** The trade must involve the use of some means of interstate commerce, such as a telephone, mail, email, national securities exchange, etc.
      6. **Remedy:** Damages are calculated as the difference between actual proceeds and what should have transpired based on the real value of the stock. These profits must be **disgorged** to the company.
   b. **10b-5 may be violated in the following four ways:**
      1. **Direct trading by an insider**
         a. An **insider** is a director, officer, shareholder, or any other **holder of material, nonpublic corporate information.**
         b. **An insider must disclose the material, nonpublic information or refrain from trading.** Failure to disclose satisfies the required fraud element of making a material omission.

2. **Tippers** (those providing insider information) are liable if **the information was shared for the improper purpose** of direct or indirect personal gain.
   a. **Personal gain** can include money, a gift, or an increase in reputation.
   b. The tipper does not have to trade in securities himself to be liable, so long as the insider information is used by another to trade.
3. **Tippees** (those receiving insider information) are liable only if **scienter** is present, such that the **tipper breached a fiduciary duty** and the **tippee knew** the duty had been breached.
4. **Misappropriators** (those obtaining corporate private information through other means) may be in breach of a duty owed to the source of the information, though typically are not in a position with a duty to disclose. (E.g., an eavesdropper, lawyer who received information for a proper purpose but then traded.)

10b-5 fact triggers:
- Officer gives a misleading press conference/statement.
- Remark overheard in public, intentionally or not intentionally.
- Officer gives inside info to lawyer who then trades or tips. Look for a professional responsibility crossover.

Exam tip: 10b-5 may be at issue whenever there is a stock transaction. There is a two-step analysis: 1) Determine if the party is in a position to be liable under 10b-5 as a direct insider, tipper, tippee, or misappropriator. 2) Establish the prima facie case. A party may be subject to 10b-5 liability in more than one way—for example, as both a tippee and a tipper, or as direct violator and a tipper. It is important to analyze each potential violation separately. Also, look for multiple parties in the question to violate 10b-5. Section 16(b) may also be at issue.

3. The **Sarbanes-Oxley** Act sets standards for publicly traded companies by creating a board that oversees public accounting firms that perform audits and creating rules pertaining to corporate financial reporting.
   a. There are **enhanced reporting requirements**, including:
      1. An **audit board** must be established by each corporation.
      2. **Senior executives** must take individual responsibility for the accuracy of financial reports.
      3. If a **filing is inaccurate** and the corporation has to restate financial reports, the CEO and CFO must **reimburse** the corporation for any incentive-based compensation received during the 12 months after the inaccurate reports were filed.

b. **Criminal penalties:** The act provides criminal penalties for:
   1. **Destroying or altering** corporate documents and/or audit records is punishable by a fine and up to 20 years in prison.
   2. **Securities fraud** is punishable up to 25 years in prison.
   3. **Whistleblowers** are afforded protection.

E. **Fundamental changes to the corporate business** or structure must be approved by a majority shareholder vote.
   1. **Typical procedure** to make a fundamental change:
      a. Board **adopts a resolution.**
      b. **Written notice** is given to shareholders.
      c. **Shareholders approve** the change by majority—all votes entitled to be cast (a higher standard than the typical quorum rule).
   2. **Types of fundamental changes**
      a. **Merger** occurs when one corporation acquires another corporation. Typically requires shareholder approval.
         1. Shareholder approval not needed where the change is not significant.
         2. Short-form merger allowed where a 90%-owned subsidiary is merged into the corporate owner.
      b. **Stock sale** occurs where one corporation purchases all shares of another corporation.
      c. **Asset sale** occurs where a company sells substantially all of its assets to another corporation.
      d. **Conversion** occurs when one entity changes corporate form—for example, from a corporation to a LLC.
      e. **Amendment** of articles or bylaws requires approval of the directors and shareholders and the amendment must be filed with the state.
      f. **Dissolution and winding up:** The last phase of a corporation is the period from the dissolution, which occurs when the corporation ceases to exist, and through the winding up period where all remaining corporate affairs are settled.
         1. **Voluntary dissolution** occurs when a corporation chooses to take the action to dissolve. This requires a majority vote by the directors and shareholders.
         2. **Administrative dissolution** occurs when the state forces a corporation to dissolve because of its administrative failures, such as the failure to pay fees or penalties, declare annual statement, maintain an agent for service, etc.
         3. **Judicial dissolution** occurs on grounds of fraud, ultra vires action, or a defective corporation; or in an action brought by minority shareholders where there is misconduct; or by creditors for an unsatisfied judgment.
   3. **Dissenter appraisal rights**: Shareholders who dissent from a proposed fundamental change may have the right to have the corporation purchase their shares.
      a. **Requirement:** Shareholder must give notice of objection and intent to demand payment before a vote is taken, deliver written

notice, cannot vote in favor of proposed action, and must demand payment in writing after the vote.

b. **Appraisal:** Shareholder receives fair market value and interest.

II. **AGENCY:** An agency relationship exists when a principal authorizes an agent to act on her behalf and **represent the principal** in dealings with third parties.

A. **Formation of principal-agent relationship** requires:

1. **Agreement** between both parties that the agent's conduct must be for the **principal's benefit**, and the principal has the **right to control** the agent.

> **Memorization tip:** Remember ABC: Agreement-Benefit-Control

a. **Distinguish from an independent contractor:** A principal has the right to control the method and manner in which an agent performs, but does not control this with an independent contractor.

b. **Subagents and borrowed agents** must meet the same agency requirements of agreement, benefit, and control.

> **Exam tip:** On an essay question, look for one of the required elements to be missing since that is typically the case.

2. **Capacity**

a. **Principal** must have capacity to contract (not be a minor) and must be mentally competent.

b. **Agent** must have minimal capacity, so an agent must be mentally competent but can be a minor.

3. **All contract formalities not required:** An agency relationship does not require consideration or a writing, unless the Statute of Frauds requires a writing (e.g., a contract regarding real property).

B. **Duties of principal and agent and remedies for breach**

1. **Principal duties**

a. **The principal owes the agent all duties imposed by their contract**, such as compensation, cooperation, indemnity, and reimbursement, and any other contractual duties imposed.

b. **Remedy for breach:** Where the principal is in breach, the agent may do any of the following:

1. **Terminate the agency** and refuse to perform further.

2. **Seek contract damages** and/or an accounting.

3. **Seek a possessory lien** for money due.

2. **Agent duties**

a. **The agent owes the principal** the fiduciary duties of:

1. **Duty of care** to act as a **reasonably prudent person** would act under similar circumstances.

  a. The **business judgment rule (BJR)** applies where the agent's duties are in a business setting and provides the presumption that the agent will act in **good faith** and in the **best interests of the principal.**
2. **Duty of loyalty:** An agent owes a duty of loyalty to the principal. An agent must put the interests of the corporation above his own interests.
  a. **No conflicts of interest**
    i. No **self-dealing,**
    ii. No **usurping the principal's business opportunity,**
    iii. No making **secret profits.**
  b. **No commingling of funds.**
3. **Duty of obedience** to follow all reasonable instructions given by the principal,
4. **Duty to communicate** relevant information that would affect the principal, and
5. Any other **express contractual** duties.

b. **Remedy for breach:** Where the agent is in breach, a principal may do any of the following:
  1. **Discharge** the agent
  2. **Withhold compensation** from the agent
  3. **Seek an accounting** or **contract remedies**, such as an action to disgorge profits, rescission, constructive trust, etc.
  4. **Seek tort damages**
  5. **Seek indemnity** for liability to third parties occasioned by the agent's wrongful actions beyond the agency scope

c. **Subagent duties**
  1. **Subagent duties** depend on whether or not the subagent is acting with authority
    a. **Acting with authority:** The subagent **owes the principal the same duties** owed by an agent.
    b. **Acting without authority:** The subagent **only owes duties to the agent.**
  2. The **agent is liable** to the principal for the subagent's breach.

d. The **agent is personally liable for contracts** with third parties in the following cases:
  1. The agent is acting with **no authority** from the principal.
  2. Principal's **identity is not revealed** (partial disclosure).
  3. Principal's **existence and identity is undisclosed.**

C. **Principal's liability for agent's contracts:** The agent's actions will bind the principal if the agent was acting under the actual or apparent authority to act for the principal. **Types of authority:**
  1. **Actual express authority** is specifically granted to the agent by the principal. It may be oral, but a writing is required if the Statute of Frauds applies.
  2. **Actual implied authority:** The agent reasonably believes the principal gave him authority because of necessity (task reasonably necessary to accomplish agency goals), custom, or prior dealings.

a. **Termination:** Actual express or implied authority may be terminated by any of the following:
   1. **Breach** of agent's fiduciary duty
   2. **Lapse** of a stated period, or a reasonable time if none is stated
   3. **Operation of law:** By the death or incapacity of either party (unless durable power of attorney exists), or bankruptcy of the principal
   4. **Changed circumstances** where it is clear the agent's services are no longer needed, such as a significant change in the market, law, or subject matter
   5. **Happening** of a specified event
   6. **Unilateral termination** by either party since agency is usually terminable at will with notice

> **Memorization tip:** Use the mnemonic BLO–CHU to memorize the six ways an agency can terminate. Blow bubble–chew gum.

3. **Apparent authority:** The agent's actions will bind the principal when the principal has provided the agent with the **appearance of authority**, on which a third party reasonably relies. The analysis centers on what occurred between the principal and the third party.
   a. **Notice requirement:** Where an agent's actual authority has terminated (unless by death or incapacity), she continues to have apparent authority to transact with known third parties with whom she has previously transacted on the principal's behalf until the third parties receive actual or constructive notice of the termination.
   b. **Written authority:** An agent may have "lingering authority" where an agent's actual authority has been terminated, but if a third party relies on written authority of the agent, the agent's apparent authority is not terminated.
      1) **Except:** Death or capacity of the principal terminates all authorities.
   c. **Agent exceeds actual authority:** The principal may still be bound if the agent is in a position that would normally allow the agent to take such action (e.g., corporate officer), or if the principal previously allowed the agent a similar excess of authority.

> **Apparent authority fact triggers:**
> - Secret instruction to agent
> - "Lingering authority" where third party not notified that agent no longer has authority
> - Action taken by a corporate officer

4. **Ratification occurs** when an agent takes action without proper authority, and the principal subsequently engages in conduct that approves the agent's action. The principal will be bound where he

has capacity, knowledge of all material facts, and accepts the agent's transaction.

5. **No authority:** Where the agent acts without actual or apparent authority, the principal is not liable on the contract and the agent is personally liable.

D. **Principal's liability for agent's torts:** A principal is liable for an agent's torts that are committed within the scope of the principal-agent relationship.

1. **Scope of principal-agent relationship:** An act is within the scope of the relationship if the conduct was of the kind the agent was hired to perform, the tort occurred on the job, and/or the agent intended his action to benefit the principal.
   a. **Except frolic or mere detour:** A principal is not liable for torts committed by an agent while the agent is substantially deviating from the planned conduct such that she is acting for her own purposes (frolic). However, a small deviation from the planned conduct (mere detour) is permissible, and the agent will still be within the scope of the agency relationship.

> <u>Exam tip:</u> When the issue of frolic or mere detour occurs on an essay question, be prepared to argue the issue both ways since it will be a close call.

2. **Independent contractors: A principal is not generally liable** for the torts of an independent contractor.
   a. **Independent contractor definition:** A principal does not control the manner and method by which an independent contractor performs, but does have the right to control the manner and method by which an agent performs.
   b. **Exceptions:** A principal is liable for the torts of an independent contractor when the conduct involves:
      1. **Ultrahazardous** activity,
      2. **Nondelegable duties**, or
      3. If **estoppel** applies where the principal held the independent contractor out as an agent.
3. **Intentional torts:** A principal is not liable for the agent's intentional torts, **except** where the conduct was:
   a. **Specifically authorized** by the principal (e.g., force is authorized),
   b. **Natural result** from the nature of the employment (e.g., a bouncer), or
   c. The tortious act was **motivated by a desire to serve** the principal.

> <u>Issue-spotting tip:</u> Agency issues usually arise where one person is acting on behalf of another person or business entity in a contract transaction.

III. PARTNERSHIP: There are two types of partnership, general and limited.

A. General partnership

1. **Definition:** A partnership is an association of two or more persons who are carrying on as co-owners of a business for profit, whether or not the parties intend to form a partnership.

> **Exam tip:** On the bar exam, determining if the parties are partners is often a close call.

2. **Formation**
   a. **No formalities required:** There are no formalities required to form a general partnership (based on contract and/or agency laws) so a partnership is found based on the **intent of the parties** to carry on a business as co-owners. **Intent of the parties can be established by:**
      1. **Contribution in exchange for profit:** The contribution of money or services in exchange for a share of profits creates a presumption that a general partnership exists. The exchange for profit is the key factor here, so an exchange for payment of a debt, rent, etc. will not create the presumption.
      2. **Common ownership:** Other indications (but not presumptions) that a partnership exists include title to property held as joint tenants or tenants in common, parties designate their relationship as a partnership, or the venture undertaken requires extensive activity by the partners.
      3. **Sharing of gross revenue** does *not* necessarily indicate the parties are partners.
   b. **California** has adopted (along with majority of states) the Revised Uniform Partnership Act (RUPA) but partners may still agree in their partnership agreement to rules not governed by RUPA and then RUPA only governs those rules not provided for in the agreement. However, certain RUPA provisions cannot be waived, such as the duty of loyalty.
   c. **Partners have a fiduciary, agency-like relationship:** Partners are bound by **contracts** entered into with authority by their co-partners, and are liable for **torts** committed by their co-partners within the scope of the partnership.
3. **Partnership assets**
   a. **Titled property** (under RUPA)
      1. **Property is deemed a partnership asset if:**
         a. **Titled** in partnership name, or
         b. It is titled in a partner's name and the instrument transferring title identifies the person's **capacity as a partner, or the existence of the partnership.**
      2. **Property is presumed a partnership asset if purchased with partnership funds.** Regardless of how title is held, property is

rebuttably presumed partnership property if purchased with partnership funds, either cash or credit.

3. **Property is not a partnership asset and is separate property if:** Property held in the name of a partner that does not indicate the person's capacity as a partner or mention the partnership, and wasn't purchased with partnership funds is presumed to be that partner's separate property, even if it is used for partnership purposes (e.g., car).

b. **Untitled property** (ownership follows common law principles)
   1. **Property is partnership property** based on the parties' **intent,** courts look at the following, if:
      a. **Partnership funds** were used to acquire, improve or maintain the property
      b. There is a **close relationship** between the property and the partnership business operations
      c. The partnership **lists it as an asset** in its books

4. **Partnership rights and duties**
   a. **Partnership rights**
      1. **Ownership:** Property acquired by the partnership is property of the partnership itself and not of the partners individually.
      2. **Transferability:** A partner is not a co-owner of partnership property and has no transferable interest in it.
         a. **Except** a partner's own share of partnership profits and surplus is transferable since they are his own personal property.
      3. **Use of property:** A partner can only use the partnership property for the benefit of the partnership.
      4. **Control:** Each partner is entitled to equal control (vote) and management of the partnership, and receives no salary for services performed (except compensation to wind up the partnership is allowed).
      5. **Profits and losses:** The default rule is that profits are shared equally and losses are shared in the same proportion as profits. For example, if the partners agree to share profits 60/40, then both profits and losses are calculated at this rate; if the partners agree only to share losses 60/40 then profits are still shared equally.
      6. **Indemnity:** A partner may be indemnified for liabilities and expenses incurred on behalf of the partnership.
   b. **Fiduciary relationship:** Partners are fiduciaries of each other and the partnership. Partners have the following fiduciary duties:
      1. **Duty of care** to use reasonable care.
         a. The **business judgment rule** applies where the agent's duties are in a business setting.
      2. **Duty of loyalty** to further the partnership interests over his own interests.
         a. **No conflicts of interest:**
            i. No **self-dealing,**

ii. No **usurping a partnership business opportunity,**
iii. No making **secret profits, or**
iv. No **competing** with the partnership

3. **Duty to disclose:** Partners must disclose any material fact regarding partnership business.
4. **Duty to account:** Partners can bring actions against other partners for losses caused by breach and may disgorge a breaching partner of profits.

5. **Partnership relations with third parties**
   a. **Debts: General partners are personally liable** for the debts of the partnership. (Although limited partners are not; see Limited Partnerships below.)
   b. **Contracts:** Each partner is an agent of the partnership for the purpose of conducting its business. The partners' authority to bind the partnership when dealing with third parties follows agency law principles:
      1. **Actual Authority:** Where the partner reasonably believes she has authority to act based on the partnership agreement or a vote by the partners, the partnership will be bound.
      2. **Apparent Authority:** Any partner may act to carry out ordinary partnership business and doing so will bind the partnership.
         a. **Except** if the partner had **no authority to act** for the partnership in the matter and the **third party actually knew or** received **proper notice** that the partner lacked such authority.
      3. **Estoppel:** If a person represents to a third party that a general partnership exists, she will be liable as if it does exist.
   c. **Torts:** The partnership members are joint and severally liable for torts committed by a partner in the scope of the partnership.
6. **Partnership liability**
   a. **Civil liability**
      1. **Contracts:** The partners are liable for all contracts entered into by a partner that is within the scope of partnership business and/or is made with authority of the partnership.
      2. **Torts:** The partners are liable for all torts committed by any partner or partnership employee that occurs within the course of partnership business or is made with authority of the partnership.
      3. **Joint and several:** Partnership liability is joint and several for all obligations. Each partner is personally liable for the entire amount of partnership obligations. However, a partner paying more than his share may seek contribution or indemnity from the other partners.
   b. **Liability of incoming partners:** Incoming partners are not personally liable for debts incurred prior to joining the partnership, but any money paid into the partnership by an incoming partner can be used by the partnership to satisfy prior debts.

c. **Liability of outgoing (dissociated) partners**
    1. A dissociating (outgoing) partner **remains liable** for partnership debts incurred prior to dissociation.
    2. A partnership **can be bound** by an act of a dissociated partner (and the dissociated partner **may be liable** for acts) undertaken within two years after dissociation if:
        a. The act **would have bound** the partnership before dissociation,
        b. The other party **reasonably believed** the dissociated partner was still a partner, and
        c. The other party **did not have notice** of dissociation.
            i. If a notice of dissociation is filed with the state all parties are deemed to have received notice within 90 days of the filing.

7. **Dissociation, Dissolution, and Winding Up**
    a. **Dissociation** occurs when a partner ceases to be a partner in the partnership.
        1. Dissociation does not necessarily terminate the partnership (unless there are only two partners).
        2. Dissociation may be voluntary, or involuntary where the other partners expel a partner.
        3. The partnership must purchase a dissociated partner's interest in the partnership.
        4. A dissociated partner may still bind the partnership and may remain liable for partnership (see section III.A.6.c.2, above).
    b. **Dissolution** occurs when the partnership stops being active and the partnership business is wound up. A partnership may dissolve for several reasons:
        1. **Voluntary dissolution** occurs when a partnership is formed for a specific purpose and the objective is achieved, or the agreement specified an end date, or when all partners agree, or in an at-will partnership when one party notifies the other.
        2. **Involuntary dissolution** can occur when the partnership is engaged in an unlawful activity, or by court decree at the request of a partner.
    c. **Winding up** is the period between the dissolution and termination of the partnership in which the remaining partners liquidate the partnership's assets to satisfy creditors, an accounting is made, and the remaining assets are distributed to the partners.
        1. **Compensation:** Partners receive compensation for winding-up activities.
        2. **Old business:** The partnership and general partners remain liable for all transactions entered into to wind up old business with existing creditors.
        3. **New business:** The partnership and general partners remain liable on new business transactions until notice of dissolution is given to creditors or until 90 days after filing a statement of dissolution with the state.

d. **Priority of distribution.** Assets are distributed in the following order:
   1. **Creditors**, including outside creditors and loans from nonpartners.
   2. **Partners who have loaned money** to the partnership or are entitled to compensation for winding-up activities.
   3. **Capital contributions** by partners.
   4. **Profits and surplus**, if any remain, are shared equally amongst the partners unless there is an agreement otherwise.

> Note: If the partnership does not have enough assets to repay a partner's capital contribution, the other partners will need to put in an equal share to satisfy that debt. Further, a partner who pays more than her share of partnership debts is entitled to contribution from the partners.

B. **Limited partnership**

1. **Definition:** A limited partnership is a partnership that has at least one general partner and at least one limited partner, which creates a two-tiered partnership structure with differing rights, duties, and liabilities for general and limited partners. The main difference is that a limited partner is only liable for the obligations of the partnership to the extent of his capital contribution and is not entitled to manage or control the partnership business.
2. **Formation:** To form a limited partnership the partners must:
   a. **File a limited partnership certificate of formation** with the state
   b. Identify the **name** of the partnership, which includes the words "limited partnership,"
   c. Provide the **names and addresses** of the agent for service of process and of each general partner, and
   d. **Maintain records:** In the state of organization the limited partnership must have an office containing records of the certificate, any partnership agreements, the partnership's tax returns for the three most current years, etc. There must also be record of the amount and description of each partner's contribution, any special distribution rights of each partner, etc.

> Exam tip: A limited partnership that is not properly formed, for example if the certificate is not filed, will be deemed a general partnership.

3. **Partnership rights and duties**
   a. **General partners** have the same rights and duties as noted above in the General partnership (see section III.A.3, above).
      1. **Indemnity:** A general partner is not entitled to a salary for services performed for the partnership, but the partnership must indemnify a general partner for liabilities incurred as a result of partnership activities.

b. **Limited partners generally have no right to act on behalf of the partnership and owe no fiduciary duties** to the partnership and are free to compete with the partnership and have interests adverse to those of the partnership unless an agreement provides otherwise. Limited partners have a right to a full accounting and to inspect the partnership books.

c. **Both general and limited partners** have the following rights:
   1. **Distribution:** Distributions are made on the basis of the partner's contribution. However, a contribution can be in the form of any benefit bestowed on the partnership including money, property, services, etc.
   2. **Consent:** A partner's contribution obligation is only excused by the consent of all partners, and is not excused by death or disability.
   3. **Transferability:** A partner's right to distributions is personal property that may be transferred.
   4. **Dissolve:** Right to apply for dissolution of the limited partnership.

4. **Partner liabilities**
   a. **General partners** are subject to the same liabilities as a regular general partner (see section III.A.5, above).
   b. **Limited partners** not liable for the obligations of the partnership itself beyond their capital contributions and generally have no right to manage the business, though they may. However, a limited partner may be found liable as a general partner if a third party has reason to believe the limited partner is actually a general partner.

5. **Dissolution**
   a. **A limited partnership will dissolve:**
      1. At the **time specified** in the limited partnership certificate.
      2. Upon **written consent** of all partners.
      3. Upon **dissociation of a general partner**, unless the agreement provides otherwise, or the partners appoint a new general partner within 90 days.
      4. Upon **judicial decree** of dissolution.
   b. **Winding up:** The limited partnership will continue to exist for the purpose of the winding up activities.
   c. **Priority of distribution:** Assets are distributed in the following order:
      1. **Creditors,** including outside creditors and partner loans.
      2. **Partners and former partners** in satisfaction of distribution previously required under the limited partnership agreement.
      3. **Capital contributions** by partners must be paid.
      4. **Partners** for the amount due under the partnership agreement, or if not specified then in proportion to their distribution share.

> **Exam tip:** Partnership has only been tested twice since it was added to the California bar exam in 2007. However, in other states that test partnership, 90% of exams focus on general partnerships.

IV. **LLP—LIMITED LIABILITY PARTNERSHIPS**

A. **Definition:** A LLP is a form of partnership where the partners are not personally liable for the obligations of the partnership.

B. **Formation:** To form a LLP a partnership must:

1. **File a statement** of qualification with the secretary of state executed by at least two partners,
2. Identify the **name and address** of the partnership, and
3. Have a partnership **name ending in LLP** or RLLP (if formed under RUPA).

C. **Liability of limited liability partners**

a. **LL partner's have no personal liability for the partnership:** All partners are not personally liable for the debts and obligations of the partnership, whether contract, tort, or otherwise.

1. Note this is different than a LP where only the limited partners are not personally liable, but the general partner is liable.

b. **LL partner will still have personal liability for his own wrongful acts.**

D. **Fiduciary obligations:** Partners owe LLP duties similar to those a director owes to a corporation, including a duty of care and duty of loyalty.

E. **Dissociation and dissolution** operate similarly to a limited partnership.

V. **LLC—LIMITED LIABILITY COMPANIES**

A. **Definition:** A LLC is a business entity that has the limited liability of a corporation combined with the tax advantages of a partnership.

B. **Formation:** To form a LLC the members must:

1. **File an "articles of organization" with the state** (which is similar to an article of incorporation),
2. Identify the **name** of LLC, and **address** of registered office and agent, and
3. Names of **all members.**
4. The LLC may also adopt an **operating agreement** identifying how the LLC is to be managed. In the absence of an agreement, the members will have an equal right to manage and control.

C. **Rights and duties of LLC members**

1. **LLC member rights**

a. **Profits and losses:** Sharing of profits and losses are **based on contributions** unless operating agreement provides otherwise.

b. **Management and control: Members typically control** the LLC, but the articles may provide for another type of management.

c. **Transferability: Management interests are not freely transferable** and members can only transfer their right to receive profits and losses, so an LLC has limited liquidity.

   2. **LLC member fiduciary duties:** Members owe the LLC and other LLC members the duty of care and duty of loyalty.

D. **Liability of LLC members:** LLC members are **not personally liable** for the obligations of the company itself beyond their own capital contributions.

E. **Dissolution:** There is a split of authority on what terminates an LLC
   1. **Traditional rule:** Dissociation of any LLC member, such as by death, retirement, resignation, bankruptcy, etc., generally causes dissolution; or
   2. **Modern trend:** Dissolution is only caused by one of the following:
      a. An event specified in the operating agreement;
      b. Consent by all members;
      c. Event that makes the enterprise unlawful; or
      d. Judicial decree.

BUSINESS ASSOCIATIONS ISSUES TESTED MATRIX

	Description of Fact Pattern	Crossover	Corps. De Facto De Jure Pierce Corp. Veil Ultra Vires	Corps. Promoters Pre-incorporation Liability	Corps. Officers & Directors Duties Duty of Care BJR Duty of Loyalty	Corps. Shareholder Rights Agreements Derivative Suits	Corps. Federal Securities Law 10b5 16b	Corps. Fundamental Change Dissolution	Agency	Partnerships General & Limited	LLP	LLC
February '11 Q5	Bob & Cate own Corp.; Bob wants to sell to sister Sally	Prof Resp			X	X		X				
July '10 Q4	ABC Computers start-up with Alfred, Beth & Charles									X	X	
February '10 Q2	ABC LLP leases offices to other lawyers	Prof Resp								X	X	
February '09 Q6	Stage Inc. is a closely held Corp. operating comedy clubs		X		X							
February '08 Q6	Albert & Barry, a librar-ian, provide law services	Prof Resp	X	X					X			
February '07 Q2	Fred & Rita own Rita's Kitchen and have 75 investors	Prof Resp		X	X	X						
July '06 Q4	B, C & D are director of Web; Web creates Adco's website on credit		X		X							
July '05 Q3	Sportco & Carole on board; Carole sells land to another	Prof Resp			X				X			
February '05 Q3	Molly & Ruth form Dryco, which is insolvent & dissolves		X	X		X		X				

Continued >

	Description of Fact Pattern	Crossover	Corps. De Facto De Jure Pierce Corp. Veil Ultra Vires	Corps. Promoters Pre-incorporation Liability	Corps. Officers & Directors Duties Duty of Care BJR Duty of Loyalty	Corps. Shareholder Rights Agreements Derivative Suits	Corps. Federal Securities Law 10b5 16b	Corps. Fundamental Change Dissolution	Agency	Partnerships General & Limited	LLP	LLC
July '03 Q1	Officer tells Lawyer corp. info for tax advice; Lawyer buys stock	Prof. Resp					X					
February '02 Q3	Acme merges with Bigco, but President Paul buys stock first				X		X	X				
February '01 Q2	Adam owns Sellco; Sellco owns Buildco., which sells houses at cost				X	X						
July '99 Q6	Sally VP at Chipco knows of new technology; she tells Laura, who tells Arnold						X					
February '99 Q4	Rentco owned 1/3 by banker Bob, who buys Plaza for $300k	Prof Resp			X							
July '98 Q5	Motco Carl sells to looter Rich of Bigco & makes mopeds				X	X						
July '98 Q3	Attorney Ann is on board of nonprofit CAP; Dave buys his kids computers	Prof Resp			X							
July '97 Q5	Artis & Ben form Compco, gift shares to Carla for marketing advice			X	X	X						

Continued >

	Description of Fact Pattern	Crossover	Corps. De Facto De Jure Pierce Corp. Veil Ultra Vires	Corps. Promoters Pre-incorporation Liability	Corps. Officers & Directors Duties Duty of Care BJR Duty of Loyalty	Corps. Shareholder Rights Agreements Derivative Suits	Corps. Federal Securities Law 10b5 16b	Corps. Fundamental Change Dissolution	Agency	Partnerships General & Limited	LLP	LLC
February '97 Q2	Graphic Pres. prohibited from selling paper; Frank buys a paper mill		X			X	X					
February '96 Q2	Art, Bob & Cora incorporate Widgco, but Art buy widgets first			X	X	X		X				
July '95 Q	Exco may sell out to Morcorp; President Dan of Exco talks to press				X	X	X	X				
February '94 Q2	Al owns Paintco; contracts for paint prior to incorporation	Contracts		X								
July '93 Q3	Al, Bob, Carl & Dan own Etco; contract for cleaning by XYZ				X	X		X				
July '90 Q6	Abby, CEO of Oilco, loudly discloses corp. info so Barb can hear						X					
February '89 Q6	HV wants to buy MCC but President Buff hates colorized films				X	X		X				
February '88 Q6	Art, president of Exco, buys all Yang stock, which his family owns				X				X			
February '87 Q1	Aco buys Tco stock; Tco CEO Dan's lawyer, Len, and son, Sam, buy stock						X					

BUSINESS ASSOCIATIONS PRACTICE ESSAYS, ANSWER GRIDS, AND SAMPLE ANSWERS

Business Associations Question 1

July 1998, Question 5

Carl owned 30% of the common stock of Motco, a corporation engaged in manufacturing high priced motorcycles. Motco has 200 shareholders. No shareholder other than Carl owned more than 2% of Motco's stock. Motco's most valuable asset has been a large plant where its internationally famous motorcycles are made.

Bigco is a corporation, all of the stock of which is owned by Albert Rich ("Rich"). Three other corporations that were recently acquired by Bigco have since become insolvent and failed. Bigco made an offer to Carl to buy all of Carl's Motco stock for $25 per share.

Before he accepted the offer, Carl received a letter from the former president of one of the three failed companies asserting that the failure had been caused by Rich "looting" the company after Bigco acquired it. The letter also stated that Bigco and Rich had been sued in an action in which it was alleged that they had dissipated the assets of all three failed companies after Bigco acquired control to raise funds for other business acquisitions. When Carl questioned Rich about this letter, he was told that the letter writer was a disgruntled former employee who had been fired for incompetence. Based on that response, Carl conducted no further inquires. If he had, he would have found that final judgments had been entered in litigation concerning Bigco's control of the three failed companies, holding Bigco and Rich liable for wrongful diversion of assets.

Carl accepted Bigco's offer. At the time of purchase, Motco's common stock was selling for $11 per share. As part of the stock sale agreement with Bigco, Carl undertook to ensure that all nine members of Motco's board of directors would resign and that Bigco's nine nominees would be elected as the replacement Motco directors, before ownership of Carl's 30% block of Motco stock passed to Bigco. The replacement of the Motco directors took place as planned.

Thereafter, Motco's new board of directors voted unanimously to convert the Motco motorcycle plant exclusively to the manufacture of motor-driven bicycles (mopeds), despite recent adverse publicity over an increasing number of moped accidents. This decision was motivated by a desire to provide an outlet for moped parts manufactured by another corporation controlled by Rich. At present, Motco's earnings from the sale of mopeds are substantially less than its former earnings from the sale of motorcycles.

Pat is a 1% shareholder of Motco. By proper procedures, she has instituted a shareholders' derivative action against Carl, Motco's new directors, and Bigco based on the events described above.

To what relief is Pat entitled in the derivative action, and on what bases and against which defendants?

Discuss.

Do not discuss federal or state securities law issues.

Business Associations Question 1 Assessment

July 1998, Question 5

This question focuses on the business association of a corporation, and in particular on the role of a controlling corporate shareholder. Though the question doesn't raise a large number of issues, there are many facts, and factual inferences that need to be used in the analysis.

This question is not organized by any calls of the question, so you will need to provide some organization yourself in order to properly address the question. The second-to-last paragraph asks specifically about an "action against Carl, Motco's new directors, and Bigco," so that is the most logical way to organize an answer. Where a question does not have specific calls there is usually some logical order that can be borrowed from the question itself, such as in this case.

Since the question itself stated that Pat brought her derivative suit "by proper procedures" there is no need to spend much time on the derivative suit issue. It is included in the grid, but as you can see it is not bolded and could have been skipped.

There are a lot of great facts to use in the analysis regarding controlling shareholder Carl's sale of the company to Rich and Bigco, such as the warning Carl received about Rich being a looter, and the facts relating to Carl's receipt of a high premium for selling his controlling share to Rich. For the analysis of the conduct of the new Motco directors there is also an abundance of facts to use, including the change of the corporate purpose from a lucrative motorcycle manufacturing plant to a much less lucrative moped manufacturing plant, the recent adverse moped publicity, Rich's other moped parts company, and the information relating to the reason behind the board making the switch. Many of these facts could also be used in the analysis of Bigco's breach of fiduciary duty as well.

In a question like this where there are a lot of facts available to use, and many of them implicate some obviously very shady behavior, be sure to make the connection in your analysis. It is not enough to recite the correct fact in the correct place in your analysis. To receive a passing score you must explain how or why the appropriate fact proves the rule or element in contention. For example, it is not enough to say that, "the board's action of converting a motorcycle plant to a moped plant was not in the best interest of the Motco shareholders." Rather, the analysis should explain *why* the facts establish the element in question, such as, "the board's action of converting a successful motorcycle plant to a less successful moped plant was not in the best interest of the company *because earnings from the sale of mopeds was substantially lower than it was from the sale of motorcycles*." At first blush the sentences look similar, but the key difference is that the first sentence requires the reader to provide the link of why the fact establishes the rule (the moped plant is less lucrative than the motorcycle plant, and making less money is not in Motco's best interest); the second sentence explains to the reader the significance of the fact pursuant to the rule so the reader need not provide his own reasoning.

Note the areas highlighted in **bold** on the corresponding grid. The bold areas highlight the issues, analysis, and conclusions that are likely **required** to receive a passing score on this question. In general, the essay grids are provided to assist you in analyzing the essays, and are much more detailed than what a student should create during the exam to organize their response to a question.

Issue	Rule	Fact Application	Conclusion
Pat v. Carl			
Shareholder derivative suit	**A shareholder may bring a derivative suit** on behalf of the corporation for harm done to the corporation. The shareholder bringing the suit must own stock and first make a demand of the directors to redress the injury, unless doing so would be futile.	Pat is a minority shareholder and is entitled to bring a derivative suit on behalf of Motco for the injuries inflicted to the company by Carl, the new directors, and Bigco. Pat may bring suit without making a demand on the board since doing so would be futile here in light of the looting allegations and duty violations of the directors (see below).	Pat may file a shareholders derivative suit.
Controlling shareholder—sale to a looter	**Traditionally a shareholder did not owe a fiduciary duty** to the corporation or shareholder. **Modern trend: Controlling shareholders (those w/enough voting strength to have a substantial impact on the corporation) owe a fiduciary duty** to the corp. and other shareholders. **Looters: Controlling shareholders have a fiduciary duty not to sell a controlling block or shares if he knows or has reason to know that purchaser intends to injure the corporation.**	**Carl is a controlling shareholder since he owned 30% of Motco stock and no other shareholder owned more than 2% of Motco's stock.** In addition, Carl had enough power to make all nine directors resign, so he clearly had voting strength to have a substantial impact on the corporation. **As a controlling shareholder, Carl has a fiduciary duty to Motco and the other shareholders.** **Rich is the sole owner of Bigco and Bigco bought all of Carl's stock, giving Bigco a controlling interest in Motco. Before the sale, Carl received a letter from the president of one of the three failed companies recently purchased by Bigco that alleged "looting," and this gave Carl reason to know that Bigco might injure Motco.** A reasonable investigation would have revealed that a court held Bigco liable for the wrongful diversion of assets of all three companies about which Carl was warned. However, **Carl made no investigation** and relied blindly on assurances from Rich, who had an obvious prejudice, that the letter writer was a disgruntled former employee. **Carl breached his fiduciary duty not to sell his controlling interest to Rich, a known looter.**	**Carl is liable for breaching fiduciary duty.**

Continued >

Issue	Rule	Fact Application	Conclusion
Controlling shareholder—sale of shares at a premium	**Sale of controlling shares at a premium is:** • Permissible if in good faith and is fair. • **Not allowed** if receiving personal benefit for the **sale of a corporate asset or corporate office.**	**Carl was paid a large premium for his shares: $14 over trading value. In exchange, Carl agreed and "undertook to ensure" that all nine directors resigned and that Bigco received majority control of the board of directors.** Carl received compensation by way of the premium for selling the corporate office. **Carl must reimburse Motco for the premium he received.**	**Carl is liable to Motco for the premium he received for the controlling stock**
Pat v. Motco			
Director's duty of care	**A director or officer owes the corporation a duty of care to act as a reasonably prudent person would act under similar circumstances.** **The business judgment rule provides that the directors must manage the corporation in good faith** and **in the best interests of the corporation** and its shareholders.	**Converting a successful motorcycle plant into a moped plant is unreasonable and not in the best interest of the corporation** and does not show due care or good faith, **especially in light of recent adverse publicity over moped accidents, which shows that this change was unsound.** **Motco would argue that it acted to provide an outlet for moped parts manufactured by another of its corporations.** However, **this argument will be unsuccessful because the action is not in the best interest of the Motco corporation.** Motco's earnings from the sale of mopeds are substantially lower than from the sale of motorcycles. **Motco's new directors** acted in bad faith to benefit Rich's corporate interests at the expense of Motco's motorcycle business and are **liable for Motco's losses.**	**Directors breached the duty of care**

Continued >

Issue	Rule	Fact Application	Conclusion
Director's duty of loyalty	**Director owes a duty of loyalty to the corporation.** A director must put the interests of the corporation above his own interests.	A director may not serve his own interests over the company. **Motco's board acted to benefit Rich's interests in another of his companies by converting the plant from motorcycles to mopeds to provide a market for his moped parts.** It is unclear if directors directly profited, but **appointment as directors is dependent on Rich** and, impliedly, the directors have an interest in promoting Rich's other business enterprises. **The directors breached their duty of loyalty.**	**Directors breached the duty of loyalty**
Pat v. Bigco			
Controlling shareholder duties	A controlling shareholder can't use the position to gain a personal benefit at the expense of the other shareholders.	Bigco (owned by Rich) bought Carl's stock to become Motco's controlling shareholder. **Rich then had Motco's original board of directors removed and elected a new board of directors who appear to act at Rich's direction and in benefit of Rich's personal interests, to the detriment of the minority shareholders, such as with the moped plant conversion that resulted in a loss.**	**Bigco is liable for losses**
Recovery	**In a shareholder derivative suit, the corporation receives the recovery, if any, and the shareholder is entitled to reimbursement for the expenses of litigation.**	Pat filed the derivative suit for the benefit of Motco. Any recovery of losses goes to Motco. Pat may recover for her reasonable expenses of litigation.	**Recovery goes to Motco and Pat receives expenses**

Business Associations Question 1 Sample Answer

July 1998, Question 5

Pat v. Carl

Shareholder Derivative Suit

A shareholder may bring a derivative suit on behalf of the corporation for harm that has been done to the corporation itself. The shareholder bringing the suit must own stock at the time the claim arose and at the time of litigation. Further, the shareholder must make a demand on the directors to redress the injury, unless doing so would be futile.

Pat is a minority shareholder of Motco with a 1% interest and is thus entitled to bring a derivative suit on behalf of Motco for any injuries inflicted to the company by Carl, the former majority shareholder, the new directors, and Bigco, the new majority shareholder. Pat may bring suit without making a demand on the board since doing so would be futile here in light of the looting allegations and violations of duty made by the directors (see below).

Controlling Shareholder—Sale to a Looter

Traditionally a shareholder did not owe a fiduciary duty to the corporation or shareholders. However, modernly a controlling shareholder does owe a fiduciary duty to the corporation and to the other shareholders. A controlling shareholder is one with enough voting strength to have a substantial impact on the corporation.

Carl was a controlling shareholder of Motco since he owned 30% of Motco stock and no other shareholder owned more than 2% of Motco's stock. In addition, Carl had enough power to make all nine directors resign, so he clearly had the voting strength to have a substantial impact on the corporation. As a controlling shareholder Carl has a fiduciary duty to Motco and the other shareholders.

Controlling shareholders have a fiduciary duty not to sell a controlling block or shares if he knows or has reason to know that purchaser intends to injure the corporation.

Rich is the sole owner of Bigco and Bigco bought all of Carl's stock, giving Bigco a 30% controlling interest in Motco. Prior to the sale, Carl received a letter from the president of one of three failed companies that had recently been purchased by Bigco. The letter accused Rich and Bigco of "looting" the other companies after Bigco acquired them. This correspondence gave Carl reason to know that Bigco might injure Motco by looting it in a similar fashion to the other three companies. Had Carl undertaken a reasonable investigation, it would have revealed that a court had held Bigco liable for the wrongful diversion of assets in all three companies about which Carl was warned. However, Carl made no investigation and instead merely asked Rich about the accusation. Carl failed to make a sufficient inquiry and relied blindly on assurances from Rich, who had an obvious prejudice, that the letter writer was simply a disgruntled former employee. Carl breached his fiduciary duty not to sale his controlling interest to Rich, a known looter.

Controlling Shareholder—Sale of Shares at a Premium

A majority shareholder may sell controlling shares at a premium so long as it is done in good faith and is fair. However, it is not permissible to sell a controlling share at a premium price to receive a personal benefit in exchange for the sale of a corporate asset or corporate office.

Carl was paid a large premium for his shares: $25 per share when the shares were trading at $11, which is a substantial $14 over trading value. In exchange for selling his interest in Motco, Carl agreed and "undertook to ensure" that all nine directors on the board resigned and that Bigco's nominees would replace them, giving Bigco majority control of the board of directors. Carl received compensation by way of the premium that was paid in exchange for selling the corporate office by means of installing nine new directors. Carl must reimburse Motco for the premium he received.

Pat v. Motco

Director's Duty of Care

A director owes the corporation a duty of care to act as a reasonably prudent person would act under similar circumstances. The business judgment rule provides that the directors must manage the corporation in good faith and in the best interests of the corporation and its shareholders.

Motco had been engaged in the successful business of manufacturing high-priced motorcycles. Once the new board of directors was installed, they voted unanimously to convert the successful motorcycle plant into a moped manufacturing plant. The board's action of converting a successful motorcycle plant to a less successful moped plant was not in the best interest of the company because earnings from the sale of mopeds was substantially lower than it was from the sale of motorcycles. This decision was unreasonable and not in the best interest of the corporation and does not demonstrate due care or good faith, especially in light of recent adverse publicity over moped accidents, which shows that this change was unsound since the demand for mopeds would likely decrease even further. Motco may argue that it acted to provide an outlet for moped parts manufactured by another of its corporations. However, this argument will be unsuccessful because the change in corporate purpose is not in the best interest of Motco. Further, Motco's earnings from the sale of mopeds are substantially lower than from the sale of motorcycles. Motco's new directors acted in bad faith by benefiting Rich's other corporate interests at the expense of Motco's motorcycle business and thus are liable for Motco's losses.

Director's Duty of Loyalty

A director owes a duty of loyalty to the corporation and may not serve his own interests over the interests of the company. Motco's board acted not to benefit Motco, but to benefit Rich's interests in another of his companies by converting the Motco plant from building motorcycles to building mopeds, and this was done to provide a market for moped parts which were supplied by another one of Rich's companies. It isn't clear if the directors directly profited in some way by taking this action—for example, if they were also on the board of the moped part company. However, each of their appointments as a Motco director is dependent on Rich since he ensured they would be placed on Motco's board and it at least appears that the directors are serving a self-interest by promoting Rich's other business enterprises. The directors breached their duty of loyalty and are liable for Motco's losses.

Pat v. Bigco

Controlling Shareholder Duties

A controlling shareholder can't use the controlling position to gain a personal benefit at the expense of the other shareholders.

Bigco, which is owned by Rich, bought Carl's stock, making Bigco the controlling shareholder of Motco. Rich then had Motco's original board of directors removed and elected a new board of directors of his choosing who appear to act at Rich's direction and for the benefit of Rich's personal interests, to the detriment of Motco and the minority shareholders, such as with the moped plant conversion, which resulted in financial losses for Motco. Bigco is in breach and is liable for Motco's losses.

Recovery

In a shareholder derivative suit the corporation receives the recovery, if any, and the shareholder is entitled to reimbursement for the expenses incurred in litigation.

Pat filed the derivative suit for the benefit of Motco. Any recovered losses go to Motco. Pat may recover for her reasonable expenses of litigation.

Business Associations Question 2

July 2010, Question 4

Alfred, Beth, and Charles orally agreed to start ABC Computers ("ABC"), a business to manufacture and sell computers. Alfred contributed $100,000 to ABC, stating to Beth and Charles that he wanted to limit his liability to that amount. Beth, who had technical expertise, contributed $50,000 to ABC. Charles contributed no money to ABC but agreed to act as salesperson. Alfred, Beth, and Charles agreed that Beth would be responsible for designing the computers, and that Charles alone would handle all computer sales.

ABC opened and quickly became successful, primarily due to Charles' effective sales techniques.

Subsequently, without the knowledge or consent of Alfred or Charles, Beth entered into a written sales contract in ABC's name with Deco, Inc. ("Deco") to sell computers manufactured by ABC at a price that was extremely favorable to Deco. Beth's sister owned Deco. When Alfred and Charles became aware of the contract, they contacted Deco and informed it that Beth had no authority to enter into sales contracts, and that ABC could not profitably sell computers at the price agreed to by Beth. ABC refused to deliver the computers, and Deco sued ABC for breach of contract.

Thereafter, Alfred became concerned about how Beth and Charles were managing ABC. He contacted Zeta, Inc. ("Zeta"), ABC's components supplier. He told Zeta's president, "Don't allow Charles to order components; he's not our technical person. That's Beth's job."

Charles later placed an order for several expensive components with Zeta. ABC refused to pay for the components, and Zeta sued ABC for breach of contract.

Not long afterwards, ABC went out of business, owing its creditors over $500,000.

1. How should ABC's debt be allocated? Discuss.
2. Is Deco likely to succeed in its lawsuit against ABC? Discuss.
3. Is Zeta likely to succeed in its lawsuit against ABC? Discuss.

Business Associations Question 2 Assessment

July 2010, Question 4

This essay question covers the business association of a partnership. In addition to the business association of a corporation, which has been tested on the California bar exam for many years, in 2007 the business associations of agency and partnership were added to the list of subjects eligible for testing. Since agency and partnership have only been eligible for testing for a few years, there are not very many practice essay questions available covering these subjects. (Question 5 in the crossover chapter also covers partnership principles.)

Partnership has only been tested twice since it was added to the California bar exam in 2007 so it's somewhat difficult to predict which topics are more frequently tested. However, in other states that test partnership, 90% of the time the exams focus on general partnerships, so there's a good chance the topic of general partnerships will be a heavily tested topic in California also.

This question focuses on a general partnership and includes issues relating to the authority of the partners to bind the partnership, the partner's fiduciary duties to the partnership, and the allocation of debts and priority of distribution when a partnership dissolves. There are many facts available to use in the analysis.

Agency has not been tested in depth since it was added as a subject in 2007. However, agency principles have come up in the context of a corporation or a partnership question, since the director of a corporation, and a partner of a partnership also have an agency relationship to the entity.

Note the areas highlighted in **bold** on the corresponding grid. The bold areas highlight the issues, analysis, and conclusions that are likely **required** to receive a passing score on this question.

Issue	Rule	Fact Application	Conclusion
Call #1			
General partnership	**A partnership is an association of two or more persons to carry on as co-owners of a business for profit. No formalities are required** and its existence is determined by the intent of the parties.	**No formalities were followed** when A, B, and C "orally agreed" to start ABC Computers, a business to manufacture and sell computers, so **it cannot be a corporation since articles of incorporation must be filed with the state.** A contributed $100,000, B contributed $50,000, and C contributed his services as a salesperson in exchange for a share of the profits, though it is unclear what profit sharing arrangement there was. **A, B, and C most likely formed a general partnership when they agreed to start ABC Computers since they formed a business to make a profit.**	**General partnership**
Partnership debt allocation	**General partners are personally liable for the debts of the partnership.** **Profits are shared equally and losses are shared in the same proportion as profits in the absence of a contrary agreement.** **Each partner is an agent of the corporation and all partners are jointly and severally liable for partnership debt.** **Assets are distributed in the following order:** 1. **Creditors.** 2. Partner loans. 3. **Capital contributions by partners.** 4. **Profits and surplus, if any remain, are shared equally among the partners unless there is an agreement otherwise.**	Since there is no specific profit sharing agreement, it is presumed that profits are shared equally. Losses are shared in the same proportion as profits, so they will also be shared equally here. **A may assert he tried to limit his liability to his initial $100,000 contribution, however for that to be effective he would have had to properly file the corporation as a limited partnership, LLP or LLC with the state. Since he did not do that, he will be considered a general partner for purposes of determining profits and losses. Further, A was actively involved in the management of the company. A will be considered a general partner.** **After paying off any creditors, A's capital contribution of $100,000 and B's of $50,000 would be repaid. Since C performed services instead of making a capital contribution, and partners are not entitled to compensation for their services, C would not receive money for his capital contribution. If any funds remain, they would be split equally among A, B, and C.**	

Continued >

Issue	Rule	Fact Application	Conclusion
Call #2			
Authority to enter into agreement	**Each partner is an agent of the partnership for the purpose of conducting its business.** Actual authority exists where the partner reasonably believes he has authority to act based on the partnership agreement or a vote by the partners, the partnership will be bound. **Apparent authority allows any partner to act to carry out ordinary partnership business and doing so will bind the partnership.** Except if the partner had no authority to act for the partnership in the matter and the third party actually knew or received proper notice that the partner lacked such authority.	To prevail for breach of contract, Deco will need to establish that B was authorized to bind the partnership. **Typically, all partners are authorized agents.** When A and C learned of the Deco contract that was very favorable to Deco, which is owned by B's sister, they informed Deco that B had no authority to enter into the contract, and refused to deliver the computers. A, B, and C agreed informally that B would design computers and C alone would handle all sales. **B would not have actual authority here since she knew that C alone would handle sales.** **Although the parties agreed to delegate tasks in this way, there was no agreement that limited the partners' authority to act on behalf of ABC. B likely at least had the apparent authority to enter into the Deco contract.** Since B is an active partner, she would seem to **have the authority to carry out ordinary partnership business,** such as selling computers, which is their business. Any limitation on B's authority was unknown to Deco so ABC will be bound on the Deco contract.	ABC will be bound to the Deco contract
Breach of duty of good faith and loyalty	**Partners have the fiduciary duties** of good faith, **loyalty,** and due care. **The duty of loyalty requires a partner to put partnership interests over his own interests. No self-dealing,** usurping a partnership opportunity, competing with the partnership, or making secret profits **is permitted.**	**B contracted with Deco, a company owned by her sister, at terms that were extremely favorable to Deco. This is a form of self-dealing because B put her own interests, in this case her familial interests, over the best interests of ABC, since the contract prevented ABC from making a profit. B's contract did not put the partnership interests first** and was not made in good faith since B knew only C was to make sales contracts. **B is likely liable for breach of the duty of good faith and loyalty.**	

Continued >

Issue	Rule	Fact Application	Conclusion
Call #3			
Authority	**Apparent authority allows any partner to act to carry out ordinary partnership business, and doing so will bind the partnership.** Except if the partner had no authority to act for the partnership in the matter and the third party actually knew or received proper notice that the partner lacked such authority.	While B is supposed to be in charge of designing the computers and C is to be in charge of sales, **since ABC has no formal agreements, each partner may share equally in the management duties and each partner has the authority to bind the partnership.** As an active partner, **C has the apparent authority to bind ABC,** at the very least. A has attempted to unilaterally limit C's ability to enter into contracts on behalf of ABC because of his concern over B and C's management, but **A does not have the authority to revoke C's power of authority.** A may have tried to put Zeta on notice that C lacked authority to contract, but his attempt was unsuccessful because A did not have the authority to revoke C's authority. Further, there is no indication that B agreed with him. In any event, ABC will be bound to the Zeta contract.	**A may not revoke C's authority**

Business Associations Question 2 Sample Answer

July 2010, Question 4

1. Debt Allocation

General Partnership

A partnership is an association of two or more persons to carry on as co-owners of a business for profit. No formalities are required to create a partnership and its existence is determined by the intent of the parties.

At the start of ABC Computers (ABC), A contributed $100,000, B contributed $50,000, and C contributed his services as a salesperson in exchange for a share of the profits, though it is unclear what profit-sharing arrangement there was between the parties. No formalities were followed when A, B, and C "orally agreed" to start ABC, a business to manufacture and sell computers. ABC cannot be a corporation since formalities must be followed to start a corporation, including that an articles of incorporation must be filed with the state, which was not done here. A, B, and C most likely formed a general partnership when they agreed to start ABC since they formed a business to make a profit.

Partnership Debt Allocation

General partners are personally liable for the debts of the partnership. Profits are shared equally and losses are shared in the same proportion as profits in the absence of a contrary agreement. Since there is no specific profit-sharing agreement for ABC, it is presumed that profits are shared equally. Losses are shared in the same proportion as profits so they will also be shared equally here.

Each partner is considered an agent of the corporation, and all partners are jointly and severally liable for all partnership debt. A may assert he tried to limit his liability to his initial $100,000 contribution since at the formation of the business he stated that fact to B and C, though he was actively involved in the management of the company. However, such an agreement will not be effective unless he properly filed the corporation as a limited partnership with the state. A LLP or LLC may have accomplished the same thing, but all forms of business entity that limit partner/owner liability require a special filing of some form with the state, which was not done here. A will be considered a general partner for purposes of determining profits and losses.

At dissolution of a partnership, the assets are distributed in the following order: first, creditors are repaid; then partner loans are repaid; then capital contributions by partners are returned; and last, if any profits and surplus remain, they are shared equally among the partners unless there is an agreement otherwise.

After paying off any creditors, A's capital contribution of $100,000, and B's capital contribution of $50,000 would be repaid. Since C performed sales services instead of making a capital contribution, and partners are not entitled to compensation for their services performed on behalf of the partnership, C would not receive money for his capital contribution. If any profits or surplus remain after the creditors are paid and A's and B's capital contributions are repaid, it would be split equally among A, B, and C.

2. Deco v. ABC

Authority to Enter into Agreement

Each partner is an agent of the partnership for the purpose of conducting partnership business. Actual authority exists where the partner reasonably believes he has authority to act based on the partnership agreement or a vote by the partners, and the partnership will be bound.

To prevail for breach of contract Deco will need to establish that B was authorized to bind the partnership to the contract. Typically, all partners are authorized agents of the partnership. A and C learned of the Deco contract entered into by B that was very favorable to Deco, and unfavorable to ABC. Further, B's sister is the owner of Deco. Subsequently, A and C informed Deco that B had no authority to enter into the contract and refused to deliver the computers pursuant to the contract.

A, B, and C agreed that B would design computers and C alone would handle all sales. B did not have actual express authority to enter into a sales contract since she knew that C alone would handle sales.

Apparent authority allows any partner to act to carry out ordinary partnership business and doing so will bind the partnership, except if the partner had no authority to act for the partnership in the matter and the third party actually knew or received proper notice that the partner lacked such authority.

Although the parties informally agreed to delegate tasks in a particular way, there was no agreement that limited the partners' authority. B likely at least had the apparent authority to enter into the Deco contract. Since B is a managing partner she would seem to have the authority to carry out ordinary partnership business, such as selling computers, which is ABC's business. Any limitation on B's authority was unknown to Deco so ABC will be bound on the Deco contract.

Breach of Duty of Good Faith

Partners have the fiduciary duties of good faith, loyalty, and due care. The duty of loyalty requires putting partnership interests over the partner's own interests. A partner may not engage is self-dealing, usurping a partnership opportunity, competing with the partnership, or making secret profits.

B contracted with Deco, a company owned by her sister, at terms that were extremely favorable to Deco and so unfavorable to ABC that ABC was unable to make a profit on the contract. This is a form of self-dealing because B put her own personal interests, in this case her familial interests, over the best interests of ABC, since the contract prevented ABC from making a profit. The contract B negotiated with Deco did not put the interest of the partnership first. Further, this contract was not made in good faith since B knew that only C was to make the sales contracts and her role was to design the computers. B is liable for the breach of the duty of good faith and loyalty.

3. Zeta v. ABC

Authority

Apparent authority allows any partner to act to carry out ordinary partnership business and doing so will bind the partnership, except if the partner had no authority to act for the partnership in the matter and the third party actually knew or received proper notice that the partner lacked such authority.

While B was supposed to be in charge of designing the computers and C was to be in charge of sales, since ABC has no formal agreements, each partner may share equally in the management duties and each partner has the authority to bind the partnership. As an active partner, C has the apparent authority to bind ABC, at the very least, for a contract that appears to be in the course of ordinary business, such as the Zeta contract for computer components. After the fact, A has attempted to unilaterally limit C's ability to enter into contracts on behalf of ABC because of his concern over B and C's management of ABC, but A does not have the authority to revoke C's power of authority. One partner may not unilaterally revoke another partner's authority. A may have tried to put Zeta on notice that C lacked authority to contract, but his attempt was unsuccessful because A did not have the authority to revoke C's authority since each partner is entitled to equal control of the partnership. Further, there is no indication that B agreed with him, or that the issue was put to partnership vote, or the subject of any agreement. In any event, ABC will be bound to the Zeta contract.

Business Associations Question 3

February 1987, Question 1

Acquirer, Inc. (Aco) and Target, Inc. (Tco) are corporations. All sales and purchases described below were conducted through a national stock exchange.

On December 1, 1986, Aco bought 120,000 Tco shares for $5 per share, thereby becoming a 12 percent Tco shareholder. Aco never previously owned any Tco stock. Aco immediately notified Tco's chief executive officer, Dan, that it had made the purchase and that it was considering a tender offer for the rest of Tco's stock at $9 per share.

The next day, Dan's personal lawyer, Len, warned Dan not to buy Tco stock until Aco's stock purchase and acquisition plans became public. On the same day, Dan told his son, Sam, about the proposed acquisition. On December 3, 1986, Len and Sam each bought 10,000 Tco shares for $5 per share.

On December 4, 1986, Aco filed appropriate disclosure documents with the Securities and Exchange Commission (SEC), and Aco and Tco separately issued press releases about the stock purchase and the proposed acquisition.

On December 5, 1986, Len and Sam each sold their 10,000 Tco shares for $8.50 per share. Aco sold its Tco shares for $9 per share on February 15, 1987.

Dan has neither sold not purchased any Tco stock since he learned of the acquisition plan.

1. What, if any, are the liabilities of Aco under SEC rule 16(b)? Discuss.
2. What, if any, are the liabilities of Dan under SEC rule 10b-5? Discuss.
3. What, if any, are the liabilities of Sam under SEC rule 10b-5? Discuss.
4. What, if any, are the liabilities of Len under SEC rule 10b-5? Discuss.

Business Associations Question 3 Assessment

February 1987, Question 1

This is another business association question that focuses on corporation issues. However, this question addresses issues concerning the federal securities laws of sections 16(b) and 10b-5.

The first call concerns a fairly simple application of the facts to a potential violation of the federal security law 16(b). However, it does test a more intricate part of the rule pertaining to 10% shareholders. As in contracts questions, it can also be important in a corporations question to pay attention to the dates. For example, the chronological timeline can be important relative to the six-month short-swing profit rule, as it is in this question.

The rest of the question concerns the federal securities law of 10b-5. There are facts that raise the issue of direct liability under 10b-5, tipper liability, and tippee liability. It is not uncommon to see a fact pattern like this where multiple facets of the 10b-5 rule are explored. For 10b-5 there is a two-step analysis: 1) Determine if the party is in a position to be liable under 10b-5 as a direct insider, tipper, tippee, or misappropriator; and 2) establish the prima facie case. A party may be potentially subject to 10b-5 liability in more than one way—for example, as both a tippee and a tipper; or as direct violator and as a tipper, as is the case in this question. It is important to analyze each potential violation separately. Also, look for multiple parties in the question to violate 10b-5, such as in this question where Dan, Sam, and Len each potentially have liability under 10b-5. The key to successful analysis is identifying the factual nuances that may lead to a different outcome under application of the rule. For example, the insider, Dan, who was the corporate CEO, shared information about a pending tender offer with both his son, Sam, and his personal lawyer, Len. While Dan did not himself trade by using the insider information, both his son and his lawyer did. The outcomes are different based on the different fiduciary positions the son and lawyer occupy in relation to the corporate insider, Dan.

The subject of business associations often crosses over with professional responsibility. Although the bar examiners didn't ask about the lawyer's ethical violations in this question, they could have since the two subjects logically intersect whenever a lawyer is one of the parties involved in a business associations essay question.

Note the areas highlighted in **bold** on the corresponding grid. The bold areas highlight the issues, analysis, and conclusions that are likely **required** to receive a passing score on this question.

Issue	Rule	Fact Application	Conclusion
Call #1			
Aco's 16(b) liability	**Any short-swing trading profits received within a six-month period by a corporate insider must be disgorged to the corporation.** Corporate insiders include shareholders owning 10% or more equity stock in the corporation. 10% shareholders must be in that position at the time of both the purchase and the sale of the shares.	**Tco stock is traded on the national exchange so the federal securities laws apply.** Aco bought 120,000 shares on December 1, 1986, and sold the 120,000 shares on February 15, 1987, for a profit of $4 per share. **Aco's purchase made it a 10% shareholder of Tco.** The purchase and sale did occur within a six-month period. However, Aco previously never owned any Tco stock prior to the purchase on December 1st and **thus was not a 10% shareholder at the time of both the purchase** and the subsequent sale, as is required for 16(b) to impose liability. Consequently, **Aco does not have liability under 16(b).**	**No 16(b) liability**
Call #2			
Dan's 10b-5 direct liability **Dan's tipper liability under 10b-5**	**Trading securities based on nonpublic corporate information is not permitted.** **Section 10b-5 provides liability for any person who employs fraud or deception in connection with the purchase or sale of any security** by means of any instrumentality of interstate commerce. Establishing fraud requires a showing of: • **Intent** to defraud • **Material misrepresentation or omission (one that a reasonable investor would consider important)**	**Dan is Tco's CEO** and he had **material corporate information** about the pending tender offer, but **since Dan never bought or sold any Tco stock trading on his insider knowledge, he cannot be directly liable under 10b-5.** **However, Dan may be liable under 10b-5 as a "tipper" for sharing inside information with Sam and Len.** Both **bought stock at a price of $5 per share knowing of a potential tender offer of $9 per share, which is material information any reasonable investor would consider important.** Reliance is presumed with a material omission. The trades were made using an instrumentality of interstate commerce since they were made on the national exchange.	**No 10b-5 liability** Probably no liability for Len **Possible liability for Sam**

Continued >

Issue	Rule	Fact Application	Conclusion
	• **Reliance** on the representation/omission • **Purchase or sale of securities** • Use of interstate commerce • **Damages** **An insider** is a director, officer, shareholder, or any other holder of **material nonpublic corporate information.** **A tipper (one providing information) is liable if the information was shared for the improper purpose of direct or indirect personal gain.**	**It appears that Dan told his personal lawyer Len about the acquisition in the course of obtaining legal advice, which is not an improper purpose, though it may have been imprudent to share the information with his personal attorney rather than a corporate attorney. Since Len warned Dan not to trade and Len had a duty of confidentiality Dan would have had a reasonable expectation that Len would not use the confidential information to make an improper trade for his own benefit.** However, **Dan likely did not have a proper purpose for recklessly sharing the insider information with his son, Sam.** Dan may have intended the information as a gift since **Dan knew that the stock price would raise to $9 from $5 a share, which any reasonable investor would consider important information.** But, Dan did not advise his son to purchase stock, and it is unclear if Dan disclosed with the intent to obtain direct or indirect personal gain. However, **there was really no proper purpose for sharing the private nonpublic information. If it can be proven Dan told Sam about the sale for his or for his son's benefit, Dan is liable under 10b-5 as a tipper** ($8.50 − $5.00 × 10,000 shares traded = $35,000 to return to Tco). [This section could have been organized in several ways.]	**No 10b-5 liability** Probably no liability for Len **Possible liability for Sam**

Continued >

Issue	Rule	Fact Application	Conclusion
Call #3			
Sam's 10b-5 liability	**A tippee (one receiving insider information) is liable only if scienter is present where the tipper breached a fiduciary duty and the tippee knew the duty had been breached.**	**As CEO, Dan clearly has a fiduciary duty to Tco, which he breached by discussing the acquisition with his son, Sam. Sam had scienter since he likely knew his father was a CEO and that the nonpublic corporate information being shared was being done in violation of Dan's fiduciary duty to Tco.** This is further established by the large size of the investment ($50,000) and timing (one day later.) **Sam is in violation of 10b-5 as a "tippee" and must be disgorged of the $35,000 profit he received** ($8.50 – $5.00 × 10,000 shares traded). Dan and Sam are both liable for insider trading regarding Sam's purchase, but Tco can only recover once.	Sam is liable for profits
Call #4			
Len's 10b-5 liability	A misappropriator **(one obtaining corporate private information through other means) may be in breach of a duty owed to the source of the information.**	**Len is likely not liable under 10b-5 as a tippee because Dan did not likely breach a fiduciary duty by discussing private corporate information with his lawyer, Len.** **However, Len is liable under 10b-5** as a misappropriator **since Len breached his own fiduciary duty to Dan by using confidential client information for his own personal benefit.** As a lawyer, Len was in a fiduciary relationship with Dan and he violated that duty by using Dan's private information for his own private gain. **Len is liable for the profits he made on the sales and must disgorge them.**	**Len is liable for profits**

Business Associations Question 4

February 2002, Question 3

Acme Corporation was a publicly traded corporation that operated shopping malls. Because of an economic slowdown, many of Acme's malls contained unrented commercial space. Additionally, the existence of surplus retail space located near many of Acme's malls prevented Acme from raising rents despite increasing costs incurred by Acme.

In June 2001, Sally, president and sole owner of Bigco, approached Paul, Acme's president. She proposed a cash-out merger, in which Bigco would purchase for cash all shares of Acme, and Acme would merge into Bigco. Sally offered $100 for each outstanding share of Acme's stock even though Acme's stock was then currently trading at $50 per share and historically had never traded higher than $60 per share.

Paul, concerned about Acme's future, decided in good faith to pursue the merger. In July 2001, before discussing the deal with anyone, Paul telephoned his broker and purchased 5000 shares of Acme at $50 per share. Paul then presented the proposed merger to Acme's board of directors and urged them to approve it. The board met, discussed the difference between the current market share price and the offered price, and, without commissioning a corporate valuation study, voted to submit the proposed deal to a shareholder vote. The shareholders overwhelmingly approved the deal because of the immediate profit they would realize on their shares. Based solely on shareholder approval, the board unanimously approved the merger, and all shareholders received cash for their shares.

In December 2001, shortly after completing the merger, Bigco closed most of the Acme malls and sold the properties at a substantial profit to a developer who intended to develop it for light industrial use.

1. Did Paul violate any federal securities laws? Discuss.
2. Did Paul breach any duties to Acme and/or its shareholders? Discuss.
3. Did the board breach any duties to Acme and/or its shareholders? Discuss.

Business Associations Question 4 Assessment

February 2002, Question 3

This business associations question covers the common corporations topics of the federal securities laws and the duties of care and loyalty.

The first two calls of the question deal with Acme's president, Paul, and his liabilities under the securities laws, 16(b) and 10b-5, and the breach of his fiduciary duties of due care and loyalty. The first call does not pose much difficulty since the facts relating to the securities violations are straightforward. Paul clearly received short-swing profits, and engaged in insider trading, so analyzing these issues is simply a matter of identifying the proper rules and the applicable facts to establish each element.

The second call deals with Paul's breach of fiduciary duties. The factual analysis is more nuanced here because while Paul acted in good faith, and the proposed merger was beneficial to the corporation, he still is likely in breach of the duty of due care because he encouraged the board to jump at what looked like a good deal without fact checking or making a reasonable investigation. The merger deal was good for Acme, but a reasonable investigation would have revealed a much better deal. Paul is also liable for the breach of the duty of loyalty because of his own considerable interest in the outcome of the merger deal because of the insider trading in which he had engaged. These two issues often arise in an essay question as an issues cluster so be on the lookout since insider trading often leads to a breach of the duty of loyalty.

The third call requires an analysis of the same facts and fiduciary duties, but on behalf of the board that went along with Paul's recommendation and approved the merger. Again, while the board can rely on some representations of the president, they are required to do what is in the best interests of the corporation and as such should have also investigated further. The facts indicate that the shareholders approved the board action, but approval by the shareholders will never absolve the board from a breach of their fiduciary duty. The shareholders have every right to rely on the board's recommendation.

Note the areas highlighted in **bold** on the corresponding grid. The bold areas highlight the issues, analysis, and conclusions that are likely **required** to receive a passing score on this question.

Issue	Rule	Fact Application	Conclusion
Call #1: Paul			
16(b)	**Any short-swing trading profits received within a six-month period by a corporate insider must be disgorged to the corporation.** Corporate insiders are officers, directors and shareholders owning 10% or more equity stock in the corporation. Trading is making a profitable purchase and sale (or sale and purchase) of company equity stock within a six-month period.	**Paul is the president of Acme, which is a publicly traded company, and is thus a corporate officer and insider.** **Paul bought 5,000 shares in July 2001 at $50 per share.** At some point Bigco purchased all of the outstanding shares of Acme stock for $100 per share, which means that Paul would have sold his shares to Acme. **It is unclear when Bigco purchased all of the Acme shares, but all of the malls Acme owned were closed down in December 2001, which occurred after the merger** (thus, when Paul would have sold all his shares). Paul made a profit by engaging in buying and selling stock within a six-month period and is thus liable for insider trading. Paul had a short swing profit of $250,000 and **this must be disgorged to the corporation.**	**Paul is in violation of 16(b)**
10b-5	**Section 10b-5 provides liability for any person who employs fraud or deception in connection with the purchase or sale of any security by means of any instrumentality of interstate commerce.** An insider is a director, officer, shareholder, or any other holder of material nonpublic corporate information. **Establishing fraud requires a showing of**	As Acme's president, Paul held material corporate nonpublic information. Paul made use of insider information regarding the proposed buyout for his own benefit. **Paul purchased 5,000 shares of Acme stock at $50 each at a time when he knew that Bigco had offered $100 per share in a proposed cash-out merger. Paul intended to deceive since he wanted to retain the profits for himself.**	**Paul is in violation of 10b-5**

Continued >

Issue	Rule	Fact Application	Conclusion
	• **Intent to defraud** • **Material misrepresentation or omission (one that a reasonable investor would consider important)** • **Reliance on the representation/ omission** • **Purchase or sale of securities** • **Use of interstate commerce** • **Damages**	**Paul failed to disclose material private corporate insider information that any investor would consider important** when he purchased shares at a reduced price for his own benefit, which is a material omission. Paul's omission was relied on by the seller of the securities, since, had Paul disclosed the insider information as he was required to do, it is very unlikely the seller would have sold to Paul at $50 per share. The stock is traded on the national exchange **and Paul made the trade by placing a telephone call to his broker, both of which are sufficient for a finding the use of interstate commerce as required under section 10b-5.** **Paul is in violation of 10b-5 and must disgorge the profits back to the corporation.**	**Paul is in violation of 10b-5**
Call #2: Paul			
Duty of care	**A director or officer owes the corporation a duty of care to act as a reasonably prudent person would act under similar circumstances.** The **business judgment rule provides that the directors must manage the corporation in good faith and in the best interests of the corporation and its shareholders.**	**Paul is an officer and director of the corporation by virtue of his position of president and as such owes a duty of care.** Paul must manage the corporation in good faith and in the best interests of the corporation as he pursues a potential merger with Bigco. At first blush **it appears that the merger would be beneficial to Acme, a company undergoing difficult times** because of the economic slowdown, which prevents Acme from leasing all of their space or increasing rents. **Further, Paul pursued the merger in good faith.**	**Paul breached the duty of care**

Continued >

Issue	Rule	Fact Application	Conclusion
		However, it **does not appear that Paul did any fact checking or investigating of alternatives, which is what a reasonable person would do,** before taking the proposed merger to the board and urging them to approve it. In addition, **the unusually high offer price should have alerted Paul that something was suspicious** and he should have investigated further. **Had Paul investigated he may have found that there was a developer interested in the properties** and Acme could have sold the properties themselves and realized a much greater profit than the sale to Bigco generated. **Paul breached his duty of care.**	**Paul breached the duty of care**
Duty of loyalty	**A director or officer owes a duty of loyalty to the corporation.** **A director or officer has a conflict of interest when he** (or a corporation he owns or has a relationship with, or his family member) **enters into a contract with the corporation or has a beneficial financial interest in a contract.**	**Paul is required to put the needs and best interests of Acme ahead of his own interests.** Once Paul engaged in improper insider trading (above) he had a conflict of interest with the corporation. **He no longer had the ability to be objective and impartial about the proposed merger since he had invested $250,000 of his own money and had a personal interest in the outcome.** **Paul is in breach of the duty of loyalty.**	**Paul breached the duty of loyalty**
Call #3: Board			
Duty of care	See above	**The board has the same fiduciary duties to the corporation and shareholders that an individual director or officer has. A reasonably prudent person would have investigated the proposed merger opportunity before signing off on it based solely on Paul's representations and urgings.** There are no facts to suggest that Paul is an expert in this area. **The board failed to commission a corporate valuation study or consider any alternatives, even after noticing the discrepancy between the offered price of $100 per share and the current value of $50 per share, which at the least should have made them suspicious.**	**The board breached the duty of care**

Continued >

Issue	Rule	Fact Application	Conclusion
		The shareholders approved the corporate action of the merger, but this does not relieve the directors of their duty of care. The shareholders are permitted to rely on the recommendation of the board, which they did here. **The board breached its duty of care.**	**The board breached the duty of care**
Duty of loyalty	See above	The board may have a conflict of interest and be engaged in self-dealing if the board members were also shareholders, though the facts do not indicate they were. **Unless they had a personal interest in the transaction, the board members are not in breach of the duty of loyalty.**	The board may have breached the duty of loyalty

Business Associations Question 5

February 1999, Question 4

Rentco, a corporation, develops and leases office buildings. Rentco's issued and outstanding shares are equally divided among Al, an attorney, Bob, president of Bank, and Carl. Rentco's three directors are Al, Bob, and Ed, who is not a shareholder. Al is also Rentco's general counsel.

The Rentco board has decided to have Rentco purchase The Plaza, an office building with highly marketable office space. At the board meeting where the decision was made, Bob was assigned the task of negotiating the purchase of The Plaza.

After the meeting, Bob discovered that Bank holds the present mortgage on The Plaza. $300,000 remains due on the mortgage loan, which is in default. Bob so advised Al and requested that Al do the legal work to foreclose the mortgage for Bank and also to form Diverco, a close corporation in which Bob will be sole shareholder. Al completed both tasks. Bob had not told Al that Bob planned to have Diverco purchase The Plaza at Bank's foreclosure sale.

At the foreclosure sale, Bob caused Diverco to purchase The Plaza for $300,000, which satisfied Bank's unpaid debt. The current market value of The Plaza is approximately $600,000.

At the next Rentco director's meeting, Bob falsely reported that he had negotiated a purchase price of $600,000 for the purchase of The Plaza by Rentco. None of the directors, including Al, asked any questions about the proposed purchase, and all voted to approve it. After the meeting, at Bob's request, Al prepared a standard real estate purchase agreement for The Plaza, naming Diverco as seller. After the closing, Bob dissolved Diverco.

Carl discovered the foregoing facts and, after making a demand on the directors that was rejected, filed a derivative action for damages against Rentco, Al, Bob, and Ed, claiming that the directors breached their fiduciary duties. Carl also filed a complaint about Al's conduct with the appropriate state bar disciplinary body.

1. Is Al, Bob, or Ed liable for breach of fiduciary duties as a Rentco director? Discuss.
2. What ethical duties, if any, has Al violated by his conduct? Discuss.

Business Associations Question 5 Assessment

February 1999, Question 4

This business associations question focuses on a corporation and the fiduciary duties that directors owe to the corporation. It is also a slight professional responsibility crossover question. Professional responsibility is a frequent crossover subject with business associations because it is easy to also test professional responsibility issues by making one of the parties a lawyer, as is the case in this question.

Similar to the format of many corporation questions, here you are tasked with identifying if the conduct of three different directors violated any duties owed to the corporation. One of the directors engaged in some pretty egregious self-dealing behavior, which makes the analysis of his fiduciary duties of care and loyalty pretty clear. Another director, who is also a lawyer and general counsel for the corporation (which explains how professional responsibility becomes involved) has knowledge of the egregious acts but does nothing in response. The third director has no knowledge of anything regarding the egregious acts, but does nothing affirmative to assert the interests of the corporation.

Since the duties of care and loyalty are analyzed under several different fact scenarios, you can demonstrate for the bar grader your nuanced understanding of the rules. The duty of care and the duty of loyalty are by far the most frequently tested topics in business associations, so be sure to have a good understanding of the rules pertaining to those fiduciary duties.

Note the areas highlighted in **bold** on the corresponding grid. The bold areas highlight the issues, analysis, and conclusions that are likely **required** to receive a passing score on this question.

Issue	Rule	Fact Application	Conclusion
Call #1			
Shareholder derivative suit	A shareholder may bring a derivative suit on behalf of the corporation for harm done to the corporation. The shareholder bringing the suit must own stock and first make a demand of the directors to redress the injury.	Carl's derivative suit is proper because he was a shareholder at the time fiduciary duties were breached and he made a demand of the directors first, which was rejected.	Shareholder derivative suit is proper
Al's duty of care	**A director or officer owes the corporation a duty of care to act as a reasonably prudent person would act under similar circumstances.** **The business judgment rule provides that the directors must manage the corporation in good faith and in the best interests of the corporation and its shareholders.**	**Al owed a duty of care to Rentco both as a director and as its general counsel.** Since Al is an attorney he may owe a higher standard of care because of his specialized legal knowledge. Al agreed to do legal work to foreclose on The Plaza, knowing that Rentco director, Bob, was Bank's president and that Bob potentially had a conflict of interest. Al should have inquired further about a potential conflict and disclosed this to the board. **Al should have investigated when he learned The Plaza had a $600,000 purchase price for Rentco** since he knew it sold for $300,000 in the foreclosure sale since he did the paperwork. It was **not reasonable or in the best interests of the corporation to fail to make appropriate inquiries** and approve a sale at more than twice the foreclosure price. Further, **Al should have told the other directors once he learned that Diverco was the seller of The Plaza since Al knew Bob was the sole shareholder of Diverco and that Bob was engaged in improper self-dealing.**	Breach of duty of care

Continued >

Issue	Rule	Fact Application	Conclusion
Al's duty to loyalty	**Director owes a duty of loyalty to the corporation. A director must put the interests of the corporation above his own interests.**	**Al may have received compensation for the legal work he performed for Bob so he may have put his interest in obtaining those fees ahead of Rentco's interests.** However, overall it doesn't appear that Al received any personal benefit from the Diverco deal, and probably lost money, so Al probably did not breach the duty of loyalty.	Could conclude either way
Bob's duty of care	See above	Bob, president of Bank, failed to disclose to the other Rentco directors that Bank owned the mortgage on The Plaza, despite having been tasked with negotiating the purchase of The Plaza. Bob asked Al to prepare the foreclosure documents and help him form Diverco, which he used to purchase The Plaza at the discount rate of $300,000 under market value. Further, **Bob lied, failed to disclose his own interest, and acted in his own interests and contrary to Rentco's when he then sold The Plaza to Rentco for $600,000.** Bob did not act in good faith. After The Plaza transaction was completed, he dissolved Diverco, further showing he only formed it to perpetuate this scheme. Even though $600,000 was market price, this will not prevent Bob from being in breach of the duty of care because of his deceptions and the personal profit he made at Rentco's expense. Bob has not acted in good faith or in the best interests of Rentco.	Breach of duty of care

Continued >

Issue	Rule	Fact Application	Conclusion
Bob's duty of loyalty	See above **No self-dealing allowed:** A director has a conflict of interest when he or a corporation he owns enters into a contract with the corporation or has a beneficial financial interest in a contract. **Usurp a business opportunity:** A director or officer **may not personally act on a business opportunity without first offering it to the corporation** where the corporation would expect to be presented the opportunity.	**Bob failed to disclose that Bank held The Plaza's mortgage and that it was in default, and that he owned Diverco and purchased The Plaza at a discount. Bob acted in his own self-interest when he purchased The Plaza through Diverco and then resold it to Rentco at a $300,000 profit.** **Bob personally usurped Rentco's opportunity to get a great deal on The Plaza property and failed to offer it to Rentco first** when clearly Rentco would expect to be presented with the opportunity since Bob had already been tasked with buying The Plaza. **Bob is in breach of the duty of loyalty** also and should disgorge his $300,000 profit to Rentco.	Breach of the duty of loyalty
Ed's duty of care	See above	Unlike Al, there is no evidence that Ed was aware of Bob's duplicitous actions and was not privy to the details about Diverco's purchase of The Plaza. He may assert that he relied on Bob's representations in good faith. However, it was **unreasonable for Ed to make no inquiry at all or to do any fact checking about the purchase of The Plaza, so Ed breached his duty.**	Ed probably in breach for nonfeasance
Ed's duty of loyalty	See above	**Ed is not in breach of the duty of loyalty because he received no benefits and had no conflicts with Rentco.**	No breach of loyalty

Continued >

Issue	Rule	Fact Application	Conclusion
Call #2			
Duty of loyalty/ conflict of interest	**A lawyer has a duty of loyalty to the client and must avoid conflicts of interest.**	Al had fiduciary duties as Rentco's general counsel. There was a potential conflict of interest that arose at the time **Al was asked to assist in the foreclosure of The Plaza and form Diverco for Bob since Rentco was Al's client, not Bob. Al should have recognized the conflict and disclosed it to all parties.** An actual conflict of interest occurred when Bob asked Al to prepare a standard real estate contract for The Plaza naming Diverco as the seller of The Plaza. **At this point Al should have withdrawn since the conflict was not resolvable.**	Breach of duty of loyalty
Duty of confidentiality	**A lawyer may not reveal any information about the representation of his client without consent.**	Al has performed legal work for Bob outside of his Rentco director role, and when he learned of Bob's plan to have Diverco sell The Plaza to Rentco, **Al had conflicting duties owned to Bob and Rentco. Al should have informed the parties to get independent legal counsel and withdrawn.**	Likely breach of duty of confidentiality
Duty of care/ competence	**A lawyer must represent all clients competently.**	**In failing to recognize the conflicts of interest, Al did not act as a reasonable attorney would act and breached his duty of competence.**	**Breached duty of competence**
Duty not to aid fraud	A lawyer may not aid a client in the commission of a fraud.	Since Al already knew Bob was the sole shareholder of Diverco **once he discovered that Diverco was the seller of The Plaza, Al knew Bob had defrauded Rentco and had done so through creating Diverco.** Since Al's services were used to facilitate the fraud, **Al should have withdrawn** at that time and recommended that Rentco seek independent counsel.	Al aided in the fraud

Business Associations Question 6

July 2005, Question 3

Alice is a director and Bob is a director and the President of Sportco, Inc. (SI), a sporting goods company. SI owns several retail stores. Larry, an attorney, has performed legal work for SI for ten years. Recently, Larry and Carole were made directors of SI. SI has a seven-person board of directors.

Prior to becoming a SI director, Carole had entered into a valid written contract with SI to sell a parcel of land to SI for $500,000. SI planned to build a retail store on the parcel. After becoming a director, Carole learned confidentially that her parcel of land would appreciate in value if she held it for a few years because it was located next to a planned mall development. At dinner at Larry's home, Carole told Larry about the planned mall development. Carole asked for, and obtained, Larry's legal opinion about getting out of her contract with SI. Later, based on Larry's suggestions, Carole asked Bob to have SI release her from the contract. She did not explain, nor did Bob inquire about, the reason for her request. Bob then orally released Carole from her contract with SI.

The next regular SI board meeting was attended only by Bob, Alice, and Larry. They passed a resolution to ratify Bob's oral release of Carole from her contract with SI. Larry never disclosed what Carole had told him about the proposed mall development.

Three years later, Carole sold her parcel of land for $850,000 to DevelopCo, which then resold it for $1 million to SI.

1. Was Bob's oral release of Carole from her contract with SI effective? Discuss.
2. Was the resolution passed by Bob, Alice, and Larry to ratify Bob's oral release valid? Discuss.
3. Did Carole breach any fiduciary duty to SI? Discuss.
4. Did Larry commit any ethical violation? Discuss.

Business Associations Question 6 Assessment

July 2005, Question 3

This question covers quite a few issues, including some that are frequently tested and some issues that are not frequently tested. In addition, the fourth call of the question concerns professional responsibility issues. Professional responsibility is a frequent crossover question and is often tested with business associations.

The first call of the question focuses on the authority of a corporate officer or director to take action on behalf of the corporation. The call requires a detailed discussion of the different types of corporate authority conferred, with a focus on analysis of actual authority and implied authority.

The second call of the question covers some less frequently tested topics, including the rules surrounding a quorum and the effect of a board resolution vote where one of the directors has a personal interest in the matter.

The third call of the question covers the frequently tested topics of a member of the board of director's fiduciary duties, with an emphasis on the duty of loyalty, and the various ways the duty of loyalty can be breached.

The fourth call of the question tests professional responsibility issues as noted above. In this question, one of the members of the board of directors has also acted as the corporate attorney and gave legal advice to another board member. As you can see, it is very easy to manipulate a business associations fact pattern to also test professional responsibility issues by having one of the parties be a lawyer, as was done here.

Note the areas highlighted in **bold** on the corresponding grid. The bold areas highlight the issues, analysis, and conclusions that are likely **required** to receive a passing score on this question.

Issue	Rule	Fact Application	Conclusion
Call #1: Bob's Oral Release			
Power as president	Corporate officers, such as the president, have authority to act on behalf of the corporation based on agency law principles.	The board of directors has the authority to oversee the management of a corporation and approve major business decisions. **As a director and the president of SI,** Bob orally agreed to release Carole from her contract to sell a parcel of land to SI for $500,000. Bob must have authority to take such an action.	Bob needs proper authority
Authority	**An officer's authority to bind the corporation may be express, inherent, or apparent.** **Actual express authority is authority specifically granted to the corporate officer by the corporation.** **Implied authority occurs where the corporate officer reasonably believes the board gave him authority.** Apparent authority occurs where the corporation has provided the officer with the appearance of authority, on which a third party reasonably relies.	**As president or a director, Bob has express authority to act where the board has formally conferred such authority. This authority can be provided in the articles of incorporation, corporate bylaws, or where the board of directors specifically agrees to delegate authority, but there is no evidence of that here.** The board did not know about Carole's intention to be released from the contract. **The board did not vote or grant Bob the express authority to bind the corporation in this matter. Bob did not have express authority to release Carole from her contract.**	**Bob did not have the authority to grant the oral release**

Continued >

Issue	Rule	Fact Application	Conclusion
		Bob was on the board of directors and was SI's president. **Though a director would not have implied authority to unilaterally act on behalf of the corporation, a corporate president would have the implied authority to bind (or unbind) the corporation for obligations that occur in the regular course of business. Here, SI only owns "several" sporting goods stores, and the contract in question was to purchase land for another location, so this would be a substantial corporate action. Since a land purchase was a major business decision for SI, Bob would not have the implied authority to act on behalf of SI.** It is unlikely that Bob would have the apparent authority to act here since Carole, as a board member herself, would know better than to think that Bob had the authority to bind SI and release Carole from the contract.	**Bob did not have the authority to grant the oral release**
Call #2: Board Resolution			
Quorum	**A quorum, which is a majority of the board of directors, must be present for board action to be valid. To take action a majority of those present at the meeting must agree to take the proposed action.**	**Binding board action can only be taken upon a majority vote where there is a quorum present. SI's board has seven directors, so four directors would be necessary to have a quorum. Since only three directors (Bob, Alice, and Larry) attended the meeting and voted to approve the resolution, their action is not binding on SI.**	**Quorum not achieved**

Continued >

Issue	Rule	Fact Application	Conclusion
Interested directors	**A quorum can only consist of board members that do not have a personal interest in the transaction.**	**Since Carole had a personal interest in the transaction to release her from her contract to sell land to SI, Carole would have to be excluded from any vote on the matter. Therefore, the resolution would have to be adopted by a quorum of the six disinterested directors, which it wasn't, so the resolution is invalid.** Further, to ratify a transaction where a director had a personal interest, as Carole does here, the board would need to be provided with all facts of the transaction, which was not done here.	**Resolution invalid**
Call #3: Carole's Fiduciary Duties			
Duty of loyalty	**A director or officer owes a duty of loyalty to the corporation. A director must put the interests of the corporation above his own interests.**	**As a director of SI, Carole owes a duty of loyalty to SI and must put the best interests of SI ahead of her own interests. Carole may not profit at the expense of the corporation.**	**Duty of loyalty owed**
Usurp corporate opportunity	**A director or officer may not personally act on a business opportunity without first offering it to the corporation where the corporation would expect to be presented the opportunity.** If the director or officer usurps a corporate opportunity, then the corporation may compel the director/officer to turn over the opportunity or disgorge profits.	**Carole sought to be released from her $500,000 land sale contract with SI because she received confidential information indicating the property value would rise and if she sold to another party she could have increased personal financial gain by selling the property at a higher price than the SI contract price of $500,000. Carole should have offered the opportunity to SI first.**	**Breach of duty of loyalty by usurping corporate opportunity**

Continued >

Issue	Rule	Fact Application	Conclusion
		Carole may argue the opportunity was in real estate and not in SI's primary business of sporting goods, however, modernly a corporate opportunity is defined broadly and SI may have chosen to earn profits by reselling the land. The director or officer may take the opportunity only after good faith rejection of the opportunity by the corporation if there was full disclosure of all material facts to a disinterested board majority. Carole did not present the opportunity to SI first or make a full disclosure of the material facts, so she may not take advantage of the corporate opportunity. Carole did sell the property for $850,000 because of the increased property value and this was SI's corporate opportunity, so Carole can be disgorged of her $350,000 profit.	**Breach of duty of loyalty by usurping corporate opportunity**
Self-dealing	A director or officer has a conflict of interest when he enters into a contract with the corporation or has a beneficial financial interest in a contract.	Carole engaged in self dealing when she sought to be released from her existing contract with SI because of the confidential information she learned, which would potentially lead to an increase in value for the parcel if she could resell it to another buyer. Self-dealing contracts are presumed unfair and voidable. Carole engaged in self-dealing at the expense of SI and thus breached her duty of loyalty to SI.	Breach of duty of loyalty by self dealing

Continued >

Issue	Rule	Fact Application	Conclusion
Duty of care	A director or officer owes the corporation a duty of care to act as a reasonably prudent person would act under similar circumstances.	Carole is in breach of her duty of care since a reasonably prudent person would have offered the opportunity to make money on the appreciating real estate parcel to the corporation.	Breach of duty of care
Duty to disclose	Directors and officers have a duty to disclose material information relevant to the corporation to board members.	Carole had a duty to disclose the confidential material information she received regarding the land appreciation to SI. This information was relevant to SI since they already had a contract with Carole to purchase the parcel and Carole also breached the duty to disclose.	Breach of duty to disclose
Call #4: Larry's Ethical Duties			
Serving on the board	A lawyer may serve on a board of directors so long as doing so does not violate any fiduciary duties owed to the corporation.	Larry worked as SI's lawyer for many years. His appointment to the board did not appear to cause any fiduciary duty violations and was permissible.	Larry originally could serve on the board
Conflict of interest	A lawyer may not represent a client where there is a conflict of interest. A concurrent conflict of interest exists if the representation of one client is directly adverse to another client.	Larry, a director of SI, has also performed legal work for SI for ten years and has a fiduciary duty to SI. Carole, also an SI director, attempted to use Larry as her personal lawyer by asking his legal advice about getting out of her contract with SI. This created a lawyer-client relationship between Carole and Larry and created both a potential conflict of interest and an actual conflict of interest since Carole's interests in getting out of her SI contract and obtaining a windfall on her parcel are clearly at odds with SI's interest. A lawyer can represent clients with a potential conflict of interest with full disclosure and consent,	Larry has a conflict of interest

Continued >

Issue	Rule	Fact Application	Conclusion
Duty of loyalty	**A director or officer owes a duty of loyalty to the corporation.**	**but not when there is an actual conflict, as exists here. Larry should have informed Carole he could not represent her and urged her to seek independent counsel. By not doing so he breached his duty of loyalty to SI.** Larry was obligated to put SI's interest first and thus should have told SI about the reason for Carole's proposed contract rescission. Larry violated the duty of loyalty by concealing this information. Further, his actions indicate he was acting in Carole's best interests, rather than SI's, by agreeing to Carole's release under the contract and not disclosing her true motives to the board. Larry should have disclosed to the board that he had a conflict of interest, without disclosing any confidential client information that Carole gave him. Further, Larry should have withdrawn from the board and probably his representation of SI.	Larry breached his duty of loyalty
Duty of competence	A lawyer shall represent the client with the legal knowledge, skill, thoroughness, and preparation reasonably necessary.	**Larry did not perform competently and failed in his duty.**	**Breach of duty of competence**
Duty to communicate	The lawyer shall promptly inform the client of any decision that affects the client's informed consent as well as reasonably consult with the client and keep him informed of the status of the case.	**Larry could not fulfill his duty to communicate to SI without breaching his duty of loyalty and confidentiality to Carole, since Carole sought legal advice from Larry. He should have withdrawn from representing both parties, and from the board.**	Probably best for Larry to keep Carole's confidence and withdraw

PART 2 CIVIL PROCEDURE

CIVIL PROCEDURE TABLE OF CONTENTS

INTRODUCTION TO CIVIL PROCEDURE

Civil procedure is a straightforward, rule-based subject that shouldn't be particularly difficult on the essay portion of the bar exam. The only potential for difficulty is that both the federal rules and the California rules are eligible for testing. Oftentimes, a legal principle operates the same and is simply called by a different name in the federal system and the California system, which is something the bar examiners seem less concerned with testing. However, the bar examiners do seem interested in testing the areas where there is a substantive difference between the federal rule and California rule. We have identified the areas where the rules differ between the federal rule and the California rule; you should be sure to know those areas well since they are frequently tested. This is true especially in an area where the application of the facts to the two different rules would lead to a different result—for example, a fact pattern where application of the traditional rule or the California primary rights theory in res judicata would lead to different outcomes.

Civil procedure is similar to contracts in that the events transpire in a predictable way. It is easiest to issue spot an exam question if you think about the civil procedure issues within the context of the life cycle of actual litigation. First, there are preliminary issues dealing with the proper court in which the action should be brought. Then there are issues that arise pretrial; the potential for a disposition of the case without a trial; issues pertaining to the trial itself; issues that arise post-trial; issues pertaining to an appeal; and, lastly, the appropriate use of a prior judgment in subsequent litigation. The issue-spotting checklist provided lists the issues in that order. However, issue spotting is typically not a challenge in civil procedure essays if you know the rules well, and the recent trend of the bar examiners has been to identify the issues for you in the call of the question.

The vast majority of the issues that will arise on an essay question will pertain to the very frequently tested topics of personal jurisdiction, subject matter jurisdiction, collateral estoppel, and res judicata. Supplemental jurisdiction, removal, venue, and joinder of parties and claims are also frequently tested topics. Make sure you are very comfortable with those concepts and can issue spot and analyze an essay dealing with those issues because if civil procedure is tested we can almost guarantee you will see several of those issues on the exam. This makes logical sense because those issues are the most susceptible to robust factual analysis, which is what the bar examiners are looking for. While there are many detailed rules in civil procedure that pertain to dates and other requirements for pleadings and discovery, and rules of that type could certainly appear on an exam, don't get hung up on them because they are typically not a fertile area for essay testing because rules of that type do not lend themselves to in-depth factual analysis, and consequently, they wouldn't be worth many points even if they were on the exam. To maximize your results, spend your limited study time practicing essays dealing with the frequently tested topics, rather than memorizing a lot of rule minutiae that you are less likely to see on an exam.

ISSUES CHECKLIST

PROPER COURT PRELIMINARY ISSUES

Personal jurisdiction (PJ)
Subject matter jurisdiction (SMJ)
Supplemental jurisdiction
Removal and remand
Venue
Notice
Choice of law

PRETRIAL PROCEDURES

Pleadings
Joinder of parties
Joinder of claims
Class action
Discovery

DISPOSITION WITHOUT TRIAL

Dismissal
Motion for summary judgment (MSJ)

TRIAL

Right to a jury
Judgment as a matter of law (JMOL)/directed verdict in Cal.

POST-TRIAL

Renewed JMOL/JNOV in Cal.
New trial
Motion to set aside judgment
Remittitur/additur

APPEAL

Final Judgment Rule (FJR) & exceptions

USE OF FINAL JUDGMENT

Res judicata (claim preclusion)
Collateral estoppel (issue preclusion)

MEMORIZATION ATTACK SHEET

PROPER COURT ISSUES

- **Personal jurisdiction (PJ)**
  - Traditional bases
    - Consent
    - Domicile in forum
    - Present & served
  - Modern: minimum contacts
    - Long-arm statute AND
      - **Cal.**: to constitutional limits
      - Specific statute: as limited
    - Nature of contacts
      - Purposeful availment
      - Foreseeable haled into court
      - Relatedness
      - Systematic & continuous
    - Fairness factors
      - Convenience
      - State's interest
      - Other interests
- **Subject matter jurisdiction (SMJ)**
  - Federal question
  - Diversity of citizenship
    - Complete diversity required
      - Person: domicile
      - Corporation: may have 2
        - Incorporation state &
        - PPB state
      - Unincorporated Assoc.: domicile of members
    - AND Exceeds $75k
- **Cal. subject matter jurisdiction**
  - Unlimited case: exceeds $25k
  - Limited case: exceeds $7,500
  - Small claims case: under $7,500
- **Supplemental jurisdiction**
  - Common nucleus of operative fact
  - Same transaction or occurrence
- **Removal jurisdiction**
  - Defendants only may remove
  - 30 days–1-year max.
- **Remand**
  - To state court if removal improper
- **Venue**
  - Claim arose
  - Defendant resides
    - **Fed.**: all Ds reside
    - **Cal.**: any D resides
  - Reside venue definition:
    - Person: domicile
    - Corp.
      - **Fed.**: where subject to personal jurisdiction
      - **Cal.**: PPB, or contract entered into, performed, or breached
  - Multi Ds: where any D resides
- **Transfer of venue**
  - **Fed.**
    - Interests of justice
    - Public factors
    - Private factors
  - **Cal.**
    - Interests of justice
    - Convenience of the parties
    - **Forum non conveniens**
  - **Fed.**: forum more appropriate
  - **Cal.**
    - Interests of justice
    - Public factors
    - Private factors
- **Notice**
  - Service of process
  - Method of service
    - Personal service
    - Substituted service
      - **Cal.**: must mail too
    - Constructive service

- **Choice of law**
  - *Erie*: balancing test
    - State substantive law
    - Fed. procedural law
  - **Cal.** conflicts of law
    - Tort: comparative impairment test
    - Contract: if choice of law clause or not determines
      - No clause: comparative impairment test
      - Yes clause: okay if reasonable basis & no Cal. conflict

PRETRIAL ISSUES

- **Pleadings**
  - **Fed.:** notice pleading
  - **Cal.:** fact pleading
- **Complaint**
  - Identify parties
  - Statement of claim
  - Demand for judgment
  - Signature
- **Response**
  - Preanswer motions
    - Motion for a more definite statement (**Cal.:** demurrer)
    - Motion to strike
      - **Cal.:** Anti-SLAPP
  - **Fed.:** 12b(6) motions
    - Lack of SMJ
    - Lack of PJ
    - Improper venue
    - Insufficient process
    - Insufficient service of process
    - Failure to state a claim
    - Failure to join an indispensable party
  - **Cal.:** Demurrer
    - Uncertain pleading
    - Liability theory unclear
    - Lack of legal capacity
    - Another case exists
    - Misjoinder of parties
    - Contract pleadings not okay
    - Certificate if required
  - **Cal.:** Motion to quash
    - Lack of PJ
    - Insufficient process
    - Insufficient service of process
  - Answer
    - Respond
    - Assert affirmative defenses
- **Amended Pleadings**
  - Relation back doctrine
    - Claims: Same conduct, transaction, or occurrence
    - Defendants
      - Same conduct, transaction, or occurrence
      - New party knew
      - Would have been named
  - **Cal.:** "Doe" amendments: 3 years if genuine ignorance of:
    - Identity of party
    - Facts giving rise
    - Law allows cause of action
- **Joinder of parties**
  - Necessary party
    - Complete relief
    - Interest harmed
    - Multiple inconsistent obligations
    - Join if
      - Personal jurisdiction, and
      - Diversity not destroyed
    - If can't join, court may
      - Dismiss, or
      - Proceed without
  - Indispensable party: dismiss
  - Impleader: D can add a 3rd party D
  - Intervention: nonparty wants to join
  - Interpleader: property holder wants single lawsuit
- **Joinder of claims**
  - Counterclaim
    - Compulsory

        - Same transaction or occurrence
        - Supplemental jurisdiction will extend
    - Permissive
        - Not same transaction or occurrence
        - Supplemental jurisdiction will <u>not</u> extend
- Cross claim: against co-party
    - Not compulsory
    - Same transaction or occurrence
    - Supplemental jurisdictions will extend
    - **Cal.**: called a "cross complaint"

◆ **Class Action**
- Numerosity
- Commonality
- Typicality
- Adequacy
- **Fed.**: type of class
    - Prejudice
    - Injunctive relief sought
    - Questions of law/fact common to class predominate
- **Fed.**: citizenship issues
    - Diversity—amount in controversy each
    - Class Action Fairness Act
        - Any class member diverse
        - Aggregate exceeds $5 million
        - 100 + class members
- **Cal.**: class action—no types
    - Ascertainable class
    - Member community interest
        - Common question of law or fact
        - Adequate representative
        - Class substantial benefit

◆ **Discovery**
- **Fed.**: Rule 26 mandatory disclosures
    - Initial disclosures
    - Expert information
    - Pretrial witnesses & documents

◆ **Discovery tools**
- Depositions
- Interrogatories
- Request for admissions
- Request to inspect & produce
- Physical or mental exam
- **Cal.**: limited cases, less discovery

◆ **Scope of discovery**
- No attorney work product

DISPOSITION WITHOUT TRIAL

◆ **Dismissal**
- Voluntary
- Involuntary
- Failure to state a claim

◆ **Default judgment**

◆ **Motion summary judgment**
- No genuine issue of material fact & entitled to judgment as matter of law

TRIAL

◆ **Right to jury trial**
- **Fed.**: legal, then equity
- **Cal.**: equity, then legal

◆ **Judgment as a matter of law**
- Reasonable people could not disagree
- Cal.: directed verdict

POST-TRIAL ISSUES

◆ **Renewed JMOL**
- Only allowed if JMOL first
- **Cal.**: called JNOV & <u>not</u> required to file DV first

◆ **Motion for new trial**

◆ **Motion to set aside judgment**

◆ **Conditional new trial on damages**
- Remittitur: damages too high
- Additur: damages too low

APPEAL

- **Final Judgment Rule (FJR)**
- **FJR exceptions**
  - Injunctions
  - Collateral issues
  - Multiple claims/parties
  - Extraordinary writ

USE OF FINAL JUDGMENT

- **Res judicata (claim)**
  - Valid & final judgment on the merits
    - **Fed.**: final when rendered
    - **Cal.**: final when appeals done
  - Actually litigated
  - Same P & same D
  - Same claim
    - **Fed.**: same transaction or occurrence
    - **Cal.**: primary rights theory
- **Collateral estoppel (issue)**
  - Valid & final judgment on the merits
    - **Fed.**: final when rendered
    - **Cal.**: final when appeals done
  - Actually litigated
  - Issue essential to judgment
  - Who can rely?
    - **Fed.**: party or privy can use
    - **Cal.**: stranger allowed if
      - Identical issues
      - Valid final judgment
      - Fair opportunity to be heard
      - Not unfair to apply
      - Party or privy if against

CIVIL PROCEDURE RULE OUTLINE

I. **PROPER COURT—PRELIMINARY ISSUES:** The first inquiry in civil procedure always centers on whether it is proper for the court selected to resolve the case at hand. To hear a case, the court must have jurisdiction over the persons involved, the subject matter of the suit, the case must be held in the proper venue, the defendant must have notice of the suit, and the proper law must be used to resolve the issues.

A. **Personal jurisdiction** means the court must have proper **jurisdiction over the parties** to an action. Personal jurisdiction will be proper where there is a sufficiently close relationship between the forum state and the defendant. There are three traditional bases that may provide personal jurisdiction. In addition, modernly, personal jurisdiction can also be found where there is a state long-arm statute authorizing the extension of jurisdiction over nonresidents and the exercise of jurisdiction is in keeping with the constitutional requirements of the minimum contacts standard.

1. **Traditional basis for personal jurisdiction** exists where the defendant
   a. **Consents** to jurisdiction in the forum state.
   b. Is **domiciled** in the forum state. A person's domicile is the state in which he intends to reside.
   c. Is **present** in the forum state when served with process.
2. **Modernly,** the **minimum contacts standard** allows personal jurisdiction over nonresidents of the forum state provided there is a **long-arm statute, and** the exercise of **jurisdiction is in keeping with the constitutional requirements of the minimum contacts standard.**
   a. A **long-arm statute** is the mechanism that gives a state the power to reach beyond its own borders and assert jurisdiction over a nonresident. There are two types of long-arm statutes:
      1. **California's long-arm statute** gives its state courts power over any person or property **up to the limits of the Constitution,** thus the minimum contacts standard is applied. California's long-arm statute permits the exercise of jurisdiction as broadly as is allowed by the U.S. Constitution, and many other states have adopted similar statutes.

> Exam tip: In an essay exam, a broad long-arm statute similar to California's is typified by language such as, "State X may exercise jurisdiction on any basis not inconsistent with the Constitution of the United States."

      2. **Specific long-arm statutes:** Some states have specific long-arm statutes that give its courts power over nonresidents **only under certain specified situations**—for example, the commission of a tort while in the state. Where a specific long-arm statute applies, the exercise of jurisdiction must satisfy that statute and also meet the constitutional requirements of the minimum contacts standard.

<u>**Exam tip:**</u> Where personal jurisdiction is not based on a traditional basis of jurisdiction, both the underlying long-arm statute and minimum contacts must be analyzed. If the long-arm statute is specific, do the analysis of the specifics of that statute and then do the minimum contacts analysis. If the state long-arm statute is co-extensive with Constitutional limits, such as California's, simply identify that fact and do the analysis under the minimum contacts portion of the answer.

b. **Nature of the defendant's contacts: A defendant must have sufficient minimum contacts with the forum state such that asserting jurisdiction over him does not offend traditional notions of fair play and substantial justice.** The minimum contacts standard determines the constitutional limit to a state's exercise of personal jurisdiction over nonresidents.

   1. **Minimum contacts:** First, assess the defendant's minimum contacts with the forum state to determine if the defendant has **purposefully availed** himself of the **benefits and protections of the state** such that it is reasonably **foreseeable that he could be haled into court** there. Additional factors to consider are

      a. **Specific jurisdiction:** The **relatedness** between the defendant's contact and plaintiff's claim. When the claim is directly related to the defendant's contact with the forum the forum state will have *specific jurisdiction* over the defendant for that claim only.

      b. **General jurisdiction:** Where the contacts with the forum state are sufficiently **systematic and continuous** *general jurisdiction* will be found and the forum state may exercise jurisdiction over the defendant for any cause of action.

<u>**Minimum contacts fact triggers:**</u>
- Advertise or solicit business in a state
- Distributor or salesperson for product in a state
- Small retail store near state border
- Awareness product is being used in a state
- Driving through a state on way to another state
- Housing state X prisoners in state Y

   2. **Fairness factors:** Next, the exercise of jurisdiction must be fair. To analyze fairness, assess:

      a. The **convenience** to the parties. Consider the location of witnesses and evidence, and the burden on the defendant to travel to the forum state.

   b. The forum **state's interest** in regulating activity within its borders and protecting its citizens.
   c. Any **other interests,** such as the plaintiff's interest in obtaining convenient and effective relief.

> **Exam tip:** Personal jurisdiction is frequently tested. If time permits, analyze the traditional basis of jurisdiction, but typically these bases will not be satisfied, and a full-fact intensive minimum contacts analysis will be required.
> **Memorization tip:** Use the mnemonic "My Parents Frequently Read Science Fiction Children's Stories Out-loud" to remember the key buzz words in the minimum contacts analysis: **M**inimum contacts, **P**urposeful availment of the benefits and protections of the state, **F**oreseeability of being haled into court, **R**elatedness between contact and claim, **S**ystematic and continuous contacts, **F**airness factors, **C**onvenience, **S**tate's interest, and **O**ther interests.

B. **Subject matter jurisdiction** means the court must have proper **jurisdiction over the subject matter of** an action. Federal courts have limited subject matter jurisdiction and may only hear cases involving federal questions or diversity of citizenship.
   1. **Federal question:** Federal district courts have subject matter jurisdiction over civil actions **arising under federal law** (e.g., U.S. Constitution, federal statutes, treaties, etc.).
   2. **Diversity of citizenship:** Federal district courts have subject matter jurisdiction over actions **between citizens of different states, and where the amount in controversy exceeds $75,000.**
      a. **Complete diversity is required.** No plaintiff may be a citizen of the same state as any defendant.
         1. A **natural person's citizenship is determined by his domicile.** A person's domicile is the state where he is **physically present** and has the **subjective intent** to make it his permanent home. Each person can only have one domicile at a time.
         2. A **corporation is a citizen** of
            a. The **state where the business is incorporated**; and
            b. The **one state where the corporation has its principal place of business** (PPB). A corporation may be the citizen of more than one state.
               i. The **PPB** is determined by the **"nerve center" test** and refers to the place where a corporation's **officers direct, control, and coordinate the corporation's activities.** Typically, this is where the corporation maintains its headquarters.
         3. **Citizenship of unincorporated associations** is determined by the citizenship of all members, including limited and general partners (e.g., Partnerships, LLCs, etc.).

4. **Citizenship of minors, decedents, and incompetents** is determined by their own citizenship, not the citizenship of their representative.

b. **The amount in controversy must exceed $75,000**, not including attorney fees.
   1. **At the time of filing:** The amount in controversy is determined at the time the action is filed.
   2. **Aggregation:** Claims can be aggregated to meet the amount if there is one plaintiff and one defendant, or if there are joint tortfeasor defendants.
      a. However, if the plaintiff recovers less than $75,000, he may have to pay the defendant's litigation costs.
      b. The value of any counterclaim cannot be aggregated to meet the exceeding $75,000 requirement.

> Note: The amount in controversy must *exceed* $75,000; not *equal* $75,000.

c. **Exceptions to federal subject matter jurisdiction:** Federal courts will not hear actions involving issuance of divorce, alimony, or child support, or to probate an estate.

3. **California state court subject matter jurisdiction:** California courts have general subject matter jurisdiction and can hear any case not within the exclusive jurisdiction of another court. **Civil cases are classified** as unlimited, limited, or small claims. If a case is misclassified, either party or the court may seek reclassification.
   a. **Unlimited civil cases** are heard in Superior Court and require an amount in controversy exceeding $25,000. There are no limitations on pleadings, discovery, or relief available, and a claimant can recover any amount.
   b. **Limited civil cases** are heard in Superior Court and require an amount in controversy over $7,500, but not exceeding $25,000. There are limitations placed on the use of process and the equitable relief available, and a claimant cannot recover more than $25,000.
   c. **Small claims cases** are heard in Small Claims Court and require that, if the plaintiff is an individual, the claim is $7,500 or less; or if the plaintiff is a business entity, the claim is $5,000 or less.
4. **Supplemental jurisdiction** applies to provide subject matter jurisdiction when an additional claim does not itself invoke federal subject matter jurisdiction, but **the additional claim shares a common nucleus of operative fact** with a claim that does properly invoke federal subject matter jurisdiction (federal question or diversity.) A common nucleus of operative fact means that the claim arises from the **same transaction or occurrence.**

> **Issue-spotting tip:** Where supplemental jurisdiction is at issue, look for subject matter jurisdiction to be at issue. In a diversity case a plaintiff cannot use supplemental jurisdiction to circumvent complete diversity requirements.

5. **Removal jurisdiction** allows the **defendant** to have a case originally filed in state court **removed to federal court** where the case could have properly been brought in either state or federal court.
   a. **Only defendants are eligible to remove** cases.
   b. **Diversity case:** In diversity cases, the defendant may not remove to federal court if he is a citizen of the forum state.
   c. **Venue:** The case can be removed to a federal district court embracing the state court where the case was originally filed.
   d. **Timing:** The defendant must remove no later than **30 days** after service of the first "removable" document (typically service of the initial pleading), but never later than one year after the initial filing.
6. **Remand:** When a defendant attempts to remove a case to federal court and the **removal is improper, the federal court can remand the case back to state court.**
   a. **Timing:** The plaintiff must move to remand the case within **30 days** of the removal, however there is no time limit if the federal court lacks subject matter jurisdiction over the case.

> **Issue-spotting tip:** Where removal and/or remand are at issue, look for subject matter jurisdiction to be at issue as well.

C. **Venue** concerns which federal district court should hear a particular case.
   1. **Venue is proper where**
      a. **Claim arose**
         1. **Federal:** Venue is always proper in the **district** where the claim arose (injury occurred or contract entered into) or where the land in dispute is located (local actions).
         2. **California:** Venue is proper in the **county** where the claim arose (injury occurred or contract entered into) or where the land in dispute is located.
      b. **Defendant resides**
         1. **Federal:** For transitory actions (not local actions), venue is proper in any district where **all defendants reside** or where a substantial part of the claim arose.
         2. **California:** Venue is proper in a county where **any defendant resides** at the time the case is filed. If no defendants reside in California, then any county is acceptable.
         3. **Definition of "reside" for venue purposes**
            a. **Natural persons reside** at their domicile.
            b. **Corporations reside**

i. **Federal:** In all districts where they are subject to **personal jurisdiction** when the case is filed.
ii. **California:** In the county where they have their **PPB**, or where a contract was entered into or performed, or where contract breach occurred, or where liability arises.

> Note: A corporation's residence for venue purposes is not defined the same way as a corporation's citizenship for diversity purposes.

c. **Multiple defendants all in the same state:** Venue is proper in any district where any defendant resides.

2. **Transfer of venue**
   a. **Federal:** Venue can only be transferred to another federal court where the case could have been filed. To determine if a transfer of venue is warranted the court will look at the **interests of justice**, including:
      1. **Public factors:** What law applies, which community should be burdened with jury service; and
      2. **Private factors:** Convenience, location of witnesses and evidence, etc.
   b. **California:** Allows for the transfer of venue to any proper county at the judge's discretion where the **interests of justice and convenience of the parties** would be served by such a transfer.
3. **Forum non conveniens**
   a. **Federal:** A court may dismiss or stay a case if there is a **far more appropriate forum elsewhere**, such as another state or country.
   b. **California:** The court will determine if another forum is more suitable under forum non conveniens by looking at the **interests of justice**, including:
      1. **Public factors:** What law applies, which community should be burdened with jury service; and
      2. **Private factors:** Convenience, location of witnesses, evidence, etc.
      3. **Note:** this is the same as the federal transfer of venue rule.

D. **Notice:** A defendant must be **properly notified** of a pending action by a reasonable method and must be given an opportunity to be heard.
1. **Service of process** means to provide a defendant with notice of a pending action by delivery to defendant of a summons (formal court notice of suit and time for response) and a copy of the complaint.
2. **Method of service**
   a. **Personal service** is always adequate and occurs when the notice is personally delivered to a defendant.
   b. **Substituted service** is usually adequate:
      1. **Federal court:** Service of process can be left at defendant's usual abode and served upon someone of suitable age and discretion who resides there; or served to defendant's authorized agent; or served by methods permitted by state law.

2. **California:** Only allows substituted service if personal service cannot be accomplished with reasonable diligence. The service of process must be left at defendant's usual abode with a competent member of the household who is at least 18 years old, and that person must be informed of the contents. The process **must also be mailed** to defendant by first class mail.
   a. **California corporation:** Service of process may be made on defendant's agent or one apparently in charge at the office during usual office hours.

c. **Constructive service:** Defendants can technically be served by registered mail, however this is only effective if the defendant agrees to waive service of process.
   1. **California** allows service by publication only if nothing else works. Plaintiff's attorney must provide an affidavit that defendant cannot be served after reasonable diligence.

E. **Choice of law in diversity actions**
   1. ***Erie* doctrine:** A federal court sitting in diversity must apply **state substantive law and federal procedural law.** The goal is to prevent forum shopping. If it is unclear whether a law is substantive or procedural, then the judge will employ a general balancing test:
      a. **Balance of interests:** The federal interest in having the federal law applied is balanced against the state interest in having the state law applied.
   2. **California conflicts of laws rule:** The following rules determine the appropriate substantive law for a federal court sitting in diversity to apply.
      a. **Tort actions:** Where two state laws are in conflict, the court evaluates the **comparative impairment to each state's interest** in having its own law applied.
      b. **Contract actions** depend on whether there is a choice of law provision in the contract.
         1. **Contracts without a choice of law provision:** The court evaluates the **comparative impairment** to each state's interest in having its own law applied.
         2. **Contracts with a choice of law provision**
            a. **No conflict:** The provision will be applied so long as it has a **reasonable basis and does not conflict** with California policies.
            b. **Conflict:** If the provision does conflict with California policies, the California law will apply if California has a **materially greater interest** in having its law applied than does the other state.

II. PRETRIAL PROCEDURES

A. **Pleadings** are the documents that set forth the claims and defenses to a case.
   1. **Purpose of pleadings:** The purpose of pleadings is to communicate with the opposing party and the court.

a. **Federal courts use notice pleading,** the goal of which is to provide the opposing party with reasonable notice of the nature and scope of the claims being asserted.
b. **California courts use fact pleading,** which is also called *code pleading* and is more specific than notice pleading.

2. **Requirements of pleadings: Rule 11** requires all attorneys or a party representing himself to sign all pleadings, written motions, and papers, certifying that the paper is proper, the legal contentions are warranted by law, and the factual contentions have evidentiary support.
   a. **Sanctions** may be imposed for violations of this rule.
      1. **Federal 21-day safe harbor:** If a motion for sanctions is served, the party has 21 days to withdraw or correct the pleadings giving rise to the sanctions.
      2. **California does not have a safe harbor rule.**
   b. Note: Rule 11 does not apply to discovery documents.
3. **Types of pleadings**
   a. **Complaint:** A complaint is used by a plaintiff to raise issues.
      1. **Federal:** A federal complaint must include
         a. **Identification of the parties**
         b. A statement of **proper subject matter jurisdiction**
         c. A **statement of the claim** showing the factual basis on which plaintiff is entitled to relief. **Notice pleading** typically only requires stating enough facts to support a plausible claim, however fraud, mistake, and special damages must be pled with specificity.
         d. A **demand for judgment.**
         e. The **signature** of the plaintiff, or his attorney.
      2. **California:** A complaint in California must include
         a. **Identification of the parties:** However, California allows plaintiffs to sue fictitious "Doe" defendants where the identity of a defendant is unknown.
         b. A **statement of the claim,** including a "statement of facts constituting a cause of action, in ordinary and concise language." Since California uses **fact pleading,** this requires pleading the specific facts supporting every element of each legal theory alleged.
         c. A **demand for judgment**, including the amount of damages sought, unless the damages sought are for actual or punitive damages for a personal injury or wrongful death action.
         d. The **signature** of the plaintiff, or his attorney.
   b. **Response: Rule 12** requires a defendant to **respond by either a motion or by an answer** within **21 days** after service of process (or within 60 days if service waived). **California** allows **30 days** to respond.
      1. **Preanswer motions**

a. **Motion for a more definite statement** is used where the complaint is too vague.
   i. **California:** This would be done by a **special demurrer** on the grounds the pleading is uncertain.

b. **Motion to strike** aimed at pleadings containing immaterial or redundant issues (e.g., demand for a jury trial when there is no right to one).
   i. **California also has an Anti-SLAPP** (Anti-Strategic Lawsuits Against Public Participation) **motion to strike** targeting suits brought to chill the valid exercise of free speech and petition. A defendant can make an Anti-SLAPP motion to strike, which shifts the burden to the plaintiff to show a probability of winning on the merits.

c. **Federal Rule 12(b) defenses** (these can be raised by a preanswer motion or in the answer)
   i. **Lack of subject matter jurisdiction:** This can be raised **anytime before all appeals are exhausted.**
   ii. **Lack of personal jurisdiction:** This must be raised in the **first response** or is deemed waived.
   iii. **Improper venue:** This must be raised in the **first response** or is deemed waived.
   iv. **Insufficient process** (something is wrong with papers): This must be raised in the **first response** or is deemed waived.
   v. **Insufficient service of process:** This must be raised in the **first response** or is deemed waived.
   vi. **Failure to state a claim** on which relief can be granted: This can be raised **anytime until the trial is concluded.**
   vii. **Failure to join an indispensable party:** This can be raised **anytime until the trial is concluded.**

d. **California demurrer** (general or special) is typically used to respond to the complaint.
   i. **General demurrer**
      (1) **Pleadings failed to state facts sufficient to constitute a cause of action.**
      (2) **Court lacks subject matter jurisdiction.**
   ii. **Special demurrer** is only allowed in cases classified as **unlimited** (thus, not allowed in those classified as limited). These issues can also be raised in the answer. A special demurrer may be based on
      (1) **Uncertain pleading** (similar to a federal motion for a more definite statement).
      (2) Complaint is unclear about **which theories of liability** are asserted against each of the defendants.
      (3) **Lack of legal capacity.**
      (4) **Existence of another case** between plaintiff and defendant on the same cause of action.
      (5) **Defect or misjoinder of parties.**

(6) Failure to plead whether a **contract** is oral or written.
(7) Failure to file a **required certificate** (e.g., for professional negligence claim).

e. **California: Motion to quash service of summons:** This is done by means of a special appearance and must be made separately from the answer. This motion must be made either **before or concurrently** with the filing of the demurrer or motion to strike or the answer, or the following defenses are deemed waived:
i. **Lack of personal jurisdiction:** <u>Unlike in federal court</u>, personal jurisdiction must be raised fairly immediately or it is waived.
ii. **Insufficient process** (something is wrong with the papers).
iii. **Insufficient service of process.**

c. **Answer:** An answer is the defendant's response to the complaint. A defendant must respond within **21 days** after service of process (or within 60 days if service waived). **California** allows **30 days** to respond.
1. **The defendant must respond to the allegations** by denying them, admitting them, or stating he lacks sufficient information to do either (failure to deny can operate as an admission).
2. **The defendant must also assert any affirmative defenses** in the answer.
a. **California:** Fact pleading requires factual detail regarding each legal element when asserting affirmative defenses.

4. **Amended pleadings:** A plaintiff has a right to amend once before the defendant responds. A defendant has a right to amend once within 21 days of serving his answer. Otherwise, a party must seek leave of court to amend, which the court will grant if justice so requires.
a. **Relation back doctrine:** Amends back to the date of the original filing.
1. **Amended claims "relate back"** (after the statute of limitations has run) if they concern the same **conduct, transaction, or occurrence** as the original pleading.
2. **Amended defendants "relate back"** if
a. They concern the **same conduct, transaction, or occurrence** as the original complaint;
b. The **new party knew** of the original action within 120 days of its filing; and
c. The new party also knew that, but for a mistake, she **would have been named** as a defendant in the original complaint.

b. **California "Doe" Amendments:** If a plaintiff substitutes a named defendant for a "Doe" defendant within **three years** of the filing it "relates back." If the original complaint contained allegations against "Doe" defendants, the plaintiff can amend and add the real defendants if the plaintiff was **genuinely ignorant** of the
1. **Identity** of the fictitiously named defendants; or

2. **The facts giving rise** to the cause of action; or
3. **The fact that the law provides** a cause of action.

> **Exam tip:** Pleadings are not typically tested outright, but the rules are eligible for testing, and the failure to state a claim upon which relief can be granted and the sufficiency of notice pleadings have been tested.

B. **Joinder of parties and claims**
   1. **Joinder of parties:** Plaintiffs and/or defendants may be joined to an existing case if the claims arise from the **same transaction or occurrence** and raise at least **one common question.** However, there still must be **subject matter jurisdiction.**
      a. **Necessary party**
         1. **Definition:** A party is a **necessary party** if
            a. The court **cannot provide complete relief** without the necessary party; or
            b. The absent party's **interest will be harmed** if he is not joined; or
            c. The absent party is **subject to multiple inconsistent obligations.**
         2. **Join:** A necessary party **must be joined if**
            a. The court has **personal jurisdiction** over him;
            b. Joining him **doesn't destroy diversity**, where diversity is the basis of federal subject matter jurisdiction.
         3. **Unable to join:** If a necessary party cannot be joined because of one of the reasons noted above, the court will consider if there is an **alternative forum** available, assess the **likelihood of prejudice**, and whether the court can shape relief to avoid the prejudice. The **court may either**
            a. **Dismiss** the case; or
            b. **Proceed** with the case without the necessary party.
      b. **Indispensable party:** A party is indispensable if complete relief cannot be provided in his absence yet he is unable to be joined to the case for some reason. When a party is indispensable the **case must be dismissed.**
      c. **Impleader** is a mechanism a **defending party** can use to **add a third party defendant** in order to seek indemnity, subrogation, or contribution.
         1. **Supplemental jurisdiction will apply** and no independent basis for subject matter jurisdiction is required.
         2. **California calls this a cross complaint,** and it is broader since it allows the addition of any claim on which the third-party defendant is liable so long as it pertains to the same transaction or occurrence.
      d. **Intervention** applies when a nonparty claims an interest in the property or transaction that is the subject of the pending lawsuit and disposition in his absence will impair his rights.

   1. **California** allows intervention if the potential intervener's interest is **direct and immediate**, and does not allow intervention if the interest is indirect and consequential.

e. **Interpleader** is an action where **one holding property** (the stakeholder) forces all potential claimants (people who claim the property) into a **single lawsuit** to avoid multiple and inconsistent litigation. There are two types of interpleader:
   1. **Statutory:** Requires only that **one claimant must be diverse** from one other claimant and the amount in controversy must be **$500** or more.
   2. **Rule 22 interpleader:** Requires that the stakeholder must be **diverse from every claimant** and the amount in controversy must **exceed $75,000.**

2. **Joinder of claims**
   a. **Counterclaim** is an offensive claim against an opposing party.
      1. **There are two types:**
         a. **Compulsory counterclaims** arise from the **same transaction or occurrence** as the plaintiff's claim and **must be raised** in the pending case or the claim is deemed waived.
            i. **Supplemental jurisdiction:** An independent basis for subject matter jurisdiction is not required since supplemental jurisdiction will extend to a compulsory counterclaim.
         b. **Permissive counterclaims** do not arise from the same transaction or occurrence and may be raised in the pending case or in a separate case.
            i. **No supplemental jurisdiction:** A permissive counterclaim must have an independent source of subject matter jurisdiction.
      2. **California uses the term cross complaint** for all third-party actions, such as counterclaims, cross claims, impleader, etc.
   b. **Cross claim** is an offensive claim against a **co-party** and must arise from the same transaction or occurrence. Cross claims are never compulsory. (This is called a *cross complaint* in California.)
      1. **Supplemental jurisdiction:** An independent basis for subject matter jurisdiction is not required since supplemental jurisdiction will extend to a cross claim.

> **Issue-spotting tip:** Where joinder of parties or claims is at issue, also look for issues of personal jurisdiction, subject matter jurisdiction, and/or supplemental jurisdiction.

C. **Class action** is a case where a representative sues on behalf of a group.
   1. **Federal court class actions**
      a. **Requirements:** A federal class action is proper if the class meets the following requirements:

1. **Numerosity:** There are too many class members for joinder to be practical;
2. **Commonality:** The questions of law or fact are common to the class;
3. **Typicality:** The representative's claims or defenses are typical of those in the class;
4. **Adequacy** of representation such that it will fairly represent the class; and
5. **Type of class:** The class must also fit within one of the following types of classes:
a. **Prejudice:** Class treatment is necessary to avoid persons participating in a fund as individuals from depleting the fund; or
b. **Injunctive or declaratory relief is sought** (e.g., employment discrimination); or
c. **Questions of law/fact common to the class predominate** over questions affecting individuals, and a class action is a superior method to resolve the issues (e.g., damages for a mass tort).

b. **Federal class action citizenship issues**
1. **Diversity action:** To determine citizenship for class actions based on diversity, the **class representative individually must establish the amount in controversy requirement**, not the class members as an aggregate.
2. **Class Action Fairness Act** (2005) applies where there isn't complete diversity and allows a federal court to hear a class action if the following requirements are met:
a. **Diversity:** Any class member is diverse from any defendant; and
b. **Aggregation:** The class claims aggregate to exceed **$5 million**; and
c. **100 members:** There are at least 100 class members.

2. **California class actions**
a. A **California class action** is allowed if there is
1. An **ascertainable class**; and
2. A **well-defined community of interest** among class members. To analyze this interest the court looks at whether
a. **Common questions of law or fact** predominate;
b. The **representative is adequate**; and
c. The class will result in **substantial benefit** to the parties and the court.

b. **Type of class:** In California there is only one type of class and distinctions are not made based on the purpose the class serves as in federal court.
c. **Notice:** Individual notice is not required and publication is an acceptable method of notice.

D. **Discovery**
1. **Discovery disclosure** requirements

a. **Federal Rule 26 requires the mandatory disclosure** of information about the pending case to the opposing party. There are three types of mandatory disclosures:
   1. **Initial disclosures** that supply information about disputed facts, including
      a. Identifying **those likely to have discoverable information** about the claim or defense;
      b. Copies or description of **tangible evidence** such as documents;
      c. A **damages computation** and supporting documentation; and
      d. Copies of applicable **insurance documents.**
   2. **Expert testimony** information, including the
      a. **Identity** of the expert,
      b. The expert's **qualifications,** and
      c. The **written report.**
   3. **Pretrial disclosures,** including a list of all nonexpert **witnesses** and a list of **documents** or exhibits.

b. **California does not require the mandatory disclosure** of information, though information may be requested.

2. **Discovery tools**

a. **Depositions:** An examination of a witness that occurs under oath and is recorded by sound, video, or stenography. Questions can be oral or written but the answers are oral.
   1. **Parties** can be deposed and **nonparties** can be deposed by means of a subpoena.
   2. **Once:** A person may not be deposed twice without court approval.
   3. **Limits**
      a. **Federal** rules permit only ten depositions and the deposition cannot exceed one 7-hour day unless the court orders otherwise.
      b. **California** has no such limits. However, California limited cases allow only one deposition by each party.

b. **Interrogatories:** Questions propounded in writing to another **party**, which must be answered in writing under oath and the responding party must respond within 30 days. Interrogatories may not be asked of nonparties.
   1. **Limits**
      a. **Federal** rules permit no more than 25 questions, including subparts, unless the court orders otherwise.
      b. **California** allows an unlimited number of form interrogatories and 35 maximum specific interrogatories, unless a court permits additional upon the filing of a "Declaration of Additional Discovery" identifying the special need.

c. **Requests for admissions** request another **party** to admit the truth of any discoverable matter. The purpose is to identify areas that are not in controversy. Requests for admission may not be asked of nonparties.

   1. **California** allows a maximum of 35 requests for admission, unless a court permits additional upon the filing of a Declaration of Additional Discovery identifying the special need.

d. **Requests to inspect and produce**

   1. **Federal:** Any party may request another **party**, or a **nonparty** with subpoena, to make available for review and copying documents, electronic copies, or other tangible items, or permit entry onto property.

   2. **California allows for a party,** but **not for a nonparty** to make requests to inspect and produce. However, the same result could be accomplished by taking the nonparty's deposition and serving a subpoena duces tecum.

e. **Physical or mental examination** of a **party** may be sought by an opposing party. A party requesting such an exam must obtain a **court order** upon a showing of **good cause** that the examination will provide information about the physical or mental condition of the party where it is **at issue.**

   1. **California** allows the defendant to have **one physical exam** of the plaintiff. Other physical or mental examinations require leave of the **court.** The attorney for the party being examined can attend the physical exam.

f. **California limited cases have limited discovery** and only allow each party a 35 maximum total for all interrogatories, inspection demands, and requests combined.

3. **Scope of discovery**

   a. **Need not be admissible:** Relevant materials can be discovered even if not admissible so long as the item is reasonably calculated to lead to the discovery of admissible evidence.

   b. **Privileged material is not discoverable**

      1. **California** requires the responding party to object with particularity, identifying the document, its author, the date, all recipients, and the specific privilege applicable.

   c. **Attorney work product is not generally discoverable**

      1. **General rule:** Work product is material **prepared in anticipation of litigation** and is generally not discoverable **unless** there is **substantial need** and the **inability to obtain** the information through other means.

      2. **Absolute privilege** applies to **mental impressions**, opinions, conclusions, and legal theories.

         a. **Federal:** Applies if generated by a **party** or **attorney** or **representative** of a party.

         b. **California:** Applies if generated by an **attorney** or his **agent.**

   d. **California Constitution recognizes a right of privacy**, which is balanced against the need for discovery.

4. **Sanctions:** For violations of discovery, sanctions may be imposed including holding a noncomplying party in **contempt, striking pleadings, imposing fees, and ordering default judgment**.

> Exam tip: The few times discovery has been tested, the issues concerned a motion to compel an exam, and the discovery of work product.

III. **DISPOSITION OF A CASE WITHOUT A TRIAL:** Sometimes a case will be resolved prior to the end of the trial.

A. **Dismissal**

1. **Voluntary dismissal:** A plaintiff may obtain one voluntary dismissal without prejudice (so it may be relitigated). The trial court also has discretion to grant a dismissal after an answer or MSJ is filed, unless substantial prejudice to the defendant would occur.
2. **Involuntary dismissal:** The court may do this at the defendant's request, or at the court's own motion. Such a dismissal is usually with prejudice, so it may not be relitigated.
3. **Dismissal for failure to state a claim** occurs in a situation where if the court assumes all allegations are true, the plaintiff still cannot win based on the face of the complaint.
   a. **California:** This is a general demurrer.
4. **California mandatory dismissal** occurs if the case is not brought to trial within five years of filing the complaint, or two years have passed from filing until the service of process.

B. **Default judgment** occurs if the defendant fails to respond within **21 days** after service federally, or **30 days** of service in California.

C. **Motion for summary judgment** (MSJ) will be ordered where the moving party can establish there is **no genuine issue of material fact and that he is entitled to judgment as a matter of law**.

1. Evidence viewed in **light most favorable to the nonmoving party**.
2. Evidence must be comprised of **firsthand knowledge** and credibility is not weighed here.
3. A **court can grant a partial** summary judgment as to one of several causes of action.

> Exam tip: Civil procedure essay exams will often phrase a call by asking if a party is entitled to a motion for summary judgment, or a dismissal. This is almost always a method employed to ask about the underlying procedural issues present in the question, such as jurisdiction or res judicata.

IV. **TRIAL**

A. **Right to a jury trial**

1. **Federal Seventh Amendment:** In federal court, the Seventh Amendment preserves the right to a jury in civil actions at law; however a judge decides issues of equity.
   a. **Legal first, then equitable:** If a case has both legal and equitable claims, the jury decides the factual legal issues first, then the judge determines the equity claim.
   b. **Demand for jury:** Plaintiff must demand in writing no later than 14 days after service of the last pleading that he is raising a jury triable issue.
   c. **Jury composition**
      1. **Each side** (not party, as in California) has **unlimited** challenges on voir dire for **cause** (bias, prejudice, related to a party), and **three peremptory** challenges (still must be used in a gender and race-neutral way).
      2. A jury may contain **6-12 jurors** with no alternates; and a **unanimous vote** is required.
2. **California:** The California Constitution grants a right to a jury trial.
   a. **Equity first, then legal:** If a case has both legal and equitable claims, the judge decides the equitable issues first, then the jury decides the legal issues.
   b. **Equitable clean-up doctrine:** Where the main purpose of a case is equitable, and the only legal issue concerns damages that are merely incidental, then the judge may hear the whole case and a jury is not required.
   c. **Jury composition**
      1. **Each party** (not each side, as in federal court) is entitled to **unlimited** challenges for **cause** (bias, prejudice, related to a party) and **six peremptory** challenges (used in a gender and race-neutral way).
      2. A jury contains **12 jurors** and alternates; and only a **three-quarters juror vote** is required (civil cases only; for criminal cases an unanimous verdict is required).

B. **Judgment as a matter of law (JMOL)** occurs when one party files a motion after the other side has been heard at trial (so a defendant can usually move twice), contending that **reasonable people could not disagree on the result,** and asks for a judgment as a matter of law. Essentially this serves to take away from the jury.
   1. **California:** This is called a *motion for a directed verdict* or a *demurrer to the evidence.*

> **Exam tip:** Civil procedure essays may ask if a party is entitled to a JMOL as a mechanism to ask about the underlying substantive claim, such as a tort.

V. **POST-TRIAL ISSUES**

A. **Renewed judgment as a matter of law (RJMOL)** occurs after the jury has reached a verdict, contending that **reasonable people could not**

disagree on the result, and asks for a judgment as a matter of law. **The losing party must have originally filed a JMOL** or they cannot later file a RJMOL.

1. **Timing**
   a. **Federal:** The motion must be made within **28 days** after entry of judgment.
   b. **California:** The motion must be made within **15 days** after mailing or service of notice of entry of judgment, or 180 days after the entry of the judgment.
2. **California:** This is called a *motion for judgment notwithstanding the verdict* (JNOV) and unlike in federal court, the losing party is **not required to make a directed verdict motion first** in order to make the JNOV motion.

B. **Motion for a new trial:** After judgment has been entered, the losing party requests a new trial based on errors made at trial.
   1. **Timing**
      a. **Federal:** The motion must be made within **28 days** after entry of judgment.
      b. **California:** The motion must be made within **15 days** after mailing or service of notice of entry of judgment, or 180 days after the entry of the judgment.
   2. **Grounds for a new trial include the following:**
      a. **Prejudicial error** at trial that makes the judgment unfair.
      b. **New evidence** that could not have been obtained for the original trial through due diligence.
      c. **Prejudicial misconduct** of a party or attorney or third party or juror.
      d. Judgment is **against the weight of the evidence.**
      e. **Excessive damages or inadequate damages.**

C. **Motion to set aside the judgment** can be based on:
   1. **Clerical errors;**
   2. **Neglectful mistakes;**
   3. **Newly discovered evidence** that could not reasonably be discovered for the original trial; or
   4. **Judgment is void.**
   5. **Timing:** A motion to set aside a judgment based on neglectful mistakes or that the judgment is void may not be brought more than one year after the judgment.

D. **Conditional New Trial on Damages: Remittitur and Additur**
   1. **Remittitur** occurs when a judge orders that the defendant will get a new trial unless the **plaintiff agrees to a reduced award** of damages where the judge finds the damages awarded by the jury were excessive.
   2. **Additur** occurs when a judge orders that the plaintiff will get a new trial unless the **defendant agrees to an increased award** of damages where the judge finds the damages awarded by the jury were insufficient.
      a. **Federal:** Additur is not permitted in federal court.
      b. **California:** Additur is permitted in California courts.

VI. **APPEAL**

A. **Final judgment rule**

1. **Final judgment rule:** Only final judgments may be appealed. A final judgment is an ultimate decision made by the trial court on the merits of an entire case.
2. **Exceptions to the final judgment rule:** Despite the final judgment rule, the following orders may be appealed:
   a. **Injunctions and some interlocutory orders.**
   b. **Trial court certifies** an interlocutory order for appeal.
   c. **Collateral orders**, such as those regarding procedural issues.
   d. **Multiple claims or parties** are involved in the case and some issues are pending, but the issue is resolved as to one claim or party and the judge expressly determines that the order as to that party is final.
      1. **California:** A judgment as to one of several parties is considered a final judgment and can be appealed. Unlike the federal rule, an express determination is not required.
   e. **Extraordinary writ:** If an order is not otherwise appealable and the circumstances are exceptional, the aggrieved party may seek a writ of mandate to compel the lower court to act, or refrain from acting.

B. **Time limits for appeals**

1. **Federal:** Must file notice of appeal within **30 days** after entry of final judgment.
2. **California:** Must file notice of appeal within **60 days** after service of notice of entry of judgment; or 180 days after entry of the judgment if no notice is served.

VII. **USE OF FINAL JUDGMENT:** Where a claim or issue has already been resolved by litigation it may be barred from being re-litigated.

A. **Res judicata (claim preclusion)** precludes relitigation of a claim that has been decided in prior litigation. A subsequent suit based on the same claim will be barred where the first claim meets the following requirements:

1. There is a **valid final judgment on the merits.**
   a. **Federal:** A judgment is final when the judgment is **rendered.**
   b. **California:** A judgment is final when the **appeals have concluded.**

> **Issue-spotting tip:** Look for facts such as a prior judgment based on failure to join a party, jurisdiction, default judgment, consent, etc.

2. The prior claim was **actually litigated or could have been** litigated.

> **Issue-spotting tip:** Look for facts such as that the underlying court heard "extensive evidence."

3. The **same plaintiff and same defendant** were parties (or privies) in the prior case and subsequent case.
   a. A **privy** is a successor in interest to the property or claim, or is a representative (e.g., trustee) of the party.
   b. **"Strangers"** to the prior litigation cannot be bound under res judicata.
4. Both the prior case and the subsequent case assert the **same claim.**
   a. **Federal:** The "same claim" means the claim derives from the **same transaction or occurrence.**
   b. **California follows the primary rights theory**, which allows a **separate cause of action** for the invasion of each primary right. Thus, a plaintiff may sue separately for personal injury and property damage, even if both occurred from the same transaction or occurrence, since under the primary rights theory they are not considered the "same claim." (E.g., a one-car accident causing both property damage and personal injury would implicate two different primary rights.)

B. **Collateral estoppel (issue preclusion)** precludes relitigation of a particular issue that has already been decided in prior litigation. A subsequent suit based on the same issue will be barred where the first claim meets the following requirements:
   1. There is a **valid final judgment on the merits.**
      a. **Federal:** A judgment is final when the judgment is **rendered.**
      b. **California:** A judgment is final when the **appeals have concluded.**
   2. The same issue was **actually litigated and necessarily determined.**
   3. The **issue was essential to the judgment** in the first case.

> **Essential issue fact triggers (this can be tricky to spot):**
> - Underlying court finds plaintiff didn't own the property in dispute, but finds defendant was not negligent anyways.
> - Underlying court finds doctor is not an agent of the hospital being sued, but finds on negligence issue anyway.
> - Look for facts that seem peripheral to a judgment.
> - Look for specific findings for the underlying judgment.

   4. Determine **who can rely** on the prior judgment
      a. **Traditionally the rule of mutuality applied** and a party asserting collateral estoppel had to be a party (or a privy) in the prior case to assert collateral estoppel in the subsequent case. Thus, a "stranger" to the first case could not use a prior judgment.
      b. **California** (and other jurisdictions where the mutuality rule is not employed) **allows a "stranger" to the prior case to rely** on a prior judgment in the following circumstances:
         1. The **issues in the two cases are identical.**
         2. There is a **valid final judgment on the merits.**
         3. The party against whom collateral estoppel is being asserted had a **fair opportunity to be heard on the critical issue** in the prior case.

4. It **would not be unfair** or inequitable to apply collateral estoppel.
5. **California** includes the additional requirement that the party against whom collateral estoppel is being asserted is a **party or in privity** with a party to the prior proceeding.

> Issue-spotting tip: If a fact pattern includes a prior judgment or lawsuit, look for res judicata and/or collateral estoppel.
>
> Exam tip: Understand res judicata and collateral estoppel since both are very frequently tested on the essay exam. Some questions will test both principles at once, while others will test one or the other. Some questions will test the principles as they apply to different parties involved in the litigation. Be sure to apply the facts to the general rule and to the California rule distinctions, which will often lead to a different result.

CIVIL PROCEDURE ISSUES TESTED MATRIX

		Crossover	Personal Jx	Subject Matter Jx	Supplemental Jx	Removal & Remand	Venue	Choice of Law (*Erie* & Cal.)	Pleadings	Joinder of Parties	Joinder of Claims	Class Action	Discovery	Without Trial (MSJ & Dismissal)	Trial (Jury JMOL/ Directed Verdict)	Post-Trial FJR/ Appeal	Res Judicata	Collateral Estoppel
July '11 Q2	Doctor performs spine surgery with metal rod on Perry	Evidence												X			X	X
July '09 Q5	Diane builds dam for camp for disadvantaged kids	Remedies Prof. Resp.															X	
July '09 Q1	Patty transports human organs, and David blocks bridge	Torts							X									
February '09 Q2	Copyco. in state A, Sally in state B injures her hand		X	X			X		X				X					
February '06 Q4	Pat & Ed v. Busco, tour bus trip of State C		X														X	X
February '04 Q6	Paul v. Tom, Danco employee & car accident		X	X	X					X	X							
February '03 Q1	Petra v. Dave & Kola over patented bottle cap		X	X		X										X		
February '02 Q1	Pam v. Danco, breach of k for paper goods			X		X									X			
July '01 Q1	Pam v. Don's Market & Rita for car accident			X			X									X		

Continued >

		Crossover	Personal Jx	Subject Matter Jx	Supplemental Jx	Removal & Remand	Venue	Choice of Law (*Erie* & Cal.)	Pleadings	Joinder of Parties	Joinder of Claims	Class Action	Discovery	Without Trial (MSJ & Dismissal)	Trial (Jury JMOL/ Directed Verdict)	Post-Trial FJR/ Appeal	Res Judicata	Collateral Estoppel
July '00 Q5	Paul v. Bigcorp & Amcorp power saw accident		X	X						X							X	
July '99 Q2	Pat v. Delta Hospital and class action for prisoner rights		X	X			X					X						
February '99 Q6	Park art importer of vases v. Wholesaler and arbitration		X	X			X											
July '98 Q2	Pat involuntarily hospitalized in state A sues pro se			X	X				X									
July '97 Q4	Danco, oil refinery built by Tom explodes in state A			X		X			X	X								
July '96 Q4	Pat v. Danco, age discrimination against salesman		X	X													X	
February '96 Q3	Dave's gym and injury to Paul	Evidence Torts													X	X		
July '95 Q6	Salesco v. Parts/ Subparts for breach of contract			X	X			X	X									
July '94 Q5	Paul injured by Manco machine sues hospital		X														X	X
February '94 Q6	Paul v. Danco explosives damage Blackacre/ Whiteacre													X	X		X	X

Continued >

		Crossover	Personal Jx	Subject Matter Jx	Supplemental Jx	Removal & Remand	Venue	Choice of Law (*Erie* & Cal.)	Pleadings	Joinder of Parties	Joinder of Claims	Class Action	Discovery	Without Trial (MSJ & Dismissal)	Trial (Jury JMOL/ Directed Verdict)	Post-Trial FJR/ Appeal	Res Judicata	Collateral Estoppel
February '93 Q1	Paulco v. Dan poor quality shipment for retail store		X					X					X					
February '92 Q5	Borrow gets car loan from Finco & payments too high				X	X				X	X			X				X
July '90 Q2	Pat gets mail order indoor hot tub & gets burned		X	X				X		X				X				
July '89 Q1	Pam injured in nursing home fire where no detectors							X					X	X				
July '88 Q4	Dan flying small plane makes forced landing on highway		X	X					X	X			X					
July '87 Q2	Pat & Dan car accident, bystander has injuries		X	X													X	X
July '86 Q2	Owner & Rider v. Trucker for car accident									X	X						X	X

CIVIL PROCEDURE PRACTICE ESSAYS, ANSWER GRIDS, AND SAMPLE ANSWERS

Civil Procedure Question 1

July 1987, Question 2

Pat, a resident of State X, was involved in an automobile accident in State Y with Dan. Pat sued Dan in State X Municipal Court alleging personal injury damages of $200,000. Dan was served with process in State Y in the manner authorized by the State X "long arm statute" which provides that the courts of State X "may exercise jurisdiction on any basis not inconsistent with the Constitution of the United States." Although he is a resident of State Y, Dan spends approximately six weekends a year in State X at a small vacation cabin in which he has a one-eighth ownership interest.

Dan moved for dismissal on the ground that Municipal Court lacked personal jurisdiction over him. The motion was denied. Dan filed an answer asserting that Pat's negligence caused the accident, and the case proceeded to trial. The jury returned a verdict in favor of Pat in the amount of $100,000. Both State X and State Y have rules making contributory negligence a complete defense in a negligence suit.

Dan appealed on the grounds that: (1) Municipal Court lacked personal jurisdiction over Dan, and (2) Municipal Court lacked jurisdiction to hear controversies exceeding $10,000. Although the jurisdictional limit for Municipal Court was $10,000, the appellate court ruled that Dan had waived his right to contest both personal jurisdiction over him in Municipal Court and Municipal Court's subject matter jurisdiction to hear the case. The appellate court affirmed the judgment and it became final.

Subsequently, Bob, a bystander who had been slightly injured in the collision, filed a complaint in State X Municipal Court against Dan and Pat for damages of $10,000, alleging negligence. Pat answered and filed a cross-complaint against Dan for damages to Pat's car arising from the collision.

Based upon the above facts, the following motions were made: Bob moved for summary judgment against Dan on the issue of negligence; Pat moved for summary judgment against Dan on the issue of negligence and for summary judgment against Bob; Dan moved for a summary judgment against Pat.

1. Was the Municipal Court correct when it ruled it had personal jurisdiction over Dan? Discuss.
2. Was the appellate court correct when it ruled Dan had waived his right to contest Municipal Court's personal jurisdiction over him and Municipal Court's subject matter jurisdiction to hear controversies exceeding $10,000? Discuss.
3. Should Bob's motion for summary judgment against Dan be granted? Discuss.

4. Should Pat's motion for summary judgment against Dan be granted? Discuss.
5. Should Pat's motion for summary judgment against Bob be granted? Discuss.
6. Should Dan's motion for summary judgment against Pat be granted? Discuss.

Civil Procedure Question 1 Assessment

July 1987, Question 2

This question is a good practice question for two reasons. First, it covers all four of the most frequently tested civil procedure concepts: personal jurisdiction, subject matter jurisdiction, res judicata, and collateral estoppel. Second, it tests two concepts, res judicata and collateral estoppel, several times each, where the analysis varies based on application of the rule to three different parties and fact situations. This is a frequent testing strategy in civil procedure and it is not uncommon to see one concept tested several times in the same essay question. Note that the call of the question asks six specific questions, so the answer should be framed to answer the questions asked. When one concept is tested several times on an exam—such as res judicata/collateral estoppel, here—the best strategy is to provide the full rule and analysis once, and jump to the key dispositive element(s) and analysis on the subsequent calls where the issue arises.

Because this question covers so much material, it is a "racehorse" question. Not all civil procedure questions are, but they can be. Since this question has six question calls it is pretty easy to identify that it is a racehorse question. If that didn't give it away, organizing the answer would have done so. With a civil procedure racehorse, it is important to practice being economical with words because many of the rules themselves use a lot of words to convey the concepts—for example, the minimum contacts rule. Since the most important part of the answer is the factual analysis, not the recitation of the rules, it is important to practice working with the language. It is best to weave the rules and analysis together in the answer where possible, and/or use "supra" within the answer to refer to rules that have already been recited earlier in the answer. For this reason, it is especially important that you know the rules well and can recite them easily.

Although it is important for every subject, it is especially important that you actually practice writing out civil procedure essay exams within timed conditions. The language is often cumbersome to work with and the analysis can be difficult to write succinctly at first, so it is crucial that you practice so you can gain speed in order to write the question response within the one-hour allotted time.

This question was administered before the bar examiners specifically stated that the California rules of civil procedure were eligible for testing on the bar exam. As of this writing, the bar examiners have yet to ask a civil procedure question that is set in California, so there is no example of such a question. Unless a question is set in California, the best approach on an exam is to apply the federal rules and note where the California rules are different, especially identifying where application of the California rule would lead to a different result.

Make note of the areas highlighted in **bold** on the corresponding grid. The bold areas highlight the issues, analysis, and conclusions that are likely **required** to receive a passing score on this question. In general, the essay grids are provided to assist you in analyzing the essays, and are much more detailed than what a student should create during the exam to organize their response to a question.

Issue	Rule	Fact Application	Conclusion
Call #1			
Personal jurisdiction	Long-arm statute **Minimum contacts:** • **Purposeful availment** • **Foreseeability** • **Relatedness** • **Systematic & continuous** • Fairness factors	Dan properly served in State Y. State X long-arm statute extends to constitutional limits, so minimum contacts test applies. **D lives in State Y and only contact w/State X is 1/8 interest in property at which he vacations 6 weekends a year, and accident is in State Y**, so unlikely D availed himself of benefits of State X regarding accident. **Not foreseeable to be haled into another state for an accident that occurred in your home state just because you have 1/8 interest in vacation home in other state.** **Accident in State Y, so no relationship between cause of action and State X.** Not continuous or systematic to **vacation in State X 6 times a year and it is unrelated to accident in State Y.** D, accident, witnesses, etc., all in State Y, not State X.	Appellate court erred
Call #2			
Waiver of personal jurisdiction	**Must object to personal jurisdiction in the first response or waived**	**D did raise the issue of lack of personal jurisdiction on the first motion he filed, so it was not waived.**	Appellate court erred
Waiver of subject matter jurisdiction (SMJ)	**Lack of SMJ may be raised anytime, including on appeal.**	**D can properly raise lack of SMJ on appeal and has not waived.**	Appellate court erred

Continued >

Issue	Rule	Fact Application	Conclusion
Call #3			
Motion for summary judgment (MSJ)	**No genuine issue of material fact and entitled to judgment as matter of law**	Appropriateness of Bob's MSJ will be determined by analysis of collateral estoppel below.	Depends on whether CE is met below
Collateral estoppel (CE)	**Traditional rule:** • Final judgment on merits • Actually litigated • Issue essential to judgment • **Mutuality: party or privy only** **Modern Cal. rule:** • **Identical issues** • **Final judgment on merits** • **Fair opportunity to be heard** • **Not unfair** • **Party CE used against party or privy to prior suit**	Jury verdict for P in previous suit, so final judgment on merits and actually litigated issue of D's negligence. Verdict based on D's negligence, so essential. **Bob not a party in prior suit, so traditionally he would be barred by CE.** **Dan's negligence for accident litigated in both.** **Jury verdict finding Dan negligent for accident** but possible jurisdictional issues (above). **Presumably,** since prior case for $200k and this case is $10k. It is unfair to let Bob use CE as a sword against D since contributory negligence is a complete defense, and D should be able to have the opportunity to litigate Bob's contributory negligence. **Dan was the defendant in the prior case.**	Traditionally, CE not allowed because Bob wasn't a party Modernly, CE would not be allowed either because it is unfair Court should not grant Bob's MSJ
Call #4			
Motion for summary judgment	No genuine issue of material fact, and entitled to judgment as matter of law	See below.	Depends on whether CE is met below

Continued >

Issue	Rule	Fact Application	Conclusion
Collateral estoppel	Traditional rule: • Final judgment on merits • Actually litigated • Issue essential to judgment • Mutuality: party or privy	**Final judgment against Dan on litigated, essential issue of Dan's negligence for the accident**. Pat and Dan were both parties, so collateral estoppel should **allow Pat to use the negligence finding against Dan.** However, Pat's claim may be barred by res judicata (see call #6). Note: Bar examiners accepted **analysis under collateral estoppel or res judicata.**	Pat's MSJ against Dan on negligence issue should be granted
Call #5			
Motion for summary judgment	No genuine issue of material fact and entitled to judgment as matter of law	See below.	Depends on whether CE is met below
Collateral estoppel	Traditional rule: • Mutuality: **party or privy** Modern Cal. rule: • **Party CE used against party or privy to prior suit**	Pat is attempting to use the prior court finding that she was not contributorily negligent for the accident against **Bob, who was not a party in the prior case. Pat will not be permitted to do so under either the traditional or modern rule.** Note: Bar examiners accepted **analysis under collateral estoppel or res judicata.**	Pat's MSJ against Bob should not be granted
Call #6			
Motion for summary judgment	No genuine issue of material fact & entitled to judgment as matter of law	See below.	Depends on whether RJ is met below

Continued >

Issue	Rule	Fact Application	Conclusion
Res judicata	Final judgment on the merits Actually litigated Same parties Same claim Majority rule: **Fed.: same T or O** Cal.: **primary rights theory**	**Jury verdict finding Dan negligent for accident** but possible jurisdictional issues (see above). Pat and Dan were parties in both actions. Under the **traditional rule, Pat would be precluded under res judicata from bringing a second suit for damages to her car since the damages occurred from the same transaction and occurrence** as the claim against Dan for personal injuries heard in the prior suit. However, if the jurisdiction follows the **primary rights theory, Pat is allowed a claim for each right invaded and each right can be asserted separately, so Pat would not be barred from bringing a subsequent suit for her property damage.**	Dan's MSJ should be granted if the jurisdiction follows the traditional rule, and denied if the primary rights theory is followed

Civil Procedure Question 1 Sample Answer

July 1987, Question 2

1. Personal Jurisdiction Over Dan

Personal Jurisdiction

The municipal court will have personal jurisdiction over Dan if there is a long-arm statute and exercising jurisdiction falls within constitutional limits.

Long-Arm Statute

A long-arm statute allows a state to reach beyond its borders and assert personal jurisdiction over a nonresident. Dan was properly served and State X's statute extends its reach to the limits of the Constitution, thus the minimum contacts test determines if personal jurisdiction over Dan is appropriate.

Minimum Contacts

Personal jurisdiction may be extended to nonresidents where there are sufficient minimum contacts with the forum state such that the defendant purposefully availed himself of the benefits and protections of the forum state and it is reasonably foreseeable that he would be haled into court. Dan is a resident of State Y, however, he spends six weekends a year in a vacation cabin in State X. Dan's one-eighth partial ownership interest in the cabin does not indicate he has availed himself of the benefits and protections of the laws of State X by sporadic vacationing in the state, nor are these contacts systematic and continuous. Further, there is no relationship between Dan's vacationing activities in State X and the car accident in his home state of State Y such that it would be foreseeable Dan would be haled into court in State X.

Bringing suit in State X also offends traditional notions of fair play and substantial justice since the fairness factors also disfavor personal jurisdiction over Dan. Since the accident happened in State Y, the injury, evidence, and witness are all in State Y, and Dan should not have to travel to defend the suit.

The court was incorrect in ruling it had personal jurisdiction over Dan.

2. Dan's Waiver of Personal Jurisdiction and Subject Matter Jurisdiction

Waiver of Personal Jurisdiction

Generally, a defendant must object to personal jurisdiction in the first response or else the issue is waived. Dan's first motion filed was a dismissal based on the ground of lack of personal jurisdiction. Therefore, Dan did not waive the issue of personal jurisdiction and the appellate court erred.

Waiver of Subject Matter Jurisdiction

Lack of subject matter jurisdiction may be raised at any time, even on appeal, and Dan raised the issue in his appeal. If in fact the Municipal Court lacks jurisdiction to hear cases over $10,000, as asserted, and Dan was sued for $200,000, the lack of jurisdiction is clear. Since subject matter jurisdiction cannot be waived and may be raised even after final judgment, the appellate court erred.

3. Bob's Motion for Summary Judgment Against Dan

Summary Judgment

Summary judgment is proper where the moving party can establish there is no genuine issue of material fact and he is entitled to judgment as a matter of law. Since Bob was not a party to the earlier lawsuit, he would have to base his motion on collateral estoppel, as analyzed below.

Collateral Estoppel (Issue Preclusion)

Collateral estoppel precludes relitigation of a particular issue that has already been decided where there is a prior judgment on the merits, the issue was actually litigated, and the issue was essential to the judgment. Traditionally, the mutuality principle requires privity between the parties. Since Bob was not a party to the original suit, he would be barred from asserting collateral estoppel under the traditional rule.

Modernly, some states, including California, allow a nonparty to assert collateral estoppel where (1) the issues are identical; (2) there was a final judgment on the merits; (3) the party against whom it is being asserted had a fair opportunity to be heard on the critical issue; (4) it would not be unfair to apply collateral estoppel; and California requires (5) the party against whom collateral estoppel is being used was a party (or privy) to the prior proceeding.

The identical issue of Dan's negligence for the accident was already decided with a valid final judgment on the merits in the prior case. Dan was a defendant in the original suit and had a fair opportunity to be heard, since that case was $200,000 in damages, and in this suit Bob is claiming a relatively paltry $10,000 in damages. However, as analyzed previously, the judgment may not be valid because of jurisdictional issues. Dan will also assert it would be unfair to apply collateral estoppel since his negligence towards Bob was not litigated and Bob's contributory negligence would be a complete defense in a negligence suit and that issue was not litigated. However, Bob will counter that Dan had a full opportunity to litigate the issue of his own negligence and Dan could have foreseen additional suits since he must have known Bob was an injured bystander. Since collateral estoppel is being asserted against Dan and he was a party in the previous case, it could be used against him, assuming it would not be unfair to do so.

Thus, even though under the modern trend collateral estoppel could be applied against Dan, it would not be fair because doing so would be unfair in light of the contributory negligence issue.

4. Pat's Motion for Summary Judgment Against Dan

Collateral Estoppel (Issue Preclusion)

Rule supra.

Pat has a prior judgment on the merits against Dan on the issue of Dan's negligence for the car accident. The issue of Dan's negligence was actually litigated, the negligence issue was essential to the judgment, and Dan and Pat were both parties in the prior action.

Pat should be permitted to use the doctrine of collateral estoppel to establish the issue of Dan's negligence for the car accident. However, Dan may be able to assert that Pat's suit should be barred by res judicata as discussed in section 6.

5. Pat's Motion for Summary Judgment Against Bob

Collateral Estoppel (Issue Preclusion)

Rule supra.

Pat is attempting to use the prior case, which determined Pat was not contributorily negligent for the accident against Bob, who was not a party to that case. Collateral estoppel may only be used against parties (or privies) from the prior case. Even though contributory negligence is a complete bar and State X has already determined that Pat was not at fault in the accident, she will be unable to use that judgment against Bob since he was not a party. Pat may not assert collateral estoppel against Bob.

Thus, the court should deny Pat's request for summary judgment against Bob.

6. Dan's Motion for Summary Judgment Against Pat

Res Judicata (Claim Preclusion)

Res judicata precludes a claim from being relitigated where there is a valid final judgment on the merits, the claim was actually litigated, the same parties were involved, and the case involves the same claim. Traditionally, the same claim means the claims derive from the same transaction or occurrence. Some states, including California, apply the primary rights doctrine, which permits separate claims for each primary right invaded.

Pat has a valid final judgment on the merits and the claim was litigated with a finding that Dan was negligent for the car accident. Pat and Dan are the same parties to the suit. Whether res judicata applies to bar Pat's suit depends on whether the jurisdiction applies the traditional rule or the primary rights rule. Under the traditional rule, Pat would be barred by res judicata from bringing a subsequent suit to assert property damage based on the same transaction and occurrence of the car accident, since it was already litigated as to Pat's personal injuries. However, if the primary rights doctrine is followed in this jurisdiction, Pat would be permitted to bring a subsequent suit to litigate the different and separate primary right of the property damage caused by the car accident, and thus res judicata would not bar her claim.

Civil Procedure Question 2

February 1992, Question 5

Borrow, a resident of State A, obtained a $12,000 car loan from Finco. Finco is incorporated and has its principal place of business in State A. When Borrow began making installment repayments against the loan, he was dismayed to learn that his required monthly payments were in an amount greater than he had expected.

Borrow brought suit against Finco in a state court in State A, asserting a claim against Finco under the federal Truth in Lending Act (TLA). TLA specifically requires lenders to disclose to a borrower in a consumer loan transaction the amount of the monthly loan payment. TLA further provides that a borrower whose rights under TLA have been violated may bring an action against the lender in a United States district court or in any other court of competent jurisdiction.

Finco filed its answer denying liability and asserting a counterclaim against Borrow under state law for recovery of the full amount owed on the loan. Finco then timely removed the suit to the United States District Court for the District of State A. In the district court Borrow moved to remand the action. The motion was denied.

Shortly thereafter Borrow moved to amend his complaint to: (1) add an additional defendant, Dealer, the company that had sold him the car; (2) allege that Dealer violated State A's Consumer Protection Law (CPL) by providing him erroneous information about the terms of his loan; and (3) allege that Dealer's CPL violation had resulted in $20,000 in damages. Dealer is incorporated in State A and conducts all its business there. The district court denied the motion to amend on the ground that the court lacked subject matter jurisdiction over Borrow's claim against Dealer.

Borrow next moved for partial summary judgment which, if granted, would preclude Finco from denying that its lending agreement violated TLA. In support of this motion Borrow offered uncontradicted evidence that in previous lawsuits brought by other borrowers in federal court, final judgments had been entered against Finco on holdings that, under circumstances identical with those in the present lawsuit, Finco's failure to make the required loan payment disclosure violated TLA. Borrow's motion was denied.

Were the district court's rulings correct as to:

1. Borrow's motion to remand? Discuss.
2. Borrow's motion to amend his complaint? Discuss.
3. Borrow's motion for partial summary judgment? Discuss.

Civil Procedure Question 2 Assessment

February 1992, Question 5

This question primarily examines the concepts of supplemental jurisdiction and collateral estoppel. This question is fairly typical for a civil procedure exam in that it tests the same concepts more than once with a slight change of facts. The concepts of supplemental jurisdiction and collateral estoppel are tested by the bar examiners somewhat frequently, however the removal and remand issues are less frequently tested and would be challenging if you didn't know the rules. Since there were not a lot of issues to cover on this question, it is important not to miss any major issues in order to receive a passing score.

On the issue of Borrow's motion to remand, there should be some discussion of the removal and remand rules and their applicability under these facts. The factual analysis is quite simple since there is a federal question here, since the TLA is a federal statute. A better answer should also have some discussion of the concepts of a compulsory counterclaim and supplemental jurisdiction as it pertains to Finco's countersuit for the full loan amount. The concepts can be blended together in the analysis so long as the issue is identified. Organizationally, since there was no particular call of the question for this issue, it could be addressed at any place in the exam so it is important to use a heading for easy identification.

There were a variety of ways the issues could be appropriately organized and addressed on the question of Borrow's motion to amend, which is exactly why it is so important to use issue headings on your answer so the bar examiners can easily find in your answer the analysis they are looking for. The answer should identify that there is no basis for federal subject matter jurisdiction for the amended complaint to add an action against Dealer. This could be addressed as a separate subject matter jurisdiction section, or included as a part of the supplemental jurisdiction analysis. The supplemental jurisdiction section could be combined to include all of the issues pertaining to supplemental jurisdiction as related to both claims and parties. The important analysis here is that the "common nucleus of operative fact" is that the claims arose from the same loan transaction.

On the call pertaining to Borrow's motion for summary judgment, the important analysis is a discussion of collateral estoppel and, in particular, the concept of the traditional rule of mutuality and the California rule not requiring mutuality since a "stranger" is trying to take advantage of the prior judgment. A thorough analysis of all of the mutuality elements is required to receive a passing score on this question.

Make note of the areas highlighted in **bold** on the corresponding grid. The bold areas highlight the issues, analysis, and conclusions that are likely **required** to receive a passing score on this question.

Issue	Rule	Fact Application	Conclusion
1. Borrow's Motion to Remand			
Removal	**A defendant may remove to federal court if the case is brought in state court and could properly be brought in federal court.**	**Here, the defendant Finco seeks to remove to federal court. A federal question is presented under the federal Truth in Lending Act (TLA), and since this is a federal statute a federal question is presented, so the original filing could have been in federal court, therefore removal was proper.**	Court didn't err; **removal was proper**
Remand	A plaintiff can file for remand back to state court where removal to federal court is improper.	There is federal subject matter jurisdiction because there is a federal question posed under the TLA, so the court properly denied the motion to remand.	Court didn't err
Compulsory counterclaim	**All counterclaims arising from the same transaction and occurrence must be raised or they are waived.**	Finco is suing for the full amount of the loan, and this action **arises from the same transaction that gave rise to the TLA loan, which is the $12,000 car loan obtained by Borrow from Finco.**	Compulsory counterclaim
Supplemental jurisdiction	**If a counterclaim is compulsory, no independent basis for federal subject matter jurisdiction is required.**	Here, Finco's counterclaim is compulsory because it arises from the same transaction or occurrence, **therefore supplemental jurisdiction will cover the claim** even though state law is the basis for Finco's claim and there is no need for an independent basis for SMJ for Finco's claim.	**Court has supplemental jurisdiction**
2. Borrow's Motion to Amend			
Subject matter jurisdiction	**Federal question or complete diversity between the parties and more than $75,000**	Here, **the suit against the dealer presents a state law claim of a violation of State A's consumer protection law, which does not pose a federal question. Additionally, all of the parties involved are citizens of State A and the claim is for less than $75,000, so the diversity requirements are defeated. There is no independent basis for subject matter jurisdiction over Borrow's amendment to add Dealer.** Borrow's motion to amend will be denied unless supplemental jurisdiction exists.	**No independent SMJ**

Continued >

Issue	Rule	Fact Application	Conclusion
Supplemental jurisdiction claims	**Common nucleus of operative fact, same T or O**	Court has discretion, but here the claim is not novel or complex, nor does the state claim predominate. **The state law claim is regarding the consumer protection law of State A, and both claims pertain to the same loan transaction, both defendant's are accused of failure to disclose loan terms appropriately**, and both claims would result in the same remedy (damages). The court probably should have allowed the amended complaint, but since the court has discretion, there was no error.	Court should allow amended complaint, but it is discretionary, so no error
Supplemental jurisdiction parties	In a diversity case, supplemental jurisdiction may not be used to circumvent the diversity requirements.	See analysis above. The original basis of jurisdiction over Finco was the federal TLA claim, and **Dealer may be added since the claim concerns a common nucleus of operative fact.** This is allowed at the discretion of the judge, so the court probably should have allowed the amended complaint. However, since court has discretion, there was no error.	Court should allow amended complaint, but it is discretionary, so no error
3. Borrow's Motion for Partial Summary Judgment			
MSJ	No genuine issue of material fact, and the moving party is entitled to judgment as a matter of law.	Requires analysis of the underlying claim	

Continued >

Issue	Rule	Fact Application	Conclusion
Collateral estoppel (CE)	**Traditional rule:** • **Final judgment on merits** • Actually litigated • Issue essential to judgment • **Mutuality: party or privy only** **Modern Cal. rule:** • Identical issues • Final judgment on merits • Fair opportunity to be heard • Not unfair • **Party CE used against party or privy to prior suit**	**Here, there is uncontradicted evidence of previous suits in federal court with final judgments against Finco "under circumstances identical to those in the present lawsuit."** **However, under the traditional mutuality rule, Borrow could not use CE as a nonparty/privity in the prior suits.** However, under the California rule There were "identical" issues per facts Final judgments were entered against Finco Presumably **Finco had a fair opportunity to be heard** **There were multiple lawsuits with the same result, lots of opportunity to be heard on the prior suits so it is fair** **And, CE is being used against Finco, who was the defendant party in the prior suits, so under the California rule CE would prevent Finco from relitigating the same nondisclosure issue and allow Borrow to use the prior judgment**	If mutuality rule not applied in the jurisdiction, collateral estoppel would be proper, so court erred in denying partial summary judgment

Civil Procedure Question 2 Sample Answer

February 1992, Question 5

1. Borrow's Motion to Remand

Removal

A defendant may move to have a case removed to federal court if the case is brought in state court and it could properly be brought in federal court. The defendant Finco seeks to remove the case to federal court, though Borrow has filed in state court. Since a federal question is presented in the case under the federal Truth in Lending Act (TLA), which is a federal statute, the original filing could have been made in federal court; therefore, removal by the defendant was proper and the court did not err.

Remand

A plaintiff can file to have a case remanded back to state court where removal to federal court is improper. Since there is federal subject matter jurisdiction on this case because there is a federal question posed under the TLA, the court properly denied the motion to remand the case to state court.

Compulsory Counterclaim

All counterclaims arising from the same transaction or occurrence must be raised or they are deemed waived. Finco has asserted a counterclaim against Borrow based on state law, and Finco is suing for the full amount of the car loan. This claim arises from the same transaction that gave rise to the federal TLA loan, which is the $12,000 car loan obtained by Borrow from Finco. Finco's counterclaim is compulsory and must be raised or deemed waived.

Supplemental Jurisdiction

If a counterclaim is compulsory because it arises from the same transaction or occurrence as the existing claim, no independent basis for federal subject matter jurisdiction is required. Here, Finco's counterclaim is compulsory because it arises from the same transaction or occurrence. Therefore, supplemental jurisdiction will extend to cover the claim even though state law is the basis for Finco's counterclaim and there is no independent basis for subject matter jurisdiction to cover Finco's claim against Borrow.

2. Borrow's Motion to Amend Complaint

Subject Matter Jurisdiction

Subject matter jurisdiction means the court must have proper jurisdiction over the subject matter of an action. Federal courts have limited subject matter jurisdiction and may only hear cases involving federal questions or diversity of citizenship, which requires complete diversity and a claim exceeding $75,000. Borrow seeks to amend his complaint to add the Dealer and assert a violation of the state Consumer Protection Law (CPL). The suit against the dealer presents a state law claim of a violation of State A's CPL, which does not pose a federal question. Additionally, all of the parties involved in the case are citizens of State A, and further, at $20,000, the claim is for less than the $75,000 required to satisfy federal diversity jurisdiction so the federal diversity requirements are defeated. There is no independent basis for subject matter jurisdiction over Borrow's amendment to add Dealer and the CPL claim. Borrow's motion to amend will be denied unless supplemental jurisdiction exists.

Supplemental Jurisdiction

Supplemental jurisdiction applies to provide subject matter jurisdiction when an additional claim does not itself invoke federal subject matter jurisdiction, but the additional claim shares a common nucleus of operative fact with a claim that does properly invoke federal subject matter jurisdiction. A "common nucleus of operative fact" means that the claim arises from the same transaction or occurrence. However, in a diversity case, supplemental jurisdiction may not be used to circumvent the diversity requirements. Here, the underlying claim by Borrow against Finco is not based on diversity and does properly invoke federal subject matter jurisdiction since it involves the federal TLA. Borrow seeks to amend to include a state law claim regarding the CPL of State A, and both claims pertain to the same $12,000 car loan transaction. Further, both defendants are accused of failure to disclose loan terms appropriately, and both claims would result in the same remedy of legal damages. The court has discretion, but here the claim is not novel or complex, nor does the state claim predominate. The court probably should have allowed the amended complaint, but since the court has discretion, there is no error.

3. Borrow's Motion for Partial Summary Judgment

Motion for Partial Summary Judgment

Summary judgment is proper where the moving party can establish there is no genuine issue of material fact and he is entitled to judgment as a matter of law. The underlying claim must be analyzed to determine if partial summary judgment is appropriate.

Collateral Estoppel (Issue Preclusion)

Collateral estoppel precludes relitigation of a particular issue that has already been decided where there is a prior judgment on the merits, the issue was actually litigated, and the issue was essential to the judgment. Traditionally, the mutuality principle requires there be privity between the parties. Here, there is uncontradicted evidence in the form of several previous lawsuits that have been decided in the favor of other borrowers, so there are final judgments on the merits on cases that were actually litigated concerning "identical" circumstances. Nonetheless, if the mutuality principle is in effect, Borrow would not be able to assert collateral estoppel against Finco since Borrow was not a party or privity to the prior lawsuits, which found that Finco's failure to make the required loan payment disclosures violated the TLA.

Modernly, some states, including California, allow a nonparty to assert collateral estoppel where (1) the issues are identical; (2) there was a final judgment on the merits; (3) the party against whom it is being asserted had a fair opportunity to be heard on the critical issue; (4) it would not be unfair to apply collateral estoppel; and California requires (5) the party against whom collateral estoppel is being used was a party (or privy) to the prior proceeding. Again, the facts were "identical" and final judgments were entered against Finco. Presumably Finco had a fair opportunity to be heard since there were multiple lawsuits with the same result, which would provide an abundance of opportunity for Finco to defend itself and be heard on the prior suits, so it is not unfair for Borrow to assert collateral estoppel. Lastly, collateral estoppel is being used against Finco, who was the defendant party in the prior suits. If the California rule is applied, collateral estoppel could be used by Borrow to prevent Finco from relitigating the same loan nondisclosure issue and Finco would be allowed to use the prior judgment to establish that issue.

Civil Procedure Question 3

February 1994, Question 6

Paul sued Danco in federal court for $100,000. He alleged that Blackacre had been damaged by Danco's negligent use of explosives. In addition, Paul sought an injunction to prohibit future blasting and timely requested trial by jury. The request for a jury trial was denied.

Danco denied that Blackacre was damaged, and claimed that Paul, who asserted ownership of Blackacre by adverse possession, was not the owner. The court heard extensive evidence and concluded that because Paul had no interest in Blackacre, and because Blackacre had not been damaged, Paul could not recover. Judgment for Danco was entered.

Owen had not been notified of Paul's suit against Danco.

Two months after judgment was entered, Owen, the true owner of Blackacre, filed a complaint in federal court against Danco, claiming damage to Blackacre from the same conduct involved in Paul's suit. Danco moved for summary judgment against Owen, asserting the defenses of res judicata and collateral estoppel. The motion was denied on the ground that there was no legal basis upon which Danco could use the doctrine of either collateral estoppel or res judicata to defend itself.

Paul sought to intervene as a plaintiff in Owen's suit, alleging that Danco's conduct damaged Whiteacre, a nearby parcel he did own but did not include in the prior suit. The court granted Paul's motion for intervention. Danco then moved for summary judgment against Paul. The motion for summary judgment was denied.

Assume that all federal jurisdictional requirements are met.

1. Did the court err in denying Paul's request for a jury trial? Discuss.
2. Did the court err in denying Danco's motion for summary judgment against Owen? Discuss.
3. Did the court err in denying Danco's motion for summary judgment against Paul? Discuss.

Civil Procedure Question 3 Assessment

February 1994, Question 6

This question primarily examines the concepts of res judicata (claim preclusion) and collateral estoppel (issue preclusion) and is fairly easy if these concepts are understood well, and difficult if they aren't. This question is fairly typical for a civil procedure exam in that it tests the same concepts more than once with a slight change of facts to alter the application. Res judicata and collateral estoppel are tested by the bar examiners frequently, while the request for a jury trial issue is an infrequently tested topic. Notice that the call of the question asks about a motion for summary judgment, but this civil procedure query is really a mechanism to get to the substantive res judicata and collateral estoppel discussion.

On the jury trial issue, it is important to include both the Seventh Amendment rule, which provides a right to a jury trial, and the application of the rule as it pertains to a case where principles of law and equity are combined. In the latter case, the federal rule is that a jury decides the legal issues first, and then the court hears the equity issues. Had the case occurred in California, the order would be reversed.

The key analysis on the res judicata issue on Danco's MSJ against Owen is identifying that Owen was not a party, a privy, or even notified of the first case, therefore his interests weren't represented in the first suit. The analysis should not be cursory since this is determinative on the issue. The important piece of analysis on the collateral estoppel issue is a discussion of the prior court's determination that Blackacre had not sustained damage from the blasting, and analysis of whether determination on that issue was essential to the judgment since Paul was ultimately found to have no interest in Blackacre.

The important analysis on the third call of the question regarding Danco's MSJ against Paul is a discussion of res judicata and analysis of the traditional rule, which provides that the same "cause of action" refers to the "same transaction and occurrence." The tricky part of the analysis is noticing that the outcome was dependent on the nature of the blasting activity. If there had been one "transaction and occurrence" of blasting that did damage to both Blackacre and Whitacre, Paul's claim would be precluded under res judicata. However, if there were additional blasting incidents, or continuing blasting activity, Paul's claim would not be precluded by res judicata. What is important here is identifying the issue that the nature of the blasting activity engaged in by Danco was determinative on the outcome here.

Make note of the areas highlighted in **bold** on the corresponding grid. The bold areas highlight the issues, analysis, and conclusions that are likely **required** to receive a passing score on this question.

Issue	Rule	Fact Application	Conclusion
1. Jury Trial			
7th Amendment	**7th Amend. preserves the right to a jury trial in federal court for suits at common law.** Where damages are claimed a jury can't be denied on the damages issue.	**Since Paul is seeking damages for injury to his land because of Danco's negligent use of explosives, this is a common law action. Paul is entitled to a jury trial for the issue of damages, which is a legal issue.**	**Court erred in denying jury trial on damages**
	Where suit involves issue of both law and equity, in federal court the legal issues go to the jury first, and then the equity claim goes to the judge. In a California court, the judge hears the equity issues first, and then the jury decides the legal issues.	Paul is requesting $100,000 in damages and injunctive relief to prohibit future blasting, so there are issues of both law and equity. The damages issue is legal and should go to the jury first, and then the Court should decide the issue of injunctive relief.	Court erred in denying jury trial on damages
2. Danco MSJ—Owen			
MSJ	**No genuine issue of material fact & entitled to judgment as matter of law**	Prior case must be analyzed to make a determination	
Res judicata (claim preclusion)	**Valid & final judgment on the merits** **Actually litigated** **Same parties** **Same Claim** Majority rule **Fed.: same T or O** **Cal.: primary rights theory**	Judgment for Danco on prior case was entered after "extensive evidence" of property ownership and concluded no damages were found. **Owen was not a party to the prior suit, was not notified, was not in privity, and his interest was not represented in the prior suit, so res judicata cannot be used.** Here, the same COA and conduct (negligent blasting) and the same piece of land are all involved, so it is the same claim	**Court correct in denying MSJ**

Continued >

Issue	Rule	Fact Application	Conclusion
Collateral estoppel (CE) (issue preclusion)	**Final judgment on merits** **Actually litigated** **Issue essential to judgment** **Mutuality: party or privy only** **Modern Cal. rule: party CE used against must be party or privy in prior suit**	The trier of fact heard "extensive evidence" and concluded both that Paul had no property interest in Blackacre and that no damage had been sustained. However, **Paul had no property interest in Blackacre, so the damages issue was not essential to the judgment since the judge did not need to make a finding on damages to resolve the case.** **Further, Owen was not a party to the prior suit, was not notified, and was not in privity, thus his interests were not represented in the prior suit. Since Owen was not a party in the prior case and had no opportunity to be heard, Danco will not be permitted to use the judgment against him using either the traditional or California rule.**	**Court correct in denying MSJ**
3. Danco MSJ—Paul			
MSJ	No genuine issue of material fact and entitled to judgment as matter of law	Prior case must be analyzed to make a determination	
Res judicata (claim preclusion)	**Valid & final judgment on the merits** **Actually litigated** **Same parties** **Same claim** Majority rule **Fed.: same T or O** Cal.: **primary rights theory**	Judgment for Danco on prior case was final and entered after "extensive evidence" of property ownership and concluded no damages were found. **Earlier suit was Paul v. Danco, and so is the current suit.**	If a new transaction or occurrence of blasting, court was correct in denying motion

Continued >

Issue	Rule	Fact Application	Conclusion
		Here, the case hinges on whether the COA in the prior suit is the same as in the subsequent suit. The COA is for the same conduct (negligent blasting), but to a different piece of property (Whiteacre). The facts are unclear: If this suit is the result of the same transaction or occurrence of blasting activity as Paul's earlier suit, res judicata would bar this subsequent suit. However, if this suit is the result of different blasting activity, the suit would not be barred. It is similarly unclear if the blasting activity invades a single primary right. **The nature of the blasting activity will control the outcome.**	If a new transaction or occurrence of blasting, court was correct in denying motion

Civil Procedure Question 4

February 2002, Question 1

Pam, a resident of State X, brought suit in state court in State X against Danco, a corporation with its principal place of business in State Y. The suit was for damages of $90,000 alleging that Danco breached a contract to supply Pam with paper goods for which she paid $90,000 in advance. In her complaint, Pam requested a jury trial. State X law provides that contract disputes for less than $200,000 must be tried to a judge.

Danco removed the case to federal court in State X. Danco moved to strike the request for a jury trial. The federal court denied the motion.

A few days before trial, Pam learned for the first time that Danco was incorporated in State X. She moved to have the case remanded to state court on this ground. The federal court denied the motion.

At trial, Pam testified that she paid for the goods but never received them. Danco admitted receiving Pam's payment and then presented evidence from its dispatcher that it had sent a truck to Pam's office with the paper goods. Danco also called as a witness Rafe, who works in a building next to Pam's office. Rafe testified he saw a truck stop at Pam's office on the day Danco claimed it delivered the goods. Rafe also testified he saw the truck driver take boxes marked "paper goods" into Pam's office that same day.

At the close of all the evidence, Pam moved for judgment as a matter of law. Danco opposed the motion, and the court denied the motion. The jury returned a verdict in favor of Pam.

Danco then moved for judgment as a matter of law, which Pam opposed. The court denied Danco's motion.

Did the court rule correctly on:

1. Danco's motion to strike the request for a jury trial? Discuss.
2. Pam's motion to have the case remanded to state court? Discuss.
3. Pam's and Danco's motions for judgment as a matter of law? Discuss.

Civil Procedure Question 4 Assessment

February 2002, Question 1

This civil procedure question is included as a practice question because it provides an example of a less typical civil procedure question covering more unusual topics. This question is difficult only because it tests some less common issues, including the right to a trial by jury, removal and remand, and the right to a judgment as a matter of law (JMOL). This question also includes the frequently tested topic of subject matter jurisdiction. The only difficulty posed by the question may be because a student may not remember the infrequently tested rules covered on the exam, or the student has not practiced trying to write such a question so it feels unfamiliar.

Since the question does not test many issues, it is important to flesh out the factual analysis using all of the facts provided in the question. This is especially true in the factual analysis of the jury trial issue, subject matter jurisdiction, and particularly the JMOL motion, which is entirely fact dependent.

This question was administered before the California rules of civil procedure were specifically tested on the California bar exam. The California rule distinctions are included on the grid so you can see how they should have been addressed.

Make note of the areas highlighted in **bold** on the corresponding grid. The bold areas highlight the issues, analysis, and conclusions that are likely **required** to receive a passing score on this question.

Issue	Rule	Fact Application	Conclusion
1. D's Motion to Strike			
Jury trial	**7th Amend. preserves right to jury in civil actions at law in federal court**	**Here, P's claim is for damages based on breach of contract, which is a civil action at law and not equity.** **Although it is in federal court because D removed the case to federal court, if the court remands it back to state court, then it would follow state laws and State X law would apply, barring a jury trial since it is only for $90,000 in damages, less than the $200,000 required by State X law.** **Since this is a civil action at law and is in federal court, P is entitled to a jury trial.**	**The court properly denied D's motion to strike**
2. P's Motion for Remand			
Remand	**A federal court can remand a case back to state court if removal was improper.**	**Here, the federal court can remand the case back to state court if the removal was improper.**	Need to analyze removal
Removal	**D can remove a case from state court to federal court if the court has subject matter jurisdiction** and personal jurisdiction.	**Need to analyze subject matter jurisdiction and personal jurisdiction to determine if removal was proper.**	**Removal improper b/c no SMJ (see below)**
Subject matter jurisdiction	**Need a federal question or diversity of citizenship** **For complete diversity, amount must exceed $75,000 & D and P must be citizens of different states.** **Citizenship of natural persons is determined by place of domicile.** **Citizenship of corporations can be dual: principal place of business and state where incorporated.**	**No federal question here since it is a breach of contract claim for damages.** **Here, P is suing D for damages of $90,000, which exceeds the $75,000 requirement.** **P is a resident of State X.** **D is a resident of State Y since its principal place of business is located in State Y; however, D is also a resident of State X since it is incorporated in State X.** **Since D and P are both citizens of State X, there is not complete diversity.**	**The court does not have subject matter jurisdiction, so removal improper—court should grant P's motion to remand, so the court erred**

Continued >

Issue	Rule	Fact Application	Conclusion
3. P & D Motion for JMOL			
JMOL—P's motion	**After the close of evidence for the other side, the moving party must show that based on the evidence before the court, no reasonable jury could find in favor of the opposing party.** (Cal.: called *directed verdict* or *demurrer to the evidence*)	**Here, P brought her JMOL after the close of all evidence, so it was acceptable from a timing perspective.** **P claims that she paid for and did not receive the paper goods she ordered from D and if the jury finds her to be credible could believe her. On the other hand, D presented evidence from the dispatcher that it sent a truck to P's office with the paper goods as well as witness testimony from Rafe that he saw the truck driver take boxes marked "paper goods" into P's office that same day, both of whom a jury could also believe rather than P if they decide to. Since a jury could reasonably believe either P or D, JMOL is improper and should not be allowed.**	**The court properly denied P's motion**
JMOL—D's motion	**After the jury reaches its verdict, the losing party can file a renewed JMOL only if it filed a JMOL during the trial.** (Cal.: called a *JNOV* and the losing party is not required to make a previous directed cerdict motion to file a JNOV)	**Here, D never filed a JMOL during the trial after the close of either P or D's case, so he cannot now file one after the jury's verdict for the first time. However, even if the JMOL had been filed timely, a jury could have reasonably believed P** because they found her more credible, even if it was only her testimony against D's dispatcher and witness testimony, so D is not entitled to a JMOL. Note: In California, the motion would be allowed, but D would still likely still lose because a reasonable person could still believe P instead of D.	**The court properly denied D's motion**

Civil Procedure Question 5

July 1999, Question 2

Pat was living in State X when he was arrested and charged with violating a State X criminal statute. Because of overcrowding in State X Penitentiary, however, Pat was forced to await trial while incarcerated in the security wing of Delta Hospital (D), a private hospital for persons with psychiatric disorders, located and incorporated in the neighboring state of Y.

Pat filed a class action complaint against D in a federal district court in State X on behalf of himself, on behalf of 25 similarly situated inmates who were incarcerated at D awaiting trial in State X and on behalf of all such future inmates. The complaint alleged violations of the State Y Prisoners' Rights Act, which guarantees prisoners, *inter alia,* the right to safe food. The complaint alleged that the food served at D was often spoiled and contaminated with vermin droppings and that, as a result, he suffered continual gastrointestinal disorders. Pat requested $70,000 in damages and an injunction prohibiting D from serving tainted food. D was properly served with a copy of the complaint.

Before D responded to the civil complaint, Pat's brother paid Pat's bail. As a result, Pat is no longer detained at D and has returned to State X.

The federal district court:

1. Denied a motion by D to dismiss for lack of jurisdiction;
2. Declined to certify the class on the ground that the class was not large enough;
3. Denied a motion by D to change venue to a federal district court in State Y; and
4. Granted a motion by D to dismiss the action as moot.

Was each of the rulings correct? Discuss.

Civil Procedure Question 5 Assessment

July 1999, Question 2

This civil procedure question requires a very thorough and detailed factual analysis on the first call of the question, which encompasses the frequently tested topics of subject matter jurisdiction, and a full personal jurisdiction analysis. There are many facts available to use in the analysis and it shouldn't be difficult to thoroughly answer the first call of the question.

Another topic covered by this question is class action certification, which is an infrequently tested topic. Though this question was asked in 1999, the grid includes information about the Class Action Fairness Act of 2005 so you can see how it would be applied had it been in effect at the time. There is also a call of the question devoted to venue, so this question provides a good opportunity to practice writing a response addressing many of the issues raised in venue since it is a topic that is somewhat frequently tested.

The last call of the question is unusual and asks if the action is moot, which is a slight crossover question with constitutional law principles. This is a good example of a question where you may be stumped by the call of the question and not quite sure how to answer the question. Even though you know what mootness is, the query may feel out of place tucked into a civil procedure question and leave you feeling doubtful about how to phrase an answer. Or sometimes you will read a question, or a call of the question, and have no idea what the question is asking. As a general rule, when in doubt about which rule to apply to the facts, do a thorough job analyzing the facts provided, which will garner some credit. Remember, you have studied really hard before sitting for the bar exam (and if you haven't you should consider postponing the exam) so if one of the questions asked on the exam that leaves you confused and uncertain about what to do, we can guarantee that almost everyone else taking the exam feels exactly the same way. Don't panic. Almost every exam has a question or call that stumps almost everyone. It happens so regularly it seems that the bar examiners must do it on purpose in order to see how the examinees can handle a curveball. Take a deep breath, realize everyone else is equally stumped, and write something lawyerly analyzing the facts. Chances are, you'll stumble onto at least part of the correct answer. Plus, if everyone taking the exam doesn't know how to a handle the question either, the bar is set really low for garnering at least partial credit.

Make note of the areas highlighted in **bold** on the corresponding grid. The bold areas highlight the issues, analysis, and conclusions that are likely **required** to receive a passing score on this question.

Issue	Rule	Fact Application	Conclusion
1. Jurisdiction			
Subject matter jurisdiction	**Need federal question or complete diversity** **Diversity—need more than $75,000 &** **P and D citizens from different states** **Natural person is a citizen of place of domicile (intend to stay there)** **Corporation/business citizen where principal place of business and incorporated (dual)** **For class actions, to determine citizenship, look only to the representative and not the class members**; Class Action Fairness Act (2005) allows federal court to hear a class action if any class member is diverse from any D and the class claims exceed $5 million.	**No federal question since P's complaint is based on violations of State Y's Prisoners' Rights Act.** **Here, P's complaint requested $70,000 which is less than the required amount of $75,000.** **P is from State X since he is only temporarily in State Y incarcerated while awaiting trial; D is a hospital located in State Y, its state of incorporation, so citizenship is diverse, but amount in controversy not met.** Here, since D is representing the class and is diverse, citizenship is acceptable, but under the CAFA, the class claims don't seem to exceed $5 million in the aggregate as 25 prisoners (and P) would not likely have $5 million in damages for contaminated food; he cannot claim damages for future inmates not yet in existence.	No SMJ
Personal jurisdiction	Traditional basis for PJ satisfied if D consents, D is domiciled in forum state, or D is present in forum state when served with process Jurisdiction may also be asserted if there is a long-arm statute and the minimum contacts test is satisfied. (Cal. long-arm statute gives power over any person or property up to constitutional limits.) **Minimum contacts** • **Purposeful availment** • **Foreseeability** • **Relatedness between the contact and P's claim** • **Systematic & Continuous**	Here, D did not consent to being sued in State X, D is not domiciled in State X, D was not present in State X. Assuming there is a long-arm statute here and it is satisfied, D will still need to meet the constitutional requirements of minimum contacts and the fairness factors. **D purposefully availed itself of State X's laws by housing State X prisoners in their hospital security wing, and it is foreseeable that one of the prisoners could assert a violation of a State Y law regarding their housing situation. The claim is related to the systematic and continuous contact of P being a prisoner of State X and State Y housing the State X prisoners.**	**Yes, PJ**

Continued >

Issue	Rule	Fact Application	Conclusion
	Fairness factors • **Convenience to parties** • **State's interest** • **Other interests** (P's interest in effective relief, judicial system's interest, interest of the states)	**The allegations of spoiled and contaminated food are the result of the contact of D accepting and feeding State X prisoners, it would be convenient to try the case in either state since State X and Y are neighboring states that are close enough to move prisoners between the two states,** State X has an interest in ensuring its prisoners, which here are still innocent as they are all awaiting trial, are treated humanely by being given safe food to eat, P and the other prisoners also have a strong interest in receiving safe and noncontaminated food while awaiting trial, and it would promote social policy of ensuring adequate housing for prisoners.	**Yes, PJ**
2. Class Certification			
Class actions	**To qualify as a class action suit, there must be:** • **Numerosity** • **Commonality** • **Typicality, and** • **The representative must be adequate** (Cal.: Allowed if there is an ascertainable class, AND a well-defined community of interest; court looks at whether common questions predominate, the representative is adequate, and the class will result in substantial benefit to the parties and the court.)	**Here, 26 prisoners could be sufficient for numerosity since having each prisoner bring a separate action would be difficult and burdensome for a court since they are all based on the commonality of food contamination and safety and it will help prevent future prisoners from bringing such a claim if the injunction is granted.** Cal.: Prisoners are an ascertainable class and have a common interest in obtaining safe food while awaiting trial, and the class will benefit the court by having one trial as opposed to several resulting in judicial efficiency.	**Class large enough so the court erred in denying class certification**

Continued >

Issue	Rule	Fact Application	Conclusion
3. Change of Venue			
Venue	**Venue is proper in any district where the claim arose; for transitory actions (not local), venue is proper in any district where all Ds reside OR a substantial part of the claim arose** Natural persons: residence equals domicile **Corp.: reside in all districts where they are subject to PJx when the case is filed** **Transfer of venue** is allowed to another federal court where the case could have been filed; court will look at interests of justice: **public factors (what law applies, what community should be burdened with jury service) and private factors (convenience, location of witnesses, evidence, etc.)**	**Here, the claim did not arise in State X since the food was served to prisoners in State Y; however, D resides in State Y for purposes of venue since it is subject to personal jurisdiction as indicated above in State X.** **Transfer of venue to State Y would be beneficial in that State Y law applies and the suit is based on State Y law.** It seems that State Y should be burdened with jury service since it is their hospital being sued for violating its own laws, but on the other hand, it is prisoners from State X so perhaps State X jury service should be utilized. **It is convenient to hear the case in State Y since D is located there as are most of the class (now P himself is in state X due to bail, but all other prisoners still in State Y)** and other witnesses such as food staff and/or doctors who diagnosed P's health issues.	**Venue proper in State X, but could reasonably be transferred to State Y, so court erred in denial**
4. D's Motion to Dismiss			
Motion to dismiss	A party can file a motion to dismiss when there is no claim	Here, D has filed a motion to dismiss based on the action being moot	Depends on below issue
Moot	**A claim is moot when it is no longer an issue, but there is an exception when it is capable of repetition yet evading review**	**D will claim that the action is moot because P is no longer served food in D since he is out on bail and in State X. However, there are still other class members being exposed to the contaminated food and it is possible that P could return there and be exposed to the spoiled food again.**	**Court erred in dismissing the case as moot**

Civil Procedure Question 6

February 2004, Question 6

Paul and Tom, both State X residents, were involved in an auto accident in State X. At the time of the accident, Tom, who was working as a delivery truck driver for Danco, was driving through State X to make a delivery to a customer located in State Y. Danco is incorporated in State Y and has its principal place of business in State Z. State Z is located adjacent to State X. Danco does no business in State X.

Paul filed a complaint against Danco in federal district court in State X on the basis of diversity jurisdiction, alleging $70,000 in property and personal injury damages. Danco was properly served with the complaint at its principal place of business.

Appearing specially in the State X federal district court, Danco filed a motion to dismiss the complaint on the grounds that the district court lacked both subject matter and personal jurisdiction and that Paul's action could not proceed without joining Tom. The district court denied Danco's motion.

Danco then filed a counterclaim against Paul to recover $20,000 in property damage to the truck Tom was driving at the time of the accident. Paul moved to dismiss Danco's counterclaim on the ground that the district court lacked supplemental jurisdiction to hear the counterclaim. The district court granted Paul's motion.

State X law provides that its courts may exercise jurisdiction over nonresidents "on any basis not inconsistent with the Constitution of the United States."

1. Did the district court rule correctly on Danco's motion to dismiss Paul's complaint? Discuss.
2. Did the district court rule correctly on Paul's motion to dismiss Danco's counterclaim? Discuss.

Civil Procedure Question 6 Assessment

February 2004, Question 6

This is a straightforward civil procedure question that covers the frequently tested topics of subject matter jurisdiction and personal jurisdiction. There are many facts to use in the minimum contacts analysis. This question also covers the joinder of a party in the first question call, and joinder is somewhat frequently tested.

This question provides a good opportunity to practice working with the most frequently tested topics in civil procedure: personal jurisdiction, subject matter jurisdiction, joinder, compulsory counterclaims, and supplemental jurisdiction. This question is not particularly difficult and covers relatively fewer issues than many other civil procedure questions. Therefore, a good and thorough analysis of all available facts is necessary to achieving a passing score.

Make note of the areas highlighted in **bold** on the corresponding grid. The bold areas highlight the issues, analysis, and conclusions that are likely **required** to receive a passing score on this question.

Issue	Rule	Fact Application	Conclusion
Call #1			
Personal jurisdiction—Danco	Traditional basis of jurisdiction Domicile Service in state Consent	No domicile or service in State X here b/c Danco has principal place of business (PPB) in State Z and is incorporated in Y; **Danco "specially" appeared** to raise the jurisdiction issue, which does not constitute Danco's consent to jurisdiction.	No traditional basis of jurisdiction
Personal jurisdiction—Danco	**Long-arm statute** **Minimum contacts:** • **Purposeful availment** • **Foreseeabilty** • **Relatedness** • **Systematic & Continuous** **Fairness factors** • **Convenience** • **State's interest** • Other's interest	Here, State X court may exercise jurisdiction over nonresidents "on any basis not inconsistent w/ Const. of U.S." so, since the **long-arm jurisdiction extends to the limits of the Constitution, so the minimum contacts test applies.** Though Danco would argue they've received no benefits or protections of State X and does no business in X, **Danco's employee was driving through State X, which is adjacent to State Z, so Danco's employee was purposely availing himself of the benefits and protections of State X by using its roads to make a product delivery. It's foreseeable Danco may have to defend** in State X for suit arising from their employee's tortious conduct. Further, **the COA, a car accident, arose directly from Danco's employee's contacts with State X**, by driving through State X on way to deliver in State Y. **Danco had no business dealings in State X** since their intended customer was in State Y, so Danco's contacts are not systematic or continuous.	**The court has personal jurisdiction over Danco**

Continued >

Issue	Rule	Fact Application	Conclusion
		The fairness factors favor litigation in State X since it would be **less costly in X since any witnesses and all events took place in X and State X law applies and it has an interest in adjudicating matters of highway safety.** Further, **Danco is a corporation** and its **PPB is located in an adjacent state** and P is an individual with a higher burden.	**The court has personal jurisdiction over Danco**
Subject matter jurisdiction—Danco	**Need a federal question or diversity of citizenship.** **For complete diversity, amount must exceed $75,000 & D and P must be citizens of different states.** **Citizenship of natural persons is determined by place of domicile.** **Citizenship of corporations can be dual: PPB and state where incorporated.**	Here, **the complaint is for $70k in damages so the amount in controversy is not satisfied.** The value of a proposed counterclaim of $20K cannot be aggregated to meet the $75k threshold. **Paul is citizen in his domicile of State X, and Danco is citizen of the state where incorporated, State Y, and the state of the PPB, State Z. Since the defendant and plaintiff are not citizens of the same state there is complete diversity.**	**SMJ is not satisfied because the claim does not satisfy the amount in controversy requirement**
Joinder of party—Tom	**Same transaction or occurrence** **But, can't destroy diversity** **Necessary party if:** • **Can't get complete relief for existing parties w/out person** • **Harm to absent party's interest** • **Absence exposes risk of inconsistent obligations**	**Tom can be joined permissively b/c the claim arose out of the same TNO, the car accident in State X.** Except, **joining Tom would defeat diversity jurisdiction** (b/c Tom is resident of X), **so he can't be joined.** Even without Tom being joined, Danco is not unduly prejudiced since they can still call Tom as a witness and Paul can get complete relief from Danco. A joint tortfeasor subject to joint and several liability is **not absolutely necessary** for adjudication, **so the case can proceed in his absence.**	No joinder because it would defeat diversity

Continued >

Issue	Rule	Fact Application	Conclusion
Call #2			
Compulsory counterclaim	**Requires common nucleus of operative fact (same T or O). Must be raised or is waived.**	**The $20k in property damage claimed here arose from same occurrence of the car accident as the underlying claim so common nucleus of operative fact. The counterclaim is compulsory and must be raised or the claim will be waived.**	**Compulsory counterclaim**
Supplemental jurisdiction	**Supplemental jurisdiction extends to compulsory counterclaims**	Don't need an independent basis for SMJ because **supplemental jurisdiction will apply to a compulsory counterclaim.**	**Supplemental jurisdiction applies**

PART 3 COMMUNITY PROPERTY

COMMUNITY PROPERTY TABLE OF CONTENTS

INTRODUCTION TO COMMUNITY PROPERTY

Community property is generally tested in only one of two formats and the rules are fairly simple, so it is a subject that is comparatively easy to handle so long as you follow a specific approach with every question. Using the approach is especially important for those students who have not taken community property as a course in law school.

The first type of fact pattern involves a couple acquiring a variety of assets, either before marriage, during marriage, and/or after separation or divorce. The assets may be earned before or during marriage, but may not vest until later. Subsequently, the couple either divorces or one spouse dies, perhaps leaving a will devising all of their property to a third party. Consequently, wills and trusts is a frequent crossover question with community property.

The second type of fact pattern will present a couple or one spouse who has incurred debt and the creditor is seeking repayment. The debt may be incurred before marriage, during marriage, or after separation or divorce, and may have been incurred for the benefit of the community or not.

Regardless of which format the question is in, community property questions are very fact driven and the chronology of events is critical to successful issue spotting and analysis. For this reason, it is useful to draw a timeline on your scratch paper, listing each event disclosed in the fact pattern. The first inquiry is always whether the couple is married or not, and if so when they were married. Pay special attention to all events that have occurred and when they occurred, such as when a marriage, separation, or divorce occurred; when an asset was acquired or debt incurred; or when any other significant event took place. Include all significant events on the timeline.

Finally, once you have created the timeline, follow the call of the question (which usually asks specifically about H and W's rights in regard to each particular asset or debt) and analyze each asset or debt using the following approach: First, identify the *source* of the asset or debt (separate property, SP, or community property, CP) and identify any original *presumption* that applies. (For example, an inheritance is presumptively separate property.) Second, identify any *actions* the parties may have taken to alter the original presumption. (For example, the parties can agree to transmute SP to CP.) Third, identify any *special classifications* that affect the original presumption. (For example, retirement pay is special and is apportioned using the time rule.) Finally, be sure to actually answer the call of the question. This seems obvious, but if the call asks what H and W's rights are regarding each asset, do the simple math and determine the answer; don't stop analyzing once you've characterized the asset or debt as community or separate property.

ISSUES CHECKLIST

RELATIONSHIP STATUS
GENERAL PRESUMPTIONS
TITLE PRESUMPTIONS
TRACING
MANAGEMENT AND CONTROL
AGREEMENTS

- Premarital
- Transmutations

SPECIAL CLASSIFICATIONS

- Personal injury
- Pension/retirement/stock options
  - Time rule
- Disability/worker's compensation
- Severance pay
- Bonuses
- Education/training
- Life insurance
- Business goodwill

PREEMPTION
CONTRIBUTIONS/IMPROVEMENTS

- <u>CP to SP</u>
  - Businesses
    - *Pereira*
    - *Van Camp*
  - CP to other spouse's SP
  - CP to spouse's own SP
  - CP pays off SP purchase price
- <u>SP to the other spouse's SP</u>
- <u>SP to CP</u>
  - Contributions/Improvements
  - Businesses

CREDIT ACQUISITIONS
DEBTS
DIVISION AND DISTRIBUTION

MEMORIZATION ATTACK SHEET

RELATIONSHIP STATUS

- **Married**
  - Valid in Cal.
  - Okay if valid in another state
- **Same-sex couples**
  - Registered same rights as married couples
- **Nonmarried couples**
  - Contracts law applies
  - If putative spouse, treat as married
    - Good faith belief
    - Estoppel may apply
- **Permanent separation**
  - Physical separation, and
  - Intent to separate

GENERAL PRESUMPTIONS

- **CP** = during marriage
- **SP** = before or after marriage, or by devise or inheritance or gift
- **QCP** = domiciled elsewhere but would be CP if in Cal.
- **QMP** = putative spouses

TITLE PRESUMPTIONS

- **MWSP** = W's name alone prior to 1975 is her SP
- **SP → jointly titled prop.**
  - <u>Death and pre-1984</u>: jointly held title is CP
    - No reimbursement
  - <u>Divorce only, 1984-1987:</u> joint tenant title by H and W is CP
    - Yes DIP reimbursement
      - Down payment
      - Improvements
      - Principal
  - <u>Divorce only, 1987 and on:</u> ANY jointly held title by H and W is CP
  - Yes, DIP reimbursement
    - Down payment
    - Improvements
    - Principal

TRACING

- **Commingled accounts**
  - Can trace SP to source
  - Burden of proof on SP proponent
  - Two tracing methods
    - <u>Exhaustion method</u>: all CP funds exhausted when property purchased
    - <u>Direct tracing</u>
      - Sufficient SP funds at time of purchase, and
      - Intent to use SP funds
  - If SP cannot be traced, account is CP
  - Tracing cannot overcome title presumption
    - Exception: bank accounts

MANAGEMENT AND CONTROL

- **Community personal property**
  - Equal power to manage CP
  - One spouse can't gift or dispose for less than fair value
  - One spouse can't sell or convey family furnishings without written consent
- **Community businesses**
  - Managing spouse can make all decisions, but must give written notice to sell
- **Community real property**
  - Both need to sign
  - Can't convey to 3rd party without other spouse consent
    - Presumed valid to BFP
    - If done, spouse has 1 yr. to set aside sale

- **Fiduciary duties**
  - Full disclosure of material facts
  - Good faith and fair dealing

AGREEMENTS

- **Premarital**
  - Effective upon marriage
  - In writing/signed by both
  - Can't waive child support
  - Voluntary/not unconscionable
  - Need full disclosure of financial obligations
  - Deemed involuntary unless
    - Independent counsel or waived in writing
    - 7 days before signing
    - Terms in writing in proficient language
    - No duress, fraud, undue influence
    - Any other factors court deems relevant
  - Laches and estoppel are available defenses
- **Transmutations**
  - Pre-1985: oral and inferred from conduct okay
  - Post-1/1/1985 need
    - Writing
    - Express declaration by
    - Adversely affected spouse
  - Exception
    - Gifts of insubstantial nature or personal
  - Not effective as to 3rd parties without notice unless recorded
  - Statements in will not admissible as evidence

SPECIAL CLASSIFICATIONS

- **Personal injury**
  - During marriage = CP
  - After marriage, injured spouse gets money as SP
  - CP gets reimbursed for expenses it paid
- **Retirement/pension/stock**
  - Earned during marriage = CP, regardless of when fully vested
  - Two approaches to divide
    - <u>Reservation of jurisdiction</u> until spouse retires
      - Other spouse can elect at time when spouse can retire
      - Use **time rule:** # yrs. married with pension/ total # yrs. pension earned = CP
    - <u>Cash out:</u> pension to employed spouse & other assets of = value to other spouse
- **Disability/worker's comp.**
  - SP or CP depends on what it replaces
- **Severance Pay**
  - If to replace earned benefits accrued when married = CP
  - If to replace lost future earnings after marriage = SP
  - **Bonuses**
  - If earned during marriage = CP
  - If earned after marriage = SP
  - Doesn't matter when paid
- **Education/training**
  - CP reimbursed if
    - It paid for education, and
    - Earning capacity substantially enhanced
  - Reimbursement reduced or modified if
    - Community substantially benefited (presumed if > 10 years)
    - Other spouse received education
    - Reduced need for spousal support

- **Life insurance**
  - Whole: lifetime coverage & accumulates cash value
    - Each estate gets % they put in
  - Term: coverage for specified term and no cash value
    - SP or CP based on latest estate to pay premium
  - Decedent can only devise 1/2 to beneficiary not their spouse, unless written waiver
- **Business goodwill**
  - Expectation of continued public patronage
  - Excess earnings method
    - Deduct fair return on business
    - Take professional's annual net earnings
    - Deduct similar professional's earnings
    - Capitalize excess earnings over marriage

PREEMPTION

- **Federal law preempts state law**

CONTRIBUTIONS/IMPROVEMENTS

- **CP to SP**
  - Businesses
    - *Pereira*: favors CP
      - Use if spouse skills is reason for growth
      - **SP = initial SP + (initial SP × RRR × # yrs.); CP = the rest**
    - *Van Camp*: favors SP
    - Use if character of business reason for growth
    - **CP = (value of spouse services × # yrs.) – actual compensation – family expenses; SP = the rest**
  - **CP to other spouse's SP:** gift presumed under majority of jurisdictions
  - **CP to your own SP:** CP reimbursed greater of amount spent on improvement or increase in value
  - **CP pays off purchase price of SP**
    - CP % = amount CP contributed to principal/ total amount of loan
    - Then, multiply this by amount of appreciation
    - Payments for interest, tax, and insurance are excluded
- **SP to other spouse's SP**
  - Reimbursed without interest for DIP
    - Down payment
    - Improvements
    - Principal
- **SP to CP**
  - Same as SP to SP above
  - Reverse *Pereira* and reverse *Van Camp* for businesses

CREDIT ACQUISITIONS

- **During marriage** = CP
- **Intent of lender** = rebut CP by showing lender relied on SP

DEBTS

- **Timing:** at time of k, tort, etc.
- **Liability** (CP, SP of each)
  - Premarital = all CP unless nondebtor has separate account without access to debtor for earnings; debtor's SP
  - Marital = all CP, debtor SP, nondebtor SP if for necessaries
  - If for benefit to comm., take from CP first

- If not for benefit to comm., take from SP first

DIVISION AND DISTRIBUTION

- **Divorce:** CP split equally
- **Death**
  - No will: all CP to spouse, 1/2-1/3 SP to spouse, depending on survivors
  - Will: can devise all SP & 1/2 of CP and QCP (but not QCP titled in survivor's name)

COMMUNITY PROPERTY RULE OUTLINE

I. **RELATIONSHIP STATUS**
   A. **Marriage between a man and a woman**
      1. **California:** A marriage is valid in California if there is a consensual civil contract between a man and woman followed by a license from the county, solemnization, and authentication.
      2. **Other jurisdictions:** California recognizes marriages between a man and woman from other jurisdictions if the marriage would be valid by the laws of that jurisdiction.
   B. **Same-sex couples**
      1. **Registered domestic partners** are afforded the **same rights and protections** as married persons.
      2. **Same-sex marriages from other jurisdictions:**
         a. **Prior to 11/5/2008:** California recognizes same-sex marriages from other jurisdictions as a **marriage.**
         b. **After 11/5/2008:** Same-sex couples married in another jurisdiction are not designated as married but are afforded the **same rights and protections** as married couples.
   C. **Nonmarried couples:**
      1. **Putative spouse:** If a **marriage is void or voidable** and the court finds that **either party or both parties** believed in **good faith** that the marriage was valid, the court will treat the party or parties as a putative spouse.
         a. **Property classification:** The property of putative spouses is treated as **community property (CP) or quasi-community property (QCP).**
         b. **Estoppel:** One may be estopped to assert the validity or invalidity of a marriage if the party making the assertion **knew** that the marriage was **not valid** or knew that it was invalid but acted as though it was valid.
            1. **Jurisdictional split:** Jurisdictions are split on how to treat a party to a void or voidable marriage where that party did not have a good faith belief the marriage was valid. Some will treat both parties as putative spouses; some will only treat the innocent party as a putative spouse.
            2. **Unmarried cohabitants** (meretricious relationships): Courts follow general **contract principles** and use resulting or constructive trusts and quasi-contract principles to allocate property for unmarried cohabitants.
   D. **Permanent separation** arises when the couple physically separates and at least **one party** has the **intent** that the separation be **permanent.**
      1. **Property classification:** After permanent separation, property of each party is treated as separate property (SP).

> <u>Exam tip:</u> Most exams indicate that H and W are married and relationship status is not at issue. Occasionally a question will include a putative spouse or contractual relationship. If the facts don't establish the existence of the marriage, address the relationship status issues before analyzing any other issues.

II. **GENERAL PRESUMPTIONS**

A. **Community property (CP)**: CP is all property, real or personal, wherever situated, acquired by a married person **during marriage** while **domiciled in California** that is not classified as separate property (SP).

B. **Separate property (SP)**: SP is property owned by either spouse **before marriage**; and/or property acquired by **gift**, **bequest**, **devise**, or **descent**; and the rents, issues, and profits obtained from any separate property.

   1. **Earnings** and accumulations are deemed SP where:
      a. **Living apart**: For a spouse **and** the minor children living with that spouse **while living separate and apart** from the other spouse, the **earnings** and accumulations are SP; or
      b. **Legal separation**: After a legal separation the earnings and accumulations are SP.
      c. **Note**: These **special rules apply to earnings** and accumulations, but not other sources of money/property.
   2. **Permanent separation**: After permanent separation, property of each party is treated as SP.

C. **Quasi-community property (QCP)**: QCP is all property, real or personal, wherever situated, acquired by either spouse while domiciled elsewhere, which **would have been CP** if it had been acquired while domiciled in California.

D. **Quasi-marital property (QMP)**: QMP is property acquired during a **void or voidable marriage**, which would have been CP or QCP if the marriage had not been void or voidable. The property of a **putative spouse** is classified as QMP.

> <u>Exam tip:</u> Once the relationship is established (if not already established in the facts), address all applicable general presumptions before moving on to analyze the assets/debts in question. Only address the general presumptions that apply to the facts. For example, if all events occurred in California, do not discuss QCP.

III. **PRESUMPTIONS INFERRED BY TITLE**

A. **Married women's special presumption (MWSP)**: Property acquired by a married woman in a **writing**, prior to **1975**, is presumed to be her SP.

   1. **Married woman and third person**: Property acquired by her and a third person results in a tenancy in common.

2. **Married woman and her spouse**: Property acquired by her and her spouse is presumed CP.

B. **Title involving expenditures of SP to benefit jointly titled property**

1. *Lucas*: At **death and prior to 1984**, all **jointly held** title by H and W is presumed to be CP with no right to reimbursement to SP without an agreement to the contrary. In other words, a gift from the SP to the CP is presumed.
2. **Anti-*Lucas* I**: At **divorce from 1/1/1984 to 12/31/1986**, property titled as **joint tenants** by husband and wife is presumed to be CP, unless there is a clear statement in the deed or a written agreement that the property is separate property, with reimbursement.
3. **Anti-*Lucas* II: At divorce from 1/1/1987 on**, any **jointly held** title by husband and wife is presumed to be CP, unless there is a clear statement in the deed or a written agreement that the property is separate property, with reimbursement.
4. **Reimbursements:** SP reimbursements (whether applicable through an agreement or anti-*Lucas*) are only allowed for expenditures made for **down payments**, payments for **improvements**, and payments that reduce the **principal** of a loan.

> **Memorization tip:** Use the mnemonic "**DIP**" to remember reimbursements apply to **D**own payments, **I**mprovements, and **P**rincipal.

> **Exam tip:** Before addressing *Lucas* and the rules following in the aftermath of *Lucas*, make sure that *title* is involved and that the title is not for bank accounts. In addition, these rules for jointly titled property only apply to situations involving death and divorce, so if the question involves a creditor seeking payment and there has been no death or divorce, then these rules do not apply.

IV. **COMMINGLED FUNDS AND TRACING**

A. **Commingled funds:** Commingling of funds does not necessarily transform or transmute the property from SP to CP if the spouse advocating SP can trace the SP portion to their SP.

B. **Burden of proof:** The burden of proof is on the spouse claiming SP, not CP, to show that each asset was acquired with SP funds.

1. **Two tracing methods** are used by courts to trace the SP:
   a. **Exhaustion method:** Requires showing that at the time the property was purchased, all community funds in a commingled account had been exhausted by community expenses, and thus **only SP funds were available** to purchase the property.
   b. **Direct tracing method:** Requires showing a direct link from the SP funds to the purchase such that there were sufficient SP funds in

the account at the time of the purchase and that the intent was to use SP funds to make the purchase.

2. **Unable to trace SP:** If it is impossible to trace the source of the property or funds in a commingled account to SP, the account will be considered community property (CP).

C. **Joint title:** Tracing cannot be used to overcome the presumption where title to property was taken jointly, **except** that tracing can be used to overcome the presumption for jointly titled **bank accounts** since bank accounts are governed by the Probate Code.

> Exam tip: When characterizing the assets/debts, first look to the initial source of funds at acquisition and then apply any general presumptions or presumptions inferred by title. Next, look at tracing issues if SP funds can be traced back to the original SP source to establish that the particular asset/debt in question is still SP.

V. MANAGEMENT AND CONTROL

A. **Community personal property**

1. **Management and control** of the community personal property belongs to **either spouse** with absolute power of disposition, other than testamentary, as they have with their separate property estate.
   a. **Except gifts:** A spouse may not make a gift, or dispose of community personal property for less than fair and reasonable value without the **written consent** of the other spouse.
2. **Family dwelling:** A spouse may not sell, convey, or encumber community personal property used in the family dwelling, furnishings, clothing of children or the other spouse without **written consent** of the other spouse.

B. **Community businesses**

1. **Management and control:** A spouse who is in charge of managing and controlling a community business can make all business decisions alone but must give **written notice of a sale** or disposition of all or substantially all of the personal property used in the business operations.

C. **Community real property**

1. **Sale or lease: Both spouses** must execute an instrument to convey or sell community real property or for leases greater than one year.
2. **Conveyance to a third person:** Conveyance of community real property by one spouse to a **bona fide purchaser** (third-person purchaser who took in good faith without knowledge) is **presumed valid**, but a conveyance to a third person **can be voided** by the other spouse **within one year** of filing of the instrument.

D. **Fiduciary duties**

1. **Full disclosure:** Each spouse has a fiduciary duty to the other spouse to **fully disclose all material facts** about community **assets and debts** as well as provide equal access to all information upon request.

2. **Good faith and fair dealing:** Each spouse has a fiduciary duty to use the highest good faith and fair dealing with each other and never take unfair advantage of the other.

> **Fiduciary duty fact triggers:**
> - One spouse sells property without the other spouse's consent
> - One spouse lies or fails to disclose information to the other spouse
> - Anytime one spouse is acting alone, consider fiduciary duty issues

VI. **AGREEMENTS**

A. **Premarital agreement:** An agreement made before marriage to become effective upon marriage.

1. **Requirements for valid premarital agreement:**
   a. **Writing required:** Premarital agreements must be in writing and **signed by both parties** and **consideration is not required.**
   b. **Enforceable:** Premarital agreements are not enforceable if they were made involuntarily, are unconscionable, or lack full disclosure.
      1. **Made involuntarily: Premarital agreements are deemed involuntary unless** the court finds that the party against whom enforcement is sought was:
         a. **Represented by independent counsel** at the time the agreement was signed **or advised** to seek independent counsel **and waived it in a separate writing;**
         b. Presented with the agreement and **advised to seek independent counsel seven calendar days** before signing it;
         c. **Fully informed in writing** of the terms and rights the party is giving up, in a language in which he is proficient (if unrepresented) and declared in writing that they received such information and from whom they received it;
         d. **Not under duress**, fraud, undue influence, and did not lack capacity; and
         e. **Any other factors** the court deems relevant.
      2. If the agreement is **unconscionable**; or
      3. The party was not provided **full disclosure** of the property or financial obligations of the other party and did not waive such disclosure in writing.
2. **Child support and spousal support**
   a. **Child support cannot be waived** by a premarital agreement.
   b. **Spousal support** can be waived by a premarital agreement if **independent counsel** represented the spouse against whom enforcement is sought at the time the agreement was signed and the provision is **not unconscionable.**
3. **Defenses to enforcement:** Equitable defenses limiting the time for enforcement, including **laches** and **estoppel** are available to either party.

B. **Transmutation:** An agreement between spouses to change the characterization of an asset. (For example, changing property from CP to SP.)
   1. **Before 1/1/1985:** Transmutations could be **oral, written, or inferred** from the conduct of the parties.
   2. **On and after 1/1/1985:** Transmutations of real or personal property must be made **in writing** by an express declaration that is made or consented to by the spouse adversely affected.
      a. **Gifts between spouses:** Transmutations do not apply to gifts between spouses that are for tangible articles of a personal nature and that are not substantial in value taking into account the marital circumstances.
   3. **Third parties:** A transmutation is not effective as to third parties without notice unless recorded.
   4. **Statements in a will:** These are not admissible as evidence of a transmutation of the property before the death of the person who made the will.

> Exam tip: After going through the relationship status (if necessary) and the presumptions and tracing issues, determine if the parties did anything to alter the characterization of the asset/debt. Typically the parties will have a transmutation or premarital agreement, so be sure to include these issues on your issues checklist.

VII. **SPECIAL CLASSIFICATIONS**

A. **Personal injury**
   1. **During marriage:** If the personal injury arose during marriage, any money received as a result of the injury is **community property** when received during the marriage.
   2. **After marriage or separation:** The money received for personal injuries are **assigned to the injured spouse**, unless the interests of justice require otherwise.
   3. **After legal separation, dissolution, or while the injured spouse was living separate from the other spouse:** Any money received is the **separate property** of the injured spouse.
   4. **Reimbursement allowed:** The community or separate property of the noninjured spouse is entitled to reimbursement from the separate property money received by the injured spouse for any expenses incurred on behalf of the injured spouse.
   5. **Liability for injury to other spouse:** The separate property of the tortfeasor spouse must be exhausted before community property may be used to discharge the liability for an injury to one spouse caused by the other spouse.

B. **Pension/retirement/stock options and other forms of retirement**
   1. **Pension plans** (and other forms of retirement) earned during marriage are CP regardless of when the pension is fully vested.

a. **Two approaches to divide pensions** are used by the courts:

1. The "**reservation of jurisdiction**" approach is used where the court reserves jurisdiction over the case until the employed spouse retires and then apportions the retirement between each spouse.
   - *a.* **Election: The nonemployed spouse** can elect to receive their share of the pension at the **earliest time** that the employed spouse could retire.
   - *b.* **Time Rule:** The CP percentage of the pension is calculated by dividing the number of years when the spouses were married, but before separation, while the pension was earned by the total number of years that the employed spouse earned the pension.

2. The "**cash-out**" approach is where the court assigns the entire pension to the employed spouse and awards other community assets, equal in value to the community interest in the retirement benefits, to the nonemployed spouse.
   - *a.* **An actuary** is used to determine the proper amount to award to the nonemployed spouse by estimating the present value of the pension.

C. **Disability/worker's compensation**: The **classification** of disability pay as SP or CP depends on what it was **intended to replace**, regardless of when it is actually paid.
   1. **Separate property:** If the disability pay is intended to replace the **spouse's retirement income after separation** or dissolution, it is SP.
   2. **Community property:** If the disability pay was **purchased with community funds** and **intended** at the time the premium was paid to **provide retirement income to the community**, then it is CP, which then **converts to pension benefits** at the age of retirement and are treated as such.

D. **Severance pay** is treated similarly to disability pay and a court will look at when the severance pay **accrued and what it replaces**.
   1. **Separate property:** If the severance pay is intended to **compensate lost future earnings after separation** or dissolution, it is SP.
   2. **Community property:** If the severance pay replaces **earned retirement benefits** from when the couple was married, or **enhances retirement** earned **during marriage**, it is CP.

E. **Bonuses** are classified based on **when they were earned** rather than when they are paid.
   1. **Separate property:** If a bonus is earned after separation or dissolution, it is SP.
   2. **Community property:** If a bonus is earned during marriage, it is CP.

F. **Education/training** is not a community asset/debt unless there is a **written agreement** to the contrary.
   1. **Reimbursement:** The community is entitled to reimbursement for **community contributions** to education/training that **substantially enhanced the earning capacity** of the party, with interest, accruing from the end of the calendar year in which the contributions were made.

2. **Reimbursement may be reduced or modified if:**
   a. The community **already substantially benefited** from the education, which is presumed after ten years;
   b. The education is **offset by the education received** by the other spouse; or

> Exam tip: Education is a frequently tested special classification. Start the analysis by stating the full general rule and then analyze both parts of the reimbursement rule. Next, state the full rule for when reimbursements may be reduced or modified and analyze those that are applicable under the facts.

   c. The education **reduced the need for spousal support** for the educated spouse.

G. **Life insurance**
1. **Whole life insurance** provides lifetime death benefit coverage and accumulates cash value.
   a. **Estate paying premium controls:** Each estate (CP and SP) has an interest to the extent that they paid the premiums.
   b. **CP interest** = amount CP contributed ÷ total amount contributed
   c. **SP interest** = amount SP contributed ÷ total amount contributed
   d. Multiply the SP and CP percentage interest by total amount of insurance to determine their respective amounts.
2. **Term life insurance** provides coverage for a specified term in exchange for the payment of a specific sum of money and does not accumulate cash value.
   a. **Estate paying premium on latest term controls:** The term policy is CP or SP depending on which estate paid the premium for the **latest term**.

> Exam tip: Generally when life insurance is tested, it is unclear from the facts whether the policy is term or whole. In that situation, analyze both and explain why it is more likely to be one or the other. For example, if the policy is paid annually, it may be more likely term insurance.

3. **Devise of CP life insurance:** To the extent the life insurance policy is CP, the decedent can only devise **one-half** to a beneficiary other than their spouse, without written consent from the spouse.

H. **Business goodwill** is the expectation of continued public patronage that stems from the built up value of one's business beyond the value of the capital stock, funds, or property.
1. **Professional practice:** When a professional practice benefits from goodwill during the marriage, the court will account to the community its share of the goodwill possessed during the marriage.
2. **Excess earnings:** The excess earnings method can be used to determine the value of the goodwill by deducting a fair return for

the business, determining the professional's annual net earnings and deducting the earnings of a similarly situated professional, and then capitalizing the excess earnings over the period of the marriage.

> **Exam tip:** Since special classifications are tested on almost every community property essay, it is crucial that you have each possible classification on your issues checklist. When one of the special classifications applies, address it after establishing the original source/presumptions. The special classification often serves to alter the original presumption.

VIII. **PREEMPTION**: Federal law preempts state law when specific types of income or liabilities are designated as the sole property of one spouse under federal law, but they otherwise would be community property under state law.

> **Issue-spotting tip:** Whenever there is any type of federal asset such as a pension or stock options or savings bonds, always address preemption. Usually a simple one- to two-line answer is sufficient. If you aren't certain whether the federal asset at issue would be preempted, mention in your response that because it is a federal asset it is possible and identify what the result would be if federal preemption applied and if it didn't.

IX. **CONTRIBUTIONS AND IMPROVEMENTS** (from one source to another)
  A. **CP contributions to SP**
    1. **Businesses:** California courts use two approaches:
      a. The ***Pereira*** approach favors the CP estate and is used by courts when the **spouse's management skills** are the primary reason for the business growth.
        1. **SP interest** = initial capital contribution to SP business + [initial capital contribution to SP business × reasonable rate of return (10%) × (# years married with business)]
        2. **CP interest** = value of business − SP interest (from above)
      b. The ***Van Camp*** approach favors the SP estate and is used by courts when the **character of the business** is the primary reason for the business growth
        1. **CP interest** = (Value of manager spouse's services × # years married) − (actual compensation) − (family expenses paid from business earnings × # years married) − CP interest; the remainder of the business value is SP
        2. **SP interest** = value of business − CP interest (from above)

> <u>Exam tip:</u> Anytime a separate property business is involved start by establishing why it is a SP business (i.e., acquired before marriage). Remember, just because a business is acquired during marriage doesn't mean it is necessarily CP. (See the fact triggers.) After establishing that the business is SP, always address <u>both</u> *Pereira* and *Van Camp* and go through each separately. Identify which approach favors each estate and explain why, and then go through the equations. If numbers are available to plug into the equations, do the calculations; if not, simply identify the appropriate equation. Finish by explaining which approach the court will likely use and why.

> <u>*Pereira/Van Camp* fact triggers:</u>
> - Business started before marriage
> - Business inherited during marriage
> - SP funds used to start business during marriage

2. **CP used to improve the other spouse's SP**
   a. **Majority rule:** A gift is presumed, unless there is an agreement to reimburse.
   b. **Minority rule:** A gift is not presumed and reimbursement is granted.

> <u>CP improving other spouse's SP fact triggers:</u>
> - Any purchase that goes with the other spouse's SP
> - Any purchase that compliments the other spouse's SP
> - Any purchase that improves the look or display of the other spouse's SP

3. **CP used to improve spouse's own SP:** When a spouse uses CP to improve that spouse's own SP, the CP is reimbursed for the amount spent on the improvement or the increase in the value to the SP, whichever is greater.
4. **CP used to pay off the purchase price of SP** (*Marriage of Moore*)
   a. **CP interest** = the amount the CP contributed to the principal ÷ total original amount of loan/balance
   b. **CP share** = the CP interest (see above) is multiplied by the amount of capital appreciation.
   c. **Excluded costs:** Payments for interest, taxes, and insurance are excluded in the calculations.

> <u>Exam tip:</u> When determining the percentage or portion of CP and SP contained in a piece of property, remember to multiply that percentage or portion by the appreciation. This step is often omitted but is necessary to identify the total amount of the property that is CP and SP, which then allows the determination of what H and W's rights are in the property.

B. **SP contributions to the other spouse's SP**
   1. **Reimbursement:** A party will be reimbursed, without interest, for contributions/improvements that can be traced from their SP to the other spouse's SP and that is used for **down payments, improvements**, and reducing the **principal** of a loan, unless there is a written waiver of the right to reimbursement or a written transmutation.

> **Memorization tip:** Use the mnemonic "**DIP**" to remember reimbursement is for Down payments, Improvements, and Principal.

C. **SP contributions to CP**
   1. **Reimbursement:** A party will be reimbursed, without interest, for contributions/improvements that can be traced from their SP to CP and that is used for **down payments, improvements**, and reducing the **principal** of a loan, unless there is a written waiver of the right to reimbursement. (Remember: "DIP.")
   2. **Businesses**: Reverse *Pereira* and *Van Camp* will apply when SP contributes to a CP business after separation/dissolution.
      a. **Reverse *Pereira***
         1. **CP Interest** = initial value of CP (at the time of separation/dissolution) + (initial value of CP × Reasonable rate of return (10%) × # years worked while separated)
         2. **SP interest** = value of the business – CP interest (above)
      b. **Reverse *Van Camp***
         1. **SP Interest** = fair salary – any salary taken during # years after separation/dissolution – CP expenses
         2. **CP interest** = the value of the business – SP interest (above)

X. **CREDIT ACQUISITIONS**
   A. **Community debt:** There is a rebuttable presumption that property acquired on credit during marriage is community property debt.
      1. **Rebut by "intent of the lender" test:** A showing that the lender relied exclusively on SP when extending credit may rebut the presumption.
      2. **Earning capacity:** If the credit is based on earning capacity, it is a community debt.

XI. **DEBTS**
   A. **Timing of debts**
      1. **Contract debt** is incurred at the time the contract is made.
      2. **Tort debt** is incurred at the time the tort occurs.
      3. **Child or spousal support debt** that doesn't arise out of the marriage is treated as a debt incurred before marriage regardless of when the court order is made or modified.
      4. **Other debts:** All other debts are incurred at the time the obligation arises.
   B. **Liability of debts**

1. **Community property is liable** for all debts incurred **before and during marriage** by either spouse, regardless of which spouse has the management and control of the property and which spouse incurred the debt.
   a. **Exception:** The **earnings** of the nondebtor spouse are not liable for **premarital debts** of the other spouse if these earnings are held in a **separate deposit account** over which the debtor spouse has no right to withdraw and the funds are not commingled with other community funds. (This exception allows the nondebtor spouse to shield his earnings, but not other sources of money.)
2. A **spouse's SP is liable** for his own debts, but not for debts of the other spouse, unless the debt was incurred during marriage and was for **necessaries of life** for the **spouse or a child**.
3. **Injury/damage:** A married person is **not liable** for injury or damage caused by the other spouse, unless the other spouse would be liable if not married.
   a. **Benefit of the community:** If the act or omission leading to injury or damage occurred during marriage for the benefit of the community, the liability should be satisfied from the **community estate first** and then the separate property of the debtor spouse.
   b. **Not for benefit of the community:** If the act or omission leading to injury or damage occurred during marriage but was not for the benefit of the community, then liability should be satisfied from the **debtor's separate property first** and the community estate second.
4. **Reimbursements** are available to either estate (CP, or either spouse's SP) if the debt is one that should have been first satisfied by another estate.

> Exam tip: When debts are involved and the entire call of the question focuses on which assets a creditor can use to satisfy a debt, it is best to address the general creditor and debt rules up front. Use the following approach: (1) Assess the type of debt, (2) when it accrued, (3) what estates are liable to pay it, and (4) in what order the property should be used to satisfy the debt. For example, address when the contract debts are incurred and what estates are liable and in what order first, then go through the specific debts from the fact pattern.

XII. **DIVISION AND DISTRIBUTION OF PROPERTY**

A. **Divorce**

1. **At divorce**, the community assets will be **equally divided** unless a special situation requires deviation from this requirement (i.e., tort liability).
2. **Real property outside California:** If it is not possible for the court to divide real property located outside the state, the court can require the parties to convey the real property or award to the party that

would have benefited from the conveyance the equivalent money value they would have received had the property been conveyed.

3. **Two marriages:** If a spouse is maintaining two marriages, courts will divide assets equally between participants or divide equally between nonguilty participants. Courts are jurisdictionally split regarding allowing the guilty party to benefit from his wrongdoing; some allow it and some don't.

B. DEATH

1. **General rule:** Upon death, **one-half** of the CP and QCP belongs to the surviving spouse and one-half belongs to the decedent's estate.
2. **Devise:** The decedent can devise **all of his SP** and his **one-half of the CP** and QCP.
   a. **QCP exception:** At death, the surviving spouse has a one-half interest in the QCP titled in the decedent's name. However, the decedent does not have an interest in the QCP titled in the survivor's name.
3. **Election by surviving spouse:** If the decedent died with a will and tried to dispose of more than his half of the CP, the surviving spouse will need to make an election between their CP rights without the will or take under the will in lieu of their CP rights.
4. **Intestacy:** If the decedent dies intestate, the surviving spouse is **automatically** entitled to the decedent's share of the CP and QCP, and to 1/3 to all of the decedent's SP (depending on whether the decedent left issue or parents surviving.)

> Exam tip: Always remember to answer the specific question call. For example, if the call asks about H and W's rights, don't simply figure out whether each of the listed assets is CP or SP or QCP, and so forth. Rather, after you have classified the types of property, proceed to distribute the property in accordance with those determinations and properly identify exactly what H and W will receive and why. Likewise, if debts are involved, identify what property H and W own in particular to determine which property the creditor should reach first to satisfy the debt, and explain why.

COMMUNITY PROPERTY ISSUES TESTED MATRIX

		Crossover	QCP	Putative Spouse/QMP	Separation	Title	*Lucas*/Anti - *Lucas*	Tracing/Com-mingled Funds	Mgmt./ Control / Gift or Sale to 3rd Party	Premarital Agreement	Transmutation/Gift	Special Classifi-cation	Time Rule	*Pereira/VanCamp* (CP to SP)	*Moore*	Improvements	Creditor Rights/ Intent of Lender	Debts/ Order of Satis-faction
July '11 Q6	H & W engaged and wait to marry for 3 yrs. to use trust					Joint title in car (not married)			X								X	X
July '10 Q6	H & W in Cal., H wealthy family with trust					JT condo/ H name cabin	X	X	X		X	stock					X	X
February '10 Q6	H & W in Cal. with prenup, rare coins				X					X	X			X				X
July '08 Q6	H & W in NY, XYZ stock	Wills/ Trusts	X			W name alone / JT			X		X	stock						
February '08 Q5	H, F in State X; H lies and moves to Cal. with W		X	X		H/W joint & separate				X	X	PI						X
July '07 Q6	H & W in Cal., H goes to law school					H name alone					X	educa-tion / goodwill						X

Continued >

		Crossover	**QCP**	**Putative Spouse/QMP**	**Separation**	**Title**	***Lucas*/Anti - *Lucas***	**Tracing/Commingled Funds**	**Mgmt./ Control / Gift or Sale to 3rd Party**	**Premarital Agreement**	**Transmutation/Gift**	**Special Classification**	**Time Rule**	***Pereira/VanCamp* (CP to SP)**	***Moore***	**Improvements**	**Creditor Rights/ Intent of Lender**	**Debts/ Order of Satisfaction**
February '07 Q4	Tom, from Cal., executed a will	Wills/ Trusts									X							
February '06 Q2	Tim & Anna try to reconcile	Wills/ Trusts								X								
July '05 Q1	H & W, Tech Co. stock				X	H name alone		X				PI /bonus / stock	X					X
July '04 Q3	Hank, avid skier, daughter Ann	Wills/ Trusts	X															
February '04 Q2	H & W in Mont., move to Cal.; H affair with A		X	X	X	TIC / H & A			X								X	X
February '03 Q6	H & W, students at X University		X			JT / H name alone	X				X	Education		X				
July '02 Q6	H & W domiciled in Ill., H lied about CL marriage			X		MWSP/ W's name alone					X					X	X	X

Continued >

		Crossover	QCP	Putative Spouse/QMP	Separation	Title	*Lucas*/Anti - *Lucas*	Tracing/Commingled Funds	Mgmt./ Control / Gift or Sale to 3rd Party	Premarital Agreement	Transmutation/Gift	Special Classification	Time Rule	*Pereira/VanCamp* (CP to SP)	*Moore*	Improvements	Creditor Rights/ Intent of Lender	Debts/ Order of Satis-faction
July '02 Q1	Theresa and Henry, child Craig	Wills/ Trusts										Life insurance	X					
February '01 Q1	H & W; H owned home before marriage					JT / W's name alone	X	X			X				X	X		
February '00 Q1	H & W married in Franklin, H engineer for Texco		X			JT	X					Bonus / stock	X				X	X
February '99 Q3	H & W married in Ill., W began law school		X		X						X	Education / bonus	X					X
July '98 Q1	H & W married in State X, W manages brokerage		X		X			X			X	Pension / disability	X	X			X	X
February '97 Q6	H, resident of Iowa, working for APEX		X			MWSP / H's name only		X	X		X	Game show / retirement / life ins.	X					
February '96 Q6	H & W; H goes to law school				X	JT / H's name alone		X	X		X	Education						X

Continued >

		Crossover	QCP	Putative Spouse/QMP	Separation	Title	*Lucas*/Anti - *Lucas*	Tracing/Com-mingled Funds	Mgmt./ Control / Gift or Sale to 3rd Party	Premarital Agreement	Transmutation/Gift	Special Classifi-cation	Time Rule	*Pereira*/*VanCamp* (CP to SP)	*Moore*	Improvements	Creditor Rights/ Intent of Lender	Debts/ Order of Satis-faction
February '95 Q3	Mike and Flo, not married but signed agreement		X		X	W's name alone		X	X		X	PI						X
July '94 Q1	Tom & Sue; Sue started Compuco				X						X	PI		X				
February '93 Q4	H & W; H run over by truck, later separate					Savings in H's name alone		X				PI / game show / disability / SS / pension	X		X			
July '92 Q1	T & W married in NY, W thought divorced			X	X	MWSP				X	X	Life insurance		X				
July '91 Q1	H, W, and H's son, S, from prior marriage					JT / H's name alone					X	Life insurance		X				X
July '90 Q3	H & W, ABDO job & landscap-ing business											PI / dis-ability / retire-ment / education	X	X	X			
February '89 Q5	H & W married in Cal., H quits as real estate agent								X		X	Life insurance	X	X				

Continued >

		Crossover	QCP	Putative Spouse/QMP	Separation	Title	*Lucas*/Anti - *Lucas*	Tracing/Com-mingled Funds	Mgmt./ Control / Gift or Sale to 3rd Party	Premarital Agreement	Transmutation/Gift	Special Classifi-cation	Time Rule	*Pereira/VanCamp* (CP to SP)	*Moore*	Improvements	Creditor Rights/ Intent of Lender	Debts/ Order of Satis-faction
February '88 Q3	W owns a small apt. building before marriage					JT	X							X	X		X	
July '87 Q6	H & W move from State X to Cal.		X			JT / H's name alone					X	PI		X			X	X
July '86 Q3	H & W, W buys office bldg					MWSP / joint account		X	X		X							
February '84 Q6	H & W, H starts XYZ Construction					MWSP / W's name alone					X	Stock		X	X			

COMMUNITY PROPERTY PRACTICE ESSAYS, ANSWER GRIDS, AND SAMPLE ANSWERS

Community Property Question 1

February 2008, Question 5

Harvey and Fiona, both residents of State X, married in 1995. Harvey abandoned Fiona after two months. Harvey then met Wendy, who was also a State X resident. He told her that he was single, and they married in State X in 1997. They orally agreed that they would live on Harvey's salary and that Wendy's salary would be saved for emergencies. They opened a checking account in both their names, into which Harvey's salary checks were deposited. Wendy opened a savings account in her name alone, into which she deposited her salary.

Harvey and Wendy moved to California in 1998. Other than closing out their State X checking account and opening a new checking account in both their names in a California bank, they maintained their original financial arrangement. In February 1999, Harvey inherited $25,000 and deposited the money into a California savings account in his name alone.

In 2004, Wendy was struck and injured by an automobile driven by Dan. Harvey and Wendy had no medical insurance. Wendy's medical bills totaled $15,000, which Harvey paid from the savings account containing his inheritance. In 2005, Wendy settled with Dan's insurance carrier for $50,000, which she deposited into the savings account that she still maintained in State X.

Very recently, Harvey learned that Fiona had died in 2006. He then told Wendy that he and Fiona had never been divorced. Wendy immediately left Harvey and moved back to State X. The savings account in State X currently contains $100,000. Under the laws of both State X and California, the marriage of Harvey and Wendy was and remained void.

1. What are Harvey's and Wendy's respective rights in:
   a) The State X savings account? Discuss.
   b) The California checking account? Discuss.
   c) The California savings account? Discuss.
2. Is Harvey entitled to reimbursement for the $15,000 that he paid for Wendy's medical expenses? Discuss.

Answer according to California law.

Community Property Question 1 Assessment

February 2008, Question 5

In community property questions, the issues usually arise in the same order they appear on the issues checklist, which is also the same order they should be addressed in an exam response, unless directed otherwise by the call of the question. Community property answers look slightly different than those of other subjects. This is because it is most efficient to first identify all of the general presumptions that are indicated by the facts. Essentially, the first paragraph of the answer will consist of a recitation of the general presumption rules with no companion analysis. However, by getting these rules out of the way in the beginning, they can be efficiently referenced throughout the answer. Once the applicable presumptions are out of the way, proceed with the following approach, which should be used on all community property questions.

First, determine if there is any issue regarding the status of the relationship between the parties. If there is—such as in this question where there is a putative spouse issue—address it first since it will impact the rest of the answer. Then, identify the applicable general presumptions. In this particular question there are four general presumptions that need to be addressed before going through the specific assets.

The next step is to approach each asset individually. The approach is covered in detail here for the first asset in the first call (State X savings account). Classify the asset based on the original presumption and then go through the checklist issues to determine if anything changes the original classification. To begin, under the general presumptions the savings account would be QMP because H and W are putative spouses, thus the account is treated as CP unless the parties did something to change this or a special classification applies.

Next, look to see if the parties did anything to alter the general presumption. First, W took title in her name alone (MWSP issue). Since events occurred post 1975, this does not actually alter the presumption, but it is an issue that you should address since the facts trigger it. Second, the parties made an oral agreement, which gives rise to transmutation. However, again the result is that it would not actually alter the presumption since there was no writing here. Next, consider if there are any special classifications. The only fact regarding the State X savings account that triggers a special classification is the deposit of personal injury settlement money. Apply the personal injury rule to reach the result that, upon dissolution, the $50,000 from W's injury would go to her as her SP for her injuries, subject to reimbursement from the CP for her medical expenses. The other $50,000 in the account would be treated as CP since the funds derive from earnings. Don't stop there; answer the question call. Go though the distribution issues and determine H and W's respective rights and answer accordingly with specificity.

Apply this approach to all assets in community property essay questions. Also, review the grid for how to approach the debt (liability) portion of the question, which will be addressed more thoroughly in another question assessment.

Note the areas highlighted in **bold** on the corresponding grid, which highlight the issues, analysis, and conclusions that are likely **required** to receive a passing score on this question. In general, the essay grids are provided to assist you in analyzing the essays, and are much more detailed than what a student should create during the exam to organize their response to a question.

Issue	Rule	Fact Application	Conclusion
Preliminary Issues			
Putative spouse	**One or both parties believes in good faith that the parties are legally married; some unknown mistake makes it illegal.** One may be estopped to assert the validity or invalidity of a marriage if they knew that the marriage was not valid or knew that it was invalid but acted as though it was valid.	**Here, W in good faith believed she was married to H as he told her he was single and they appeared to get married in 1997. Thus, until she found out the truth in 2006, she and H were putative spouses.**	**H and W putative spouses—QMP implicated**
General Presumptions			
CP	**CP is property, other than separate property, acquired by either spouse during marriage. All assets acquired during marriage are presumptively CP.**		
SP	**All property acquired before or after marriage or after permanent separation, or by gift, devise, or bequest is presumed to be SP.**		
QCP	**QCP is property acquired while the couple was domiciled in a non-CP state, which would have been classified as CP had it been acquired under the same circumstances in California.**	QCP will be treated like CP	
QMP	**QMP is property acquired during a void or voidable marriage, which would have been CP or QCP if the marriage had not been void or voidable.**	QMP will be treated like CP	

Continued >

Issue	Rule	Fact Application	Conclusion
Prenuptial agreement or transmutation	Must comply with the SOF (but can use estoppel or reliance to get around) Deemed involuntary unless: 1. Represented by independent counsel at time agreement was signed or advised to seek independent counsel and waived in a separate writing 2. Presented with agreement 7 days before signing and told to seek independent counsel 3. If unrepresented, one must be fully informed in writing of the terms and rights they are giving up, in a language in which the party is proficient 4. No duress, fraud, undue influence 5. Anything else the court deems relevant	None of these elements appear to be met here as there is no writing or independent representation by H and W that they would live on H's salary and save W's for emergencies **(if oral agreement before marriage).** **Also: No transmutation at all because no writing and after 1985 (if oral agreement after marriage).**	No prenuptial agreement and no transmutation
1a. State X Savings Account			
QMP/CP	See above	Earnings during marriage are CP; QMP here.	
Title/MWSP	Prior to 1975, title in W's name alone indicated her SP	Here, after 1975, so no MWSP; **title in W's name alone will not change QMP to SP**	No MWSP
Transmutation	Transmutations are agreements between spouses to change the character of an asset. Before 1/1/1985: transmutations could be oral, written, or inferred from conduct of parties **Post 1/1/1985: need a signed declaration, in writing**, by spouse adversely affected expressly stating that a change in ownership is being made OR the gift must be insubstantial in nature—of a personal nature	Here, arguably since H knew W opened the State X savings acct. in her name alone, he agreed to a transmutation to her SP, but since they agreed that it would be used for emergencies for presumably both of them and **there is no writing, there is no transmutation.**	**No transmutation**

Continued >

Issue	Rule	Fact Application	Conclusion
Personal injury	**If COA arose during marriage: CP** If COA arose before or after marriage: SP (community entitled to reimbursement if medical bills were paid out of community funds) **On divorce: injured spouse's SP** unless the interests of justice require otherwise, but **community entitled to reimbursement**	**Here, the $50,000 deposit into the State X account was QMP since W was injured during their putative spouse marriage, but at dissolution in 2006 it will become her SP since she was the injured spouse.** **The remaining $50,000 is QMP because it was W's earnings.** The community (H's SP here) will be entitled to reimbursement for medical expenses, as discussed below in Q2.	**W gets $50k from her personal injury, and W and H each get $25k from other $50k in account**
1b. Cal. Checking Account			
QMP and CP and QCP	See above	**Since H's earnings were to be deposited into this new checking account and it was in both H and W's names, it is QMP, treated as CP. Any State X earnings that may be transferred to this account would be QCP/QMP.**	**H and W each get 1/2**
Transmutation	See above	Since in both names, no indication that there was a change in the character of the account as QMP.	H and W each get 1/2
1c. Cal Savings Account			
SP	See above	**H inherited the money in the savings account, so it is presumed to be his SP; the account was in his name alone and no appearance that funds were commingled, so still his SP.**	**H's SP**

Continued >

Issue	Rule	Fact Application	Conclusion
2. Medical Expenses			
Debts	The CP and debtor's SP are liable for debts incurred during marriage, and nondebtor's SP if for necessaries.	Here, the medical expenses were incurred during the putative marriage, so the community is liable and W's SP. If medical treatment were necessary for W's life, then H's SP would be liable too.	CP and W's SP liable
Order of satisfaction	If to benefit the community, take from community first, otherwise debtor's SP.	Here, **should take from H's SP last since there were sufficient community funds to draw from and some community funds were specifically reserved for "emergencies."**	CP first, then H's SP
Personal injury	At divorce, the injured spouse receives the money from personal injuries, but the community may be entitled to reimbursement.	Here, since W will get her personal injury settlement, the community will be **entitled to reimbursement for her $15,000 expenses.** But since H's SP paid, H should be reimbursed. This is true even if debt was for necessaries because the community or W's SP should pay for those medical expenses first before taking from H's SP since it was a debt that benefited W more than H. Further, **they maintained W's savings account for "emergencies," which had sufficient funds to pay this expense before taking from H's SP.**	**H reimbursed**

Community Property Question 1 Sample Answer

February 2008, Question 5

California is a community property state. All property, real or personal, wherever situated, acquired by a married person during marriage while domiciled in California that is not classified as separate property, is presumed to be community property (CP). Property owned by either spouse before marriage, or after permanent separation, or by gift, devise, or bequest, is presumed to be separate property (SP).

Quasi-community property (QCP) is that acquired while a couple are domiciled in a noncommunity property state, which would have been classified as CP had it been acquired in the same circumstances in California. Quasi-marital property (QMP) is property acquired during a void or voidable marriage, which would have been CP or QCP if the marriage had been valid.

1. H and W's Respective Rights

Putative Spouse

Before determining H and W's respective rights in the assets and liabilities of the parties it is necessary to characterize the nature of their relationship. Where one or both parties to a relationship believes in good faith that the parties are legally married and some unknown mistake makes the marriage illegal, they are considered putative spouses. The property of putative spouses is treated as if it is CP or QCP. While H knew he wasn't actually divorced from Fiona, W believed in good faith that she and H were married since H told her he was single and H and W had a wedding in 1997. Until such time as W found out the truth in 2006, she and H are considered putative spouses. Therefore, the property acquired during the putative marriage is QMP and will be treated like CP.

Prenuptial Agreement

Parties may orally agree about many things, but a prenuptial agreement that changes the classification of property, or where one spouse gives up rights to property must meet several requirements. Such an agreement will be deemed involuntary unless the impacted party is represented by independent counsel at the time the agreement is signed (or waived in writing), presented with the agreement seven days before signing, fully informed in writing of the terms and rights that are being given up, and there may not be fraud or duress. Since the agreement that H and W would live on H's salary and save W's earnings for emergencies was oral and did not meet any of these requirements, it will not be enforceable. Even if it were in writing, it is unclear that deciding to use W's earnings for emergencies designates it as her SP since having an emergency fund would benefit both spouses. All of the property from the putative marriage will be deemed QMP.

1a. State X Savings Account

The money in the State X savings account is comprised of W's salary, and a $50,000 settlement from a 2004 car accident that injured W. W's earnings during the putative marriage are QMP, so they will be treated as CP. The funds deposited from the car accident settlement would also be considered QMP and treated as CP because the cause of action arose during the putative marriage. However, at the time of the dissolution in 2006, a personal injury award will become the SP of W, since she was the injured party.

W took title to the savings account in her name alone, however taking title in a woman's name alone will not change the classification from QMP to SP. Prior to 1975 taking title in a woman's name alone created a presumption the property was SP, but that rule does not apply here since these events occurred in 1995 and later.

A transmutation is an agreement between spouses to change the character of an asset. Oral transmutations were valid prior to 1985, but after January 1, 1985, a valid transmutation required a declaration signed by the adversely affected spouse, unless the gift was insubstantial in nature. W's earnings are not insubstantial so a written transmutation is required, and there is not one here so the State X savings account is QMP.

W will receive the $50,000 traceable to the personal injury settlement (subject to reimbursement discussed below), and the other $50,000 in the State X savings account is QMP and will be treated like CP; H and W are each entitled to a one-half share of $25,000 each.

1b. California Checking Account

H's earnings from his job that were earned during the putative marriage were deposited into the California checking account. Earnings are presumed to be QMP. Any earnings that were transferred from the State X account are likewise considered QMP. Further, the checking account was titled in both H and W's names, which further supports the classification as QMP, which was in both H and W's name. This is QMP and treated like CP for purposes of disposition. Consequently, H and W are each entitled to one-half of the balance.

1c. California Savings Account

H inherited $25,000 and deposited it in the California savings account during the putative marriage. However, an inheritance is presumed to be SP unless it appears the funds were commingled with the community funds (or QMP). Here, H kept the inheritance in a separate savings account titled in his own name so it retains its classification of SP, and H is entitled to 100% of the money in the California savings account.

2. Medical Expenses

The community—in this case, the QMP—is liable for debts incurred during the marriage, and the nondebtor's SP may even be liable when the debt was incurred for necessaries. Here, the medical expenses and ensuing debt were incurred during the putative marriage, so the community is liable, and W's SP is liable. If the medical treatment W received was necessary for the maintenance of life, it would be considered necessary and H's SP would also be liable for the debt.

If the debt was incurred for the benefit of the community, payment first comes from the community, then the debtor spouse's SP and then the other spouse (so long as it was for a necessary item). Here, H paid for W's debt with his SP funds from the California savings account when there were sufficient community funds available to pay the $15,000 debt. For example, the State X savings account had

$100,000 available for "emergencies" so the debt could have been paid with those QMP funds. Further, W received a $50,000 settlement for the accident, which should have been able to cover the $15,000 in direct medical expenses attributable to the personal injury suffered in the car accident. Assuming there were sufficient community funds available to pay for the medical debt, as it appears there were, H should be reimbursed for the $15,000 he paid in W's medical bills.

Community Property Question 2

February 2001, Question 1

In 1980, Herb married Wanda, and the couple took up residence in a California home, which Herb had purchased in 1979.

Herb had bought the home for $50,000 by making a $5,000 down payment and signing a promissory note for the balance. At the time of the marriage, the outstanding balance on this note was $44,000. During the next 20 years, the couple paid off the note by making payments from their combined salaries. The home now has a fair market value of $200,000.

In 1985, Wanda sold for $10,000 a watercolor she had painted that year. She and Herb orally agreed that the $10,000 would be her sole and separate property. Wanda invested the $10,000 in a mutual fund in her name alone. The current value of the mutual fund is now $45,000.

In 1985, Herb and Wanda bought a vacation cabin on the California Coast for $75,000. They made a down payment of $25,000 with community property funds, and both signed a note secured by a deed of trust on the cabin for the balance. Title to the cabin was taken in the names of both Herb and Wanda "as joint tenants."

Shortly afterward, Herb inherited a large sum of money from his mother and used $50,000 of his inheritance to pay off the note on the cabin. In 2000, Herb and Wanda added a room to the cabin at a cost of $20,000, which Herb paid out of the funds he had inherited. The current fair market value of the cabin is $150,000.

In 2001, Wanda instituted a dissolution proceeding. What are Herb's and Wanda's respective rights to:

1. The home? Discuss.
2. The mutual fund? Discuss.
3. The cabin? Discuss.

Answer according to California law.

Community Property Question 2 Assessment

February 2001, Question 1

This is a very straightforward question since H and W were married and domiciled in California, so there are no relationship issues to consider. As in contracts, the chronology of events is very important in community property questions. Sketch out a brief timeline of events to keep all the details straight.

Once you've organized your answer, you will notice there is actually a manageable amount of assets and issues to consider. When this happens and you notice there aren't quite so many issues to address, take a moment and run the fact pattern back through the issues checklist to see if you missed any issues. Also, look to see if there are any "homeless" facts from the fact pattern that are left unused that may raise an issue, or be used to bulk up some of the analysis. More often than not you probably missed something important. This question presents the more unusual case—where you find that you indeed had identified all of the issues and can proceed to writing out your answer (while thanking your lucky stars that you received at least one manageable question on the bar exam).

When drafting the answer, begin with the general presumptions for CP and SP and move immediately to the assets. On the first asset, the home, you will notice there are some odd fractions in the calculations, such as the community taking a 44/50 share of the home value. This is not unusual for a community property question. Calculators aren't allowed on the exam but don't worry, it's perfectly acceptable to note the fractional interest without actually doing the calculation. If the numbers are easy to work with feel free to complete the calculations, but the bar examiners seem very understanding of the idea that bar examinees are planning to be lawyers, not mathematicians.

On the second asset, where the watercolor earnings are used to buy the mutual fund, the date becomes pivotal to the analysis. Many issues within community property have different rules depending on when the event occurred, which is why a timeline is so useful. After January 1, 1985, a writing is required for a valid transmutation. Notice that since this event occurred in 1985 and there is no writing, the rule is not satisfied; however, it is still necessary to analyze the issue. Remember, your job on the bar exam is to identify and analyze all issues raised by the facts, whether they are then proven or disproven.

Finally, make note of the areas highlighted in **bold** on the corresponding grid. The bold areas highlight the issues, analysis, and conclusions that are likely **required** to receive a passing score on this question.

Issue	Rule	Fact Application	Conclusion
General Presumptions			
Community property	**CP is property, other than separate property, acquired by either spouse during marriage. All assets acquired during marriage are presumptively CP.**		
Separate property	**All property acquired before or after marriage or after permanent separation, or by gift, devise, or bequest is presumed to be SP.**		
1. The Home			
SP	See above	**Since H purchased the home in 1979 prior to marriage, it is presumed to be his SP. Further, his $5,000 down payment is his SP, as is the $1,000 he must have paid down on the promissory note.**	H's SP
CP pays off SP	CP payments that pay off purchase price of SP (***Marriage of Moore***) **Amount principal reduced / Original Amt. of loan = CP interest**	**Since, the community paid off the $44,000 balance of the promissory note, it will be reimbursed for it according to *Moore*.** **44,000 / 50,000 = CP interest** (88%) (of which each gets half) **6,000 / 50,000 = H's SP interest**	**H gets 6/50 of the $200,000, and H and W will split the 44/50 of the $200,000**
2. The Mutual Fund			
CP	See above	**Since W painted the watercolor during marriage with her work, skill, and effort, the earnings from it are presumed to be CP.**	

Continued >

Issue	Rule	Fact Application	Conclusion
Transmutation	Transmutations are agreements between spouses to change the character of an asset. **Before 1/1/1985: transmutations could be oral, written, or inferred from conduct of parties.** **Post 1/1/1985: need a signed declaration, in writing, by spouse adversely affected expressly stating that a change in ownership is being made** OR the gift must be insubstantial in nature—of a personal nature	**Since the oral agreement to make the $10,000 earnings from W's watercolor W's SP was in 1985, it needed to be in writing to be enforceable; it was not, as it was oral.** The only exception to this would be if it was an insubstantial gift, but since $10,000 is not a personal gift and 1/5 of the amount of their house's value around that time, it is likely not insubstantial.	**CP, so H and W each get $22,500 for the mutual funds**
Tracing	Courts can trace the funds used for the expenditure to their original source	Here, the mutual funds were purchased with the CP funds from the watercolor, so still CP.	Still CP
Title/MWSP	Title in W's name alone presumes her SP if prior to 1975	Here, after 1975, so **title in W's name alone will not overcome CP presumption** without a writing for transmutation.	Still CP
3. The Cabin			
CP	See above	**Since H and W acquired the cabin in Cal. while married, it is presumed to be CP.**	CP
Transmutation	See above	Although H may assert that 2/3 of the cabin is his SP since he used his SP inheritance to pay off the deed, there is no writing to indicate such a transmutation and it is after 1985, so H's SP funds will be considered a gift to the community to pay off the deed.	Still CP

Continued >

Issue	Rule	Fact Application	Conclusion
Title (*Lucas*)	**JT title presumed to be CP** **SP reimbursed for DIP (down payment, improvement, principal)**	**Here, since H and W took title as joint tenants, this further presumes that the cabin is CP. However, H's $20,000 of SP that he used to add a room is likely an improvement since it improved the cabin in size and likely value, so he will be entitled to reimbursement for this improvement expense. Further, assuming the $50,000 payment paid down principal since he paid it off then, that too would be reimbursed to H's SP. If any of the $50,000 paid off interest or taxes, it would not be reimbursed.**	Still CP **H reimbursed for $70,000** **Remaining $80,000 split between H and W ($40,000 each)**

Community Property Question 2 Sample Answer

February 2001, Question 1

California is a community property state. All property, real or personal, wherever situated, acquired by a married person during marriage while domiciled in California that is not classified as separate property, is presumed to be community property (CP). Property owned by either spouse before marriage, or after permanent separation, or by gift, devise, or bequest, is presumed to be separate property (SP).

1. The Home

If a home is purchased with both SP and CP funds, at dissolution the SP and CP estates will receive a pro rata share of the home's value. Since H purchased the home in 1979, which is before the date of the marriage, it is presumed to be H's separate property. The home's original value was $50,000, and the $5,000 down payment and the $1,000 paid towards the promissory note were both made with H's SP funds before the marriage in 1980. After the marriage, the CP funds coming from H and W's combined salaries were used to pay off the balance of $44,000 owing on the promissory note. Where CP payments are used to pay off the purchase price of a home originally purchased with SP funds, the CP interest is the amount the principal has been reduced, divided by the original amount of the loan. The community is entitled to receive $44,000 (reduction in principal) divided by $50,000 (original amount of loan), which is a 44/50 interest in the home.

Each spouse is entitled to receive one-half of the CP interest of 44/50 of the home's current value of $200,000. H is also entitled to receive his SP share of 6/50 of the $200,000 current home value.

2. The Mutual Fund

The funds used to purchase the mutual fund originated from $10,000 earned by W's work, skill, and effort expended during the marriage in painting a watercolor, so the earnings from the sale of the watercolor, used here to buy a mutual fund, are presumed to be CP. However, H and W orally agreed that the $10,000 earned from the watercolor sale would be W's sole and separate property. Prior to 1985 an oral transmutation between spouses agreeing to change the character of an asset were valid. However, a transmutation made on or after January 1, 1985, requires a written, signed declaration by the adversely affected spouse expressly stating that the change of ownership is being made, unless the transmutation relates to an insubstantial gift. Here, the oral agreement between H and W occurred in 1985, so their agreement to make W's $10,000 earning her SP must be in writing in order to be enforceable. However, it is not in writing so it is not enforceable. The $10,000 earnings are unlikely to qualify as the exception for an insubstantial gift since it is hard to argue $10,000 is insubstantial when it comprises 1/5 the value of their home at the time.

Courts can trace the funds used for an expenditure to their original source. Since the mutual fund was purchased with CP funds from the watercolor sale, the mutual fund is CP.

The fact that W took title in her name alone is not dispositive to the characterization of the property as separate or community. If a woman took title in her name alone prior to 1975 there was a presumption the asset was her SP. However, this occurred after 1975 so taking title in W's name alone cannot overcome the presumption that the property is CP.

The mutual fund purchased with the $10,000 is now worth $45,000 and is CP so each spouse is entitled to a one-half share of the $45,000.

3. The Cabin

The cabin was purchased in California during the time H and W were married so the cabin is presumed to be CP. The $75,000 cabin was purchased with a $25,000 down payment made with CP funds and a $50,000 loan. H and W also took title as joint tenants, furthering the presumption that the cabin is CP. H then paid off the loan with SP funds he received from an inheritance. However, when SP funds are used to pay down a loan on a CP asset, the SP funds are considered a gift to the community unless there is a transmutation. This occurred after 1985 so there must be a written transmutation to change the characterization of the property to H's SP, and there is no written transmutation here so the cabin remains CP. However, when SP is used for making down payments, improvements, or reducing the principal on a loan for a CP property, the SP is entitled to reimbursement. To the extent H's $50,000 was used to pay down the principal on the cabin loan, H is entitled to reimbursement. He is not entitled to reimbursement to the extent the money was used for interest on the loan or taxes.

H also used $20,000 SP funds to make an addition of a room onto the cabin. This likely increased the value of the cabin by making it larger and more valuable and is thus an improvement, so H is entitled to reimbursement for the $20,000 also.

The fair market value of the cabin is $150,000. Once H receives reimbursement for the $50,000 SP payment on the loan (assuming it all went to paying principal) and the $20,000 SP payment for the addition, there is a remaining value of $80,000, which is CP and should be split equally between H and W.

Community Property Question 3

July 1990, Question 3

All of the following events occurred in California.

Shortly after he graduated from college in 1957, Harry purchased a home for $40,000, taking title in his name. Harry's father gave him the $10,000 down payment and Harry borrowed the balance of the purchase price on a note secured by a 30-year mortgage for the remainder. A month later, Harry married Wilma and began work for ABDO Corporation. Harry made all mortgage payments from his ABDO earnings. The house is now worth $500,000.

A homemaker until their children were grown, Wilma enrolled in a local public university and in 1983 earned a professional credential in landscape architecture. Her tuition and other educational costs were paid by Harry from his ABDO earnings.

In 1984, using a $50,000 inheritance from her father, Wilma established a remarkably successful landscape business, Flora, Inc. In 1990, Wilma was offered $600,000 for Flora even though the physical assets were worth only $50,000. Wilma rejected the offer.

In 1990, Harry was permanently and totally disabled in a hunting accident. In satisfaction of his claim for personal injuries, he received a $400,000 settlement, which he used to purchase a portfolio of corporate stocks now worth $600,000.

Harry can no longer work at ABDO because of his disability. He now receives ABDO disability benefits, which provide two-thirds of his monthly pre-injury salary. The disability payments will continue until 1995 when Harry turns 60. He will then receive ABDO early retirement benefits, which will be three-fourths of his pre-injury monthly salary.

Harry and Wilma have decided to obtain a dissolution of their marriage.

1. How should the following assets be classified and distributed on dissolution:
   a. The house? Discuss.
   b. Flora, Inc.? Discuss.
   c. The corporate stocks? Discuss.
   d. The ABDO disability payments? Discuss.
   e. The future ABDO retirement benefit payments? Discuss.
2. Should any adjustment in the distribution be made in order to reflect the cost and value of Wilma's education? Discuss.

Community Property Question 3 Assessment

July 1990, Question 3

This question tests several of the special classifications and the distribution of many different assets at marriage dissolution. At first glance it is apparent there is a lot of material to cover in just one hour, so time management is key to a successful answer. As always, organize your answer on scratch paper before you begin writing the answer. As you write the answer, be careful to allocate your time appropriately to ensure you are able to answer all of the question calls.

The easiest mistake to make on this exam is addressing W's education within the discussion of Flora, Inc. When analyzing Flora, Inc., the issue is whether the business is CP or SP and what amount of money each spouse will receive from it. W's education is not relevant to this issue. Although her education enabled her to open this business by providing her with the necessary training in landscaping, it has nothing to do with the classification of the business and distribution to each spouse. Further, the second call of the question specifically asks about the impact of W's education on the distribution, so this is where her education should be addressed. This is a good reminder why it is important to always read the full fact pattern, including all question calls, and organize before writing.

The analysis of Flora, Inc. presents some challenges. Start by identifying the original source of funds and the general presumptions. Students often mistakenly classify this business as CP because it was acquired during marriage. However, it was acquired with SP funds from W's inheritance, so it is W's SP business since the funds to start Flora, Inc. can be traced to her SP inheritance regardless of whether she was married. Unfortunately, making this mistake would lead you to miss the *Pereira* and *Van Camp* issue and analysis, which are required to pass this question. This is why it is so important to slow down enough to think things through when organizing your answer. One important missed issue can lead to a failing answer.

Another issue that leaves students perplexed is the ABDO retirement issue and application of the time rule. It is not clear in the fact pattern the exact date that the parties divorced. However, a careful reading of the facts explains that H was disabled in 1990 and will receive disability payments until 1995. This question was given in July 1990 (the question date is at the top of each question), so if H was disabled in 1990 and W is now seeking dissolution, the dissolution itself must be in 1990. If you missed this and were unable to properly calculate the time rule, you should have still identified the time rule as applicable, stated the dissolution would have occurred between 1990 and 1995, and analyzed it to the best of your ability.

Finally, make note of the areas highlighted in **bold** on the corresponding grid. The bold areas highlight the issues, analysis, and conclusions that are likely **required** to receive a passing score on this question.

Issue	Rule	Fact Application	Conclusion
General Presumptions			
Community property	**CP is property, other than separate property, acquired by either spouse during marriage. All assets acquired during marriage are presumptively CP.**		
Separate property	**All property acquired before or after marriage or after permanent separation, or by gift, devise, or bequest, is presumed to be SP.**		
1a. The House			
SP	See above	House presumed SP because H purchased it prior to marriage.	
CP pays off SP (Moore)	**When CP pays off the purchase price of SP the community is entitled to reimbursement** as follows: Amount principal reduced/Original amount = CP interest Note: **the court can deviate from this and award the entire house to one of the parties and give the other spouse other community assets to compensate for their share**	Here, **the community helped to pay off H's house, which is his SP because H had a 30-yr. mortgage to pay down $30,000 of the house, and he paid all mortgage payments from his ABDO earnings, which are CP**. Since it has been more than 30 years and his earnings paid off "all" mortgage payments, the community should be compensated for its interest as follows: **30,000/40,000 = 3/4 CP interest; the SP paid 10,000/40,000 = 1/4 SP interest** Since the house is now worth $500,000, 1/4 of it ($125,000) will be H's SP and 3/4 of it will be CP ($375,000).	H gets $125k + 1/2 of $375k; W gets 1/2 of $375k

Continued >

Issue	Rule	Fact Application	Conclusion
1b. Flora, Inc.			
SP	See above	Since W started Flora, Inc. with money she inherited from her father, it is a SP business	
SP enhanced by CP	***Pereira*: tends to favor community; use when spouse's management and skills are primary reason for growth of business** **Initial SP contribution + [initial SP contribution × reasonable rate of return × # years married with business] = SP; remainder CP** ***Van Camp*: tends to favor separate estate; use when character of business is the primary reason for the growth** **(Value of manager spouse's services × # years) — (Actual compensation) — (family expenses × # years) = CP; remainder SP**	Pereira: 50,000 + (50,000 × 10% × 6 years) = 80,000 SP; remainder (600,000 – 80,000) = 520,000 CP • This assumes H and W sought dissolution in 1990 when the business was offered the $600,000. (It is definitely prior to 1995 since H will continue to receive disability until that time.) *Van Camp*: No facts to this equation **Here, if W's expertise in landscaping is the reason for the growth of the business, the court will use *Pereira*. This is likely the case since assets are only worth $50k, meaning goodwill likely responsible for other $550k—W's efforts thus community labor**	**Court likely to use *Pereira*** with H receiving $260k and W $340k
1c. Corp. Stocks			
CP	See above	Since the stocks were acquired during marriage they are presumptively CP unless a special classification alters this.	

Continued >

Issue	Rule	Fact Application	Conclusion
Personal injury	**If COA arose during marriage: CP; if COA arose before or after marriage: SP** **On divorce: injured spouse's SP unless the interests of justice require otherwise, but community entitled to reimbursement**	**Here, the injury seems to have occurred during marriage, making the settlement CP.** **Since H and W are getting divorced, the settlement (traceable to the stocks) will become his SP, but the community is entitled to reimbursement for any expenses it paid for his injury.**	H gets stocks worth $600k but community may be reimbursed if it spent money on injury
1d. ABDO Disability			
CP	See above	Disabled during marriage, so CP unless special classification.	
Disability pay	**Classification as SP or CP depends on what it is intended to replace** (it does not matter when it is earned)	Here, **the disability pay is intended to replace earnings since H was totally and permanently disabled and can no longer work and the disability provides 2/3 of his monthly pre-injury salary; thus, payments during marriage are CP and after divorce are H's SP.**	During marriage, CP; after marriage, H's SP
1e. Future ABDO Retirement			
CP and SP	See above	Retirement accrued during marriage CP and after marriage SP	
Time Rule	**Total pension/stock X # years of marriage while pension earned / Total # years pension earned = CP** **The court can retain jx until 1995 and distribute the retirement then or deviate from the time rule and assign the entire pension to the earning spouse and another community asset of equal value to the other spouse**	H worked for ABDO for all 33 years of marriage (assuming dissolution in 1990) making this entire amount CP, but if he continues to accrue the benefits from 1990 to 1995 then this portion will be his SP Total retirement x 33/38 = CP and then 5/38 would be H's SP	Mostly CP but part SP if still accrues after marriage but before 1995

Continued >

Issue	Rule	Fact Application	Conclusion
2. W's Education			
Education	**Education is never CP** **The community is entitled to reimbursement if it paid for the education and the education substantially enhanced the earning capacity of the educated spouse** **Defenses to reimbursement (could be denied or simply reduced)** **1. Community already substantially benefited from the education (presumed if > 10 years since education obtained)** **2. Other spouse also received a community funded education/training, or** **3. Education reduced the need for spousal support for the educated spouse**	Here, W's professional credential is landscaping and is her SP. **The community may be entitled to reimbursement because it paid for the education from H's ABDO earnings, and the education likely enhanced her earning capacity since she was a homemaker previously and now is able to earn money by opening her own landscaping business.** **Defenses:** **1. If 1990 is year of dissolution, the education was only obtained 7 years ago but the community may have already substantially benefited because her business has been successful over the past 6 years, as indicated by the $600,000 offer.** **2. Not applicable.** **3. Need for spousal support likely reduced since she can now support herself with her successful business.**	W's SP but community may be reimbursed, but unlikely since strong defenses for reimbursement

Community Property Question 4

July 1992, Question 1

Tony and Wanda were married in New York in 1959. They separate in 1963, and Wanda moved to California. In 1964, Tony represented to Wanda that he had divorced her. Believing Tony, Wanda became engaged to Hap. Shortly before their duly licensed and witnessed 1965 marriage in California, Wanda and Hap orally agreed, among other things, that any insurance proceeds either might collect during their marriage would be their community property.

Six months after their marriage, Wanda received $100,000 as the beneficiary of her deceased father's life insurance policy. She deposited the $100,000 in a stock brokerage account titled in her name alone. The account was managed for her by a financial consultant, and now has a value of $300,000.

In 1980, Hap received a $200,000 inheritance from his mother, with which he purchased a restaurant. Hap has continuously managed the restaurant. It is highly rated for its food, décor, and service. Last month, Hap was offered $1,000,000 for the restaurant.

In 1988, Wanda's employer purchased for her and has continued to pay all premiums on a $500,000 life insurance policy. Wanda's insurance beneficiary designation is: "my surviving husband."

Last week Wanda died in a work-related accident. Wanda's will, duly executed in 1980, leaves all her community property to Hap, and all her separate property to her sister, Betty.

Tony has reappeared and can prove that despite his representation to Wanda, they were never divorced.

What are Hap's rights?

a. In the stock brokerage account? Discuss.
b. In the restaurant? Discuss.
c. In Wanda's life insurance proceeds? Discuss.

Answer according to California law.

Community Property Question 4 Assessment

July 1992, Question 1

This question covers some issues that have been previously covered in other questions, and some new special classifications of life insurance and bonuses. The biggest problem with this question is the putative spouse issue since it potentially effects the distribution of all of W's assets, and the identity of her designated beneficiary under her insurance policy is not clear. Don't let a monkey wrench like this rattle you. Take a deep breath and handle each issue one at a time.

This question raises a distribution issue since W's will left her CP to H and her SP to her sister. Since W is allowed to dispose of her one-half of the CP and all of her SP, this is a proper devise. As a putative spouse, H would take all of the CP (his half and her half) and W's sister would take all of her SP. Now, focus on the call of the question. The call only asks about H's rights, but to make that determination you must analyze if anything goes to Tony or W's sister because those assets would be excluded from H's recovery. However, the answer to the overall call of the question can be directed to what H will receive.

Another issue here is the possibility of a prenuptial agreement since prior to marriage both H and W agreed to make all insurance proceeds CP. If the dates in the question were more recent, you would need to go through all the factors in the premarital agreement rules section. However, the examiners were not looking for this issue here since the parties made their agreement in 1965 and the "deemed involuntary unless" rule was not in effect until 1988. For extra practice, it is a good idea to review the rule here under these facts by treating this question as a current question under which this rule would apply. This will allow you to see how the analysis is organized and operates. That way, if you see the premarital agreement issue on the bar exam, you will have already practiced writing it out.

Since time management is always an issue on the bar exam, you should always try to write out the essays under timed conditions rather than just issue spotting and organizing them. Use the grids to review your essays to see if you spotted all issues, properly identified all rules, and used all applicable facts. But, if you merely check your organized answer with the grid, you will not know if you could have written out the entire essay within the allotted hour and, in particular, if you can properly analyze the issues by linking the facts to the corresponding rule elements in a coherent analytical sentence.

Finally, make note of the areas highlighted in **bold** on the corresponding grid. The bold areas highlight the issues, analysis, and conclusions that are likely **required** to receive a passing score on this question.

Issue	Rule	Fact Application	Conclusion
General presumptions	**Community property is property, other than separate property, acquired by either spouse during marriage. All assets acquired during marriage are presumptively CP.** **All property acquired before or after marriage or after permanent separation, or by gift, devise, or bequest is presumed to be SP.** Quasi-marital property is property acquired during a void or voidable marriage, which would have been CP or QCP if the marriage had not been void or voidable. QMP is treated like CP.		
Putative spouse	**One or both parties believe in good faith that the parties are legally married; some unknown mistake makes it illegal.** (Looks at the objective reasonableness of belief.)	Here, H and W were never legally married because Tony lied to W; Tony and W were never divorced. **W and H both believed in good faith that they were married as W believed Tony about the divorce and W and H had a duly licensed and witnessed wedding.** Due to Tony and W never being divorced (an unknown mistake to both W and H), W and H current marriage is illegal. You could have further explored whether objectively reasonable—never received divorce papers, signed anything, etc.—which probably would have boosted the score by 5 points here	W and H are putative spouses (this implicates QMP)

Continued >

Issue	Rule	Fact Application	Conclusion
Permanent separation	Actual physical separation AND intent to permanently separate communicated to the other	Here, Tony and W were physically separated in 1963 when W moved to California. Intent to permanently separate shown by Tony telling W they were divorced, and W becoming engaged (and she thought) married to H.	Tony and W permanently separated
a. Stock Account			
SP	See above	**Here, W inherited her father's life insurance policy, which is SP because it is inherited.**	
Transmutation	An **agreement between spouses** to change the character of an asset or series of assets. **Before 1/1/1985, transmutations could be oral**, written, or inferred from conduct of parties; after that date, they need to be in writing.	Here, W and H orally agreed prior to 1985 that any insurance proceeds they collected would be CP, but **this was prior to their marriage and thus is not a valid transmutation since transmutations are during marriage between spouses**.	**No transmutation**
Prenuptial agreement	Current rule (from *Bonds* case—deemed involuntary unless . . .) not in effect until 1988 wouldn't apply here.	Even if it were after 1988 that they made this agreement, it was **not in writing** and neither party was represented so the current factors would not be met anyway.	**No valid prenuptial agreement**
MWSP	Property taken in W's name alone prior to 1975 creates a presumption that it is her SP.	Here, W took title to stock in her name alone in 1965 or 1966, creating a presumption that it is her SP (and no transmutation as indicated above).	Remains W's SP, so goes to Betty
Pereira/Van Camp	A court may invoke *Pereira* and/or *Van Camp* if SP is possibly enhanced by community labor.	Since money for stock inherited, it is SP; but here, community did not enhance the SP because the account was managed by a financial consultant, not by the labor of W; so the community was not responsible for the increase in the value and likely would not benefit at all.	W's SP, so still **goes to Betty**

Continued >

Issue	Rule	Fact Application	Conclusion
b. Restaurant			
SP	See above	Money inherited so SP, can use tracing to establish restaurant purchased with inherited money	SP business
SP enhanced by CP	*Pereira*: tends to favor the community; **use when the spouse's management skills are the primary reason for the growth** **Formula: Initial SP contribution + [initial SP contribution × reasonable rate of return × # years] = SP interest; remainder is CP** *Van Camp*: tends to favor SP estate; **use when the character of the business is the primary reason for growth** **Formula: [Value of manager spouse's services × # years married] − [actual compensation] − [family expenses paid × # years married] = CP; remainder is SP**	Here, the restaurant was purchased with SP funds so it is a SP business, but the community is entitled to its share for enhancing the business. ***Pereira* is likely to be used because the business has flourished with Hal's continuous management and labor**, both community assets; he likely chose décor and food, and manages the service, which likely have helped with its success. Community should be compensated for his skills here. 200,000 + [200,000 x 10% × 1980 until W's death] = SP (H's) The remainder would be CP (or treated as such because really QMP) – since W left all CP to Hal, he would take all of it anyway No indication business was successful due to it being a restaurant or any particular type that is not related to H and his services, so likely it wouldn't apply; there are no facts to fill in formula either, but **would all be H's anyway since W left all CP to H.**	**All SP and CP in restaurant would go to H**
c. Life Insurance			
CP	**CP presumption**	**Since her life insurance policy was taken during marriage (putative spouse here), it is presumptively CP (really QMP)**; since her employer paid for the premiums it is similar to bonuses and earnings here.	

Continued >

Issue	Rule	Fact Application	Conclusion
Life insurance	Term v. whole: look to see which estate paid latest term v. each estate benefits to the extent it paid	Here, neither the community nor separate estates paid because W's employer paid, so need to treat insurance like earnings or bonuses.	
Earnings/ bonuses	If they are intended to reward the employee for their hard work, they are community assets; if as a gift, they are the employee's SP	Here, it is not clear whether the insurance was as gift or earnings, but most likely treated like earnings for her working there and being an employee, so community asset; more likely that the employer did this for all employees as part of their employment plan, not just as a bonus for one specific employee. **W left her policy proceeds to "my surviving husband," who is currently Tony with Hap being a putative spouse.** Arguably, this could mean Tony because she did not put Hap's name there when despite him being her then-current husband (in belief). However, **the court is likely to construe the language to mean Hap, as W in good faith thought she was married to Hap and that he would be her surviving husband since she was (in her mind and physical being) married to Hap in 1988 when her employer purchased the policy and was still with H at the time of her death** and she could have left it general in the event she later in life got another divorce.	Life insurance will be QMP—treated like CP; also H was the named beneficiary, which is the same result as if treated like CP; so all of W's policy proceeds will go to H
Conclusion		Court would also likely apply estoppel to Tony to prevent him from being able to recover for any of the W's assets.	Overall, Hap will receive everything with the restaurant and the life insurance proceeds, but nothing for the stock, as that will go to Betty

Community Property Question 5

February 1997, Question 6

In 1974, Hugh (H), a resident of Iowa, a non-community property state, began working there for Apex. Apex has an employee retirement plan which gives to each employee who retires after 20 years of continuous employment with the company the option of receiving either a lifetime monthly pension payment or an actuarially equivalent single lump sum payment. H eventually retired from Apex in 1994.

In 1977, H obtained a credit card which carried with it, free of extra charge, a $200,000 travel accident life insurance benefit on each commercial aviation flight ticket purchased with the credit card. The annual charge for the credit card was paid each year by H from his Apex salary and, after his retirement in 1994, from wages of a part-time job he held.

In 1983, H married Wendy (W) in Iowa, and H and W went to California on their honeymoon. While there, they visited a television studio where W appeared on a quiz show and won a condominium in California worth $100,000. W took title to the condominium in her name alone. After their return to Iowa, H and W decided to move to California and live in the condominium. Apex had offices in California, and H arranged to be transferred there. H and W moved into the condominium in 1984.

In 1990, H received a sizeable bonus from Apex in recognition of his extraordinary work for the firm in 1989. Unknown to W, H used the bonus as a down payment on the purchase of an office building in California, taking title in his name alone. In November 1994, he sold the building for a small profit to a purchaser who paid full value and who was aware that H was married. The building has since increased substantially in value because of the announcement of the construction of a new shopping center nearby.

When H retired from Apex in 1994, he chose the lump sum payment option available under his retirement plan and received $200,000 in cash which he used to buy U.S. Savings Bonds. He had the bonds registered, "H, Pay on Death to George." Under the applicable federal statute, such designation means that H is the owner of the bond, but it is "payable on death" of H to George (G), who is H's brother.

In January 1995, H was killed on a flight to visit G. The credit card company's insurance carrier paid $200,000 to H's estate. H's will confirmed to W her interest in their community property and quasi-community property and gave all property over which he had power of testamentary disposition to G.

What are the rights of W and G to each of the following properties?

1. The condominium? Discuss.
2. The office building? Discuss.
3. The bonds? Discuss.
4. The life insurance proceeds? Discuss.

Answer according to California law.

Community Property Question 5 Assessment

February 1997, Question 6

Wills and trusts is a frequent crossover subject with community property. This question tests some of the wills rules. However, all wills and trusts issues that persistently arise in community property exams are also included in the community property rules outline.

This question requires an understanding of the QCP rules since the parties start their marriage in the noncommunity property state of Iowa, and then move to the community property state of California. The first call of this question poses a unique classification issue since W won the condo as a prize on a game show. W had to participate in the game show and use her skill or knowledge or luck to win. Winnings of this nature are treated like earnings or gambling winnings and are considered CP (or QCP).

The next issue is related and is easy to miss: It is absolutely imperative to pay attention to where the parties are domiciled before classifying property. When W won the condominium, she and H were domiciled in Iowa and visiting California on their honeymoon. Thus, the condominium is not CP, but QCP. The distinction is extremely important because there is a small nuance in the QCP rule that is applicable here. At death, the surviving spouse has a one-half interest in the QCP titled in the decedent's name, but the decedent does not have a right to QCP titled in the survivor spouse's name. This is an example of where the technique of highlighting or underlining the facts as they are used pays off. Notice that the fact pattern stated that W took title to the condo in her name alone. Why is that fact included in the fact pattern? That fact is there so you can spot the issue of how QCP is treated differently at death depending on who is the surviving spouse. If you find you haven't used a fact in the fact pattern, always take a moment to ask yourself what you can do with that fact. There aren't many red herrings in bar essays. If you haven't used a fact, you've probably missed a key issue or analysis.

This question is particularly detailed with many facts, all of which go to specific issues. The management and control of property is another issue raised by the fact that H sold the CP office building to a third party. Many facts go to this issue, including the purchaser's knowledge that H was married. The U.S. Savings Bonds raise the issue of federal preemption since any U.S. asset implicates federal law. Use all available facts in your analysis for maximum points.

This question is a good example of why it is so important to carefully read the facts. Any mistake along the way, such as classifying the game show winnings as W's SP, or missing the QCP issue and classifying the condo as CP, or missing the QCP titled in survivor's name rule, will result in missed issues and/or the wrong result. Careful attention to detail while organizing your answer will likely prevent those mistakes. But, if you miss the issues because you didn't know the rules, you need to study the rules.

Finally, make note of the areas highlighted in **bold** on the corresponding grid. The bold areas highlight the issues, analysis, and conclusions that are likely **required** to receive a passing score on this question.

Issue	Rule	Fact Application	Conclusion
General presumptions	CP is property, other than separate property, acquired by either spouse during marriage. **All assets acquired during marriage are presumptively CP.** **All property acquired before or after marriage or after permanent separation, or by gift, devise, or bequest, is presumed to be SP.** **QCP is property acquired while the couple was domiciled in a non-CP state, which would have been classified as CP had it been acquired under the same circumstances in California.**		
1. Condominium			
QCP	See above **For QCP, the surviving spouse has a 1/2 interest in the QCP titled in the decedent's name. However, the decedent does NOT have an interest in the QCP titled in the survivor's name.**	**Here, since the game show winnings were acquired while the couple was married and domiciled in Iowa, they are QCP because they would have been CP had they been domiciled in Cal. at the time.** Winnings are due to W's work and skill on the game show, which are community assets while married. Since H died, **he does not have any rights in the QCP** titled in W's name since only surviving spouses have interest in QCP property titled in the other spouse's name.	**W gets entire condo; G nothing**
MWSP	Prior to 1975, property titled in W's name alone presumed to be her SP.	Here, the condo won from the game show was worth $100,000 and was titled in W's name alone, but after 1975 (it was 1983) so not presumed to be her SP.	No MWSP

Continued >

Issue	Rule	Fact Application	Conclusion
2. Office Building			
CP presumption		Presumed CP because it was acquired while domiciled in Cal. during marriage from H's work.	**CP**
Special classification: bonus	Look to see if employer provided bonus for good work (community labor) or if more like a personal gift (possibly SP).	Here, bonus was for H's extraordinary work so likely a community asset/earning.	Bonus CP
Title: H's name alone	Transmutation after 1985 requires writing; title not dispositive unless jointly titled	Here, no writing so still treated like CP; it is not H's SP since W never agreed in writing to make it H's SP.	No transmutation
Sale to 3rd party	**One spouse cannot transfer, gift, or sell CP to a 3rd party without the other spouse's written consent; other spouse can void transfer** (if real property, there is a 1-year statute of limitations with BFP's). H can will away his half of the CP as he wishes.	Here, **W never consented to transfer, and the purchaser was on notice as he was aware that H was married**, so purchaser would not be considered a BFP; and **there is no written consent from W to sell property so she can void the transfer** any time. W entitled to her half of the CP, and George can get H's half of the CP that he willed away.	W and G each get 1/2
3. Bonds		Here, the bonds were from retirement where for the first 9 years H was not married and the last 11 he was making part SP and part CP	
Special classification: **retirement**	**Use time rule to apportion for SP and CP interests.** **Total retirement × # years married/total # years = CP; remainder is SP**	200,000 × 9/20 = 90,000 SP 200,000 – 90,000 = 110,000 CP (1/2 to W and 1/2 to George) – 55,000 each	G would get \$145k, and W would get \$55k, unless preempted

Continued >

Issue	Rule	Fact Application	Conclusion
Preemption	**Federal rule trumps state rule.**	**Here, since the savings bonds are U.S. Savings Bonds, the federal laws for bonds (title controls) would preempt Cal. community property laws, so it is likely G would take all bonds under federal rule.**	G likely takes all bonds
4. Life Insurance			
CP and SP presumptions	See above	**Possibly SP since the credit card was obtained prior to marriage in 1977, but the premiums were paid during marriage** since they were paid each year from H's salary. So the year he died, the community paid for the card.	CP, so W and G would each get $100k
Life insurance	**Term: latest estate to pay receives** Whole: CP and SP both take amount they contributed; use time rule **to apportion** **The other spouse may not defeat the surviving spouse's share of the life insurance by naming another beneficiary.**	Here, **CP since H's salary paid the latest payment for the fee for the card. Because the card fee was paid each year, it is more like term life insurance.** Community paid latest premium so CP.	W and G each get $100k

Community Property Question 6

February 2000, Question 1

H and W were married in 1985 in Franklin, a non-community property state. H worked as an engineer for Texco beginning in 1975. W worked as a bookkeeper. During his employment with Texco, H received annual bonuses in the form of Texco stock. By 1990, H owned 1,000 shares of Texco.

In 1990, H accepted a job offer from Calco, a California-based engineering firm, and H and W moved to California. In 1991, H and W purchased a condominium for $200,000, taking title as "H and W, husband and wife, as joint tenants with right of survivorship." W paid the $50,000 down payment with money she had recently inherited, and H and W obtained a $150,000 loan secured by a deed of trust for the balance of the purchase price. H made the monthly principal and interest payments on the loan out of his Calco earnings.

In 1999, W, who had found a bookkeeping job shortly after moving to California, was charged with embezzling $50,000 from that employer. W admitted spending the $50,000 on cocaine. W retained Lawyer, who negotiated a plea bargain pursuant to which W pled guilty, was placed on three years probation, and was ordered to make full restitution. W also underwent treatment at DrugStop, a drug treatment facility, at a cost of $10,000. Lawyer charged W $5,000 to handle her case.

H had no knowledge of either W's embezzlement or cocaine habit until her arrest. H has filed for dissolution of the marriage. The condominium is currently valued at $300,000 with a $50,000 balance on the mortgage.

What are H and W's respective rights and liabilities with regard to:

1. The 1,000 shares of Texco stock? Discuss.
2. The condominium? Discuss.
3. The attorney's fees, restitution, and expenses for the DrugStop treatment? Discuss.

Answer according to California law.

Community Property Question 6 Assessment

February 2000, Question 1

This question has an entire call devoted to the debts of the parties. Start the answer to the debt question call by first addressing the general rules for debts, such as when they are incurred, which estates are liable, and in what order the various estates will need to pay the debt. Doing this as an introduction will save time because the information can then be incorporated as each specific debt is addressed. Then use the following approach to analyze each debt: (1) Assess the type of debt, (2) when it accrued, (3) what estates are liable to pay it, and (4) in what order the property should be used to satisfy the debt.

For example, for the first debt mentioned (attorney's fee) quickly analyze that it is a contract debt that was incurred at the time it was made, which was during marriage. Since it is a debt incurred during marriage, to satisfy the debt all CP is liable as well as the debtor spouse's SP and the nondebtor spouse's SP (but only if the contract was for necessaries). Since hiring an attorney is not a necessary item that sustains life, H's SP will not be liable for the debt. Then, analyze if the debt was incurred in benefit of the community in order to determine the order of satisfaction. Since the purpose of the debt was to pay for an attorney to defend on the embezzlement charge and embezzling funds to buy cocaine does not benefit the community, satisfaction should come from W's SP first and then the CP.

Follow the same approach to analyze each specific debt. The challenging part of the last debt is determining if W's stay at DrugStop was for necessaries, which would then make H's SP liable. You should argue both ways here. It is important to mention that for $10,000 she is likely receiving room and board as well as drug treatment, so arguably it is for the necessaries of food and shelter, making H's SP liable for the debt. However, since the debt was not for the benefit of the community, H's SP would be the last source to draw from because W's SP would first be liable, then the CP, and H's SP is last.

This question also tests the concept of credit acquisitions, which is rather straightforward but necessary to address. Be sure to use your issues checklist to avoid missing issues such as this because many of them are easy to overlook. Also, notice that stock is treated like pensions and retirement, and the time rule is used for apportioning the stock the same way it operates for regular pensions and retirement benefits.

Finally, make note of the areas highlighted in **bold** on the corresponding grid. The bold areas highlight the issues, analysis, and conclusions that are likely **required** to receive a passing score on this question.

Issue	Rule	Fact Application	Conclusion
General presumptions	**CP is property, other than separate property, acquired by either spouse during marriage. All assets acquired during marriage are presumptively CP.** **All property acquired before or after marriage or after permanent separation, or by gift, devise, or bequest, is presumed to be SP.** **QCP is property acquired while the couple was domiciled in a non-CP state, which would have been classified as CP had it been acquired under the same circumstances in California.**		
Call #1: Texco Stock			
SP and QCP presumptions	See above	Stock acquired prior to marriage presumed to be SP, and stock acquired during marriage presumed to be QCP since acquired while H and W were married in a non–community property state because it would be CP if in Cal. since acquired during marriage.	
Special classification: **stock**	For stock, it does not matter when it was dispensed or is exercisable; **for stock earned before and during marriage, use the time rule to apportion.**	Here, **the stock was earned before and during marriage so the time rule would be used** to determine the CP and SP allocations.	
Time rule	**Total stock × # years of marriage while pension earned/total # years pension earned = CP**	**1,000 shares × 5 years/15 years = 1,000 × 1/3 = CP share of stock** **1/3 of stock is CP, so W and H each get a 1/2 share of that, which is 1/6 each.** **The remaining 2/3 of stock is H's SP.**	H gets 5/6 and W 1/6 of 1,000 shares

Continued >

Issue	Rule	Fact Application	Conclusion
Call #2: Condominium			
SP and CP presumption	See above	Since W paid for part of the condo with inherited money, 1/4 of it would presumptively be her SP; the remainder was purchased by both H and W in Cal. and is presumed to be CP.	
Credit acquisitions	**If taken during marriage, presumed to be CP debt.** **May rebut by showing lender relied exclusively on SP when lending credit/granting loan (intent of lender test).**	Here, the loan was taken during marriage in Cal., so it is presumed to be CP debt. The loan was for H and W as joints tenants with **no indication that SP earnings or money was used by lender to grant the $150,000 loan**. The fact that **H's earnings, which are CP, paid the principal and interest** further support it was a community debt and not separate.	$150k loan is CP debt
Title: anti-*Lucas*	At divorce, post-1984, **jointly held title presumed to be CP.** **SP entitled to reimbursement for DIP (down payments, improvements, and principal—not for interest and appreciation), unless written agreement to the contrary.**	Here, H is seeking a dissolution of marriage after 1984, making their jointly held title presumptively CP. Since **H and W are both listed on title as joint tenants for the condo, the entire condo is presumed to be CP** despite W contributing $50,000 as SP down payment, but **her SP contribution is entitled to reimbursement for the $50,000 down payment.** Any interest or appreciation made on the $50,000 would not be reimbursed as there is no written agreement indicating such agreement. The community would pay off the remainder of the $50,000 mortgage out of the $300,000 value and reimburse W her $50,000 SP down payment, leaving $200,000 to split between H and W.	W gets $150k; H gets $100k

Continued >

Issue	Rule	Fact Application	Conclusion
Call #3: Attorney's Fees			
Debts	Creditor can generally reach anything the debtor has a right to manage and control.		
Type of debt	For contractual debts, the debt is incurred at the time of contract formation.	Here, the attorney fees are likely contractual with an attorney and W, and the **lawyer was retained during marriage, so the debt was a debt incurred during marriage.**	
Satisfaction	**Community property is liable for both spouses' premarital debts and all debts incurred during marriage.** **The non-debtor's SP is only liable for debts incurred during the marriage if it was for necessaries.** **If the debt was for the benefit of the community, take from the community first; if not, then from debtor spouse's SP.**	Since the attorney fees are a debt incurred during marriage, all CP is liable for this debt. Since an attorney is not necessary for life necessaries, H's SP would not be liable. **The debt was not for the benefit of the community, but rather W's drug problems, which destroyed the community; H not even aware until her arrest, so the debt should be paid from W's SP first, and then the community.** Since W has $50,000 SP from the condo, she should be able to pay the $5,000 attorney fees out of her SP funds.	W's SP first, and then CP if necessary to pay $5k attorney fees
Call #3: Restitution			
Debts	See above		
Type of debt	For criminal or tort debts, the debt occurs at the time of the tort or crime	Here, the debt owed for restitution **occurred at the time of the tort of embezzlement, which was during marriage.**	

Continued >

Issue	Rule	Fact Application	Conclusion
Satisfaction	**See above**	All CP and W's SP are liable since debt was incurred during marriage; since **not for the benefit of the community because destroyed marriage and H not aware until W's arrest, H's SP will not be liable and W's SP funds should be used first to pay the debt and then the CP.** Since W has to pay attorney fees, too, as indicated above, she may not have enough money to pay off both $50,000 restitution and $5,000 attorney fees with her $50,000 SP so part of debts will need to come from CP.	W's SP first, and then the CP to pay $50k restitution
Call #3: Drug Stop Treatment			
Debts	Creditor can generally reach anything the debtor has a right to manage and control		
Type of debt	See above for contractual debt rule	Here, likely contracted to **receive treatment, which was during marriage.**	
Satisfaction	**See above**	**Here, W likely received food and shelter while in treatment, making the debt for necessaries, too, so H's SP would be liable for this debt as well as all of W's SP and the CP.** Not for benefit of community because marriage ended over it, so don't take from CP first. **Take from W's SP first, then CP, then H's SP**; since CP has more than $10,000 in condo and stock, H's SP likely will not need to be used.	W's SP first, then CP, then H's SP if necessary

PART 4 CONSTITUTIONAL LAW

CONSTITUTIONAL LAW TABLE OF CONTENTS

INTRODUCTION TO CONSTITUTIONAL LAW

Constitutional law essays are similar to torts essays in that they are typically very fact intensive and require the full use of all applicable facts and factual inferences with comparatively fewer issues to analyze. Although a "racehorse" question with many issues can arise, it is less common. Rather, current testing trends indicate that the examiners are looking for in-depth analysis and are less concerned with assessing the skill of issue spotting on constitutional law questions.

Constitutional law essays tend to focus heavily on the issues pertaining to individual rights (equal protection, due process, freedom of speech, etc.). Many of the rules contained in the "Constitutional Law Rule Outline" are rarely essay tested—though they certainly could be—but they are heavily tested on the MBE portion of the bar exam.

Sometimes a constitutional law essay will have open-ended question calls and not indicate the specific issues to be addressed. This type of question will often ask what claims arising under the Constitution a party may bring, or what constitutional challenges a party can assert. To organize your answer, use your issues checklist to aid you in spotting all of the issues and avoid missing easily overlooked minor issues such as "State Action."

Some constitutional law questions will only ask about one issue. When the call is limited to one issue, the key points stem from the in-depth analysis of each rule element. Consequently, a very detailed understanding of the elements of each rule is necessary. Studying the fact triggers provided in the outline can aid your understanding of how a rule arises and how it functions in various factual situations. When the call is specific there is no need to write out your issues checklist. Rather, write out the rule elements for the identified issue and align the corresponding facts to the elements as you go through the fact pattern line by line.

Constitutional law essays usually require the use of logical inferences when analyzing the elements. For example, a fact pattern will not usually identify the government's interest applicable to a scrutiny level for equal protection, or any issue requiring such analysis. You must infer from the facts what a reasonable governmental interest would be when analyzing this prong of the scrutiny test. The same use of logical inferences also applies to analyzing whether there are reasonable alternatives. Give a few examples for maximum points.

Finally, it is useful to have a predetermined approach to apply to each of the constitutional law issues. If you know in advance how to approach each issue, it will enable you to wisely spend your valuable exam time analyzing the issues. Constitutional law doesn't lend itself to being tested as a crossover with other subjects, with the exception of criminal procedure. The Rules Outline presents the issues in the order they are best approached on an exam, unless directed otherwise by the question call.

ISSUES CHECKLIST

JUSTICIABILITY

Case or controversy
Standing
Ripe
Moot
11th Amendment

STATE ACTION

STATE POWER

FEDERAL POWERS

Congress
Judiciary
Executive

LIMITATIONS ON STATE POWER

Preemption
DCC
Privileges and Immunities Clause
Contracts Clause

LIMITATIONS ON FEDERAL POWER

10th Amendment
Improper delegation of legislative power

STATE AND FEDERAL POWER LIMITATIONS

- 1st Amend.—religion
- 1st Amend.—speech
- Freedom of association
- Due Process Clause
  - Substantive
  - Procedural
- Equal Protection Clause
- Takings

MEMORIZATION ATTACK SHEET

JUSTICIABILITY

- Case/controversy
  - Actual dispute
  - No political questions
- **Standing**
  - Individual
    - Injury
    - Causation
    - Redressability
  - 3rd party
  - Organizational
  - Taxpayer
- **Timeliness**
  - Ripe (not too early)
  - Moot (not too late)
- 11th Amendment
  - Cannot sue state
  - Bars actions for damages
  - Cities and counties okay

STATE ACTION

- Traditional public function, or
- Govt. entanglement

STATES POWER

- **10th Amendment**
  - Powers not delegated to fed. govt. saved for states

FEDERAL POWERS

- **Congress**
  - Can regulate **commerce** if:
    - Interstate
      - Channels
      - Instrumentalities
      - Persons & things moving
      - Activities with substantial effect
    - Intrastate (purely local)
      - Economic
        - Rational belief
        - Substantial economic effect
      - Noneconomic
        - Direct & substantial effect
  - Tax and spend
  - War
  - Naturalization/bankrupt.
  - Necessary and proper—if rationally related
- **Judiciary**
  - Cases under Constitution
  - Admiralty/2 states/citizens of diff. states
  - Not if independent and adequate state grounds
- **Executive**
  - Carry out laws
  - Executive order
  - Treaties
  - Appointments
  - Foreign affairs
  - Pardon federal offenses
  - Veto bills—but no line- item
  - Executive privilege is qualified: weigh govt. interest

LIMITATIONS ON STATE POWER

- **Supremacy Clause**
  - State law conflicts with
  - fed. law—preempted
- **Dormant Commerce Clause**
  - Discriminatory, or
  - Undue burden
  - If discriminatory on its face, must be:
    - Necessary to
    - Important noneconomic govt. interest
  - If not discriminatory on its face, then:
    - Rational basis applied
  - Balance burden v. benefit
  - Exceptions
    - Market participant
    - Congress's consent

- **Privileges/Immunities Clause**
  - State cannot discriminate against noncitizens
  - Unless substantially related and no less discriminatory alternatives
  - Rights fundamental to national unity
  - Corps. are not citizens
- **Contracts Clause**
  - Public: reasonably related and necessary to important public interest
  - Private: rational basis

LIMITATIONS ON STATE AND FED.

- **1st Amend. religion**
  - **Free Exercise Clause**
    - Can't burden religion
    - Unless compelling govt. interest
    - Generally applicable laws are okay
  - **Establishment Clause**
    - Can't endorse/favor religion
    - Incidental effect okay if benefits for wide variety
    - Sect preference: strict scrutiny
    - No sect preference need:
      - Secular purpose
      - Primary effect is not to advance/inhibit religion
      - No govt. entanglement
- **1st Amend. free speech**
  - **Content-based**: strict scrutiny
  - **Less protected speech**
    - Obscenity
      - Prurient interest
      - Patently offensive
      - Lacks L.A.P.S.
  - Misrepresentation/defamation
    - Imminent lawless action
    - Fighting words
  - **Content-neutral**
    - Significant govt. interest
    - Narrowly tailored
    - Open alternative channels
  - **Time, place, manner**
    - Public: Content neutral
      - Significant govt. interest
      - Narrowly tailored
      - Open alternative channels
    - Limited public: specific group/discussion when open, same test as public forum
    - Designated public: open for a specific purpose same test as public forum
    - Nonpublic: rational basis
      - Legitimate govt. interest
      - Rationally related
      - Open alternative channels
  - **Commercial speech**
    - Substantial govt. interest
    - Directly advances it
    - Reasonably tailored
  - **Symbolic speech**
    - Within constitutional power
    - Important govt. interest
    - Unrelated to speech
    - Prohibits no more speech than necessary
  - **Reasonable limitations**
    - Vague: not clearly defined
    - Overbroad: punishes both protected & unprotected speech
    - Unfettered discretion: no defined standards
  - **Prior restraints**
    - Stop speech before it occurs; unconstitutional unless:
      - Serious public harm
      - Narrowly drawn
      - Final determination
- **Freedom of association**
  - Freedoms protected by 1st Am. and not social
  - Compelling govt. interest
  - Least restrictive means
- **Substantive due process**

  - Deprive life, liberty, property interest
  - Fundamental right = strict scrutiny
  - No fundamental right = rational basis
- **Procedural due process**
  - Fair process prior to deprivation of life, liberty, or property
  - Judicial: hearing, counsel, call witnesses, trial, appeal
  - Nonjudicial: balance private int. and risk of error v. govt. interest
- **Equal Protection Clause**
  - Different treatment
    - On its face
    - As applied
  - **Levels of review**
    - Strict scrutiny
      - Necessary to
      - Compelling govt. interest
    - Intermediate scrutiny
      - Substantially related
      - Important govt. interest
    - Rational basis
      - Rationally related
      - Legitimate govt. interest
  - **Classifications**
    - Supsect: race, national origin, state alienage
    - Quasi-supsect: gender and legitimacy
    - Nonsuspect: social; economic; other
    - EPC—fundamental rights
  - **Level of review required**
    - Suspect = strict scrutiny
    - Quasi-suspect = intermediate scrutiny
    - Nonsuspect = rational basis test
    - EPC fund. right = strict scrutiny
- **Takings Clause**
  - Cannot take private property
  - For public use
  - Without just compensation
  - Public use = rationally related
  - Just compensation = market value of property
  - Per se taking if:
    - Permanent physical invasion
    - No economic value left
  - Not per se taking: court considers:
    - Economic impact
    - Interference with investment-backed expectations
    - Character of govt. action

CONSTITUTIONAL LAW RULE OUTLINE

I. **JUSTICIABILITY IN FEDERAL COURT:** The following justiciability issues may arise

   A. **Case or controversy:** There must be an actual case or controversy in dispute.

      1. **Declaratory judgments** are permitted. Declaratory judgments are those that state the legal effect of a regulation or the conduct of parties in regard to a controversy.
      2. **Advisory opinions** are not permitted.

   B. **Political questions** may not be heard by federal courts. If the issue is committed to another branch of the federal government (president or Congress) or if there are no manageable standards by which the court can resolve the issue, the federal court won't hear it.

   C. **Standing**

      1. **Individual standing** requires a plaintiff to prove:
         a. An actual or imminent **injury**,
         b. The injury is **caused** by the conduct complained of, and
         c. It is likely that the injury will be **redressed** by a favorable decision.
      2. **Third-party standing** requires the plaintiff to prove he has:
         a. **Individual standing**, and
         b. A **special relationship** between the plaintiff and the third party, **or**
         c. That it is **difficult for the third party** to assert his own rights.
      3. **Organizational standing** requires:
         a. The **members have standing** in their own right,
         b. The interests asserted are **related to the organization's purpose**, and
         c. The case **does not require participation** of individual members.
      4. **A federal taxpayer has standing** to sue over a federal tax or spending program that violates the Establishment Clause.

> Exam tip: Standing is almost always at issue when an individual or group challenges a statute or regulation. A plaintiff must establish standing prior to having the case heard, so logically it is one of the first issues that should be discussed. However, whether it is a major issue or minor issue depends on the quantity of facts available to use in the analysis.

   D. **Timeliness: ripeness and mootness**

      1. **Ripeness:** A case will not be heard if there is not yet a live controversy or immediate threat of harm (future wrong).
      2. **Mootness:** A case will not be heard if a live controversy existed at the time the complaint was filed but has since been eliminated.
         a. **Except** the case will not be found moot if:
            1. The controversy is **capable of repetition, yet evading review**—e.g., abortion litigation—or
            2. **Voluntary cessation** of the activity by the defendant.

> **Exam tip:** Timeliness is rarely an exam issue, and if it is, it is usually a minor issue so be brief. Ripeness tends to be an issue when the claimant is seeking declaratory relief or when a statute has been enacted but not yet enforced. Otherwise, these are minor issues that need only minimal attention.

E. The **Eleventh Amendment** provides **immunity to the states** from any federal suit against any one of the states by citizens of another state or a foreign state.
   1. **Actions that have been barred** include actions for damages by citizens of the same state.
   2. **Actions that are not barred** include suits by states or the federal government against other states, suits against subdivisions of the state (such as cities and counties), suits seeking injunctions against state officials, and suits against states that occur in state courts.
   3. **States have sovereign immunity** from private damage suits brought against the state in the state's own courts.

II. **STATE ACTION:** For an action to violate the Constitution, there must be **government involvement** with the challenged action.
   A. **Private actor:** The action of a private actor can qualify as state action if:
      1. Performing functions that are **traditionally public functions** (e.g., parks, prisons, elections); or
      2. Where the **state is heavily involved** in the activity, such as by commanding, encouraging, or being entangled with the activity.

> **Exam tip:** State action is an often-overlooked issue that is worth valuable points and can usually be adequately addressed in one or two sentences. Addressing this issue informs the grader that you understand the claimant must establish that "state action" is present before such action can violate any constitutional rights.

III. **POWER RESERVED TO THE STATES**
   A. **Federalism:** The federal government and state governments coexist.
   B. The **Tenth Amendment** provides that the powers not delegated to the federal government or prohibited by the Constitution are reserved to the states. Therefore, Congress can't compel a city or state to pass a law.

IV. **FEDERAL POWERS:** There are three branches comprising the federal government—the legislative branch (Congress), the judicial branch, and the executive branch (president).
   A. **Congress has limited, enumerated powers** granted by the Constitution. Consequently, there must be a **source of power** for any congressional action. Congress has the following enumerated powers:

1. **Regulate commerce:** This includes interstate commerce, intrastate commerce, commerce with foreign nations, and commerce with the Indian Tribes. This is a very broad source of power that encompasses many activities.
   a. **Interstate activity regulations:** Congress may regulate the:
      1. **Channels** of interstate commerce (e.g., roads, rivers, etc.);
      2. **Instrumentalities** of interstate commerce (e.g., trucks, boats, wires, internet, etc.);
      3. **Persons and things** moving in interstate commerce; and
      4. **Activities that substantially affect** interstate commerce.
   b. **Intrastate activity regulations** (purely local activity)
      1. **Commercial or economic activity:** May be regulated if there is a **rational basis** to believe that the activity will cause a **substantial economic effect** on interstate commerce, or if there is a **substantial cumulative economic affect** (e.g., include growing wheat or marijuana).
      2. **Noncommercial or noneconomic activity:** May be regulated if the activity has a **direct and substantial affect** on interstate commerce. Less deference is given to Congress's power to regulate noncommercial activity.
2. The **Taxing and Spending Clause** gives Congress the right to tax and spend for the general welfare of the United States. The allocation of conditional funding must be done unambiguously and cannot be excessively coercive.
3. The **war powers grant** Congress the power to declare war and to raise and support the armed forces.
4. **Naturalization and bankruptcy:** Congress has the power to establish uniform laws of naturalization and bankruptcy.
5. **Post–Civil War Amendments:** Congress has the power to enforce the post–Civil War Amendments such as the Thirteenth Amendment's abolition of slavery, the Fourteenth Amendment's establishment of equal rights for all natural citizens, and the Fifteenth Amendment's right to vote irrespective of race or color.
6. The **Necessary and Proper Clause** grants Congress broad authority to enact laws that shall be necessary and proper to execute any of their enumerated powers. The law need only be **rationally related** to the implementation of a constitutionally enumerated power.

> Exam tip: Most essays involve actions by state governments and not the federal government. However, should you receive an essay that involves congressional action, quickly write a mini-issues checklist of Congress's powers. Then, also consider all possible limitations on power applicable to the federal government, and remember the Tenth Amendment powers that are reserved to the states, which also serve to limit the federal government's power.

B. **Judiciary**
   1. **Federal judicial power** allows federal courts to review cases:
      a. **Arising under the Constitution** or the laws of the United States;
      b. **Admiralty;**
      c. Between **two or more states;**
      d. Between **citizens of different states;** and
      e. Between a state or its citizens and a **foreign country or foreign citizen.**
   2. **Exception: independent and adequate state grounds.** The Supreme Court will not review a case where there are independent and adequate state law grounds for the state court's decision, even if there is a federal question involved.

C. **Executive branch: powers of the president**
   1. **Execution of laws** made by Congress.
   2. **Supervise the executive branch,** including federal agencies, by issuing an executive order.
      a. **Executive orders** are valid unless they are inconsistent with a congressional statute or some specific provision of the Constitution itself.
   3. **Make treaties** with **foreign nations,** subject to two-thirds Senate approval.
   4. **Speak for the United States in foreign policy** and negotiate executive agreements with foreign countries.
   5. **Appoint ambassadors.**
   6. **Appoint top-level federal officers** subject to Senate approval (e.g., federal judges and cabinet members).
   7. **Issue pardons** for federal offenses, except cases of impeachment.
   8. **Veto a bill passed by Congress** in its entirety (a line-item veto is unconstitutional) by sending it back to Congress unsigned with a message stating the reasons for rejection.
   9. Under **executive privilege,** the president has a qualified right to refuse to disclose confidential information relating to his performance of his duties. It is qualified to the extent that other compelling governmental interests may outweigh the president's right to refuse to disclose information.

> <u>Exam tip:</u> It is rare to have an essay that focuses on executive branch actions. However, it is useful to memorize a mini-issues checklist of all executive powers, just as you do for congressional powers, in the event that you receive an essay question involving an action by the executive branch.

V. LIMITATIONS ON STATE POWER

A. The **Supremacy Clause** states that the Constitution is the supreme law of the land. Any state law that **directly conflicts** with federal law, **impedes the objectives** of federal law, or regulates an **area traditionally occupied** by Congress, will be **preempted** by federal law.
   1. **Conflict preemption:** Where a state law is inconsistent with a valid federal law covering the same subject matter, the state law is invalid.

2. **Field preemption:** Where the federal government intends to "**occupy the entire field**" the states cannot even regulate in that field.

B. The **Dormant Commerce Clause** (DCC) restricts the states and local governments from regulating activity that affects interstate commerce if the regulation is (1) discriminatory or (2) unduly burdensome.

1. **Discriminatory:** A regulation that is **facially discriminatory** against out-of-towners (protectionist to local interests) will only be permitted if it is **necessary** to achieve an **important noneconomic governmental interest** such that there are **no reasonable nondiscriminatory alternatives.** Facially discriminatory regulations are virtually **per se violations** of the DCC.
   a. The term "**out-of-towners**" refers to a favoring of **local interests** over nonlocal interests and need not apply literally to favoring one state over another, but can apply to towns and localities as well.
2. **Undue burden:** A regulation that **unduly burdens** interstate commerce will be permitted if it is **rationally related** to a **legitimate government interest**, and the **burden imposed on interstate commerce must be outweighed by the benefits** to the state. This is essentially a rational basis test plus balancing.
3. **Exceptions**
   a. **Market participant:** When the state is not acting as a regulator, but rather owns or operates a business, it may favor local interests over nonlocal interests.
   b. **Congressional consent** to the regulation.

> Exam tip: Remember, there must be "state action." If federal governmental action is involved, the *Commerce Clause* is at issue, if state government action is involved, the *Dormant Commerce Clause* is at issue. The call of the question may ask generally about the Commerce Clause and not make this distinction.

> Issue-spotting tip: Where a state regulation discriminates against out-of-towners, an equal protection issue is raised in addition to DCC because potentially similarly situated people are being treated differently.

> Dormant Commerce Clause fact triggers:
> - State legislation requiring all individuals/companies to do something
> - State legislation requirements for some companies and not others
> - State legislation giving discounts to some companies and not others
> - City banning or limiting out-of-towner use/access to state facilities

C. The **Privileges and Immunities Clause** of Article IV prevents a state or city from discriminating against **noncitizens** regarding rights **fundamental to national unity.**
   1. **Rights fundamental to national unity** focus on one's right to support oneself such as the right to be employed, engage in business, or practice one's profession.
   2. **Corporations and aliens are not considered citizens** for this rule so they will not be afforded protection.
   3. **Test is rigorous scrutiny:** Discrimination against noncitizens will only be allowed if the noncitizens are a **peculiar source of evil** and the discrimination is **substantially related** to this evil and there are **no less discriminatory alternative** means available.

> Exam tip: Thus far, on the bar exam this issue has always arisen when a corporation is involved so the Article IV Privileges and Immunities Clause did not apply. After recitation of the rule, one line of analysis indicating that a company was involved, thus making the clause inapplicable, is sufficient.

D. The **Contracts Clause** prevents state governments from passing laws that retroactively and substantially impair existing contracts.
   1. **Public contracts:** If the state is trying to avoid its **own** financial obligations, the law must satisfy **intermediate scrutiny.** The law must be **reasonably related** and **necessary** to serve an **important public purpose.**
   2. **Private contracts:** If the state is substantially impairing private contracts, the law must satisfy the **rational basis test.** The law must be **reasonably related** to serve a **legitimate public interest.**

> Exam tip: Whenever you have an essay with a state acting through a city, government official, or any such mechanism that would constitute state action for the purpose of raising a constitutional issue, always double check the action pursuant to the four limitations on state power.

VI. LIMITATIONS ON FEDERAL POWER

A. The **Tenth Amendment** reserves to the states all powers not delegated to the federal government by the Constitution.
   1. The federal government **cannot commandeer the states** by imposing targeted or coercive duties on state legislators or officials (such as ordering the passage of a law), but it can impose regulatory statutes of generally applicable laws that apply to both private and state actors.

B. **Improper delegation of legislative power**
   1. **Legislative authority:** Congress **cannot delegate** its legislative authority to make law.
   2. **Regulatory authority:** Congress **can delegate** regulatory powers to other branches of the government if there are **intelligible principles** that govern the exercise of the delegated authority.

VII. **LIMITATIONS ON FEDERAL AND STATE POWER—INDIVIDUAL RIGHTS:** The following constitutional protections apply to all federal and state governmental actions and provide **individual rights** for the people.

A. **Freedom of Religion** is a First Amendment limitation on Congress's actions and is also applicable to the states through the Fourteenth Amendment. There are two clauses.

1. The **Free Exercise Clause** bars any law that prohibits or seriously burdens the free exercise of religion.
   a. **Except: A law of general applicability** that does **not intentionally burden** religious beliefs and **advances important public interests** is allowable.
2. The **Establishment Clause** prohibits laws respecting the establishment of religion. The government can't endorse or favor specific religious groups.
   a. **Incidentally favoring** one religion over another in an attempt to benefit a wide variety of people is allowable.
   b. **Sect preference:** If the government action contains a sect preference, **strict scrutiny** applies and the action must be **narrowly tailored** to achieve a **compelling government interest**.
   c. **No sect preference:** If the government action contains no sect: preference, it must satisfy the ***Lemon* test** and the action must
      1. Have a **secular purpose**,
      2. Have a **primary secular effect**, which neither advances or inhibits religion, and
      3. Not foster **excessive government entanglement** with religion.

> **Exam tip:** Every time religion has been tested, it has been necessary to discuss both the Establishment Clause and the Free Exercise Clause.

B. **Freedom of Speech:** The First Amendment protects an individual's right to free speech and is applicable to the states through the Fourteenth Amendment.

1. **Two classes of speech:** Speech prohibitions can be content-based or content-neutral and the rules vary depending on this distinction.
   a. **Content-based** speech regulations are those that forbid the communicative impact of the expression.
      1. **Strict scrutiny** applies to content-based restrictions and they are rarely allowed. The regulation must be **necessary** (narrowly tailored) to achieve a **compelling governmental interest.**

> **Content-based fact triggers:**
> - Banning events promoting particular views
> - Banning specific content or types of content
> - Banning a specific action or conduct
> - Banning the sale of specific items

2. **Unprotected categories** of speech include obscenity, fraudulent misrepresentation and defamation, advocacy of imminent lawless action, and fighting words. For the unprotected categories of speech the only requirement is that the government must **regulate in a content-neutral way.**
   a. **Obscenity:** Speech is considered obscene if it describes or depicts sexual conduct that, taken as a whole, by the average person:
      i. Appeals to **prurient interest** in sex (under a community standard);
      ii. Is **patently offensive** (under a community standard); and
      iii. **Lacks serious literary, artistic, political, or scientific** value (under a national reasonable person standard).
   b. **Misrepresentation and defamation** are torts and are covered in detail in the Torts Rules Outline.
   c. **Imminent lawless action:** The government can ban speech advocating imminent lawless action if it is **intended to incite** or produce imminent lawless action and is **likely** to produce such action.
   d. **Fighting words** are words that are likely to cause the listener to commit an act of violence. However, causing another to be angry alone is insufficient.

> Exam tip: In 2010 the Supreme Court used the language above to describe both designated and limited public forums. Some federal courts have used these terms interchangeably, as have some law professors. Since this is a newer ruling, we suggest you distinguish the limited public forum and the designated public forum on an exam response, if applicable, to demonstrate your understanding of the distinction.

b. **Content-neutral** speech (or communicative conduct) regulations are those where the regulation is aimed at something other than the communicative impact of the expression.
   1. **Intermediate review:** Such regulations are allowed if
      a. They serve a **significant government interest,**
      b. Are **narrowly tailored** to serve that interest, and
      c. Leave open **alternative channels** of communication.

> Content-neutral fact triggers:
> - Denying activities at certain times or days
> - Limiting activities in certain places
> - Limiting activities to use certain methods (e.g., sound equipment)
> - Excluding people from visiting or attending events
> - Requiring activities to take place in designated areas
> - Banning activities or conduct in specific locations

2. **Time, place, and manner** restrictions on speech (or communicative conduct) are analyzed based on the type of forum in which the speech or conduct occurs.
   a. **Public forums** are forums that are generally open to the public and subject to **intermediate review:**
      i. They serve a **significant government interest,**
      ii. Are **narrowly tailored** to serve that interest, and
      iii. Leave open **alternative channels** of communication.
   b. **Limited public forums** are forums that are opened for limited use by certain groups or discussion of certain subjects. When they are open they are subject to **intermediate review:**
      i. They serve a **significant government interest,**
      ii. Are **narrowly tailored** to serve that interest, and
      iii. Leave open **alternative channels** of communication.
   c. **Designated public forums (unlimited public forums)** are forums that are not traditionally open to the public, but are opened up to the public at large for a specific purpose. When they are open they are subject to **intermediate review:**
      i. They serve a **significant government interest,**
      ii. Are **narrowly tailored** to serve that interest, and
      iii. Leave open **alternative channels** of communication.
   d. **Nonpublic forums** are forums that are closed to the public. The regulation must be:
      i. **Content neutral,**
      ii. Serve a **legitimate government interest,**
      iii. Be a **reasonably related** interest, and
      iv. Leave open **alternative channels** of communication.

2. **Commercial Speech:** The government may restrict commercial speech (advertising) only if the regulation serves a **substantial government** interest, **directly advances that interest**, and is **reasonably tailored** to serve that interest.
3. **Symbolic Speech:** The government may restrict symbolic speech, which is the freedom not to speak or the freedom to communicate an idea by use of a symbol or communicative conduct, if the regulation is:
   a. Within the **constitutional power** of the government to enact,
   b. Furthers an **important governmental interest** unrelated to the suppression of speech (content-neutral), and
   c. **Prohibits no more speech** than necessary.
4. **Limitations on free speech regulations**
   a. **Vagueness:** A speech regulation is unconstitutionally vague if it is so unclearly defined that a **reasonable person would have to guess** at its meaning.
   b. **Overbreadth:** A speech regulation is unconstitutionally overbroad if it bans **both protected speech and unprotected speech**.
   c. **Unfettered discretion:** A regulation, licensing scheme, or permit regulation is unconstitutional if it leaves unfettered discretion

to the decisionmaker by not setting forth **narrow and specific grounds** for denying a permit, **or** where the permit mechanism is **not closely tailored to the regulation's objective**. Further, the regulation must be a reasonable means of maintaining public order.

5. **Prior restraints** prevent speech from being heard **before it even occurs**. These are rarely allowed and carry a heavy presumption of unconstitutionality. A prior restraint is only allowed where the government can show that some **irreparable or serious harm** to the public will occur and then there must be **narrowly drawn standards** and a final determination of the validity of the restraint.
   a. **Collateral bar rule:** Under the collateral bar rule, if a prior restraint is issued, one cannot violate it and then defend oneself by asserting that the action is unconstitutional, even if this is correct.

> Prior Restraint fact triggers:
> - Discretion to allow or deny the use of facilities
> - Banning the release, display, or sale of things before review
> - Denying permits for various activities
> - Preventing the publication or disclosure of information

> Exam tip: When free speech is at issue, write out a mini-issues checklist including all possible speech issues. First, identify the state action. Next, look at whether the regulation is content-based or content-neutral, and then apply the appropriate test. If it is arguably either, then analyze both. For example, if the regulation limits the viewing of specific content, but only at certain times of the day, apply both tests. Lastly, consider all other potential speech issues, such as obscenity, overbreadth, prior restraint, commercial speech, etc.

C. **Freedom of association:** First Amendment case law recognizes an individual's right to freely associate with other individuals in groups.
   1. **Public job or benefit:** Freedom of association also prevents the government from denying a public benefit or job based on a person's association.
   2. Freedom of association only applies to freedoms protected by the **First Amendment** and is not for social purposes.
   3. The **government can only prevent freedom of association** or require individuals to associate in regard to First Amendment freedoms if there is a **compelling governmental interest** that cannot be achieved by **less restrictive means**.

D. **Due Process** binds the states through the Fourteenth Amendment, and the federal government through the Fifth Amendment.

1. **Substantive Due Process (SDP)** limits the government's ability to regulate certain areas of human life, such as the substantive interests in life, liberty, or property. (Regulates one's **personal autonomy and privacy**.)
   a. **Rights subject to SDP** are either fundamental or nonfundamental.
      1. **Fundamental rights:** Under SDP this refers to rights relating to marriage, living with one's family, child bearing and child rearing.
         a. **Strict scrutiny** applies to fundamental rights under SDP. The government action must be **necessary** to achieve a **compelling** government objective.
      2. **Nonfundamental rights:** Under SDP this applies to everything else, but typically social and economic regulations.
         a. **Rational basis test** applies to nonfundamental rights under SDP. The government action need only be **rationally related** to achieve a **legitimate** government objective. The burden of proof attaches to the challenger of the government action.

> **Substantive Due Process fact triggers:**
> - Bills requiring specific individuals to do something in violation of their fundamental rights (e.g., mandatory sterilization)
> - Denying benefits or permits to individuals or groups
> - Penalizing companies or individuals financially
> - Preventing individuals from their right to take part in activities

2. **Procedural Due Process (PDP)** requires the government to use **fair process** before depriving a person of life, liberty, or property.
   a. **Life, liberty, or property interests**
      1. **Liberty interest:** Includes physical liberty as well as intangible liberties, such as the right to drive, raise a family, etc.
      2. **Property interest:** Includes real property, personal property, government employment, government licenses, and government benefits that one is already receiving.
   b. **Process due**
      1. **For judicial proceedings** this includes the right to a hearing, counsel, call witnesses, a fair trial, and appeal.
      2. **For nonjudicial proceedings** this involves a **balancing test** by the court to weigh:
         a. The **private interest** that will be affected by the government action,
         b. The **risk of error** due to the procedural safeguards used and the possibility of substitute procedural safeguards, and
         c. The **government's interest** in fiscal and administrative burdens that the substitute procedural safeguards would cause, including the public interest.

E. The **Equal Protection Clause (EPC)** of the Fourteenth Amendment (applicable to the federal government through the Fifth Amendment DPC) prohibits the government from **treating similarly situated persons differently.**
   1. **Different treatment for similarly situated people**
      a. **Violation on its face:** The government treats people differently in a statute or regulation.
      b. **Violation as applied:** If the government treats people differently through the administration of a statute.
      c. **Intentionally different treatment** is required for heightened review (strict scrutiny and intermediate scrutiny) under EPC, and not just the incidental burdening effect.
   2. **Three levels of review can apply to EPC**
      a. **Strict scrutiny** requires the government to prove that the classification is **necessary** to achieve a **compelling** government interest.
      b. **Intermediate scrutiny** requires the government to prove that the classification is **substantially related** to achieve an **important** government interest.
      c. **Rational basis (low-level scrutiny)** requires the classification is **rationally related** to a **legitimate** government interest. The burden of proof is on the challenger of the classification.
   3. **Classification scheme:** EPC is at issue when people are treated differently based on classifications.
      a. **Suspect classifications** only include those based on **race, national origin,** and state **alienage** (not a U.S. citizen) and are subject to **strict scrutiny.**
      b. **Quasi-suspect classifications** only include those based on **gender** and **illegitimacy** and are subject to **intermediate scrutiny.**
      c. **Nonsuspect classifications** include everything else, including those based on nonsuspect and nonfundamental rights, such as economic and social welfare and are subject to **rational basis** review.
      d. **EPC fundamental rights:** The fundamental rights under the EPC are subject to **strict scrutiny** and limited to:
         1. **Voting** in state and local elections, except special purpose districts.
         2. Being a **political candidate.**
         3. Having **access to the courts.**
         4. **Migrating from state to state.**
         5. **Note:** The fundamental rights subject to strict scrutiny under EPC are different from the fundamental rights subject to strict scrutiny under SDP.
   4. **Level of review required**
      a. **Suspect classifications** and **EPC fundamental rights** receive **strict scrutiny** and thus require **intent** on the part of the government to treat individuals differently. **Strict scrutiny** requires the government to prove that the classification is **necessary** to achieve a **compelling** government interest.

b. **Quasi-suspect** classifications receive **intermediate scrutiny** and require **intent** on the part of the government to treat individuals differently. Intermediate scrutiny requires the government to prove that the classification is substantially related to achieve an important government interest.

c. **Non-suspect** classifications receive **rational basis review**. Rational basis (low-level scrutiny) requires the classification is rationally related to a legitimate government interest. The burden of proof is on the challenger of the classification.

> <u>Exam tip:</u> When analyzing EPC, after finding "state action" determine who is being treated differently and why (classification scheme). Determine the level of review that applies to that type of classification scheme. Then, analyze the level of review under the facts and using factual inferences (particularly to determine the government objective). Be aware that it is possible for more than one type of classification to apply, requiring analysis of each applicable level of review (e.g., gender and age, or an EPC fundamental right and an economic reason). Lastly, analyze the government's intent to discriminate if strict or intermediate scrutiny applies.

> <u>Equal Protection Clause fact triggers:</u>
> - Treating individuals differently for any reason
> - Denying benefits or funds to select individuals
> - Charging more money to certain people for anything
> - Prohibiting access to events to certain individuals
> - Only allowing select companies to conduct business

F. The **Takings Clause** of the Fifth Amendment provides that **private property** may not be **taken for public use** without **just compensation**.

1. **Public use** is satisfied if the state's use of the property is **rationally related** to a conceivable public purpose and can include public benefit rather than actual public usage.
2. **Just compensation** is measured by the market value of the property at the time of the taking.
3. **"Per se" takings:** Regulatory actions are "per se" takings if there is a
   a. Permanent **physical invasion**, or
   b. Denial of **all economically beneficial use** of property.
4. **Non–"per se" takings:** To determine if a regulatory action is a taking, the court will consider:
   a. The **economic impact** on the claimant,
   b. The extent to which it has **interfered with investment-backed expectations**, and
   c. The **character** of the government action.

CONSTITUTIONAL LAW ISSUES TESTED MATRIX

		Crossovers	Ripe/Moot	Standing	11th Amend.	State Action	Federal Powers/ Govt. Branches	Federal Preemption	DCC	P&I Clause	K's Clause	1st Amend. Religion	1st Amend. Speech Content-Based v. Neutral	Speech- Vague/ Overbroad/ Unfettered Discretion	Prior Restraint	Symbolic Speech	SDP	PDP	EP	Takings Clause
February '11 Q2	Charles enlisted in the U.S. Army and changes religion											X								
February '10 Q4	Paula wants to develop 100 acres of protected wetlands																			X
July '09 Q4	Statute, Congress, U.S. Sec. Transp. want safe highways			X			Congress												X	
July '08 Q2	Antiterrorism acts, the president & Homeland Security						Executive	X			X									
July '07 Q4	Dan stood on capital steps, lights a fire & kills a pedestrian	Criminal Procedure				X							X			X				
February '07 Q5	City ordinance bans tobacco ads to prevent smoking			X		X							X	X						
July '06 Q2	Columbia County has porn ordinance; Videorama sues		X	X		X							X	X	X					

Continued >

		Crossovers	Ripe/Moot	Standing	11th Amend.	State Action	Federal Powers/ Govt. Branches	Federal Preemption	DCC	P&I Clause	K's Clause	1st Amend. Religion	1st Amend. Speech Content-Based v. Neutral	Speech-Vague/ Overbroad/ Unfettered Discretion	Prior Restraint	Symbolic Speech	SDP	PDP	EP	Takings Clause
February '06 Q3	Mike has 30-yr. master lease and subleases to others	Real Property				X													X	X
February '05 Q1	State X statute requires gasahol			X		X			X	X							X	X	X	
July '04 Q2	State X passes an antiloitering statute			X		X							X	X						
February '04 Q5	NHTSA restricts radar detectors on big trucks			X		X		X	X											
February '03 Q5	Paul wants to be a cheerleader; sues Rural Univ.			X		X												X	X	
February '02 Q5	Assembly of Future Life has unpopular beliefs		X	X		X											X	X	X	X
July '01 Q4	Ada denied jail chaplain job because woman and religion			X	X	X						X							X	
July '00 Q4	Ruth the reporter observes illegal dog fight	Criminal Procedure		X		X							X						X	

Continued >

		Crossovers	Ripe/Moot	Standing	11th Amend.	State Action	Federal Powers/ Govt. Branches	Federal Preemption	DCC	P&I Clause	K's Clause	1st Amend. Religion	1st Amend. Speech Content-Based v. Neutral	Speech-Vague/ Overbroad/ Unfettered Discretion	Prior Restraint	Symbolic Speech	SDP	PDP	EP	Takings Clause
February '98 Q2	Escapee Hyde kidnaps Vic & wants manifesto published			X		X							X							X
July '97 Q2	Ordinance taxes new residents $500 if 2 + kids		X	X											X		X	X	X	
July '96 Q2	Ida, HUD, Congress; lead paint testing & removal plan			X			Congress													
July '95 Q2	Alternative education for pregnant students		X	X		X											X		X	
July '94 Q2	Ricks County Jail, females refused jailer positions			X	X	X													X	
February '94 Q5	Trial of serial killer; Pat publishes juror info			X		X							X		X				X	
February '92 Q2	ANI wants to develop, but zoning restrictions					X														X
July '91 Q2	CATS wants to protest taxes & Kate is naked					X							X	X	X	X				

Continued >

		Crossovers	Ripe/Moot	Standing	11th Amend.	State Action	Federal Powers/ Govt. Branches	Federal Preemption	DCC	P&I Clause	K's Clause	1st Amend. Religion	1st Amend. Speech Content-Based v. Neutral	Speech-Vague/ Overbroad/ Unfettered Discretion	Prior Restraint	Symbolic Speech	SDP	PDP	EP	Takings Clause
February '91 Q2	City-owned landfill & NAWT protests ordinance			X		X			X	X	X								X	
February '90 Q2	RMBA has interest rates ordinance w/ local fee discount		X	X		X		X	X	X	X						X	X	X	X
February '89 Q4	State X owns an office building but leases ground floor				X								X	X						
J '88 Q2	SAFDC limits fund recipients based on reproduction																X	X	X	
F '87 Q2	Pacific Home TV Movie Control Act limits R movies		X	X		X		X	X		X		X	X	X				X	
J '85 Q2	Val wants graduation rescheduled		X	X		X						X	X		X			X	X	

CONSTITUTIONAL LAW PRACTICE ESSAYS, ANSWER GRIDS, AND SAMPLE ANSWERS

Constitutional Law Question 1

July 1985, Question 4

The County Board of Education (Board) seeks your advice as Board's legal counsel regarding two current problems:

1. The public high school in the county district has scheduled graduation ceremonies for a Saturday morning, as has been the custom for all schools in the District. This year's senior class valedictorian, Val, holds religious beliefs that prevent her from attending the graduation ceremony because Saturday is the Sabbath day observed by her religion. Val has demanded that Board reschedule the graduation so she can attend and deliver the traditional valedictory address.
2. Board has had a policy of permitting community groups to use the high school auditorium for evening and weekend meetings at a modest rental fee. Now NFO, a local organization that advocates racial and religious discrimination, has applied for use of the auditorium for a major recruiting meeting on April 20. Persons and groups opposed to what they characterize as the "extremist" views of NFO are demanding that Board reject the application "out of hand, without giving it or even appearing to give it serious consideration." The local police chief also opposes the application on the basis of "hard intelligence" that some militant "anti-fascists" plan to remove NFO members from the school auditorium by physical force if the meeting takes place.

Both Val and NFO have delivered letters to Board invoking "rights under the U.S. Constitution" in support of their respective demand and application.

What issues arising under the U.S. Constitution are presented by:

1. The demand of Val? Discuss.
2. The application of NFO? Discuss.

Constitutional Law Question 1 Assessment

July 1985, Question 4

Although this is an older question, it is still very representative of a "racehorse" constitutional law question. Since it addresses several issues, both minor and major, it is extremely important that you adequately organize your answer on scratch paper prior to writing it out. This enables you to know which issues are minor and which are major so you can plan your writing time accordingly.

For example, any time you have to analyze a level of scrutiny, that analysis often takes longer to write out than an analysis of issues that have straightforward elements, like standing. Analyzing the levels of scrutiny requires more inferences, examples, and reasoning than simple elemental rules like standing. Consequently, those issues are often worth more points on a question.

This question is particularly intensive in that it tests all aspects of the First Amendment in one question. You have to address religion, free speech, and the implied freedom of association. This last issue has rarely been tested on the essay portion of the bar exam, but this question is a good example of how it does arise when it is tested. Thus, any time people are being prevented from meeting with those they wish to meet with, you should consider freedom of association as a possible issue. The free speech and religion issues are easy to spot since the facts speak to religion and the ability of both Val and NFO to express themselves verbally.

Remember, in a question like this you should write a more detailed issues checklist regarding all possible limitations on state powers so you don't miss any issues. Also, since there are so many issues to address in one hour, it is probably necessary to do a more cursory IRAC on the minor issues. It is better to analyze all the issues, even if some are in a truncated format, than to omit some issues and lose all the points applicable to that issue. Since the majority of points on the exam are contained in the analysis, you may need to analyze the rule by combining it with the factual analysis in order to finish the exam in a timely manner. This is especially true with multiple-issue racehorse questions.

If you missed any of the issues, review your issues checklists and add fact triggers to help you see how the facts can raise specific issues. Also, be sure to rewrite the question and/or any particular issues you miss. We recommend this for all essays to ensure that you have written every type of issue in essay format prior to sitting for the bar exam. Practice may not make perfect, but it will sure help you pass the exam. Being comfortable with writing out all possible issues gives you the mindset, muscle memory, and confidence you need to succeed on this exam.

Finally, make note of the areas highlighted in **bold** on the corresponding grid. The bold areas highlight the issues, analysis, and conclusions that are likely **required** to receive a passing score on this question. In general, the essay grids are provided to assist you in analyzing the essays, and are much more detailed than what a student should create during the exam to organize their response to a question.

Issue	Rule	Fact Application	Conclusion
V's Demands			
Standing	Injury Causation Redressable	Val cannot attend graduation or give valedictorian speech due to date of graduation. Caused by Board policy to hold all graduations on Saturday. Redressable if date of ceremony is changed.	V has standing
State action	Need to bring claim under Constitution; traditional public function or heavy gov. entanglement required.	County Board of Education implementing policy, so part of state/govt. entanglement.	State action exists
First Amendment Free Exercise Clause Establishment Clause	**(Incorporated to states through 14th Amend.)** **Govt. cannot prohibit or seriously burden the exercise of religion but may regulate if law of general applicability, which does not intentionally burden, and advances important public interests.** **Prohibits laws respecting the est. of religion.** **Govt. law that incidentally favors one religion over another but is designed to benefit a wide variety of people is fine.** **If no sect preference, law is valid if** **1. It has a secular purpose** **2. Its primary effect neither advances nor inhibits religion** **3. It does not produce excessive govt. entanglement with religion**	**V punished because she cannot attend graduation but state regulating all schools/students by having graduation on Sat., so it is a law of general applicability.** **Also, there is an important public interest of having graduation at a time and day when it is easier for parents and families to attend; since most people work on weekdays, weekends are likely a good time for most people.** **V will argue that the law prohibits her from observing her religious beliefs and the establishment of her religion, but it is an incidental burden/favor to other religions since it is designed to benefit the majority of families to enable them to attend graduation without work conflicts and other scheduling issues.** **No sect preference here.** **1. Policy here makes planning easier for all involved.** **2. Secondary effect on religion not primary effect as primary effect is likely to allow parental attendance and have all schools on same schedule.** **3. No excessive entanglement here.**	**No Free Exercise Clause violation No Est. Clause violation**

Continued >

Issue	Rule	Fact Application	Conclusion
Free Speech Content neutral Time, place, manner Public or limited public forum or designated forum	**Regulation is not about content of speech itself but timing of it—day it occurs. Open to public or occasionally open to public-at-large for a specific purpose (designated public forum) or to a specific group or discussion (limited public). 1. Content neutral 2. Narrowly tailored to serve signif. govt. interest 3. Leaves open channels of communication**	**Policy here regulates activity and time of speech, not content of speech itself, so content neutral. Graduation open to public attendance likely in public area since at a public school; but may be designated public forum if at school and only open to public at large for the graduation. 1. About time of speech not its content. 2. Significant state interest in finding a day when most parents can attend, but could also do Sunday or evening so may not be narrowly tailored. 3. Either V must go on Sat. to give speech or she will not be able to, so no likely other channel for her to communicate her speech (maybe via video feed from home).**	Likely a free speech violation
Equal Protection	**Prohibits similarly situated persons from being treated differently. If nonsuspect class, do rational basis review. Rationally related to legitimate govt. interest.**	**Here, V is treated equally to all other persons in that all students must attend on Saturday, so likely no discrimination at all. V could argue she's being treated differently based on her religion, but timing is not prohibiting her from practicing her religion, so not a 1st Amend. fundamental right issue; rather, it interferes with her religious beliefs and ability to follow those. State intent is to provide a day when most parents can attend, making planning easier and the same for all schools (legitimate reason); having it held on Saturdays is rationally related to this govt. interest because most people can likely attend then.**	**No Equal Protection violation**

Continued >

Issue	Rule	Fact Application	Conclusion
NFO's Application			
Standing / organizational	Members have standing. Interests germane to org. purpose. No individual participation required.	Members injured if cannot have meeting, caused if Board does not allow meeting, redressable if meeting allowed; interest in having meeting to advance org. purpose by recruiting other members, can seek injunctive or declaratory relief for meeting without member participation.	NFO will have standing
State action	Significant state involvement or public function.	County Board of Education acting by considering preventing use of auditorium.	State action exists
Ripeness	Need harm or immediate threat of harm.	Board hasn't decided whether to let NFO use school, but injury imminent if Board does not let them use the school.	Yes, ripe
Procedural Due Process	Cannot deprive of life, liberty, or property without due process—typically notice and hearing **Process required for nonjudicial proceedings involves balancing test by the court to weigh private interest that will be affected by the govt. action**, risk of error due to **procedural safeguards** used, and possibility of substitute procedural safeguards, and the **government's interest in fiscal and administrative burdens** that the substitute procedural safeguards would cause, including public interest	Possible freedom of speech violation without opportunity to be heard. **Interest to NFO to promote their beliefs and recruit. If NFO could be heard, it could relay how important a meeting is and why; could write out message. State interest based on hard intelligence that physical force will be used—will cost state money and resources, but not that difficult, costly, or time consuming to afford NFO a hearing. Also if Board acts "out of hand" without giving it much attention and rejects NFO application, then NFO wouldn't have any opportunity to be heard and the risk of error would be great to them.**	**Procedural Due Process violation**

Continued >

Issue	Rule	Fact Application	Conclusion
Free speech/ content-based	Restriction based on content of speech. Strict scrutiny—narrowly tailored to achieve a compelling govt. interest; least restrictive means.	NFO possibly banned from auditorium based on content of their beliefs. Govt. interest: likely compelling to prevent violence, use of physical force. Not narrowly tailored/least restrictive means because could require extra money to pay for guards, limit numbers, prevent any physical touching, etc., rather than ban meeting.	Free speech violation
Prior restraint	Prevents speech from being heard before it occurs. Govt. must show that some irreparable or serious harm to the public, narrowly drawn standards, and a final determination of the validity of the restraint.	NFO meeting has not occurred yet, so no speech yet. Serious harm to the public may occur here because of public danger and use of physical force. There are no standards used here; Board appears to have unfettered discretion. No injunction sought and no prompt and final determination made.	Prior restraint violation
Less protected speech	Imminent lawless action	Here, antifascists plan to remove NFO members from school, but this is non- (or anti-) NFO members that would be possibly committing lawless action, not NFO members.	Not less protected speech
Equal Protection	See above If based on free speech (fund. right), do S.S.—narrowly tailored to a compelling govt. interest.	Treats groups who want to use the auditorium differently based on the type of speech. Use strict scrutiny because free speech involved. See content-based analysis above.	Equal Protection violation

Continued >

Issue	Rule	Fact Application	Conclusion
Freedom of association	Freedom of association only applies to freedoms protected by the 1st Amend. and not for social purposes. Right is not absolute and may be infringed by compelling govt. interests if infringements are the least restrictive means.	Here, state would be prohibiting a politically unpopular group, NFO, from expressing and meeting in regard to their extreme religious and racial views, and free speech is part of 1st Amend. protection. Govt. interest: likely compelling to prevent violence, use of physical force. Does not use least restrictive means because could require extra money to pay for guards, prevent any physical touching at all, etc., rather than banning meeting.	Freedom of association violation

Constitutional Law 1 Sample Answer
July 1985, Question 2

1. Val's Demand

Standing

Plaintiff must establish she has an injury in fact that was caused by the state action and that her harm is redressable. Val has standing because she will be injured by Board's custom of holding all graduations on Saturday since she will be unable to attend graduation or give her speech, but if the date of is changed she can attend, making her injury redressable.

State Action

Constitutional limitations generally only apply to state action, and here there is state action because a county school district is entangled by their implementation of a policy.

First Amendment

The First Amendment is incorporated to the states through the Fourteenth Amendment.

Free Exercise Clause

The Free Exercise Clause bars any law that prohibits or seriously burdens the free exercise of religion, except for laws of general applicability. Here, the state custom required all graduation ceremonies to be held on the same Saturday so it is a law of general applicability. The purpose of the rule is not to intentionally burden religion, but rather to make the event easier for the district to plan and coordinate. Further, the custom serves the important public interest of holding graduations on a predictable day when it is easiest for most families to attend because it is not a typical workday, so there is no Free Exercise Clause violation.

Establishment Clause

The Establishment Clause prohibits laws respecting the establishment of religion. A state action without sect preference is allowable if it has a secular purpose, a secular effect, and it does not produce excessive government entanglement with religion. Val will argue the Board custom of holding graduation on Saturday has the effect of inhibiting her religious beliefs while favoring those who hold their Sabbath on other days. However, the Board will argue that the purpose of holding all graduations on Saturday is secular because it was done to streamline planning and allow parental attendance. The restriction has only a secondary effect on religion, and the primary purpose of the custom is secular. Further, the state action is not excessively entangled with any religion. There is no violation of the Establishment Clause.

Free Speech

The regulation here is content neutral since it does not concern the content of speech at all, but rather the timing when a particular speech can take place.

Forum

The valediction is to be given at a public school graduation, which is likely open to the public and held in a public area, so it is probably a public forum. It may be a designated public forum if the location at the school is only open to the public at large for the graduation ceremony.

Time, Place, and Manner

Whether a public or limited public forum, a valid time, place, and manner regulation will be upheld if it is content neutral, narrowly tailored to serve a significant government interest, and leaves open alternative channels of communication. The custom of holding graduations on Saturday appears to be content neutral because it concerns the day the speech is given not the words spoken. This custom seems to be tailored to the purpose of efficiency for the Board in having all graduations on the same day, and there is a government interest in providing a graduation day that is convenient for most graduates and their families. However, since the event could be held on an evening or Sunday and fulfill the same interest, it may not be sufficiently narrowly tailored. Val will assert that she has no alternate channels of communication since as the class valedictorian; she either gives her valedictory address at this graduation or does not have the opportunity to speak at all. Though it may be possible to do a video feed from home, there are probably not alternative channels. Thus, Val may have a valid challenge on free speech grounds.

Equal Protection

The Equal Protection Clause prohibits similarly situated persons from being treated differently by the state. Val may argue that she is being discriminated against for her religious beliefs since those who hold the Sabbath on another day are favored by the state custom. However, religious classifications are only subject to the rational basis test under equal protection. The government regulation need only be rationally related to a legitimate government interest.

Val will argue that the Board custom is discriminatory of her religious beliefs by having the graduation on a Saturday rather than on a Sunday when she could attend. However, since the school regulation did not treat Val any differently than any other graduate, regardless of religious affiliation, there isn't discrimination. Further, holding the graduation on Saturday serves the legitimate interest of providing a day where most parents can attend, and that holding all district graduations on the same day made planning and coordination easier, which is rationally related to the interest of holding a memorable graduation ceremony for most students, so there is no equal protection violation.

2. NFO's Application

Standing

Organizations have standing where the members would have standing, the interest is germane to the organizational purpose, and individual participation is not required. The NFO members would be injured by the Board's refusal to allow their meeting since they want to advance the organization's purpose by increasing their recruiting efforts. The injury is redressable since NFO can seek declaratory relief without individual member participation.

State Action

Since the County Board of Education is run by the state, any actions taken by them would qualify as state action.

Ripeness

A case will not be heard if there is not yet a live controversy or immediate threat of harm.

The Board has not decided whether NFO can use the auditorium and therefore the issue is not ripe, however the injury is imminent if the Board does not let NFO hold their meeting and the court should grant relief now to avoid the subsequent harm.

Procedural Due Process

The state must provide fair process before depriving an individual of their life, liberty, or property. Here, there is a possible deprivation of free speech without the opportunity to have due process. For a nonjudicial proceeding there is a balancing test to weigh the private interest affected by the state action, the risk of error due to the procedural safeguards used, possible substitute procedural safeguards, the government's interest in fiscal and administrative burdens that the substitute procedural safeguards would cause, and the public interest. NFO's interest is in the recruiting of new members and promotion of their beliefs. If NFO had the opportunity to be heard they could explain the importance of such a meeting. The state interest here is based on hard intelligence that physical force will be used, which will cost money and resources to protect against. However, affording a hearing is not dangerous, time consuming, or costly. Also if the Board acts "out of hand, without giving or even appearing to give serious consideration," to NFO's application to use the auditorium, NFO wouldn't have the opportunity to be heard and the risk of error is great. While it is possible the Board's actions would be justified based on the police chief's "hard intelligence" that militia groups plan to remove NFO forcefully, NFO is still entitled to be heard and their procedural due process rights have been violated.

Free Speech

Content-Based Restriction

It is presumptively unconstitutional to place burdens on speech because of its content, and they are subject to strict scrutiny. Here, the Board's action is a content-based speech restriction since it is attempting to prevent NFO from meeting in the auditorium in order to silence NFO's "extremist" views of advocating racial and religious discrimination. The government interest is likely compelling since it is to prevent violence directed at NFO. However, not allowing NFO to speak is not narrowly tailored and the least restrictive means of serving the government interest since they could require extra security guards, or limit attendance, or take other precautionary measures besides banning the meeting.

Prior Restraint

Prior restraint prevents speech before it can be heard. The government must show irreparable harm to the public, narrowly drawn standards, and a final determination on the restraint's validity. The NFO meeting has yet to occur so this would be a prior restraint on NFO's speech. There is potential harm to the public (supra) but there are no standards at all, let alone narrowly drawn ones. The Board has unfettered discretion to issue or deny permits, which is improper. Thus far, no final determination has been sought.

Imminent Lawlessness

Speech inciting imminent lawless action is not protected; however, it is the antifascists who plan to behave violently, not the NFO members. Since it is the antifascists who have expressed intent to be violent and the NFO has not encouraged this, the speech of NFO is protected.

Equal Protection

Free speech is a fundamental right so strict scrutiny applies. See content-based free speech analysis supra. The Board is in violation of the Equal Protection Clause.

Freedom of Association

First Amendment case law recognizes an individual's right to freely associate with other individuals in groups, which NFO is attempting to do here with the recruitment meeting. This right may be abridged if there are compelling government interests unrelated to the suppression of ideas, which cannot be achieved through less restrictive means. However, as discussed supra, less restrictive means are available.

Constitutional Law Question 2

February 2005, Question 1

A State X statute prohibits the retail sale of any gasoline that does not include at least 10 percent ethanol, an alcohol produced from grain, which, when mixed with gasoline, produces a substance known as "gasohol." The statute is based on the following legislative findings: (1) the use of gasohol will conserve domestic supplies of petroleum; (2) gasohol burns more cleanly than pure gasoline, thereby reducing atmospheric pollution; and (3) the use of gasohol will expand the market for grains from which ethanol is produced.

State X is the nation's largest producer of grain used for making ethanol. There are no oil wells or refineries in the state.

Oilco is an international petroleum company doing business in State X as a major retailer of gasoline. Oilco does not dispute the legislative findings underlying the statute or the facts concerning State X's grain production and lack of oil wells and refineries. Oilco, however, has produced reliable evidence showing that, since the statute was enacted, its sales and profits in State X have decreased substantially because of its limited capacity to produce gasohol.

Can Oilco successfully assert that the statute violates any of the following provisions of the United States Constitution: (1) the Commerce Clause, (2) the Equal Protection Clause, (3) the Due Process Clause, and (4) the Privileges and Immunities Clause? Discuss.

Constitutional Law Question 2 Assessment

February 2005, Question 1

This is a question that students often enjoy seeing because they know immediately that it is a constitutional law question by reading the call, and they also know they do not have to do much issue spotting because the call is so specific. While "enjoyable" is perhaps not the best word to describe this type of question, it is certainly less stressful and more calming to approach it when you immediately know the subject and the issues you are being asked to address. In a situation like this, there is no need to write out your issues checklist. Rather, after you have read the facts, you should begin by writing out your elements to the identified rules.

Note that it is still important to read the facts through once first before writing out the rules and beginning to match up the facts on your outline. Although the first question call asks about the Commerce Clause, without reading the facts, you have no way of knowing whether it is state government action implicating the Dormant Commerce Clause, or federal government action implicating the regular Commerce Clause. A quick read of the facts reveals that State X is the government actor and the Dormant Commerce Clause is at issue.

This question is also very useful to illustrate the importance of organizing your answers entirely prior to writing out the essay. It is generally necessary to spend 15 minutes organizing the essay and 45 minutes writing the essay. Once you have organized your answer, but before you have started writing, you can determine which issues are worth the most points and spend your time accordingly. For example, in this question, call four is worth the least amount on this question. This is because this issue can be easily addressed by providing an issue heading, concisely stating the rule, and then adding one sentence of analysis quickly dismissing the issue by stating that the Privileges and Immunities Clause does not apply because Oilco is a corporation and is therefore not considered a citizen for purposes of this clause. Lastly, conclude by answering the specific call that Oilco will not be able to successfully assert that this statute violated the Privileges and Immunities Clause.

Once you have your answer organized with an outline on scratch paper, you should be able to easily see that there were far fewer facts to the analysis of call 4 than to the others. You will know before writing that this issue is worth the least number of points and, therefore, not to spend nearly as much time writing out that issue as the Dormant Commerce Clause issue. It is common for issues with more rules and/or rule elements to be worth more points because there are more facts available to analyze with the elements. You can easily see from glancing at the grid below which issues are likely worth more points on this question because the facts are voluminous. You should be able to do this with your outline of the answer you've organized on scratch paper. We recommend putting a star next to the big issues to help you pace yourself as you are writing so you can easily identify where to "go big" with the analysis on a major issue and where to truncate the IRAC on a minor issue.

Note the areas highlighted in **bold** on the corresponding grid. The bold areas highlight the issues, analysis, and conclusions that are likely **required** to receive a passing score on this question.

Issue	Rule	Fact Application	Conclusion
Standing	**Injury, causation, redressability**	**Injury: O's sales and profits decreased** substantially because of its limited capacity to produce gasohol. **Causation: This is caused by the State X statute,** which requires O to have 10% ethanol in gasoline. **Redressability: If the statute is unconstitutional, O can sell its non-gasohol gasoline** and increase sales again.	**O has standing**
Ripeness	Need harm or immediate threat of harm	O was harmed by substantial losses in profits and sales.	Ripe
State action	**Significant state involvement or exclusive public function**	**Here, State X acted through legislation; need to show state action to bring a claim under the Constitution.**	**State action exists**
(1) **Commerce Clause**	**Under the Dormant Commerce Clause, the state cannot regulate interstate commerce if (1) it is discriminatory or (2) unduly burdensome**. If the regulation is facially discriminatory, **it must be necessary to an important, noneconomic govt. interest** with no reasonable nondiscriminatory alternatives. **For burden, look at state's interest v. burden on interstate commerce** **Exceptions: market participant**, Congress consents	**Discriminatory: Statute does not discriminate on its face, but the statute does favor State X–produced gasohol over out-of-state since State X is the nation's largest grain producer and it does not have any oil wells and refineries. Further, the state interest/favoritism is shown by the fact that requiring 10% ethanol made from grains will expand the market for grains from which ethanol is produced, which will further benefit State X.** However, it does regulate all gasoline producers the same, possibly indicating that it is not discriminatory. Noneconomic state interest: Arguably, the interest is merely economic as this statute will expand grain market and produce more money for State X through the sale of its grain to make gasohol, but **the statute will help produce more clean-burning fuel and thereby reduce pollution,** indicating that the state interest is actually not purely economic [Note: only one state-released answer talked about this "unless . . . noneconomic . . . " part of the rule.]	Both state-released answers came to different conclusions here

Continued >

Issue	Rule	Fact Application	Conclusion
		Nondiscriminatory options: State X has legislative findings with definite reasons for why it has the statute, none of which O can dispute, indicating it is necessary for State X to have the statute. However, the statute could phase out pure gasoline to gasohol over time, rather than instantaneously. [Note: Only one state-released answer addressed this part of rule as well.] **Market participant: Not clear that state is acting as a market participant by selling or buying, so this exception will fail.** Undue burden: **Although O will still be able to sell its gasoline in other states, it is suffering substantial losses and profits by not being able to sell adequate amounts of gasohol in State X**, thus placing an undue burden on interstate commerce. **State X does have multiple benefits by requiring ethanol as indicated above**, but if many gas retailers are suffering similar problems with using gasohol, then it is likely that the burden will be undue and will have a major impact on interstate commerce.	Both state-released answers came to different conclusions here
(2) Equal Protection Clause	**Prohibits similarly situated persons from being treated differently.** **Nonsuspect class: rational basis—rationally related to a legitimate state interest**	**Here, gasoline retailers are being treated differently based on whether they use gasohol or not in State X retail.** **Treatment based on using grain and making ethanol v. not using it is a nonsuspect class as it does not involve race, alienage, or gender.** **State interest (see above): Increases market for grain, lowers pollution, conserves petroleum—all of which are legitimate state interests.** **Rationally related: By requiring ethanol use, all of these interests will be met as indicated by the legislative findings, and the fact that O does not dispute these findings indicates they must be true and reliable.**	**No Equal Protection violation**

Continued >

Issue	Rule	Fact Application	Conclusion
(3) Due Process Clause	**Substantive Due Process: deprivation of life, liberty, or property** **If no fundamental right is involved, use rational basis test—see above.** **Procedural Due Process:** requires notice and a hearing prior to taking away the life, liberty, or property of an individual.	Here, deprivation of property right—selling gasoline. **The right to sell gasoline is not a fundamental right, so rational basis is used.** **See above (in Equal Protection analysis) for rational basis analysis.** Here, there was likely notice and opportunity to be heard as State X passed the statute through legislation and even has legislative findings to support the statute.	**No Substantive Due Process violation** No Procedural Due Process violation
(4) Privileges and Immunities Clause	**The city or state cannot discriminate against noncitizens** unless the state has a substantial justification and there are no less discriminatory, alternative means available. Only protects fundamental rights **Corporations and aliens are not considered citizens for purposes of the P & I Clause.**	**Here, O is an international company and, as such, is not considered a citizen for purposes of the Privileges and the Immunities Clause.**	**No Privileges and Immunities Clause violation**

Constitutional Law 2 Sample Answer
February 2005, Question 1

Standing
To establish standing to bring suit Oilco must demonstrate they have suffered an injury, it was caused by the defendant's action, and that it is redressable. Oilco has been injured since their sales and profits have decreased substantially because of their limited capacity to produce gasohol. This injury is caused by State X's statute requiring 10% ethanol in gasoline, and it is redressable because if the statute is found unconstitutional Oilco can go back to selling their non-gasohol gasoline and increase sales.

Ripeness
To bring suit the case must be ripe for adjudication and there must be an immediate threat of harm, which can be shown here since O has substantial sales losses.

State Action
To bring suit Oilco must show state action by significant state involvement or performance of a public function to bring any claim under the Constitution. Here, State X has acted through legislation so there is state action.

1. Commerce Clause
Pursuant to the Dormant Commerce Clause a state cannot regulate interstate commerce if it is discriminatory or unduly burdensome, unless it furthers an important noneconomic state interest and there are no reasonable nondiscriminatory alternatives. The statute here does not discriminate on its face, but it does favor State X–produced gasohol over out-of-state products since State X does not have any oil wells or refineries within the state but is the nation's largest grain producer, and grain is a key ingredient in ethanol, which State X gasoline is now required to contain in the amount of 10% in accordance with the statute. Requiring the gas to contain 10% ethanol, which is made from grains primarily produced in State X, favors local interests by expanding the market for ethanol grains, which thereby discriminates against out-of-state gasoline producers. While the statute regulates all gasoline producers whether in-state or out-of-state in the same way, this statue has the effect of favoring local interests economically by expanding the market for a local product, and thus it is likely discriminatory.

State X may argue that even if the statute is discriminatory it serves a noneconomic state interest and there are no reasonable alternatives, so it is allowable. As indicated by the legislative findings, the statute will help produce more clean-burning fuel and thereby reduce pollution and conserve natural resources, so it does not have a purely economic purpose, though it will also have the economic effect of stimulating demand for State X grain. There does not seem to be a reasonable alternative to the statute since State X has legislative findings with definite reasons supporting the statute that are not protectionist of State X businesses. The only possible alternative might be a gradual phasing in of the statute, rather than an instantaneous implementation.

There is also an exception to the Dormant Commerce Clause where the state is acting as a market participant. However, it does not appear that the state is in the business of buying or selling the ethanol, rather the state is legislating so this exception will not apply.

To establish if the statute is unduly burdensome the state's interest is weighed against the burden on interstate commerce. Although as an international company Oilco is able to sell their normal gasoline in other states, they are suffering substantial financial losses by not being able to sell their normal gasoline in State X, which places an undue burden on interstate commerce. While State X has a valid interest in having ethanol added to the gasoline as indicated above, if many gas retailers are suffering similar problems to Oilco, the cumulative effect of the burden on interstate commerce may outweigh the state's interest in producing clean-burning fuel.

2. Equal Protection

The Equal Protection Clause prohibits similarly situated persons from being treated differently. Here, gasoline retailers are being treated differently depending on whether they sell gasohol in State X. The classification scheme pertains to using grain and ethanol in the production of gasoline, and the rational basis test will apply since this is not a suspect class because it does not pertain to race, alienage, gender, or illegitimacy. The state action must be rationally related to a legitimate state interest to not violate equal protection. The state interest is a legitimate one, as discussed above (pollution, conservation, etc.). By requiring ethanol added to the gasoline, all of the state's interests will be satisfied, and this result is supported by the legislative findings. Further, Oilco does not dispute these findings, so they are likely true and reliable; thus, the statute here is rationally related to the state's legitimate interest and there is no Equal Protection Clause violation.

3. Due Process Clause

Substantive due process limits the government's ability to regulate certain areas of human life, typically regarding personal autonomy and privacy. If a fundamental privacy right is not involved, the rational basis test applies. The State X statute does apply equally to all companies, but the right to sell gasoline is an economic right and not a fundamental right, so the rational basis test will apply. See Equal Protection supra for the application of the rational basis test. There is no Substantive Due Process Clause violation.

Procedural due process requires that fair processes be implemented before the state takes away a life, liberty, or property interest. Here, since the statute was passed through the legislative process and there are legislative factual findings in support of the statute, it is likely that there was an adequate opportunity for Oilco to be heard. There is no Procedural Due Process Clause violation.

4. Privileges and Immunities Clause

A state cannot discriminate against noncitizens unless the state has a substantial justification and there are no less discriminatory alternative means available. This clause only applies to fundamental rights that pertain to national unity and, most importantly, does not protect aliens and corporations since they are not considered citizens under this clause. Oilco is an international company and, as such, is not considered a citizen eligible for protection under the Privileges and Immunities Clause, therefore there is no violation.

Constitutional Law Question 3

February 2002, Question 5

The growth of City has recently accelerated, putting stress on municipal infrastructure. City's water supply, roads, sewers, and schools are all operating in excess of designed capacity.

The Assembly of Future Life was organized in City not long ago. Its members adhere to certain unpopular religious beliefs. City gave the Assembly preliminary zoning approval for plans to build a worship center on a one-acre parcel of real property the Assembly owned within City's borders. The Assembly's plans incorporated a dwelling for its minister. Soon after the preliminary zoning approval, newspapers in City featured articles about the Assembly and its members' beliefs.

After these newspaper articles appeared, City adopted a "slow growth" ordinance providing for an annual lottery to allocate up to 50 building permits, with applicants for certain "priority status" dwellings entitled to participate first. Priority status dwellings were defined as: (1) affordable housing; (2) housing on five-acre lots with available sewer and water connections; or (3) housing with final zoning approval as of the date the ordinance was adopted. Only after all applicants for priority status dwellings had received permits in the lottery could other applicants participate.

Over 500 applicants for priority status dwellings participated in the first annual lottery. Realizing that its opportunity to participate in a lottery could be years away, the Assembly submitted an application for retroactive final zoning approval and a building permit. City denied the application.

The Assembly brought suit in federal district court against City, alleging that: (1) City's ordinance was invalid under the due process, equal protection, and takings clauses of the U.S. Constitution; and (2) City's denial of the Assembly's application was invalid under the due process clause of the U.S. Constitution.

What arguments can the Assembly reasonably make in support of its allegations and is each argument likely to succeed? Discuss.

Constitutional Law Question 3 Assessment

February 2002, Question 5

This question is rather specific in that it enables you to quickly identify the subject and the necessary issues. As for the previous question, you would not need to write out your issues checklist. Notice that the call of the question asks you to focus on the arguments that the Assembly can reasonably make in support of its allegations, so be sure that you are analyzing Assembly's side as you tackle each issue. Of course, to adequately argue Assembly's side, you should also anticipate City's arguments and how Assembly would respond to those arguments.

This question often confuses students for two reasons. First, students often do not know whether to address Substantive Due Process or Procedural Due Process when the call refers to Due Process in general. The answer depends on what is at issue. Was there a deprivation relating to personal autonomy or privacy? If so, go through Substantive Due Process. Or, was there a problem with the process itself? If so, go through Procedural Due Process. However, if it is unclear whether there was a process issue, you may want to quickly address Procedural Due Process, but don't spend that much time on it, which is exactly what one of the state-released answers did here on the first question call.

The second problem students have with this question is that they discuss the same Due Process issue for the first and second call. The examiners would not ask about Due Process separately in two separate calls if they were asking about exactly the same issue. So, it is not acceptable on this question to simply say "see above." Rather, for the first call, the focus is on City's ordinance, which means you need to focus on whether the ordinance itself violates Due Process. Also, you could have quickly addressed Procedural Due Process because it is likely to infer that there is some type of notice and hearing before ordinances are adopted. The second call of the question focuses on the Due Process involved with City denying Assembly's application in particular, rather than the validity of the ordinance itself. This call does lend itself to both types of Due Process analysis. Always be very careful to know exactly what each call is asking and don't assume that if it asks about the same issue in two calls that the analysis is the same.

This question also tests the Takings Clause. When analyzing Takings issues, you often need to go through both the "per se" taking rules and the non-"per se" taking rules in order to earn all available points. Also, some bar exam questions (as you can see in the Matrix at the end of this part) have tested only the issue of takings with one call devoted to a total taking (per se) and the other call devoted to a partial taking (non-per se) so be sure you know both rules well.

Finally, make note of the areas highlighted in **bold** on the corresponding grid. The bold areas highlight the issues, analysis, and conclusions that are likely **required** to receive a passing score on this question.

Issue	Rule	Fact Application	Conclusion
Allegation (1)			
Standing	**Individual standing: injury, causation, redressability** **Organizational standing:** individual members need standing (per rule above), germane to organizational purpose, and no individual participation is required.	**Here, Assembly is injured, as it cannot receive a permit to build its worship center due to the slow growth ordinance, which would be remedied if the ordinance were deemed unconstitutional.** For organization: Members have standing (see above); germane to organizational purpose because the center will help them with their interests in regard to their religious beliefs; and no participation required because simply seeking declaratory relief, and the organization will receive the permit, not the individual members.	**Yes, standing**
Ripeness	Harm or immediate threat of harm	Here, arguably Assembly has not been harmed yet because it could receive its permit after the lottery, but this is unlikely based on the priority levels; since Assembly is not a priority, harm is immediate because Assembly will not get a permit to build their center under the current ordinance structure.	Yes, ripe
State action	Significant state involvement or traditional public function	Here, the City is a government actor and it enacted the ordinance at issue, which constitutes significant state involvement.	Yes, state action
Substantive Due Process	Deprivation of life, liberty, property **If based on a fundamental right → strict scrutiny (necessary to achieve a compelling govt. interest)** **If based on a nonfundamental right → rational basis (rationally related to a legitimate govt. interest)**	Here, the ordinance deprives individuals of their right to property—in this case, to build. **Assembly will argue ordinance interferes with their fundamental right to religion under the 1st Amend. by prohibiting them from practicing their religion, which would warrant strict scrutiny. However the ordinance does not prohibit them from practicing their religion because they are still free to practice and worship**; it only prohibits them from building the structure in which they want to worship. Since the ordinance simply prohibits them from building a building and receiving a permit, **it is not about their religion, but the building, which would receive a rational basis test.**	**Ordinance does not violate Substantive Due Process**

Continued >

Issue	Rule	Fact Application	Conclusion
		Legitimate govt. interest: Preserving the govt. infrastructure since the growth of City has recently accelerated; it is a legitimate interest since the growth is putting stress on the infrastructure and the govt. has a legitimate interest in protecting this infrastructure so the City has adequate water supply, roads, sewers, and schools given they are already operating in excess of designed capacity. **Rationally related: By limiting building development, City can stabilize and maintain control of its infrastructure; also, the ordinance gives priority to preexisting infrastructure** so as not to put further strain on the infrastructure because priority is given to those with available water and sewer connections and those who already obtained approval, avoiding new building that would require additional water and sewer and resources not accounted for. If S.S were applied: Even if compelling to maintain infrastructure, not narrowly tailored and necessary because they could still allow building for buildings not yet built if already approved, which would still affect the infrastructure; also, by allowing the new affordable housing and housing on 5-acre lots, it could bring in many more apt.-type buildings and more people, which would actually cause more strain on the infrastructure and use even more water, sewer, etc., than perhaps a church building that doesn't have numerous persons living there nor use as much sewer and water.	**Ordinance does not violate Substantive Due Process**
Procedural Due Process	Need notice and hearing before life, liberty, or property taken by govt. (intentional, not negligent).	Here, arguably the govt. is taking away Assembly's property right since it cannot build on its land as it is desires, and it did have preliminary zoning approval to build there. However, is it likely that the ordinance itself did go through some notice and hearing before becoming an ordinance—the community likely knew about it prior to it being adopted and had an opportunity to object or state their concerns, but the facts are silent here so it is possible that no notice or hearing was provided to the community or Assembly prior to the adoption of the ordinance.	Possible Procedural Due Process violation

Continued >

Issue	Rule	Fact Application	Conclusion
Equal Protection	Requires that similarly situated persons be treated similarly. **Suspect class: 1st Amend. fundamental right → strict scrutiny** (necessary to achieve a compelling govt. interest and uses least restrictive means) **Quasi-suspect: gender → Intermediate scrutiny (substantially related to an important govt. interest)** **Nonsuspect: all other → rational basis (rationally related to a legitimate govt. interest)** **For strict and intermediate scrutiny, need to prove intent.**	Here, the ordinance gives priority to persons who are building affordable housing, or already have existing sewer and water connections, or final approval; does not allow permits for others unless they win lottery. **This is discriminatory on its face, but not in regard to religion or a fundamental right; Assembly will argue it is intended to discriminate against it based on its religious views because City passed the ordinance after the newspaper articles appeared about Assembly and its religious views.** **However**, the ordinance affects everyone—not just Assembly and its religion—it would equally apply to any type of religion that wanted to build a building or worship center; thus, **it will receive rational basis review as the discrimination is between certain types of housing and permits, giving it a rational basis test.** **See above for rational basis analysis.**	No Equal Protection violation
Takings	**Private property may not be taken for public use without just compensation.** Public use—rationally related to a conceivable public purpose **There is a per se taking if there is a permanent physical invasion or the denial of all economic value.** **To determine if a regulatory action is a taking that does not meet the per se requirements, the court will consider (1) economic impact of the regulation on claimant, (2) the extent to which the regulation interfered with investment-backed expectations, and (3) character of govt. action.**	**Assembly will argue the value of their land has been taken away as there is no viable use for their land since they only wanted a worship center, and without that the land is useless to them.** **However, Assembly is still free to use the land for other non-building uses and can still worship on the land without a building or use the land for other purposes.** **Economic impact on claimant could be great if they need to rent another facility and are unable to do anything productive with theirs; expectations and investment made for the sole purpose of building a worship center there, so they cannot do what was intended and planned. However, govt. has a very important and possibly compelling govt. interest in protecting and slowing down its growing infrastructure, so limiting the permits may aid in this slow growth and will likely benefit the public at large by slowing down the infrastructure so that everyone has sufficient water, resources, and facilities usage.**	State-released answers concluded differently here; either way is sufficient so long as you analyze the necessary factors and see both sides

Continued >

Issue	Rule	Fact Application	Conclusion
Allegation (2)			
Procedural Due Process	**See above**	Here, Assembly did not receive notice or hearing regarding its denial of a permit after being given the preliminary zoning approval. Here, Assembly was not heard on its issue of final approval; rather, it just has to adhere to the ordinance and follow the priority list, of which they are not at the top of the priority list. Nor does the ordinance provide for a hearing—rather, it just has a lottery and decides on its own. However, just because Assembly had preliminary approval does not indicate they would have received final approval or a permit even without the ordinance; as such, there was not yet a property right attached since they purchased the land without knowing that they would definitely be able to build their worship center. [Note: Both state-released answers were very different here. You only needed to analyze the rule somewhat and you were fine.]	Likely no violation
Substantive Due Process	See above	Here, it is unclear why the City denied Assembly's retroactive permit. **Assembly will argue City denied permit due to their religious beliefs because it was after the newspaper articles and after the ordinance; however, the better argument is that it was because building additional buildings would harm their infrastructure** and could lead to others who also obtained preliminary approval to want their buildings built and cause many other buildings on top of the priority and lottery ones. **If based on religion, do strict scrutiny review (see above).** **If based on building/infrastructure, do rational basis review (see above).** (More likely the case since not about their specific religion but more likely about the infrastructure.)	No violation

Constitutional Law Question 4

July 2006, Question 2

In an effort to "clean up Columbia County," the County Board of Supervisors recently passed an ordinance, providing as follows:

"(1) A Review Panel is hereby established to review all sexually graphic material prior to sale by any person or entity in Columbia County.

(2) Subject to subsection (3), no person or entity in Columbia County may sell any sexually graphic material.

(3) A person or entity in Columbia County may sell an item of sexually graphic material if (a) the person or entity first submits the item to the Review Panel and (b) the Review Panel, in the exercise of its sole discretion, determines that the item is not pornographic.

(4) Any person or entity in Columbia County that fails to comply with subsection (2) or (3) is guilty of a misdemeanor, and is punishable by incarceration in jail for one year or by imposition of a $5,000 fine, or by both."

Videorama, Inc., a local video store, has brought an action claiming that the ordinance violates the First Amendment to the United States Constitution.

What arguments may Videorama, Inc. reasonably make in support of its claim, and is it likely to succeed? Discuss.

Constitutional Law Question 4 Assessment

July 2006, Question 2

This question is a full-blown free speech question. If you start by reading the call, you are unable to even determine which subject the question pertains to because the call merely asks about the arguments Videorama may make in support of its claim and whether it will succeed. However, a quick glance at the preceding sentence tells you that the claim is for a violation of the First Amendment. Now you know you are dealing with constitutional law. Nonetheless, at this point, you don't know which issue(s) within the First Amendment are applicable. A quick reading of the facts, with your fact triggers in mind, should quickly lead you to free speech.

Therefore, there is no need to write out your entire constitutional law issues checklist since free speech is only one issue on the main issues checklist. This is the type of question where you need to utilize your mini-issues checklist that you memorized specifically for free speech questions. In this checklist, you should have all possible issues relating to speech, including those that are required to make a claim under the First Amendment at all, such as standing and state action. This more detailed speech checklist will help you avoid missing easily overlooked issues, such as prior restraint, which can lead to missing a lot of points.

Once you have spotted all the issues and noted the corresponding rules, you will need to analyze the issues, as you do with many constitutional law questions, by using logical inferences and giving two or three examples to support your arguments. For example, the facts state that the goal of the ordinance was to "clean up Columbia County." When analyzing the government's interest for your content-based speech issue, you need to infer the reason why removing sexually graphic material might help "clean up" the county. Both state-released passing answers argued that perhaps there is an interest in preventing children from being exposed to these materials. This is the type of logical inference you need to make to maximize your analysis points.

Further, when discussing whether the ordinance is necessary to achieve this governmental interest, both state-released passing answers gave examples of other less restrictive means the government could take to clean up the county, such as imposing zoning laws and age requirements. When analyzing which other means may be available, always try to think of two or three examples to support your argument in order to earn maximum points. A good answer to this question should be filled with inferences and examples that are necessary to properly and adequately analyze the issues. For example, the analysis of the issues vagueness and overbreadth also required the use of examples that are not contained in the facts to explain why the ordinance is perhaps vague and overbroad.

Finally, make note of the areas highlighted in **bold** on the corresponding grid. The bold areas highlight the issues, analysis, and conclusions that are likely **required** to receive a passing score on this question.

Issue	Rule	Fact Application	Conclusion
Standing	Injury Causation Redressability	V is likely to incur imminent injury if selling videos with sexually graphic material because ordinance passed and they are likely in violation and can be fined or owner imprisoned; or financially injured by not being able to sell these videos. Injury caused by ordinance because without ordinance they could sell any videos. Redressable because if ordinance is unconstitutional they will not have to comply and can continue business unaffected.	Yes, standing
State action	**Need state action to bring a challenge under the Constitution.** **Govt. agents performing traditionally public functions, or state is heavily entangled in activity.**	**Challenges asserted under the First Amendment so state action is necessary to assert these challenges** **Here, local state government, Columbia County, through its state County Board of Supervisors, passed the ordinance so the state is heavily entangled**	**Yes, state action**
1st Amend. free speech	Applies to states via 14th Amend. and protects an individual's right to free speech.		
Content-based speech	**Forbids communication of specific expressions.** **Subject to strict scrutiny: regulation must be necessary to a compelling govt. interest, unless less-protected speech.**	**Here, the ordinance forbids material that is sexually graphic, which is in regard to the content of the material.** **Govt. interest is to clean up the county, so arguably compelling if children are being exposed to pornographic or sexually graphic material that is not appropriate for them.** **Ordinance is not necessary to achieve this govt. interest, though, because County could prevent children from seeing this through other means such as [must give some examples]** limiting the area in which these materials can be sold so that only adults can view them, or not allowing these materials to be sold within a specific distance to parks and schools or areas that children frequent, zoning laws, age requirements, etc.	**Content-based and govt. fails strict scrutiny test, so ordinance violates 1st Amend.**

Continued >

Issue	Rule	Fact Application	Conclusion
Obscenity	**Speech is considered obscene if it describes or depicts sexual conduct that, taken as a whole, by the average person** **1. appeals to prurient interest in sex (under a community standard),** **2. is patently offensive to a community standard, and** **3. lacks serious literary, artistic, political, or scientific value (under a national reasonable person standard).**	1. **It is unclear if the sexually graphic content of the materials that V rents/sells appeals the prurient interest in sex**; arguably it might if people seek out that material for sexual purposes. However, people might buy movies that have scenes that contain sexually graphic material that don't appeal to this interest. 2. If sufficient numbers of the public are buying these types of materials, they likely aren't too offensive. Also, if it were that offensive, V likely wouldn't sell enough to cause them any injury under the ordinance. 3. **Some sexually graphic materials do have scientific value such as [give examples]** movies on anatomy or childbirth; also, some movies are artistic in nature and have sexually graphic content as part of the artistry.	Not obscene
Reasonable limitations	**Vague: unclearly defined; fails to give reasonable notice to ordinary person** **Overbroad: punishes or restricts speech protected under the 1st Amend.** Unfettered discretion: no narrow and specific standards for denying request	**Ordinance not clearly defined because there is no definition for what constitutes sexually graphic material; this could be [any examples would suffice here but you need some]** complete nudity, partial nudity, single persons, multiple persons, sexual actions beyond nudity, and so forth. **Ordinance is overbroad in that it restricts some protected speech such as some R movies**; or videos involving childbirth that people have the right to view; or science videos involving anatomy, which people have the right to view as well **[need to give some example of what is restricted that might be protected].** Unfettered discretion because there are no narrow standards for the review board to use to determine whether to allow the sale of the materials or not; rather, it is at their sole discretion.	**All reasonable limitations are violated, so 1st Amend. violated**

Continued >

Issue	Rule	Fact Application	Conclusion
Prior restraint	**Prevents speech before it occurs.** **Govt. must show that** **1. irreparable or serious harm to the public will occur** **2. narrowly drawn standards** **3. final determination of the validity**	**Here, the materials are prevented from being sold prior to being sold, so it is a prior restraint.** 1. Irreparable or serious harm could be damage to children or some other harm that the county is addressing to "clean up" the county. **2. There are no standards at all here for this ordinance to guide the review panel to allow or deny the materials.** **3. No final determination as to the validity of the ordinance has been sought or determined and challengers have no right to appeal it.**	Yes, prior restraint, so ordinance violates 1st Amend.
Collateral bar rule	If a prior restraint is issued, one cannot violate it and then defend oneself by asserting that the action is unconstitutional, even if they are correct.	Even if the ordinance is found to be unconstitutional, V must still obey it and seek recourse through the courts first.	

Constitutional Law Question 5

July 2009, Question 4

In a recent statute, Congress authorized the United States Secretary of Transportation "to do everything necessary and appropriate to ensure safe streets and highways." Subsequently, the Secretary issued the following regulations:

> Regulation A, which requires all instructors of persons seeking commercial driving licenses to be certified by federal examiners. The regulation details the criteria for certification, which require a minimum number of years of experience as a commercial driver and a minimum score on a test of basic communication skills.
>
> Regulation B, which requires that every bus in commercial service be equipped with seatbelts for every seat.
>
> Regulation C, which provides that states failing to implement adequate measures to ensure that bus seatbelts are actually used will forfeit 10 percent of previously appropriated federal funds that assist states with highway construction.

The State Driving Academy, which is a state agency that offers driving instruction to persons seeking commercial driving licenses, is considering challenging the validity of Regulation A under the United States Constitution. The Capitol City Transit Company, which is a private corporation that operates buses within the city limits of Capitol City, is considering challenging the validity of Regulation B under the United States Constitution. The State Highway Department, another state agency, is considering challenging the validity of Regulation C under the United States Constitution.

1. What constitutional challenge may the State Driving Academy bring against Regulation A, and is it likely to succeed? Discuss.
2. What constitutional challenge may the Capitol City Transport Company bring against Regulation B, and is it likely to succeed? Discuss.
3. What constitutional challenge may the State Highway Department bring against Regulation C, and is it likely to succeed? Discuss.

Constitutional Law Question 5 Assessment

July 2009, Question 4

This is one of those rare constitutional law questions that tests congressional (federal) action rather than state action. When you approach this question and begin to write out your issues checklist, there is no need to write out all of the limitations on the state because they are totally inapplicable. However, since Congress is acting, you will need to write out your own mini-issues checklist for Congress's powers. Then, you need to specifically focus on the limitations that only apply to the federal government as well as those limitations that apply to both the federal and state governments.

Without having some knowledge of Congress's enumerated powers, you would not be able to properly issue spot this question or adequately analyze the issues. The Commerce Clause issue requires a full analysis of the federal Commerce Clause and knowledge of the specific rules that apply to commercial or economic regulations, as opposed to noneconomic regulations. Further, standing needs to be addressed with each call and each party since without standing they would not be able to challenge any of the regulations.

This constitutional law question is noticeably different from the typical question that tests the constitutional law concepts through the prism of a state actor. Seeing a question like this puts you on notice of the level of detail and sheer breadth of knowledge you are required to know in order to pass the California Bar Exam. You not only need to know 17 individual subjects (if you break down each subject into its own category), but you also need to know all of the issues included in the checklists provided and in the rules outlines. Further, you need to not only understand the rules with depth, but also be able to write out each of the rules in sentence format. This is why it is so important to not only memorize the rules from the Memorization Attack Sheets, but also to truly understand their meaning and practice writing the rules out in sentence format to have handy and ready for use on the essays.

In another unusual question that was somewhat similar to this one, the state bar examiners tested the executive branch acting to impose a regulation, as opposed to a state or Congress. That question (and questions covering any other constitutional law issues not covered in these questions) can be found in the crossover questions section. To fully prepare for the bar exam, you should be writing out every one of these essays in timed sessions rather than just outlining and issue spotting them. You should also write out the practice essays in the crossover section to see how the various subjects can relate to one another and combine in a question. If timing is an issue at first, that is normal and to be expected since you often don't have all of your rules memorized and understood at the beginning of your bar studies. Focus on the writing aspect of exam taking, including spotting all of the issues, organization, and using all of the facts. Your timing will improve as you practice writing out more essays and become familiar with how each issue applies to a given set of facts.

As with the other essays, make note of the areas highlighted in **bold** on the corresponding grid. The bold areas highlight the issues, analysis, and conclusions that are likely **required** to receive a passing score on this question.

Issue	Rule	Fact Application	Conclusion
Call #1: State Driving Academy			
Standing	Injury Causation Redressability	Injured because will need to have all instructors to be certified, which will cost money and they cannot continue to use instructors that aren't certified until they become certified. Caused by Regulation A as before they didn't need to be certified. Redressable because if Regulation A was unconstitutional, they wouldn't need to have all instructors certified.	Yes, standing
Commerce Clause	Congress can regulate the (1) use of channels of interstate commerce, (2) instrumentalities of interstate commerce, and (3) persons/things in interstate commerce, and activities that substantially affect interstate commerce. For commercial or economic activity, Congress can regulate if it has a rational basis to believe the activity will have a substantial effect on interstate commerce or if there is a substantial cumulative economic effect.	Here, Congress is regulating commercial driving instruction, which involves the instrumentalities and persons in interstate commerce. It is rational to believe that if you have set criteria for licenses and certifying instructors that train commercial drivers, the certified drivers will then be more careful and drive more safely since they will have been trained by drivers with a set number of years of experience who met a minimum score and thus can effectively communicate how to drive to others they are instructing. Also, the safety of highways has a substantial effect on interstate commerce since it involves all parts of interstate commerce.	No violation of Commerce Clause

Continued >

Issue	Rule	Fact Application	Conclusion
Delegation of powers	**Congress can delegate regulatory powers to other branches if there are intelligible principles to govern.**	**Here, Congress delegated the power to ensure safe streets and highways to the U.S. Secy. of Transportation, another branch of government; although the authority seems broad, the regulation has specific standards and principles to use in governing.**	**Delegation proper**
10th Amend.	**The federal government cannot commandeer the states by imposing targeted or coercive duties on state legislators or officials, but it can impose regulatory statutes that are of general applicable law that applies to both private and state actors.**	**Here, the Regulation does impose a duty on state officials since it is a state agency that instructs the drivers, but it applies to both private and state actors and is of general applicability to all commercial drivers in training seeking a license.**	**No 10th Amend. violation**
Conclusion			**State Driving unlikely to succeed**
Call #2: Capital City Transport			
Standing	See above	Injured because Capital City Transport will need to expend money installing seat belts in all of its buses; caused by Regulation B and would not need to install them if Regulation was unconstitutional.	Yes, standing
Commerce Clause	**See above**	Since the buses are instrumentalities of interstate commerce, Congress can regulate them. **It is rational that if seat belts are installed in buses, there will be fewer injuries in accidents with buses, and thus safety on highways will be improved.** It will also substantially affect, in the aggregate, interstate commerce since buses carry thousands of people over time on the highways.	**No Commerce Clause violation**

Continued >

Issue	Rule	Fact Application	Conclusion
Delegation of powers	See above	Similar to above and likely allowed.	Delegation proper
State action	**Need to bring constitutional claim; traditional public function or heavy entanglement.**	**Here, federal regulation is involved, which was authorized by Congress, a branch of the government.**	**Yes, state action**
Equal Protection	**Prohibits the government from treating similarly situated persons differently.** **For nonsuspect classifications, the regulation must be rationally related to a legitimate govt. interest.**	**Here, the Regulation is treating commercial buses differently from noncommercial buses by only requiring seat belts in commercial buses.** **Nonsuspect class because not based on race, ethnicity, gender, or legitimacy. Ensuring safety on streets and highways is a legitimate govt. interest because it should be protecting citizens.** **It is also rationally related because by using seat belts, fewer injuries are likely to occur when accidents happen on streets and highways.**	**No Equal Protection violation**
Conclusion			**Capital City unlikely to succeed**
Call #3: State Highway Department			
Standing	See above	Injured because they have to implement measures or they lose money; caused by Regulation C and wouldn't be an issue if Regulation C was unconstitutional.	Yes, standing

Continued >

Issue	Rule	Fact Application	Conclusion
Tax and Spend Clause	**Congress can tax and spend for the general welfare of the U.S. and can allocate conditional funding** if done unambiguously and **not excessively coercive.**	**Here, Congress is conditioning funding,** but not unambiguously since the Regulations specifically detail what states must do, in that they must see that seat belts in buses are used. **Also, the condition will only take away 10% of funding, which is not excessively coercive since it is such a small amount.**	**No Tax and Spend violation by Congress**
Delegation of power	**See above**	**Same as above.**	
Conclusion			**State Hwy. Dept. unlikely to succeed**

Constitutional Law Question 6

July 2001, Question 4

To prepare herself for a spiritual calling to serve as a pastor at City's jail, Ada enrolled in a nondenominational bible school. After graduating, Ada advised the pastor of her own church that she was ready to commence a ministry and asked that her church ordain her. While sympathetic to her ambition, Ada's pastor accurately advised her that their church did not ordain women.

Ada began going to City's jail during visiting hours and developed an effective ministry with prisoners, particularly women inmates who increasingly sought her counsel. Ada noticed that ordained ministers who visited the jail received special privileges denied to her.

Dan, the jail supervisor, told Ada that ministers who were ordained and endorsed by a recognized religious group were designated "jail chaplains" and, as such, were permitted access to the jail during nonvisiting hours. He told Ada that she too could be designated a jail chaplain if she obtained a letter from a recognized religious group stating that it had ordained her as a minister and had endorsed her for such work.

Ada replied that her church was not part of any recognized religious group and would not ordain her anyway because she was a woman. She asked Dan nonetheless to designate her a jail chaplain because of the effectiveness of her work.

Dan refused to designate Ada a jail chaplain or to allow her the access enjoyed by jail chaplains. He acted pursuant to jail regulations adopted to avoid security risks and staff involvement in making determinations as to who was really a "minister."

Ada has brought suit in federal court to obtain an injunction requiring that she be designated a jail chaplain or be granted access to City's jail equivalent to those who have been designated jail chaplains. Ada's complaint is based on the grounds that the refusal to designate her a jail chaplain violates rights guaranteed to her and the prisoners by the First Amendment to the U.S. Constitution and also violates rights guaranteed to her by the equal protection clause of the Fourteenth Amendment to the U.S. Constitution.

How should Ada's suit be decided? Discuss.

Constitutional Law Question 6 Assessment

July 2001, Question 4

This constitutional law question depicts how to approach a typical First Amendment religion question. When religion is tested, you should analyze the Free Exercise Clause and the Establishment Clause, though it doesn't matter which clause you do first. Be sure to know the rules for each clause. Typically, in most Establishment Clause issues, there is no sect preference in the regulation, which then requires application of the corresponding three-part test.

Constitutional law questions are similar to torts in that they are usually full of facts to use in the analysis and have many two-sided arguments, and you often have to make logical inferences to fully analyze the government's interest when analyzing many of the tests and levels of scrutiny. In this question, the facts actually tell you one of the government interests, which include security and staffing concerns at the jail, but you should still elaborate further by making logical inferences. For example, you can explain why staffing is a "compelling" government interest by logically inferring that the staffing of prison guards is likely higher on days when the prison is open to visitors because of increased security concerns. Thus, when there is no general visitation, there are likely fewer guards, which explains the need for having fewer visitors able to access prisoners to avoid higher risks involved in potential prisoner fights and/or altercations when in transit to visitation areas. This is one example of a logical inference that strengthens your analysis and earns you maximum points.

This question also tests Equal Protection in a complex manner. Because more than one type of classification scheme is utilized, several levels of scrutiny must be analyzed. In addition, the classification schemes involved are not clear-cut and can be argued by both sides. Ada will assert she is being treated differently based on the fundamental right of her religious beliefs (which she will argue since the government always has difficulty meeting the strict scrutiny test), while the prison will argue that the different treatment is merely based on her title as an ordained or not ordained minister. In addition, Ada can argue she is being treated differently based on her gender since women are not ordained. However, City can rebut that while the jail has the regulation in place, it is Ada's church that is discriminating based on gender, not the prison. It is also worth noting that whenever you have analyzed a level of scrutiny for one issue and another issue requires the application of the same test to the same situation, you can save time by directing the grader to "see above."

Always remember to follow the call of the question specifically. This question asks how her suit should be decided and identifies that her suit is based only on First Amendment and Equal Protection grounds. Don't waste time addressing unrelated issues, such as Due Process. Also, it's important to demonstrate that you fully understand how the laws operate by first addressing the standing and state action issues, because without those two preliminary issues being satisfied, Ada can't even get to the First Amendment or Equal Protection issues.

Finally, make note of the areas highlighted in **bold** on the corresponding grid. The bold areas highlight the issues, analysis, and conclusions that are likely **required** to receive a passing score on this question.

Issue	Rule	Fact Application	Conclusion
Standing	**Individual** • **Injury** • **Causation** • **Redressability** **3rd party** • **Individual standing** • Special relationship between claimant and 3rd party *or* difficult for 3rd party to assert [Both state-released answers had slightly different rules here but both addressed the issue and analyzed their rules.]	**Individual** • **Ada suffers injury as she doesn't receive same privileges as ministers, including right to visit during non-visiting hours.** • **Inability to visit during non-visiting hours and be recognized as a minister is caused by the imposition of the adopted jail regulations.** • **If injunction granted, Ada would be permitted to visit during non-visiting hours and receive same special privileges as ministers.** 3rd Party • Individual standing established above. • **Ada has a special relationship with the prisoners as some of the female inmates increasingly seek her counsel; not difficult for inmates to assert as they can bring their own constitutional claims themselves**, but this standing test is an "or" test here so first prong met is sufficient.	**Ada has standing**
11th Amend.	Private party cannot sue state.	Here, Ada is seeking an injunction against the city jail and possibly Dan, not the state itself.	No 11th Amendment bar
State action	**Need state govt. action to bring a claim under the U.S. Constitution.**	**Here, the state's city jail has adopted jail regulations, which is a subdivision of the state, and Dan is a state government employee.**	**State action exists**
1st Amend.—religion	1st Amend. of the U.S. Constitution applicable to the states through the 14th Amend.		

Continued >

Issue	Rule	Fact Application	Conclusion
Free Exercise Clause	**Cannot punish someone on the basis of religious beliefs unless compelling govt. interest that is narrowly tailored.** **Can regulate conduct, even if it includes religious conduct, if it is a law of general application.**	**Arguably, the regulation punishes on the basis of religion as there are exceptions for some ministers and not others based on which churches ordain their ministers and which do not. Further, only ministers from "recognized" religious groups are designated as jail chaplains, indicating that some ministers are punished based on their religion.** **The govt. interest would be to maintain the safety of the prison and staff and avoid security risks** by allowing too many people to visit during non-visiting hours when it is likely that there are fewer guards/staff working. But this is likely not compelling because there is no indication that non-ordained or non-recognized ministers pose a greater threat to security than those who are ordained or recognized; although it would keep the number of visitors down, that is not the primary interest and that could be furthered by doing background checks and physical searches, so **not narrowly tailored.** **Possibly a law of general application in that it restricts visiting hours to everyone who is not a jail chaplain, but for the reasons above it really doesn't apply to all and distinguishes ordained ministers and recognized religions.**	**Regulations violate Free Exercise Clause**

Continued >

Issue	Rule	Fact Application	Conclusion
Establishment Clause	Cannot favor or burden religious groups, but incidental burden or favoritism is fine. If a law contains a sect preference, it must be narrowly tailored to promote a compelling govt. interest. **If a law contains no sect preference, it is valid if it has a secular purpose, it's primary effect neither advances nor inhibits religion, and it does not produce excessive govt. entanglement with religion.**	Here, there is no sect preference, so the three-factor *Lemon* test will need to be examined. **Secular purpose: Reduces number of visitors during non-visiting hours, which reduces security risks and staffing needs.** Primary effect: Arguably not to advance or inhibit religion as it applies to all religious visitors, but since it **distinguishes between recognized v. not recognized and ordained v. not ordained, it does inhibit and advance certain religions, depending on whether they ordain all of their ministers and whether their religion is recognized.** Govt. entanglement: **The govt.,** through the city jail supervisors, decides whether someone is a minister or not for purposes of being a jail chaplain; there is no indication as to what standards, if any, the jail uses to **determine which religious groups are recognized and which are not, indicating the jail determines this, implicating govt. entanglement**	**Regulations violate Establishment Clause**
1st Amend.—free speech	Content based v. content neutral If content neutral, look to time, place, and manner restrictions. Nonpublic forum: govt. may regulate if viewpoint neutral and reasonably related to a legitimate govt. purpose	Here, regulations are content neutral as they are not regulating what content the ministers can or cannot relay to the prisoners, but rather the time in which they can. Nonpublic since jails are typically closed to the public.	No Free Speech violation

Continued >

Issue	Rule	Fact Application	Conclusion
		Viewpoint neutral as it doesn't restrict on a particular viewpoint. Legitimate govt. interest: Security of prison, staffing concerns, safety. Reasonably related: By keeping number of non-visiting hours visitors reduced, less chance of security risks or staffing problems, and ministers can still minister through visiting hours.	No Free Speech violation
Equal Protection	Prohibits similarly situated persons from being treated differently. **Suspect class: 1st Amend. fundamental right → strict scrutiny** (necessary to achieve a compelling govt. interest and uses least restrictive means) **Quasi-suspect: gender → intermediate scrutiny (substantially related to an important govt. interest)** **Nonsuspect: all other → rational basis (rationally related to a legitimate govt. interest)** **For strict and intermediate scrutiny, need to prove intent** on part of govt. to discriminate.	Here, Ada is being treated differently than jail chaplains based on her 1st Amend. right to religion, her gender, and whether her religion is recognized and she is ordained. Suspect: Religion—see 1st Amend. religion violations above. (No compelling govt. interest and not necessary as could use other means such as background check. **See above** for further reasons.) **Intent: On its face, as it distinguishes between ordained and not ordained and recognized religions and not recognized religions.** **Quasi-suspect: Gender—some churches would not ordain women, so some women of some religions could never be jail chaplains. Govt. interest—argue both ways here; same with substantially related, but note that the prison is not the one refusing to ordain her, it is her church, but the prison does have the requirement and will not change it.**	Regulations violate Equal Protection Clause

Continued >

Issue	Rule	Fact Application	Conclusion
		Intent: Not on its face because some women can be jail chaplains if their churches will ordain them; not in its application either as some women can be jail chaplains. **Motive behind law based on staffing and security, not women v. men**, and not the jail who distinguishes between men and women but rather the churches themselves. The effect alone is insufficient. **Nonsuspect: Title (ordained v. not ordained)—govt. interest and rationally related (reasonable). See analysis above for free speech nonpublic forum.**	Regulations violate Equal Protection Clause

PART 5 CONTRACTS

CONTRACTS TABLE OF CONTENTS

CONTRACTS INTRODUCTION

There is a life cycle to any contract and events unfold chronologically in a predicable way. This makes issue spotting contracts exams easier than other subjects because certain issues will be raised at certain points in the contracting process. If you know to look for them at that point, you will not miss spotting the issues raised by an essay question. After reading a contracts essay question, it may be helpful to sketch out a brief timeline of events in chronological order with the dates of the communications and what transpired on each date to assist you in issue spotting the exam. Consider each communication or event in order since chronology of events is particularly important in analyzing contracts.

A well-organized issue-spotting checklist is an essential tool to aid in spotting all of the issues that can arise in a contracts essay question. The Contracts Issues Checklist follows the lifecycle of a contract and presents the issues in the likely logical order they would arise and be spotted on an essay question. Memorize this checklist and use it to assist you in spotting the issues.

First is the contract formation stage, and the potential issues arising consist of issues related to the applicable law governing the agreement, offer, acceptance, contract terms, adequacy of consideration, and/or promissory estoppel. Other issues that will be identifiable at the contracting stage of the essay are Statute of Frauds problems, parol evidence, misrepresentation, unconscionability, or mistake.

Typically, in a contracts fact pattern, communications or conduct will occur after the contract is entered into. Any communication that occurs after the contract is established must either pertain to a new contract, a potential modification of the contract at hand, or an issue related to breach. The issues that can be raised by these communications are the waiver of conditions, the parol evidence rule, contract modification, and any issues relating to third parties to the contract.

There are also issues that arise at the point of the breach. The materiality of the breach is often at issue and should be analyzed. Anticipatory repudiation, violation of warranty, and accord and satisfaction will also be identifiable at this point, if present at all.

Facts that raise potential defenses to a contract's enforcement can arise at any time in the contracting process, so look for them as you go through the fact pattern. Sometimes as essay question will ask you to frame your response in the context of the defenses available to one of the contracting parties, rather than in the context of affirmatively proving up the contract. Remember, any failure of the underlying contract can operate as a defense to the contract's enforcement. In addition, consider the traditional contract defenses of impossibility, impracticability, and frustration of purpose.

After the breach has been established an essay answer often requires a full discussion of remedies, including damages, and perhaps restitution and/or specific performance. Contracts questions are often crossover questions, particularly with remedies.

ISSUES CHECKLIST

APPLICABLE LAW

CONTRACT FORMATION

Offer/termination of offer
Acceptance
Contract terms
Consideration/promissory estoppel

DEFENSES TO CONTRACT FORMATION (ARISING AT TIME OF CONTRACTING)

SOF (Statute of Frauds)
Misrepresentation/fraud
Unconscionability
Mistake

CONTRACT TERMS & OTHER PERFORMANCE ISSUES

Conditions/waiver of conditions
PER (Parol Evidence Rule)
Modification
Third-party issues (TPB/assignment/delegation/novation)

BREACH

Material v. minor
Anticipatory repudiation
Warranties
Accord & satisfaction

DEFENSES TO CONTRACT ENFORCEMENT (ARISING LATER)

Any issue with contract validity
Condition precedent not met
Impossibility/impracticability/frustration of purpose

REMEDIES

Damages (foreseeable, certain, duty to mitigate)
Restitution
Specific performance

MEMORIZATION ATTACK SHEET

APPLICABLE LAW

- ♦ **UCC**
  - Goods (movable)
  - Merchant
- ♦ **Common law**
- ♦ **Predominance test**

CONTRACT FORMATION

- ♦ **Offer**
  - Intent
  - Definite terms (QTIPS)
  - Communicated to offeree
- ♦ **Irrevocable offers**
  - UCC firm offers
    - Merchants
    - Signed writing
    - 3-month max.
  - Option contract
  - Detrimental reliance
- ♦ **Acceptance**
  - Within reasonable time
  - Only in response
  - C/L mirror image rule
- ♦ **Termination of power to accept**
  - Rejection
  - Counteroffer
  - Revocation
  - Lapse of time
  - Death or incapacity
- ♦ **Mailbox rule** (dispatch)
- ♦ **Mailbox rule *exceptions*:**
  - Offer says otherwise
  - Option k: upon receipt
  - Both acceptance & rejection
    - Rejection 1st: acceptance if received 1st
    - Acceptance 1st: on dispatch
- ♦ **Acceptance varies (UCC)**
  - Added terms
    - 1 not a merchant: then proposal only
    - Both merchants: then add the term, except
      - Offer limited to its terms expressly
      - Material alteration
      - Objection within reasonable time
  - Conflicting terms
    - Knock-out rule
    - UCC gap fillers
- ♦ **Consideration**
  - Illusory promise
  - Requirements contract
  - Output contract
  - Promissory estoppel

DEFENSES TO FORMATION

- ♦ **SOF** (Mr. Dog)
  - Marriage
  - Real property
  - Debt of another
    - Except "main purpose"
  - One year
  - Goods $500 or more
- ♦ **SOF writing requirement**
  - Essential terms
  - Signed party charged
  - **Exception:** merchant's confirming memo
    - 2 merchants
    - 1 receives confirmation
    - Both are bound
    - Unless objection within 10 days
  - **Exception:** promissory estoppel
- ♦ **Misrepresentation/fraud**
- ♦ **Unconscionability**
- ♦ **Mistake**
  - Basic assumption
  - Material effect
  - Risk not imposed on party claiming

K TERMS/PERFORMANCE

- ♦ **Conditions**
  - Express: strict compliance
  - Constructive: substantial compliance

- **Waiver of conditions**
  - Keeping the benefit
  - Failure to insist on compliance
- **PER**
  - Partial integration
    - PE not to contradict
    - PE okay to supplement
  - Total Integration
    - PE not to contradict
    - PE not to supplement
- **PER exceptions** (PER does not apply)
  - Subsequent communications
  - K formation defect evidence
  - Condition precedent to k effectiveness
  - Interpret ambiguous terms
    - Course of performance
    - Course of dealing
    - Usage of trade
- **Contract modification**
  - C/L
    - Mutual assent
    - Consideration
  - UCC
    - Mutual assent
    - Good faith
    - No consideration required
- **3rd-party beneficiary**
  - Intended (can sue)
  - Incidental (can't sue)
- **Assignment:** transfers rights
  - No consideration required
  - Gratuitous assignment okay
  - Assignee stands in shoes
  - Can't if material change
- **Delegation:** transfers duties
  - Delegator remains liable
  - Can't delegate if duty of skill
- **Novation**
  - Obligee accepts new performance
  - Terminates delegator liability

BREACH

- **Material v. Minor**
  - Receive substantial benefit?
  - Extent of part performance
  - Willfulness of breach
  - Time not of essence unless contracted for
- **UCC: Perfect tender rule**
  - Reject the whole
  - Accept the whole
  - Accept a commercial unit
  - **Except:** does not apply to installment k's
- **Seller's right to cure** (UCC)
  - Notice
    - Timely new tender
- **Divisible contract**
  - Agreed equivalents
  - Operates as separate k's
- **Anticipatory repudiation**
  - Unequivocal expression
  - Won't perform
  - Before performance due
  - Nonrepudiating party can
    - Sue immediately
    - Suspend performance
    - Urge performance
  - Right to demand adequate assurances
    - Reasonable grounds for insecurity
    - In writing
    - Okay to suspend performance pending assurances
- **Warranties**
  - Express
  - Implied warranty of merchantability
  - Fitness for particular purpose
  - Implied good faith & fair dealing
- **Accord**
  - Agree to substitute performance
  - Doesn't discharge original k
- **Satisfaction**
  - Performance of the accord
  - Discharges both k's

DEFENSES

- **Contract defenses**
  - No mutual assent
  - Lack of consideration
  - No writing & writing was required
  - Misrepresentation/fraud/duress
  - Unconscionability
  - Lack of capacity
  - Illegality of contract
  - Condition precedent not met
- **Impossibility**
- **Impracticability**
- **Frustration of purpose**

REMEDIES

- **Damages limitations**
  - Foreseeability
  - Duty to mitigate
  - Certainty
- **Expectation damages**
  - As if k performed
- **Consequential damages**
  - Direct foreseeable consequences
  - Unique to plaintiff
- **Reliance damages**
  - As if k was never made
- **Liquidated damages**
  - Difficult to calculate
  - Reasonable approximation of damages
  - Only measure used if okay
- **Nominal damages**
- **No punitive damages in k**
- **Quasi-contract**
  - D derived a benefit
  - Unfair to allow D to keep
- **Replevin** (personal prop)
- **Ejectment** (real prop)
- **Reformation** (rewrites k)
- **Rescission** (undo k)
- **Specific performance**
  - Contract is valid
  - K conditions satisfied
  - Inadequate legal remedy
    - Damages too speculative
    - Insolvent D
    - Multiplicity of suits
    - Property is unique
  - Mutuality of performance
  - Feasibility of enforcement
  - No defenses
    - Laches
    - Unclean hands
    - Other k defenses

CONTRACTS RULE OUTLINE

I. **APPLICABLE LAW TO GOVERN THE CONTRACT**
   A. **Introduction to contracts**
      1. **Contract definition:** A contract is a bargained-for exchange, for which the law provides a remedy if it is breached.
      2. **Objective theory:** The objective theory of contracts provides that a party's conduct is judged by how a *reasonable person* would interpret the conduct of that party.
      3. **Applicable law:** The applicable law governing a contract depends upon the subject matter of the contract.
         a. **UCC:** The Uniform Commercial Code (UCC) governs contracts for the sale of goods.
         b. **Common law:** The common law governs all other contracts except those for the sale of goods.
   B. **Uniform Commercial Code (UCC):** Article 2 of the UCC governs contracts for the **sale of goods.** Special UCC provisions apply when one or more parties are merchants. As a general principle, the UCC interprets more liberally than common law and endeavors to find a contract exists where possible.
      1. **Goods** are defined as movable, **tangible property**.
      2. **Merchant:** A merchant is one who **deals in goods of the kind**, or one holding oneself out as having special knowledge or skills regarding the practices or goods involved in the contract. Merchant is construed broadly.
   C. **Common law** applies to all contracts that do not involve the sale of goods. Typically this involves contracts for the provision of services, or relating to real property.
   D. **Predominance test:** Where a contract includes **both goods and the provision of services,** the predominance test determines if UCC or common law governs the contract. Determine the **predominant purpose** for the contract as a whole and the law governing that area provides the applicable law for the entire contract.

> <u>Exam tip:</u> The application of the predominance test will likely have lots of factual analysis and a two-sided argument without a clear answer. If so, throughout your analysis of the rest of the issues, be sure to analyze the facts using both the UCC and the common law where the two rules differ.

II. **CONTRACT FORMATION:** A valid contract requires **mutual assent, which consists of an offer and acceptance, and consideration.** Once the offer is accepted the parties have a contract.

A. **Offer:** An offer is a **manifestation of willingness to enter into a bargain.** An offer requires a demonstration of **intent** to enter into a contract, **definite and certain terms,** and **communication to the offeree.**
   1. **Intent:** The words or conduct of the offeror (the person making the offer) must demonstrate a present intent to enter into a contract. An objective reasonable person standard is used to analyze.
      a. **Language:** The language used by the offeror can help establish the offeror's intent. While precise language, such as "I offer," clearly establishes an offer, it is not required. The **objective standard** of how a reasonable person would interpret the language is used to determine intent.
      b. **Context:** The context in which an offer is made can help establish intent.
         1. **Offers in jest:** An offer made in jest is not a valid offer.
         2. **Preliminary negotiations:** A party's language may invite preliminary negotiations but lack present willingness to contract (e.g., "I'm thinking of selling my car" or "I'd consider taking $5,000 for my car.")
            a. **Solicitation of bids** is likely preliminary negotiations.
            b. **Advertisements** are typically invitations to deal and not offers to sell.
               i. **Exception:** Ads containing **words of commitment** and where the **offeree can be identified** with specificity can be sufficiently definite to be an offer.
            c. **Catalogs** with specified goods and prices are typically an invitation to deal, not an offer.
   2. **Definite and certain terms:** The offer must contain definite and certain terms such that the **content of the bargain can be determined** and enforced. (The parties can communicate back and forth, which as a whole provides the essential terms, and the court may supply some missing terms.)
      a. **Quantity:** The quantity term must be stated or ascertainable.
      b. **Time of performance** can be a missing term supplied by the court as a "reasonable" time.
      c. **Identity of the parties:** The parties must be identified.
      d. **Price:** Price must be stated for real estate contracts. However, the UCC provides "reasonable price at the time of delivery" if missing.
      e. **Subject matter** must be identified clearly.

> <u>Memorization tip:</u> Use **QTIPS** to memorize the essential terms of a valid contract: **Q**uantity, **T**ime of performance, **I**dentity of the parties, **P**rice, and **S**ubject matter.

   3. **Communicated to the offeree:** An offer must be communicated to the offeree, such that the **offeree has knowledge** of the offer.

B. **Acceptance:** An acceptance is the **manifestation of assent to the terms of the offer.** This can be by **words** (oral or written) creating an express contract, or by **conduct** creating an implied-in-fact contract.

1. **Two methods of acceptance:** The offeror is the master of the offer and thus proscribes the method by which his offer can be accepted.
   a. **Bilateral:** A bilateral contract is where **both parties make promises** to perform.
   b. **Unilateral:** A unilateral contract exchanges the **offeror's promise** for the **offeree's actual performance** of the requested act.
2. **Power of acceptance:** The power of acceptance is subject to some limitations:
   a. **Timing:** Acceptance must be within a **"reasonable time."**
   b. **Only by offeree:** Only by a person at **whom the offer is directed** may accept.
   c. **Only in response to an offer:** The offeree must know of the offer before accepting. (E.g.: Where a reward has been offered, a person performing the requested act without knowing about the reward cannot "accept" by his performance.)
   d. **Manner of acceptance:** An offer must be accepted in the **manner required by the offer.** But, if no method is specified, acceptance can be by **any "reasonable" means.**
   e. **Objective standard:** Acceptance by performance is judged by an objective standard.
3. **Termination of the power to accept** (five ways)
   a. **Rejection:** An outright rejection of the offer by the offeree.
   b. **Counteroffer:** A counteroffer is an offer made by the offeree to the offeror regarding the same subject matter as the original offer but contains different terms. It is a **rejection** and a **new offer.**
      1. **Distinguish counteroffer from inquiry:** Inquiring about the possibility of another deal will not serve as a counteroffer and rejection. Analyze the language used (e.g., "Would you take less . . . ?" is an inquiry not a counteroffer).
   c. **Revocation:** An offeror can revoke an ordinary offer at any time before acceptance, which serves to terminate the power of acceptance. A revocation can be:
      1. **Direct or indirect.**
      2. **Unambiguous words or conduct** that is inconsistent with the intention to contract (e.g., selling the good that is the subject of the contract to another party).
      3. **Of which the offeree is aware:** The offeree need only be made aware of words or conduct of the offeror that indicates the offer was revoked.
      4. **Exception: irrevocable offers.** Some offers are irrevocable:
         a. **UCC "firm offers"** are irrevocable even without consideration. "Firm offers" require the following:
            i. **Made by a merchant** (one dealing in goods of the kind).
            ii. **Signed writing:** In writing and signed.
            iii. **Gives assurance it will be held open** for a specified time, during which it's irrevocable.
            iv. **Three-month limit on irrevocability:** No offer can be irrevocable for longer than three months without

consideration. Even if a "firm offer" states it will remain open for longer than three months, it will only be irrevocable for three months. But, the offer is *not automatically revoked after three months*. So, for the first three months the offeror cannot revoke the offer, but after three months the offeror *can* revoke his offer. If he *does not revoke* his offer *it will remain open* and can still be accepted.

b. **Option contract:** An option contract is one where the offeror grants the offeree an "option" to enter into a contract for a specified period of time and promises the offer will be held open during that time. **Consideration is required** for an option contract. The offer will be **irrevocable for the stated option period.**

c. **Detrimental reliance and partial performance:** An offer will be temporarily irrevocable if the offeree has made preparations to perform in reasonable detrimental reliance on the offer, or has performed in part.

i. **Unilateral contract:** Once performance has begun the offer is temporarily irrevocable.

ii. **Bilateral contract:** Making preparations to perform may make the offer irrevocable if justice requires (e.g., subcontractor bids).

d. **Lapse of time:** The offeror can set a **time limit** for acceptance, **or** if none is stated it remains open only for a **"reasonable" time**. Once the time has passed, the offer lapses and may not be accepted. An oral offer typically lapses at the end of the conversation.

e. **Death or incapacity of either party:** If either the offeror or offeree dies or loses the legal capacity to enter into a contract, the power to accept an outstanding offer is **terminated automatically**.

4. **When an acceptance is effective**

a. **Mailbox rule:** The mailbox rule provides an **acceptance is effective** upon **proper dispatch**.

1. **Proper dispatch** requires that the offeree no longer has control or possession of the acceptance, such as with a properly mailed letter.

b. **Mailbox rule exceptions:**

1. Where the **offer itself provides otherwise,** the terms of the offer control.

2. **Option contract is effective upon receipt.**

3. **If both an acceptance and a rejection sent,** the rule depends on which was dispatched first.

a. **Rejection dispatched first,** the acceptance will only become **effective if it is received first.**

b. **Acceptance dispatched first** is **effective on dispatch** in accordance with the normal rule.

5. **Acceptance varying from offer: The rule** depends on if common law or the UCC applies.

a. **Common law "mirror image" rule:** An acceptance must be a precise mirror image of the offer. If the response conflicts at all with the terms of the offer, or adds new terms, the purported acceptance is a **rejection and counteroffer.**
b. **UCC:** Any "expression of acceptance" or "written confirmation" will act as an **acceptance even if terms are "additional to or different from"** those contained in the offer. The outcome here depends on if the terms are additional or conflicting to those in the offer.
    1. **Additional terms in the acceptance:** The **"battle of the forms"** rule determines the outcome and depends on if one or both parties are merchants.
        a. **If one party or more is not a merchant**, any additional term is a **proposal** and will not become a part of the contract unless the other party assents.
        b. **If both parties are merchants,** the additional term **automatically becomes a part of the contract** subject to a few **exceptions** (term won't be added if):
            i. **Offer expressly limits acceptance to its terms.**
            ii. **Material alteration** with added term (e.g., warranty disclaimer).
            iii. **Objection:** If the offeror objects to the additional term within a **reasonable time.**
    2. **Conflicting terms** will cancel each other out.
        a. **Knock-out rule:** Conflicting terms cancel each other out and **neither enters the contract.** The contract then consists of the agreed-to terms, and the court will supply missing terms if needed.
        b. **UCC:** The contract then consists of the agreed-to terms and **UCC gap fillers** will supply the missing terms as follows:
            i. **Price "reasonable price** at the time of delivery."
            ii. **Place of delivery:** buyer must **pick up the goods** from the seller.
            iii. **Time for shipment** is a **"reasonable time."**
            iv. **Time for payment:** Payment is **due upon receipt** of goods. Thus, no credit is extended.
        c. **Common law:** The contract then consists of the agreed-to terms and the court may supply missing terms on a "reasonable basis" if necessary.

6. **Acceptance by shipping goods:** Unless the offer specifies otherwise, an offer to buy goods may be accepted by shipping the goods (e.g., a "purchase order" sent to the seller and the seller fills the order). The offer is accepted by promptly shipping **conforming or nonconforming** goods.
    a. **Shipping conforming goods is an acceptance.**
    b. **Shipping nonconforming goods:** The effect of shipping nonconforming goods depends upon whether the seller acknowledges the nonconformity of the shipment.

1. **Shipment without acknowledging nonconformity:** The offer has been **accepted and breached** simultaneously.
2. **Shipment with acknowledging nonconformity:** This is an "accommodation" to the buyer and **will not serve as an acceptance.** Rather, the seller is making a **counteroffer** that the buyer is then free to accept or reject.

> **Exam tip:** **Mutual assent** is frequently tested on the bar exam. Some questions will state the parties have a valid contract so mutual assent is not at issue. If so, do not waste time establishing the contract, just identify the parties and terms of the contract and move on to the issues raised in the question. Where mutual assent is an issue requiring depth of analysis, there will typically be a series of communications (oral or written) between the parties. It is helpful to sketch out a brief **timeline** in chronological order, noting the dates of each communication and what transpired on each date. Analyze each communication in order to determine if a contract has formed. First, **look for an offer**. Determine if the first communication is an offer. If it's not, consider if the next communication is an offer (because it can't be an acceptance). If the first communication is an offer, look to the next communication to determine if it's an **acceptance** or **a rejection and counteroffer**. Continue looking at each communication until you find an offer and acceptance. Any communication that occurs **after** the valid acceptance must pertain either to a new contract, a potential modification of the contract at hand, or an issue related to breach.

C. **Consideration** is a bargained-for exchange of legal detriment and can be a promise to do an act, or forbearance from doing an act one is otherwise entitled to do.
   1. **Illusory promise:** An illusory promise is one **not supported by consideration** and is thus not enforceable. The promisor appears to promise something, but in fact does not commit to do anything at all. (E.g.: A's promise to buy as many widgets as he wants is illusory because A can say he doesn't want any widgets and thus wouldn't have to perform.)
   2. **Requirements and output contracts** can appear illusory but are not because the **implied obligation of good faith** requires both parties to use their best efforts to supply the goods and promote their sale.
      a. **Requirements contracts:** In requirements contracts the parties agree the seller will be the **exclusive source of all of the buyer's requirements** for a particular item for a specified period of time.
      b. **Output contracts:** In an output contract the buyer agrees to buy **all of the seller's output** of a particular item for a specified period of time.

> <u>Exam tip:</u> Should a requirements or output contract be at issue on an essay question, analyze the facts under the rules and explain **why** the contract is not illusory.

3. **Inadequate consideration examples:** A court will not inquire into the adequacy of consideration, but some types of promises do not provide adequate consideration.
   a. **Gifts:** A promise to make a gift is unenforceable.
   b. **Sham or nominal consideration** is insufficient, but it must be very obvious since the court is reluctant to inquire into the adequacy of consideration.
   c. **Past consideration:** A promise to pay for a benefit received in the past will **not provide current consideration** on a new bargain subject to **two exceptions:**
      1. **New promise to pay a past debt** can provide valid consideration if it is made in writing or partially performed.
      2. **New promise to pay for benefits previously received** at the promisor's request or in an emergency can be binding without consideration.
   d. **Preexisting duty rule:** The preexisting duty rule provides that a promise to do something one is already legally obligated to do will **not provide consideration** for a new bargain.

D. **Promissory estoppel:** A promise that foreseeably (to the promisor) induces reliance, and is actually relied upon, may be enforceable to prevent injustice, even without consideration.
   1. **Substitute for consideration:** Promissory estoppel serves as a substitute for consideration.
   2. **Recovery limited to reliance damages**, so the plaintiff will not get the benefit of the bargain, but rather will be put in the position he would have been in if the promise was never made.

> <u>Exam tip:</u> If a contract is lacking consideration, consider if promissory estoppel could make the promise enforceable. The recovery is higher with a valid contract, but promissory estoppel is a good alternative where consideration is lacking.

III. **DEFENSES TO CONTRACT FORMATION:** These may arise at the time of contracting.
   A. The **Statute of Frauds (SOF)** provides that certain types of contracts are unenforceable unless they are in writing.
      1. **Five categories** of contracts "fall within" the SOF.
         a. **Marriage:** A contract made upon consideration of marriage, such as a promise to do or not do something if we marry.
         b. **Real property:** The sale of an interest in land (e.g., sale, mortgage, leases, or easements of at least one-year duration).
         c. Promise to pay the **debt of another** (suretyship).

d. **One year:** A contract incapable of being fully performed within one year of the making. Time starts to run at the making of the contract, not how long it takes to perform under the contract. Performance must be literally impossible (e.g., contract to perform a concert on a date over one year after the date of contracting).
e. **Sale of Goods of $500 or more.**

> <u>Memorization tip:</u> Use **Mr. Dog** to memorize the five categories of contracts to which the SOF applies: **M**arriage, **R**eal Property, **D**ebt of another, **O**ne-year, **G**oods.

2. **SOF Exceptions** apply to each of the five categories of contracts covered by the SOF and an oral contract would be enforceable if:
   a. Made **in consideration of marriage** consisting of *mutual promises to marry.*
   b. Made for an interest in **real estate** where the *conveyance* has been made, or *performed in part* will be enforceable.
   c. To pay the **debt of another** where the *"main purpose"* of the agreement is the *promisor's own economic interest.*
   d. **The contract can't be performed in one year, but full performance has occurred.** (This is true even if it takes longer than one year for the party to have tendered performance.)
   e. **Sale of goods $500 or more where:**
      1. **Specially manufactured goods** are not suitable for sale to others.
      2. **Admission** in a pleading or court testimony.
      3. **Goods are accepted or paid for.**
3. **SOF writing requirement:** There must only be one or more writings that combined include the **essential terms** of the contract (including the subject matter) and that is **signed by the party to be charged.** The writing need not be addressed to or sent to the other party. Thus, a writing can be held against one party (the party who signed it) and not the other. The writing requirement is subject to two exceptions.
   a. **Exception:** The **merchant's confirming memo** allows a writing to be enforced against both the *signer and recipient* where it is
      1. **Between two merchants.**
      2. **One party receives signed confirmation.**
      3. **Both parties will be bound.**
      4. **Except if the recipient objects within ten days of receipt.**
   b. **Exception:** A **promissory estoppel** theory where a party detrimentally relied on the agreement. (This only allows a plaintiff to recover to the extent necessary to prevent injustice.)

> **Exam tip:** The SOF operates as a defense to enforcement of an oral contract. When analyzing the SOF use the following approach: (1) Does the contract **fall within the SOF** (Mr. Dog)? (2) Do any of the Mr. Dog SOF **exceptions** apply? (3) Does the **writing satisfy the SOF?** (Consider whether the writing includes the essential terms and is signed by party to be charged or if there is a proper merchant's confirming memo.) (4) Can the doctrine of promissory estoppel be applied to enforce the oral contract?

B. A **misrepresentation** may serve as a defense where one party makes a misrepresentation prior to the other signing the contract.
   1. The **state of mind** of the party making the misrepresentation need not be intentional; it can be done negligently or even innocently.
   2. **Material fact:** It must pertain to a material fact, not an opinion.
   3. **Justifiable and actual reliance:** It must be justifiable to rely on the misrepresentation and the party must in fact rely on the misrepresentation.

C. **Unconscionability:** If the court finds a contract term so unfavorable it is unconscionable, the court may decline to enforce the contract or any unconscionable part of the contract. Unconscionability is assessed at the time of contract formation.

D. A **mistake** is a belief not in accord with the facts and can be mutual or unilateral.
   1. A **mutual mistake** is one made by both parties to the contract. A contract can be avoided for mutual mistake if:
      a. **Basic assumption:** The mistake is to a basic assumption; and
      b. **Material effect:** The mistake has a material effect on the deal; and
      c. **Risk:** The risk of mistake is not imposed on the party seeking to avoid the contract.
   2. A **unilateral mistake** is one made by only one party to the deal. The mistaken party must show the three factors for mutual mistake, and
      a. The other party **knew,** or should have known of the mistake, **or**
      b. The enforcement of the contract would be **unconscionable.**

IV. CONTRACT TERMS AND OTHER PERFORMANCE ISSUES

A. **Conditions:** A condition is an event that must occur before performance of the other party is due. If it does not occur, performance of the second party is excused. Conditions can be express or constructive.
   1. **Express:** An express condition is created by the language of the parties demonstrating the intent to have a condition (e.g., "upon condition that").
   2. **Constructive:** A constructive condition is one supplied by the court for fairness. Each parties' performance is generally a constructive condition to the subsequent performance required by the other party.

3. **Compliance with conditions**
   a. **Express conditions** require strict compliance.
   b. **Constructive conditions** only require substantial performance.
4. **Waiver of conditions:** The party the condition is intended to benefit always has the power to waive it. Waiver can occur by:
   a. **Benefit:** Receiving and keeping a benefit, **or**
   b. **Failure to insist on compliance** can operate as a waiver.
   c. A **waiver can be retracted** unless the other party detrimentally relied.

B. **Parol Evidence Rule (PER):** The PER limits the extent to which evidence of discussions or writings made **prior to, or contemporaneous with,** the signed written contract can be admitted and **considered as part of the agreement.** It depends on whether the writing is a total integration or partial integration.
1. **Partial integration** is one intended to be the **final expression** of the agreement, but ***not* intended to include all details** of the parties' agreement.
   a. **PER is *not*** allowed to **contradict** a term in the partial integration.
   b. **PER *is*** allowed to **supplement** a term in the partial integration.
2. **Total integration** is one that not only is the **final expression** of the agreement, but is also **intended to include all details** of the agreement.
   a. **PER is *not*** allowed to **contradict** a term in the total integration.
   b. **PER is *not*** allowed to **supplement** a term in the total integration.
3. **PER exceptions:** The PER will not apply to bar certain types of evidence.
   a. **Subsequent communications:** The PER does not bar evidence of subsequent communications of the parties occurring after the time of contracting.
   b. **Contract formation defects:** The PER does not bar evidence of contract formation defects (e.g., allegations of fraud, duress, mistake, lack of consideration, illegality, or anything that would make the contract void).
   c. **Conditions precedent to the contract's effectiveness:** The PER does not bar evidence of conditions precedent to contract's effectiveness. This exception applies to a situation where the parties agree that the **contract itself will not take force** until some stated condition is met. (E.g.: A contract is negotiated between A and B, but the parties orally agree the contract will not be in effect until B's board of trustees votes to approve the contract. PER will not bar the introduction of evidence regarding the condition that the board of trustees must approve the contract because that is a condition precedent to the contract's effectiveness.)
   d. **Ambiguous terms:** The PER does not bar evidence regarding the interpretation of ambiguous contract terms. The UCC provides the following rules to aid in contract interpretation:

1. **Course of performance** refers to evidence of the conduct of these parties regarding the contract at hand. (Best, if available.)
2. **Course of dealing** refers to evidence of the conduct of these parties regarding past contracts between them. (Second best.)
3. **Usage of trade** refers to evidence of the meaning others in the same industry and/or locality would attach to a term. (Least persuasive.)

> **Exam tip:** Whether an agreement is a total or partial integration can be a tricky call. Since there will rarely be a clear answer as to what the contracting parties intended, be prepared on an essay to analyze the PER both ways. Chronology is very important in contracts questions and is critical in analyzing the PER. If communication occurs **after** the writing, analyze it under PER, explain that the PER does not bar such evidence, and also consider if there is a contract modification or an anticipatory repudiation at issue under the facts since these issues may also arise.

C. **Contract modification**
   1. **Oral contract modifications:** Oral contract modifications are generally allowed.
      a. **Statute of Frauds (SOF):** With an oral contract modification, if the contract as modified falls within the **SOF**, the **modification must be in writing.** Where the modification must be in writing and isn't, the modification is unenforceable, and the original contract stands and is enforceable.
   2. **Contract modification requirements** differ depending on whether the contract is subject to the common law or the UCC.
      a. **Common law:** At common law, **mutual assent** and **consideration is required.**
      b. **UCC:** Under the UCC, **mutual assent** and **good faith** is required, but **consideration is *not* required.**

> **Issue-spotting tip:** If the modification must be in writing and isn't, the original contract stands and the modification is not enforceable. However, consider whether any facts give rise to an analysis of **detrimental reliance** (material change in position in reliance on the modification) as a way to enforce the modified contract. In addition, whenever there are communications that occur subsequent to contracting, analyze PER in addition to the potential contract modification analysis.

D. **Contracts of two or more parties**
   1. **Third-party beneficiary** is a person whom the promisor intends to benefit by the contract but who is not already a party to the contract.

a. **Intended beneficiary:** An intended beneficiary is one intended by the promisor to benefit from the contract. An intended third-party beneficiary **can sue** to enforce the contract. There are two types of intended beneficiaries.
   1. **Creditor beneficiary:** This is a third party whom the promisor intends to benefit because the promisor owes him money.
   2. **Donee beneficiary:** This is a third-party beneficiary the promisor intends to give a gift.

b. **Incidental beneficiary:** An incidental beneficiary is one who **indirectly benefits** from the contract, but that result is not the intent of the promisor. An incidental third-party beneficiary **cannot sue** to enforce a contract (e.g., an adjacent property owner to a large planned development is an incidental beneficiary).

2. **Assignment and/or delegation** concern a transfer of rights or duties owed under the contract to a third person.
   a. **Assignment:** An assignment is when a party to an existing contract **transfers her rights** under the contract to a third person. The assignor assigns to the assignee the performance due under the contract from the obligor. The general rule is that all rights are assignable.
      1. **No consideration** is required.
      2. A **gratuitous assignment** (gift) is allowed.
      3. The **assignee "stands in the shoes"** of the assignor and takes subject to all defenses, set-offs, and counterclaims the assignor has.
      4. **Exception: Can't assign if material change** in duty/risk.
   b. **Delegation** is when a party to an existing contract appoints to a third person the duties owed under the contract. The delegator appoints to the delegatee the performance due under the contract to the obligee. The general rule is that all duties can be delegated.
      1. **Delegator** (party owing performance) **remains liable.**
      2. **Exception: Can't delegate duties of skill** or judgment.
      3. **Novation:** A novation occurs when the obligee (the one receiving performance) **expressly agrees to accept** the performance of the delegatee (the new performer) instead of the delegator (the original performer). A **novation terminates the liability of the delegator.**

V. BREACH OF CONTRACT ISSUES

A. **Material breach under common law:** A contract breach is material where there was **not substantial performance** on the contract. The following are factors to consider in the analysis:
   1. Party **did not receive substantial bargain** of benefit.
   2. **Extent of any part performance.**
   3. **Willfulness of breach:** The more intentional it is, the more likely it's a material breach.
   4. **Time is not of the essence** in a contract unless specifically agreed to, and thus a delay will not amount to a material breach.

B. **Material breach under UCC:** The rules for breach are different under the UCC.
   1. **Perfect tender:** The "perfect tender" rule applies to contracts for a **single delivery** and provides that if the goods tendered **fail to conform** to the contract in any respect, the buyer has three choices:
      a. **Reject the whole** within a reasonable time; **or**
      b. **Accept the whole; or**
      c. **Accept any commercial unit and reject the rest.**
   2. **Exception—installment contracts:** The "perfect tender" rule does not apply to installment contracts where the parties have contracted for more than one delivery.

> Exam tip: One way an offer can be accepted is by the shipment of nonconforming goods. When this happens, it is both an acceptance of the offer and a simultaneous breach of the same contract because the goods tendered fail under the "perfect tender" rule, so look for these issues to go together.

   3. **Seller's right to cure:** The buyer's right to reject nonconforming goods is subject to the seller's right to cure the defect. A seller may cure the defect any time before performance is due, with the following provisions:
      a. **Notice:** The seller must give notice to the buyer; **and**
      b. **New tender:** The seller must make a new tender within the time for performance. The seller may even make a new tender after the time for performance if the seller has a reasonable belief this would be acceptable to the buyer.
   4. **Divisible contract:** A divisible contract is one where the parties have divided up their performance into **agreed equivalents**, which means that each corresponding part performance is roughly equal to the corresponding part compensation. (E.g.: A and B agree that B will paint 15 identical cars of A for $500 each.)
      a. **Breach of a divisible contract:** For purposes of breach, each agreed equivalent operates as a separate contract.

C. **Minor breach:** If a breach is not material, it is a minor breach and the nonbreaching party may recover damages but must still perform.

> Exam tip: Always analyze if a breach is material or minor. There is rarely a clear answer, so use all the facts and argue both ways where appropriate.

D. **Anticipatory repudiation:** An anticipatory repudiation is an **unequivocal** expression by a party, occurring **before the time for performance** is due, that she **will not perform** under the contract.
   1. **Nonrepudiating party response:** Once a party has anticipatorily repudiated, the nonrepudiating party can take three courses of action:

   a. **Sue immediately:** Sue immediately for breach even though the time to perform under the contract has not yet passed; **or**
   b. **Suspend performance:** Suspend performance and wait until performance is due to sue; **or**
   c. **Urge performance:** The nonrepudiating party may urge performance under the contract and sue later if their efforts are futile.
2. **Right to demand adequate assurances:** Where the conduct of a party is not unequivocal enough to rise to the level of an anticipatory repudiation, but does cause **reasonable grounds for insecurity** about their forthcoming performance, the insecure party can **demand adequate assurances** of due performance. This must be done in **writing** and he may **suspend his own performance** until receiving adequate assurances.

> **Issue-spotting tip:** Several issues tend to cluster with **anticipatory repudiation.** Look for **PER** and/or **contract modification** and/or the **right to demand adequate assurances.**

E. **Warranties:** There are several contract warranties that may be violated.
   1. **Express:** An express warranty is made explicitly.
   2. **Implied warranty of merchantability** warrants that goods will be fit for the ordinary purpose for which such goods are used.
   3. **Warranty of fitness for a particular purpose** only applies where the buyer relies on the seller's judgment to select appropriate goods for a stated purpose.
   4. **Implied covenant of good faith and fair dealing** is inherent in every contract.

F. **Accord and satisfaction**
   1. **Accord:** An accord is an agreement where one party promises to **render substitute performance** and the other promises to **accept that substitute** in discharge of the existing duty. It does not discharge the obligation under the original agreement until the substitute performance has been completed (a satisfaction).
   2. **Satisfaction:** A satisfaction is the **performance of the accord,** which then discharges both the original agreement and the accord.

VI. **DEFENSES TO ENFORCEMENT:** These can arise at any time in the contract life cycle. A defense **discharges the duty to perform** under the contract.

A. **Contract defenses:** Though not "defenses" in the traditional sense, any failure of the underlying contract can operate as a defense, such as
   1. **No mutual assent.**
   2. **Lack of consideration.**
   3. **No writing, where a writing is required by the SOF.**
   4. **Misrepresentation, fraud, or duress** at the time of contracting.
      a. **Misrepresentation/fraud** (from the Torts Outline).
      b. **Undue influence/duress:** Extreme pressure or coercion that leads to invalidation of the contract.
   5. **Unconscionability:** Unfairness at the time of contracting.

6. **Lack of capacity** to contract because of **minority** or **mental incapacity** (not being of sound mind).
7. **Illegality of contract.**
8. **Condition precedent not met:** When one party must satisfy a condition before the other party's performance is due, and the condition has not been satisfied, it serves as a defense to the nonperformance of the second party.

B. **Impossibility** occurs when a supervening, unforeseeable event makes performance **impossible** and thus discharges performance. The event must be one that **neither party assumed the risk** of, and performance must be literally impossible. Typically, this can happen three ways:
   1. **Destruction** of the contract subject matter, or the means of performance proscribed in the contract.
   2. **Death or incapacity** of a person required to perform under the contract.
   3. **Supervening illegality:** The subject of the contract was legal at the time of contracting, but now it isn't.

C. **Impracticability** occurs when the occurrence of an event the parties assumed would not occur makes performance **extremely and unreasonably difficult.** The event must concern a **basic assumption** of the contract and the parties must not have **allocated the risk** of that event to the party seeking to use this defense.

D. **Frustration of purpose** occurs when a party's purpose for entering the contract is destroyed by supervening events. Both parties **must know the purpose** of the contract; the event must **not be reasonably foreseeable**; and **frustration is total.**

> <u>Exam tip:</u> Think very broadly for defenses to a contract. All potential problems with the underlying contract can serve as a defense to the contract itself. Impossibility, impracticability, and frustration of purpose are an issues cluster. Discuss all three under the facts and demonstrate your understanding of the differences between the three doctrines.

VII. CONTRACT REMEDIES

A. **Measure of damages**
   1. **Potential damage limitation issues:** The concepts below have the potential to limit a damages award.
      a. **Foreseeability:** Damages must be foreseeable by a reasonable person at the time of contracting, or if the damages are unusual the defendant needs actual notice of their possibility.
      b. **Duty to mitigate losses:** This comes up most frequently in consequential damages for a sales contract where the buyer does not try to "cover" by obtaining goods from an alternate supplier.
      c. **Certainty:** Damages must be able to be calculated with certainty, and not too speculative (e.g., lost profits for a new business).

2. **Expectation damages** compensate a plaintiff for the **value of the benefit plaintiff expected to receive** from the contract. Expectation damages put the plaintiff in the position he would have been in if the contract was performed. (Also called *compensatory damages*.)
3. **UCC expectation damages formulas**
   a. **Buyer's UCC damages—seller has goods and seller in breach**
      1. **If the buyer covered:** Damages are the difference between the contract price and the cover price.
      2. **If the buyer did not cover:** Damages are the difference between the contract price and the market price at the time the buyer learned of the breach.
      3. **In addition,** with either method the buyer can also recover **consequential damages** and **incidental damages.**
   b. **Seller's UCC damages—seller has goods and buyer in breach**
      1. **If the seller resold the goods:** Damages are the difference between the contract price and the resale price.
      2. **If the seller did not resell the goods:** Damages are the difference between the contract price and the market price.
      3. **Seller is a "lost volume" seller:** A "lost volume" seller can recover lost profits if seller:
         a. Has a big enough **supply to make both** the contracted sale and the resale;
         b. Would have **likely made both** sales; and
         c. Would have made a **profit on both** sales.
      4. **In addition**, the seller may also recover for **incidental damages, but *not* consequential damages.**
   c. **Buyer's UCC damages—buyer has goods and seller in breach:** Typically seller has tendered defective goods and the buyer has kept them. Damages are the difference between perfect goods and the value as tendered.
   d. **Seller's UCC damages—buyer has goods and buyer in breach:** The measure of damages is the full contract price.
4. **Consequential damages** compensate for damages that are a direct and foreseeable consequence of the contract nonperformance and are unique to each plaintiff (e.g., lost profits).
5. **Reliance damages** put the plaintiff in the position he would have been in had the contract never been made. They are used primarily where there is a contract but the expectation damages are too uncertain to calculate.
6. **Liquidated damages** are damages in an amount stipulated to in the contract. They are allowable when actual damages are **difficult to calculate,** and the amount agreed to is a **reasonable approximation** of the anticipated loss from a breach. The clause can't appear punitive and, if proper, provides the **only measure of damages recoverable** for breach.
7. **Nominal damages** are awarded where the plaintiff's rights have been violated but no financial loss has been sustained.
8. **Punitive damages** are **not awarded** for a standard breach of contract.

> **Exam tip:** The most frequently tested damages are expectation, consequential, and the potential limitations on damages (foreseeability, duty to mitigate, and certainty).

B. **Legal restitutionary remedies**
   1. **Quasi-contract** is not actually a "contract" at all; rather, it is a contract implied in law to prevent injustice where there is no enforceable contract but some relief is fair because the defendant has derived a benefit and it would be unfair to allow defendant to keep that benefit without paying money to the plaintiff in restitution. Typical situations are:
      a. **No attempt to contract,** but defendant derived a benefit.
      b. **Unenforceable contract.**
      c. **Plaintiff in material breach** but defendant received a benefit.

> **Quasi-contract fact triggers:**
> - D allows construction (e.g., fence, garage) and says nothing
> - Contract fails (e.g., firm offer expires) but advertising in reliance
> - Contract fails (e.g., condition precedent not met) but partial performance (e.g., software program)
> - Contract fails (e.g., indefinite terms) but full performance

   2. **Replevin** applies when the plaintiff wants her personal property returned.
   3. **Ejectment** applies when the plaintiff wants her real property returned.

C. **Equitable restitutionary remedies**
   1. **Reformation** rewrites a contract to accurately reflect the agreement of the parties where the writing is in error, such as a scrivener's error.
   2. **Rescission** permits a party to undo a bargain.
   3. **Grounds for rescission or reformation:** Allowed where a contract has resulted from fraud, misrepresentation, duress, or mistake.

D. **Specific performance** applies where a party is ordered by the court to render the promised performance under the contract (permanent injunction in contract).
   1. **Valid contract** is required (including definite and certain terms).
   2. **Conditions** imposed on the plaintiff must be satisfied.
   3. **Inadequate legal remedy:** Money damages can be inadequate because:
      a. **Certainty:** The monetary value of the damages can't be calculated with certainty.
         1. **Too speculative** and uncertain to calculate.
         2. **Defendant insolvent** so a damages award is worthless.
         3. **Multiplicity of lawsuits:** because the breach gives rise to an ongoing problem or multiplicity of lawsuits.

   b. **Property in question is unique**
      1. **Real property:** Real property is always unique.
      2. **Special personal property:** Where the item is rare or has special personal significance, such as a family bible.
4. **Mutuality of performance:** Both parties must be eligible to have their performance under the contract ordered by the court.
5. **Feasibility of enforcement:** The order must be feasible for the court to enforce.
   a. **Jurisdiction issues:** Present a problem where the actions to be supervised are out of the court's jurisdiction and contempt power.
   b. **Court supervision issues**
      1. **Multiple series of events** poses greater potential problems.
      2. **Act requiring skill, taste, or judgment.**
      3. **Personal services** (involuntary servitude concerns).
6. **No applicable defenses**
   a. **Traditional equitable remedy defenses**
      1. **Laches** is an unreasonable delay that is prejudicial to the defendant.
      2. **Unclean hands:** The plaintiff is engaging in unfair dealing in the disputed transaction.
   b. **Other contract defenses:** Any failure of the contract operates as a defense that will prevent specific performance including mistake, misrepresentation, failed consideration, lack of capacity, SOF, and sale to a "bona fide purchaser" (one who took for value without notice of the situation that gives rise to the dispute).

> Memorization tip: Memorize the specific performance elements with the sentence "chocolate cheesecake is my favorite dessert." Each element should be established, but you should provide more expansive analysis on the elements that have more facts available to use in the analysis.

CONTRACTS ISSUES TESTED MATRIX

		Crossover	Offer	Accept	Consideration/ Prommisory Estoppel	K Terms/ PER	Conditions/ Waiver	K Modification	Anticipatory Repudiation	SOF/ Other Defenses	DisCharge/ Excuse of Perf.	Performance/ Breach or Warranty	Third-Party Issues	Dmgs./Quasi-K	Specific Perf.
July '11 Q3	Al gives Dr. Betty his office building		X	X	X					X					
February '10 Q4	Lou, partner of firm, and Chris, the paralegal	Remedies	X	X	X		X			X				X	X
February '10 Q1	Pat & Danco k for 4 computer programs				X	X	X	X	X					X	
February '09 Q5	Developer & Highlands parcel					X	X				X	X		X	
July '08 Q4	Barry & rare phaeton car	Remedies							X					X	X
July '08 Q3	Owner & Builder; redwood fence		X	X									X	X	
July '07 Q5	Paula, art acquisition & Monay painting	Remedies			X					X					X
July '06 Q3	Resi-Clean & cleaning services		X	X	X	X	X				X	X		X	
February '06 Q5	Marla, Larry & widget buyer	Prof. Resp.	X	X	X					X					
July '05 Q5	Stan & Barb contract for 100 acres	Remedies				X	X		X	X				X	X
July '05 Q2	Developer, ASI, MPI	Real Property											X		

Continued >

		Crossover	Offer	Accept	Consideration/ Prommisory Estoppel	K Terms/ PER	Conditions/ Waiver	K Modification	Anticipatory Repudiation	SOF/ Other Defenses	DisCharge/ Excuse of Perf.	Performance/ Breach or Warranty	Third-Party Issues	Dmgs./Quasi-K	Specific Perf.
February '05 Q2	PC & Mart; Model X computers		X	X	X					X		X		X	
July '02 Q4	Travelco & golf vacation to Scotland		X	X	X					X	X			X	
February '02 Q2	Berelli & special Tabor tomatoes	Remedies			X	X								X	X
February '01 Q6	Owens/Carter & new garage						X				X	X		X	
February '00 Q5	Seller & Buyer; 10,000 tires		X	X	X							X			
July '99 Q3	Susan, Felix & telephone software	Prof. Resp. Torts				X									X
February '99 Q5	News/Maker/Boss & printing presses		X	X	X				X	X	X			X	X
February '98 Q1	Maker/Carrier & transportation svc	Remedies	X	X	X	X				X		X		X	X
February '96 Q1	Ace & exterior house painting					X	X	X			X	X		X	
July '95 Q1	Lab/Disco & hazardous waste	Prof. Resp.				X	X				X	X			
February '95 Q1	Neptune/Seafood & 250 lbs. salmon								X		X			X	X
February '94 Q2	Al, PaintCo. & latex paint	Business Assoc.						X		X		X	X	X	
February '94 Q4	Fidelity & Bildco	Remedies Torts										X		X	

Continued >

		Crossover	Offer	Accept	Consideration/ Prommisory Estoppel	K Terms/ PER	Conditions/ Waiver	K Modification	Anticipatory Repudiation	SOF/ Other Defenses	DisCharge/ Excuse of Perf.	Performance/ Breach or Warranty	Third-Party Issues	Dmgs./Quasi-K	Specific Perf.
February '93 Q6	Delta/Pratt & installing 6 coolers		X	X		X					X	X		X	
February '92 Q3	Natl. Bank/Pam & wrongful discharge					X		X				X		X	X
July '91 Q5	BoxCo./MovingCo. & cardboard boxes		X	X	X	X				X		X			
February '91 Q6	Tech. Univ. & Data; air quality equip		X	X	X			X	X	X	X				X
February '90 Q6	Joe & his wealthy brother, Steve	Remedies	X	X	X					X					
February '90 Q1	Bilder & custom built houses										X	X		X	X
July '88 Q3	Owen & Cobb remodel	Remedies					X			X	X	X		X	
July '87 Q3	Sam, Whiteacre, Blackacre	Remedies								X		X	X	X	
February '87 Q6	Clark & Jones; political pens		X	X		X		X	X	X	X				
February '86 Q4	Buyer & Seller; turbine		X	X	X	X		X	X	X				X	X

CONTRACTS PRACTICE ESSAYS, ANSWER GRIDS, AND SAMPLE ANSWERS

Contracts Question 1

February 2005, Question 2

PC manufactures computers. Mart operates electronics stores.

On August 1, after some preliminary discussions, PC sent a fax on PC letterhead to Mart stating:

> We agree to fill any orders during the next six months for our Model X computer (maximum of 4,000 units) at $1,500 each.

On August 10, Mart responded with a fax stating:

> We're pleased to accept your proposal. Our stores will conduct an advertising campaign to introduce the Model X computer to our customers.

On September 10, Mart mailed an order to PC for 1,000 Model X computers. PC subsequently delivered them. Mart arranged with local newspapers for advertisements touting the Model X. The advertising was effective, and the 1,000 units were sold by the end of October.

On November 2, Mart mailed a letter to PC stating:

> Business is excellent. Pursuant to our agreement, we order 2,000 more units.

On November 3, before receiving Mart's November 2 letter, PC sent the following fax to Mart:

> We have named Wholesaler as our exclusive distributor. All orders must now be negotiated through Wholesaler.

After Mart received the fax from PC, it contacted Wholesaler to determine the status of its order. Wholesaler responded that it would supply Mart with all the Model X computers that Mart wanted, but at a price of $1,700 each.

On November 15, Mart sent a fax to PC stating:

> We insist on delivery of our November 2 order for 2,000 units of Model X at the contract price of $1,500 each. We also hereby exercise our right to purchase the remaining 1,000 units of Model X at that contract price.

PC continues to insist that all orders must be negotiated through Wholesaler, which still refuses to sell the Model X computers for less than $1,700 each.

1. If Mart buys the 2,000 Model X computers ordered on November 2 from Wholesaler for $1,700 each, can it recover the $200 per unit price differential from PC? Discuss.
2. Is Mart entitled to buy the 1,000 Model X computers ordered on November 15 for $1,500 each? Discuss.

Contracts Question 1 Assessment

February 2005, Question 2

Properly issue spotting and analyzing a contracts essay question requires keen attention to detail. It is very important to have a detailed understanding of the chronology of events that transpire in a contracts essay question. This essay question is a very good example of why it is so important to be detail oriented with the fact pattern (and also to know the contracts rules cold). During the 15 to 20 minutes allocated to organizing your essay answer it is essential to slow down and not make a mistake in your understanding of the facts, because doing so can cause you to miss spotting a key issue.

This UCC-based contracts essay question is typical in that there are a series of communications between the parties and you must analyze the legal import of each communication. It might be helpful to jot down a timeline to keep track of the dates, and what transpired on each date. It might also be helpful to jot down on the top of your scratch paper who is who (PC = manufacturer, Mart = store). It seems obvious, but during an exam, with the stress time pressure, it is easy to get confused on who the parties are, especially with a longer fact pattern like this one. Analyze each communication in order to determine if a contract has formed. First, look for an offer. Determine if the first communication is an offer. If it's not, consider whether the next communication is an offer (because it can't be an acceptance). If the first communication is an offer, look to the next communication to determine whether it's an acceptance, or a rejection and counteroffer. Continue looking at each communication until you find an offer and acceptance. This fact pattern is unusual in that the offer is a "firm offer" so the buyer can continue to accept on the offer, which is promised to remain open for six months, to a maximum order of 4,000 computers.

To properly analyze this question it was imperative to know the nuances of the "firm offer" rule. The "firm offer" rule requires that where a merchant has provided a written offer and has given assurances, the offer will be held open for a stated period, and the offer must be held open for the stated time period, but not to exceed three months. However, after three months the offer is not automatically revoked but is simply revocable. Should the offeror not revoke the offer, it will remain open and subject to acceptance. It is also necessary to understand the mailbox rule, which provides that an acceptance is effective upon proper dispatch.

Typically, any communication that occurs after a valid acceptance must pertain either to a new contract, a potential modification of the contract at hand, or an issue related to breach. Here, the subsequent communication from PC that all orders must be placed through their exclusive distributor can be analyzed as a revocation, and as an anticipatory repudiation.

Though the two calls of the question are very specific to remedies, it is clear that the entire sequence of events must be analyzed in order to properly answer the two calls. The question is actually more of a contracts question that touches on remedies than a true crossover question.

Make note of the areas highlighted in **bold** on the corresponding grid. The bold areas highlight the issues, analysis, and conclusions that are likely **required** to receive a passing score on this question. In general, the essay grids are provided to assist you in analyzing the essays, and are much more detailed than what a student should create during the exam to organize their response to a question.

Issue	Rule	Fact Application	Conclusion
Applicable law	• **UCC applies to the sale of goods (tangible moveable items).** • **Merchants: those who regularly deal in goods of the kind.** • Common law applies to all other agreements.	• **Here, k to sell/buy Model X computers, which are moveable goods.** • **Mart regularly deals in computers since it operates electronic stores; PC does as well since it manufactures computers.**	**UCC applies** Special merchant provisions also apply
Offer v. advertisement	• **Present intent to be bound** • **Certain and definite terms** • Identified offeree	• PC showed intent to be bound by faxing letter directly to Mart, agreeing to fill any orders after both parties had preliminary discussions. • **Terms: max. of 4,000 units; subject matter: Model X computers; time: during next 6 months; both parties identified (fax to Mart by PC); and price ($1,500 each)** • Identified offeree: fax directly to Mart • Not an advertisement because specific to Mart and quantity indicated.	**Yes, offer**
Firm offer	Written offer signed by a merchant giving assurances offer will be kept open—irrevocable without consideration for stated time (not to exceed 3 months).	Here, offer by PC on its letterhead, which suffices as signature under UCC, assured Mart offer to fill any orders would be open for 6 months, even though only irrevocable for 3 months (up to Nov. 1). PC could have revoked offer after the 3 months (since it stated open for 6 months) but PC didn't revoke offer after Nov. 1, so offer still open.	Yes, firm offer still open
Acceptance	Assent to terms; UCC does not require mirror image.	• Here, **Mart assenting to terms by responding with a fax on Aug. 10 that it accepts PC's proposal** and plans to advertise. • Mart further showed assent by ordering 1,000 computers on Sept. 10, and 2,000 on Nov. 2nd by means of a letter.	**Yes, acceptance**

Continued >

Issue	Rule	Fact Application	Conclusion
Mailbox rule	**Acceptance effective upon proper dispatch.**	**Here, Mart's Nov. 2nd letter to buy 2,000 more computers was sent prior to PC's notification** on Nov. 3rd that orders need go through Wholesaler. Further, means were proper because ordered by letter previously.	**Nov. 2nd acceptance valid**
Revocation	By words or conduct; **effective when received** unless firm offer or foreseeable and detrimental reliance.	• Here, **revocation on Nov. 3rd** when PC indicated Wholesaler now their exclusive distributor was not PC. • Nov. 3rd, after 3-month max. period for firm offer (started Aug. 1st) so okay to revoke, but Mart already accepted another order for 2,000 more on Nov. 2nd, so cannot revoke after accepted. • Also, Mart foreseeably and detrimentally relied by advertising in newspapers and made this clear to PC in its Aug. 10 fax.	Revocation effective Nov. 3rd but not for orders already submitted, and may have reliance for remaining orders
Consideration	**Bargained-for exchange**	**Money exchanged for computers,** but Mart not obligated to purchase any computers, so arguably no consideration until Sept. 10 when Mart actually ordered computers.	Yes, consideration
Statute of Frauds	**Contracts for sale of goods over $500 need writing signed by party to be charged.**	**PC, party to be charged, sent a fax on its letterhead, which will suffice under the UCC for a writing**, and Mart subsequently responded in writing by fax and letter.	SOF satisfied
Anticipatory repudiation	Unequivocal expression; party will not perform prior to time for performance.	Here, PC indicated on Nov. 3rd (before all performance is due) it would not perform by fulfilling up to 4,000 units as promised for next 6 months (when **6-month period not up yet**).	Yes, anticipatory repudiation

Continued >

Issue	Rule	Fact Application	Conclusion
Breach	Material: nonbreaching party does not receive substantial benefit.	Here, purpose of k was for Mart to get up to 4,000 computers at a set price; it only received 1/4 of these, so it did not substantially benefit	Yes, material breach
Call #1: **Damages/cover**	Under UCC, buyer can "cover" & purchase replacement goods, recovering difference in price when breach.	Here, Mart can order remaining 3,000 computers and **pay $1,700, rather than originally agreed $1,500 and seek the $200 difference for each of the 2,000 units it ordered on Nov. 2nd** since it already accepted prior to PC's revocation of their offer.	**Mart can cover and seek difference for Nov. 2nd order**
Call #2: Quasi-contract	**Detrimental reliance** (above) **or quasi-contract** (to avoid unjust enrichment)	Revocation effective on Nov. 3rd prior to Mart trying to accept remaining order for 1,000 more computers and after 3-month max. for firm offer, but arguably Mart foreseeably and detrimentally relied as indicated above and PC benefited by Mart's advertising and selling its computers (**needed one of these arguments**).	Mart can get last 1,000 for $1,500 (**could have gone either way**)

Contracts Question 1 Sample Answer

February 2005, Question 2

Applicable Law

The UCC applies to the sale of goods, which are tangible, movable items. The common law applies to all other agreements. The contract here is for the purchase of Model X computers, which are movable goods so the UCC applies.

There are some special provisions in the UCC that apply to merchants. Merchants are those who regularly deal in goods of the kind. Mart regularly deals in computers since it operates an electronics store, and PC does as well since it manufactures computers for sale. Both parties are merchants and the special UCC provisions for merchants will apply to the transaction.

Offer

A valid offer must include the present intent to be bound, definite and certain terms, and be communicated to an identified offeree. PC demonstrated their intent to be bound by faxing a letter directly to Mart (the identified offeree), after the parties held preliminary discussions, communicating their intent to fill any order made pursuant to the fax. The communication is an offer and not an advertisement since it is specific to Mart and the key terms are indicated. The terms of the contract are sufficiently definite and certain and include the quantity terms of up to a maximum of 4,000 units; the subject matter of the Model X computers; the time for performance is during the subsequent six months; both parties are identified since PC sent a fax to Mart; and the price term is $1,500 per computer.

Firm Offer

A firm offer is a written offer signed by a merchant, which gives assurances that the offer will remain open (and subject to acceptance) for a stated time period. Such an offer is irrevocable even in the absence of consideration for the stated time, but not to exceed three months. Here, PC has communicated on letterhead, which is sufficient to qualify as a "signed" writing under the UCC. PC assures Mart the offer will remain open for six months. According to the UCC such an offer is only irrevocable for three months, which is up to Nov. 1 here. Therefore PC could have revoked their firm offer after Nov. 1 if they chose to, even though the stated term is six months, but since PC did not revoke, the offer it remained open and subject to acceptance.

Acceptance

An acceptance is an assent to the terms of an offer. Under the UCC a mirror image acceptance is not required. Mart assented to the terms of PC's offer by responding with a fax on Aug. 10 that they were accepting PC's proposal and were planning an advertising campaign to promote the sale of the Model X computers. Mart further showed assent by ordering 1,000 computers on Sept. 10 and an additional 2,000 units on Nov. 2 by means of a letter. Mart has accepted PC's offer.

Mailbox Rule

An acceptance becomes effective upon proper dispatch. Mart sent a letter to PC on Nov. 2 agreeing to purchase 2,000 more computers pursuant to the open offer of Aug. 1. A letter is a proper method of dispatch here because no other method of acceptance was specified and Mart had successfully used this method of communication previously to accept. This letter was sent prior to Mart receiving PC's fax of Nov. 3 informing Mart that all future orders needed to be placed through Wholesaler. Therefore, the acceptance of Nov. 2 is effective.

Revocation

An offer can be revoked through words, or conduct that is inconsistent with the offer remaining open. A revocation is effective upon receipt and can be revoked at any time unless it is a firm offer or there is foreseeable detrimental reliance. Here, PC revoked the open firm offer on Nov. 3 by stating in their fax that Wholesaler was now their exclusive distributor and they would not be accepting orders directly. There was a firm offer here, but no firm offer can be revocable for a period longer than three months under the UCC. Therefore, the three-month period of irrevocability expired on Nov. 1, so PC was able to revoke their open offer and did so here by their words, informing Mart that they now had an exclusive distributor who would take all new orders, which was conduct inconsistent with the offer still remaining open for acceptance. As noted above, Mart had already effectively accepted another order for 2,000 units prior to the revocation, so that transaction will stand. Mart can also argue that they detrimentally relied on the offer remaining open and that doing so was foreseeable to PC since they were informed of Mart's advertising campaign.

Consideration

A valid contract requires a bargained-for exchange. Here, money is being exchanged for computers, so there is valid consideration. However, Mart was not obligated to buy any computers under the original deal, so consideration wasn't present until Mart placed their order.

Statute of Frauds

The Statute of Frauds requires that contracts for the sale of goods of $500 or more must be in writing and signed by the party to be charged. PC is the party to be charged here, and PC sent a fax on its letterhead, which is sufficient to satisfy the writing requirement under the UCC. Mart also responded in writing and can be charged under the contract.

Anticipatory Repudiation

An anticipatory repudiation is the unequivocal expression by one party that they will not perform under the contract, which is given prior to the time performance is due. PC indicated on Nov. 3, which is before performance was due, that they would not perform on the open offer by fulfilling the 4,000 units as promised when the six-month open offer period was not yet expired. This was the unequivocal expression by PC they were not intending to perform under the contract and is an anticipatory repudiation.

Breach

A breach is material if the nonbreaching party does not receive the substantial benefit of the bargain. The purpose of the bargain was for Mart to purchase up to 4,000 Model X computers at a set price and Mart only received 1/4 of the amount promised, so they did not substantially benefit and the breach is material.

1. Damages/Cover

Under the UCC, a buyer can "cover" and purchase replacement goods and recover the difference in price where there is a breach. Mart can order the remaining quantity under the contract of 3,000 Model X computers at $1,700, rather than the agreed-on price of $1,500 and seek the $200 difference per computer for the 2,000 computers ordered on Nov. 2, since Mart had already accepted prior to PC's revocation of their offer. Mart will receive the $200 cost difference for the Nov. 2 order of 2,000 units.

2. Quasi-contract/Detrimental Reliance

Mart may also try to recover in quasi-contract for their foreseeable detrimental reliance on PC's promise to keep the offer open for six months. The revocation was effective on Nov. 3, which is prior to Mart's attempting to accept the offer for the remaining 1,000 units remaining under the contract. Mart will assert that they detrimentally relied on the promise of an open offer by expending money on an advertising campaign and that this reliance was foreseeable to PC because PC informed them on Aug. 10 of their plan to commence with an advertising campaign to promote the Model X computer in accordance with the proposal. It is likely Mart will also be able to recover for the $200 differential for the final order of 1,000 computers based on a detrimental reliance theory.

Contracts Question 2

February 1996, Question 1

On June 1, 1994, Owner signed a contract with Ace Painting to paint the exterior of Owner's house by September 1, 1994 for a contract price of $4,700. On July 1, Owner called Ace by telephone and told Ace that it was particularly important that the house be painted by September 1 because his employer had transferred him and he was putting the house up for sale.

The weather was unusually rainy, and Ace fell behind on all of its painting jobs. Ace could have hired additional painters or subcontracted out some of its jobs to stay on schedule, but Ace would have lost money on several jobs. Ace did not finish painting Owner's house until September 20. As a consequence, Owner did not list the house for sale until September 21.

The house stood empty, and Owner made no effort to rent or otherwise make use of it, until it was finally sold in May 1995. Most realtors in the area agree, and would testify, that the "selling season" in the area runs from May 1 to October 1 and that Owner's house would have been more likely to be sold in 1994 if it had been painted and ready to show by September 1.

Owner has refused to pay Ace for the work. Ace has sued Owner for $4,700. Owner denies liability and counterclaims against Ace for $6,000, asserting that the delay in Ace's completion was the cause of his missing the "selling season." The interest payments on the mortgage on Owner's house from October 1994 to May 1995 totaled $6,000.

What claims and defenses may Owner and Ace reasonably assert against each other and what is the likelihood of success on each? Discuss.

Contracts Question 2 Assessment

February 1996, Question 1

This is a typical example of a common law-based contracts essay question. This contract is for the provision of services—painting a home—and thus the common law rules apply.

Mutual assent is frequently tested on the bar exam with a detailed fact scenario requiring analysis of multiple communications between the parties. This question is an example of an essay question where mutual assent is not at issue since the fact pattern states the parties "signed a contract." Do not waste time establishing the existence of the contract; simply identify the applicable law, parties, and contract terms and move on to the issues raised in the question.

This is another good example of a fact pattern where communication between the parties occurs after the contract is entered into. As always, chronology is very important in contracts questions. If communication occurs after the writing (here, the contract was entered into on June 1), analyze it under the Parol Evidence Rule and explain that the Parol Evidence Rule does not bar such evidence because it only bars communications prior to or contemporaneous with the writing. Also, consider whether there is a contract modification or an anticipatory repudiation at issue under the facts since these issues tend to cluster together where there is a subsequent communication. Here, the facts give rise to a contract modification analysis.

Again, it is essential that you know and understand the nuances of the contracts rules, especially any rules that are applied differently under the UCC and at common law. The common law governs this contract, and the rule at common law is that contract modifications require mutual assent and consideration. Under the UCC, contract modifications only require mutual assent and good faith, but do not require consideration. In order to receive a passing grade on this question, it is essential that this rule be applied correctly.

Another key rule of law tested under this fact pattern is the general principle that time is not of the essence in a contract unless specifically contracted for. In the original contract, the parties agreed to a completion date for the house-painting project. Simply stating a completion date in the contract is not the same thing as a contract that explicitly makes "time of the essence" as an express condition of the contract, which then requires strict compliance. Since the due date need not be strictly complied with, the effect of Ace Painting's delay in completing the project was merely a minor breach of the contract and not a material breach.

It is worth noting that the defenses of impossibility, impracticability, and frustration of purpose are all raised under this fact pattern. These defenses are usually an issue cluster, and where you spot one, typically all three should be analyzed under the facts in order to demonstrate your understanding of the differences between the three doctrines.

Make note of the areas highlighted in **bold** on the corresponding grid. The bold areas highlight the issues, analysis, and conclusions that are likely **required** to receive a passing score on this question.

Issue	Rule	Fact Application	Conclusion
Applicable law	• UCC applies to goods. • CL applies to other k's.	Here, k to paint house (provide a service) so common law governs.	Common law governs
Formation of k	Offer, acceptance, consideration	Here, O "signed a contract" with A, so all formation requirements met.	Valid k
Parol Evidence Rule (PER)	**Agreements prior to or contemporaneous with k are inadmissible to change k terms.**	**Here, O called A on July 1 (after contract date of June 1) indicating that it was particularly important for house to be painted by Sept. 1. Since after contract, PER doesn't bar and it is admissible.**	Call on July 1 admissible
Modification	**At common law, k modifications require mutual assent and consideration.**	**O tried to modify contract by making time of the essence (indicating it is a material term, which would make not finishing on time a major breach when typically finishing later is merely a minor breach); problem is no mutual assent or new consideration, so invalid.**	No modification to make time of the essence
Express condition	Event that must occur before performance of the other party is due.	Express condition for A to finish painting O's house by Sept. 1. A did not do so, and so unless condition excused/discharged, A will be in breach.	Yes, express condition
Duty to perform—**discharge by unforeseen events**	• **Impossibility—supervening, unforeseeable event (objective std.) makes performance literally impossible.** • **Impracticability**—occurrence **of an event the parties assumed would not occur makes performance extremely and unreasonably difficult.** • **Frustration of purpose—purpose for entering the contract is destroyed by supervening events.**	• **Here, the rain was not a supervening, unforeseeable event, as rain is always somewhat foreseeable given that weather can always change unexpectedly. Although it was unusually rainy, likely not completely unforeseeable; "unusually" also indicates it could sometimes rain, just not so much, and any rain would hinder painting. Also, A could have still finished by hiring additional painters or subcontracting jobs, so not objectively impossible.**	Duty to perform not discharged

Continued >

Issue	Rule	Fact Application	Conclusion
		• **Here, possibly extremely and unreasonably difficult to finish because hiring additional painters or subcontracting jobs could cost A extreme expense, but likely wouldn't take that many painters or additional help to finish earlier, as without help they were only 19 days late. Could have hired help for a few days and likely been on time without unreasonable difficulty or expense.** • **Purpose of contract not frustrated as house was still painted and O still listed house for sale.** Also, Ace did not know at time of contracting that purpose was to sell house.	Duty to perform not discharged
Breach by A	• Major: nonbreaching party does not receive substantial benefit of bargain • Minor: nonbreaching party does receive substantial benefit of bargain	Here, O did receive substantial benefit as he contracted for house to be painted (ultimate goal); A was not aware of reason to paint at time of contract, nor desire to sell, so O received what he ultimately bargained for—a painted house. Time was not of the essence, so **failure to paint on time is a minor breach as it was a reasonably minor delay (19 days).**	Minor breach by A
Compensatory **damages**	**Expectation damages (less any incidental damages)**	**Here, A expects to be paid for painting house—$4,700. A should be paid since breach was minor, less any incidental damages O can prove.**	A gets $4,700, less incidentals

Continued >

Issue	Rule	Fact Application	Conclusion
Consequential damages	**Damages that are direct and foreseeable consequence of k nonperformance and are unique to each plaintiff.** **Requires** • **Foreseeable** • **Duty to mitigate** • **Certain**	• **Damages not direct because O can't prove that house did not sell because O finished painting 19 days late (no causation).** • **Here, O's damages for $6,000 not foreseeable at time of k formation as A was not aware then that O needed to move, sell house, and list on day of completion.** • **O didn't try to mitigate by listing without painting finished or by trying to rent it during time it didn't sell.** • **Damages not certain—even if house painted on time and during selling season, no guarantee his house would have sold.**	O does not get $6,000
Quasi-contract	Award value of benefit conferred to avoid unjust enrichment.	Even if A breached, he would be entitled the value of the benefit conferred as O would be unjustly enriched if his house were painted for free.	

Contracts Question 2 Sample Answer

February 1996, Question 1

Applicable Law

The UCC applies to contracts for the sale of goods, and the common law applies to all other contracts. The contract is for house painting, which is a service; therefore, the common law governs this contract.

Contract Formation

A valid contract requires an offer, an acceptance, and consideration. Here O "signed a contract" with A, so all of the contract formation requirements are met.

Parol Evidence Rule (PER)

The PER provides that any agreements made prior to or contemporaneous with the contract are inadmissible to prove the contents of a contract. O called A on July 1, which is after the contract date of June 1, and told A that it was very important his house was painted by Sept. 1 because he was putting his house up for sale. Since this communication occurred after the contract, and not prior to or contemporaneously, the PER will not bar its introduction and it is admissible.

Modification

At common law, all contract modifications require mutual assent and consideration. O tried to modify an existing contract by making time of the essence by having a firm finish date of Sept. 1, when that term was not contained in the original contract. Time is not typically of the essence unless it is specifically contracted for, so missing a due date on a normal contract would constitute a minor contract breach; whereas, if time is of the essence, it would constitute a major breach. However, here there was no mutual assent to the added contract term regarding timeliness and there was no new consideration provided for the modification, so the attempted modification by O is invalid.

Express Condition

An express condition is an event that must occur before the performance of the other party is due. There was an express condition in the original contract that the house painting would be finished by Sept. 1. A did not comply with the condition, so unless the condition is excused or discharged A will be in breach of contract.

Impossibility

The defense of impossibility arises when supervening and unforeseeable events make performance under the contract literally impossible. While the weather was unusually rainy, it cannot be considered supervening and unforeseeable since a change in weather conditions is always foreseeable. Further, since the weather was "unusually" rainy it indicates rain is not unheard of in this locale, which may then be unforeseeable. Rather, it is just not common in the amounts seen, which is typical of unpredictable weather, and any amount of rainfall in this location would be something an outside house painter would be aware of. In addition, performance was not literally impossible because A could have hired additional painters or subcontracted the job to get the project finished on time, so performance was not impossible

Impracticability

The defense of impracticability occurs when an event occurs, the occurrence of which the parties assumed would not occur, and it makes performance extremely and unreasonably difficult. While it's possible that the unusual rain made the job extremely and unreasonably difficult to complete because hiring extra workers or subcontractors could be extremely costly, it is unlikely. It wouldn't have probably taken that many extra workers to finish the job on time since as they were they were only 19 days late in completion. Further, house painting is not such highly skilled work that it would likely be prohibitively expensive to hire extra workers for a few days, so performance was not impracticable.

Frustration of Purpose

The defense of frustration of purpose applies when the underlying purpose for contracting is destroyed by supervening events. The purpose for contracting is not frustrated here since the house was still painted and it was still listed for sale, although not as timely as O would have liked. Also, at the time of contracting, A did not know that the purpose of the house painting contract was so that O could list the house for sale, so the purpose was not frustrated and this defense will not apply.

Breach

A major breach occurs when the nonbreaching party does not receive the substantial benefit of the bargain. A minor breach occurs when the nonbreaching party does receive the substantial benefit of the bargain. O did receive the substantial benefit of the bargain because he contracted to have his house painted, which was the ultimate contract goal, and his house was painted. At the time of contracting, A was unaware of O's purpose of putting the home up for sale by a certain date. Therefore, A received what he bargained for, a painted house. Time was not specifically made of the essence in the original contract so A's failure to paint the house by the due date of Sept. 1 was a minor breach, since 19 days was not an unreasonably long delay. Therefore, A is in minor breach because O received the substantial benefit of the bargain.

Compensatory Damages

Compensatory damages compensate a party for their expectation as if the contract had been performed. A expects to be paid for painting the house at the price of $4,700, which A should be awarded since the breach is minor, less any incidental damages.

Consequential Damages

A party may also recover damages that are a direct and foreseeable consequence of the nonperformance of the contract. O will try to recover for the $6,000 loss for missing the selling season because of A's delay in completion. The damages are not directly attributed to the delay because O can't prove the cause of the house not selling until May was because the house painting was completed 19 days late. O's damages are not foreseeable to A because A was not aware at the time of contracting that O needed to move, sell the home, and planned to list it for sale on the day of completion. O didn't make any attempt to mitigate his damages by listing the home before the paint job was completed or by trying to rent the home while it was on the market for eight months. Lastly, the damages for the delay in selling the home are not certain because even if the house had been painted on time and was available during the selling season there is no guarantee the home would have sold. O will not be able to recover for the $6,000 because he is unable to prove causation, foreseeability, and certainty, and he did nothing to mitigate his losses.

Quasi-contract

An award in quasi-contract provides the value of the benefit conferred to avoid unjust enrichment. Even if A was in major breach, he would still be able to recover the benefit conferred on O because otherwise O would be unjustly enriched if his house were painted for free.

Contracts Question 3

February 2006, Question 5

Marla is a manufacturer of widgets. Larry is a lawyer who regularly represents Marla in legal matters relating to her manufacturing business. Larry is also the sole owner and operator of a business called Supply Source ("SS"), in which he acts as an independent broker of surplus goods. SS is operated independently from Larry's law practice and from a separate office.

At a time when the market for widgets was suffering from over-supply, Marla called Larry at his SS office. During their telephone conversation, Marla told Larry that, if he could find a buyer for her excess inventory of 100,000 widgets, Larry could keep anything he obtained over $1.00 per widget. Although Marla thought it unlikely that Larry would be able to sell them for more than $1.25 per widget, she said, ". . . and, if you get more than $1.25 each, we'll talk about how to split the excess." Larry replied, "Okay," and undertook to market the widgets.

During a brief period when market demand for widgets increased, Larry found a buyer, Ben. In a written agreement with Larry, Ben agreed to purchase all 100,000 widgets for $2.50 each. Ben paid Larry $250,000. Larry then sent Marla a check for $100,000 with a cover letter stating, "I have sold all of the 100,000 widgets to Ben. Here is your $100,000 as we agreed."

When Marla learned that Ben had paid $2.50 per widget, she called Larry and said, "You lied to me about what you got for the widgets. I don't think the deal we made over the telephone is enforceable. I want you to send me the other $150,000 you received from Ben, and then we'll talk about a reasonable commission for you. But right now, we don't have a deal." Larry refused to remit any part of the $150,000 to Marla.

1. To what extent, if any, is the agreement between Larry and Marla enforceable? Discuss.
2. In his conduct toward Marla, what ethical violations, if any, has Larry committed? Discuss.

Contracts Question 3 Assessment

February 2006, Question 5

Sometimes a bar exam essay question will come along that has a "deal-breaker" issue contained in it. Deal-breaker issues are usually tricky to spot and require more thought than usual. Where there is a deal-breaker issue, a panicked reading of the facts and frantic essay writing will almost certainly lead to failure.

This contracts question is a good example of a question with a tricky deal-breaker issue in it. There is no easy way to know if there is a deal-breaker issue in a question. As always, let the facts guide you. Slow down and carefully read the facts. If there is a fact that seems odd or unusual, take a moment to think it through and figure out why that fact is in the question. Essay questions are very carefully drafted. Consequently, there are usually never any "red-herring" type facts. Each fact is contained in the question for a reason, and you need to figure out what that reason is.

We always recommend that students read the question through once without making any notes to get a feel for the story. Doing so also prevents jumping to conclusions and heading down the wrong path. This question provides an excellent example of how reading too fast and jumping to conclusions can lead to a failing essay. The first sentence of the question states that Marla manufactures widgets. A student may read that sentence and jump to the conclusion that widgets are goods and, therefore, the UCC governs the contract, jotting down "UCC" in the margin or on the scratch paper and proceeding to the next sentence. But that is incorrect. Further reading of the question reveals that while Marla manufactures widgets, she is contracting with Larry to provide the broker service of finding a buyer for her surplus widgets. Thus, Larry is providing a service (finding a buyer) not purchasing widgets (goods), so the common law governs the contract. During the extreme time pressure of the exam it is easy to miss such a subtle distinction. But a reading of paragraph two should cause a student to stop and question what the contract is about because the deal outlined is unusual or atypical. Usually a contract is for one party to sell something and the other to buy it. However, this deal is more complicated than that, so it should cause you to slow down and figure out what is really going on. Don't become distracted by focusing on the details provided regarding the contract terms. Always be clear about what the basis of the bargain is and affirmatively decide which law governs the contract. Once you figure out that the common law applies, the rest of the question is pretty easy. It is worth noting that it is important to identify the Statute of Frauds as a potential issue, even though the conclusion is that it's inapplicable. Remember: Use the facts to prove, or disprove, an issue.

Though the contracts issues are much more heavily weighted, this question is actually a crossover question because one of the calls of the question pertains to professional responsibility (PR). Even if you haven't started reviewing the PR rules at this point in your studies, you should have enough knowledge of the rules to muddle through this question since the PR issues aren't particularly difficult. It is certain that PR will be tested on every California bar exam so a mini-review of PR here is helpful.

Make note of the areas highlighted in **bold** on the corresponding grid. The bold areas highlight the issues, analysis, and conclusions that are likely **required** to receive a passing score on this question.

Issue	Rule	Fact Application	Conclusion
Call #1 (enforceable agreement)			
Applicable law	• UCC applies to goods. • CL to other k's.	**Here, goods are involved because M manufactures widgets, *but* contract is for L's services as broker to perform the service of finding M a buyer for her surplus widgets. M is not selling goods to L, so CL applies.** **[Note: One state-released answer discussed this concept within a SOF discussion, but still discussed the ultimate issue that CL not UCC applies.]**	CL governs
Offer	• **Present intent to be bound** • **Definite and certain terms** • **Identified offeree**	• M showed intent to be bound by calling L at SS office. M wanted to get rid of excess widgets she could not sell herself; offers L a share of profit to find buyer. • **Definite and certain terms: quantity of 100,000 widgets, L keeps amount between $1 and $1.25 per widget; they will discuss later amounts over $1.25, if any. Possibly uncertain terms due to this later discussion, but more likely, since they agreed to later discuss, that they could later determine a fair amount to split excess of $1.25, and a court could use analogy of UCC (even though not UCC) to find a "reasonable" price here for excess in the event they could not agree.** • Identifiable offeree is L as she called him at his SS office.	Yes, offer
Acceptance	**Unilateral k requires performance to accept.**	**Here, unilateral contract because M seeking L to perform by finding her a buyer. L did perform by finding Ben to buy all widgets for $2.50 per widget.**	Yes, acceptance
Consideration	**Bargained-for exchange**	**M agreed to share part of profit on widget sale with L; L agreed to perform the service of finding a buyer for the widgets.**	Yes, consideration

Continued >

Issue	Rule	Fact Application	Conclusion
Defenses: SOF	**Sale of goods over $500 needs a writing.**	**Here, goods themselves not being sold between M and L—their contract not for sale of goods, but rather for L to find buyer for M—so contract between M and L not for sale of goods.**	SOF not applicable
Quasi-contract	Court can award value of benefit conferred to one party to avoid unjust enrichment.	Here, even if offer not valid above (due to indefinite terms) and no valid contract, court would still award L fair market value or reasonable share of profits to avoid M's unjust enrichment. Same principle applies to M for excess over $1.25 that L kept; M should get a fair share of that.	Quasi-k would apply if k not valid
Call #2 (ethical violations)			
Duty of loyalty/conflict (business transaction with client)	**L must not enter a business transaction with a client unless** • **Terms are fair and reasonable to the client** • **Terms fully disclosed in writing to client** • **Client advised in writing to seek independent counsel** • **Client gives informed consent in writing**	Here, L, a lawyer, entered agreement with a client, M, as he regularly represents her regarding her manufacturing business. • Terms were likely fair and reasonable to client as M made the terms herself. • Terms not in writing as this was an oral contract over the phone. Also, not all terms fully disclosed because of ambiguity of share if price exceeds $1.25. • **Client not advised to seek independent counsel.** • **Client didn't give informed consent in writing.**	L breached ethical duty
Duties of honesty/communication	L owes a duty to communicate with client and be honest with client and public at large.	**Here, L did not disclose excess he made over $1.25 and refused to give M any part of this when they agreed to discuss how to split the excess at a later time.**	L breached ethical duties

Contracts Question 4

July 2005, Question 5

Stan and Barb entered into a valid written contract whereby (1) Stan agreed to convey to Barb 100 acres of agricultural land and water rights in an adjacent stream, and (2) Barb agreed to pay Stan $100,000. When Stan and Barb were negotiating the deal, Stan said, "You know I want to make sure that this property will still be used for farming and not developed." Barb replied simply, "Well, I can certainly understand your feelings." In fact, Barb intended to develop the land as a resort.

The conveyance was to take place on June 1. On May 15, Stan called Barb and told her the deal was off. Stan said that a third party, Tom, had offered him $130,000 for the land. Stan also said that he had discovered that Barb intended to develop the land.

On May 16, Barb discovered that Stan has title to only 90 of the 100 acres specified, and that he does not have water rights in the adjacent stream.

Barb still wishes to purchase the property. However, it will cost her $15,000 to purchase the water rights from the true owner of those rights.

What equitable and contractual remedies, if any, may Barb seek, what defenses, if any, may Stan assert, and what is the likely outcome on each? Discuss.

Contracts Question 4 Assessment

July 2005, Question 5

This question has many facts that can be used for dual purposes and to make multiple arguments. This makes this essay a little challenging to organize because there are many issues that can be raised and some facts raise issues that don't fit neatly into predetermined legal categories. The key to succeeding on a question like this is to read the facts carefully. Assess each fact separately and consider all the potential issues it raises. Remember, a fact may have more than one use in an essay.

To further complicate the issue, the call of the question asks about 1) the remedies Barb may seek, and 2) the defenses Stan will assert. Logically, it makes more sense to handle the questions in the opposite order because of the life cycle of a contract. While it's nice to structure the answer to respond to the query as posed, don't waste time or energy worrying about how to order your response. But be certain to signpost each legal issue with an issue heading so the bar grader can find your analysis of the issue.

You will notice on this question that there are several issues that could logically be addressed at several different places. For example, the issue of price abatement (because the property was 90 acres not 100 acres) could be raised under that heading (e.g., "Abatement"), or addressed as part of the marketable title analysis (e.g., "Marketable Title"), or addressed as a subtopic in the remedies discussion (e.g., "Damages—10 Acres"). The important thing is that the factual analysis is contained in the answer and that there is a heading descriptive enough for the bar grader to find it. If you are unsure of which legal issue to use as a heading, use a factual description (e.g., "The Stream").

There are also some factual issues raised that could appropriately be analyzed under several different legal principles. For example, Barb's failure to comply with Stan's wishes regarding the future use of the property could be analyzed as a potential failure for Barb to satisfy a condition of the contract, or as a misrepresentation, or as a rescission or reformation based on the alleged misrepresentation. Essentially, the factual analysis is the same under any of the theories, and any of the legal theories are fine to utilize as a legal framework. What is most important is the corresponding factual analysis. If you aren't certain which is the best legal issue to use, just pick one, use a good heading, and do a good job with the factual analysis. To be thorough, it's also wise to briefly mention the other legal theories you've spotted, but don't waste a lot of time being duplicative in the analysis.

Make note of the areas highlighted in **bold** on the corresponding grid. The bold areas highlight the issues, analysis, and conclusions that are likely **required** to receive a passing score on this question.

Issue	Rule	Fact Application	Conclusion
Barb v. Stan			
Valid contract	Offer, acceptance, consideration	Barb and Stan entered into a "valid written contract" for 100 acres.	Valid contract
Anticipatory Repudiation	**Unequivocal expression party will not perform prior to time for performance.** Nonrepudiating party may • Treat k as repudiated and sue immediately. • Suspend performance and sue when performance is due. • Urge performance and sue if unsuccessful.	**Here, on May 15 Stan called Barb and said the deal was off—an unequivocal expression that Stan was not going to perform prior to closing date of June 1.** Barb can seek any of the three options now that Stan anticipatorily repudiated the contract. Since she still wants the land, her best choice is to treat the contract as repudisated and sue immediately.	Yes, Stan anticipatorily repudiated k
Specific performance	• **Valid k (certain terms)** • **Conditions met** • **Inadequate legal remedy** • **Mutuality** • **Feasibility** • **No defenses (laches, unclean hands)**	• **Valid written contract with certain terms: Barb pays $100k in exchange for Stan's 100 acres of land and water rights in the stream.** • **Barb has met all conditions** (but see contrary argument below). • **Land is unique so inadequate legal remedy.** • **Both can perform (B to pay and S to deliver land) so mutuality fine [only needed in some jurisdictions today].** • **Court can enforce/supervise by making Stan deliver title—property and Stan are within court's jurisdiction.** • **Defenses: laches—no unreasonable delay by Barb; unclean hands (see below in Stan's defenses; need to argue both sides).**	Court should grant specific performance

Continued >

Issue	Rule	Fact Application	Conclusion
Marketable title (**abatement** in price)	Seller needs to provide marketable title.	Here, Stan did not own 100 acres (only 90) and did not have water rights, so title not accurate and marketable. **Court could abate price for 90 acres**; since worth $100k for 100 acres, **court could give Barb 90 acres for $90k, less the $15k she needs to pay for water rights.** **[Note: Price abatement could have been discussed within another issue, such as damages, but it should have been addressed somewhere within your answer.]**	Title not marketable; abate price
Expectation damages	Put P in same position as if contract had been performed.	**Value of land puts Barb in same position, so if worth $130k (since Stan said could sell for that as is) then Barb should get the $30k difference between the market price and the contract price, plus $15k to obtain the water rights.** But, since land is unique, specific performance would be the preferred remedy over damages.	Barb could get damages
Stan's Defenses			
Unclean hands	**Unfair dealings regarding transaction being sued upon**	**Arguably, here, Barb acted unfairly since, when Stan told her he wanted the land to remain farmland, Barb told him she understood his feelings, yet she actually intended to develop the property into a resort. However, she didn't lie about her intentions nor did she promise him she would maintain it as farmland. Rather, she responded vaguely that she understood his feelings, not that she would act as he so desired. Also. the intended use of land not in contract.**	Better answer would find no unclean hands

Continued >

Issue	Rule	Fact Application	Conclusion
Condition not satisfied [could label as *rescission* or *reformation*]	All conditions must be satisfied by both sides to be valid; if not, could rescind k or need to reform k.	Here, Stan might consider the **use of the land as farmland to be a condition,** as he indicated his intention as such. However, **use of land was not part of contract so could not be express condition**, unless oral negotiation part of contract. (Need to see if comments about land use would be part of contract. [See PER below or could discuss it now.])	K valid; no condition unless PER allows in evidence
PER	Cannot introduce evidence of agreement made prior to or contemporaneous with k.	Here, **statements about land use were made when negotiating the deal—before contract—**so the statements would not come in as evidence, and so contract still valid as is without conditions as to land use. **[Note: Could have addressed PER within another issue, but needed to mention factually on the exam.]**	PER bars evidence, so k still valid—no conditions
Misrepresentation	Fraud or material misrepresentations make k void.	Here, Barb didn't inform Stan about her intentions of using land for resort, but did not lie or tell him anything about how she planned to use the land, so there was no material misrepresentation, as she was not required to tell him how she would use the land.	No misrepresentation

Contracts Question 5

February 2000, Question 5

In January, in response to an inquiry, Seller sent Buyer a letter offering to sell 10,000 tires, assorted sizes to be selected by Seller and delivered at the rate of 1,000 each month for ten months. This letter stated the price for each size and specified that payment was due on delivery of each shipment. Buyer sent a letter agreeing to purchase 10,000 tires, assortment to be specified by Buyer. Buyer's letter contained its standard provision that any disputes arising under the agreement were to be resolved by commercial arbitration. The letter also contained Buyer's specification of the size assortment for the first month's shipment of tires.

On February 1, Seller's driver arrived with the first installment, which consisted of the assortment specified in Buyer's letter. The driver left the tires without asking for payment. Four days later Buyer sent Seller a check for the first installment and a letter specifying the assortment for the second installment. On March 1, Seller's driver arrived with the second installment, again containing the assortment specified in Buyer's letter. Again the driver left the tires without getting payment.

Three days later Buyer sent a check for the second installment and specifications for the third installment. On April 1, Seller's driver arrived, but the assortment was not exactly what Buyer had specified. Buyer accepted the tires anyway and seven days later sent a check for the third installment, along with specifications for the fourth installment.

On May 1, Seller's driver arrived, again with an assortment that was not exactly what Buyer had specified. Buyer agreed to take delivery, but Seller's driver insisted on payment. When Buyer was unable to pay, Seller's driver refused to leave the tires and took them back to Seller's warehouse.

Buyer called Seller to complain about the driver's refusal to leave the tires and insisted upon immediate redelivery. Buyer said he would pay "as usual, a few days after delivery." Seller refused and told Buyer, "If you don't like it, why don't you take me to arbitration?" Buyer replied, "Look, I have no intention of arbitrating this dispute. But I'm not accepting that last shipment unless it meets my specifications precisely and unless you allow me the same leeway for payment as with past shipments."

Seller sued Buyer for breach of contract. Buyer simultaneously filed a counterclaim against Seller and moved the court for an order staying the suit and compelling arbitration. Seller opposed the motion.

1. How should the court rule on the motion for an order staying the suit and compelling arbitration? Discuss.
2. What are the rights and obligations of Seller and Buyer, and who should prevail on the merits of the litigation? Discuss.

Contracts Question 5 Assessment

February 2000, Question 5

This is a complicated UCC-based contracts question. Both calls of the question are framed somewhat atypically. In addition, this essay tests some more unusual concepts, including a sophisticated battle of the forms situation where one additional term (arbitration clause) and one conflicting term (which party selects the tire assortment) are added to the contract in the acceptance letter. There is also an express term that has not been complied with, which raises the issue of conditions and their waiver. In short, there is a lot going on in this question. Take a deep breath and carefully read the question. Sketch out a brief timeline to help keep track of the facts. Issue spot the question first. Take a moment to figure out how to best present the issues to thoroughly respond to the calls of the question before you begin writing.

The first call of the question is unusual. The question is framed as if it is asking about a procedural issue of a stay and an order to compel arbitration. However, this is just a mechanism sometimes used on essay questions as a means of asking for analysis of the underlying substantive issues. (This also occurs in civil procedure where the call of the question will ask whether the court should grant a motion for summary judgment, which is just a means of asking about the underlying substantive issues.) A careful reading of the question reveals that what is actually at issue is a more complicated formation issue centered on a battle of the forms analysis of the underlying installment contract. This is because the only way to determine if the arbitration clause is controlling is to analyze whether the arbitration clause Buyer included in their acceptance letter became a part of the contract and is thus enforceable.

The second call of the question asks about the rights and obligations of Seller and Buyer. This calls for a full discussion of the issues pertaining to 1) the time payment was due under the contract, and 2) which party was to select the tire assortment for each shipment. Buyer's noncompliance with the contract term that payment was due upon delivery led to a fairly simple analysis of contract conditions, and the waiver of conditions. The analysis related to the tire selection is a continuation of the battle of the forms analysis since Buyer's acceptance letter contained two additional and conflicting terms. The arbitration clause is an additional term to the contract (addressed in call one). The tire selection clause added in Buyer's acceptance is in direct conflict with the term in the original offer and needs to be addressed in call two. These issues could be addressed in a variety of ways: headings by performance and breach (as in the attached grid), or headings organized by each contract term (payment/tire selection), or headings organized by the underlying rules analyzed, and so forth. The key is using the available facts to analyze the issues. The conclusions could go either way on both issues, depending on the factual analysis. So long as you see both sides to the issues and your conclusions are consistent with your analysis, the conclusion isn't important.

Make note of the areas highlighted in **bold** on the corresponding grid. The bold areas highlight the issues, analysis, and conclusions that are likely **required** to receive a passing score on this question.

Issue	Rule	Fact Application	Conclusion
Call #1 (Arbitration Clause Valid?)	Need to decide if term in k valid to see if court should compel arbitration		
Applicable law	• **UCC governs goods** (CL all other ks). • Goods: moveable, tangible objects. • Merchants: those who regularly deal with goods of the kind.	**Here, tires are moveable goods, so UCC applies.** S and B appear to both regularly buy/sell tires so both are merchants.	UCC applies, as do special merchant rules
Offer	• Present intent to be bound • Definite and certain terms • Identified offeree	• Here, in Jan., S sent a letter to B "offering" to sell tires—shows S's intent to sell tires to B. • Terms: 10,000 tires per month for 10 months, prices for each size in letter, assorted sizes to be determined by S, and payment due on delivery. • Letter to B, the identifiable offeree.	Yes, offer

Acceptance	Under UCC, acceptance does not need to mirror terms of offer.
	Battle of the forms (UCC § 2-207)
	Between merchants, additional terms become part of k unless
	• **Offer limits acceptance to it terms**
	• **Material alteration**
	• **Offeror rejects new terms within reasonable time**
		• Here, B sent letter to S agreeing to purchase tires, but he added/altered a few terms of the offer.
		• Different/added terms:
		  • B stated tire assortment to be specified by B (not S as S's offer stated); changed term [discussed below because not necessary to determine if court should compel arbitration]
		  • **Disputes handled via arbitration (not in original offer)—additional term**
		• **S neither limited acceptance in the offer nor rejected either of these alterations/additions, but they may materially alter the agreement.**
		• **Arbitration clause: Since these clauses are so standard today, it may not materially affect the agreement. However, some courts find that this change does materially affect the agreement if they end in a binding decision with no right to appeal.**
			Yes, acceptance BUT new terms added
			Arbitration clause likely valid; court should stay motion and compel arbitration [can conclude either way]

Continued >

Issue	Rule	Fact Application	Conclusion
Consideration	Bargained-for exchange	S delivers tires and B pays money for tires.	Yes, consideration
Call #2 (Rights/Obligations)			
Performance (as to **payment due on delivery by B**)	Condition: event that must occur before performance of the other party is due. **Waiver of condition** • Failure to insist on compliance can operate as a waiver . • Waiver can be retracted unless detrimental reliance.	• Condition (payment due on delivery): Once S delivers tires, B has absolute duty in contract to pay at that time. • Here, S waived timely payment by **accepting late payment for Feb., Mar., and Apr. installments (1/3 of the contract, basically 3 out of 10 installments), letting B pay for each delivery 3-7 days after delivery**; but S can retract this waiver. However, arguably, B detrimentally relied on the custom of being able to pay late and didn't have money ready on May 1 without notice of retraction.	S likely waived condition for B to pay upon delivery, so S should leave tires without payment
Performance (as to tire selection term)	**Knock-out rule: conflicting terms added to the k cancel each other out** and neither enters the k; k consists of the terms on which the parties agree and UCC gap fillers [Some jurisdictions use additional term rule above.] **Waiver**—see above for conditions waived	• **Since S's offer says S controls tire selection, and B's acceptance says B controls tire selection, under knock-out rule, conflicting terms knock each other out**, and the court would use **UCC gap fillers and the conduct** of the parties. The court can look at the **course of performance** between the parties under this contract or usage of trade in the industry. First two deliveries (Feb., Mar.) complied with B's specifications. In Apr. and May, B specified the tire assortment. The 3rd shipment didn't comply exactly with B's specifications but B accepted the shipment. Likely B can continue to select. • If a court uses the rule for term additions, S didn't object, but the tire selection change might materially alter the contract since tires are the subject matter of the contract, so it is a major term.	Likely the tire selection term is knocked out by the knock-out rule; through course of performance, B can continue to select

Continued >

Issue	Rule	Fact Application	Conclusion
Breach (by S) (tire selection)	Under UCC, for installment k's, B may declare total breach only if defects in installment substantially impair the value of entire k.	• Here, **S could have waived right to choose tires by letting B choose tires** for Feb. and Mar., but then S didn't follow B's Apr. specifications and B accepted anyway; likely put B on notice of waiver retraction that B would no longer let B decide specifications. **Since changed term is likely part of the contract, S is in breach for not letting B choose tires and failing to deliver tires. S needs to deliver tires owed** and for the remaining installments on the contract.	S needs to deliver tires B selects
Breach (by B) (nonpayment)	Must comply with k terms.	**B must pay, as failure to pay substantially impairs contract; but B doesn't have to pay until 3-7 days after delivery since S waived right to immediate payment.**	B must pay 3-7 days after delivery

Contracts Question 6

July 2011, Question 3

Betty is a physician. One of her patients was an elderly man named Al. Betty treated Al for Alzheimer's disease, but since she believed he was destitute, she never charged him for her services.

One day Al said to Betty, "I want to pay you back for all you have done over the years. If you will care for me for the rest of my life, I will give you my office building. I'm frightened because I have no heirs and you are the only one who cares for me. I need to know now that I can depend on you." Betty doubted that Al owned any office building, but said nothing in response and just completed her examination of Al and gave him some medication.

Two years passed. Al's health worsened and Betty continued to treat him. Betty forgot about Al's statement regarding the office building.

One day Betty learned that Al was indeed the owner of the office building. Betty immediately wrote a note to Al stating, "I accept your offer and promise to provide you with medical services for the rest of your life." Betty signed the note, put it into a stamped envelope addressed to Al, and placed the envelope outside her front door to be picked up by her mail carrier when he arrived to deliver the next day's mail.

Al died in his sleep that night. The mail carrier picked up Betty's letter the following morning and it was delivered to Al's home a day later. The services rendered by Betty to Al over the last two years were worth several thousand dollars; the office building is worth millions of dollars.

Does Betty have an enforceable contract for the transfer of the office building? Discuss.

Contracts Question 6 Assessment

July 2011, Question 3

This contracts question focuses on basic contract formation and applicable defenses. One problem that often arises with formation questions is that students forget to bring up the applicable defenses. On this particular question, the defenses were worth 20% of the available points for this question. Thus, if you forgot to go through the applicable defenses, you would have earned a maximum of 80, assuming all other issues discussed were perfect. For this reason, it is imperative to use an issues checklist to assist you in issue spotting. In particular, when you write out your issues checklist and realize this question is about formation, you should then write out each possible defense on your checklist rather than just writing the word "defenses." This will help you to see all possible applicable defenses.

Another challenge that students face on this question is deciphering when they need to discuss both sides of an argument. For example, in the offer analysis, many students mistakenly analyze the offer while seeing only one side. They quickly find that Al had the intent to be bound and that the terms were certain and definite. However, a better answer correctly analyzes both sides of this issue by carefully reading the facts. A careful read of the facts indicates that Al wanted Betty to "care" for him for the "rest of" his life. These terms are not exactly clear because the care required for an Alzheimer's patient in the present might not involve the same type of care required ten years down the line. Likewise, if the rest of the Al's life is one year versus ten years, that makes a big difference in their contract in terms of what Al is bargaining for. Thus, in order to receive the maximum number of points for this question, a careful use of the facts should lead you to argue both sides in terms of the adequacy of the offer.

Similarly, this essay question also requires you to determine the order in which you should address the issues. Generally, formation questions are simple in that you only discuss the basic rules of offer, acceptance, and consideration. However, in this question it is unclear whether Al wanted Betty to promise to care for him—thus creating a bilateral contract—or whether he wanted her to simply perform and care for him—which would create a unilateral contract. Thus, the best way to organize the answer would be to first address the applicable law and offer, and then discuss whether the contract is unilateral or bilateral (you could argue both ways here) before proceeding to discuss acceptance by performance, acceptance under the mailbox rule, and so forth. Since your analysis under those types of acceptance would depend on the type of contract, you should first address the type of contract. If you did not discuss unilateral and bilateral contracts, then you should add those issues to your issues checklist to ensure you don't miss them on future essays.

Finally, make note of the areas highlighted in **bold** on the corresponding grid. The bold areas highlight the issues, analysis, and conclusions that were likely **required** to receive a passing score on this question.

Issues	Rules	Key Facts	Conclusion
Applicable law	**UCC for goods** **Common law for services**	**Service to care for a patient, so common law.**	**Common law applies**
Offer	**Manifestation of willingness to enter a bargain:** • **Intent to be bound** • **Certain and definite terms** • **Communicated to offeree**	**A arguably intended to be bound because he offered to give B his office building for her to care for him for the rest of his life.** However, he arguably only wanted to pay her back as he stated, which would be expressing gratitude and not an intent to offer the building to make a contract for the future. The terms "care for" and "rest of my life" are not exactly clear because the care could change over the years, and it isn't clear how long Al will live. **A communicated to B, as he told her directly.**	Likely an offer
Type of contract	**Unilateral:** offeror's promise is in exchange for the offeree's actual performance. **Bilateral:** both parties make promises to perform.	**The fact that he needed to "know now" indicates that it was most likely a promise he wanted from B, but he also specifically said he wanted her to "care for" him, indicating performance.** [Argue both ways and explain why you think one side is the better argument.]	Could conclude either way
Termination of offer	**Lapse of offer: reasonable time to respond**	**Two years, if bilateral contract, would likely be an unreasonable amount of time to respond to an offer.** But if unilateral, B had been treating him from the time of the offer; the problem is that she was already treating him before and arguably did not treat him thereafter in response to the offer, as she was already doing so anyway.	**Likely offer terminated due to lapse of time**

Continued >

Issues	Rules	Key Facts	Conclusion
Acceptance by mailbox rule	**Acceptance is effective upon proper dispatch.** Proper dispatch involves offeree no longer having control/ possession.	Although **B put a note with her signed acceptance in a stamped envelope addressed to A** outside her front door, she still had control and access to the response up until the mail carrier picked it up, as she could access the letter since it was just outside her door as opposed to at the post office or in a mailbox to which she had no access once the letter was deposited. Since **A died before the mail carrier picked up her letter,** the offer was not accepted prior to A's death, which would terminate the offer.	No acceptance by the mailbox rule
	Acceptance by performance: objective standard	Here, B was already performing prior to the offer, so it isn't clear that her continued performance was in response to the offer, especially since she didn't believe A owned the building, which would indicate she was performing to be kind and not based on the offer.	No acceptance by performance likely
Consideration	**Bargained-for exchange of legal detriment** **Past consideration: a promise to pay for a benefit received in the past is not effective** Preexisting duty: promise to do something one is already legally obligated to do will not provide consideration for a new bargain	**Exchange of an office building for medical care.** Only could work if B's argument is based on acceptance by promise because **past services and a preexisting legal obligation would prevent the care from being applicable to care already being performed and/or care in which the doctor already had a duty to perform since existing patient—especially since A stated that he wanted to pay B for the work she had done over the years and B doubted A owned the building.**	Could conclude either way depending on whether you found unilateral or bilateral contract
Promissory estoppel	Promise that foreseeably induces reliance	As stated above, B was already performing and did not even believe A owned the building, so her continued care was not in reliance of expecting the building.	No promissory estoppel

Continued >

Issues	Rules	Key Facts	Conclusion
Statute of Frauds	**Need writing for contracts involving the sale of an interest in land** **Terms in writing and signed by the party to be charged**	**Here, office building so there is an interest in land and the writing is not signed by A, the party to be charged.**	**SOF valid defense**
Capacity	Need to be of a sound mind	**A had Alzheimer's disease but clearly recalled** property and that he had no heirs.	Al had capacity
Undue influence/ duress	Extreme pressure or coercion that leads to invalidation of the contract	**A was in fear of no care if he didn't offer land, and B in position of power to give medical care, but Al came to her with this idea on his own volition.**	Likely no undue influence/duress
Unconscionability	Unfairness at time of contract	Possibly no option for A because he was elderly and needed care and had no heirs, but unlikely since B did nothing to make his offer unfair and B didn't initiate idea and her care was worth several thousand dollars.	Contract not unconscionable

PART 6 CRIMES

CRIMINAL LAW TABLE OF CONTENTS

CRIMINAL PROCEDURE TABLE OF CONTENTS

INTRODUCTION TO CRIMES

This chapter covers both criminal law and criminal procedure. Although you likely took these as two distinct courses in law school, we have combined them here because that is the way they are primarily tested on the California bar exam. Criminal procedure is frequently the subject of a crossover question and often crosses with evidence or constitutional law.

The key to both criminal law and criminal procedure is in the approach to the most heavily tested topics, which include murder and the search and seizure provisions of the Fourth Amendment. It is imperative to approach each specific issue in the appropriate order when you organize and write out your essays to ensure that you don't inadvertently omit any key elements or steps that are crucial and can affect the entire conclusion, so pay close attention to the order in which each particular element or step is addressed in the outline.

While issues checklists and fact triggers are extremely useful for many subjects, they are not as helpful for these subjects. Generally, the calls of the questions are specific and typically direct you to discuss murder and any lesser included offenses, or specifically indicate that the defendant is alleging a violation of his Fourth, Fifth, or Sixth Amendment rights. Thus, it is important to not only know the rules and their elements, but also to know specifically what rights are covered by each of the applicable amendments. For example, you must know that *Miranda* rights are invoked under the Fifth Amendment. Likewise, you must know that murder's lesser-included offenses can include offenses such as voluntary and involuntary manslaughter. While the calls tend to be comparatively more specific in crimes essay questions, you are required to know how the issues interrelate in order to properly spot all of the issues.

While fact triggers can be extremely useful for many other subjects, in criminal law it is a bit more simplified. For instance, if there is a dead person, you probably need to address murder. Issue spotting is generally straightforward on crimes essays because the facts are obvious and the calls are specific. Nonetheless, it is still a good idea to memorize the issues checklist and pay attention to the fact triggers to ensure success in the rare event that you receive an open-ended question call. We have also included specific issue-spotting checklists for certain topics.

What is critical to success on a crimes essay, in addition to knowing how to approach each specific issue, is having a full understanding of how the rules apply. This is one subject where rote memorization—without a clear understanding of how and why the rules apply, and the subtle distinctions between the rules—can lead to trouble. For example, the bar examiners can create a fact pattern that raises both conspiracy and accomplice liability as issues. However, if you don't understand the difference between the two issues, you may either inadvertently omit one issue from your response or analyze both issues in the same way, even though the rules have slightly different requirements.

ISSUES CHECKLIST

CRIMINAL LAW

- **Crimes Against the Person**
  - Assault
  - Battery
  - Mayhem
  - Kidnapping
  - Rape
  - Homicide
- **Theft Crimes**
  - Larceny
  - Embezzlement
  - False pretenses
  - Robbery
  - Extortion
  - Theft
  - Burglary
  - Receipt of stolen property
  - Arson
- **Incomplete Crimes**
  - Solicitation
  - Attempt
  - Conspiracy
  - Merger
- **Accomplice Liability**
- **Defenses**
  - Self-defense
  - Defense of others
  - Defense of property
  - Insanity
  - Intoxication
  - Necessity
  - Mistake
  - Entrapment

CRIMINAL PROCEDURE

- **Fourth Amendment**
  - Arrest
  - Routine stops
  - Search and seizure
    - Exceptions
      - SILA
      - Plain view
      - Automobile
      - Consent
      - Exigent circumstances
      - Stop and frisk
- **Fifth Amendment**
  - *Miranda* warnings
  - Right to counsel
  - Right against self-incrimination
  - Double jeopardy
  - Due process
- **Sixth Amendment**
  - Right to counsel
  - Right to confront witnesses
  - Right to jury
  - Right to speedy trial
- **Exclusionary Rule**
- **Good Faith Warrant Exception**
- **Confessions/Identification**
  - Voluntariness
  - Due process
  - Pleas
- **Eighth Amendment**
  - Bail
  - Sentencing

MEMORIZATION ATTACK SHEET

CRIMES AGAINST PERSONS

- **Assault**
  - Attempt to commit battery, or
  - Intent to place another in fear of imminent injury
- **Battery**
  - Intentional or reckless
  - Causing
  - Injury or offensive touching
- **Mayhem**
  - Permanent dismemberment of body
- **Kidnapping**
  - Unlawful confinement
  - Move or conceal in secret place
- **Rape**
  - Unlawful sexual intercourse
  - Not spouse
  - No consent
- **Murder**
  - Unlawful killing
  - With malice (4 ways)
    - Intent to kill
      - Presumed if deadly weapon
    - Intent to commit grievous bodily injury
    - Reckless indifference
    - Felony murder rule
      - Natural and probable consequence
      - During commission
      - Not liable if co-felon killed by nonfelon
  - Actual and proximate cause
  - Intent can transfer
- **Voluntary manslaughter**
  - Adequate provocation
  - D in fact provoked
  - No time to cool off, and
  - D did not cool off
  - OR imperfect self-defense
- **Involuntary manslaughter**
  - Gross negligence
  - D disregards substantial danger of serious harm/death
  - OR misdemeanor manslaughter
- **Degrees of murder**
  - **1st degree**
    - Premeditation, and
    - Deliberate
    - OR felony murder rule (FMR)—dangerous felonies
  - **2nd degree**
    - All murders that not 1st degree or manslaughter
- **Defenses**—see below

THEFT CRIMES

- **Larceny**
  - Trespassory taking and carrying away
  - Of personal property
  - Of another
  - With intent to steal
- **Embezzlement**
  - Fraudulent conversion
  - Of personal property
  - Of another
  - By one in lawful possession
- **False pretenses**
  - D knowingly makes
  - False representation
  - Past or present fact
  - Causes another to
  - Convey title
- **Robbery**
  - Larceny elements, and
  - Property taken from person or their presence
  - Through force or fear
- **Extortion**
  - Threat of future harm
  - Deprive owner of property
- **Theft**
  - Illegal taking
  - Of another's property

- **Burglary**
  - Breaking and entering
  - Of dwelling house
  - Nighttime
  - Intent to commit felony
- **Receipt of stolen property**
  - Knowingly
  - Receive, conceal, or dispose of
  - Stolen property
- **Arson**
  - Malicious burning
  - Dwelling house
  - Of another

INCOMPLETE CRIMES

- **Solicitation**
  - Request or encourage
  - Another to commit a crime
  - Intent that they do so
  - Merges into actual crime
- **Conspiracy**
  - Agreement
  - Two or more people
  - Intent to commit unlawful act
  - Majority require overt act
  - Co-conspirator liable if
    - Foreseeable
    - In furtherance of objective
  - Does not merge
- **Attempt**
  - Intent to commit crime
  - Affirmative act (beyond mere preparation)
  - Merges into actual crime

ACCOMPLICE LIABILITY

- Principal—commits crime
- Accomplice
  - Aids, abets, encourages
  - Carrying out of a crime
  - Doesn't commit actual crime
  - Liable for additional crimes of accomplices if:
    - Foreseeable
- Accessory after the fact
  - Obstruction of justice

DEFENSES

- **Self-defense**
  - Reasonable force
- **Defense of others**
  - Reasonable belief
  - Reasonable force
- **Defense of property**
  - Reasonable force
  - No deadly force
- **Insanity**
  - *M'Naghten* test
    - D has mental disease
    - D can't understand, or
    - D doesn't know wrong
  - Irresistible impulse
    - D has mental disease
    - D unable to control conduct
  - *Durham* test
    - Conduct product of mental illness
  - Model Penal Code
    - D lacks capacity
    - D cannot appreciate criminality or conform
- **Intoxication**
  - Voluntary
    - Negates specific intent
  - Involuntary
    - Possible defense to all
- **Necessity**
  - Reasonable belief
  - Necessary to avoid
  - Imminent and greater injury to society
- **Mistake**
  - Of fact
    - Negates specific intent
    - Negates general intent if mistake reasonable
  - Of law
    - No defense
- **Impossibility**
  - Factual
    - D makes mistake about an issue of fact
    - No defense

- Legal
  - D thinks act is criminal but it isn't
  - Valid defense
- **Entrapment**
  - Law enforcement
  - Induces D to commit crime
  - D wasn't predisposed to commit crime

FOURTH AMENDMENT

- **Arrest**
  - Need warrant if in home
  - Warrant based on probable cause
  - Probable cause is reasonable belief
- **Routine stops okay**
  - Automobile stop
    - Reasonable suspicion
    - Objective standard
  - Fixed checkpoints for compliance with laws
  - Stop and frisk (see below)
- **Search and seizure**
  - Govt. action required
  - Expectation of privacy
  - Warrant based on
    - Probable cause
      - Connected
      - Found in place
    - Neutral magistrate
    - Description
    - Knock and announce
  - No warrant needs exception
    - SILA
      - Lawful arrest
      - Area within access/immediate control
      - Protective sweep ok
    - Plain View
      - Legitimately on premises
    - Automobile
      - Probable cause
      - Impound
    - Consent
      - Voluntarily
      - Totality of circumstances
    - Exigent circumstances
      - Destruction of evidence likely
      - Injury to persons
      - Hot pursuit
    - Stop and Frisk
      - Reasonable suspicion
      - Articulable facts
      - Pat down for weapons okay

FIFTH AMENDMENT

- ***Miranda* warnings**
  - Right to remain silent
  - Anything he says can be used against him
  - Right to attorney
    - Custodial
    - Interrogation by police
      - Likely to elicit incriminating response
      - Suspect must know police are questioning
    - Exception: public safety
    - Cannot re-*Mirandize* until 14 days later
- **Waiver of *Miranda***
  - Voluntarily
  - Knowingly, intelligently
- **Right to Counsel (*Miranda*)**
  - Unambiguous request by accused to invoke
  - Police must cease all questioning
- **Right against self-incrimination**
  - Only to testimony, or
  - Communicative evidence
  - Could expose him to criminal liability
- **Double jeopardy**
  - Cannot be tried for same offense twice
  - Applicable if jury or 1st witness sworn in
- **Due process**
  - Voluntary confessions
  - No unnecessarily suggestive ID

SIXTH AMENDMENT

- **Right to counsel**
  - Post-charge
  - Line-up, show-up, or sentencing
  - Not for photo id, handwriting, fingerprints, physical evidence
  - Ineffective assistance
    - Counsel performance deficient
    - Based on reasonably competent attorney
    - Different result if not deficient
  - D can waive right
- **Right to confront witnesses**
  - Adverse/hostile witness
  - Compel testimony or cross-examine
  - Only for testimonial statements
    - Nontestimonial if ongoing emergency
  - Co-defendants
    - Redact statement, or
    - Other D takes stand
- **Right to jury trial**
  - For serious offenses
  - With potential for > 6 months in jail
  - D can waive right
  - At least 6 jurors
  - 6 jurors: unanimous
  - Federal crime: unanimous
  - 12 jurors: majority
  - Need impartial jury
  - Jury not fair cross-section if D can prove
    - Group excluded is distinctive
    - # in representitive group not reasonable compared to # in community
    - Systematic exclusion
- **Right to speedy trial**
  - Case-by-case decision
  - Court balances:
    - Length of delay
    - Reason for delay
    - Prejudice to D
    - Time and manner in which D asserted right
- **Right to preliminary hearing**
  - Need probable cause if not established
  - Within 30 days of arrest
  - D can waive right

EXCLUSIONARY RULE

- **Judge-made doctrine**
  - Can't use evidence if found in violation D's 4th, 5th, or 6th Amend. rights
  - D needs standing—his own rights violated only
- **Fruit of the poisonous tree**
  - Other evidence stemming from violation inadmissible too
  - Exceptions
    - Independent source
    - Inevitable discovery
    - Purged taint
- **Can still use evidence**
  - To impeach
  - In civil or parole hearings
- **Good faith warrant exception**
  - Improper warrant results in 4th Amend. violation
    - Evidence not barred if officers act in good faith
    - Except lie/no probable cause

CONFESSION/ID/MISC.

- **Voluntary confessions**
  - No police coercion
  - Totality of circumstances
  - Mental illness irrelevant
- **Due process: identification**
  - No unnecessarily suggestive ID of the defendant
  - Totality of circumstances
  - ID unfair to D
- **Plea bargain**
  - Voluntary, intelligent
  - No obligation to plea
  - Judge doesn't have to accept

EIGHTH AMENDMENT

- **Bail**
  - Not excessive/unduly high
  - Court considers:
    - Seriousness of offense
    - Weight of evidence against D
    - D's financial obligations
    - D's character
- **Cruel/unusual punishment**
  - Penalty cannot be grossly disproportionate to crime
  - No death if mentally retarded or minor
  - Victim statements allowed during penalty phase
  - Jury considers mitigating circumstances against death

CRIMINAL LAW RULE OUTLINE

I. **CRIMES AGAINST THE PERSON**
   A. **Assault** is either an attempt to commit a battery or the intent to place another in fear of imminent injury.
   B. **Battery** is the intentional or reckless causing of a bodily injury or an offensive touching to another.
   C. **Mayhem** is the permanent dismemberment or disablement of a bodily part.
   D. **Kidnapping** is the unlawful confinement of another, involving movement or concealment in a secret place.
   E. **Rape** is the unlawful sexual intercourse of a female, not one's wife, without her consent.
   F. **Homicide** is the unlawful taking of the life of another. The two types of homicide are murder and manslaughter.
      1. **Murder** is the unlawful killing of another person with malice aforethought.
         a. **Malice** is the requisite mental state for murder and can be established by:
            1. An **intent to kill** (desire to kill or knowledge to a substantial certainty death will occur);
               a. Use of a **deadly weapon** or instrument creates the inference of an intent to kill.
            2. An **intent to commit grievous bodily injury;**
            3. A **reckless indifference** to the value of human life (also known as "depraved heart" murder); or
            4. An **intent to commit a dangerous felony,** known as the **felony murder rule.**
               a. The intent to commit certain dangerous felonies supplies the malice requirement for murder where death is a **natural and probable consequence** of defendant's conduct and occurs **during the commission** of the felony, even if the death is accidental.
                  i. **Death of co-felon:** The majority of courts hold that a defendant is not liable for the death of a co-felon when a **nonfelon kills** the co-felon during commission of the felony (e.g., a co-felon is killed by a police officer).
                  ii. **Death of bystander:** Courts are split as to whether a defendant is liable for murder when the victim, or a police officer, kills a bystander during the commission of the felony.
               b. **Inherently dangerous felonies:** The felony murder rule typically applies to the following inherently dangerous felonies:
                  i. Burglary
                  ii. Arson

    iii. Rape
    iv. Robbery
    v. Kidnapping

b. **Causation:** The defendant's conduct must also be the **cause in fact** and the **proximate cause** of the death.

> Exam tip: Generally, causation is a minor issue that can be addressed in one or two sentences. However, when the defendant did not do the actual killing, always argue both sides of the causation issue. For example, where the victim kills herself, a third-party kills the victim, or the killing was not contemplated or was far removed from events.

c. **Intent can transfer** for murder (just like in torts).

d. **"Fleeing felon":** Under the "fleeing felon standard," a law enforcement officer can use deadly force against a fleeing felon if:
   1. The use of deadly force is **necessary to prevent the felon's escape;**
   2. The fleeing felon has **threatened the officer with a weapon** or the officer has probable cause to believe that the felon has **committed a crime** involving the infliction or threatened infliction of serious physical harm; and
   3. The officer gives the felon some **warning** of the imminent use of deadly force, if feasible.

2. **Manslaughter:** In most states there are two types of manslaughter, voluntary and involuntary.
   a. **Voluntary manslaughter:** There are two types of voluntary manslaughter—heat of passion and imperfect self-defense.
      1. **Heat of passion:** Murder can be reduced to **voluntary manslaughter** if the defendant killed in the heat of passion and the following requirements are met:
         a. **Reasonable provocation:** He acted in response to a provocation that would cause a reasonable person to lose self-control,
         b. **Acted in heat of passion:** Defendant was in fact provoked at the time he acted,
         c. **No cooling off time:** There was insufficient time for a reasonable person to cool off between the provocation and the killing, and
         d. **Defendant did not cool off:** The defendant did not in fact cool off by the time he killed.
      2. **Imperfect self-defense:** Murder may also be reduced to **voluntary manslaughter** if the defendant kills under an unreasonable mistake about the need for self-defense.
   b. **Involuntary manslaughter** can arise two ways.
      1. **Gross negligence:** Involuntary manslaughter arises when a person's behavior is grossly negligent and the conduct results in the death of another. Gross negligence is the disregard of a very substantial danger of serious bodily harm or death.

2. **Misdemeanor-manslaughter:** Involuntary manslaughter also arises when the defendant commits a **misdemeanor** and a death occurs accidentally during its commission.

3. **First-degree murder** can arise two ways.
   a. **Premeditation and deliberation:** First-degree murder applies when the killing was the result of premeditation and deliberation—in other words, where the defendant acted in a cool and dispassionate manner and had time to reflect upon the idea of killing, even if only for a moment.
   b. **Enumerated inherently dangerous felony** under an application of the felony murder rule, such as the felonies of arson, robbery, burglary, rape, mayhem, or kidnapping.
4. **Second-degree murder:** If the murder does not rise to the level of first-degree murder and is not reduced to manslaughter, the defendant will be guilty of second-degree murder.

> **Issue-spotting tip:** If the defendant did not actually kill the victim himself, always consider his possible liability for murder as an accomplice, as a co-conspirator, or through application of the felony murder rule.

5. **Defenses** may apply to murder (see section V below for defenses).

> **Exam tip:** To analyze a fact pattern with a killing start by defining murder. Next, list all four types of malice and analyze those that are applicable to the facts. Next consider whether manslaughter or criminal negligence apply, which will reduce the murder charge. If manslaughter does not apply, then analyze whether the murder will be first or second degree. Lastly, consider any applicable defenses.

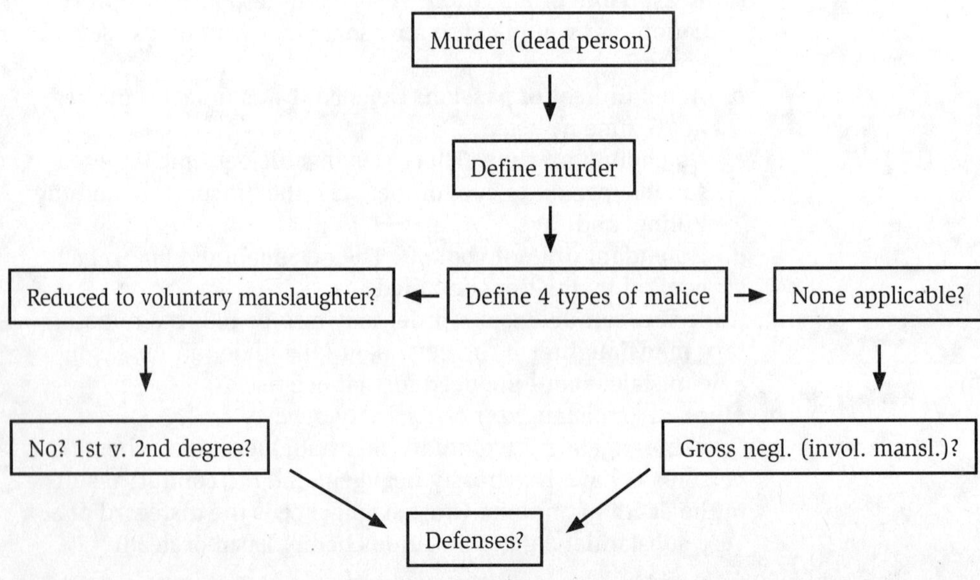

II. THEFT CRIMES

A. **Larceny** is the trespassory taking and carrying away of personal property of another with the intent to steal.

B. **Embezzlement** is the fraudulent conversion of personal property of another by one who is already in lawful possession of that property.

> Exam tip: For embezzlement, the embezzler always has lawful possession; whereas for larceny, the person taking the property does not have lawful possession.

C. **False pretenses** occurs when the defendant knowingly makes a false representation of a past or present material fact, which causes the person to whom it was made to convey title to the misrepresenter who intends to defraud.

> Exam tip: If the defendant is tricked into giving up possession, it could be larceny (by trick) as opposed to false pretenses because no title has passed.

D. **Robbery** is a larceny (see section II.A above) and in addition the property has been taken from the person or presence of the owner through force, or by placing the owner in fear.

E. **Extortion** is a threat of future harm to deprive an owner of his property.

F. **Theft** is the illegal taking of another person's property.

G. **Burglary** is a breaking and entering of the dwelling house of another at nighttime with intent to commit a felony therein.

H. **Receipt of stolen property** is a crime when one knowingly receives, conceals, or disposes of stolen property.

I. **Arson** is the malicious burning of the dwelling of another.

> Exam tip: Theft crimes are rarely tested on the essay portion of the exam, though they are a frequently tested on the MBE.

III. SOLICITATION, CONSPIRACY, AND ATTEMPT

A. **Solicitation** occurs when one requests or encourages another to commit a crime with the intent that the person solicited does commit the crime, regardless of whether they agree to do so.

B. **Conspiracy** is an agreement between two or more persons who intend to commit an unlawful act or a lawful act by unlawful means.

1. The **agreement can be implied or inferred** and does not require that all persons commit the actual act.
2. **Mere knowledge is insufficient** to establish the intent necessary to commit the unlawful act.
3. **Conspiracy is complete when**
   a. At **common law**, the conspiracy occurred the moment the agreement was made, but. . .

   b. The **majority of jurisdictions now require an overt act**, which can be as little as preparation, to form the conspiracy.
4. A **unilateral conspiracy** is allowed modernly, such that the party who agrees to commit the unlawful act can be convicted of conspiracy even if the other party does not agree to the conspiracy.
5. **Liability for crimes of co-conspirators:** Conspirators are liable for the crimes of co-conspirators if the crimes were committed **in furtherance of the objective** and were **reasonably foreseeable.**
6. **Defenses**
   a. **Withdrawal:** Once the agreement is made and the conspiracy is formed, one cannot withdraw from the conspiracy liability, but they can withdraw for purposes of future crimes of co-conspirators if they communicate their withdrawal to co-conspirators (federal law allows communications to authorities as well) and take an affirmative action to withdraw.
   b. **Impossibility** is not a defense (see section III.E below).

C. **Attempt** is an act done with intent to commit a crime and an affirmative act, or substantial step, in furtherance of the intent to commit the crime, beyond mere preparation.

D. **Merger**
1. **Solicitation and attempt merge** into the actual crime so they cannot be charged in addition to the actual crime.
2. **Conspiracy does not merge** into the actual crime and can be charged in addition to the actual crime.

> **Incomplete crimes fact triggers:**
> - More than one person in fact pattern
> - Hiring another person for any reason
> - Multiple parties taking part in an activity, even if not all parties are aware of the details
> - One person helping out another

E. **Defenses**
1. **Factual impossibility** is **not** a defense (see section V below).
2. **Legal impossibility** is a defense (see section V below).

> **Issue-spotting tip:** When the facts make conspiracy an issue, always consider accomplice liability as well since they often arise together.

IV. **ACCOMPLICE LIABILITY**

A. **Principal:** A principal is one who commits the actual crime.

B. **Accomplice:** An accomplice is one who **aids, abets, assists, or encourages** the carrying out of a crime, but does not commit the actual crime.
1. The **accomplice is liable** for **the crime** he assisted or encouraged if the principal carried out the crime.

2. **Mere knowledge is insufficient** to establish the intent to aid or encourage in the crime.
3. **Additional crimes:** Accomplices are **liable for additional crimes** committed by the principal in the course of committing the intended crime, so long as the crimes were a **natural and probable consequence** (foreseeable).

C. **Accessory after the fact** is an accomplice who knowingly gives assistance to a felon, for the purpose of helping him avoid apprehension following commission of a crime. Modernly, an accessory after the fact is charged with obstruction of justice.

D. **Defenses**

1. **Withdrawal:** An accomplice **can withdraw** before the crime is committed.

> Exam tip: Know the difference between accomplice liability and conspirator liability. Often on exams, differing outcomes may result in terms of the defendant's liability when analyzing these two issues based on the actions of other accomplices or co-conspirators.

V. **DEFENSES**

A. **Self-defense:** A person has a right to apply self-defense against unlawful force if reasonable force is used; deadly force may only be used in response to deadly force.

1. **Imperfect self-defense:** Where a person uses self-defense resulting in death and had made an unreasonable mistake about the need to do so, murder charges can be reduced to charges of voluntary manslaughter.

B. **Defense of others:** It is permissible to use reasonable force to defend another when one reasonably believes that the other person would be justified in using such force and the amount of force used is reasonable.

1. **Minority rule: "Stands in shoes,"** which means a party may only defend another if the person being defended was justified in using self-defense.

C. **Defense of property** allows an individual to use a **reasonable amount of force**, though never deadly force, to protect his real or personal property.

D. **Defense of insanity:** Depending on the jurisdiction, there are various tests for insanity.

1. ***M'Naghten* test:** The defendant must show that he suffered from a mental disease causing a defect in his reasoning powers that resulted in him not understanding the nature and quality of his act or that he did not know that his act was wrong.
2. **Irresistible impulse test:** The defendant must show that he was unable to control his conduct due to a mental illness.
3. ***Durham* test:** The defendant must show that his conduct was the product of a mental illness. (This standard is broader than the other two tests above.)

4. **Model Penal Code:** The defendant must show that he lacked substantial capacity to appreciate the criminality of his conduct or conform his conduct to the requirements of the law. (This is a blend of the other three tests.)

> Exam tip: Whenever insanity or the defendant's mental stability is at issue, be sure to go through all four types of insanity. Use headings and IRAC each one separately.

E. **Intoxication**
   1. **Voluntary, self-induced intoxication** is only a defense to specific intent crimes (first-degree murder, assault, incomplete crimes, property crimes) such that the intoxication may have prevented the defendant from formulating the requisite specific intent.
   2. **Involuntary intoxication** is treated as an illness and may be a defense to all crimes, as it negates the intent to commit the crime when an intoxicating substance is ingested unknowingly or under duress.

F. **Necessity** may be a defense if the defendant reasonably believed that commission of the crime was necessary to avoid an imminent and greater injury to society than that involved in the crime.

G. **Mistake**
   1. A **mistake of fact** may negate a specific intent crime as well as malice, and may negate a general intent crime if the mistake was reasonable.
   2. A **mistake of law** is generally not a defense.

H. **Impossibility**
   1. **Factual impossibility** arises when the defendant makes a mistake concerning an issue of fact. This is not a valid defense.
   2. **Legal impossibility** arises when the defendant incorrectly believes that what he is doing is criminal when it is not. This is a valid defense.

I. **Entrapment** exists where a law enforcement official, or someone cooperating with him, induces the defendant to commit the crime that he wasn't otherwise predisposed to commit.

CRIMINAL PROCEDURE RULE OUTLINE

I. THE **FOURTH AMENDMENT** protects individuals against unreasonable searches and seizures of property and against unlawful arrests.
   A. **Arrest**
      1. **Warrant:** An arrest warrant is generally not required for an arrest unless a person is arrested in his home.
         a. **Probable cause required:** An arrest warrant must be issued based on probable cause, which is a reasonable belief that the person violated the law.
   B. A **routine stop** by the government is typically permitted.
      1. **Automobile stop:** The police may randomly stop automobiles if there is a reasonable suspicion or wrongdoing based on an objective standard.
      2. **Checkpoints:** The police may set up fixed checkpoints to test for compliance with laws relating to driving or if special law enforcement needs are involved, such as immigration.
      3. **Stop and frisk:** Police may also stop and frisk individuals without arresting them (see section I.C.4.f below).
   C. **Search and seizure of property:** A search warrant is required for government search and seizure of property that is located where one has a reasonable expectation of privacy because a person has a right to be free from unreasonable search and seizure.
      1. **Government action required:** There must be government action (as opposed to private) for the Fourth Amendment search and seizure protections to apply.
      2. **Reasonable expectation of privacy:** The defendant must have a reasonable expectation of privacy in the property or place being searched or seized for the Fourth Amendment protection to apply. One has a reasonable expectation of privacy in his home and its curtilage (i.e., surrounding buildings, such as a garage).
      3. **Warrant is required:** Where a person has a reasonable expectation of privacy, the police need a search warrant based on probable cause to search and seize property. A warrant must be:
         a. **Based on probable cause:** Probable cause is established where it is reasonable that the items to be searched:
            1. Are **connected with criminal activities,** and
            2. **Will be found in the place** to be searched.
         b. **Issued by a neutral magistrate:** The search warrant is issued based on facts presented to a neutral and detached magistrate.
         c. **Description:** The search warrant must contain a particular description of the **premises to be searched**, and the **items to be seized.**
         d. **Knock and announce before execution:** To execute the search warrant, the police must knock and announce themselves before entering the premises. If there is no response, the police can enter and seize the items described but may not exceed the scope of the warrant.

Search and seizure fact triggers:
- Police search a home
- Police search a car
- Police search clothing on a person
- Police search a person's belongings
- Police arrest a person anywhere with or without a warrant
- Police stop a person in a car or on foot for violating a law

4. **Exceptions to the warrant requirement:** If the police conduct a search or seizure without a valid search warrant, there may be an applicable exception.
   a. **Search incident to a lawful arrest (SILA):** When the police are making a lawful arrest, they may search the area within the arrestee's immediate control (his wingspan).
      1. **Protective sweep:** Under SILA, police may also conduct a protective sweep of all or part of the premises where the arrestee is arrested if they have a reasonable belief based on specific and articulable facts that other dangerous individuals may be present.
      2. **Vehicle:** Under SILA, the police can search a car and its compartments if it is reasonable to believe that the arrestee might access the vehicle at the time of the search or the vehicle contains evidence of the offense of the arrest.
   b. **Plain view:** The police may make a warrantless search if they see an object or contraband in plain view so long as they are legitimately on the premises or have a right to be in the position to obtain the view.
   c. **Automobile:** If police have **probable cause** to believe that a vehicle contains contraband, they may search the whole automobile and any container therein.
      1. If the driver is arrested, the police may **impound the car**, transport it to the station house, and search it there without a warrant.

Issue-spotting tip: Although the police may not search a suspect's vehicle compartments under SILA, if the suspect does not have access to the car (such as if the suspect is held in a police car), the police can still get around a Fourth Amendment violation under the automobile exception if they have probable cause. So, consider both of these exceptions when an automobile is involved, and remember that without an arrest, SILA will not be applicable.

   d. **Consent:** The police may make a warrantless search if the person whose premises, items, or person will be searched voluntarily consents.

e. **Exigent circumstances:** The police may conduct a search or seizure without a warrant if they have probable cause and it is necessary to:
   1. Prevent imminent **destruction of evidence**
   2. Prevent imminent **injury to persons**, or
   3. Search for a felony suspect in **hot pursuit** that the police reasonably believe has entered particular premises.

f. **Stop and frisk:** A police officer may **stop and frisk** a person if the police have a reasonable suspicion of criminal activity or involvement that is supported by articulable facts.
   1. The brief detention may include a pat-down search for weapons if the suspect appears dangerous and armed, but the police may not search for contraband or evidence.

> <u>Memorization tip:</u> Use the mnemonic **SPACES** to remember the exceptions for the warrant requirement (**S**earch incident to a lawful arrest, **P**lain view, **A**utomobile, **C**onsent, **E**xigent circumstances, and **S**top and frisk). On most exams, the police will search a home or car without a warrant, thus requiring analysis of the applicable exceptions. Also, as discussed in section IV below, if there is a defective warrant, consider the good faith exception below.

II. **FIFTH AMENDMENT**

A. ***Miranda*:** When a suspect is taken into custody by the police and is under interrogation, his confession will be admissible against him only if he has received the requisite *Miranda* warnings, informing him that he has the right to remain silent, that anything he says can be used against him, that he has the right to have an attorney present, and if he cannot afford an attorney, one will be appointed for him.

1. ***Miranda* warnings apply to custodial interrogations.**
   a. **Custodial:** A suspect is in custody when a reasonable person would believe that he is not free to leave.
   b. **Interrogation** includes words or actions by the police that they should know are reasonably likely to elicit an incriminating response from the suspect.
      1. **Suspect must be aware:** A custodial interrogation does not occur when a suspect speaks to an undercover agent or government informant and the suspect does not know that he is speaking to a law enforcement officer, even if the suspect is in jail.
2. **Public safety exception:** *Miranda* warnings **do not apply** to questioning that is reasonably prompted by a concern for public safety.
3. **Re-*Mirandize*:** Once the suspect has unambiguously invoked his rights under *Miranda*, the **police cannot re-*Mirandize* the suspect** in an attempt to get the suspect to speak unless there has been a sufficient break in custody (14 days deemed sufficient).

<u>Miranda fact triggers:</u>

- Police place an informant with the suspect (whether he works for the government or not)
- Police give Miranda rights or re-Mirandize a suspect
- Police question a suspect at any time
- Suspect confesses
- Suspect placed in a line-up

<u>Exam tip:</u> Remember that just because a set of facts triggers the issue of *Miranda* doesn't mean that *Miranda* has been violated. Rather, it is just an indicator that you need to discuss the issue and explain why the suspect's *Miranda* rights were or were not violated.

4. **Waiver of *Miranda*:** A suspect may waive his *Miranda* rights, expressly or impliedly, but such a waiver is only admissible if it is voluntarily, knowingly, and intelligently made. Mere silence is insufficient to demonstrate a waiver.

B. **Fifth Amendment right to counsel under *Miranda*:** When the accused unambiguously indicates that he wishes to speak to counsel, the police are required to cease all questioning until the suspect has consulted a lawyer, and the lawyer must be present while any further questioning occurs.

<u>Exam tip:</u> Remember that even if a suspect's confession was obtained in violation of Miranda, it only limits the confession from being introduced in the prosecution's case-in-chief, but it is still admissible to impeach the suspect defendant. Compare and contrast this with confessions that are not voluntary and are the result of police coercion, which cannot be used to impeach the defendant.

C. **Fifth Amendment right against self-incrimination:** This right protects a criminal defendant from compulsion to give testimony or communicative evidence that could expose him to criminal liability.

<u>Exam tip:</u> Remember to focus on whether the statement or evidence is testimonial or communicative and not physical evidence. Physical evidence such as fingerprinting, line-ups, blood samples, photographs, and other identification procedures are not protected by the Fifth Amendment right against self-incrimination.

D. **Fifth Amendment double jeopardy:** This protects an individual from being tried for the same offense twice after jeopardy attaches. Jeopardy attaches when the jury has been impaneled and sworn for a jury trial, or when the first witness has been sworn for a bench trial.

E. **Fifth Amendment due process**, which is applicable to the states through the Fourteenth Amendment, requires that:
   1. **Confessions be made voluntarily**, and
   2. **Identifications** are not unnecessarily suggestive and so conducive to mistaken identification that it is unfair to the defendant. (See section V below.)

III. SIXTH AMENDMENT

A. **Right to effective counsel:** A suspect against whom formal criminal proceedings have been commenced has a right to effective counsel at any post-charge line-up or show-up, including sentencing. This right does not apply to photo identifications, or when police take physical evidence from a suspect such as handwriting samples or fingerprints.
   1. **Standard of effectiveness:** To establish ineffective assistance of counsel, the defendant must prove that counsel's performance was deficient in that counsel **did not act as a reasonably competent attorney** would have acted, and that this deficiency was prejudicial such that, but for the deficiency, the **result would have been different.**
   2. **Attorney substitution:** A court will allow the defendant to substitute his attorney if the interests of justice so require, taking into account any conflicts, the interests of the defendant and the court, and the timeliness of the request.
   3. **Self-representation:** The defendant is permitted to knowingly and intelligently **waive his right to counsel** and represent himself.

B. **Right to confront adverse witnesses:** The Sixth Amendment allows a defendant in a criminal prosecution the right to confront adverse witnesses.
   1. **Compel testimony:** The right to confront includes issuing subpoenas to compel testimony of an adverse or hostile witness, as well as to **cross-examine** hostile witnesses.
   2. **Testimonial statements:** The prosecution may not admit testimonial statements by a third person against the defendant unless the declarant is available for cross-examination either at the time the statement was made or during trial.
      a. **Statements are nontestimonial when** made in the course of police interrogation under circumstances objectively indicating that the primary purpose of the interrogation is to enable police assistance to meet an ongoing emergency, such as a 911 call.
      b. **Statements are testimonial when** the circumstances indicate that there is no ongoing emergency, and that the primary purpose of the interrogation is to establish or prove past events potentially relevant to later criminal prosecution.

3. **Joint co-defendants** can raise "right to confront" issues.
   a. **Confession of one co-defendant:** Where two defendants are jointly tried and one of them confesses, the right to confront adverse witnesses prohibits use of that statement against the other defendant unless the statement can be redacted or the co-defendant who made the statement takes the stand and subjects himself to cross-examination.
   b. **Severance of joint trial:** Where co-defendants are charged for the same crime, courts prefer joint trials for judicial economy, but will sever the co-defendants if a joint trial would result in substantial prejudice to one of the defendants.

> **"Right to confront" fact triggers:**
> - Co-defendants
> - Witness does not take the stand
> - Witness dies
> - Witness cannot be found

C. **Right to a jury trial:** Criminal defendants have the right to a jury trial for serious offenses that have a potential sentence of greater than six months.
   1. **Waiver permitted:** The defendant may voluntarily, knowingly, and intelligently waive his right to a jury trial.
   2. **Number of jurors required:** Juries must consist of **at least six persons** and can consist of twelve persons.
      a. **Six-person jury:** In a six-person jury, a **unanimous verdict** is required.
      b. **Federal criminal trial:** A **unanimous verdict** is required.
      c. **Twelve-person jury:** In a twelve-person state jury, **only a substantial majority** is required for a conviction.
   3. **Impartial jurors:** A jury must be impartial, consisting of a fair cross-section of a community.
      a. A **jury does not consist of a fair cross-section of a community** if the defendant can prove that:
         1. The group alleged to be excluded is a **distinctive group** in the community;
         2. The representation of this group in venires from which juries are selected is **not fair** and reasonable **in relation to the number of such persons in the community**; and
         3. This underrepresentation is due to **systematic exclusion** of the group in the jury-selection process.
   4. **Voir dire:** During voir dire each side (not party) has **unlimited strikes for cause** (bias, prejudice, related to a party, etc.) and **three peremptory strikes** that may be used for any reason, so long as the reason is gender and race neutral.
   5. **Discrimination not permitted:** The equal protection clause of the Fourteenth Amendment prevents the state or any state actor,

including the court, from intentionally discriminating against a distinctive group in selection of the jury pool.

D. **The right to a speedy trial:** The Sixth Amendment right to a speedy trial is viewed on a case-by-case basis with the court balancing the following factors:
   1. The length of the delay;
   2. The reason for the delay;
   3. The prejudice to the defendant as a result of the delay; and
   4. The time and manner in which the defendant asserted his right.

E. **Right to a preliminary hearing:** A defendant who pleads not guilty has a right to a preliminary hearing if probable cause has not been established, within 30 days of their arrest, unless he waives such right. (The rules for preliminary hearings vary among jurisdictions.)

IV. THE EXCLUSIONARY RULE AND GOOD FAITH WARRANT EXCEPTION

A. **The exclusionary rule** is a judge-made rule that **prohibits the prosecution from introducing evidence** obtained in violation of a defendant's Fourth, Fifth, or Sixth Amendment rights.
   1. **Standing required:** The defendant must have standing to assert the exclusionary rule, such that the evidence wrongfully obtained must have been in violation of the defendant's own constitutional rights and not any third persons.
   2. **"Fruit of the poisonous tree":** Evidence wrongfully obtained is inadmissible as the "fruit of the poisonous tree"—in other words, evidence that is found as a result of the original wrongfully obtained evidence—subject to the following **exceptions:**
      a. **Independent source:** The evidence obtained could have been obtained from an independent source separate from the illegal source; or
      b. **Inevitable discovery:** The evidence obtained would inevitably have been discovered by other police techniques, had it not first been obtained through illegal discovery; or
      c. **Purged taint:** There are a sufficient number of additional factors that intervened between the original illegality and the final discovery that the link is too tenuous, such that the intervening factors have purged the taint of the illegal discovery.
   3. **Allowed for impeachment:** Illegally obtained evidence may still be used to impeach the defendant, defense witnesses, or grand jury witnesses.
   4. **Allowed during civil hearings or parole proceedings:** Illegally obtained evidence is allowed in civil hearings or parole proceedings.

> **Exam tip:** Whenever there is a possible Fourth, Fifth, or Sixth Amendment violation, consider the potential application of the exclusionary rule and briefly mention it. Be certain that the defendant has "standing" and is the one whose rights were violated and not a third person. Analyze any exceptions that might allow the evidence to come in, despite a violation. Lastly, mention that the evidence can still be used to impeach the defendant.

B. **The good faith warrant exception:** Where an officer acts in reasonable reliance on a facially valid search warrant issued by a proper magistrate and the warrant is ultimately found to be unsupported by probable cause, the exclusionary rule will not apply and the evidence will not be barred.
   1. **Exception:** The good faith warrant exception does not apply (and thus the evidence will be excluded under the exclusionary rule) where:
      a. **The affiant knew the information he was providing in the affidavit was false,** or he would have known except for his reckless disregard of the truth.
      b. **There was a lack of probable cause** such that the magistrate's reliance on the affidavit was unreasonable.

V. ADDITIONAL CONFESSION, IDENTIFICATION, AND MISCELLANEOUS ISSUES

A. **Confessions must be voluntary:** Under the Fourteenth Amendment, confessions must be made voluntarily without police coercion, in light of the totality of the circumstances, with the court considering the susceptibility of the suspect and the environment and methods used.
   1. **Nongovernmental coercion:** A confession obtained by nongovernmental coercion is admissible.
   2. **Confession by person who is mentally ill:** A confession made by a person suffering from mental illness is admissible.
   3. **Police coercion:** Where a confession is the result of police coercion, the prosecution cannot use it during its case-in-chief *or* to impeach the defendant. This rule is in contrast to a confession obtained in violation of *Miranda,* which is still admissible for impeachment purposes.

B. **Due process in identification:** A defendant's due process rights are violated if an identification of the defendant based on the totality of the circumstances is unnecessarily suggestive and so conducive to mistaken identification that it is unfair to the defendant.

> **Due process fact triggers:**
> - Defendant is identified on the way to any court hearing or show-up
> - Defendant is identified alone or not in a line-up
> - Defendant and the witness are at the same location at the same time
> - Defendant is distinct in some way from others in a line-up

C. **Plea bargains:** A defendant can settle by plea bargain to receive a less serious charge or a lighter sentence if he is competent, understands the charge, and understands the consequences of the plea.
   1. **Voluntary and intelligently:** Plea bargains must be made voluntarily and intelligently; in open court and on record.
   2. The prosecutor has **no obligation to agree to a plea** and the **judge can refuse** to accept the guilty plea if he thinks the defendant didn't commit the crime.

> **Issue-spotting tip:** This outline is organized by Amendment since most essays ask whether the defendant's Fourth, Fifth, or Sixth Amendment rights have been violated. Thus, you should memorize all issues that stem from each Amendment. However, memorize the following mini-issues checklist for issues that arise in conjunction with one another when a defendant confesses.
> - Voluntariness
> - Due process
> - Miranda
> - Waiver of Miranda
> - Fifth Amendment right to counsel

VI. **EIGHTH AMENDMENT**

A. **Bail:** The Eighth Amendment requires that **bail shall not be excessive or unduly high** based on several factors, including the following:
   1. The **seriousness** of the offense;
   2. The **weight of the evidence** against the defendant;
   3. The defendant's **financial abilities**; and
   4. The defendant's **character**.

B. **Cruel and unusual punishment:** The Eighth Amendment prohibits cruel and unusual punishment by preventing the penalty imposed on the defendant from being grossly disproportionate to the seriousness of crime.
   1. **A defendant cannot be sentenced to death** if:
      a. At least one juror finds the defendant is **mentally retarded**; or
      b. He is a **minor** at the time of the crime.
   2. **Victim impact statements** during the penalty phase do not violate a defendant's Eighth Amendment right against cruel and unusual punishment.
   3. **Mitigating circumstances:** When considering a death penalty, the jury shall consider mitigating circumstances such as the defendant's age, capacity, previous criminal liability, duress, other defendants' involvement, and any other factors that mitigate against imposition of a death sentence.

CRIMES ISSUES TESTED MATRIX

		Crossover Subject	Murder Manslaughter	Other Crimes	Conspiracy Accomplice Liability	Attempt Solicitation	4th Amend. Arrest Search & Seizure	5th Amend. *Miranda* Counsel Self-incrimination	6th Amend. Right to Counsel Right to Confront Speedy Trial	6th Amend. Right to Jury Juror Issues	Exclusionary Rule	Voluntary Confessions Pleas	Due Process Or Pre-trial issues	8th Amend. Penalty Sentencing	Defenses
July '11 Q1	Vicky sells computers; Dan tries to steal them with Eric's pickup			Several	X	X									
July '10 Q5	Harriet on porch, Don walks up with gun & she thinks it's a toy			Kidnapping		X	X				X	X			X
July '09 Q6	Polly, uniformed police officer, stops speeding car with cocaine						X	X	X						
February '08 Q3	Dan's neighborhood overrun by gangs, but Dan refuses to join		X					X	X		X				X
July '07 Q4	Dan stood on the capital steps, lights a fire & kills a pedestrian	Con. Law	X			X									X
February '07 Q3	Dan, mental patient, kills V in grocery store after he was insulted		X												X

Continued >

		Crossover Subject	Murder Manslaughter	Other Crimes	Conspiracy Accomplice Liability	Attempt Solicitation	4th Amend. Arrest Search & Seizure	5th Amend. *Miranda* Counsel Self-incrimination	6th Amend. Right to Counsel Right to Confront Speedy Trial	6th Amend. Right to Jury Juror Issues	Exclusionary Rule	Voluntary Confessions Pleas	Due Process Or Pre-trial issues	8th Amend. Penalty Sentencing	Defenses
February '06 Q6	Deft saw officer Oscar attempt to arrest Friend, who was resisting arrest						X	X	X		X		X		X
July '04 Q1	Dan, Art & Bert rob Vince's Store; Vince kills Art		X	Extortion/ Stolen Prop.	X				X						
February '04 Q1	Bank robbed at 1:00 pm by man with a shotgun and an accent						X	X			X				
February '03 Q3	Don is a passenger in V's car; takes a drug and kills V	Evidence	X					X	X				X		X
February '01 Q3	Duce & Cody arrested for armed robbery and both confess						X	X	X						
July '00 Q4	Ruth the reporter observes illegal dog fight	Con. Law						X							
February '00 Q6	Picasso sketch taken from museum and purchased in Switzerland	Evidence					X	X	X						

Continued >

		Crossover Subject	Murder Manslaughter	Other Crimes	Conspiracy Accomplice Liability	Attempt Solicitation	4th Amend. Arrest Search & Seizure	5th Amend. *Miranda* Counsel Self-incrimination	6th Amend. Right to Counsel Right to Confront Speedy Trial	6th Amend. Right to Jury Juror Issues	Exclusionary Rule	Voluntary Confessions Pleas	Due Process Or Pre-trial issues	8th Amend. Penalty Sentencing	Defenses
July '99 Q1	Al, Bob & Charlie plan to import 50 cases whiskey without paying proper duty	Prof. Resp.		Theft	X	X									X
February '99 Q2	Deft is a suspected cash courier for narcotics based on wiretap						X	X				X			
July '97 Q6	Don found Vic assaulting Don's wife and vows revenge		X		X										
July '96 Q3	Bicycle messengers used by Dan to deliver packages and heroin	Prof. Resp.		Drug Sales	X										
February '96 Q5	Art and Bill kidnap V; Art rapes V and V kills herself		X	Rape	X			X	X			X			X
February '95 Q5	Officer Jones arrests Dan Deft in red sports car for robbery						X	X	X				X		
July '94 Q3	Jane, police officer not in uniform, arrests Al in dark alley		X							X				X	X

Continued >

		Crossover Subject	Murder Manslaughter	Other Crimes	Conspiracy Accomplice Liability	Attempt Solicitation	4th Amend. Arrest Search & Seizure	5th Amend. *Miranda* Counsel Self-incrimination	6th Amend. Right to Counsel Right to Confront Speedy Trial	6th Amend. Right to Jury Juror Issues	Exclusionary Rule	Voluntary Confessions Pleas	Due Process Or Pre-trial issues	8th Amend. Penalty Sentencing	Defenses
J ’93 Q2	Bart failed to pay Deft for cocaine; Deft confesses to Snitch						X	X	X			X			
F ’93 Q2	Deft has mental illness and becomes enraged at landlord Vic					X			X			X	X		X
J ’92 Q5	Art & Bill transporting illegal drugs; Carl is private bodyguard		X		X										X
J ’90 Q1	Police enter Bob’s mobile home without a warrant						X		X				X		
F ’90 Q5	Wit identifies Deft at his arraignment; Deft represents himself								X	X		X	X		
J ’88 Q5	Al & Bill give a ride to Clara and then rape her		X		X					X				X	
F ’84 Q5	Rape prosecution against Roe	Evidence						X							

CRIMES PRACTICE ESSAYS, ANSWER GRIDS, AND SAMPLE ANSWERS

Crimes Question 1

February 1996, Question 5

Art and Bill agreed to kidnap Vickie and to make a ransom demand of her parents. Because he knew that Art had been convicted of a forcible sexual offense in the past, Bill insisted that Art agree that no harm would be inflicted on Vickie. Art assured Bill that he would not harm her.

Art and Bill kidnapped Vickie, locked her in a room in Art's home, and communicated a $100,000 ransom demand to Vickie's parents. Her parents promptly contacted the police, who were unsuccessful in efforts to locate and rescue Vickie.

Several days after the kidnapping, Art raped Vickie. Despondent over the confinement and mortified by the rape, Vickie killed herself only hours after the rape. Bill was not present and had no knowledge of the rape or suicide until Art told him that Vickie had killed herself shortly after Art had raped her. Art also told Bill that he was going to dispose of Vickie's body. Bill immediately turned himself in to the police. He then told the police: a) about the kidnapping in detail; b) what Art had said about the rape and suicide; and c) that Art had said he was going to dispose of Vickie's body.

Police arrested Bill, went to Art's home where they found Vickie's body, and arrested Art.

Based on the above facts:

1. On what theory or theories of liability might Bill be convicted of rape? Discuss.
2. Are Art and Bill, or either of them, guilty of the murder of Vickie? If so, is the offense first or second degree murder? Discuss.
3. Is Bill's statement to the police, or any part of it, admissible at a joint trial of Bill and Art if neither testifies? Assume all proper objections are made. Discuss.

Crimes Question 1 Assessment

February 1996, Question 5

This is a rather complex crimes question that requires a full understanding—by applying principles of co-conspirator or accomplice liability—of how one can be liable for a crime he didn't actually commit. Students often mistakenly dismiss Bill for rape and both Bill and Art for murder under the incorrect assumption that since they didn't actually commit the crime they cannot be charged. As you see in the following Issue Grid and Sample Answer, though, this is not correct. In addition, students often don't pay close attention to the felony murder rule and often overlook the fact that the rape was not ongoing when Vickie killed herself, making the felony rule inapplicable for that felony. However, since the kidnapping was still ongoing, the felony murder rule would apply to that felony. Always pay close attention to the details regarding which crimes were occurring at the time of the death, which parties contributed to the death, and how they contributed.

This question also requires an analysis of murder. It's best to follow the approach outlined in the rules by starting out with the general rule for murder; next, identify the four ways to establish malice; and lastly, analyze those that are applicable. In addition, be sure to carefully follow the call of the question by addressing whether the murder can be first or second degree. One particular element that must be analyzed here is causation. Although causation is rarely an issue on murder essays, this fact pattern is a great example of the type of facts that will put causation in issue since neither Art nor Bill actually killed Vickie since she committed suicide. Anytime someone other than the defendant actually does the killing or commits the act that kills the victim, always discuss causation with more detail than you otherwise would, and argue both sides. Typically, the conclusion does not matter so long as you identify the competing arguments and explain how you arrived at your conclusion.

The third call of the question involves a few criminal procedure issues, which are comparatively minor. After organizing your entire answer, you should be able to determine which calls and issues will be weighted the most. To do this, you need to see which issues have the most rule elements and/or facts that correspond to those issues and rules. These issues will be worth more points than minor issues that have very minimal rules and/or few facts that correspond to them. Before writing out your essay, apportion your time accordingly. For example, on this exam, if you have 45 minutes left to write after organizing your answer, you would know that the second call requires the most analysis, and the first call is the next-most fact intensive one. You should plan to spend approximately 20 minutes analyzing call two, 15 minutes on call one, and 10 minutes on call three. These numbers are not set in stone but are guidelines as to how you should apportion your time to completely answer the question and garner the most possible points.

Finally, make note of the areas highlighted in **bold** on the corresponding grid. The bold areas highlight the issues, analysis, and conclusions that are likely **required** to receive a passing score on this question. In general, the essay grids are provided to assist you in analyzing the essays, and are much more detailed than what a student should create during the exam to organize their response to a question.

Issue	Rule	Fact Application	Conclusion
B's Liability for Rape			
Conspiracy	Conspiracy requires • An agreement • Between two or more persons • Intent to commit an unlawful act The majority of jurisdictions require an overt act.	Both A and B agreed to kidnap V. There are two of them. The intent to kidnap one for ransom is unlawful. Here, they committed more than an overt act by actually kidnapping her and seeking the ransom.	B liable for conspiracy
Co-conspirator liability	Co-conspirators liable if crimes were • Foreseeable, and • In furtherance of the objective.	B knew that A had been convicted of a prior sexual offense, which makes it possible and likely foreseeable that if A were alone with a girl that he could sexually offend her. Since the goal of the conspiracy was to get ransom money by kidnapping V, A raping V would not help further the goal of getting money. But, arguably, if V's parents knew she was raped, this could encourage them to pay sooner so as to avoid future harms, but unlikely since it had been several days and they were not able to come up with the money and promptly contacted the police.	B not liable for A raping V
Accomplice liability	Aids, abets, assists, or encourages the carrying out of a crime, but does not commit the actual crime. Liable for other accomplice's acts if foreseeable criminal acts of another.	Arguably B aided or abetted in A raping V, as he allowed A to be left alone with V knowing of A's past sexual offenses making another sexual offense foreseeable. Although B told A not to harm V, this could arguably show that he knew something bad was possible since he felt the need to warn A in the first place and address the issue; also, he helped lock V in A's home making it more likely and foreseeable that A could harm V.	B liable for rape under accomplice liability

Continued >

Issue	Rule	Fact Application	Conclusion
Withdrawal	**One can withdraw before the crime.**	**Here, the rape and killing already occurred, so it was too late.**	**No defense**
Murder Liability			
Murder	**Murder is the unlawful killing of another person with malice aforethought.** **Malice can be proven by** • **An intent to kill (desire or knowledge to a substantial certainty),** • **An intent to commit grievous bodily injury,** • **A reckless indifference to the value of human life, or** • **An intent to commit a dangerous felony.** Under the **felony murder rule**, malice is implied if death was a natural and probable consequence of D's conduct, and death occurred during commission of the felony, even if death was accidental and independent from the felony. **The D's conduct must also be the cause in fact and the proximate cause of the death.**	Here, V was killed, but the question is whether it was unlawful in that she took her own life rather than A or B taking her life, but they helped put her in the position that resulted in her death. **For malice:** There is nothing here to show either A or B intended to kill V as killing her would likely not give them any ransom money at all. A and B didn't actually inflict the injury that directly caused the death either; although A raped V, neither A nor B injured V, killing her directly. **Arguably, raping a kidnapped V may lead them to think they cannot escape and will die anyway and thus is reckless disregard for life since people often die when faced with kidnapping and rape situations, even if by their own hand.** **FMR/rape, but death did not occur during the commission of that felony since rape was completed at the time V killed herself hours later; but kidnapping was ongoing and that is an inherently dangerous felony.**	Could conclude either way based on causation analysis

Continued >

Issue	Rule	Fact Application	Conclusion
		Further, as V was raped and could think she was never going to live or get out of her situation, it is natural and probable consequence that V's two very dire situations—kidnap and rape over a short period of time—could cause one to become unstable and suicidal. **But for V being kidnapped and raped and despondent and mortified, she would not have killed herself.** See above for foreseeability; also, it is foreseeable that a victim that has been kidnapped and raped several days after the kidnapping with no indication help is ever going to come would kill herself. **[Argue both ways here.]** Also, V killed herself only hours after the rape indicating there was no break in the chain of causation. **Since both A and B are liable for the underlying felony, they will be liable for the murder as well.**	
1st v. 2nd Degree	1st degree is premeditated and deliberate (D is dispassionate and reflected on the idea to kill), or **via FMR if an enumerated inherently dangerous felony.** All other murder: 2nd degree	Here, neither A nor B intended or planned on V killing herself; in fact, B wasn't expecting this at all, which is why he turned himself in to the police once he realized how far things went. **Here, since kidnapping is an enumerated inherently dangerous felony, A and B could be convicted of 1st degree murder under the FMR.** If not, 2nd degree.	**1st degree murder**

Continued >

Issue	Rule	Fact Application	Conclusion
B's Statements			
Voluntariness	**Confession must be voluntarily made** in light of totality of the circumstances.	**B went to the police on his own volition and confessed without any police coercion.**	**Statement voluntary**
5th Amend.: *Miranda*	To receive *Miranda* warnings, D must be in custodial interrogation.	Here, B not in custody as he was free to leave since **he voluntarily went to the police on his own.** No interrogation since B told police everything rather than them asking him questions. No *Miranda* violation	**No 5th Amend. violation**
6th Amend.: right to confront	**D has a right to confront adverse co-D witnesses through cross-examination, or the statement must be redacted or the co-D must take the stand.**	**Here, since B's statement implicates A, it cannot be used against A unless it is redacted as to his involvement or B testifies, which he is not doing here; the statement can be used against B though, but the portions in reference to A must be redacted.**	**Statement admissible if redacted**

Crimes Question 1 Sample Answer

February 1996, Question 5

1. B's Liability for Rape

Conspiracy

A conspiracy is an agreement between two or more persons with the intent to commit an unlawful act, or a lawful act by unlawful means. The majority of jurisdictions also require an overt act, which can be mere preparation.

Here, both A and B agreed to kidnap V, which is an unlawful act that involves two people. Further, they committed more than an overt act by actually kidnapping her and seeking the ransom from her parents.

Thus, B is liable for conspiracy for kidnapping and may be liable for the crimes committed by co-conspirators.

Co-conspirator Liability

Conspirators are liable for the crimes of co-conspirators if the crimes committed were reasonably foreseeable and were committed in furtherance of the objective.

Here, B knew that A had been convicted of a prior sexual offense, which makes it possible and likely foreseeable that if A were alone with another female that he could sexually offend her. Further, since A's previous offense was a conviction and not just an allegation or charge, this makes it more probable and foreseeable that A could commit a similar crime again.

Although B may argue that A raping V was not foreseeable since A assured B that he would not harm V, the mere fact that B felt the need to seek assurances from A shows that he knew some form of harm to V was possible. Further, the fact that V was being held in A's home made it more foreseeable that A could harm V as he would be alone with her.

Despite the fact that it was foreseeable that A would rape V, the prosecution will have a difficult time showing that A raping V was in furtherance of the conspiracy objective. Arguably, since the goal of the conspiracy was to get ransom money from kidnapping V, A raping V would not help further the goal of getting money.

It is possible that if V's parents knew she was raped, this could encourage them to pay sooner so as to avoid future harms to her, but this is unlikely since it had been several days since A and B kidnapped V and her parents were still not able to procure the money. In fact, they promptly contacted the police indicating they did not have the ability to pay the ransom to get their daughter back.

Thus, the rape was not in furtherance of the objective and B will not be liable for A raping V as a co-conspirator.

Accomplice Liability

An accomplice is one who aids, abets, assists, or encourages the carrying out of a crime, but does not commit the actual crime. An accomplice is liable for additional crimes committed during the course of committing the intended crime to the same extent as the principal if the crimes were the natural and probable (foreseeable) consequence of the conduct.

Here, B aided and abetted in A raping V since he allowed her to be left alone with A, knowing of A's prior sexual convictions. Although B told A not to harm V, this could arguably show that he knew some harm to V was possible since he felt the need to warn A in the first place. Further, he helped lock V in A's home, making it more probable and foreseeable that A could harm V since A had the opportunity to be alone with her. In addition, the rape occurred during the commission of the kidnapping as the kidnapping was still ongoing at the time of the rape, which is why V was still being held in A's home.

Therefore, B will be liable for rape as an accomplice.

Withdrawal

An accomplice can withdraw before the crime is committed. Here, the crime of kidnapping, the rape, and the killing all already occurred before B went to the police, making his attempted withdrawal untimely and ineffective. Thus, B is still liable for rape, as there are no valid defenses to negate the crime.

2. A and B's Murder Liability for V's Death

Murder

Murder is the unlawful killing of another person with malice aforethought. Malice can be proven by (1) an intent to kill (desire or knowledge to a substantial certainty), (2) an intent to commit grievous bodily injury, (3) a reckless indifference to the value of human life, or (4) an intent to commit a dangerous felony.

Intent to Kill

There is nothing to indicate that either A or B intended to kill V or desired or knew with substantial certainty that she would kill herself, since killing her or her death would not further their goal of obtaining ransom money.

Intent to Commit Grievous Bodily Injury

Although A and B intended to kidnap V, they did not agree to harm her physically. However, A did commit grievous bodily injury to V by raping her. However, the rape did not result in her death as she killed herself several hours after the rape was completed. Since neither A nor B actually inflicted the injury that resulted in her death, it is unlikely that they will be responsible for her murder under this theory of malice.

Reckless Indifference to the Value of Human Life

Arguably, raping a kidnapped victim may lead the victim to think she cannot escape and will die anyway, which could result in death by suicide. Since suicide is not unheard of for rape victims, the fact that V was kidnapped for several days and raped could indicate that A's raping her was conduct that exhibited a reckless disregard for life since people often commit suicide when faced with dire situations and are despondent and mortified, as V was here. Further, since B is liable for both the kidnapping and rape, he too could be liable under this theory of malice.

Felony Murder Rule

Under the felony murder rule, malice is implied if the death was a natural and probable consequence of the defendant's conduct, even if accidental and the death occurred during the commission of the felony and was independent from the felony.

Here, although both rape and kidnapping are felonies, the death did not occur during the commission of the rape since that felony ended prior to V's death. However, the kidnapping was ongoing and V killed herself during the commission of that crime.

Further, as V was raped and could reasonably think that she was not going to survive, coupled with the fact that she was despondent and mortified over the kidnapping and rape, it is a natural and probable consequence that a victim who was kidnapped and raped over a short period of time could become mentally unstable and suicidal.

Thus, both A and B will be liable for murder under this theory of malice as well.

Causation

The defendant's conduct must also be the cause in fact and the proximate cause of the death.

Actual Cause

Actual cause requires that the death be directly caused from the harm inflicted, such that the harm inflicted is the "but for" cause of the death.

But for V being kidnapped and raped and despondent and mortified over the two crimes, she would not have killed herself.

Proximate Cause

Proximate cause requires that the resulting death be a foreseeable result.

See above for foreseeability discussions. In addition, although A and B will argue that V's action was an intervening force cutting off their liability, it was still foreseeable that a victim in this situation would become suicidal, as discussed above. Further since she killed herself only hours after being raped and during the kidnapping, there is no break in causation or link between the actions of A and B and her resulting death.

Thus, A and B are the cause of V's death.

First-Degree Murder

First-degree murder is found when D's actions are premeditated and deliberate or when a defendant is found guilty under the felony murder rule for an enumerated inherently dangerous felony, which includes kidnapping.

Here, neither A nor B intended or planned on V killing herself at any point. In fact, B wasn't expecting this at all, which is why he turned himself in to the police once he realized that events occurred beyond what he contemplated. However, since kidnapping is an enumerated inherently dangerous felony, A and B can both be convicted of first-degree murder under the felony murder rule.

Thus, A and B are liable for first-degree murder.

Second-Degree Murder

If murder is not first degree or reduced to manslaughter, the defendant will be found guilty of second-degree murder.

Here, since A and B are both likely guilty of first-degree murder through the felony murder rule, they will not be guilty of second-degree murder.

3. B's Statements

Voluntariness

Confessions must be made voluntarily without police coercion, in light of the totality of the circumstances.

Here, B went to the police on his own volition and confessed without any police coercion. Further, he was likely confessing since the events went beyond what he contemplated and he knew that V's death was serious, which further indicates that his own conscience, rather than police questioning, is what prompted him to confess.

Thus, B's statement and confession were voluntary.

Fifth Amendment: *Miranda*

To receive *Miranda* warnings, D must be in custodial interrogation.

Custody

A person is in custody if he reasonably believes that he is not free to leave.

Here, B was not in custody as he was free to leave since he voluntarily went to the police and was not brought there or asked to go there.

Interrogation

Interrogation includes any words or actions by the police that they should know are reasonably likely to elicit an incriminating response from the suspect.

Here, the police did not interrogate B since he voluntarily told police everything without them asking him questions or trying to elicit his responses.

Thus, there is no Fifth Amendment violation for failure to provide B with a *Miranda* warning.

Sixth Amendment: Right to Confront Adverse Witnesses

The Sixth Amendment allows a defendant in a criminal proceeding the right to confront adverse witnesses. The prosecution may not admit testimonial statements against the defendant by a third person unless the defendant has an opportunity to cross-examine the witness.

Here, B's statements will be admitted against him and A in a joint trial. Since B made the statements, they may be used against him. However, since his statements implicate A for kidnapping and raping V, as well as planning for and disposing her body, these statements are testimonial and would adversely affect A. Since, B will not be testifying, A would not have an opportunity to cross-examine B as to the statements.

Redaction

The prosecution can admit evidence that implicates a joint defendant if they can redact the statement or the co-defendant takes the stand.

Since B will not be testifying, the prosecution will need to redact the statement or it will be inadmissible during the joint trial.

Crimes Question 2

July 2009, Question 6

Polly, a uniformed police officer, observed a speeding car weaving in and out of traffic in violation of the Vehicle Code. Polly pursued the car in her marked patrol vehicle and activated its flashing lights. The car pulled over. Polly asked Dave, the driver, for his driver's license and the car's registration certificate, both of which he handed to her. Although the documents appeared to be in order, Polly instructed Dave and his passenger, Ted: "Stay here. I'll be back in a second." Polly then walked to her patrol vehicle to check for any outstanding arrest warrants against Dave.

As she was walking, Polly looked back and saw that Ted appeared to be slipping something under his seat. Polly returned to Dave's car, opened the passenger side door, looked under the seat, and saw a paper lunch bag. Polly pulled the bag out, opened it, and found five small bundles of what she recognized as cocaine.

Polly arrested Dave and Ted, took them to the police station, and gave them *Miranda* warnings. Dave refused to answer any questions. Ted, however, waived his *Miranda* rights, and stated: "I did not know what was inside the bag or how the bag got into the car. I did not see the bag before Dave and I got out of the car for lunch. We left the windows of the car open because of the heat. I did not see the bag until you stopped us. It was just lying there on the floor mat, so I put it under the seat to clear the mat for my feet."

Dave and Ted have been charged jointly with possession of cocaine. Dave and Ted have each retained an attorney. A week before trial, Dave has become dissatisfied with his attorney and wants to discharge him in favor of a new attorney he hopes to select soon.

What arguments might Dave raise under the United States Constitution in support of each of the following motions, and how are they likely to fare:

1. A motion to suppress the cocaine? Discuss.
2. A motion to suppress Ted's statement or, in the alternative, for a separate trial? Discuss.
3. A motion to discharge his present attorney and to substitute a new attorney in his place?

Discuss.

Crimes Question 2 Assessment

July 2009, Question 6

This criminal procedure question is typical and covers Fourth Amendment search and seizure issues, which is a heavily tested area within criminal procedure. Be methodical and follow all steps when organizing a response that incorporates the Fourth Amendment since analysis of the issue(s) at each step is required to receive the maximum points on the essay. Otherwise, it is easy to forget obvious issues, such as the requirement that you need government action for the Fourth Amendment to apply. Although the state action requirement is obviously met (since Polly is a police officer), you must still address it in your answer, and the failure to do so will result in missing easy points.

Also, if mnemonics work well for you, remember the mnemonic SPACES for the exceptions to a warrantless search. On most exams that test the Fourth Amendment, the facts will include a warrantless search. On the rare occasion when the fact pattern includes a search warrant, it will probably be improperly executed, thus raising the issue of the good faith exception. Just be sure that you don't use the good faith exception to an improperly executed warrant as one of the exceptions applicable to a warrantless search. It is crucial that you understand which exceptions apply to each factual situation. Pay especially close attention to whether there was a warrant for the arrest or search and, if there was, whether it was properly executed since this is the determinative issue from which all of the other issues flow.

It is important to fully understand the distinction between the search incident to a lawful arrest (SILA) exception and the automobile exception. Students often don't fully comprehend the differences between the two exceptions. Remember that for SILA to apply, there must be a lawful arrest; whereas, lawful arrest is not required for the automobile exception to apply. Similarly, under SILA the police cannot search the compartments within a car if the suspect does not have access to them, such as when the suspect is in the back of the police car or handcuffed. However, under the automobile exception, the police can search the car compartments if there is probable cause to believe that they contain contraband. Keep these distinctions in mind because when one of them is inapplicable, the other one may apply.

Finally, remember that although you only need one exception to admit the evidence under a warrantless search, the bar examiners expect an IRAC of every possible exception where there are corresponding facts. Thus, even if SILA is met, don't stop there. Go through all possible remaining exceptions that might be applicable or that have facts that correspond to them. This will ensure that you receive maximum points by using all facts and spotting all issues.

To see which issues are of greater weight on this essay, make note of the areas highlighted in **bold** on the corresponding grid. The bold areas highlight the issues, analysis, and conclusions that are likely **required** to receive a passing score on this question.

Issue	Rule	Fact Application	Conclusion
Call #1: Motion to Suppress Cocaine			
4th Amend.	4th Amend. protects individuals against unreasonable searches and seizures of property and against unlawful arrests.	Here, there was a search of Dave's car and thus a 4th Amend. analysis is warranted.	
Govt. action	There must be government action (as opposed to private) for the 4th Amend. search and seizure protections to apply.	Here, Polly, a uniformed police officer, who works for the government, searched Dave's car, found the cocaine, and arrested Dave and Ted.	Yes, govt. action
Standing	**D must have a reasonable expectation of privacy in the property or place being searched or seized.**	**Here, Dave has a reasonable expectation of privacy in his car since most individuals do not allow random people to access their car, especially compartments and storage not in plain view.**	**Dave has standing**
Search warrant	Generally, police need a **search warrant based on probable cause**, in which it is reasonable that places to be searched are connected with criminal activities and items will be found in places to be searched.	**Here, Polly did not have a search warrant at the time she searched Dave's car and found the cocaine. Thus, Dave will argue that the search was invalid and violated his 4th Amend. rights.**	**No warrant**
Routine auto stop	The police may **randomly stop automobiles if there is a reasonable suspicion of wrongdoing** based on an objective standard.	**Here, Polly stopped Dave's car because it was speeding and weaving in and out of traffic in violation of the Vehicle Code, thus giving her a reasonable suspicion that he was violating the traffic laws.**	**Routine stop permissible**
Exception to warrantless search	**If police conduct a search or seizure without a valid search warrant, there must be an applicable exception.**	**Since Polly did not have a search warrant to search Dave's car, Dave can argue that evidence of the cocaine should be suppressed.**	**Need warrant exception**
SILA	When police are making a lawful arrest, they may search area within the arrestee's immediate control.	Here, the police made a lawful arrest, but not until after Polly searched Dave's car and found the cocaine. Thus, this exception will not be applicable.	No SILA exception

Continued >

Issue	Rule	Fact Application	Conclusion
Plain view	Police may make warrantless search if they see an object or contraband when they are legitimately on premises or have a right to be in position to have view.	Here, the bag was not in plain view because it was under the passenger seat. In fact, Polly didn't even know what Ted slipped under the seat and had to open his door to access it, proving that it was not in plain view. Further, the cocaine was inside the paper bag and not visible even under the seat.	No plain view exception
Automobile	**If police have probable cause to believe that a vehicle contains contraband, they may search whole automobile and any container therein.** If driver is arrested, police may impound car, transport it to the station house, and search it there without a warrant.	Here, Dave will argue that Polly did not have probable cause to believe that the car contained contraband because he was speeding and weaving in and out of traffic, which is a routine traffic violation that is not typically associated with cocaine or contraband. However, Polly can argue that when drivers speed and weave in and out of traffic, they could be drunk or under the influence of drugs, and, coupled with the fact that she saw Ted slip something under the seat, it gave her probable cause or reasonable belief that there was contraband under the seat, which could have been the reason for the unsafe driving. **Since Polly had no idea what Ted was placing under the seat and Ted was not the one who was driving, it is unlikely that her belief that there was contraband was reasonable.** Further, she then saw a paper lunch bag, which would not likely be associated with alcohol or contraband as it relates to Dave violating the traffic laws.	**No automobile exception**
Consent	Police may make warrantless search if person whose premises, items, or person will be searched voluntarily consented considering the totality of the circumstances.	Here, Dave did not consent to his car being searched. Instead, Polly just opened the passenger door where Ted was seated, looked under the seat, saw the bag, pulled it out, and opened it without permission from either Dave or Ted.	No consent exception

Continued >

Issue	Rule	Fact Application	Conclusion
Exigent circumstances	The police may conduct a search or seizure without a warrant if they have probable cause and it is necessary to • Prevent imminent destruction of evidence • Prevent imminent injury to persons, or • Search for a felony suspect in hot pursuit that the police reasonably believe has entered particular premises.	Here, Polly would not have probable cause to believe that Dave or Ted would destroy the evidence because she didn't even know it existed until after she searched. Nor would she reasonably suspect, from a routine traffic stop, that it existed to begin with. Further, there is no danger to persons or a hot pursuit in progress.	No exigent circum-stances exception
Stop and frisk	**Police officer may stop and frisk a person if police have reasonable suspicion of criminal activity or involvement that is supported by articulable facts.** **Brief detention may include pat-down search for weapons if the suspect appears dangerous and armed, but may not search for contraband or evidence.**	**Here, although the stop may be reasonable due to the speeding, the search was not reasonable as there was no reasonable suspicion of criminal activity other than traffic violations.** **Also, the detention gave Polly no reason to assume Dave and Ted were armed or dangerous as they did not act inappropriately, but rather provided her with the documents she requested, such as Dave's license and registration.**	**No stop and frisk exception**
Exclusionary rule	Exclusionary rule is a judge-made rule that **prohibits prosecution from introducing evidence** obtained in violation of a D's 4th, 5th, or 6th Amend. rights. **D must have standing** to assert exclusionary rule, such that evidence obtained must have been in violation of D's own constitutional rights and not any third person's.	**Here, since the cocaine was obtained in violation of Dave's 4th Amend. rights, it will be excluded.** **Also, Dave has standing as it was his car that was searched and the evidence is now being used against him.**	**Cocaine suppressed**

Continued >

Issue	Rule	Fact Application	Conclusion
Call #2: Suppress Ted's Statement/Separate Trial			
6th Amend.: right to confront	**Prosecution may not admit testimonial statements by a third person against D unless the declarant is available for cross-examination either at the time statement was made or during trial.** Statements are testimonial when circumstances indicate no ongoing emergency, and that primary purpose of interrogation is to establish or prove past events potentially relevant to later criminal prosecution. **Where two Ds are jointly tried and one of them confesses, right to confront adverse witnesses prohibits use of that statement unless the statement can be redacted or the co-D who made the statement takes the stand and subjects himself to cross-examination.**	**Here, Ted's statement that he didn't know what was in the bag or how it got into the car and that it just appeared there after lunch when they left the windows down due to the heat is testimonial because it was made in response to questions by police at the police station, which can prove events relevant to the charge of cocaine, which was found in the bag.** **The problem here is that if Ted doesn't take the stand to testify, which he may not since he is a co-defendant, Dave has the right to cross-examine him about the statement, which is not possible if Ted doesn't testify.** However, arguably, the statement is not adverse to Dave since it doesn't implicate Dave. Rather, it indicates that neither Dave nor Ted had anything to do with the cocaine and that it was likely placed in the car when they were at lunch since there was easy access and the windows were rolled down. On the other hand, it can be inferred that if Ted had nothing to do with the paper bag in Dave's car, then the jury may find that it must have been Dave. Since this interpretation is possible, the court might suppress Ted's statement.	Court is likely to suppress Ted's statement
Severance	Where co-Ds are charged for the same crime, courts prefer joint trials for judicial economy, but will **sever the co-Ds** if a joint trial would result in substantial prejudice to one of the Ds.	As discussed above, Ted's statement doesn't directly implicate Dave and in fact, it tends to indicate that someone else is to blame for the bag being put in the car, which would not result in any prejudice to Dave, especially not substantial prejudice. **If Ted and Dave implicate each other, then a new trial would be necessary as the testimony from each would violate the 6th Amend. rights of the other, and each would have the right to cross-examine the other.**	Court will not likely sever the co-defendants based on Ted's statement

Continued >

Issue	Rule	Fact Application	Conclusion
Call #3: Motion to Discharge/Substitute Attorney			
Right to effective counsel	Suspect against whom formal criminal proceedings have been commenced has **right to effective counsel** at any post-charge line-up or show-up.	**Here, Dave retained an attorney, rather than having one appointed to him, but this does not mean that he cannot replace this attorney with another attorney. The problem here is that he has become dissatisfied with his attorney the week before trial for unknown reasons.** **Although he has the right to an attorney of his choice, the court will need to consider whether it is fair to substitute new counsel at this stage of the proceedings.**	**Yes, right to effective counsel**
Right to substitute attorney	A court will allow D to **substitute attorney if interests of justice** so require, taking into account any conflicts, the interests of D and the court, and timeliness of request.	**Here, it is unclear why Dave has become dissatisfied with his attorney so it is difficult to determine whether the court would grant his motion. However, since trial is scheduled to begin in one week** and there doesn't appear to be any major conflict or concern from the facts, **it is unlikely that the court would substitute the attorney as this would affect and delay Ted as well as Dave and would not be efficient for the courts since the court already scheduled the trial for those dates.**	**Unlikely court will grant motion for new attorney**

Crimes Question 2 Sample Answer

July 2009, Question 6

1. Motion to Suppress Cocaine

Fourth Amendment

The Fourth (4th) Amendment protects individuals against unreasonable searches and seizures of property and arrest. Here, there was a search Dave's car and thus a 4th Amendment analysis is warranted.

Government Action

There must be government action in order for the 4th Amendment search and seizure protections to apply. Here, Polly, a uniformed police officer, who works for the government, searched Dave's car, found the cocaine, and arrested Dave and Ted. Therefore, there is government action.

Standing

The defendant must have a reasonable expectation of privacy in the property or place being searched or seized.

Here, Dave has a reasonable expectation of privacy in his car since most individuals do not allow random people to access their car, especially compartments and storage areas not in plain view. Therefore, Dave has standing to asset a violation under the 4th Amendment.

Search Warrant

Generally, the police need a search warrant based on probable cause, in which it is reasonable that the items to be searched are connected with criminal activities and the items will be found in the place to be searched.

Here, Polly did not have a search warrant at the time she searched Dave's car and found the cocaine. Thus, Dave will argue that the search was invalid and violated his 4th Amendment rights.

Routine Automobile Stop

The police may randomly stop automobiles if there is a reasonable suspicion or wrongdoing based on an objective standard.

Here, Polly stopped Dave's car because it was speeding and weaving in and out of traffic in violation of the Vehicle Code, thus giving her a reasonable suspicion that is was violating the traffic laws. Thus, the initial automobile stop was permissible.

Exceptions to a Warrantless Search

If the police conduct a search or seizure without a valid search warrant, there must be an applicable exception. Since Polly did not have a search warrant to search Dave's car, Dave can argue that evidence of the cocaine should be suppressed, barring any valid exceptions.

SILA

When the police are making a lawful arrest, they may search the area within the arrestee's immediate control. Here, the police made a lawful arrest, but not until after Polly searched Dave's car and found the cocaine. Thus, this exception will not be applicable.

Plain View

The police may make a warrantless search if they see an object or contraband when they are legitimately on the premises or have a right to be in the position to have the view.

Here, the bag was not in plain view because it was under the passenger seat. In fact, Polly didn't even know what Ted slipped under the seat and had to open his door to access it, proving that it was not in plain view. Further, the cocaine was inside the paper lunch bag and not visible even under the seat. Therefore, this exception will not apply.

Automobile

If the police have probable cause to believe that a vehicle contains contraband, they may search the whole automobile and any container therein. Further, if the driver is arrested, the police may impound the car, transport it to the station house, and search it there without a warrant.

Here, Dave will argue that Polly did not have probable cause to believe that the car contained contraband because he was speeding and weaving in and out of traffic, which is a routine traffic violation that is not typically associated with cocaine or contraband.

However, Polly can argue that when drivers speed and weave in and out of traffic, they could be drunk or under the influence of drugs. This possibility, coupled with the fact that she saw Ted slip something under the seat, gave her probable cause or a reasonable belief that there was contraband under the seat, which could have been the reason for the unsafe driving.

Overall, since Polly had no idea what Ted was placing under the seat and Ted was not the one who was driving, it is unlikely that her belief that there was contraband was reasonable. Further, she then saw a paper lunch bag, which would not likely be associated with alcohol or contraband as it relates to Dave violating the traffic laws. Therefore, this exception will not be applicable.

Consent

The police may make a warrantless search if the person whose premises, items, or person will be searched voluntarily consented considering the totality of the circumstances. Here, Dave did not consent to his car being searched. Instead, Polly just opened the passenger door where Ted was seated, looked under the seat, saw the bag, pulled it out, and opened it without permission from either Dave or Ted. Thus, there was no consent.

Exigent Circumstances

The police may conduct a search or seizure without a warrant if they have probable cause and the search is necessary to prevent imminent destruction of evidence, imminent injury to persons, or if they are pursuing a felony suspect and reasonably believe the suspect in hot pursuit has entered particular premises.

Here, Polly would not have probable cause to believe that Dave or Ted would destroy the evidence because she didn't even know it existed until after she searched under the seat. Nor would she reasonably suspect that it existed to begin with from a routine traffic stop since they were not being chased for drugs, but rather for typical traffic violations. Further, there is no danger to persons or a hot pursuit in progress.

Thus, there are no exigent circumstances that would allow a warrantless search.

Stop and Frisk

A police officer may stop and frisk a person if the police have a reasonable suspicion of criminal activity or involvement that is supported by articulable facts. The brief detention may include a pat-down search for weapons if the suspect appears dangerous and armed, but may not search for contraband or evidence.

Here, although the stop may be reasonable due to the speeding and weaving in and out of traffic, the search was not reasonable as there was no reasonable suspicion of criminal activity other than typical traffic violations.

Also, the detention gave Polly no reason to assume Dave and Ted were armed or dangerous since they did not act inappropriately, but rather provided her with the documents she requested, such as Dave's license and registration. Thus, the stop and frisk exception is inapplicable.

Exclusionary Rule

The exclusionary rule is a judge-made rule that prohibits the prosecution from introducing evidence obtained in violation of a defendant's 4th, 5th, or 6th Amendment rights. The defendant must have standing to assert the exclusionary rule such that the evidence obtained must have been in violation of the defendant's own constitutional rights and not any third persons.

Here, since the cocaine was obtained in violation of Dave's 4th Amendment rights, it will be excluded. Also, Dave has standing since it was his car that was searched and the evidence is now being used against him.

Overall, Dave will be successful in his motion and the cocaine will be suppressed as it was seized in violation of his 4th Amendment rights.

2. Suppress Ted's Statement or Separate Trial

Sixth Amendment Right to Confront Adverse Witnesses

The prosecution may not admit testimonial statements by a third person against the defendant unless the declarant is available for cross-examination either at the time the statement was made or during trial. Statements are testimonial when the circumstances indicate that there is no ongoing emergency, and that the primary purpose of the interrogation is to establish or prove past events potentially relevant to later criminal prosecution.

Here, Ted's statement that he didn't know what was in the bag or how it got into the car and that it just appeared there after lunch when they left the windows down due to the heat is testimonial because it was made in response to questions by police at the police station which can prove events relevant to the charge of cocaine, which was found in the bag.

Thus, Ted's statement invokes the Sixth (6th) Amendment.

Co-defendants

Where two defendants are jointly tried and one of them confesses, the right to confront adverse witnesses prohibits use of that statement unless the statement can be redacted or the co-defendant who made the statement takes the stand and subjects himself to cross-examination.

The problem here is that if Ted doesn't take the stand to testify, which is his right as a co-defendant, Dave will not be able to cross-examine him regarding his statement.

However, arguably, the statement is not adverse to Dave since it doesn't implicate Dave. Rather, it indicates that neither Dave nor Ted had anything to do with the cocaine and that it was likely placed in the car when they were at lunch since there was easy access and the windows were rolled down.

Although Dave will likely argue that a reasonable juror could infer from Ted's statement that if Ted had nothing to do with the paper bag in Dave's car, then it must have been Dave's cocaine since the jurors may not believe that some random person placed the bag under the seat when the windows were rolled down. Since this interpretation is possible and Dave would not have a chance to cross-examine Ted, the court will likely suppress Ted's statement.

Severance

Where co-defendants are charged for the same crime, courts prefer joint trials for judicial economy but will sever the co-defendants if a joint trial would result in substantial prejudice to one of the defendants.

As discussed above, Ted's statement doesn't directly implicate Dave and in fact, it tends to indicate that someone else is to blame for the bag being put in the car, which would not result in any prejudice to Dave, especially not substantial prejudice.

However, if Ted and Dave implicate each other, separate trials could be necessary as the testimony from each would violate their 6th Amendment rights to confront each other.

Overall, the court will not likely sever the co-defendants based on Ted's statement, but rather just suppress it.

3. Motion to Discharge/Substitute Attorney

Right to Effective Counsel

A suspect against whom formal criminal proceedings have been commenced has a right to effective counsel at any post-charge line-up or show-up.

Here, Dave retained an attorney, rather than have one appointed to him, but this does not mean that he cannot replace this attorney with another attorney. The problem here is that he has become dissatisfied with his attorney the week before trial for unknown reasons.

Although he has the right to an attorney of his choice, the court will need to consider whether it is fair to substitute new counsel at this stage of the proceedings.

Right to Substitute Attorney

A court will allow the defendant to substitute their attorney if the interests of justice so require, taking into account any conflicts, the interests of the defendant and the court, and the timeliness of the request.

Here, it is unclear why Dave has become dissatisfied with his attorney, so it is difficult to determine if the court would grant his motion. However, since trial is scheduled to begin in one week and there doesn't appear to be any major conflict or concern from the facts, it is unlikely that the court would substitute the attorney as this would affect and delay Ted as well as Dave and would not be efficient for the courts since the court already scheduled the trial for those dates.

Thus, given the timing of the request, it is unlikely that the court will grant Dave's motion for a new attorney, barring any serious conflict or problem.

Crimes Question 3

February 2003, Question 3

Don was a passenger in Vic's car. While driving in a desolate mountain area, Vic stopped and offered Don an hallucinogenic drug. Don refused, but Vic said if Don wished to stay in the car, he would have to join Vic in using the drug. Fearing that he would be abandoned in freezing temperatures many miles from the nearest town, Don ingested the drug.

While under the influence of the drug, Don killed Vic, left the body beside the road, and drove Vic's car to town. Later he was arrested by police officers who had discovered Vic's body. Don has no recall of the events between the time he ingested the drug and his arrest.

After Don was arraigned on a charge of first degree murder, the police learned that Wes had witnessed the killing. Aware that Don had been arraigned and was scheduled for a preliminary hearing at the courthouse on that day, police officers took Wes to the courthouse for the express purpose of having him attempt to identify the killer from photographs of several suspects. As Wes walked into the courthouse with one of the officers, he encountered Don and his lawyer. Without any request by the officer, Wes told the officer he recognized Don as the killer. Don's attorney was advised of Wes's statement to the officer, of the circumstances in which it was made, and of the officer's expected testimony at trial that Wes had identified Don in this manner.

Don moved to exclude evidence of the courthouse identification by Wes on grounds that the identification procedure violated Don's federal constitutional rights to counsel and due process of law and that the officer's testimony about the identification would be inadmissible hearsay. The court denied the motion.

At trial, Don testified about the events preceding Vic's death and his total lack of recall of the killing.

1. Did the court err in denying Don's motion? Discuss.
2. If the jury believes Don's testimony, can it properly convict Don of:
   (a) First degree murder? Discuss.
   (b) Second degree murder? Discuss.

Crimes Question 3 Assessment

February 2003, Question 3

This is a typical criminal procedure/criminal law crossover question in that it tests the right to counsel within the context of a murder scenario. This type of fact pattern is very common. In fact, 60% of all murder questions arise in conjunction with a Sixth Amendment issue. In addition, many times there are suspect identifications or confessions involved in murder fact patterns that raise issues under the Fifth and/or Sixth Amendments.

This question is rather straightforward in that you did not need to issue spot or write out your issues checklist. The facts clearly state on what grounds Don moved to exclude the evidence in the first call. If you missed any of these issues, it is likely because you did not pay close attention to the facts and you need to slow down and underline or highlight the facts as you read them. Further, whenever a call asks you about whether the court erred in denying a motion (in any essay question), you should always refer back to the facts to see what the motion was and on what grounds the motion was denied. This will ensure that you do not miss any issues.

As to the second call of the question, it clearly requires a discussion of murder, and you should approach this issue just as you did in previous questions: starting out by defining murder and then identifying the four ways to establish malice. After completing that analysis, you should then analyze the requirements for first- and second-degree murder. It is crucial to always remember to analyze any applicable defenses. If you tend to forget to analyze defenses, then you should alter your checklist to include a listing of all possible defenses that can apply to each issue, and quickly write them out on your scratch paper when you get an essay that deals with a particular issue. This will help you get in the habit of going through all of the defenses that can apply to all issues and will help you to avoid missing them. This is especially important because in a question like this, there are specific facts that lead to a discussion of the defenses, which can affect the entire outcome of whether Don is guilty of murder or not.

It is also worth noting that on questions like this it is not important which conclusion you come to, but rather that you clearly state and adequately support your conclusion. Whenever you have an issue that can logically be argued two ways, you will find that the state-released passing answers often come to different conclusions on that issue. The key is that both passing answers argue both sides of the issue and then explain why the author thought one side was the stronger argument.

Finally, to determine whether you spotted and analyzed the major issues and properly allocated your time to the various issues, make note of the areas highlighted in **bold** on the corresponding grid. The bold areas highlight the issues, analysis, and conclusions that are likely **required** to receive a passing score on this question.

Issue	Rule	Fact Application	Conclusion
Call #1			
6th Amend.: right to counsel	**A suspect against whom formal criminal proceedings have been commenced has a right to effective counsel at any post-charge line-up or show-up, including** sentencing (not needed for photo identifications, or when police take physical evidence such as handwriting or fingerprints).	**Formal charges have been filed since Don was attending his preliminary hearing, so Don had a right to counsel.** A line-up is a critical stage in the proceeding, though a photo-identification procedure is not critical. Since the police were "aware" that Don was being arraigned on the day they brought Wes, the witness, by the courthouse, it seems suspicious and may indicate bad faith. But if it is true that the police went to the courthouse for the "express purpose" of conducting the photo line-up it would demonstrate good faith, and they did not prompt Wes to make the identification; rather, he volunteered it upon seeing Don. **Don was accompanied by his lawyer, so he was not denied the right to counsel,** though the lack of notice and the element of surprise may have precluded preparation by the counsel. The court likely did not err.	Can conclude either way
Due process	**D's due process rights are violated if identification of the defendant based on totality of the circumstances is unnecessarily suggestive and so conducive to mistaken identification that it is unfair to D.**	**Wes was brought by the courthouse to review a photo line-up on the day Don was scheduled to have his preliminary hearing. Don's presence with his attorney may be unduly prejudicial and impermissibly suggestive that he is a criminal**. Further, **there were no procedural safeguards, such as those imposed during a normal line-up where there are other choices.** However, Wes made the identification spontaneously so there was nothing suggestive about it since Wes didn't know Don would be present. The chance of error in a spontaneous identification is not likely. Also, in a courthouse there are likely to be several defendants and people in the vicinity, so Wes's identification of Don was not likely impermissibly suggestive in violation of due process.	Can conclude either way

Continued >

Issue	Rule	Fact Application	Conclusion
Hearsay	**Out-of-court statement offered for the truth of matter asserted is inadmissible unless an exception applies.**	The officer's testimony concerns an **out-of-court statement made in the courthouse hallway by Wes and is offered for its truth, that Wes identified Don as the killer.** It will be excluded unless an exception applies.	**Hearsay**
Prior statement of identification	Prior identification of a person made after perceiving him is substantively admissible if declarant testifies at trial.	Assuming Wes is available to testify, the prior identification is admissible. **[It is essential to identify some applicable hearsay exception,** such as present sense impression or party admission, even though no other exceptions are effective. Missing the prior statement of identification is not fatal.]	Could conclude either way
Call #2			
Murder	**Murder is the unlawful killing of a human being with malice aforethought.** **Malice can be proven by intent to kill, intent to commit grievous bodily injury, reckless indifference to the value of human life, or intent to commit a dangerous felony.**	There are no facts here regarding the means and manner of Vic's death, though Don killed Vic and left his body beside the road. Since **Don was under the influence** of a hallucinogenic drug, **he has no recollection of events from the time he took the drug until the time of his arrest.** Don may have been so intoxicated he was unable to form the specific intent to kill, commit grievous bodily injury, or have reckless disregard for the value to human life.	D not liable for common law murder
First-degree murder	**Premeditated and deliberate murder** (need specific intent to kill); or felony murder if one of the enumerated felonies (arson, robbery, burglary, rape, mayhem, kidnapping)	As noted above, **Don was so intoxicated it is possible he was unable to premeditate or deliberate as required of first-degree murder.**	**Not guilty of 1st degree murder**

Continued >

Issue	Rule	Fact Application	Conclusion
Second-degree murder	**All other murders**—not determined, as above, to be 1st degree, voluntary manslaughter, or involuntary manslaughter—**are 2nd-degree murder.**	Don did kill Vic so there was a homicide here. If the killing wasn't justified, and/or the intoxication defense is ineffective (see below) Don will be guilty of second-degree murder.	Guilty, unless a defense is effective
Involuntary intoxication	Involuntary intoxication may provide a criminal defense where intoxicating substance is ingested unknowingly, or under duress, and may be treated as an illness.	Don refused to ingest the drug, which indicates **he may have had awareness of the type of drug it was**. However, **Don will argue he was forced to take the drug under duress** because Vic **threatened to kick him out of the car in a desolate mountain area, in freezing temperatures, many miles from the nearest town.** This may have put Don in reasonable fear for his life with no reasonable choice but to take the drug. Involuntary intoxication may provide a defense to murder since Don was **too intoxicated to have an awareness of what was going on, or form the requisite intent for any type of murder, and was not responsible for his state of intoxication.** If treated as an illness—like insanity—Don could show that at the time he didn't know his actions were wrong as he didn't know what he was doing, that he couldn't control his actions or appreciate them, or that his conduct was the product of being on the drug, all of which would negate the specific intent to kill.	Involuntary intoxication is likely an effective defense
Voluntary intoxication	**Voluntary intoxication is not a defense to murder, however it may provide a defense to the ability to form specific intent.**	If Don is considered to be voluntarily intoxicated, Don may still have a defense. **Since he was virtually unconscious, Don may not have been able to form specific intent.** Should malice or premeditation be established, voluntary intoxication might be a mitigating factor, lessening the crime to voluntary manslaughter.	Don may have reduced culpability

Crimes Question 4

July 1993, Question 2

Police officers believed that Deft had assaulted Bart because Bart failed to pay Deft for cocaine Deft sold to Bart. The officers obtained a valid warrant for the arrest of Deft on an assault charge. They went to Deft's apartment and arrested Deft at the front door when he responded to their knock. The officers then walked through the apartment and, in a rear bedroom, saw drug paraphernalia which they left in place.

A police officer advised Deft of his *Miranda* rights. Deft immediately stated: "I do not want to talk to you." Deft was booked and placed in a cell with Snitch, an inmate who was known by the jailers to be an informant. Snitch asked Deft why he had been arrested and engaged Deft in a conversation about drug sales during which Deft made statements incriminating himself concerning drug trafficking. Snitch promptly related Deft's statements to jail personnel.

Police then obtained a warrant authorizing a search of Deft's apartment for cocaine and drug paraphernalia. The affidavit in support of the warrant recited that Deft had sold cocaine to Bart. The affidavit also recited that a police officer had seen drug paraphernalia in Deft's apartment. The affidavit did not disclose Deft's statements to Snitch or the circumstances in which police observed the drug paraphernalia. Officers who executed the search warrant seized the drug paraphernalia and cocaine which they also found in the apartment.

Deft has been charged with possession of cocaine and drug paraphernalia under applicable state laws.

1. Deft has moved to exclude from evidence his statements to Snitch. Deft claims his statements were involuntary, were elicited after he invoked his *Miranda* rights, and were obtained in the absence of counsel. He argues that admission of the evidence would violate his rights under the Fifth and Sixth Amendments to the United States Constitution. What arguments should the prosecutor make in opposition to the motion, and how should the court rule on the motion? Discuss.
2. Deft has also moved to exclude any testimony regarding the police officers' initial observations of drug paraphernalia in Deft's home and to exclude the items seized in the search made pursuant to the search warrant. What arguments based on the Fourth Amendment to the United States Constitution should Deft make in opposition to the motion, and how should the court rule on the motion? Discuss.

Crimes Question 4 Assessment

July 1993, Question 2

You will notice that the first call of this question is very specific. It specifically tells you that Deft is challenging the admissibility of evidence because of violations of the Fifth and Sixth Amendments and that his statements were involuntary. Each issue identified must be addressed. There are two areas that students struggle with on this call. First, the question tests some of the smaller, more nuanced part of the rules—such as that Snitch does not work for the government, and that Deft was only arrested as opposed to charged. Since some of the criminal procedure rules are so nuanced, it requires a careful reading of the facts to ensure adequate and proper analysis. Second, the call of the question focuses on what arguments the prosecutor should make. To fully understand what arguments the prosecutor should make, you need to analyze both sides of each issue and to properly identify what arguments and counterarguments the prosecutor will make. It is important to recognize what is being asked in the call of the questions and phrase your answer accordingly to solve the problem posed.

The second call tells you that Deft is challenging the admissibility of evidence based on violations of the Fourth Amendment right against unlawful search and seizure. This call does require you to issue spot and identify which rules are at issue pursuant to the Fourth Amendment. To properly issue spot this question, go through the same approach you did in previous questions and use a mini-checklist of all exceptions to ensure you don't miss spotting the issues. The nuance rule tested on call two involves the exceptions to the good faith rule, which itself is an exception to the exclusionary rule. These particular exceptions are rarely tested on the exam, but you still need to know them in the event that they do arise, as they did in this question. Thus, it is best to memorize all rules rather than just the major ones that are always tested.

Further, both calls ask you how the court should rule, so be sure to frame your answer accordingly. Answer the specific questions being asked by providing a conclusion of how the court should rule on each issue raised, and of course, include why you reached the conclusion you did.

Finally, make note of the areas highlighted in **bold** on the corresponding grid. The bold areas highlight the issues, analysis, and conclusions that are likely **required** to receive a passing score on this question.

Issue	Rule	Fact Application	Conclusion
Call #1: Statements to Snitch			
14th Amend.: **voluntariness**	**Confessions must be made voluntarily without police coercion, in light of the totality of the circumstances,** with the court considering the susceptibility of the suspect and the environment and methods used.	**The prosecution will argue that there is no evidence of any official involvement or coercion in obtaining Deft's statement** because Snitch seemed to be acting under his own initiative. Snitch merely began a conversation with Deft, and Deft proceeded to tell Snitch about his drug trafficking activities. Deft would argue that the police purposely placed a known informant in his cell, which constitutes police action. However, as the prosecution will argue, this is not enough government action to make Snitch a government agent, especially because Snitch does not work for the government.	**Deft's statement was made voluntarily—evidence is allowed**
5th Amend.: *Miranda*	**A person subject to a custodial interrogation is entitled to receive the warnings required under *Miranda*.** Custodial interrogation does not occur when a suspect speaks to an undercover agent or government informant and suspect does not know they are speaking to a law enforcement officer, even if the suspect is in jail.	**Deft was arrested and in custody and received the required *Miranda* warnings. Once a defendant invokes his *Miranda* rights, they must be honored. Once Deft invoked his rights, the police were correct to stop the interrogation.** **Though Snitch was known to be an informant, the prosecution will successfully argue that he was not a police agent and thus there was no custodial interrogation.**	**No violation of 5th Amend.—evidence is allowed**
6th Amend.: right to counsel	**A criminal defendant has the right to counsel after formal criminal proceedings have been filed at any line-up or show-up.**	**The prosecution will show that since Deft had only been arrested and booked, and formal criminal proceedings had not yet been filed, the 6th Amend. is inapplicable.** Further, the 6th Amend. right to counsel only applies to the charged offense—which would be assault here—not to any crimes like the drug crimes that hadn't been charged.	**No violation of 6th Amend.—evidence is allowed**

Continued >

Issue	Rule	Fact Application	Conclusion
Call #2: Officers' Observations			
4th Amend.	**4th Amend. protects against unreasonable search and seizure where there is government action, and property or place searched or seized is one in which D has reasonable expectation of privacy.**	There is government action here since the observations were made by police officers. Further, **Deft will assert that he has a reasonable expectation within his home,** and here, **the police made their observation in Deft's apartment.** There is an expectation that there will not be a government intrusion but officers' observation was of a back bedroom of Deft's home, with Deft arrested at the front door, **so the search here will not be valid unless there is a valid warrant or an exception applies.**	**Warrant or exception required**
Warrantless search	Warrantless search is only allowed if it falls under an exception to warrant requirement.	Since there was no warrant for the search an exception must apply (see below).	Need exception
Search incident to lawful arrest (SILA)	**When police are making lawful arrest, they may search area within the arrestee's immediate control.** **Police may also conduct protective sweep of all or part of premises if they have a reasonable belief**, based on specific and articulable facts, **that other dangerous individuals may be present.**	The police had a valid arrest warrant for Deft on assault charges. The police are permitted to search the area within Deft's immediate control, in the interest of officer safety, for weapons or evidence he may destroy. **However, Deft will argue that he was arrested at the front door of his apartment on an assault charge, which does not involve co-conspirators,** not a drug charge. **It does not appear that the officers believed an accomplice was present on the scene**, so when the officers walked through the entire apartment and observed drug paraphernalia in a back bedroom **they exceeded the scope of a permissible search.** Absent a belief that other dangerous individuals were present, the officers were not entitled to view the contraband in the back bedroom and Deft prevails.	Could conclude either way

Continued >

Issue	Rule	Fact Application	Conclusion
Plain view	**Police may make a warrantless search if they see an object or contraband when they are legitimately on premises or have a right to be in the position to have the view.**	**If the officers entered Deft's apartment to conduct a legitimate protective sweep, their observations of the drug paraphernalia in the back bedroom are admissible.** In addition, they secured the premises and obtained a warrant before seizing the evidence. However, Deft will argue that the officers were not lawfully engaged in a protective sweep because they were not legitimately entitled to be in the location from which the view was obtained, and their observations will not be admissible because they arrested him at the front door for an assault charge, not for a drug-related charge.	Could conclude either way
Call #3: Search Warrant Evidence			
4th Amend.	See rule above	The police are government actors and there is a reasonable expectation of privacy in one's home. Here, however, the police have a warrant. (See below.)	
Validity of warrant	**Valid warrant must be** issued by neutral magistrate, **based on probable cause,** describe the place to be searched, and items to be seized.	Here, the affidavit recited Bart's claim that Deft sold cocaine to Bart, and that drug paraphernalia were observed in Deft's home. **This is conclusory information and inadequate as it does not identify the basis and reliability of the information.** Deft will argue that Bart is unreliable and the warrant omitted material information, such as that the observation of the paraphernalia was the result of an improper search and the suspect circumstances of Deft's statement to Snitch (though these statements will be admissible). Under a totality of circumstances test, there was probably insufficient probable cause.	Can conclude either way

Continued >

Issue	Rule	Fact Application	Conclusion
Exclusionary rule	Exclusionary rule is a judge-made rule that **prohibits prosecution from introducing evidence** obtained in violation of a defendant's 4th, 5th, or 6th Amend. rights.	Here, the seizure of the evidence was in violation of Deft's 4th Amend. rights, so it will be excluded under the exclusionary rule unless an exception applies.	Evidence can be excluded unless exception applies
Good faith exception	**Exclusionary rule does not bar evidence that was obtained by officers acting in reasonable reliance on a search warrant issued by a proper magistrate but ultimately found to be unsupported by probable cause** This **exception does not apply where** • affiant knew the information he was providing in the affidavit was false or would have known except for his reckless disregard, OR • when where the magistrate relied on an **affidavit that was so lacking in indicia of probable cause** as to render his belief in the affidavit unreasonable	Assuming the warrant was invalid, the evidence may still be allowed under the good faith exception to the warrant requirement. There is no evidence the police acted in anything other than good faith in executing the warrant. **However, the warrant may be found to be so lacking in the basis for probable clause that the good faith exception won't apply because of the manner in which it was obtained, in that the officers omitted material facts about the circumstances in which the evidence was initially viewed.** Further, if the affiant was the same officers that made the illegal search to begin with and then recklessly disregarded the truth on the affidavit, then it is likely that the good faith exception would not apply.	Can conclude either way

Crimes Question 5

July 1999, Question 1

Al, Bob, and Charlie planned to bring 50 cases of whiskey ashore from a ship anchored in the harbor near their town and sell it to a local bar owner. They believed the whiskey had been produced abroad and was subject to a federal import duty. They also knew that smuggling items into this country without paying duty required by the Tariff Act is a crime. In fact, however, the whiskey in this shipment had been produced in the United States.

The three met at Al's house on Monday and agreed to bring the whiskey ashore by rowboat on Friday night. On Wednesday, however, Bob called Al to say that he and his wife were going to visit relatives that weekend and Bob would not be able to help bring the whiskey ashore. Al said that was all right, that he and Charlie could handle the boat and the whiskey, but that Bob would naturally be cut out of the profits on this job.

When Charlie learned from Al that there would be just the two of them he became apprehensive, but he was afraid of what Al might do to him if he tried to back out. Therefore, on Thursday, Charlie informed the police of Al's plan and did not show up on Friday night. Al was arrested on Friday night as he came ashore, alone, with the whiskey and was loading it into a truck he had stolen from a nearby Coast Guard parking lot.

Al, Bob, and Charlie have been charged with theft of the truck and conspiracy to import dutiable goods without payment of duty.

Al has also been charged with attempt to import dutiable goods without payment of duty. He has told Len, his attorney, that he plans to testify that he knew all along that the whiskey was produced in the United States.

Based on the above facts:

1. Should Al, Bob, or Charlie be convicted of:
   a. Conspiracy to violate the Tariff Act? Discuss.
   b. Theft of the truck? Discuss.
2. Should Al be convicted of attempt to import dutiable goods without payment of duty in violation of the Tariff Act? Discuss.
3. If Al insists on testifying that he knew the whiskey was produced in the United States, what, if anything, should Len do? Discuss.

Crimes Question 5 Assessment

July 1999, Question 1

This question is rather difficult because it is a crossover question with professional responsibility and it tests some of the more difficult defenses involved in criminal law. To do well, you have to have a good understanding of how the defenses apply to facts, rather than just having the rules memorized.

The simple part of this question is that the criminal law issues are specifically asked about in the calls, so issue spotting the crimes is not necessary. The question does not specifically tell you to discuss defenses or which defenses are applicable, but discussing defenses is essential to properly analyzing the facts and answering the questions posed. Thus, you should write out a mini-checklist of all defenses applicable to crimes questions to ensure you do not overlook any. If you tend to forget to discuss defenses, you should always write them out as part of the checklist with every question. Also, remember that the bar examiners expect you to address defenses regardless of whether they specifically ask about them. The reason for this is because you cannot be convicted of a crime if there is a valid defense. Thus, to answer the calls of the question posed here, you must consider defenses.

As to the professional responsibility crossover question, this call is rather limited since Len the lawyer does not come into the fact pattern until the last sentence, and then, only with regard to Al's plan to testify. Thus, your inquiry here is limited to that one fact and what an attorney should do when a defendant wants to testify. So, for this call, you don't need to write out your entire professional responsibility issues checklist to answer the question. However, you do need to know the rules that apply when a defendant plans to take the stand and possibly lie under oath.

A final point on questions like these: Make sure you apportion your time appropriately. Often, students forget to allocate their time after they are done organizing their answer, but before writing out the answer. Here, as you will see by looking at your organized answer, all three calls are not likely given the same weight in scoring. There are many more issues to discuss in call one than in the other two calls. This is because there are three parties to consider and two different crimes, as well as any applicable defenses for each. Compare that with call two, which has only one party and one crime, and call three, which discusses just one fact and two issues. Thus, the amount of time you spend on call one should be significantly longer than the time spent on call two or three.

Finally, be sure to make note of the areas highlighted in **bold** on the corresponding grid. The bold areas highlight the issues, analysis, and conclusions that are likely **required** to receive a passing score on this question.

Issue	Rule	Fact Application	Conclusion
Call #1.a: A, B, C Conspiracy			
Conspiracy	**Conspiracy is an agreement between two or more persons who intend to commit an unlawful act** or a lawful act by unlawful means. The agreement can be implied or inferred and does not require that all persons commit the actual act. **At common law, conspiracy occurred the moment the agreement was made, but the majority of jurisdictions now require an overt act,** which can be as little as preparation, to form the conspiracy.	**Here, there are two or more people, as A, B, and C all agreed to bring the whiskey ashore. They also agreed to commit an unlawful act because importing goods without paying duty violated the Tariff Act, so they agreed to violate the law.** **The overt act could be when A stole the truck, which is clearly an overt act to load the whiskey into it. However, B and C may have withdrawn prior to the overt act. (See below.)** However, the mere preparation of them holding a meeting could suffice as an overt act if they did anything more than agree to commit the act at that time.	**A, B, and C should be convicted of conspiracy, barring any defenses**
Mistake of fact	**Mistake of fact** negates any specific intent crime, as well as malice and general intent crimes if the mistake was reasonable.	**Here, A, B, and C were mistaken in their belief that the whiskey was imported. Thus, although they intended to commit a crime and import the whiskey without paying duty, the importing would not be a crime because the whiskey was produced in the United States. However, they still had the intent to commit a crime, so this defense would not be applicable.**	**Mistake of fact is not a valid defense**

Continued >

Issue	Rule	Fact Application	Conclusion
Withdrawal	**Once the agreement is made and the conspiracy formed, one cannot withdraw from liability for the conspiracy, but can withdraw for purposes of future crimes of co-conspirators,** if they communicate their withdrawal to co-conspirators (federal law allows communication to authorities as well) and take an affirmative action to withdraw.	As to B: **Under the majority rule, arguably B withdrew before the overt act as he called A on Wednesday, and it isn't clear when A stole the truck. Most likely A stole it on Friday as it would have been reported or found if before Wednesday, so B likely withdrew prior to the overt act, and thus the conspiracy was not yet formed under the majority law.** As to C: **C might also have withdrawn if the overt act didn't occur until Friday because he contacted the police on Thursday.** **The problem is that C didn't communicate his withdrawal to A, but rather to the police. This would suffice under federal law, but likely not under common law.**	**Under common law, A, B, and C would be convicted of conspiracy; under majority rule, they may not be, depending on when A stole truck**
Impossibility	**Factual impossibility** arises when D makes a mistake concerning an issue of fact; not a valid defense. **Legal impossibility** arises when D incorrectly believes that what he is doing is criminal when it is not; a valid defense.	Here, A, B, and C did not believe that what they were doing was criminal when it wasn't because importing goods without paying duty is a crime. However, they believed that the whiskey they were bringing ashore was imported when it was not, thus the crime was factually impossible although it was legally possible had it been imported. Since factual impossibility is not a valid defense, this defense will fail as well.	**Impossibility not a valid defense**

Continued >

Issue	Rule	Fact Application	Conclusion
Call #1.b: A, B, C Theft			
Theft	**Theft** is the illegal taking of another person's property.	Here, A stole the truck from the Coast Guard parking lot, which belonged to the Coast Guard, not him.	**A is guilty of theft**
Co-conspirator liability	Conspirators are **liable for crimes of co-conspirators if crimes were committed in furtherance of objective** and were reasonably foreseeable.	Here, it is foreseeable that Al would steal a truck since they would need something in which to transport the whiskey after they carried it ashore. **Stealing the truck also furthered the objective of the conspiracy, which was to sell the whiskey to local bar owners, as they could transport it to the bar owners by using the truck to load it and transport it.** **As discussed above, both B and C did possibly withdraw prior to the theft of the truck, depending on when A stole the truck, as B called A and A acknowledged his withdrawal by cutting him out of the profits and C informed the police, who arrested A.**	**If truck stolen on Friday, both B and C withdrew in time and are not liable for theft**
Call #2: Al Attempt			
Attempt	**Attempt is an act done with intent to commit a crime and an affirmative act, or substantial step, in furtherance of intent to commit crime** (beyond mere preparation).	**Here, A attempted to commit a crime as he attempted to import whiskey without paying the duty. The fact that it was not imported whiskey is not relevant, as he still intended to commit a crime, whether he could or not.**	**A can be convicted of attempt**

Continued >

Issue	Rule	Fact Application	Conclusion
Impossibility	See rule above	See above.	Not a valid defense
Call #3: Len's Ethical Obligations			
Duty of confidentiality	L must not reveal anything related to the representation of a client without their consent.	**Here, L cannot reveal to anyone anything A has disclosed to him without obtaining A's consent.**	**L cannot reveal A's confidences**
Duty of candor	**No falsifying testimony or evidence or counseling or assisting a witness to do so.** **If client in a criminal matter wants to lie, attorney must allow him to testify due to 5th Amend., but should not ask questions—let him testify in narrative.** If a witness wants to lie, refuse to put him on the stand.	**Here, L cannot prevent A from taking the stand, but he should advise him to tell the truth, and if L knows A is lying, he should not ask him any questions but just allow A to narrate.** L may attempt to withdraw, but this will depend on how close they are to trial and whether there are any conflicts involved.	**L must allow A to testify, but cannot ask questions**

Crimes Question 6

July 1994, Question 3

Jane, a police officer who was not in uniform, attempted to make a lawful arrest of Al for distribution of a controlled substance. Doug, who did not know either Al or Jane, arrived on the scene, a poorly lit alley and did not realize that Jane was a police officer. Because Jane was wearing civilian clothes and holding a gun on Al, Doug thought Jane was robbing Al.

Doug ran up and shoved Jane away from Al, who fled down the alley. Jane fired a shot at Al, killing Al. Doug then wrested the gun from Jane and shot Jane, killing Jane.

Doug was indicted for murder of Jane under a statute that mandates imposition of the death penalty for first degree murder of a peace officer who is in the performance of her duties. During jury selection, over Doug's repeated objections, the prosecutor used his peremptory challenges to remove all African-Americans and death penalty opponents from the jury.

1. What factual and legal defenses are available to Doug and, if they are accepted by the jury, of what crime, if any, should Doug be convicted? Discuss.
2. If Doug is convicted, how should the appellate court rule on an argument that the prosecutor's actions during jury selection denied Doug rights under the Sixth and or Fourteenth Amendments to the United States Constitution? Discuss.
3. If Doug is convicted of first degree murder as charged and the jury is instructed that it has no discretion as to penalty, would imposition of the death penalty violate Doug's rights under the Eighth Amendment to the United States Constitution? Discuss.
4. Did Jane act lawfully when she shot Al? Discuss.

Crimes Question 6 Assessment

July 1994, Question 3

This question is not the typical crimes question for a variety of reasons. First, it tests numerous rules that are rarely tested, including the Eighth Amendment right against cruel and unusual punishment, the use of peremptory challenges in a voir dire proceeding (which can arguably be construed as a civil procedure issue), and the use of lethal force by a police officer in civilian clothes. Second, the first call specifically asks about the "defenses" that are available to Doug. This is difficult because some students might not read closely and make the mistake of discussing the crimes as their primary focus, rather than briefly mentioning the crimes as a mechanism to introduce the discussion of the applicable defenses. On this question, the answer should focus on the defenses in accordance with the call of the question. However, you must first determine briefly what crimes are at issue so that you know which defenses are applicable.

Since this question covers several issues that are infrequently essay tested, this is a good practice question to see what you would do if faced with an essay question where you may not recall the rule. Hopefully, you will remember all of the less frequently essay tested rules from your MBE preparations since the more nuanced rules tend to show up frequently on the MBE portion of the bar exam. However, if you cannot remember a rule, then you need to make one up that is logical when considering the available facts that pertain to the issue. For example, when it comes to the issue of an officer using lethal force, common sense would dictate that police officers are not allowed to shoot to kill without limitations. Therefore, you know that there must be some limit. Since Jane was in civilian clothes and Al was unarmed and fled the scene, Al did not pose a danger to Jane and probably did not know Jane was an officer. In this situation, after considering these facts, you would then draft a rule that perhaps discussed the need for the felon to be a danger to the officer before the officer could shoot him. This is not the precise "fleeing felon" rule, but it's close enough to earn you some points on the issue since you would still analyze the facts and apply them to a logical, if imperfect, rule. When you can't remember a rule, the worst thing you can do is avoid discussing the issue. Rather, create a rule using your common sense and from the inferences you can make from the facts provided; then, analyze the facts to the created rule just as you would normally do. Focus on the factual analysis to receive at least partial credit on the issue.

Finally, be sure to make note of the areas highlighted in **bold** on the corresponding grid. The bold areas highlight the issues, analysis, and conclusions that are likely **required** to receive a passing score on this question.

Issue	Rule	Fact Application	Conclusion
Call #1			
Murder	Murder is unlawful killing of another person with malice aforethought. Malice can be proven by • An intent to kill (inferred when a deadly weapon is used to kill) • An intent to commit grievous bodily injury • A reckless indifference to value of human life or • An intent to commit a dangerous felony First degree is premeditated and deliberate. Second degree is all other unless voluntary manslaughter.	Here, the question asks about defenses, but before looking at defenses available, it is necessary to determine which crimes are at issue so you can address the applicable defenses to those crimes: • Since Doug shot and killed Jane, murder and/or manslaughter would be at issue. • It can be inferred that Doug intended to kill Jane because he used a gun, which is a deadly weapon; at a minimum, he intended to inflict grievous bodily injury as guns are known to cause serious injury or death. • The death was not premeditated because the only fact that prompted Doug to act was when he suddenly saw Jane holding a gun to Al. Also, he did not appear to have the intent to kill Jane until after she shot Al, indicating that it wasn't deliberate and planned. So, the murder would not be 1st degree murder, if it is murder.	Look at defenses for murder
Defense of others	**Defense of others is permissible when one reasonably believes that 3rd party would be justified in using such force, and force used is reasonable.** Minority rule "stand in shoes": a party may only defend another if person being defended was justified in using self-defense.	**Here, Doug reasonably believed that Jane was robbing Al since Jane was not wearing her police uniform and was holding a gun on Al. However, Al did not have the right to defend himself since he was being lawfully arrested for use of a controlled substance. But, since Jane was not wearing a uniform, it would have still been reasonable for Doug to believe that Al had the right to use force. Further, the force allowed would be deadly since Jane appeared to be using deadly force on Al since she shot and killed Al.** **The problem arises with the fact that Al was already dead at the time Doug shot Jane, so Al no longer needed defending.** In a jurisdiction applying the minority rule, Doug would have no privilege of defense of others since Al was not privileged to defend himself because Jane was making a lawful arrest.	**Defense of others not a valid defense**

Continued >

Issue	Rule	Fact Application	Conclusion
Self-defense	**A person has a right to apply self-defense against unlawful force if he exerts reasonable force, and may only resort to deadly force if the danger being resisted is also deadly force.** **An imperfect self-defense resulting in death that is based on an unreasonable mistake can reduce a murder charge to voluntary manslaughter.**	**Here, Doug may have reasonably feared that Jane would shoot and kill him like she did Al since Doug was unaware of the fact that Jane was a police officer. In this situation, he would be able to use force to defend himself.** **However, he used deadly force by shooting her after he had already disarmed her, so at that time deadly force was not being exerted on him. Further, there is no indication that Jane was aiming the gun toward Doug or that Doug feared for his life to warrant his use of deadly force.** **Here, it is likely that Doug's mistake was reasonable at first because Jane was not in uniform and it appeared as though she was robbing Al at gunpoint. Further, since Jane then shot and killed Al, Doug may have reasonably believed that his life was in danger as well. But once he disarmed Jane, his belief that his life was in danger was likely unreasonable.**	**Self-defense is not a valid defense** **Possible imperfect self-defense**
Voluntary manslaughter	**Murder can be reduced to voluntary manslaughter if D killed in the heat of passion** when he • Acted in response to a provocation that would cause a reasonable person to lose self-control, • D was in fact provoked at the time he acted, • There was insufficient time for D to cool off between the provocation and the killing, and • D did not in fact cool off by the time he killed.	Arguably, Jane didn't do anything to provoke Doug since she was trying to arrest Al. However, the provocation could be the use of deadly force by Jane against Al. But the fact that Al is a stranger to Doug might make a reasonable person not lose self-control when trying to defend a stranger, as opposed to a family member. Although Doug did appear to be provoked to defend Al, it may not have been reasonable since there was no relationship between Doug and Al. There was not likely sufficient time for Doug to cool down because the events all seemed to occur relatively quickly. Further, Doug did not in fact cool down as he wrested the gun away from Jane and then killed her rather instantly.	**No voluntary manslaughter, unless an imperfect self-defense**

Continued >

Issue	Rule	Fact Application	Conclusion
Mistake of fact	**Mistake of fact** negates any specific intent crime, as well as malice and general intent crimes if the mistake was reasonable.	**Here, as discussed above, Doug's mistaken belief that Jane was robbing Al at gunpoint is reasonable since Jane was not in her police uniform. This could negate a specific intent murder crime and, likely, general intent murder.** **The problem would still arise when Doug killed Jane after Al was no longer in danger (as he was dead) and Jane was disarmed after Doug wrested the gun away from her.** This mistake can also possibly negate the death penalty imposed under the statute for killing a police officer that is in the performance of her duties since Doug did not know that Jane was a police officer and had a possible imperfect defense due to this mistake.	No mistake of fact likely for killing
Answer to call			D may be guilty of 2nd degree murder or vol. manslaughter
Call #2			
6th Amend.: right to jury	Under 6th Amend., criminal Ds have the **right to a jury trial** for serious offenses that have a potential sentence of greater than six months **Jury must be impartial,** consisting of a fair cross-section of a community.	Here, Doug was indicted for murder, which under the current statute warrants a death penalty sentence, thereby giving Doug the right to a jury trial. If the community has African-Americans in it, then a jury completely devoid of African-Americans would not be representative of a fair cross-section of the community and would violate the 6th Amend.	**6th Amend. violation, so appellate court should rule in Doug's favor**

Continued >

Issue	Rule	Fact Application	Conclusion
	Each side (not party) has unlimited strikes on voir dire for cause (bias, prejudice, related to a party), and 3 **peremptory strikes** (still **must be used in a gender and race neutral way**).	**Here, the prosecutor used his peremptory challenges to remove all African-Americans, which is not a permissible use, as it was not done in a race-neutral way.** **However, the prosecutor can remove biased jurors, such as those who are opponents of the death penalty.**	**6th Amend. violation, so appellate court should rule in Doug's favor**
14th Amend.	**Equal Protection Clause of 14th Amend.** prevents state or any state actor, including the court, from intentionally discriminating against a distinctive group in selecting a jury pool.	**Here, the prosecutor is discriminating against African-Americans by removing all of them from the jury, especially since he has discriminated against this distinct group only.**	**14th Amend. violation, so appellate court should rule in Doug's favor**
Call #3			
8th Amend.: punishment	8th Amend. prohibits **cruel and unusual punishment** by preventing the penalty imposed on D to be grossly disproportionate to seriousness of crime. **When considering death penalty, jury shall consider mitigating circumstances,** such as D's age, capacity, previous criminal liability, duress, other Ds' involvement, and any other factors that mitigate against imposition of a death sentence.	Here, imposition of the death penalty if Doug reasonably thought that Jane was robbing Al at gunpoint would be grossly disproportionate to the crime since he would have mitigating circumstances that would not warrant the death penalty. **Further, the jury should consider these mitigating circumstances prior to Doug being sentenced automatically to the death penalty since the statute would violate his 8th Amend. rights since the mitigating circumstances, such as his reasonable mistake, would not be considered.**	8th Amend. violation

Continued >

Issue	Rule	Fact Application	Conclusion
Call #4			
Fleeing felon standard	Under "fleeing felon standard," **law enforcement officer can use deadly force against a fleeing felon if**: (1) **use of deadly force is necessary** to prevent felon's escape, (2) **fleeing felon has threatened officer** with a weapon or officer has probable cause to believe that felon has committed a crime involving infliction or threatened infliction of serious physical harm, and (3) officer gives felon some warning of the imminent use of deadly force, if feasible.	Here, Jane, as a police officer, can use deadly force to prevent a felon's escape in certain circumstances. Since Al was fleeing down the alley, Jane could have used her gun to stop Al, but **she was not threatened with a weapon by Al nor had Al committed a crime that caused physical harm to another. Rather, Al was being arrested for distribution of a controlled substance.** Further, Jane did not warn Al she was going to use deadly force.	**Jane did not act lawfully when she shot Al**

PART 7 EVIDENCE

EVIDENCE TABLE OF CONTENTS

INTRODUCTION TO EVIDENCE

Evidence essay questions feel different than questions in other subjects. Evidence questions are almost always "racehorse style" with a great many issues tested (sometimes as many as 25 or more) but with comparatively thin factual analysis. The two main skills being tested with an evidence question (besides knowledge of evidence, of course) are 1) issue spotting, and 2) time management.

First, in order to pass evidence essay questions, it is imperative that you spot all of the issues, and there will be a great many. Evidence requires a more detailed checklist than other subjects to successfully issue spot the question. There are two reasons for this: 1) There are more legal issues in evidence compared to other subjects, and 2) the issues don't necessarily jump out at you; you have to go looking for them. For this reason, it is best to have a detailed checklist and "run" each piece of evidence through the checklist looking for pertinent issues while organizing your answer. Obviously this approach takes time and you won't be fast at it the first few times you do it. Like any skill you are trying to develop, the more you practice, the better you get. It is essential to practice answering evidence essay questions under timed conditions to get the hang of it.

The other important skill being tested with an evidence essay question is time management. One hour goes by quickly when faced with an essay containing 25 to 30 legal issues. Even though there is a lot to write, and it is tempting to start right away, 15 to 20 minutes of the one-hour allotted time should be spent organizing the essay in order to properly spot all of the issues. Though some rules will have more elements than others, the depth of analysis (meaning the amount of factual analysis and factual inferences available to use in the analysis of any one issue) is likely to be similar from issue to issue. This makes pacing yourself somewhat easier because you don't need to worry about going from deep analysis to shallow analysis as you move from issue to issue. Typically, evidence is uniformly comprised of comparatively shallow analysis. Therefore, the goal is to write at a sufficient pace to cover all of the issues in the allotted time. Again, practicing a truncated analysis is essential because you will not know the level of detail you can use to cover 25 to 30 issues in an hour until you try to do it. The worst thing you can do is not finish your answer (which will cause you to fail the question), or go over the one-hour allotted time (which will cause you to fail the following question) so you must practice successfully completing an evidence essay in one hour.

Evidence essays can look different than other essays. They will often arise in one of two ways: (1) as a series of paragraphs discussing some items of evidence, or (2) as a transcript of "Questions and Answers," each of which represents various evidentiary issues. Evidence questions are rarely crossover questions, but it can happen.

The evidence rules in this outline are based on the Federal Rules of Evidence (FRE) or federal common law. Where the law in California (California Evidence Code, or CEC) differs from the federal rules, it will be noted. If it is not so noted, assume the California rules and federal rules are the same. Pay special attention to the areas of law where the California rule is different than the federal rule because those are favorite testing areas.

ISSUES CHECKLIST

RELEVANCE

Logical
Legal (balancing test)
Prop. 8 (and exemptions)

PUBLIC POLICY EXCLUSIONS

Subsequent remedial measures
Liability insurance
Offers to: pay medical bills/settle/plead guilty

WITNESS ON THE STAND

Competency/personal knowledge
Form of the question objections (NUCALF)
Opinion (lay or expert)

PRIVILEGES (ATTORNEY-CLIENT/DR.-PATIENT/PSYCHOTHERAPIST-PATIENT/MARITAL)

CHARACTER

Character "at issue"
Civil or criminal
Other purpose (I PIK A MOP)

IMPEACHMENT

HEARSAY

Nonhearsay purpose
Hearsay exceptions:
- Admissions
- Witness statements
  - Medical diagnosis and treatment
  - Then-existing state of mind
  - PSI (present sense impression)
  - Excited utterance
- **Prior statement of available witness**
  - PIS (prior inconsistent statement)/PCS (prior consistent statement)
  - Prior identification
- **Documents**
  - Past recollection recorded
  - Business records
  - Public records
- **Declarant unavailable**
  - Former testimony
  - Dying declaration
  - Declaration against interest

DOCUMENTS ADMITTED INTO EVIDENCE

Relevance
Authentication
Best evidence rule
Hearsay exceptions

JUDICIAL NOTICE

MEMORIZATION ATTACK SHEET

RELEVANCE

- ♦ **Logical**
  - Prove or disprove a material fact
  - CEC: disputed fact
- ♦ **Legal**
  - Probative v. prejudice balancing test
- ♦ **Prop. 8 (Cal. Crim. Court)**
  - D opens door to character
  - Rape shield laws
  - Media member
  - Court may exclude (§ 352)
  - Secondary Evidence Rule
  - Hearsay
  - Exclusionary rules of U.S. Constitution
  - Exclusionary rules of Cal. post-1982
  - Privileges

PUBLIC POLICY EXCEPTIONS

- ♦ **Subsequent remedial measures**
  - Except
    - Ownership & control
    - Precautions infeasible
    - Other party destroyed evidence
- ♦ **Liability insurance**
  - Except
    - Ownership & control
    - Impeachment
    - Admission
- ♦ **Offers medical expenses**
  - FRE exception: admission
  - CEC exception: none
- ♦ **Settlement offer**
  - Disputed claim only
  - CEC: applies to mediation also
- ♦ **Offers to plead**
  - Cal. exception: Prop. 8 may allow
- ♦ **Cal. expression of sympathy**
  - Except: admission of fault

WITNESS EXAMINATION

- ♦ **Personal knowledge required**
- ♦ **Objection: form of the question**
  - Narrative
  - Unresponsive
  - Compound
  - Argumentative
  - Leading
  - Assumes Facts not in evidence
- ♦ **Present recollection refreshed**
  - W shown item to refresh
  - W then testifies from memory
- ♦ **Lay opinion**
  - FRE: not scientific or specialized knowledge
- ♦ **Expert opinion**
  - Assists trier of fact
  - W qualifies as expert
  - Opinion based on sufficient facts
  - Reliable principles used
    - FRE: *Daubert* standard
    - CEC: *Kelly/Frye* standard
  - Applied principles reliably

PRIVILEGES

- ♦ **Attorney-client**
  - Client: person or corporation
  - Confidential communications (intended as confidential)
  - Professional services is purpose of communication
  - Holder: client
  - Lasts until
    - FRE: after death
    - CEC: estate settled
  - Exceptions
    - Further crime or fraud
    - Dispute w/lawyer

- CEC: prevent death/serious bodily injury

- **Doctor-patient**
  - FRE: no Dr.-patient privilege
  - CEC: communication made for diagnosis & treatment only
- **Psychotherapist-patient**
  - Fed. & Cal. both allow
- **Self-incrimination**
- **Marital adverse testimony**
  - During marriage
  - Holder: witness spouse
  - Fed.: criminal only
  - Except: cases between spouses
- **Marital confidential communication**
  - During & after marriage
  - Holder: both spouses
  - Except: cases between spouses
- **CEC-only privileges**
  - Counselor-victim
  - Clergy-penitent
  - News reporters

CHARACTER EVIDENCE

- **3 types of character evidence**
  - Reputation
  - Opinion
  - Specific acts
- **Civil Court rules**
  - Not for conduct in conformity
  - Except: character "at issue"
  - FRE exception: sexual assault/child molestation
  - Rape shield: rape/sex assault
    - FRE: if probative value substantially outweighs prejudice; reputation only if P puts reputation in issue
    - CEC: only to prove P's sexual conduct w/the D
- **Criminal Court rules: D's character**
  - D must "open door"
  - Pertinent character trait only
  - If D on stand: truthfulness
  - Except: P can open door in sexual assault/child molestation
  - FRE exception: if D offers on V character, prosecution can match for D
  - CEC excepttion: if D offers on V's *violent* character, Prosecution can match for D
  - CEC exception: domestic violence/elder abuse
- **Criminal Court rules: V's character**
  - D must "open door"
  - Pertinent character trait only
  - Except: rape shield rules apply
  - FRE exception: D offers that V 1st aggressor, Prosecution can rebut that V peaceful (rep./opin.)
- **D's character: form of evidence**
  - Direct: no specific acts
  - Cross (to rebut)
    - FRE: all 3 forms, but no extrinsic evidence allowed
    - CEC: no specific acts
- **V's character: form of evidence**
  - Direct
    - FRE: no specific acts
    - CEC: all 3 forms allowed
  - Cross: all 3 forms allowed
  - FRE exception: D offers that V 1st aggressor, Prosecution can rebut that V peaceful (rep./opin.)
  - Rape shield
    - No reputation/opinion
    - Specific acts only for
      - 3rd-party source of semen/injury
      - Prior consent w/D
    - CEC: reasonable belief of consent

- **Other purpose character**
  - Intent
  - Preparation
  - Identity of perpetrator, M.O.
  - Knowledge of fact or event
  - Absence of mistake/accident
  - Motive
  - Opportunity
  - Plan or scheme
- **Habit or custom**
- **Similar happenings**

IMPEACHMENT

- **Character for truthfulness**
  - Reputation & opinion okay
  - Specific acts
    - FRE: okay, but no extrinsic evid. allowed
    - CEC
      - Civil: allowed
      - Criminal: not allowed
  - Criminal conviction
    - Crimen falsi: unless 10 years old
    - Felony
      - Criminal D: okay if probative value outweighs prejudicial effect
      - Others: okay unless prejudicial effect substantially outweighs probative value
    - Misdemeanor
      - FRE: not allowed
      - CEC
        - Civil: not allowed
        - Criminal: if moral turpitude
- **Prior inconsistent statement**
  - Extrinsic evidence allowed, must explain or deny
- **Bias**
  - Extrinsic evidence allowed, must explain or deny
- **Sensory or mental defect**
- **Contradiction by another W**
- **Rehab impeached witness**
  - Meet the attack
  - Good character if attacked
  - Prior consistent statement
- **Bolstering the witness**
  - FRE: not allowed
  - CEC: allowed

HEARSAY & EXCEPTIONS

- **Hearsay:** Out of court statement; offered for truth of matter asserted
- **Nonhearsay purpose**
  - Effect on listener/reader
  - Declarant's state of mind
  - Legally operative fact
- **Admissions:** any statement
  - **Party admissions**
  - **Adoptive:** manifest belief in truth of statement
  - **Vicarious:** employee or agent statement in course of relationship
  - CEC: employee negligence only
  - **Co-conspirator:** during & in furtherance of the conspiracy
- **Witness statements: other hearsay exceptions**
  - **Medical purpose diagnosis & treatment**
    - Cause okay, but not fault
    - CEC: child abuse victim only
  - **State of mind:** then-existing mental, emotional, physical state
  - **Present sense impression**
    - Describe event/condition
    - While perceiving
    - CEC: describing declarant's own conduct only
  - **Excited utterance**
    - Startling event
    - Statement made while under stress of event
- **Prior statement of available W's**
  - **Prior inconsistent statement**
  - **Prior consistent statement**
  - **Prior identification**

- **Document exceptions**
  - **Past recollection recorded**
    - Firsthand knowledge
    - Fresh @ time of recording
    - W recollection impaired now
    - Record accurate @ time made
  - **Business record**
    - Business activity
    - Regular practice to keep
    - Firsthand knowledge
    - Business duty to report
    - Timely @ time made
  - **Public record**
    - Agency record of own acts
    - Matters observed w/duty to report
    - Investigative reports
    - FRE: not against criminal D
  - **Learned writings**
- **Declarant unavailable exceptions**
  - **Unavailbilty** is established by
    - Privileged
    - Death or illness
    - Can't procure W reasonably
    - Witness refuses to testify
    - Witness can't remember
  - **Former testimony**
    - Civil case only
      - FRE: predecessor in interest only
      - CEC: similar interest in prior proceeding & deposition in same proceeding allowed
  - **Dying declaration**
    - Re: circumstances of death
    - While believing death imminent
    - FRE: civil & criminal homicide only & death not required
    - CEC: death required & allows "OJ" exception for physical abuse
  - **Declaration against interest**
    - Financial or penal interest
    - CEC: social interest, too
  - **Forfeiture by wrongdoing**
- **Residual "catch-all" exception**

DOCUMENTS

- **Establish relevance**
- **Authentication**
  - Real evidence: distinct characteristic or chain of title
  - Demonstrative: fair representation
  - Writings/recordings
  - Self-authenticating documents
- **Best evidence rule (Cal.: SER)**
  - Original or copy
- **Summaries of voluminous writings**

JUDICIAL NOTICE

- **Judicial notice allowed if**
  - Not subject to reasonable dispute
  - Generally known in jurisdiction
  - Capable of accurate & ready determination

EVIDENCE RULE OUTLINE

I. **PRELIMINARY EVIDENCE CONCEPTS**
   A. **Direct or circumstantial:** Evidence can be direct or circumstantial
      1. **Direct evidence** can automatically resolve an issue.
      2. **Circumstantial evidence** only resolves an issue if additional reasoning is used.
   B. **Type of evidence:** Evidence can come in **several forms.**
      1. **Testimonial evidence** is when a witness makes an assertion in court.
      2. **Real evidence** is the actual thing involved in the case (e.g., gun).
      3. **Demonstrative evidence** is a tangible item that illustrates a concept (e.g., map of accident scene).

II. **RELEVANCE:** Only relevant evidence may be admitted.
   A. **Logical relevance definition**
      1. **FRE:** Evidence is relevant if it has any tendency to prove or disprove a **material fact.**
      2. **CEC:** Evidence is relevant if it tends to be material to a **disputed fact.**
   B. **Legal relevance exclusion:** Otherwise relevant evidence may be excluded if its **probative value is substantially outweighed by the danger of unfair prejudice**, confusion of issues, misleading the jury, or wasting time. (FRE 403; CEC 352)

> <u>Exam tip:</u> On an essay, for each piece of evidence always first determine if the evidence is **logically relevant**. But, only analyze if the evidence is **legally relevant** where there is the potential for the evidence to have an unfairly prejudicial effect. (E.g.: Where character evidence is allowed for a purpose other than to show conduct in conformity—such as to show motive or identity—a public policy exclusion exception, where the meaning of the evidence is ambiguous or could be unfairly seen in a negative light, etc.)

   C. **California Proposition 8** provides that in **criminal** trials in California state courts, all relevant evidence is admissible, even if objectionable under the CEC, subject to a few special exemptions. (Cal. Const. Amend., 1982, "Victims' Bill of Rights.")
      1. **Exemptions to Proposition 8**
         a. **<u>D</u>efendant** still must **"open the door"** to bring in evidence of his own character before the prosecution can do so.
         b. **<u>R</u>ape shield laws** still limit evidence of a victim's character.
         c. **<u>M</u>ember of media** still can't be held in contempt for refusing to reveal confidential news source, etc.
         d. **<u>C</u>ourt** still has the **power to exclude** evidence if the probative value is substantially outweighed by the danger of unfair prejudice, confusion of issues, misleading the jury, or wasting time. (CEC 352 still applies.)

e. **Secondary evidence rule** still applies
f. **Hearsay** may still not be admitted, unless subject to an exception.
g. **Exclusionary rules** based on the **U.S. Constitution** still apply (e.g., *Miranda*, Confrontation Clause, etc.).
h. **Exclusionary rules** that were adopted by the **California legislature** with a 2/3 vote after 1982 still apply. (1982 is the year Prop. 8 passed.)
i. **Privileges** that already existed in 1982 still apply (e.g., attorney-client, professional, and both marital privileges).

> Memorization tip: Use the mnemonic **DR** Mammal **C**ounts **SHEEP** to remember the nine Prop. 8 exemptions.

> Exam tip: If the essay concerns a **criminal case** in **California court** do the following for each piece of evidence: 1) Apply the ordinary rules of evidence (general CEC rules of evidence and objections); 2) explain that despite the ordinary rules, Prop. 8 permits the admission of all relevant evidence unless one of the nine exemptions applies; and 3) determine whether any of the Prop. 8 exemptions will serve to exclude the evidence. (Be sure to always consider if the court will exclude for unfair prejudice under CEC 352.)

III. **PUBLIC POLICY EXCLUSIONS:** Otherwise-relevant evidence can be excluded for public policy reasons. This is because as a society we want to encourage certain types of behaviors.

A. **Subsequent remedial measures**

1. **General rule:** Evidence of safety measures, or repairs performed after an accident, are **not admissible to prove culpable conduct.**
   a. **FRE only:** In addition, in a **products liability** action, evidence of safety measures are inadmissible to show defective product design.
2. **Exception:** Evidence of subsequent remedial measures **is admissible to establish:**
   a. **Ownership or control:** Show ownership or control of an instrumentality; or
   b. **Precaution not feasible:** To **rebut** a claim that the precaution was not feasible; or
   c. **Destruction of evidence:** That the **other party** destroyed evidence.

B. **Liability insurance**

1. **General rule:** Evidence of liability insurance is **not admissible to prove culpable conduct** (such as negligence or defendant's ability to pay a judgment). The purpose of the policy exclusion is that evidence of insurance may have a tendency to suggest the defendant has deep pockets to pay for any injuries, or tends to be negligent and that is why he carries insurance.

2. **Exception:** Evidence of liability insurance **is admissible to establish:**
   a. **Ownership or control:** Showing ownership or control of an instrumentality is allowed (e.g., the liability policy is held by the car owner); or
   b. **Impeachment**; or
   c. **Admission: A statement of fault** made in conjunction with a statement regarding the possession of liability insurance is **admissible.** For example, the statement "I have plenty of insurance" said after an injury-producing accident may be admitted as evidence that the declarant felt he was at fault for the injury.

C. **Offers to pay medical expenses**
   1. **General rule:** Offers to pay medical, hospital, or similar expenses occasioned by an injury are **not admissible to prove liability** for that injury. The reason for this rule is that we don't want to discourage people from offering to pay medical expenses because of the fear it is the equivalent of an admission of guilt.
   2. **FRE-only exception: Collateral admissions of fact** made during an offer to pay medical expenses **are admissible.** (But, not under the CEC.)

D. **Settlement offers:** An offer to settle a claim and related statements are **not admissible to prove the claim's validity, liability, or amount.**
   1. **Disputed claim only:** This rule only applies to a claim that is **disputed as to validity or amount.** It does not apply if a claim has not yet been made.

> **Issue-spotting tip:** Look for a declarant to blurt out a settlement offer at the scene of an accident before it is clear there is a disputed claim.

   2. **CEC: Mediation proceeding** discussions are also **not admissible.**

E. **Offer to plead guilty:** An **offer to plead** guilty to a crime, and **all related statements** made during plea negotiations, are **not admissible to prove** that a **criminal defendant** is **guilty, or a consciousness of guilt.**
   1. **California exception:** Such statements may come in under Prop. 8.

F. **Expressions of sympathy—CEC only:** Evidence of expressions of sympathy are **not admissible in civil actions** that are related to the **death or suffering** of an accident victim, but **statements of fault** made in connection with the sympathy **are admissible**.

IV. **WITNESS EXAMINATION** (Witness on the Stand)

A. **Flow of testimony**
   1. **Direct examination:** The questioner may not ask leading questions unless the witness is "hostile." A leading question is one that is framed to suggest the desired answer.
   2. **Cross examination:** Leading questions are usually permitted, and cross examination is limited to the subject matter of the direct examination.
   3. **Re-direct examination** is limited to the subject matter of the cross examination.

4. **Re-cross examination** is limited to the subject matter of the re-direct examination.

B. **Competency:** A witness must have **personal knowledge** of the matter about which he is to testify, and must declare that he will **testify truthfully**.

C. **Role of the judge**
   1. The trial judge may **call witnesses** and may **ask questions** of any witness.
   2. **CEC:** A judge presiding at a trial is **incompetent to testify** at that trial, provided a party objects (same for a juror).

D. **Objections to the form of the question** (or answer)
   1. **Narrative:** Questions calling for a narrative are too broad (e.g., "So, what happened?").
   2. **Unresponsive:** The witness answer is unresponsive to the question.
      a. **CEC:** A motion to strike can be made by either party, not just the examining party.
   3. **Compound:** Two questions are contained in one question (e.g., "Did you beat your wife and steal your neighbor's money?").
   4. **Argumentative:** The question is unnecessarily combative (e.g., "Do you really expect the jury to believe this nonsense?").
   5. **Leading** (on direct): The question itself suggests the answer the questioner desires (e.g., "Isn't it true that Ace's has been fixing prices?").
   6. **Facts:** Assumes facts not in evidence (e.g., "When did you make your will?" when there is no evidence the witness ever made a will).

> <u>Memorization tip:</u> Use the mnemonic **NUCALF** to remember the form of the question objections.

E. **Present recollection refreshed** is a technique that allows any **item** (photo, document, etc.) to be used to **refresh a witness's memory** where the witness's recollection is currently uncertain. Once shown the item, the witness must then **testify from his refreshed memory**.
   1. **Not evidence:** The item used to refresh is not considered evidence and may even be otherwise inadmissible evidence.
   2. **Right to inspect:** The adversary has a right to inspect the item, cross examine, and introduce pertinent portions into evidence.
   3. **CEC:** Whether the refreshing is done before or during trial by means of a document, the **writing must be produced** or testimony is stricken unless the document is unavailable.

> <u>Issue-spotting tip:</u> **Present recollection refreshed** is often confused with past recollection recorded. With present recollection refreshed the item shown to the witness is a memory stimulus, which then allows the witness to *testify entirely from memory*. **Past recollection recorded** (see section X.D.1) is a hearsay exception and applies when the document consulted *does not actually refresh* the witness's memory, so the document is then read into the record.

F. **Opinion testimony**
   1. **Lay opinion** is admissible if rationally based on the witness's perceptions and is **helpful to the trier of fact.** These are not legal conclusions, but opinions (e.g., estimating driving speed, identity of a person, value of property, familiarity of handwriting, physical condition, etc.).
      a. **FRE only:** Lay opinion may **not** be based on scientific or **specialized knowledge.**
   2. **Expert opinion**
      a. **Requirements for an expert opinion to be admissible:**
         1. Specialized knowledge will **assist the trier of fact** in understanding the evidence or determining a fact;
         2. The witness must be **qualified as an expert** by knowledge, skill, experience, training, or education;
         3. The testimony must be **based on sufficient facts** or data;
         4. The testimony must be the product of **reliable principles** and methods; and
         5. The witness must have **applied the principles reliably** to the facts of the case.
      b. **Basis for the expert's opinion** may be based on:
         1. The expert's **firsthand knowledge;**
         2. The expert's **observation of prior witnesses;** or
         3. A **hypothetical question** posed by counsel.
      c. **Reliable principles and methods**
         1. **FRE: The *Daubert/Kumho*** standard requires:
            a. **Peer reviewed and published** in scientific journals,
            b. **Tested** and subject to retesting,
            c. **Low error rate,** and
            d. ***Reasonable level of acceptance.***
         2. **CEC: The *Kelly/Frye*** standard requires that:
            a. The proponent must prove that the **underlying scientific theory** and the instruments it uses,
            b. It has been ***generally accepted as valid*** and reliable in the relevant scientific field.
            c. **Exception:** The standard **does not apply to medical and nonscientific** testimony.

V. **PRIVILEGES**

A. A **privilege** provides testimonial protection for certain relationships.
   1. **Federal privilege rules** apply in federal court for criminal, federal question, or federal law cases. The **federal common law applies** since there is no FRE regarding privileges.
   2. **State privilege rules** apply in federal court diversity jurisdiction, or in state court.

B. **Types of privileges**
   1. **Attorney-client:** A **client has a right** not to disclose any **confidential communication** between the attorney and the client relating to the **professional relationship.**

a. **Client:** A client can be a **corporation**, as well as an **individual.**
   1. **Federal common law:** Applies to **employees/agents if authorized** by the corporation to make the communication to the lawyer.
   2. **CEC:** Applies to **employees/agents** if the natural person to speak to the lawyer on behalf of the corporation, or the employee did something for which the corporation may be held liable and the corporation instructed her to tell its lawyer what happened. (As applied, both FRE and CEC rules yield the same result.)

b. **Confidential communications:** The communication must be **intended** to be confidential.
   1. Presence of a **third party** may serve to waive the privilege.
   2. **Does not apply to physical evidence** turned over to the lawyer, only to communications.
   3. **CEC only:** Allows **holder to stop eavesdroppers** and other wrongful interceptors from revealing information.

c. **Professional services:** The communication must be made for the **purpose of facilitating legal services**, though a fee need not be paid.

d. **Holder of the privilege:** Only the **client holds the privilege** and the lawyer may assert it on the client's behalf.

e. **Privilege lasts until:**
   1. **Federal common law: After death,** with the exception of a will contest.
   2. **CEC:** Privilege evaporates when the dead client's **estate has been fully distributed** and his personal representative has been discharged.

f. **Exceptions:** The privilege does not apply if:
   1. **Crime or fraud:** The communication was used to further crime of fraud; or
   2. **Dispute with lawyer:** Relates to a dispute between the lawyer and client; or
   3. **Two or more parties consult** on a matter of common interest and the communication is offered by one against another; or
   4. **CEC only:** Lawyer reasonably believes the disclosure is **necessary to prevent a crime** that is likely to result in **death** or **substantial bodily harm.**

2. **Doctor-patient privilege**

a. **Federal common law:** There is **no federal doctor-patient privilege,** except for the special case of psychotherapists (see section V.B.3 below).

b. **CEC:** Applies only to communications made to medical personnel for the **purpose of medical diagnosis and treatment.**
   1. **Exceptions:** The privilege does not apply if:
      a. **Patient puts his physical condition in issue.**
      b. Doctor's assistance was **sought to aid wrongdoing.**
      c. **Dispute** between **doctor and patient.**

   d. Information the **doctor is required to report.**
   e. **Commitment, competency, or license revocation** proceedings.

3. **Psychotherapist-patient and social worker-client privilege**
   a. **Federal common law:** There is a federal psychotherapist-patient privilege for confidential communications.
   b. **CEC:** Confidential communications made to a licensed **psychotherapist or social worker** are privileged.
      1. **Exceptions:** The privilege does not apply if:
      a. **Patient puts his mental condition in issue.**
      b. Services were **sought to aid wrongdoing.**
      c. **Dispute** between **therapist/social worker and patient.**
      d. Patient is a **danger to self and others.**
      e. **Therapist is court appointed.**
      f. Patient is a **minor and possible crime victim.**
4. **Self-incrimination:** The Fifth Amendment provides that no person shall be compelled to be a witness against himself.
5. **Marital privileges:** There are two types of marital privileges.
   a. **Adverse testimony privilege (testimonial immunity):** One spouse **cannot be compelled** to testify against the other spouse.
      1. **Duration:** It can only be **claimed during the marriage** but covers information **learned before or during** the marriage.
      2. **Holder: Only the witness spouse** holds the privilege.
      3. **Federal common law:** Applies to **criminal** cases only.
      4. **CEC:** Applies to **criminal and civil cases** and the spouse is privileged from being called to the witness stand.
      5. **Exception:** Does not apply in **actions between the spouses** or in cases involving crimes against the testifying spouse or either spouse's children.
      6. **Effect:** Invoking the privilege makes the spouse **unavailable for hearsay purposes.**
   b. **Confidential communications privilege:** One spouse **may not disclose** the confidential communications of the other **made during the marriage.**
      1. **Duration:** The **privilege survives the marriage**, but only covers statements (not acts) made during marriage.
      2. **Holder: Both spouses** may assert the privilege not to disclose and **may prevent the other spouse** from disclosing.
      3. **Exception:** Does not apply in actions **between the spouses** or in cases involving crimes against the testifying spouse or either spouse's children.
      4. **Effect:** Invoking the privilege makes the spouse **unavailable for hearsay purposes.**
6. **CEC-only privileges**
   a. **Counselor-victim** privilege for confidential communications between a counselor and a victim of sexual assault or domestic violence.
   b. **Clergy-penitent** privilege for penitential communications.

c. **News reporters** are immune from contempt of court for refusal to disclose sources.

> <u>Exam tip:</u> For an essay exam where a privilege is at issue, establish the following: (1) the relationship, (2) that the communication is confidential, (3) which party holds the privilege, and (4) if any exceptions apply.

VI. CHARACTER EVIDENCE

A. **Form of character evidence:** There are three methods of proving character.
   1. **Reputation:** Testimony regarding one's reputation in the community.
   2. **Opinion:** Testimony regarding the witness's opinion of the person.
   3. **Specific acts** engaged in by the person, which are presented in court.

B. **Civil court character evidence**
   1. **Rules**
      a. **General rule:** Character evidence is generally **not admissible to prove conduct in conformity** with that character trait on a particular occasion.
      b. **Character "at issue" exception:** Character evidence is admissible where character **"at issue" and is an essential element** of the case.

> <u>Character "at issue" fact triggers:</u>
> - Wrongful death (because a person's value is dependent on their character)
> - Negligent entrustment
> - Defamation (because a person's character matters when assessing reputational damage)

      c. **FRE exception:** Cases based on **sexual assault or child molestation. (CEC has no such exception.)**
      d. **Rape shield provisions:** Rape and sexual assault cases have special rules, known as "rape shield" provisions, which generally disallow evidence of a rape or sexual assault **victim's past sexual conduct.**
         1. **FRE:** Reputation, opinion, and specific acts evidence are only admissible if the **probative value substantially outweighs the danger of unfair prejudice.** Plaintiff must put her reputation in issue for reputation evidence to be admitted. (A higher standard than typical balancing test.)
         2. **CEC:** Defendant cannot offer evidence of plaintiff's prior sexual conduct unless to prove **prior sexual conduct with the defendant.**
   2. **Form of evidence:** All three forms of evidence (reputation, opinion, and specific acts) are generally allowed.

C. **Criminal court character evidence**

1. **Rules:** Where allowable, the character trait must always be **pertinent** to the case, but the rules for admission differ depending on whose character it is.
    a. **Defendant's character**
        1. **General rule: Only the defendant can "open the door"** to evidence of a **pertinent** character trait, but once opened, the prosecution can rebut.
        2. **Exceptions** to general rule
            a. **FRE and CEC: Prosecution can be the first to offer** character **"propensity"** evidence in **sexual assault or child molestation** cases.
            b. **FRE only:** Where the **defendant offers** evidence of the **victim's character,** prosecution can offer evidence that the defendant has the same character trait.
            c. **CEC only:** Where the **defendant offers** evidence of the **victim's violent character,** prosecution can offer evidence that the defendant has violent character. (Note: CEC rule is narrower than FRE counterpart.)
            d. **CEC only:** In prosecution for **domestic violence or elder abuse,** prosecution may offer evidence that the defendant committed other acts of domestic violence or elder abuse.
        3. **Credibility:** A **defendant testifying on the stand** only puts his **credibility** at issue, but not necessarily his general character.
    b. **Victim's character**
        1. **General rule: Only the defendant can "open the door"** to evidence of a **victim's pertinent** character trait, but once opened, the prosecution can rebut.
        2. **FRE-only exception:** If **defendant claims** or offers evidence that the **victim** was the **first aggressor**, the prosecution may offer evidence of the **victim's character for peacefulness**.
        3. **Rape and sexual assault case special rules:** "Rape shield" provisions generally disallow evidence of a rape or sexual assault victim's past sexual conduct (subject to the form of evidence rules that follow).
2. **Form of evidence** allowed depends on whose character trait it is and if it is raised during direct or cross examination.
    a. **Defendant's character**
        1. **Direct examination:** No specific acts are allowed to show character, only reputation and opinion evidence.
        2. **Cross examination** (to rebut character evidence)
            a. **FRE:** All three forms of evidence are allowed. But, while specific acts may be asked about, extrinsic evidence regarding the specific act is not allowed, so the prosecutor is stuck with the witness's answer.
            b. **CEC:** No specific acts evidence is allowed to show the defendant's character (subject to Prop. 8).

b. **Victim's character**
   1. **Direct examination**
      a. **FRE:** Only **reputation and opinion** evidence are allowed to show character; **no specific acts** evidence is allowed.
      b. **CEC: All three** forms of evidence are allowed (reputation, opinion, and specific acts).
   2. **Cross examination** (to rebut character evidence): **All three** forms of evidence (reputation, opinion, and specific acts) are allowed (FRE and CEC).
   3. **FRE-only exception:** If the **defendant claims** or offers evidence that the **victim was the first aggressor**, the prosecution may offer evidence of the victim's character for peacefulness only by **reputation and opinion** evidence.
   4. **Rape and sexual assault case special rules:** "Rape shield" provisions generally disallow evidence of a rape or sexual assault victim's past sexual conduct.
      a. **Reputation and opinion** evidence are always inadmissible.
      b. **Specific acts** are only admissible to prove
         i. **Third party** is the source of semen or injury to the victim; or
         ii. **Prior acts** of consensual intercourse **with the defendant**; or
         iii. **Constitutionally** required.
      c. **CEC only: Defendant can offer** victim's prior sexual conduct to show he **reasonably believed she consented**, but not to show that she did consent.

D. **"Other purpose" evidence allowed:** Evidence of other crimes, wrongs, or specific bad acts **are not admissible to show conduct in conformity**, but may be used to show proof of some other relevant factor such as:
   1. **Intent** to commit the act.
   2. **Preparation** to commit the act.
   3. **Identity** of the perpetrator, including M.O. (modus operandi).
   4. **Knowledge** of some fact or event.
   5. **Absence** of mistake or accident.
   6. **Motive** to commit the crime.
   7. **Opportunity** to commit the act.
   8. **Plan** or scheme.

> Memorization tip: Use the mnemonic **I PIK A MOP** to remember the "other purposes" that specific acts character evidence may be admitted to prove.
> Issue-spotting tip: Where character evidence is allowable for "other purposes," always do the **legal relevance balancing test** to determine if the evidence should be excluded because it is too prejudicial.

<u>Exam tip:</u> Character evidence can be challenging to analyze so always consider and discuss the following issues:

1. Determine if the case is civil or criminal. If criminal, is the evidence regarding the defendant or the victim? Apply the rules.
2. Identify the form of the evidence presented (reputation, opinion, specific acts) and if it is admissible in that form.
3. Determine if there is an "other purpose" for admitting the evidence? If so identify it and do the legal relevance balancing test.

<u>Character evidence fact triggers:</u>

- Prior conviction of any kind
- Evidence someone is a liar (e.g., lied on tax return, perjury case)
- Evidence someone is a bad guy (e.g., violent, shady bookkeeping practices, abusive to family/friends, sells drugs, sexual misconduct, prior malpractice cases)

VII. **OTHER CIRCUMSTANTIAL EVIDENCE**

A. **Habit and custom** is a **regular response to a repeated situation** and is admissible to show conduct in conformity.

1. **Applies to individuals and businesses.**
    a. **Person:** Evidence of a person's habit is admissible to show the person **acted in accordance** with the habit on a particular occasion (e.g., driver who always fastens her seatbelt before driving).
    b. **Business practices:** The routine practice of an organization is admissible to show the **practice was followed** by the business on a particular occasion (e.g., outgoing mail placed in the outbox is collected and mailed everyday at 3 p.m.).
2. **Three factors** are considered to determine if habit or character evidence:
    a. The more **specific** the behavior, the more likely it's habit.
    b. The more **regular** the behavior, the more likely it's habit.
    c. The more **unreflective or semi-automatic**, the more likely it's habit.

B. **Similar happenings:** Evidence that similar happenings that occurred in the past (or failed to occur) are allowed if the events are **substantially similar**. Typically used to show prior accident or injury, or the absence of a past accident or injury.

VIII. IMPEACHMENT

A. **Impeachment:** A witness's credibility may be impeached by cross examination (or on direct, if witness is "hostile"), or with the proper foundation, by extrinsic evidence (i.e., other witnesses). Either party may impeach a witness.

1. **Five main ways to impeach:**
    a. **Character for truthfulness:** This can be shown by reputation and opinion, past crimes, past bad acts. (See section VIII.A.2 below.)
    b. **Prior inconsistent statement (PIS)**
        1. **Extrinsic evidence** may be used to prove the PIS if
            a. The witness who made the PIS is given an opportunity to **explain or deny**, and
            b. The proponent of the PIS is given an opportunity to **interrogate** the impeaching witness.
        2. **FRE limitation: If not given under oath,** the PIS can only be used for **impeachment** purposes. (CEC does not have this limitation.)
    c. **Bias:** A witness may be impeached by a showing of bias, self-interest, or motive.
        1. **Extrinsic evidence** is allowed if the witness is given an opportunity to **explain or deny.**
    d. **Sensory or mental defect:** A witness may be impeached by showing that his capacity to observe or remember is impaired.
    e. **Contradiction of testimony by another witness.** However, this rule is limited and can't concern a collateral matter. A collateral matter would be contradiction on a fact not material to case, but only contradicts the witness.
2. **Impeaching witness's *character for truthfulness*.** (From VIII.A.1.a above. Note that this is accomplished through character evidence regarding truthfulness, so be mindful of the character evidence rules discussed above.)
    a. **Reputation and opinion regarding truthfulness is allowed,** but inquiry into any specific acts that led to the witness's opinion or the person's reputation is not allowed.
    b. **Specific bad acts that bear on truthfulness**
        1. **FRE: Specific bad acts** that are probative of ***truthfulness*** may be inquired into on **cross examination** but are always subject to the legal relevance balancing test.
            a. The question must be made in good faith.
            b. **Extrinsic evidence is not allowed** to prove the bad act, so essentially the questioner is stuck with the answer received from the witness.
        2. **CEC**
            a. **Civil court: Prohibits** the extrinsic evidence and the initial cross examination.
            b. **Criminal court:** Prop. 8 **permits** both the initial cross examination and the extrinsic evidence (subject to the legal relevance balancing test).

c. **Impeaching with criminal conviction**
   1. **Crimen falsi (FRE):** All convictions (felonies and misdemeanors) for crimes involving a **false statement** are admissible and the judge may not exclude under the legal relevance balancing test, unless the conviction (e.g., forgery, perjury, embezzlement, etc.) is more than ten years old.
   2. **Felony conviction**
      a. **FRE:** A balancing test is used to determine admissibility, depending on witness status.
         i. **Witness is criminal defendant:** The conviction is admissible only if the probative value outweighs its prejudicial effect.
         ii. **Other witness:** The conviction is admissible unless the prejudicial effect *substantially* outweighs the probative value.
      b. **CEC: Felony convictions** are admissible if:
         i. It has **not been expunged**, pardoned, etc.
         ii. The felony involves **moral turpitude**, and
         iii. Subject to legal relevance balancing test.
   3. **Misdemeanor convictions**
      a. **FRE:** Misdemeanors that are not crimen falsi are **not admissible to impeach.**
      b. **CEC**
         i. **Civil court: Misdemeanors cannot be used** to impeach a witness
         ii. **Criminal court:** Misdemeanors can only be used if it involves **moral turpitude.**
   4. **Old convictions** may not be used if **more than ten years** have elapsed from both the conviction and the prison term, unless specific facts make the probative value of the conviction substantially outweigh the prejudicial effect.

<u>**Impeachment evidence fact triggers:**</u>
- Character evidence at issue
- Prior conviction of any kind
- Prior bad behavior (e.g., sell drugs, accused of sexual misconduct, bad driving, accused of excessive force)

3. **Rehabilitating impeached witnesses**
   a. **Must meet the attack:** The rehabilitating evidence must support the witness's credibility in the same respect as the attack.
   b. **Good character:** Can show witness's good character where evidence of his **character for untruthfulness** has been shown.
   c. A **prior consistent statement (PCS)** can be used to rebut an express or implied charge of recent fabrication, or that witness's testimony was the product of improper motive.

B. **Bolstering the witness**

1. **FRE: Bolstering is not allowed.** A lawyer may not offer evidence supporting a witness's credibility until it has been attacked.
2. **CEC: Bolstering is allowed**. Either side may offer evidence supporting a witness's credibility before it has been attacked.

IX. **HEARSAY IS INADMISSIBLE** UNLESS AN EXCEPTION APPLIES.

A. **Hearsay** is an **out-of-court statement** offered for the **truth of the matter** asserted.

1. **"Out of court"** means that the declarant must make the statement at some time and place other than while testifying at the trial or hearing.
   a. This includes a declarant repeating his own prior out-of-court statement.
2. The **statement** can be oral or written, or even nonverbal conduct if it is intended as an assertion.
3. **Truth of the matter:** Offered for the truth of matter asserted.

B. **Nonhearsay purpose: An out of court statement may be nonhearsay because it is not being offered for truth** of the matter asserted such as in the following situations where evidence is offered to show:

1. **Effect on listener or reader**, such as being put on notice, having certain knowledge, had a certain emotion, or behaved reasonably or unreasonably.
2. **Declarant's state of mind**
   a. **Knowledge** of facts, or
   b. **Mental state** (e.g., declarant stating "I'm Abraham Lincoln" is offered not to prove its truth, but that the delarant is delusional).
3. **Legally operative fact.** A statement that itself has legal significance (e.g., solicitation, defamation, words establishing a contract).

> <u>Nonhearsay purpose fact triggers:</u>
> - Put someone on notice (e.g., brakes are bad, drill bit is defective)
> - Knowledge/Mental state (e.g., information that provides motive for subsequent act)

> **<u>Issue-spotting tip:</u>** Where statements that would otherwise be hearsay are being admitted because the statement is not being offered for its truth, but rather for the purpose of establishing one of the exceptions above, always do the **legal relevance prejudicial balancing test.** There is always a danger of unfair prejudice when evidence is admissible for one purpose but not another.

C. **Multiple hearsay** occurs where an out-of-court statement quotes or paraphrases another out-of-court statement. **Each level of hearsay must fall within an exception** to be admissible.

> **Multiple hearsay fact triggers:**
> - Police report including bystander or witness statement
> - Work order containing mechanic's observations
> - Surgical report containing observation of medical personnel
> - Witness testifying what another person told him a third party said

D. **Policy:** The following policies behind the hearsay rule and hearsay exceptions can provide key points of analysis in an essay question.
   1. **Rule purpose:** The purpose of the hearsay rule is that some communications are suspect because of the **danger of misinterpretation** without the speaker present to clarify. The hearsay dangers are ambiguity, insincerity, incorrect memory, and inaccurate perception.
   2. **Exception purpose:** The purpose of the hearsay exceptions is that where circumstances provide an **aura of authenticity** to a statement, it should be admissible.

X. HEARSAY EXCEPTIONS AND EXCLUSIONS

A. **Admissions** are excluded from hearsay and will be admitted.
   1. **Party admission:** A party admission is **any statement** made by a party, and it may be offered against him. The statement need not be against declarant's interest.
      a. **CEC** calls this a hearsay "exception" not "exemption."
   2. **Adoptive admission:** An adoptive admission is a statement made by another where the party **knows of its content** and voluntarily **manifests belief in the truth** of the statement by words or action.
      a. **Silent adoptive admission:** Adoptive admission can be made by silence if a **reasonable person would have spoken up**, but always subject to the Fifth Amendment right to remain silent. For example, if at an accident scene one party says, "it's all your fault," this may be an adoptive admission by silence because a reasonable person would have refuted the statement if he was not at fault.
   3. **Vicarious admission:** A vicarious or representative admission can arise two ways.
      a. **Explicit authorization:** A statement made by an authorized spokesperson of party.
      b. **Employee or agent:** A statement made by an agent/employee of the party concerning a transaction within the **scope of the agent/employee relationship**, and made **during the existence** of the relationship.
         1. **CEC is more narrow:** A statement by an employee of a party is a party admission of employer only where **negligent conduct of that employee** is the basis for employer's liability in a case of respondeat superior.
   4. **Co-conspirator admissions** are statements made **during course** of the conspiracy and **in furtherance** of conspiracy.

a. **Confrontation Clause:** However, a co-conspirator admission is subject to the confrontation clause requirement that a defendant is allowed to confront his accusers, so if the co-conspirator refuses to testify, the co-conspirator admission will not be admitted.

B. **Spontaneous, excited, or contemporaneous statement hearsay exceptions**
   1. **Medical diagnosis or treatment statements:** A statement made for the **purpose** of medical diagnosis or treatment is admissible.
      a. Statement may be made by **third person** if to help obtain treatment.
      b. Statement may include the **cause** of the condition, but **not statements of fault.**
      c. **CEC:** Statement of **past physical condition** is only admissible if made to obtain medical diagnosis and treatment by a **child abuse victim.**
   2. **Statement of then-existing mental, emotional, or physical condition** is admissible to show the condition or state of mind.
      a. **Does not apply to a statement of memory or belief.**
   3. **Present sense impression (PSI)**: A statement is admissible if describing or **explaining an event** or condition and **made while declarant was perceiving** the event or condition or immediately thereafter.
      a. **CEC contemporaneous statement:** Applies to a statement explaining **conduct of the declarant** and made **while the declarant engaged in that conduct** (narrower than FRE).
   4. **Excited utterance:** A statement is admissible if relating to a **startling event** or condition and **made while the declarant was still under the stress** of excitement caused by the event or condition.

<u>Excited utterance fact triggers:</u>
- Any statement followed by an exclamation mark
- Witness to a car accident
- Descriptions such as that someone is angry or shouting

C. **Prior statements of available witnesses**
   1. **Prior inconsistent statement (PIS)**: A PIS is **substantively admissible**, not merely for impeachment purposes, if:
      a. **Oath:** The PIS was made under oath as part of a formal proceeding.
      b. **Cross examination:** The declarant is subject to cross examination concerning the PIS.
   2. **Prior consistent statement (PCS)**: A PCS is only admissible **substantively** if offered to **rebut a charge** of recent fabrication, or improper motive. It need not be made under oath.
   3. **Prior identification** of a person, made after perceiving the person, is **substantively admissible** if the **declarant testifies** at trial.

D. **Document hearsay exceptions**

1. **Past recollection recorded:** If a witness **cannot testify from memory,** a party may **introduce** a written record of an event.
   a. **Requirements** must be satisfied
      1. **Firsthand knowledge** of the sponsoring witness.
      2. Events were **fresh in the memory** when record was made.
      3. Witness now has **impaired recollection.**
      4. Record was **accurate when written.**
   b. **Document read to jury:** The writing itself is not admissible but may be read to the jury.

> <u>**Issue-spotting tip:**</u> **Past recollection recorded** applies when the document consulted to refresh memory *does not actually refresh* the witness's memory, so if it otherwise qualifies, the document is then read into the record. **Present recollection refreshed** allows an item to be shown to the witness as a memory stimulus, which then allows the witness to testify entirely from memory.

2. **Business record** is admissible where a sponsoring witness establishes the record was kept in the course of **regularly conducted business activity.**
   a. **Business activity** includes events, conditions, opinion, or diagnosis.
      1. **CEC:** Does not allow opinions or diagnoses.
   b. **Regular practice** to keep such a record.
   c. **Personal knowledge:** Made by a person with personal knowledge.
      1. **Firsthand knowledge** by original supplier of information.
      2. **Business duty to report:** The record must be made by one with a business duty to report.

> <u>**Exam tip:**</u> Look for information contained in reports that is provided by those without a business duty to report, such as an accident witness.

   d. **Timeliness:** Made at or near time of matters indicated
3. **Public records and reports** are admissible if within one of the following categories:
   a. **Agency's record of its own activities.**
   b. **Matters observed in the line of duty** and under a duty to report.
   c. **Investigative reports** with factual findings resulting from investigations made.
   d. **Criminal case limitation—FRE only: Criminal prosecution** cannot use matters **observed by police officers** or police investigations against a criminal defendant. (CEC does not have the limitation.)

> <u>Issue-spotting tip:</u> Multiple hearsay problems are often found in business records or public records. The first level of hearsay is the record itself; the second level of hearsay can occur where the record contains information provided by another person. Remember, each level of hearsay must have a hearsay exception in order for the evidence to be admitted.

4. **Learned writings and commercial publications**
   a. **FRE:** Admissible if called to the attention of an expert witness and established as **reliable authority**.
   b. **CEC:** Admissible only for facts of **general notoriety and interest**.

E. **Declarant unavailable hearsay exceptions**
1. **Witness unavailable:** The witness's unavailability must be established in one of the following ways:
   a. **Privileged** from testifying.
   b. **Death or illness** prevents witness from testifying.
   c. **Reasonable means** can't procure the witness.
   d. **Witness refuses to testify** despite a court order.
      1. **CEC** requires refusal be made out of fear.
   e. **Witness unable to remember.**
      1. **CEC** requires total memory loss.
2. **Four hearsay exceptions requiring unavailability**
   a. **Former restimony:** Former testimony is admissible where the party against whom the testimony is now offered had, during the earlier hearing or deposition, an opportunity to examine that person and a **similar motive to develop the testimony**.
      1. **Civil cases only**
         a. **FRE only:** Allows **predecessor in interest** to have been present in earlier proceeding to develop testimony.
         b. **CEC only:** Allows if **anyone with a similar interest** was present in earlier proceeding, or it is being offered against the person who offered it on her own behalf in the earlier proceeding, or against a successor in interest of such person.
         c. **CEC only: Deposition** testimony given in the **same civil action** is admissible for all purposes if deponent is unavailable at trial or lives more than 150 miles from the courthouse.
   b. **Dying declaration:** A dying declaration is admissible where a statement is made by a declarant, while **believing his death was imminent**, and is concerning the cause or **circumstances of his impending death**.
      1. **FRE:** Only allowed in civil and criminal homicide cases, and declarant **need only be unavailable**, not dead.
      2. **CEC:** Applies to all civil and criminal cases and declarant must **actually be dead**.

   3. **CEC "OJ" Exception—statement describing physical abuse:** Applies to allow a statement made at or near the time of injury or threat, describing infliction or threat of physical abuse, in writing, recorded, or made to police or medical professional, under trustworthy circumstances.
  c. **Declaration against interest:** A declaration against interest is admissible if, **at the time** it was made, it was against the **declarant's financial or penal interest.**
   1. **FRE:** If offered to **exculpate** the accused, there must be **corroborating evidence.**
   2. **CEC:** Includes a statement against one's **social interest.**
   3. Note: The Confrontation Clause may keep the statement out of evidence.
  d. **Forfeiture by wrongdoing:** A hearsay exception will apply where a party has engaged in **witness tampering** intended to make the witness unavailable.

F. **Residual "catch-all" hearsay exception:** An otherwise hearsay statement may be admissible if **trustworthy**, is regarding a **material fact**, is **more probative** on the point than other evidence, and **notice** is given to the opposing side.

> <u>**Memorization tip:**</u> Hearsay exceptions is the second-most frequently tested evidence principle (after relevance). To aid memorization of the hearsay exceptions, group them into categories:
> - Four admissions (party, adoptive, vicarious, co-conspirator)
> - Four witness statements (medical, then-existing state, PSI, excited utterance)
> - Three prior statements of available witnesses (PIS, PCS, Prior Identification)
> - Four documents (PRR, business, public, learned writing)
> - Four declarant unavailable (former testimony, dying declaration, declaration against interest, forfeiture by wrongdoing).
>
> <u>**Exam tip:**</u> To properly analyze a piece of evidence, always include each hearsay exception that potentially applies under the facts.

XI. DOCUMENTS, REAL EVIDENCE, AND DEMONSTRATIVE EVIDENCE

A. **Relevance:** All documentary evidence must be relevant in order to be admissible.

B. **Authentication:** All evidence, other than testimony, must be authenticated as genuine in order to be admitted. Authentication is proof that the item **is what the proponent claims** it is.
 1. **Methods of authentication**
  a. **Real evidence:** Can be authenticated by **distinctive characteristics** or **chain of custody.**

b. **Demonstrative evidence** must be a **fair representation.**
c. **Writings and recordings** can be authenticated by admissions, eyewitness testimony, handwriting verifications (expert or nonexpert with personal knowledge, or trier of fact with sample comparisons), circumstantial evidence (e.g., postmark, address), etc.
   1. **Ancient documents**
      a. FRE: 20 years
      b. CEC: 30 years
d. **Self-authenticating documents: Certified copies** of public records (e.g., deeds), official publications, newspapers, and periodicals.
   1. **FRE only: Business records** and **trade** inscriptions.
   2. **CEC only:** Signature of **notary** or domestic public employee.

<u>Authentication fact triggers:</u>
- Phone call, especially if voice disguised or muffled
- Greeting card with signature found by a third party
- Signature on letter
- Report of any kind

C. **Best evidence rule (FRE) and secondary evidence rule (CEC):** To prove the **contents** of a writing (including photos, X-rays, recordings), the original writing must be produced. **Machine duplicates are also allowed** unless the authenticity of the original is disputed.
   1. If **original or photocopy is unavailable:** Oral testimony is admissible, and the CEC even allows handwritten duplicates.
   2. **Best evidence rule (BER) does not apply** when the fact to be proved exists independently of the writing (e.g., witness can testify from personal knowledge), where writing is collateral (minor), voluminous records, or public records.
D. **Summaries of voluminous writings:** If original documents are so voluminous that they can't be conveniently introduced into evidence, a summary may be introduced through a sponsoring witness.

<u>Exam tip:</u> Whenever a document is being introduced into evidence always analyze the following four issues: 1) relevance, 2) authentication, 3) BER, and 4) hearsay and any applicable hearsay exceptions.

XII. **PROCEDURAL ISSUES**
   A. **Burdens of proof:** There are two different burdens of proof.
      1. **Burden of production:** Where a party has the burden of production, that party must come forward with the **evidence to establish that fact** or issue.
      2. **Burden of persuasion:** The evidence must be sufficient to establish the issue.
         a. **Civil case:** The burden typically rests with the **plaintiff** and usually is to a **preponderance of the evidence** standard.

b. **Criminal case:** The burden of persuasion rests with the **prosecution** and is **beyond a reasonable doubt.**

B. **Presumptions** are inferences that the jury must draw from a set of facts.

1. A **civil case presumption** operates to shift the burden of **producing evidence** (not persuasion) to the opposing party.
   a. Examples of rebuttable presumptions: mail delivery, legitimacy, sanity, that a death is not suicide, death from seven years' absence, etc.
2. **There is no criminal case presumption.** The burden of production and persuasion is always on the prosecution to prove every element of a crime beyond a reasonable doubt.

C. **Judge and jury allocations**

1. The **judge** decides issues of **law.**
2. The **jury** decides issues of **fact.**

XIII. JUDICIAL NOTICE

A. **Judicial notice** is the process of establishing facts without presenting evidence. The court can take judicial notice of facts **not subject to reasonable dispute** because they are either

a. **Generally known** within the jurisdiction, or
b. Capable of **accurate and ready determination** by a source whose accuracy cannot be reasonably questioned.

B. **Instructions and judicial discretion**

1. **FRE:** A party **must request judicial notice** to **compel** judicial notice. If not requested, the court has discretion to take judicial notice. Judicial notice can occur at any time even on appeal.
   a. **Civil case:** The jury **must accept** noticed fact.
   b. **Criminal case:** The jury **may accept** the noticed fact.
2. **CEC:** Whether requested or not, the court **must take judicial notice of matters generally known** within jurisdiction. CEC does not distinguish between civil and criminal.

EVIDENCE ISSUES TESTED MATRIX

		Crossover	Relevance	Prop. 8	Policy Exclusions	Personal Knowledge	Form of Questions	Lay Opinion	Expert Opinion	Privileges	Character & Habit	Impeachment	Hearsay & Exceptions	Authentication	BER / SER	Judicial Notice
July '11 Q2	Doctor performs Perry's back surgery	Civ. Proc.	X							X						
February '11 Q6	Green's Grocery & lottery ticket w/wrong #s	Remedy	X										X			
July '10 Q3	David & Vic fight; Vic has heart attack		X	X		X					X	X	X	X		
July '09 Q3	Paula & Dan in a car accident		X	X	X	X		X	X				X	X	X	
February '09 Q3	Dustin commits robbery; ex-wife Wendy on stand		X	X		X	X	X		X			X			
July '07 Q3	Dave, Mechanic, bad brakes & car accident		X			X		X					X		X	
February '07 Q6	Officer Will, Calvin's cocaine, & Donna's car		X			X			X		X		X	X	X	
July '05 Q4	Dan charged with arson of failing business		X			X					X		X	X	X	

Continued >

		Crossover	Relevance	Prop. 8	Policy Exclusions	Personal Knowledge	Form of Questions	Lay Opinion	Expert Opinion	Privileges	Character & Habit	Impeachment	Hearsay & Exceptions	Authentication	BER / SER	Judicial Notice
July '04 Q4	Victor on fire from gaso-line; Dan charged		X			X	X				X		X		X	X
July '03 Q3	Dan assaults off-duty policeman in bar fight		X			X	X				X	X	X		X	
February '02 Q6	Phil v. Dirk, the barber, for hair loss		X		X	X			X				X	X	X	X
July '01 Q3	Walker v. TruckCo for car accident		X			X	X	X					X			
July '00 Q1	Dan sells heroin @ Guy's Bar		X				X				X	X	X	X	X	
February '00 Q6	Picasso sketch taken from museum	Crimes											X			
July '99 Q4	Mary v. Dr. Jones & wobbly drill bit in back surgery		X		X	X	X	X			X	X	X		X	
July '98 Q6	Dunn, Empire Trucking Co. & car accident		X		X	X	X	X				X	X		X	
February '98 Q3	Don, armed assault on Victor & tells Bernice		X			X				X	X	X	X	X	X	
July '97 Q1	Dave sells cocaine & Carl Smith is witness		X			X	X				X	X	X		X	
July '96 Q1	Don, fistfight in boardinghouse & kills Vic		X			X					X	X	X	X		

Continued >

		Crossover	Relevance	Prop. 8	Policy Exclusions	Personal Knowledge	Form of Questions	Lay Opinion	Expert Opinion	Privileges	Character & Habit	Impeachment	Hearsay & Exceptions	Authentication	BER / SER	Judicial Notice
February '96 Q3	Dave's gym & injury to Paul	Civ. Proc. Torts	X				X					X	X	X	X	
July '94 Q4	Don & Phil in car accident; Officer Jones		X		X	X	X	X	X		X	X	X	X	X	
February '93 Q3	Mary's husband killed car accident with Truckco		X		X	X	X				X	X	X	X	X	
July '92 Q3	Dan charged w/ killing Vickie, w/red scarf		X			X					X	X	X	X	X	X
February '92 Q6	Paul v. Don, tort action for stab wounds		X				X						X	X		
July '91 Q4	Pam hit by Carl, Dan's pizza driver		X		X	X							X	X	X	
July '90 Q4	Dave, waiter at Bill's café charged arson		X			X		X	X		X	X	X			X
July '88 Q1	Superhealth Pharmacy & Dee's morphine		X							X	X	X	X			
July '87 Q1	Don hits Paul, Vicky injured & dies in surgery		X			X		X		X	X		X			

EVIDENCE PRACTICE ESSAYS, ANSWER GRIDS, AND SAMPLE ANSWERS

Evidence Question 1

February 1993, Question 3

Mary sued Trucking Company (TruckCo) for the wrongful death of her husband, Hal. Hal was killed when a log truck driven by Boyd crossed the center line and struck Hal's car. Boyd was severely injured and died a week later from complications. TruckCo asserts that Boyd was an independent contractor hauling logs for TruckCo and not a TruckCo employee. At the trial by jury, the following occurred:

1. Plaintiff called Tom, TruckCo's president, as a hostile witness. Plaintiff asked the following question: "Didn't you call Mary the day after the crash, tell her that it was Boyd's fault, and offer to pay Hal's funeral expenses?"
2. Plaintiff then asked Tom: "Didn't TruckCo have a liability insurance policy covering the truck driven by Boyd at the time of the collision?"
3. Plaintiff called Officer Reno. Reno testified that Boyd had given him a statement after the crash. Reno then read the following from his report: "Boyd stated he fell asleep at the wheel and ran over the center line."
4. Mary testified that Hal loved her and was a kind and considerate spouse. Defendant then called Smith, Mary and Hal's longtime neighbor, and asked Smith the following: "What was Hal's reputation in the community, prior to the crash, for fighting with Mary?" Plaintiff's objection was sustained. If allowed to testify, Smith would have testified that Hal had a reputation for being quarrelsome and physically violent with Mary.

Assume that in each instance all appropriate objections were made.

1. Was the question asked in paragraph 1 objectionable? Discuss.
2. Was the question asked in paragraph 2 objectionable? Discuss.
3. Should Reno have been permitted to read from his report as set forth in paragraph 3? Discuss.
4. Was the objection in paragraph 4 properly sustained? Discuss.

Evidence Question 1 Assessment

February 1993, Question 3

Evidence essays are usually "racehorse" questions where a large quantity of issues must be covered. This evidence question is no exception and has 19 separate issues that needed to be analyzed, plus other potential issues that could logically be discussed but were not required in order to pass the essay. In addition to testing the rules for evidence, evidence essay questions also put your issue-spotting ability and time management skills to the test. Evidence requires the use of a more detailed checklist than usual since spotting all of the important issues is essential to passing and because there are so many issues tested and they aren't always easy to spot.

Spend a full 15 to 20 minutes organizing your answer before you begin to write. In those 15 to 20 minutes, create a brief outline on scratch paper to assist you in writing your answer. Use lots of abbreviations to do it quickly, and leave lots of white space on the scratch paper to make it easy to follow. First, ask yourself a few important questions and jot down the answers at the top of your scratch paper: Is the case civil or criminal, and in federal or California court? If you can't tell, you'll need to answer using both rules and point out the rule differences where applicable. What is the underlying cause of action, crime, or defense? You will use this information each time you analyze why a piece of evidence is relevant. (E.g.: "Underlying cause of action is negligence. A party's statement admitting fault for a car accident tends to establish breach.")

Next, organize the question into sections based on the call of the question, and/or by piece of evidence. In this question you would break it down into four sections based on the four separate calls of the question, with each call of the question corresponding to a piece of evidence. (E.g: "Call #1, Tom's statement to Mary.") Take each piece of evidence and "run" it through your issues checklist. By that, we mean go issue by issue through the checklist and decide if each issue applies to that piece of evidence. Logical relevance is always an issue, so jot that down as the first issue and note the corresponding fact that will be used in the analysis (e.g., "log. rel.—Trucko liable."). Then, continue with all the other issues: public policy exclusions ("settlement offer—no claim yet"; "offer to pay meds—funeral expenses"); witness on the stand ("leading Q—okay because hostile"); privileges ("character, and impeachment don't apply"); hearsay ("on phone & to prove liability"); and hearsay exceptions ("admission—Tom Co. president"). Then do the same thing for calls 2, 3, and 4. Now that you've spotted all the issues and know which facts to use in the analysis, you are ready to write your answer from the outline you've created on the scratch paper.

While most of the issues are easy to spot, there is one tricky "deal breaker" issue on this question that is essential to passing this essay: The last call of the question (and that is likely not by accident) brings up the sophisticated issue that a wrongful death suit puts the decedent's character "at issue" because the quality of his character has a bearing on damages, and thus the normal rules barring character evidence do not apply. Although evidence questions usually tend to contain an abundance of issues but more shallow analysis, this tricky issue is an exception to that general rule.

Make note of the areas highlighted in **bold** on the corresponding grid. The bold areas highlight the issues, analysis, and conclusions that are likely **required** to receive a passing score on this question. In general, the essay grids are provided to assist you in analyzing the essays, and are much more detailed than what a student should create during the exam to organize their response to a question.

Call	Issue	Rule	Fact Application	Conclusion
1				
	Relevance: logical	**Relevant if it has any tendency to prove or disprove a material fact.**	Tom's statement would tend to **prove Truckco's liability under a respondeat superior theory since Boyd's at fault for the accident.**	**Relevant**
	Leading Q (or misleading Q or compound Q)	**Suggests the answer to the question**; allowed on direct w/ "hostile" witness.	Truckco is a party opponent and so is **hostile witness,** so **leading Q allowed.** And, here, said, "didn't you . . . ," which suggests the answer.	Leading
	Public policy excl.: settlement offers	**Not allowed to show liability**, but must have "claim" first.	**Public policy excludes offers to settle because it would otherwise inhibit settlement offers if they could be used against the offeror later.** Tom called Mary the next day so it appears no "claim" filed, so allowed. (Could argue offer to pay for medications instead.)	Not excluded for policy reasons because no claim filed
	Public policy excl.: offer to pay med. expenses	**Not admissible to show liability, but admissions made are admissible.**	**Same public policy argument** as above. Here, **offer to pay** funeral expenses is similar to medical or hospital expenses so **can't admit to show liability.**	**Not admissible**
	Legal relevance	Relevant evidence may be excluded if its probative value is substantially outweighed by dangers of unfair prejudice, etc.	Here, probative value of showing Truckco's liability for the accident that killed Hal. But, it is highly prejudicial because public interest discourages policy that chills settlement offers/offers to pay medical expenses.	Legally relevant—prejudicial value doesn't substantially o/w probative value
	Hearsay	**An out-of-court statement offered for the truth of the matter asserted.**	**Out of court: Because statement was made on the phone.** **Truth of matter asserted: That Boyd caused Hal's death so Truckco will pay expenses.**	**Hearsay & excluded unless exception**

Continued >

Call	Issue	Rule	Fact Application	Conclusion
	Party admission Vicarious admission	Party opponent statement is admissible. Statement by agent/employee of a party concerning a transaction w/in scope of agent/employee relationship & made during relationship.	Here, **Tom is an employee (president) of party Truckco and, as president, is authorized to speak for Truckco** since a typical duty of a company president would be to handle litigation and be the company spokesperson, **so this is a** vicarious **admission.**	Vicarious **admission**
2				
	Relevance	See above	**Tends to prove Boyd is an employee of Truckco and thus Truckco is liable.**	**Relevant**
	Leading question	See above	Suggests answer, but hostile witness (see above).	Leading;
	Public policy excl.: liability insurance	**Not allowed to show negligence, but allowed to show ownership/control.**	**Public policy excludes evidence of insurance because of the danger that it will imply the defendant has deep pockets to pay or has insurance because he's careless. But, it is admissible to show that Truckco owned the truck involved and that Boyd was Truckco's employee.**	**Admissible to show Truckco's ownership & control of truck**
	Legal relevance	See above	Probative value of showing that Boyd is an employee outweighs **prejudicial effect of implying negligence because of insurance or deep pockets to pay.**	Legally relevant
3				
	Relevance	See above	Tends to show **Boyd breached duty of care to Hal.**	Relevant
	Personal knowledge	See above	Reno had no personal knowledge of Boyd statement.	No personal knowl.

Continued >

Call	Issue	Rule	Fact Application	Conclusion
	Hearsay Double hearsay	See above	**Out of court: Because report** **For truth: regarding accident causation** **Two levels: 1) Boyd's statement; 2) Reno's report**	**Excluded, unless exception**
	Party admission **Vicarious admission**	See above See above	If Boyd is an employee of Truckco, Boyd's statement is a vicarious admission of Truckco because as a driver an accident was in course and scope; statement was made during employment.	Admission of party opponent
	Hearsay exception: declaration against interest	**Statement against one's financial or penal interest when made & declarant unavailable.**	**Since Boyd is dead, he is unavailable and the statement has the ring of truth because it's against Boyd's own financial interest since he accepts blame** and admits he fell asleep at the wheel.	**Declaration against interest**
	Hearsay exception: excited utterance	**Relating to a startling event while under stress of excitement.**	**Being involved in a fatal car accident is a startling event, the statement relates to the accident's causation, and the statement was made soon after at the accident scene while still under stress.**	**Excited utterance**
	Present sense impression (PSI)	A statement describing an event while perceiving the event, or soon after.	Could qualify as PSI if statement was made very soon after perceiving the event of the accident.	PSI
	Hearsay exception: business record	**A record of regular business activity, regular practice to keep record, made by one w/ a biz duty to report, near event time.**	**While it otherwise qualifies, the statement from Boyd contained in the police report will not qualify as business record exception because Boyd had no business duty to make a report. However the officer's observations are okay if normal to make such a report and done near time of accident.**	Business record for officer, **but not Boyd's statement**

Continued >

Call	Issue	Rule	Fact Application	Conclusion
	Past recollection recorded	Can read a document into evidence where: • Witness had knowledge • Fresh in memory @ time • Can't remember now • Made timely & accurate	If officer is allowed to read the report into evidence, it must meet the rule requirements for a past recollection recorded.	Okay with proper foundation
4				
	Relevance	See above	**Tends to prove amount of damages for the wrongful death claim.**	**Relevant**
	Personal knowledge		Neighbor testifying from personal knowledge of Hal.	Personal knowl.
	Character evidence: character trait "at issue"	**Character evidence is generally not allowed to show conduct in conformity, except where "at issue."**	**Here, character trait of Hal being a good husband is "at issue" because damages would include his value as a spouse. A good husband is worth more than a lousy one, so Hal's "quarrelsome" and "violent" nature pertains to the damages issue.**	Character allowed
	Legal relevance	See above	Highly probative to know Hal is quarrelsome and violent and, while prejudicial, not unduly so where character is at issue.	Relevant
	Impeachment	Can impeach w/ testimony that contradicts witness.	This will be allowed as impeachment evidence by a witness, Smith, regarding the reputation of Hal, that **directly contradicts Mary's testimony about Hal's value as a loving, kind, and considerate spouse.**	Allowed

Evidence Question 1 Sample Answer

February 1993, Question 3

1. Paragraph 1

Logical Relevance

Evidence is relevant if it has any tendency to prove or disprove a material fact. Tom's statement would tend to prove Truckco's liability under a respondeat superior theory since their employee Boyd is at fault for the accident, and so it is relevant.

Leading Question

A leading question suggests the answer and is not permissible on direct examination, except with a hostile witness, which Truckco is as the party opponent.

Settlement Offer

Offers of settlement are not admissible to show liability where there is a claim. Public policy interest excludes offers to settle because otherwise it would inhibit resolution by settlement if the offers could later be used against a person. Tom called Mary the day after the accident so there may not have been a claim, and if so it is admissible.

Offer to Pay Medical Bills

Offers to pay medical bills are not admissible to show liability, but admissions made in conjunction are admissible. For the same policy reasons above offers to pay medical bill, and, likewise, expenses such as funeral expenses are not admissible to show liability, so this statement is inadmissible.

Legal Relevance

Otherwise-relevant evidence may be excluded if the probative value is substantially outweighed by the danger of unfair prejudice. Here, there is probative value in showing that Truckco is liable for Hal's death, but this is also highly prejudicial because public interest discourages policies that chill settlement offers or offers to pay medical bills. Nonetheless, the evidence is legally relevant.

Hearsay

Hearsay is an out-of-court statement offered for the truth of the matter asserted. Tom's statement was made out of court on the phone and offered to prove the truth that their employee Boyd was responsible for the accident that killed Hal. This is hearsay and excluded unless an exception applies.

Party Admission/Vicarious

A statement by a party opponent is admissible. A statement by an employee of a party concerning a matter within the scope of and during their employment will be a vicarious admission of the party. Tom is Truckco's employee; he is president and within the course of his duties as president would be authorized to speak for Truckco regarding litigation, so Tom's statement is a vicarious admission of Truckco.

2. Paragraph 2

Relevance

The question tends to prove Boyd is an employee of Truckco, and thus, they are liable for the accident, so it is relevant.

Leading Question

The form of the question tends to suggest the answer, but Tom is a hostile witness so this is allowable.

Liability Insurance

Liability insurance is not admissible to show negligence but may be admitted to establish ownership or control of an instrumentality. Public policy interest excludes evidence of liability insurance because of the dangers associated with implying that only a careless defendant carries insurance or that there are deep pockets available to pay a damages award. But, liability insurance is admissible to show ownership or control of the truck involved in the accident and that Boyd is Truckco's employee, so it would be admissible for that purpose.

Legal Relevance

The probative value of showing that Boyd is Truckco's employee and Truckco owns the truck outweighs any prejudicial effect of implying that Truckco is a careless company or that they have deep pockets to pay a damages award.

3. Paragraph 3

Relevance

Officer Reno's statement tends to show Boyd breached his duty of care to Hal and is relevant.

Personal Knowledge

It appears that Reno has no personal knowledge of Boyd's statement, which is required for testimony since he is reading from his report.

Double Hearsay

Where there is hearsay contained within hearsay, each level of hearsay must be subject to an exception or the entire statement/report is excluded. There are two levels of hearsay here because there is 1) Boyd's statement, in 2) Reno's written report.

Party Admission/Vicarious

If Boyd is an employee of Truckco, his statement is a vicarious admission of Truckco because, as a driver, an accident occurred during the course and scope of his employment as it was made during his employment.

Declaration Against Interest

A hearsay exception is available for statements made against one's own financial or penal interests and is admissible if the declarant is unavailable. Since Boyd died from his injuries in the accident he is unavailable and, further, his statement has the ring of truth to it because it is against his own financial interests to accept blame for the accident and admit that he fell asleep at the wheel of the truck. Boyd's statement will be admissible as a declaration against interest.

Excited Utterance

A hearsay exception applies to excited utterances, which relate to a startling event and are made while still under the stress of excitement from the event. Being involved in a fatal car accident is a startling event, and Boyd's statement here relates to the causation of the accident, which is the startling event. Further, Boyd's statement was made soon after the accident while still at the scene, so it was made while under the stress of the event so it is admissible as an excited utterance.

Present Sense Impression

Present sense impression (PSI) is a hearsay exception for statements made describing an event while perceiving the event or immediately thereafter. Boyd's statement could come in as a PSI if it was made very close in time after perceiving the accident.

Business Record

A hearsay exception exists for business records, which are records of regularly conducted business activity, where it is the regular practice to keep the record, made by one with a business duty to report, and done near the time of the event. While Officer Reno's report otherwise qualifies, the statement from Boyd, which is contained in the police report, will not qualify as a business record because Boyd was under no business duty to report the accident events. However, Officer Reno's observations are admissible if it was normal for him to make such a report and it was done near the time of the accident.

Past Recollection Recorded

A document can be read into evidence where the witness had knowledge of the event, it was fresh in memory at the time it was made, the witness can't remember the information now, and the record was timely and accurate when made. If Officer Reno is allowed to read the report into evidence, they will need to establish it meets the requirements for a past recollection recorded outlined here.

4. Paragraph 4

Relevance

Mary's testimony about Hal tends to prove the amount of damages for the wrongful death claim and is relevant.

Personal Knowledge

The neighbor is testifying from his personal knowledge of Hal.

Character

Character evidence is generally not admissible to show conduct in conformity with the character trait, except it is allowed where character is "at issue." Hal's character trait of being a good husband is at issue because in a wrongful death claim Mary will be compensated for his value as a spouse, and a good and loving husband is worth more monetarily than a lousy husband. Hal's quarrelsome and violent nature is at issue in a wrongful death case because it pertains directly to damages and should be admitted.

Legal Relevance

Hal's value as a quarrelsome and violent husband is highly probative and, while it is prejudicial, it is not unduly so because character is directly at issue.

Impeachment

Another witness's contradicting statements can be used to impeach a witness. The neighbor's testimony will also be allowed in as impeachment evidence against Mary since his testimony regarding Hal's reputation directly contradicts Mary's testimony that Hal was a loving, kind, and considerate spouse.

Evidence Question 2

July 2009, Question 3

While driving their cars, Paula and Dan collided and each suffered personal injuries and property damage. Paula sued Dan for negligence in a California state court and Dan filed a cross-complaint for negligence against Paula. At the ensuing jury trial, Paula testified that she was driving to meet her husband, Hank, and that Dan drove his car into hers. Paula also testified that, as she and Dan were waiting for an ambulance immediately following the accident, Dan said, "I have plenty of insurance to cover your injuries." Paula further testified that, three hours after the accident, when a physician at the hospital to which she was taken asked her how she was feeling, she said, "My right leg hurts the most, all because that idiot Dan failed to yield the right-of-way."

Officer, who was the investigating police officer who responded to the accident, was unavailable at the trial. The court granted a motion by Paula to admit Officer's accident report into evidence. Officer's accident report states: "When I arrived at the scene three minutes after the accident occurred, an unnamed bystander immediately came up to me and stated that Dan pulled right out into the path of Paula's car. Based on this information, my interviews with Paula and Dan, and the skid-marks, I conclude that Dan caused the accident." Officer prepared his accident report shortly after the accident.

In his case-in-chief, Dan called a paramedic who had treated Paula at the scene of the accident. Dan showed the paramedic a greeting card, and the paramedic testified that he had found the card in Paula's pocket as he was treating her. The court granted a motion by Dan to admit the card into evidence. The card states: "Dearest Paula, Hurry home from work as fast as you can today. We need to get an early start on our weekend trip to the mountains! Love, Hank."

Dan testified that, as he and Paula were waiting for the ambulance immediately following the accident, Wilma handed him a note. Wilma had been identified as a witness during discovery, but had died before she could be deposed. The court granted a motion by Dan to admit the note into evidence. The note says: "I saw the whole thing. Paula was speeding. She was definitely negligent."

Assuming all appropriate objections were timely made, should the court have admitted:

1. Dan's statement to Paula about insurance? Discuss.
2. Paula's statement to the physician? Discuss.
3. Officer's accident report relating to:
   a. The unnamed bystander's statement? Discuss.
   b. Officer's conclusion and its basis? Discuss.
4. Hank's greeting card? Discuss.
5. Wilma's note? Discuss.

Answer according to California law.

Evidence Question 2 Assessment

July 2009, Question 3

This question is one of the most difficult evidence questions, but it is still a good practice question because it represents the first time (and one of only a few times) that California evidence has been tested on the essay exam. Prior to 2007, only federal rules of evidence were eligible for essay testing. In 2007, the California rules of evidence were also eligible for essay testing. Fortunately, most of the rules are similar. But, when studying, pay special attention to those areas where the rules are different because they are favorite testing areas.

You will note that at the very end of the question it states, "Answer according to California law." Where the question instructs you to answer according to California law, do so. If the question occurs in federal court applying federal law, answer using only the federal rules. If it isn't clear from the question which rules to apply, the safest way to answer is to use the federal rules and point out where the California rules are different.

This is a super racehorse question since there are more than 30 issues to analyze. However, not all of the potential analysis is critical to succeeding on this question. Once again, successful issue spotting is the key to a passing score, as you can see by noting the bold areas in the attached grid.

Though we typically recommend using a traditional IRAC format for essay answers, evidence essays do not lend themselves to using a perfect IRAC format—there simply isn't a sufficient amount of time. Practice weaving together the rules, factual analysis, and conclusion in one or two sentences (depending on the complexity) and doing a truncated analysis.

When organizing the essay, make note of the areas where there actually is some substance to the factual analysis. This will typically be in those areas where there are a lot of facts to use, or something pivotal is happening. If you aren't sure, asking yourself what the point of each paragraph is should help to sharpen your focus. We suggest using a symbol, like a star, to identify those areas for yourself on your outline. For example, in this question the key analytical focus should be on a few big issues: the prejudicial impact of the statement regarding liability insurance in call 1; the possible ways of getting the statement made to the doctor into evidence in call 2; the double hearsay, the spontaneous bystander statement (because there were so many facts to use right on point), and the officer's lack of foundation as an expert in call 3; the nonhearsay purpose for entering the card in call 4; and the improper lay opinion regarding an ultimate issue in call 5. When writing, pay a bit more attention to the analysis in these areas. For all other issues the analysis should be truncated. Where there is a multi-part rule but only facts pertaining to one of the elements are available, it is advisable on this type of racehorse question to jump straight to the point. Minor issues can be properly dispatched with one well-written sentence.

Make note of the areas highlighted in **bold** on the corresponding grid. The bold areas highlight the issues, analysis, and conclusions that are likely **required** to receive a passing score on this question.

Issue	Rule	Fact Application	Conclusion
Prop. 8	**In a Cal. criminal case, all relevant evidence is admissible unless exempt.**	**Here, it is not a criminal case, but civil, so Prop. 8 is not applicable.**	Prop. 8 not applicable
Call #1 (D Stmt. to P)			
Logical relevance	**Relevant if material to a disputed fact.**	**Shows that D is likely at fault (disputed fact) if he thought his insurance would need to pay.**	Logically relevant
Legal relevance	**Probative value v. unfair prejudice**	**It was probative to prove D was possibly at fault, but could prejudice a jury because insurance means ability to pay.** [Note: One state-released answer argued this under admission analysis.]	Legally relevant because doesn't rise to unfair prejudice level
Public policy exclusion: liability insurance	**Inadmissible to prove culpable conduct.** (Admissible to prove ownership, control, or as part of an admission.)	**Statement is not admissible to prove D was negligent or at fault,** but can admit if it shows D's admission of fault (since he expected his insurance to pay).	Not admissible for culpable conduct, but okay if admission
Public policy exclusion: offer to pay medical	**Offers to pay medical bills and any admissions made with the offer are inadmissible.**	It was likely not an offer to pay medical bills, but rather just an acknowledgment that P has insurance.	Not an offer to pay medical, so not excluded
Personal knowledge	Must have personal knowledge of facts.	P was there and D made statement to P.	P has personal knowl.
Hearsay	**Out-of-court statement offered to prove the truth of the matter asserted is inadmissible.**	Here, D's statement was made out of court, but was not likely offered to prove the truth that he had insurance; rather, offered to show that he was likely at fault and believed his insurance would pay due to his fault.	Likely not hearsay
Spontaneous statement	Made at or near time of startling event.	Car accident is a startling event and statement was made immediately after.	Hearsay exception

Continued >

Issue	Rule	Fact Application	Conclusion
Hearsay exception: admission	**Party admission:** any statement by a party offered by a party opponent.	**Here, statement was made by P, a party, by D, a party opponent, so it is an admission.**	Even if hearsay, admissible as it is admission
Answer call of Q		Could have concluded either way depending on above issues	Either way is okay
Call #2 (P Stmt. to Dr.)			
Logical relevance	See above	**Shows P's injuries and that D was at fault (disputed fact) because he failed to yield the right of way.**	Logically relevant
Legal relevance	See above	First part of statement (leg hurt) was probative to show P damages and not prejudicial as that was her injury. Second part of statement (D not yielding) could be prejudicial as it implicates he is at fault and not very probative in that it needs to be verified and need his side of story.	Prejudicial, so likely would not come in [one answer came to opposite conclusion]
Personal knowledge	See above	P made statement so she is aware of it.	Personal knowledge
Hearsay	See above	• **Statement to physician made out of court** at the hospital, and • Statement 1: P's leg injury offered to prove damage for negl., • Statement 2: D didn't yield the right of way offered to prove D breached duty, so • **Both statements offered to prove truth**, so inadmissible hearsay.	Both statements inadmissible hearsay unless exception applies
Hearsay exception: spontaneous statement	**Hearsay statement relating to a startling event or condition is admissible when made while declarant was still under the stress of excitement caused by the event or condition.**	• Here, since P was injured and at hospital, P could still be under the stress of excitement caused by accident. • While **car accident is a startling event, P's statement to Dr. was 3 hours after the accident, so possibly not still under the stress of the accident**; likely would have calmed down by then.	Could conclude either way, but likely not still under excitement of accident

Continued >

Issue	Rule	Fact Application	Conclusion
Hearsay exception: state of mind or physical cond. **Medical treatment**	• **Hearsay statement of declarant's then-existing physical condition is admissible to show the physical cond.** • **CEC narrow if made for diagnosis or treatment—declarant must be a minor describing child abuse/neglect.**	• Statement 1 (leg hurts): Made at hospital in response to physician question—likely so physician could treat her; thus, in Cal., **response would not come in as P was not a minor describing child abuse/neglect.** • Statement 2 (D not yielding right of way): Not about physical condition or medical treatment, so not applicable.	Possible exception for 1st part of statement; not for 2nd part
Hearsay exception: contemp. statement	Explaining conduct of declarant made while the declarant was engaged in the conduct.	Statement was made 3 hours after accident, not during conduct, but, perhaps during conduct of receiving medical treatment and describing feelings.	Could go either way
Answer call of Q		Court likely improperly admitted the statement	No
Call #3 (O's Accident Rpt.): a. Bystander Stmt.			
Logical relevance	See above	Shows D at fault (disputed fact).	Relevant
Legal relevance	See above	**Probative to show D more likely at fault**, but could be prejudicial as D cannot cross-examine O as to investigation methods and report since O is unavailable at trial.	Prejudicial [one answer came to opposite conclusion]
Personal knowledge	Witness must have personal knowledge of facts.	Bystander was at scene of accident and witnessed it, so personal knowledge.	Personal knowledge
Hearsay (double)	See above—need exceptions for both levels	Statement was out of court at scene of accident and offered to prove truth that D was at fault (two statements—bystander and report itself).	Hearsay—inadmissible unless exception

Continued >

Issue	Rule	Fact Application	Conclusion
Hearsay exception: public records	Hearsay record of a public office is **admissible if** (i) record describes activities of the office, (ii) **record describes matters observed pursuant to duty imposed by law**, or (iii) factual findings from investigation	Here, record made by O, who had a duty to report details of accident, but the bystander was not under a duty to report any details, so statement by bystander would not come in through report.	No public record exception
Hearsay exception: business record	Hearsay admissible if it is (1) records a business activity event, (2) regular practice to keep record, (3) made by a person with knowledge, (4) at or near time of matters indicated.	Here, police report record of accident kept in course of business, but usually police reports are not admissible under business records as CEC doesn't allow opinions or diagnosis, and report contains police officer opinion of what occurred.	No business record exception
Spontaneous statement	See above	**Bystander immediately came to O, and O arrived at scene only 3 minutes after accident, so bystander likely still under excitement of accident.**	Hearsay exception, so admissible
Contemporaneous statement	See above	Here, accident did not involve bystander conduct, so statement not made while bystander was involved in any conduct.	No exception
Call #3 (O's Accident Rpt.): b. O's Conclusion			
Relevance	See above	Proves D is at fault; see above for prejudicial statement.	See above
Lay opinion	**Admissible only if rationally based on the witness's perceptions and helpful to the trier of the fact.**	Here, O's opinion is rationally based on perception of interviewing witnesses, skid marks, and accident scene evidence; also helps jury understand where the cars skidded and what others witnessed.	Admissible as lay opinion

Continued >

Issue	Rule	Fact Application	Conclusion
Expert opinion	**Expert opinion is admissible if (1) assists trier of fact, (2) witness is qualified, (3) based on sufficient facts, (4) used reliable principle and methods, and (5) applied principles reliably to facts of case.** (*Kelly/Frye* standard doesn't apply to nonscientific testimony.)	Here, (1) assists jury as indicated above in lay opinion; (2) police office may be qualified to determine skid marks as investigating officer, **but no indication he properly analyzed the skidmarks or was qualified expert**; (3) not clear whether O report was based on sufficient facts but had skidmarks and witness statements; (4) unclear if O used reliable principle; (5) not clear if applied principles reliably.	**Not expert opinion**
Hearsay	See above	Statement was made out of court shortly after accident and offered to prove truth that O thought D was at fault.	Hearsay inadmissible unless exception
Public record exception	See above	O under duty to report his conclusions and based on factual findings (interviews, skid marks, etc.), so they likely could come in.	
Answer call of Q		Hearsay exception, but may be too prejudicial so court improperly admitted report.	Likely too prejudicial to admit
Call #4 (H Greeting Card)			
Relevance	See above	**Show P may have been at fault, not D (disputed fact).**	Relevant
Hearsay/ Nonhearsay	**See above**	**Statement was made on card out of court, but not to show P and H were going to get an early start on weekend, but to show effect on reader since P may have been speeding to get home.**	Not hearsay
Authentication	**Proof that the document is what the proponent claims it to be.**	Paramedic found note but can't verify that it is in fact a note from H; he can only verify that he found it in P's pocket and its contents, but can't verify H wrote it or that its contents were true.	Likely not authenticated

Continued >

Issue	Rule	Fact Application	Conclusion
Secondary evidence rule	Original writing must be produced.	Actual card admitted	SER okay
Answer call of Q		Court improperly admitted card	Shouldn't have admit
Call #5 (W's Note)			
Logical relevance	See above	Show that P may have been at fault due to speeding (disputed fact).	Relevant
Legal relevance	See above	It was probative to show that P may have been at fault, but prejudicial for the same reason. Note was conclusory and P has no opportunity to cross-examine W, as W is dead.	Prejudicial [one answer came to opposite conclusion]
Personal knowledge	See above	D cannot verify that W wrote the note or observed the accident, only that he received it from her.	No personal knowledge
Hearsay	See above	**W's statement was made out of court at accident scene, and offered to prove P was speeding and at fault (truth of matter).**	Hearsay
Spontaneous stmt.	See above	Unclear if made at accident during time of event.	Hearsay exception
Lay opinion	See above	Statement 1: W observed whole thing, so based on her perception; it's likely one can tell if a car is speeding based on other cars or their own speed, but unsure how W knew or observed P speeding, but would be helpful to jury to know if P seemed to be going faster than a normal car should have been going. **Statement 2: W can't make judgment if P was negligent because that is for a jury to decide, not based on W's perception.**	1st statement likely ok as lay opinion 2nd statement not ok
Authentication	**See above**	**W personally handed note to D, who can testify as to such,** but cannot verify that W wrote note.	Likely not authenticated
Secondary evid. rule	See above	Here, actual note admitted.	SER okay
Answer call of Q		Court improperly admitted note.	Shouldn't have admit

Evidence Question 2 Sample Answer

July 2009, Question 3

Prop. 8

All relevant evidence is admissible in a Cal. criminal case, but this is a civil case so Prop. 8 doesn't apply.

Question 1

Logical Relevance

Evidence is relevant if it is material to a disputed fact, and the insurance comment is material to the disputed fact of fault so it's relevant.

Legal Relevance

Relevant evidence may be excluded if its probative value is outweighed by the danger of unfair prejudice. Insurance availability could be probative of fault and, while prejudicial because one could think defendant has deep pockets to pay since insured, it is not unfairly so.

Liability Insurance

Evidence of liability insurance is not admissible to show fault but is allowed to show ownership or control or as part of an admission. For public policy reasons, Dan's statement regarding insurance is not admissible to show culpability, but the court can admit the admission of fault aspect of the statement, which can be inferred from Dan's expectation of paying for damages with his insurance.

Offers to Pay Medicals

Evidence of an offer to pay medical bills and any corresponding admissions are inadmissible for public policy reasons. It is unlikely Dan's statement was an offer to pay medical bills here, but more likely that it was an acknowledgement that he has insurance available to pay.

Personal Knowledge

Paula was present at the scene and has personal knowledge of Dan's statement so she can testify.

Hearsay

Hearsay is an out-of-court statement offered for the truth of the matter asserted and is inadmissible unless subject to an exception. Dan's statement was made out of court at the accident scene but is likely being offered not to prove Dan actually has insurance, but that Dan felt responsible for the accident, so the statement is likely not hearsay.

Spontaneous Statement

A spontaneous statement is a hearsay exception where it is made at or near the time of a startling event and while still under the stress from the event. Dan's statement was made at the startling event of the accident scene, and if the statement is hearsay this exception will apply.

Admission

Any statement made by a party opponent may be admitted. Dan is the party opponent to Paula so his statement at the scene is an admission and admissible.

Dan's statement regarding the insurance should be admitted.

Question 2

Logical Relevance

P's statement to the doctor tends to show the disputed facts of the extent of her injuries and that Dan is as fault for failure to yield.

Legal Relevance

While somewhat probative, the statement about Dan being at fault is also somewhat prejudicial since it establishes the ultimate issue in the case, but it will likely still be admitted. The statement about the leg injury is not prejudicial and allowable.

Personal Knowledge

P's statement is made from her own experience and observation so she has personal knowledge.

Hearsay

P's statement was made out of court at the hospital. The part about the leg injury is offered for its truth about the extent of her injury. The part about D's failure to yield is also offered for its truth that D was at fault in the accident. Both statements are hearsay and inadmissible unless an exception applies.

Spontaneous Statement

Since P was injured in the accident and her statement was made when she was transported to the hospital by ambulance, she may have still been under the stress of the startling event of the car accident. However, the statement occurred three hours after the accident, so it is likely she had sufficient time to calm down and was not still under the excitement so this hearsay exception will not apply.

State of Mind

This provides a hearsay exception for statements of declarant's then-existing state of mind/bodily condition. In California, the exception is narrowed to statements made for purpose of diagnosis and treatment or it must be a minor child describing child abuse, which is inapplicable here.

Contemporaneous Statement

There is a hearsay exception for one explaining her conduct, if the statement is made at the time declarant is engaged in the conduct. Since P's statement was made three hours after the accident, it was not made at the time P was engaged in the conduct, so this exception will not apply.

There is no applicable hearsay exception so the court likely improperly admitted P's statement.

Question 3

a. Bystander Statement

Logical Relevance

The bystander statement is relevant to help establish the disputed fact of accident fault.

Legal Relevance

The bystander statement is probative to show D is more likely at fault; however, it is somewhat prejudicial since D can't cross examine O as to the contents of the report since O is unavailable. Nonetheless, the statement is relevant.

Personal Knowledge

The bystander has personal knowledge since she was an eyewitness to the accident.

Hearsay—Double

There are two levels of hearsay: 1) Bystander statement contained in 2) O's report. Both were made out of court at the scene of the accident and offered for their truth of D's fault for the accident. Each hearsay level must have an exception or the statement/report won't be admissible as hearsay.

Public Records

Record of a public office is admissible if it describes the office activities, describes matters observed pursuant to a duty, or reports investigative findings. Here, O had a duty to prepare his investigation report, but the bystander was under no such duty to report on the accident, so the bystander statement won't qualify under the public records hearsay exception.

Business Records

A business record can also be an exception to the hearsay rule. While the police report records a normal business event, which is a regular practice, made by one with knowledge, and made timely, under the California rule, the record does not qualify if it contains opinions or diagnosis. Since O's report contains opinions, it is inadmissible under this exception also.

Spontaneous Statement

The bystander was on the scene, and when O arrived three minutes after the accident, the bystander immediately gave her statement and was likely still under the excitement of the startling accident that had just occurred. Therefore, Bystander's statement is admissible as a spontaneous statement.

Contemporaneous Statement

Since the accident did not involve any conduct of the bystander, her statement cannot come in as a contemporaneous statement describing her own conduct.

b. O's Conclusion

Relevance

O's conclusions help prove the disputed fact of fault for the accident. Legal relevance is supra.

Lay Opinion

Lay opinion is admissible only if rationally based on witness's perception and is helpful to the trier of fact. O's opinion is based on his perception of interviewing witnesses, observing the scene, skid marks and other accident scene evidence, and would help the jury understand where the cars skidded, and what others witnessed. It is admissible lay opinion.

Expert Opinion

An expert opinion is permissible if it assists the trier of fact, the witness is qualified, the opinion is based on sufficient facts, reliable principles were used, and they were applied reliably to the case facts. A police officer is likely qualified to render an opinion of skid marks, but there is no evidence here he was qualified as an expert or properly analyzed the skid marks. It is unclear if O's report was based on sufficient facts, used reliable principles, or applied them reliably to the facts of the case, but it did contain witness statements and skid mark analysis. Without more details, O's opinion is insufficient as expert testimony.

Hearsay

The report was made out of court and offered for its truth of O's observations regarding accident fault, which were contained in the report, so it is inadmissible unless an exception applies.

Public Record

O was under a business duty to prepare the report and include his findings and observations, so the report should be admissible under the public record exception.

Question 4

Relevance

The greeting card is relevant to establish the disputed fact of fault for the accident because it may show that P was at fault, not D.

Hearsay

The statement is made as an inscription on a greeting card, which is out of court. However, it is not being offered for its truth, that P and H were going to get an early start on the weekend, but rather is being offered to show that P may have been speeding in a rush to get home to start the weekend.

Authentication

In order to be admitted, all documents must be authenticated that they are what they purport to be. The paramedic found the card in P's pocket, but other than that can't verify that H wrote it or that the contents were true, so it will not be admitted since it can't be authenticated.

Secondary Evidence Rule

An original writing must be produced, which can be done here as the actual card was admitted. However, the court should not have admitted the card since it was not properly authenticated.

Question 5

Logical Relevance

W's note is relevant to establish the disputed fact of fault for the accident.

Legal Relevance

W's note is probative of fault but is unduly prejudicial because it is conclusory as to fault and there is no opportunity to question W since she is dead and unavailable to testify.

Personal Knowledge

The note appears to be based on W's observations at the scene.

Hearsay

W's note was made out of court and is being offered for the truth that P was at fault for causing the accident by speeding. The note is inadmissible hearsay unless an exception applies.

Spontaneous Statement

It is unclear if the note was made while under the stress of the startling car accident, so it can't come in as a spontaneous statement.

Lay Opinion

W's statement that she observed the accident and P was speeding is based on her perception, and lay people can typically estimate car speed, though it's unclear the method she used to do so. It is helpful for the jury to know P's car was going fast, so this opinion is acceptable as evidence. W's statement that P was negligent should not be admitted because it is an improper lay opinion since it goes to the ultimate issue the jury is to decide.

Authentication

W personally handed the note to D, and D can so testify. However, D has no way to verify that W actually wrote the note, so it can likely not be properly authenticated.

Secondary Evidence Rule

The original was admitted, so the secondary evidence rule is satisfied. However, the court improperly admitted the note since it couldn't be properly authenticated and was unduly prejudicial.

Evidence Question 3

July 2005, Question 4

Dan was charged with arson. The prosecution attempted to prove that he burned down his failing business to get the insurance proceeds. It is uncontested that the fire was started with gasoline. At a jury trial, the following occurred:

The prosecution called Neighbor, who testified that fifteen minutes after the fire broke out, he saw a blue Corvette speed from the scene.

The prosecution next called Detective Pry. Pry testified that he checked Motor Vehicle Department records and found that a blue Corvette was registered to Dan. Pry also testified that he observed a blue Corvette in the driveway of Dan's house.

The prosecution then called Scribe, the bookkeeper for Dan's business. Scribe testified that, two months before the fire, Dan told Scribe to record some phony accounts receivable to increase his chances of obtaining a loan from Bank. Scribe then testified that she created and recorded an account receivable from a fictitious entity in the amount of $250,000, but that Bank denied the loan anyway. Scribe further testified that, two days after the fire, Dan again told her to create some phony accounts receivable, but that she refused to do so.

The prosecution called Jan, the night janitor at Dan's business, to testify that the evening before the fire, as Jan was walking past Dan's office, Jan heard a male voice say, "Gasoline is the best fire starter." Jan knew Dan's voice, but because the office door was closed and the voice muffled, Jan could not testify that the voice was Dan's.

Assume that, in each instance, all appropriate objections were made.

Should the court have admitted:

1. Detective Pry's testimony? Discuss.
2. Scribe's testimony? Discuss.
3. Jan's testimony? Discuss.

Evidence Question 3 Assessment

July 2005, Question 4

Since California evidence is a new area of testing and has only been eligible for testing since 2007, most of the practice questions and sample answers don't include California evidence. The following question is from 2005, but the attached answer grid has been altered to include the California rules along with the federal rules so you can test yourself on how to format a question that covers both the federal rules and the California rules in one question. Remember, the California rules only apply to the essay portion of the bar exam, not the MBE. The MBE still only tests the federal rules.

This question covers some really typical evidence ground: logical and legal relevance, character evidence, the best evidence rule, authentication, business records, hearsay, and hearsay exceptions. However, it manages to cover a lot of ground since each of the three items of evidence has multiple corresponding legal issues. Further, it covers some favorite testing topics is unusual ways.

The business record hearsay exception is tested, but all of the analysis comes from logical inferences the student must make about how the DMV operates. This would be an easy issue to miss spotting because not only is the factual analysis entirely made from inferences, but also the ultimate conclusion is that the business record hearsay exception does not apply because the report itself is not even being admitted into evidence. Rather, the report was simply referenced by the testifying witness, Detective Fry. Even though the business record exception clearly does not apply to witness testimony, it is still an important issue to spot. Remember, your job is to use the facts to prove or disprove the existence of a legal issue.

The character evidence issue is a bit tricky because it tests the exception to the general rule that character evidence is inadmissible to prove conduct in conformity. Here, the evidence was being admitted to show possible motive to commit the arson, which is admissible. Remember: When character evidence is being allowed in subject to an exception, it always raises the issue of the legal relevance balancing test because it will always be prejudicial.

Both calls 2 and 3 test the exception to the hearsay rule where an out-of-court statement is not considered hearsay if it is not being offered for the truth of the matter asserted. That concept is sometimes difficult to conceptualize, and this question gives two nice examples of the concept in action.

Make note of the areas highlighted in **bold** on the corresponding grid. The bold areas highlight the issues, analysis, and conclusions that are likely **required** to receive a passing score on this question.

Issue	Rule	Fact Application	Conclusion
Call #1: Det. Pry's Testimony			
Prop. 8	Criminal trials in Cal.: all relevant evidence is admissible even if objection under CEC, except for: D open door first in character evidence, legal relevance, SER, hearsay. Time saver: on exam, only name the applicable Prop. 8 exceptions.	Here, criminal trial so all CEC objections discussed below may result in evidence still being admissible under Prop. 8 unless it falls into one of the exceptions.	
Logical relevance	**Relevant if it tends to prove or disprove a material fact.** CEC fact must be in dispute.	What Pry learned from checking DMV records **tends to prove that D did commit arson** because Neighbor already testified that 15 minutes after fire, he saw a blue Corvette, and **if D owned a blue Corvette** and the failing business, **it is likely he started the fire**. **The fact that Pry observed a blue Corvette in the driveway also tends to prove that D owned a blue Corvette, and since this car was seen leaving D's business right after fire, he likely started it.** CEC: The fact as to who owned the blue Corvette that likely started fire is in dispute.	**Logically relevant**
Legal relevance	**Relevant evidence can still be excluded if its probative value is substantially outweighed by its prejudicial value.**	Although many people own blue Corvettes—causing it to be somewhat prejudicial to D just because he owns one, too—it is **very probative to identify the arsonist, as that car was seen speeding away from the scene** of the fire 15 minutes after it started, and so it's not unfairly prejudicial.	**Legally relevant**
Personal knowledge Competency	**Witness needs to have personal knowledge about the matter about which he is testifying.**	**Pry read the DMV reports himself and personally observed a blue Corvette in D's driveway, indicating that he had personal knowledge.**	**Pry has personal knowledge**

Continued >

Issue	Rule	Fact Application	Conclusion
Best evidence rule CEC = Secondary ER	**To prove the terms of a writing, the original writing must be produced** if terms of writing are material.	**Pry's testimony should have been excluded since the actual DMV records regarding the registered owner of the blue Corvette were not produced and should have been.**	**BER violated, so testimony as to DMV records should not be admitted**
Hearsay	**An out-of-court statement offered to prove the truth of the matter asserted.**	**DMV records are statements made by DMV employees who prepared the reports by transcribing them, and they are offered to prove the truth that D owned a blue Corvette, which is what the prosecution is asserting**	**DMV report is hearsay**
Business record hearsay exception	**Hearsay admissible if it is (1) record of business activity event,** (2) regular practice to keep record, **(3) made by a person with knowledge,** (4) at or near time of matters indicated.	**Here, the DMV reports are recorded by DMV employees, who have a duty to record such information, and the DMV regularly keeps these records in its ordinary course of business. However, the report itself was not admitted so there is no record to except under hearsay; rather, only Pry's testimony, not the business record itself.**	**Exception would apply to actual record, but record not in evidence**
Official/public record hearsay exception	Record of a public office is **admissible if** (i) record describes activities of the office, (ii) **record describes matters observed pursuant to duty imposed by law**, or (iii) factual findings from investigation (FRE: criminal prosecution cannot use last two factors; CEC: no limitations on prosecution)	DMV records describe activities of the office as the office notes any changes when people buy and sell vehicles, change addresses, and make other changes; DMV is also likely under a duty by law to accurately report information on vehicles, but cannot use this in a criminal prosecution (although, can be used in Cal.). Problem is that document itself is not in evidence, so this would not work.	**Would be valid public record exception if record admitted into evidence, but it's not so no exception**
Conclusion: Call #1		**Pry's testimony about DMV reports should not be admitted, but observation about car in driveway should be admitted.**	**Observation of car admissible**

Continued >

Issue	Rule	Fact Application	Conclusion
Call #2: Scribe's Testimony			
Logical relevance	**See above**	**Scribe's testimony would tend to show that D did have a reason or motive to commit arson because he was financially distraught, as can be shown by his desire to commit or aid another to commit a crime to help relieve him of his financial troubles.**	**Logically relevant**
Legal relevance	**See above**	**Prejudicial because jury can infer that D's dishonest nature and bad acts in the past will lead them to believe that he did burn down his business—for the same reasons he tried to convince the bookkeeper to break the law.** However, probative value likely outweighs the prejudicial nature of the testimony because it tends to show D's motive for the arson.	Could conclude either way here
Personal knowledge Competency	**See above**	**D personally told Scribe the information to which she is testifying, and she herself prepared the account records as requested by D.**	**Scribe has personal knowledge**
Character evidence	**In a criminal case, evidence of D's character can only be opened by D**; but once opened by D, prosecution can rebut. **But, character evidence allowed to show intent, preparation, identity, knowledge, absence of mistake, motive, opportunity, plan.**	Criminal case because D is charged with arson. D did not open door, but **prior bad acts involving bookkeeper tend to show his motive for financial relief to start fire**, as well as his intent—likely to burn down the business to get money to help his financial situation.	**Character evidence allowed**

Continued >

Issue	Rule	Fact Application	Conclusion
Hearsay	**See above**	**Not hearsay because it is being offered to show D had a motive by showing that he planned other schemes to get money to alleviate his financial troubles** by telling Scribe to record phony records, when Scribe did record phony records, and when D told her again to create phony records. **Also could go to state of mind to show he was desperate to get money.**	**Not hearsay**
Admission	**Even if court found it was hearsay, an admission by a party opponent makes it nonhearsay.** CEC says hearsay "exception," not "exemption."	**Admission because it applies to any statement (here about shady banking and bookkeeping) made by party opponent (Dan) to the prosecution.**	**Admission = hearsay exemption**
Conclusion: Call #2		Could conclude either way depending on legal relevance conclusion.	Either way
Call #3: Jan's Testimony			
Logical relevance	See above	**Tends to prove that D knew gasoline was best to start a fire, indicating he likely was involved with the fire that erupted after his comment.** CEC: Disputed fact as to who started fire.	**Logically relevant**
Legal relevance	See above	Not very prejudicial because D can argue that Neighbor cannot identify him with certainty because didn't see him, but **very probative because indicates D likely knew about fire, especially since gasoline was used and D had motive.**	**Legally relevant**

Continued >

Issue	Rule	Fact Application	Conclusion
Personal knowledge Competency	See above	**Jan personally heard the statement because she was there and is familiar with D's voice.**	**Jan has personal knowledge**
Authentication	**Need to authenticate that voice heard is who it purports to be; can be person familiar with voice**; or look at circumstantial evidence involving certain facts that only a particular person would have knowledge of. The jury decides if voice is what it purports to be.	**Jan is familiar with D's voice because she is the night janitor in D's building. However, because the door was closed and the voice muffled, she was not able to testify that the voice was D's, so arguably, she could not authenticate the voice she heard.** **However, the other facts and circumstances, such as Jan hearing a male voice when D is male, inside of D's office could lead a jury to conclude that it was D's voice.**	**Likely D's voice authenticated, but jury decides, so testimony can be admitted**
Hearsay	**See above**	**Nonhearsay because offered not for truth of matter but rather for state of mind as to D's mind or effect on listener—that D had knowledge about how to start a fire in the exact manner in which the building did burn, not the fact that gasoline is best way to start a fire.**	**Nonhearsay**
Admission	See above	Admission by party opponent if statement was made by Dan.	Hearsay exemption (CEC: exception)
Conclusion: Call #3		**Jan's testimony should be admitted.**	**Testimony should be admitted**

Evidence Question 4

July 1999, Question 4

Mary Smith sued Dr. Jones, alleging that Jones negligently performed surgery on her back, leaving her partly paralyzed. In her case-in-chief, Mary called the defendant, Dr. Jones, as her witness. The following questions were asked and answers given:

[1] Q. Now, you did not test the drill before you used it on Mary Smith's vertebrae, did you?
[2] A. No. That's not part of our procedure. We don't ordinarily do that.
[3] Q. Well, since Mary's operation, you now test these drills immediately before using them, don't you?
A. Yes.
[4] Q. Just before you inserted the drill into my client's spine, you heard Nurse Clark say "The drill bit looks wobbly," didn't you?
A. No. I did not.
Q. Let me show what has been marked as plaintiff's exhibit number 10. [Tendering document] This is the surgical report written by Nurse Clark, isn't it?
A. Yes.
[5] Q. In her report she wrote: "At time of insertion I said the drill bit looked wobbly," didn't she?
A. Yes. That's her opinion.
Q. Okay, speaking of opinions, you are familiar with the book, *General Surgical Techniques* by Tompkins, aren't you?
A. Yes.
Q. And it is authoritative, isn't it?
A. Some people think so.
[6] Q. And this book says, at page 255, "Always test drill bits before using them in spinal surgery," doesn't it?
A. I guess so, but again that's his opinion.
Q. Now, you've had some trouble yourself in the past?
A. What do you mean?
[7] Q. Well, you were accused by two patients of having sexually abused them, weren't you?
A. That was all a lot of nonsense.
[8] Q. But you do admit that in two other operations which you performed in 1993 the drill bit which you were using slipped during back surgery, causing injury to your patients?
A. Accidents do happen.

What objection or objections could Dr. Jones' attorney reasonably have made to the question or answer at each of the places indicated above by the numbers in the left-hand margin, and how should the court have ruled in each instance? Discuss.

Evidence Question 4 Assessment

July 1999, Question 4

This question is an example of a transcript style evidence question, which consists of a series of questions posed to a witness and the witness's answers to those questions. Pay special attention to the details in the introductory paragraph, which will tell you what type of case it is, who the participants are, and where the case is procedurally. In this particular case, Mary Smith is suing Dr. Jones in civil court for negligence (medical malpractice). Plaintiff Smith is presenting her case in chief and has called Defendant Dr. Jones to the witness stand for questioning. This information helps to establish the players and the sequence of the case and should be noted at the top of your scratch paper as you outline your answer. For example, since the case is for negligence, to be relevant all of the evidence presented must have a tendency to prove or disprove a material fact, which would be an element of negligence (duty, breach, causation, or damages).

The call of the question asks for the proper objections Defendant Dr. Jones's attorney can make at each of the numbered places in the transcript, and how the court should rule. Evidence questions typically involve some role-playing and feel a bit like a real court situation where you are tasked with quickly identifying all possible objections (issue spotting), quickly explaining how the facts apply to the rule (analysis), and deciding how the court should rule (conclusion).

Like most evidence questions, this question is a racehorse. There are eight separate numbered areas in the transcript to analyze. You can assume there will be more than one issue for each of the eight sections, so there are at least sixteen issues. Issues regarding the "form of the question" are typically present in a transcript style question, so be sure to look for them. Aside from the form of the question objections, this question covers typical evidence issues, including relevance, the public policy exclusion of subsequent remedial measures, hearsay and hearsay exceptions, and character evidence.

This question dates from 1999 and thus before California evidence was tested. However, the attached answer grid has been altered to include the California rules along with the federal rules so you can test yourself on how to format a question that covers both the federal rules and the California rules.

Make note of the areas highlighted in **bold** on the corresponding grid. The bold areas highlight the issues, analysis, and conclusions that are likely **required** to receive a passing score on this question.

Issue	Rule	Fact Application	Conclusion
1			
Logical relevance	**Evidence is relevant if it has any tendency to prove or disprove a material fact.** CEC: fact must be in dispute.	**A reasonable doctor would use procedures** of testing the drill before conducting surgery, **and this would tend to prove negligence in not doing so.** [Can address in call 1 or 2.]	Overruled
Leading question	**Question suggests the answer; allowed on direct w/ "hostile" witness.**	**Dr. Jones is hostile since party opponent (defendant) and called by plaintiff.**	**Overruled**
Argumentative/ misleading	**Question is combative, or unduly confusing.**	**Question contains a double negative, but is not confusing.**	Sustained
2			
Unresponsive	**Answer is unresponsive to the question.**	Answer describes procedure and **gives more information than asked for in the question. Plaintiff should move to strike the answer after "no."**	**Sustained** and answer stricken after "no"
3			
Logical relevance	See above	**Shows it was negligent to not to test drill bit before surgery since Dr. Jones does now,** and this is a negligence case.	Overruled
Legal relevance	Relevant evidence can still be excluded if its probative value is substantially outweighed by its prejudicial value.	Public policy reasons will exclude the evidence because of its prejudicial value.	Sustained
Public policy exclusion: subsequent remedial measures	**Evidence of subsequent safety measures, or repairs performed after an accident, are inadmissible to prove culpable conduct, but are allowed to show ownership or control.**	**Safety measures taken subsequent to the accident are inadmissible to prove culpable conduct because public policy** disfavors squelching safety improvements out of a fear that it would be seen as an admission of fault. **No issue of ownership or control here, so evidence excluded.**	**Sustained**

Continued >

Issue	Rule	Fact Application	Conclusion
4			
Logical relevance	See above	Statement of nurse demonstrates that doctor negligently and knowingly used a wobbly drill bit during the surgery.	Overruled
Hearsay	**An out-of-court statement offered for the truth of the matter asserted.**	**Out of court because statement was made in the operating room;** if offered for truth of showing drill was wobbly, it is hearsay and excluded unless there is an exception.	**Sustained, unless exception applies**
Nonhearsay: effect on hearer	Nonhearsay if offered for effect on hearer, not truth.	If offered to show Dr. Jones heard the warning about the wobbly drill and then failed to act reasonably, it may be admissible.	Overruled
Party admission	**Any statement by a party is admissible.** (FRE: nonhearsay; Cal.: exception)	**It is likely nurse was a hospital employee and thus not a party.**	**Inadmissible**
Vicarious admission	Authorized statement, **or one made by employee/agent concerning & during scope of employment.**	**If the nurse was an employee of Dr. Jones, this statement could be a vicarious admission and admissible against Dr. Jones.**	Inadmissible
Adoptive admission by silence	An adoptive admission (voluntary manifestation of truth of statement) made by conduct (silence, if unreasonable to be silent).	A reasonable doctor would have objected to the description of the drill bit as wobbly if it wasn't true since surgery was commencing using the drill bit.	Admissible
Present sense impression	**A statement describing or explaining an event** or condition and **made while perceiving the event** or condition or immediately thereafter.	**Nurse commented on the condition of the drill while perceiving the drill wobble; thus, it is admissible as a present sense impression.**	**Admissible**

Continued >

Issue	Rule	Fact Application	Conclusion
5			
Logical relevance	See above	Nurse's surgical report can show the drill bit was wobbly to establish negligence or that Dr. Jones is lying.	Overruled
Authentication	**Writing must be authenticated as genuine to be admissible.**	Report must be authenticated, and Dr. Jones has the knowledge to establish the surgical report is genuine.	Overruled
Best evidence rule	To prove contents of a writing the original must be introduced (copy okay, usually).	Here, it appears that the report itself is being introduced since it is marked as "exhibit #10."	Sustained
Hearsay (double)	See above **Each level of hearsay must have an exception to be admissible.**	**Here, out-of-court statement because it is from a hospital surgical report** and is offered for truth that drill bit is wobbly. **Two levels of hearsay: the statement and the report itself. As noted above, the operating room statement is admissible as a present sense impression.**	**Sustained, unless an exception**
Hearsay exception: business records	**A record made in the regular practice of business, by one w/ a business duty to report, made near event time.**	**A surgical report is probably a normal record made in the regularly conducted business of the hospital. The surgical nurse would likely have a business duty to report, so if made near time of the surgery it is admissible.**	**Admissible**
6			
Logical relevance	See above	Shows Dr. Jones unreasonable and negligent in not following the *General Surgical Techniques* procedures.	Overruled
Hearsay	See above	**Statement** is in a book and **offered for the truth that drill bits should be tested before surgery.**	Sustained, unless an exception

Continued >

Issue	Rule	Fact Application	Conclusion
Hearsay exception: learned writings	**Scientific texts and treatises may be admitted for substantive truth if reliable authority.** CEC: only permits facts of general interest.	**If authoritative nature of treatise is verified, probably admissible. Unclear if this is the case w/answer "some people think so."** May be okay to use treatise to impeach Dr. Jones. California rule is probably too narrow to allow this in.	Overruled
7			
Logical relevance	See above	Sexual misconduct w/ other patients likely not relevant to negligent back surgery, but may be used to impeach.	Sustained
Impeachment character evidence	**Character evidence is generally not allowed to show conduct in conformity. FRE: can impeach w/prior bad acts regarding truthfulness, but not with extrinsic evidence.** CEC: Can't use to impeach.	**Sexual misconduct is not related to negligent back surgery or the character trait of truthfulness.** Further, these are only accusations, not convictions. This is inadmissible.	**Sustained**
Legal relevance	Otherwise-relevant evidence may be excluded if its probative value is substantially outweighed by dangers of undue prejudice, etc.	Here, if this were somehow logically relevant it would not pass the test of legal relevance since these are only accusations, not convictions, and not highly probative. Further, allegations of sexual misconduct with patients would be highly inflammatory and prejudicial.	Sustained

Continued >

Issue	Rule	Fact Application	Conclusion
8			
Logical relevance	See above	Prior accidents of the same mechanism of injury have a tendency to prove both duty and breach.	Overruled
Similar happenings	Evidence of similar events is not generally admissible, except where "substantially similar."	Seems substantially similar if both accidents were also regarding a drill slippage during back surgery; this case is back surgery with a "wobbly" drill bit.	Overruled
Impeachment character evidence	See above	**Can't use prior acts of negligence as evidence that Dr. Jones has character trait of negligence and acted in conformity with it on this occasion.** This is not regarding the character trait of truthfulness, so it can't be used for impeachment purposes either.	**Sustained**

Evidence Question 5

February 2002, Question 6

Phil sued Dirk, a barber, seeking damages for personal injuries resulting from a hair treatment Dirk performed on Phil. The complaint alleged that most of Phil's hair fell out as a result of the treatment. At a jury trial, the following occurred:

A. Phil's attorney called Wit to testify that the type of hair loss suffered by Phil was abnormal. Before Wit could testify, the judge stated that he had been a trained barber prior to going to law school. He took judicial notice that this type of hair loss was not normal and instructed the jury accordingly.

B. Phil testified that, right after he discovered his hair loss, he called Dirk and told Dirk what had happened. Phil testified that Dirk then said: (1) "I knew I put too many chemicals in the solution I used on you, so won't you take $1,000 in settlement?" (2) "I fixed the solution and now have it corrected." (3) "Don't worry because Insco, my insurance company, told me that it will take care of everything."

C. Phil produced a letter at trial addressed to him bearing the signature "Dirk." The letter states that Dirk used an improper solution containing too many chemicals on Phil for his hair treatment. Phil testified that he received this letter through the mail about a week after the incident at the barbershop. The court admitted the letter into evidence.

D. In his defense, Dirk called Chemist, who testified as an expert witness that he applied to his own hair the same solution that had been used on Phil and that he suffered no loss of hair.

Assume that, in each instance, all appropriate objections were made. Did the court err in:

1. Taking judicial notice and instructing the jury on hair loss? Discuss.
2. Admitting Phil's testimony regarding Dirk's statements? Discuss.
3. Admitting the letter produced by Phil? Discuss.
4. Admitting Chemist's testimony? Discuss.

Evidence Question 5 Assessment

February 2002, Question 6

This evidence essay question is typical in many ways but is a great practice question because it also poses some challenges. The question covers a less common topic—judicial notice—and covers several of the public policy exceptions to relevance. Many bar questions are formatted like this one in that they cover a particular area of law in depth by slightly altering the facts so your answer can demonstrate your facility with the rules and their nuances.

The first challenge is an organizational one. Paragraph B contains three numbered statements that Dirk said to Phil during their phone conversation. Call two of the question asks if the court erred in admitting Dirk's statements. Whenever the facts are broken down into paragraphs, or into numbered statements like this one, it is always easiest to work with the material by analyzing each piece of information separately. The danger in doing otherwise is that it is easy to miss spotting all of the issues when working with the statements as a group. Once the three statements from paragraph B are separated and analyzed it is very easy to see that they share some issues (relevance, hearsay, party admission) but, while each statement raises the issue of public policy exclusions, each statement raises a different exclusion (settlement offers, subsequent remedial repairs, liability insurance). Once the statements have been separated and organized on your scratch paper, you can easily see where you can make an efficient use of "supra" to streamline your analysis. Another approach would be to use headings to indicate where the three statements are being analyzed together (relevance, hearsay, party admission), and where they are being analyzed separately (the three public policy exclusions).

The second challenge posed by this question is time management. When this question was originally administered, it was the last essay question of the exam (day three, question six) and the last question call (number four) covers the lengthy rule for expert witnesses. Not only does the rule have multiple elements, but also the analysis is fairly sophisticated. The proposed expert was an expert in chemistry, but his testimony was regarding hair loss. Further, the methodology used to form his opinion was to test the chemical solution on his own head and report his findings. You don't have to know a lot about the scientific method to realize that method can't be reliable! It isn't a particularly difficult issue to spot, even for a student fuzzy on the rule or suffering from fatigue. The challenge is in managing your time—both throughout the exam, so there is a full hour to devote to the question, and throughout the question, so there is enough time to properly answer call four. This question also provides a great example of why organizing your answer before you start writing is so important. If you organize before you start writing, you will unravel the problem posed by call two (three statements in one question) before you start writing, and you will realize that call four is going to take some time to write. You can then apportion your time and pace yourself accordingly.

This question dates from 2002 and thus before California evidence was tested. However, the attached answer grid has been altered to include the California rules along with the federal rules so you can test yourself on how to format a question that covers both the federal rules and the California rules.

Make note of the areas highlighted in **bold** on the corresponding grid. The bold areas highlight the issues, analysis, and conclusions that are likely **required** to receive a passing score on this question.

Issue	Rule	Fact Application	Conclusion
Call #1			
Judicial notice	**The court can take judicial notice of facts not subject to reasonable dispute,** either generally known or capable of accurate and ready determination.	**It is not easily verifiable or universally known that this type of hair loss is not normal and so an inappropriate topic for judicial notice. The Judge's personal experience as a barber is not a proper use of judicial notice.**	**Court erred**
Call #2: Stmt. 1—Settle			
Logical relevance	**Evidence is relevant if it has any tendency to prove or disprove a material fact.** CEC: fact must be in dispute.	Dirk's negligence is at issue, so an offer to settle the claim has a **tendency to prove his responsibility for Phil's injuries.**	**Relevant**
Legal relevance	Relevant evidence can still be excluded if its probative value is substantially outweighed by its prejudicial value.	The probative value is not outweighed by any prejudicial effect here because the public policy exclusion applies.	Relevant
Public policy exclusion: settlement offer	**Not allowed to show liability, but must have a disputed "claim" first** (liability or amount).	**Assuming there is a disputed claim here,** since Dirk's statement regarding settlement for $1,000 was made in response to Phil's phone call notifying Dirk of the hair loss trouble, **this statement is inadmissible to show liability.**	**Excluded, court erred in admitting**
Hearsay	**An out-of-court statement offered for the truth of the matter asserted.**	This statement was made out of court on the telephone and is offered for its truth—that Dirk made a settlement offer and implicitly admitted liability—so it is inadmissible unless an exception applies.	**Hearsay, unless exception**
Party admission	**Any statement by a party opponent is admissible.** FRE: nonhearsay; CEC: exception	Dirk admitted that he put too many chemicals in the solution used on Phil. **The statement is admissible as a party admission.**	Allowed as an admission, but see above

Continued >

Issue	Rule	Fact Application	Conclusion
Call #2: Stmt. 2—Solution Fix			
Logical relevance	See above	Dirk's negligence is at issue and testimony that the solution had to be fixed implies something was wrong with it and **tends to show Dirk's negligence.**	**Relevant**
Public policy exclusion: subsequent remedial measures	**Evidence of subsequent safety measures, or repairs performed after an accident, are inadmissible to prove culpable conduct,** but are allowed to show ownership or control, or (FRE) to show defective product design.	**Public policy excludes** testimony of subsequent remedial measures because of the chilling effect on people fixing defective products or conditions. **The only purpose of the testimony is to show Dirk's liability. Therefore, the statement that the solution needed to be fixed is inadmissible.** If Dirk claims the solution wasn't his or that fixing it was impossible, the statement is admissible.	**Excluded, court erred in admitting**
Hearsay	See above	Statement is made out of court on the telephone and offered to prove that solution needing fixing, **so it is inadmissible unless an exception applies.**	**Hearsay, unless exception**
Party admission	See above	Dirk admitted the solution was now fixed and the **statement is admissible as a party admission.**	Allowed, so court didn't err, but see above
Call #2: Stmt. 3—Insurance			
Logical relevance	See above	Dirk implied he was responsible, which **tends to show his fault for the injury to Phil.**	**Relevant**
Public policy exclusion: liability insurance	**Not allowed to show liability,** but an admission made is allowed.	**Public policy excludes evidence of insurance** because of the danger it will imply the defendant has deep pockets to pay or has insurance because he's careless, so **Dirk's statement regarding his insurance is inadmissible.**	**Excluded, court erred in admitting**

Continued >

Issue	Rule	Fact Application	Conclusion
Hearsay (double)	See above Need exceptions for each level to be admissible.	Dirk's statement is made out of court on the telephone and offered for the truth that he is at fault for Phil's injuries. There are two levels of hearsay: 1) Insurance Co.'s statement to Dirk; 2) Dirk's repeating of their statement to Phil.	**Hearsay, not allowed**
Party admission	See above	As analyzed supra, **Dirk's statement can come in as a party admission.**	Allowed, so court didn't err
Call #3			
Logical relevance	See above	The letter has a **tendency to show that Dirk is liable** since he admitted using an improper solution.	Relevant
Authentication	**Proof that the document is what the proponent claims it to be.**	**Dirk's signature would have to be authenticated**	Must be authenticated
Best evidence rule	Original writing must be produced. CEC: secondary evidence rule	The letter is being admitted so this rule is complied with.	Allowed
Hearsay	See above	The letter was written out of court and is offered for the truth that Dirk used too many chemicals in the solution, causing Phil's hair loss.	**Hearsay**
Party admission	See above	**Dirk's statement** that the solution was improperly prepared **is a party admission** and is admissible as such.	Allowed, so court didn't err
Call #4			
Logical relevance	See above	Has a tendency to show the solution Dirk used was responsible for Phil's hair loss.	Relevant

Continued >

Issue	Rule	Fact Application	Conclusion
Expert opinion	**Expert opinion is admissible if:** **1) assists trier of fact,** **2) witness is qualified,** **3) based on sufficient facts,** **4) used reliable principles and methods, and** **5) applied principles reliably to facts of case.**	1) Expert testimony would assist trier of fact because hair chemicals are outside common knowledge. 2) **Witness has no specialized knowledge of hair loss, and is only an expert in chemistry.** 3) **Personal observation and use of the product on oneself is not an appropriate scientific method.** 4) **Opinion was inappropriately based on personal experience, not scientific method.** 5) Not applied reliably to the case.	Court erred in admitting

Evidence Question 6

February 1998, Question 3

Don is being prosecuted criminally for committing an armed assault against Victor. The evidentiary issues presented in his jury trial are based upon the following chronology of events:

1. June 5, 1985: Don was convicted of bribery and received a three-year sentence which he served in full without parole;
2. June 1, 1997: Victor was assaulted, allegedly by Dan;
3. June 4, 1997: Victor identified Don from a lineup as the person who assaulted him (Victor);
4. June 6, 1997: Don was arrested and charged with the assault of Victor;
5. August 1, 1997: Don confessed privately to his long-time fiancée, Bernice, that he (Don) is the one who assaulted Victor;
6. August 15, 1997: Detective Phillips, who had been present at the June 4 lineup, testified at a preliminary hearing that Victor identified Don at the June 4 lineup, and Phillips was cross-examined by Don's attorney;
7. September 1, 1997: Don and Bernice were married;
8. September 15, 1997: Detective Phillips was shot and killed in a hunting accident;
9. October 1, 1997: Don, again privately, confessed to Bernice that he (Don) is the one who assaulted Victor;
10. November 1, 1997: Don and Bernice were divorced;
11. December 1, 1997: The case against Don comes to trial;
12. December 1, 1997: Victor testifies at trial, remembers making a lineup identification, but cannot make an in-court identification;
13. December 3, 1997: The prosecution seeks to introduce a certified transcript of the preliminary hearing testimony of Detective Phillips;
14. December 4, 1997: The prosecution calls Bernice, seeking to have her testify to the August 1 and October 1 confessions of Don, and both Bernice and Don raise marital privilege objections;
15. December 8, 1997: The prosecution calls a witness, seeking testimony as to Victor's reputation for peacefulness in his community;
16. December 9, 1997: The prosecution rests; and
17. December 10, 1997: Don testifies in his own defense, and on cross-examination the prosecution seeks to impeach Don with his 1985 bribery conviction.

Assuming that all appropriate objections were made, should the court admit the evidence offered by the prosecution in numbers 13, 14, 15, and 17, as specified above? Discuss.

Evidence Question 6 Assessment

February 1998, Question 3

At first glance, this question seems similar to the transcript style evidence question. However, unlike the transcript style question, which consists of a series of questions posed to a witness and the witness's answers to those questions, this type of question lists a series of events in chronological order—generally starting with some initial criminal act, charge, or conviction, and ending with events surrounding the trial itself. Further, the transcript style questions often involve a call that asks you to identify the proper objections an attorney can make in regard to the questions posed to the witness and the witness's answer. In this question, though, you are told to assume that all appropriate objections were made. Thus, your focus when spotting issues should be centered on the reasons why the court should or should not admit the evidence rather than every objection that should have been made.

It is important to remember that you often must analyze the "objections" to see if the court should admit the evidence. For example, even if the proper objection to hearsay was made, which you are told to assume it was, you still need to analyze the possible exceptions to see if the court should admit the evidence despite the hearsay objection. Don't mistakenly believe that because the objections have been made, you need not discuss hearsay, relevance, and so on. If you avoided analysis of all issues for which an objection can be made, you wouldn't discuss any issues.

On this type of question, you need to analyze with more in depth than the typical transcript style question because this question only focuses on four specific events compared to the seven to nine specific questions and answers contained in a typical transcript style question. Here, each specific event requires a detailed analysis of the major issue. In one event, there is multiple hearsay, and for that analysis you need an exception to each layer of hearsay. Another event focuses on both types of marital privilege. The third event focuses on character evidence, and the fourth on impeachment. To pass this question, you need to provide a detailed analysis on each of these issues within each event. And, on every evidence question, always remember to discuss the relevance of each piece of purported evidence.

This question also tests a few hearsay exceptions and exemptions that the previous questions did not, such as prior identification and former testimony. You should do as many practice questions as you can to see all of the different types of hearsay exceptions and exemptions as possible. Further, this question, unlike the previous questions, tests the marital privileges.

Finally, answer the call of the question by stating whether the court should admit the evidence. Made note of the areas highlighted in **bold** on the corresponding grid. The bold areas highlight the issues, analysis, and conclusions that are likely **required** to receive a passing score on this question.

Issue	Rule	Fact Application	Conclusion
# 13. Transcript of Det. Phillips			
Logical relevance	**Evidence is relevant if it has any tendency to prove or disprove a material fact.**	**Shows that V identified D as aggressor and that D likely did assault V.**	**Relevant**
Authentication	**Writing must be authenticated as genuine to be admissible.** Certified documents are self-authenticating.	Here, the transcript is certified, so it is a self-authenticating writing.	Document authenticated
Best evidence rule	To prove contents of a writing, the original must be introduced (copy okay, usually); BER does not apply to public records.	Here, the transcript is a certified public record of a preliminary hearing, so the BER would not bar admitting this transcript.	BER not violated
Hearsay (multiple)	**Out-of-court statement offered to prove the truth of the matter asserted.** **Multiple: each level of hearsay needs an exemption or exception to be admissible (3 levels here).**	**1) Prior ID made out of court at line-up and offered to prove that V identified D as the assailant.** 2) Transcript itself made out of court to prove that V identified D. **3) Det. Philips testimony made out of court (since not in this court) and is offered to prove that V identified D as the assailant.**	**All hearsay, unless exceptions**
Exemption: Prior ID	**Not hearsay** if statement of identification of a person made after perceiving the person.	V made out-of-court ID, which is classified as nonhearsay because it was at the line-up after perceiving D assaulting him. Note: also okay since D can cross-examine V and V testified at trial (so no 6th Amend. issues).	**ID nonhearsay**

Continued >

Issue	Rule	Fact Application	Conclusion
Exception: Public records	Hearsay record of a public office is admissible if (i) record describes activities of the office, (ii) record describes matters observed pursuant to duty imposed by law, or (iii) factual findings from investigation.	Here, making a transcript as a court reporter is likely part of the office activities of a court reporter.	Hearsay exception met
Exception: Former testimony	**If declarant unavailable and party against whom testimony is now being offered had opportunity to examine that person and motive to examine similar, and declarant was under oath.**	**Here, Det. Philips is unavailable since he was shot and killed in a hunting accident. D's attorney also cross examined Det. Phillips previously when he testified and motive was the same, since the defense didn't want V to ID D. Also, Det. was under oath, as at a hearing.**	**Hearsay exception met**
Conclusion: #13			Court should admit evidence
# 14. Bernice's Testimony			
Logical relevance	**See above**	**Proves that D likely committed the assault against V.**	**Relevant**
Spousal testimonial immunity	**One spouse cannot be compelled to testify against the other spouse; only the witness spouse can invoke the privilege and it can only be claimed during marriage, but can include information learned before or during marriage.**	**Although Bernice (the testifying spouse) claimed the privilege, and the confession by D occurred both before and during marriage, they were divorced prior to trial, so she can no longer claim this privilege.**	**Privilege not valid**
Confidential marital communications	**Communications made in reliance upon the intimacy of the marital relationship are privileged; both spouses may assert; it only covers statements made during marriage, but does survive the marriage.**	**Only the October confession was made during marriage and privately. The Aug. confession was only during engagement, and so while the Oct. one would be privileged, the Aug. one would not.**	**Oct. confession privileged; Aug. not**

Continued >

Issue	Rule	Fact Application	Conclusion
Hearsay	**See above**	**D's confessions to B were made out of court and are now offered to prove that D assaulted V.**	**Hearsay, unless exception**
Hearsay exemption: admission by party opponent	**Not hearsay if made by a party opponent.**	**Here, statement is by D, who is a party opponent to the prosecution.**	**Nonhearsay**
Conclusion: #14			**Court should admit Bernice Aug. testimony**
# 15. Testimony About Victor's Reputation			
Relevance	**See above**	**Unless D is claiming self-defense, V's peacefulness does not tend to prove any material fact.**	**Likely not relevant**
Victim's character	**D must first present character issues before the prosecution can rebut.**	**Since prosecution is going first and the defense has not yet presented its case, the prosecution cannot introduce evidence as to V's peacefulness.** If D claimed self-defense, then the D may have already potentially opened this door, allowing the prosecution to show V's character in order to prove that D wasn't acting in self-defense since V is peaceful.	**Should not come in**
Conclusion: #15			Court should not admit witness testimony
# 17. Impeachment by Don's Bribery Conviction			
Relevance	See above	By D taking the stand, his credibility is at issue, indicating that a conviction of bribery might prove he is a liar.	Relevant

Continued >

Issue	Rule	Fact Application	Conclusion
Impeachment	**A witness may be impeached by any party by cross examination. Convictions for crimes involving dishonesty or false statements are also admissible (both misdemeanors and felonies); need to balance probative v. prejudicial value if more than 10 years; if not dishonest, then must be felony.**	**Here, D may be impeached by the prosecution since he is being cross examined. Bribery likely is a crime involving dishonesty since one is acting in an improper and deceitful way to alter the behavior of another. Even if not involving dishonesty, D's bribery conviction is likely a felony since it was punishable by a 3-yr. sentence (> 1 yr.). Conviction is probative to show D may be a liar (reduces his credibility). It is prejudicial as it may imply D is not a good person, leading jury to convict based on past behavior. However, since conviction was more than 10 years ago and a completely unrelated crime, the jury will not likely convict him here based on that crime.**	**Prosecution can use conviction to impeach D**
Authentication	See above	Likely can get a certified copy, or it is a public record, so fine.	Authenticated
Best evidence rule	See above	Public record, so likely it is fine.	BER no bar
Hearsay/nonhearsay purpose	See above	Conviction made out of court but not offered to prove that he was convicted of bribery, but rather for impeachment purposes.	Not hearsay
Conclusion: #17			Court should admit conviction

PART 8 PROFESSIONAL RESPONSIBILITY

PROFESSIONAL RESPONSIBILITY TABLE OF CONTENTS

INTRODUCTION TO PROFESSIONAL RESPONSIBILITY

Professional responsibility is one subject that always, without fail, is tested on every single bar exam. Often, it comprises an entire essay question; sometimes it is covered both on its own and as a crossover question on the same exam. If this subject does arise as a crossover question, it is often in conjunction with business associations. However, as you can see in the following Issues Tested Matrix, the examiners have managed to cross over professional responsibility with nearly every subject eligible for testing. To fully prepare for this subject, it is recommended that you write out several essays covering all of the possible tested issues since it is guaranteed to show up on your bar exam in one format or another.

A unique trait to professional responsibility essays is that the conclusion ***does*** matter. Unlike other subjects where the conclusion is rarely important, professional responsibility generally requires you to reach the correct conclusion in order to receive full credit on an issue.

You will notice that the rules are stated in the outline in a more general way, which is how they appear in the rules. However, when using the rules in an essay, you can customize or tweak the rule so that it applies more directly to the factual situation. Since professional responsibility tests both the ABA and California rules, you must know both and be able to distinguish between them. This is extremely important since you must follow the directions in the call of the question, which usually asks you to distinguish the two sources of law. Thus, where there is a distinction between the two rules, you must identify the distinction and specifically refer to the rule as being either ABA or California in your essay answer so it is clear to the examiners which source of law you are analyzing. Although you don't need to identify the source of the rule with particularity, the examiners test your knowledge of the California Rules of Professional Conduct, relevant sections of the California Business and Professions Code, and leading federal and state case law on the subject, in addition to the ABA Model Rules of Professional Conduct and ABA Model Code of Professional Responsibility. Since 2006, all professional responsibility essays have specifically asked the examinees to answer according to California and ABA authorities. The rules contained in the following outline only apply to the ABA if the rule is labeled "ABA only"; and the rule only applies to California if labeled "California rules." All other rules are substantially the same for both the ABA and California.

On professional responsibility essays, the calls are often very broad, asking you to identify any ethical violations; so using the issues checklist is crucial to success on this subject. It is often necessary to issue spot by reviewing on its own each "action" the attorney takes. For example, you may need to spot all issues that arise when the attorney begins to represent two clients who do not share the same interest. This single "action" can lead to multiple issues, such as duty of loyalty (conflict of interest), duty of care, withdrawal, and so on. Then, the attorney might help one party do something, which could give rise to a whole different set of issues. Therefore, unlike other subjects, in professional responsibility looking at each "action" individually, rather than looking at the entire fact pattern collectively, generally spots the issues. As a result, you often have answers that break down the essay by the attorney "action" (with headings for each action), followed by issue headings for the potential ethical violations within that action.

ISSUES CHECKLIST

LAWYER-CLIENT RELATIONSHIP

Loyalty
- Conflicts of interest
  - Two clients
  - Current client and another
  - Business transactions
  - Government employee
  - Gifts/interest
  - Financial assistance
  - Compensation by 3rd parties
  - Organizational clients
  - Imputed disqualification

Communication
Scope
Confidentiality
Attorney-client privilege
Fees
- Reasonable
- Contingent
- Fee splitting
- Referral fees

Competence/care
Diligence
Safekeeping property
Relationship/sexual relations
Withdrawal

PROFESSIONAL INTEGRITY

Advertising/solicitation
Fairness
- Communication with represented parties
- To court/opposing counsel
- Trial publicity
- Prosecutor duties

Unauthorized practice of law
Reporting ethical violations
To public/profession
- Illegal/improper conduct
- Frivolous claims/threats of action

MEMORIZATION ATTACK SHEET

CONFLICT OF INTEREST

- ♦ **Current clients**
  - Conflict of interest if one client's interest is directly adverse to another
  - Need written informed consent
- ♦ **Aggregate settlements**
  - L cannot make for 2 or more clients
- ♦ **Current client and 3rd party**
  - Conflict of interest if significant risk that
  - Representation materially limited by
  - L's responsibility to any 3rd party
- ♦ **Exceptions to concurrent conflicts (ABA)**
  - L's reasonable belief
  - Not prohibited by law
  - Claims not against each other
  - Informed written consent
- ♦ **Exceptions to concurrent conflicts (Cal.)**
  - Informed written consent
  - Only need written disclosure (not consent) if:
    - Conflict between L and party/witness
    - Same matter as client
    - Substantial effect on L's representation
- ♦ **Cal. okay if L represents insured and insurer**
- ♦ **Business transactions okay if:**
  - Terms fair/reasonable
  - Terms fully disclosed in writing to client
  - Advised to seek independent counsel
  - Informed written consent
- ♦ **Former govt. employee**
  - May not represent in private
  - If L participated personally & substantially
  - Unless informed written consent
- ♦ **Gifts**
  - L can't solicit substantial gifts
  - Prepare an instrument that gives gifts
  - Unless related
  - Cal.: L can accept if fair
- ♦ **Proprietary interest**
  - L cannot acquire
  - Unless lien for fees or contingency in civil case
- ♦ **Financial assistance (ABA)**
  - Only for advancing
  - Court costs/litigation expenses
  - In contingency cases
  - Or indigent clients
- ♦ **Financial assistance (Cal.)**
  - After employment
  - Okay to loan if written IOU
- ♦ Compensation by 3rd party
  - Informed consent
  - No interference with L & client
  - Information remains confidential
- ♦ **Organization**
  - L acts for best interest of organization only
  - If L knows associated person engaged in wrongdoing
  - Likely to result in substantial injury to organization
  - L refers to internal higher authority
  - ABA only: if needed, refer to outside authority
  - Cal. only: if needed, resign; no outside referral
- ♦ **Imputed disqualification**

- Conflict for L applies to entire firm, unless:
  - Based on L's personal interest, or
  - Former client and firm
  - Timely screened
  - Written notice to former client/certify compliance
- Client can waive

♦ **L terminates firm**
- Firm okay to represent client with interest adverse
- To previous client of L
- Unless matter substantially the same, and
- Any remaining firm L has confidential information

DUTY TO COMMUNICATE

♦ Promptly inform client
♦ About settlement, offers, pleas
♦ Status of case

SCOPE OF REPRESENTATION

♦ L takes actions & legal strategy to represent client
♦ Client decides substantive issues: pleas, offers, settlements, jury trial issue

DUTY OF CONFIDENTIALITY

♦ **L cannot reveal information relating to representation, unless:**
- Informed consent
- Impliedly authorized (ABA)
- L reasonably believes necessary to:
  - Prevent death or substantial bodily injury
    - Cal:
      Disclosure optional
      - Try to dissuade first
      - Inform client of planned reveal
  - Prevent crime/fraud of financial injury (ABA)
  - Mitigate/rectify substantial financial injury (ABA)
- Secure legal advice (ABA)
- Establish defense for L (ABA)
- Comply with law (ABA)

ATTORNEY-CLIENT PRIVILEGE

♦ **Attorney-client**
- Person or corporation
- Confidential communication is intended
- Professional service is purpose
- Holder: client
- Lasts until:
  - FRE: after death
  - CEC: estate settled
- Exceptions:
  - Further crime or fraud
  - Dispute w/lawyer
  - CEC: prevent death/serious bodily injury

FEES

♦ **ABA: reasonable fees**
♦ **Cal.: not unconscionable fees**
- Time limitations
- Experience, reputation, ability
- Nature and length of relationship
- Time, labor, novelty, difficulty
- Fee customarily charged
- Likelihood to preclude other employment
- Amount involved/results obtained
- Whether fixed or contingent fee
  (Think TENT FLAW)

♦ **Fee agreements**
- How fee calculated
- Nature of services
- Responsibilities of L & client

- Fee agreements > $1,000 Cal.
  - In writing, unless:
    - Corporate client
    - Client waives writing in writing
    - Emergency
    - Previous client & similar service
- **Fee disputes: Arbitration**
  - Cal. requires/ABA encourages
- **Contingency fee agreement**
  - In writing
  - Signed by client (and L in Cal.)
  - Method for fee and %
  - Expenses to deduct & when
  - Cal.: also related matters not covered in agreement
  - Cal.: negotiable unless health care (set % then)
  - ABA: not for domestic/ criminal cases
  - Cal.: domestic okay if does not promote divorce
- **Division of Fees**
  - Prohibited with non-L
  - With Ls, okay if:
    - Proportionate to work
    - Client agrees in writing
    - ABA: total fee reasonable
    - Cal.: total fee not unconscionable & full disclosure
- **Referrals**
  - Don't give value, unless
    - Qualified referral service
    - Approved by authority
  - Cal.: okay if not for consideration, promise for future/ continue
  - Reciprocal okay if not exclusive and client informed

DUTY OF COMPETENCE/CARE

- Knowledge, skill, thoroughness
- Cal. includes diligence and mental, physical, emotional ability
- Cal.: okay to associate with competent attorney or become one
- ABA: duty of diligence separate

SAFEKEEPING PROPERTY

- Client property separate from L's
- Accounting kept for 5 yrs.

SEXUAL RELATIONS

- Okay if preexisting, consensual
- Cal.: if not preexisting, okay but no:
  - Require/demand for representation
  - Coerce, intimidate, or use undue influence
  - Continue if makes incompetent

WITHDRAWAL

- **Shall if:**
  - Violation of rules
  - Mental/physical condition
  - ABA: discharged
  - Cal.: knows clients' action to harrass
- **May if:**
  - Fraud/crime using L
  - Client's action repugnant to L
  - Client fails to fulfill obligation
  - Good cause
  - ABA: no materially adverse effect on client
  - ABA: unreasonable financial burden on L
  - Cal.: client has no good faith; unreasonable; can't work with co-counsel

ADVERTISING/SOLICITATION

- **No false/misleading communication**
- **No live or in-person soliciting**
- **Cal. presumes invalid if:**
  - Guaranty, warranties, results
  - Testimonial without disclaimer

- Delivery to potential client not in correct mental, etc., state
- Delivery to accident/hospital
- Dramatization not labeled
- No fee without recovery label unless client cost disclosed

♦ **Name/address required**
♦ **Labeled as advertising**
♦ **Specialist if approved**

FAIRNESS

♦ Represented parties need L
♦ No falsity, tamper evidence, etc.
♦ No influence jurors, judge
♦ No extrajudicial statement if material prejudice proceedings
♦ Prosecutors give D exculpatory evidence

UNAUTHORIZED PRACTICE

♦ No partnering with non-L
♦ Liable for other L prof. resp. if ratify or supervise and could mitigate

REPORTING ETHICAL VIOLATIONS

♦ Must report another L violation
♦ Cal.: permits but not required

DUTY TO PUBLIC/PROFESSION

♦ No fraud/crime/frivolous claims
♦ Cal.: no harass/threaten

PROFESSIONAL RESPONSIBILITY RULE OUTLINE

I. **LAWYER-CLIENT RELATIONSHIP**

A. **Duty of loyalty:** A lawyer has a duty of loyalty to his client that requires the lawyer to put the **interest of his client above all other interests** and to avoid any conflicts of interest.

B. **Conflict of interest:** A lawyer must avoid all conflicts of interest with his client.

1. **Concurrent conflict of interest:** The general rule is that a lawyer may not represent a client where there is a conflict of interest. A concurrent conflict of interest can arise several ways.
   a. **Between current clients:** A concurrent conflict of interest exists if the representation of **one client is directly adverse to another client.**
   b. **Between current client and another:** A concurrent conflict of interest exists if there is a **significant risk** that the representation of one or more clients will be **materially limited** by the lawyer's **responsibilities** to **another client**, a **former client**, or a **third person** or by a **personal interest** of the lawyer.
   c. **Exception to concurrent conflicts of interest (ABA only): A lawyer may still represent the client** where there is a concurrent conflict **if:**
      1. The lawyer **reasonably believes** that the lawyer will be able to provide competent and diligent representation to each affected client without an adverse affect,
      2. The representation is **not prohibited by law,**
      3. The clients are **not asserting a claim against each other** in the same litigation, and
      4. Each client gives **informed written consent.**
   d. **Exception to conflicts of interest (California rules)**
      1. **Informed written consent:** A lawyer may still represent the client where there is a concurrent (actual) or potential conflict with the client's **informed written consent.**
      2. Written disclosure: A lawyer may still represent the client with **only written disclosure** of the conflict where the conflict arises from the **lawyer's relationship** (legal, personal, etc.) with a **party or witness** in the **same matter** as the client's that would substantially affect the lawyer's representation.
         a. **Cal. difference from ABA rule:** Written consent by the client or reasonable belief there will not be an adverse affect is not necessary under the California rule, but is required under the ABA.
2. **No aggregate settlements:** A lawyer who represents **two or more clients** shall not participate in making an aggregate settlement of the claims of or against the clients or, in a criminal case, an aggregate agreement as to guilt or pleas, unless each client gives **informed written consent.**

3. **Insurance (California rule):** Lawyers are permitted to represent both **insurers and insureds** whereby the insurer has the contractual right to unilaterally select counsel for the insured, resulting in no conflict of interest.
4. **Business transactions:** A lawyer **shall not enter into a business transaction** with a client or knowingly acquire an interest adverse to the client **unless:**
   a. The **terms are fair** and reasonable to the client,
   b. The **terms are fully disclosed in writing** to the client in a manner that can be understood by the client,
   c. The client is advised in writing to **seek independent counsel**, and
   d. The **client gives informed written consent** to the essential terms including whether the lawyer is representing the client in the transaction.
5. **Former government employee:** A lawyer who has formerly served as a government employee **shall not represent** a client in connection with a matter in which the lawyer participated **personally and substantially** as a government employee unless the governmental agency gives **informed written consent.**

> **Issue-spotting tip:** The imputed disqualification rules also apply here. See section I.C. below.

6. **Solicitation of gifts**
   a. **ABA rule:** A lawyer **shall not solicit any substantial gift** from a client **or prepare an instrument** that gives the lawyer a gift unless the lawyer is **related** to the client.
   b. **California rule:** A lawyer **may accept a gift** if it is **fair** and there is **no undue influence.**
7. **Proprietary interest:** A lawyer **shall not acquire a proprietary interest** in the cause of action or subject matter of litigation **unless it is**
   a. To acquire a **lien to secure the lawyer's fees**, or
   b. To contract with a client for a **reasonable contingency fee** in a civil case.
8. **Advances to client**
   a. **ABA only:** A lawyer **shall not provide financial assistance** to a client in connection with litigation, **with the exception of**
      1. **Contingency cases:** A lawyer may advance **court costs and expenses of litigation** in contingency cases, the repayment of which is dependent on the case outcome, and
      2. **Indigent clients:** A lawyer can advance **court costs and expenses of litigation** on behalf of indigent clients.
   b. **California rule:** A lawyer may **lend** money to the client after employment if the client promises in **writing to repay** the loan.
9. **Compensation from third parties:** A lawyer **shall not** accept compensation from third parties to represent the client **unless**
   a. The client gives **informed consent,**

b. There is **no interference** with the lawyer's independent professional judgment or with the lawyer-client relationship, and
c. Information relating to the representation remains **confidential**.

10. **Organizational client:** A lawyer employed by an organization represents the organization and must act in the **best interest of the organization.**
    a. **Report to a higher authority:** If the lawyer knows that an **officer, employee, or other person** associated with the organization is engaged in (or intends to) action that is likely to result in substantial injury to the organization, the lawyer shall **refer the matter to higher authority** in the organization, unless the lawyer reasonably believes that it is not in the best interest of the organization to do so.
        1. **Failure to act: If the highest authority fails to take action** and the lawyer reasonably believes the violation will result in substantial injury to the organization
            a. **ABA only:** The lawyer **may reveal information**, regardless of confidentiality, if such disclosure is **necessary to prevent the injury.**
            b. **California rules:** The lawyer **may not disclose information outside** the organization; rather it recommends the lawyer to **urge reconsideration** of the matter to the higher authorities within the organization or **resign** from representation.
    b. **Representation of organization's individuals:** A lawyer **may represent the organization and its officers**, directors, employees, shareholders, or other constituents if all four exceptions required for representation of those with concurrent conflicts are met (see I.B.1.c above).

11. **No limiting malpractice liability**
    a. **ABA only:** An attorney **may not agree to limit** the lawyer's liability to the client without advising the client in writing to **seek independent legal counsel** regarding settlement of such a claim.
    b. **California rules do not allow** a lawyer to prospectively limit liability to a client.

<u>Exam tip:</u> Conflicts of interest are the most heavily tested issues on professional responsibility essays. Be sure to first start by looking at what type of conflict exists; then, determine whether it is potential or actual conflict. Next, identify the corresponding ABA and California rules. It is best to analyze each required element in its own paragraph and possibly with its own heading if there is a lot of analysis for each element (such as analysis of the issue if the lawyer reasonably believes he can represent the client). Also, be sure to identify whether the rule is California only. You may want to start off your essay by explaining that all rules are for both California and ABA unless otherwise noted.

Conflict of interest fact triggers:
- L represents a corporation, and others involved with the corporation contact L about an issue related to the corporation
- L represents multiple parties
- L represents one party and drafts a document for someone involved with the other party
- L is on the board for a corporation and acts as its attorney
- L is friends with the client
- L has an interest in the subject matter in which he is assisting the client or his interest is opposite the client's

C. **Imputed disqualification:** Imputed disqualification occurs when any conflict of interest exists for an attorney, which results in **all attorneys in his firm being disqualified** from representing the client since all attorneys share the conflict, **unless:**
   1. The prohibition is based on a **personal interest** of the disqualified lawyer and does not present a **significant risk** of **materially limiting** the representation by the other attorneys, or
   2. The prohibition is based on a **former client** and arises out of the disqualified lawyer's association with a **prior firm**, and the lawyer is **timely screened** from any participation in the matter and the former client is provided **written notice** of the above as well as certifications of compliance with the screening procedures.
   3. A **client can waive** any imputed disqualification with **informed written consent.**

D. **Lawyer terminates firm:** When a lawyer has terminated an association with a firm, the firm **may thereafter represent** a person with **interests materially adverse** to those of a client represented by the formerly associated lawyer **unless:**
   1. The matter is **substantially the same**, and
   2. Any remaining lawyer has **confidential information** that is material to the matter.

E. **Duty to communicate:** The lawyer shall promptly inform the client of any decision that affects the client's informed consent as well as reasonably consult with the client and keep him informed of the status of the case.

F. **Scope of representation:** A lawyer may take actions to represent the client, but the lawyer must abide by the **client's substantive decision** to settle, plea, or waive jury trial after the lawyer has consulted with the client. The **lawyer** is responsible for employing the appropriate **legal strategy.**

Issue-spotting tip: Often when the lawyer fails to inform the client about a possible settlement, offer, or plea, it invokes both the issues of the scope of the representation and the lawyer's duty to communicate. As a result, if scope is involved, always address the duty to communicate as well.

G. **Duty of confidentiality:** A lawyer **shall not reveal** information relating to the representation of a client **unless:**
   1. The client gives **informed consent,**
   2. The disclosure is **impliedly authorized** to represent the client (**ABA only**),
   3. The lawyer **reasonably believes the disclosure is necessary** to
      a. Prevent reasonably certain **death or substantial bodily harm (disclosure is optional in California)**,
         1. **California rule:** The lawyer must first make a good faith effort to **persuade the client** not to commit the criminal act and **inform** the client of the lawyer's ability to reveal the information.
      b. Prevent the client from **committing a crime or fraud** that is reasonably certain to result in **substantial injury to the financial interests** or property of another and the client is or has **used the lawyer's services** to do so (**ABA only**), or
      c. **Mitigate or rectify substantial injury** to the financial interests or property of another that is reasonably certain to result or has resulted **from using the lawyer's services** to further commission of the crime (**ABA only**),
   4. **Secure legal advice** about the lawyer's compliance with these rules (**ABA only**), or
   5. **Establish a claim or defense** on behalf of the lawyer in a **controversy between the lawyer and the client,** or in defense of the conduct the client was involved in with the lawyer's services (**ABA only**), or
   6. **Comply with another law** or court order (**ABA only**).

> **Exam tip:** There are quite a few distinctions between the ABA and California rules regarding confidentiality. Remember that California is extremely strict with regard to confidentiality, much more so than the ABA. Also, whenever there is a conflict of interest between clients or an organization and one of its constituents, always raise the duty of confidentiality since it is always a possible violation since the lawyer can accidentally disclose information from one client to the other in these situations. Many exams often raise the issue even if the lawyer has yet to disclose any information. Thus, even if the call asks what violations the lawyer has committed, it is best to raise the issue to let the exam grader know there is a likelihood of disclosure and the lawyer could easily violate the duty of confidentiality in that situation.

H. **Attorney-client privilege:** A client has a right not to have disclosed any confidential communication between the attorney and the client relating to the professional relationship.
   1. A **corporation** can be the client, as well as an individual.
      a. **Federal common law:** Applies to **employees/agents if authorized** by the corporation to make the communication to the lawyer.

b. **California Evidence Code (CEC):** Applies to employees/agents if the **natural person to speak to the lawyer** on behalf of the corporation, or the employee did something for which the corporation may be held liable and the corporation instructed her to tell its lawyer what happened. (As applied, both FRE and CEC yield the same result.)

2. **Confidential communications:** The communication must be **intended** to be confidential.
   a. The presence of a **third party** may serve to **waive** the privilege.
   b. **Does not apply to physical evidence** turned over to the lawyer—only to communications.
   c. **CEC only:** Allows holder to stop **eavesdroppers** and other wrongful inceptors from revealing confidential information.
3. **Professional services:** The communication must be made for the **purpose of facilitating legal services**, though a fee need not be paid.
4. **Holder of the privilege:** Only the **client holds the privilege** and the lawyer may assert it on the client's behalf.
5. **Privilege lasts until:**
   a. **Federal common law: After death**, with the exception of a will contest.
   b. **CEC:** Privilege evaporates when the dead client's **estate has been fully distributed** and his personal representative has been discharged.
6. **Exceptions:** The attorney client privilege **does not apply** if:
   a. Used to **further crime of fraud**; or
   b. Relates to a **dispute between the lawyer and client**; or
   c. **Two or more parties** consult on a matter of common interest and the communication is offered by one against another; or
   d. **CEC only:** Lawyer **reasonably** believes the disclosure is **necessary to prevent a crime** that is likely to result in **death or substantial bodily harm.**

> <u>Exam tip:</u> The duty of confidentiality applies regardless of whether the client requests it, and applies to communications that could reasonably lead to the discovery of confidential information; whereas the attorney-client privilege is much more narrow and only applies when the lawyer or client will be testifying about confidential communications and it only applies to those communications pertaining to the legal services.

I. **Fees**
   1. **Reasonable fees:** All fees must be **reasonable** considering the following factors (**ABA only**):
      a. **Time limitations** imposed by the client or circumstances,
      b. **Experience**, reputation, and ability of the lawyer, and

c. **Nature** and length of the relationship with the client,
d. **Time and labor**, novelty and difficulty, and skill required,
e. **Fee customarily charged** in the locality for similar services,
f. **Likelihood** that the acceptance will preclude other employment,
g. **Amount involved** and results obtained,
h. **Whether** the fee is fixed or contingent.

2. **California rule:** Fees may **not be illegal or unconscionable** based on the same factors as reasonableness above for the ABA.

> **Memorization tip:** Since there are so many factors, think of **TENT FLAW** to remember the ABA reasonable/California unconscionable factors should this issue arise on an essay. Think of yourself camping and having a tent mishap . . . picture it now.

3. **Fee agreements must state:**
   a. How the fee is **calculated;**
   b. The general **nature of the legal services**; and
   c. The **responsibilities** of the lawyer and the client.
4. **California rule** requires all fee agreements **over $1,000 to be in writing unless** the client is a **corporation**, the agreement was made during an **emergency**, the client **waives** the writing in writing, the services are for a **previous client with similar services** in which the fee can be implied.
5. **Arbitration: California requires** a lawyer to submit to **arbitration for fee disputes,** whereas the **ABA only encourages it.**
6. **Contingency fee agreements:** A contingency fee agreement, which is a fee agreement in which the fee is dependent on the outcome of the matter, must
   a. Be in **writing,**
   b. Be **signed by the client** (**California rules** require the agreement to be **signed by both** the lawyer and client with each having a copy),
   c. State the **method by which the fee is to be determined,** including percentages in the event of a settlement, trial, or appeal,
   d. State the **litigation and other expenses to be deducted** from the recovery, and
   e. State whether such expenses are to be deducted **before or after the contingent fee is calculated** (**California rules** look at how disbursements and costs will affect the contingency fee and client's recovery and if the client will have to pay any related matters not covered by the agreement).
   f. **California rules** also require that the agreement state that the **fee is negotiable** (**unless** the claim is for **negligence against a health care provider**, in which case, the first $50,000 can be 40%, the next $50,000 would be 33.33%, the next $500,000 would be 25%, and 15% for any excess beyond that).

g. **Domestic or criminal cases:** A lawyer **may not** enter into a **contingent fee agreement** in a **domestic relations** matter or a **criminal case.**
   1. **California rules allow** contingency fees on a very limited basis in domestic cases based on the circumstances of the situation and **only if it does not promote divorce.**

7. **Division of fees between lawyers** who are not in the same firm may be made only if
   a. The **division is proportionate** to the services performed by each lawyer or each lawyer assumes joint responsibility for the representation,
   b. The client agrees to the division and **consents in writing,** and
   c. The total fee is **reasonable.**
   d. **California rules** allow division between lawyers if the client **consents** in writing after full disclosure and the total fee is **not unconscionable.**
8. **No sharing fees with non-lawyers:** A lawyer may not share legal fees with a non-lawyer.
9. **No "finder's fee" allowed:** A lawyer **shall not give anything of value to a person** for recommending the lawyer's services unless it is a **qualified referral service** that has been approved by an appropriate regulatory authority.
   a. **California rule allows a lawyer to make a gift** of gratuity for a recommendation resulting in employment if the gift was not offered or given as consideration of a promise, agreement or understanding that the referral would be forthcoming or continue in the future.
10. A **reciprocal referral agreement** between lawyers is permissible if it is **not exclusive** and the client is **informed** of the agreement.

J. **Duties of competence/care:** A lawyer shall represent the client with the legal **knowledge, skill, thoroughness** and **preparation** reasonably necessary.
   1. **California rule:** A lawyer's duty to act competently **includes diligence** and mental, physical, and emotional ability.
   2. **California rule:** Allows a lawyer to associate or **consult with another competent lawyer** or **acquire the necessary skills** to become competent before performance is required.

K. **Duty of diligence:** A lawyer shall act with reasonable diligence and promptness in representing a client.

L. **Safekeeping property:** A lawyer shall hold property of clients or third persons connected with a representation **separate from the lawyer's own property** and must **keep accounting records** for five years.

M. **Sexual relations with clients:** A lawyer **shall not** have sexual relations with a client **unless a consensual sexual relationship existed before** the lawyer-client relationship commenced.
   1. **California rule allows consensual sexual relations** with a client as long as the lawyer does not:

   a. **Require or demand** sexual relations with a client as a condition of representation,
   b. **Coerce,** intimidate, or exert undue influence on client; or
   c. Represent a client if the sexual relations cause the lawyer to **perform incompetently.**
   d. Note: These restrictions do not apply if there is a preexisting sexual relationship that predates the attorney client relationship.

N. **Withdrawal:**
   1. **Mandatory withdrawal:** A lawyer **shall withdraw** from representation if
      a. The representation will result in a **violation of the rules** of professional conduct or other law;
      b. The lawyer's **mental or physical condition** materially impairs the lawyer's ability to represent the client; or
      c. The lawyer is **discharged (ABA only).**
      d. **California rule requires withdrawal** if the lawyer **knows or should know** that the client is bringing an action **without probable cause** or to **harass or maliciously injure** a person.
   2. **Permissive withdrawal:** A lawyer **may withdraw** from representation if
      a. He can do so **without material adverse effect** on the interests of the client **(ABA only),**
      b. The client persists in action involving the lawyer's services that the **lawyer reasonably believes is fraudulent or criminal,**
      c. The client has used the lawyer's services to **perpetrate a crime or fraud,**
      d. The clients insists upon taking **action that the lawyer considers repugnant** or with which the lawyer has a fundamental disagreement,
      e. The **client fails substantially to fulfill an obligation** to the lawyer regarding the lawyer's services and has been given **reasonable warning** that the lawyer will withdraw unless the obligation is fulfilled,
      f. The representation will result in an **unreasonable financial burden** on the lawyer **(ABA only),** or
      g. Other **good cause** exists.
      h. **California rule permits withdrawal** where
         1. The client **insists** on presenting claims or defenses that **cannot be supported by good faith,**
         2. The client engages in **conduct that makes it unreasonably difficult** for the lawyer to represent him, or
         3. The lawyer is **unable to work with co-counsel.**
   3. **Duty to client upon permissive withdrawal:** When the court grants permission for withdrawal, the attorney shall protect the client's interests and
      a. Provide the client with **reasonable notice** to allow time to seek other counsel;
      b. **Surrender papers and property** (the lawyer may retain a copy); and

c. **Refund any advanced payments** not yet earned.

> <u>Exam tip:</u> Anytime the lawyer has violated a rule of professional responsibility or engaged in any of the activities that support withdrawal, you should mention withdrawal briefly and explain why the attorney may want to withdraw and whether it would be permissive or mandatory.

II. PROFESSIONAL INTEGRITY

A. Advertising/solicitation

1. **Truth required:** A lawyer **shall not make false or misleading communication** about the lawyer or the lawyer's services.
2. **Advertising allowed:** A lawyer may advertise services through written, recorded or electronic communication, including public media, unless the prospective client has made it known to the lawyer of his desire to not be solicited. All advertisements must:
   a. Contain the **name and office address** of at least one lawyer responsible for its content.
   b. **Be labeled advertising material:** All written, recorded, or electronic communications must include the words "Advertising Material" on the outside of the envelope and at the beginning and end of any recorded or electronic communication.
      1. **California rule** requires that a correct **copy** of the communications be retained for two years.
      2. **California rule** requires that it be labeled as a communication or solicitation such as "advertisement" or "newsletter," but **does not require any exact words** to be used, so long as the words are in 12-point print on the first page.
3. **No direct solicitation:** A lawyer may not conduct in-person, live telephone, or real-time electronic contact.
   a. **California rule presumes the following communications to be in violation of the rules:**
      1. **Guarantees**, warranties, or predictions regarding results.
      2. **Testimonials** or endorsements without a disclaimer that it is not a guarantee, warranty, or prediction of results.
      3. **Delivery to a potential client** that the lawyer knows or should reasonably know is in such a **fragile** physical, emotional, or mental state that he could not exercise reasonable judgment.
      4. **Transmissions at the scene of an accident** or en route to the hospital or at the hospital or care facility.
      5. Communications that contain a **dramatization,** without a disclaimer that it is a dramatization.
      6. **"No fee without recovery"** communications, unless it also states whether the client will be liable for costs.
4. **Specialists:** A lawyer shall not imply or state that he is certified as a specialist in a particular field of law, unless:

   a. The lawyer has been **certified as a specialist** by the ABA or a state-approved organization, and
      1. **California rule** requires it to be an organization certified or **accredited by the California State Bar.**
   b. The **name of the certifying organization is clearly identified** in the communication.

B. **Duty of fairness:** A lawyer has a **general duty of fairness to third parties, opposing counsel,** and the **court.**
   1. **Represented parties:** A lawyer **shall not communicate with parties the lawyer knows to be represented** by another lawyer **unless** the other lawyer has **consented** or the communication is **authorized** by law or court order.
   2. **Duty of fairness to the court:** A lawyer shall not knowingly
      a. **Make a false statement** of fact or law to a tribunal or fail to correct a false statement of material fact or law previously made,
      b. **Fail to disclose adverse legal authority,** or
      c. **Offer evidence that the lawyer knows to be false.**
      d. A lawyer who knows the **client intends to engage in fraudulent or criminal activity** shall take reasonable remedial measures, including, if necessary, disclosure to the tribunal.
   3. **Duty of fairness to opposing counsel:** As to the opposing counsel and party, a lawyer **shall not:**
      a. **Unlawfully obstruct evidence,** or destroy or conceal documents or other material;
      b. **Disobey the court rules;**
      c. **Make a frivolous discovery request** or fail to reasonably comply with discovery requests;
      d. **Assert personal opinions** during trial; or
      e. **Request others to refrain from giving relevant information** unless a relative or agent of client.
   4. **Duty of decorum to the tribunal:** A lawyer **shall not:**
      a. **Seek to influence jurors,** judges, or other officials,
      b. **Communicate ex-parte** with such persons during proceedings,
      c. **Communicate with jurors** after they are discharged if they don't want to communicate.
   5. **Duty not to suppress evidence: California rules prohibit a lawyer from suppressing any evidence** that the lawyer or the lawyer's client has a legal obligation to reveal or produce.
   6. **Extrajudicial statements:** A lawyer who is participating in an investigation or litigation or a matter **shall not make** an extrajudicial statement that the lawyer knows or reasonably should know will be **publicly disseminated** and have a **substantial likelihood of materially prejudicing** the proceeding.
      a. The lawyer **may state** the **claim, offense,** or **defense** involved; the information in the **public records;** that an **investigation is in progress; requests for information; warnings** of danger; and the **status of the accused** in a criminal case.

7. **Prosecutors** shall
   a. **Refrain from prosecuting** charges that are **not supported by probable cause,**
   b. Make **timely disclosure** to the defense of all **exculpatory evidence,** and
   c. **Refrain from making extrajudicial statements** that have a **substantial likelihood** of heightening **public condemnation** of the accused.

> Exam tip: Anytime a lawyer takes any action that may disadvantage another party, opposing counsel, or alter evidence, consider application of the duty of fairness. If there is an action occurring in the facts that is not specified in the rules above but seems questionable, mention the duty of fairness. Use common sense to determine what you think the lawyer should do and what you would do as an ethical lawyer. Label the discussion "Duty of Fairness" and analyze why the actions are or are not fair and/or ethical to others.

C. **Unauthorized practice of law/liability for others**
   1. **No practice with a non-lawyer:** A lawyer **shall not practice** with or form a partnership or association authorized to practice law with a non-lawyer.
   2. **Responsible for ratification and supervised lawyers:** A lawyer shall be **responsible for another lawyer's violation** of the Rules of Professional Conduct if the lawyer knowingly **ratifies the conduct** or is a partner or has **direct supervisory authority** over the other lawyer and could have **mitigated** the consequences.

D. **Duty to report ethical violations**
   1. A **lawyer who knows that another lawyer** has committed a violation of the Rules of Professional Conduct that raises a substantial question as to that lawyer's honesty, trustworthiness, or fitness as a lawyer **shall** inform the appropriate professional authority.
   2. **California rule permits, but does not require,** the reporting of ethical violations.

E. **Duty to the public/profession**
   1. **No criminal conduct:** A lawyer **shall not** counsel a client to engage, or assist a client, in criminal or fraudulent conduct, but may counsel the client to discuss the legal consequences and assist them in making a good faith effort to understand the law.
   2. **No frivolous claims:** A lawyer **shall not bring or defend** a proceeding unless there is a **basis in law and fact** for doing so that is not frivolous.
   3. **No harassing: The California rules** prohibit a lawyer from seeking, accepting, or continuing employment to conduct a defense or case without probable cause or for the purpose of **harassing or maliciously injuring any person.**

4. **No threats: The California rules prohibit a lawyer from threatening** to present criminal, administrative, or disciplinary charges to obtain an unfair advantage in a civil dispute.

> **<u>Exam tip:</u>** Similar to the broad scope of the duty of fairness, anytime a lawyer acts inappropriately in a fact pattern, you should also address the lawyer's duty to the public/profession. Use common sense to determine what you think the lawyer should do and what you would do as an ethical lawyer. Label the discussion "Duty to the Public/Profession" and analyze why the actions are or are not fair and/or ethical to others.

PROFESSIONAL RESPONSIBILITY ISSUES TESTED MATRIX

		Crossover	Duty of Loyalty/ Conflicts	Duty to Communicate / Scope of Representation	Duty of Confidentiality	Attorney-Client Privilege	Fees & Splitting/ Gifts/Loans	Duties of Competence/Care/ Diligence	Attorney-Client Relationship/ Sexual Relations	Withdraw / File Return	Solicitation/ Advertising	Fairness to Parties/ Counsel/Court	Unauthorized Practice Law/Report Ethics Violation	Duties to Public / Profession
July '11 Q4	Austin, physician, becomes lawyer		X		X			X				X	X	
February '11 Q5	Bob owns 51% of Corp; Cate owns 30%	Bus. Assoc.	X		X			X						
July '10 Q2	Hazardous waste, tax attorney Anne		X	X	X	X	X	X						
February '10 Q2	ABC LLP leased offices to attorneys	Bus. Assoc.	X		X			X						
July '09 Q5	Diane builds dam for childrens' camp	Civ. Pro. / Remedies			X	X								
July '09 Q2	Attorney Alex & Dusty, movie actor											X		X
February '09 Q1	Betty, ABC, Lucy Lawyer, XYZ		X		X		X	X						
July '08 Q1	Alex, solo law practice, Booker		X		X		X	X					X	
February '08 Q6	Attorney Albert and Barry form Lawco	Bus. Assoc.					X						X	
February '08 Q2	Acme Paint, Lawyer June, lead in paint		X		X					X				
February '07 Q2	Rita and Fred form Rita's Kitchen	Bus. Assoc.	X		X			X						

Continued >

		Crossover	Duty of Loyalty/ Conflicts	Duty to Communicate / Scope of Representation	Duty of Confidentiality	Attorney-Client Privilege	Fees & Splitting/ Gifts/Loans	Duties of Competence/Care/ Diligence	Attorney-Client Relationship/ Sexual Relations	Withdraw / File Return	Solicitation/ Advertising	Fairness to Parties/ Counsel/Court	Unauthorized Practice Law/Report Ethics Violation	Duties to Public / Profession
July '06 Q5	Client hit by truck driven by Driver		X	X			X	X	X					
February '06 Q5	Larry represents Marla; widgets	Contracts	X	X								X		X
July '05 Q6	Lawyer Lou dates Client Sally		X	X			X		X		X	X		
July '05 Q3	Lawyer works for SI and helps Carole	Bus. Assoc.	X	X	X			X						
February '05 Q4	Ann, Officer Patty, employment discr.	Evidence				X		X				X		X
July '04 Q5	L, 10 yrs. as Deputy District Attorney						X	X			X	X		X
February '04 Q3	L represents Sis in divorce, Dad's estate		X		X		X	X				X		
July '03 Q5	L employed by ChemCorp.		X		X					X				X
July '03 Q1	D contacts L for tax advice; L buys stock	Bus. Assoc.	X		X							X		X
February '03 Q4	L hired by City, later works for W & Z		X		X		X							
July '02 Q3	Betty, son Todd, Attorney Alice		X	X			X	X				X		
February '02 Q4	Richard, trust; wife Alicia is attorney	Wills and Trusts	X	X	X			X				X		X
July '01 Q5	Attorney Ann represents Harry	Torts										X		X

Continued >

		Crossover	Duty of Loyalty/ Conflicts	Duty to Communicate / Scope of Representation	Duty of Confidentiality	Attorney-Client Privilege	Fees & Splitting/ Gifts/Loans	Duties of Competence/Care/ Diligence	Attorney-Client Relationship/ Sexual Relations	Withdraw / File Return	Solicitation/ Advertising	Fairness to Parties/ Counsel/Court	Unauthorized Practice Law/Report Ethics Violation	Duties to Public / Profession
February '01 Q5	Jones & Smith ads and fees						X				X			
July '99 Q3	Susan, Felix, Larry, Telecom	Contracts	X		X			X				X		
July '99 Q1	Al, Bob, Charlie, whiskey	Crimes			X					X				X
February '99 Q4	Rentco, Attorney Al, Bob & Carl	Bus. Assoc.	X		X			X						X
July '98 Q3	Attorney Ann is a member of CAP	Bus. Assoc.	X		X							X		X
February '98 Q4	L is Donna's attorney, helps Stan	Real Prop.	X	X										
July '97 Q3	Attorney Ann writes letter to Tenant		X	X			X		X		X			
February '97 Q5	David charged with murder and robbery				X	X				X				X
July '96 Q3	Dan uses heroin bicycle messengers	Crimes												X
July '95 Q1	Lab's hazardous waste products	Contracts										X		X
February '95 Q4	May represented Int'l Banker's Union		X	X			X							
February '94 Q1	Knowles represents bank robber Baker				X			X				X		X
July '93 Q6	Ted, a resident of Cal., executed a will	Wills and Trusts	X											

Continued >

		Crossover	Duty of Loyalty/ Conflicts	Duty to Communicate / Scope of Representation	Duty of Confidentiality	Attorney-Client Privilege	Fees & Splitting/ Gifts/Loans	Duties of Competence/Care/ Diligence	Attorney-Client Relationship/ Sexual Relations	Withdraw / File Return	Solicitation/ Advertising	Fairness to Parties/ Counsel/Court	Unauthorized Practice Law/Report Ethics Violation	Duties to Public / Profession
July '93 Q4	Attorney represents wife in divorce		X				X	X		X				
February '93 Q5	Owen's son's birthday party; Petey, pool	Torts	X		X			X						
February '92 Q4	Amy's Restaurant, repair work on exit	Torts												X
July '91 Q6	An old bus explodes, kids killed/injured		X		X		X							
July '90 Q5	Dr. is a nationally recognized surgeon		X	X	X		X	X						
February '90 Q3	O is treasurer for Bank; L is counsel		X		X	X				X				

PROFESSIONAL RESPONSIBILITY PRACTICE ESSAYS, ANSWER GRIDS, AND SAMPLE ANSWERS

Professional Responsibility Question 1

July 2006, Question 5

Lawyer represents Client, who sustained serious injuries when she was hit by a truck driven by Driver. Lawyer and Client entered into a valid, written contingency fee agreement, whereby Lawyer would receive one-third of any recovery to Client related to the truck accident. Because Client was indigent, however, Lawyer orally agreed to advance Client's litigation expenses and to lend her $1,000 monthly in living expenses that he would recoup from any eventual settlement. Lawyer did not tell Client that he had written a letter to Physician, Client's doctor, assuring Physician full payment of her medical expenses from the accident out of the recovery in the case.

Unfortunately, Driver had strong legal defenses to defeat the claim, and the case would not settle for the amount Lawyer initially forecast. Counsel for Driver finally offered $15,000 to settle the case without conceding liability. By this time, Lawyer had advanced $5,000 in litigation and living expenses, and Client had incurred $5,000 in medical expenses.

Client was reluctant to accept the offer. Realizing, however, that this case could drag on indefinitely with little chance of substantial recovery, Lawyer took Client out for an expensive dinner, at which they shared two bottles of wine. Afterward Lawyer took Client to Lawyer's apartment where they engaged in consensual sexual relations.

Later that evening Lawyer persuaded Client to accept the settlement offer by agreeing to give her the net proceeds after his contingency fee and the amounts he had advanced were deducted and not to pay Physician anything.

The next week, Lawyer distributed the net proceeds to Client as agreed.

What ethical violations, if any, has Lawyer committed?

Answer according to California and ABA authorities to the extent there is any difference among them.

Professional Responsibility Question 1 Assessment

July 2006, Question 5

Professional responsibility is the most frequently tested subject on the California bar exam, and we can almost guarantee that you will see at least one professional responsibility essay question. Sometimes professional responsibility will be tested in the form of a crossover question, but sometimes there will be a full professional responsibility question as well as a crossover question. It is wise to be well prepared and know the professional responsibility rules cold.

In recent years the bar examiners seem very interested in exploring the differences between the ABA Model Rules, the ABA Code, and the California professional responsibility rules as contained in the California Rules of Professional Conduct, relevant sections of the California Business and Professions Code, and leading federal and state case law. Be certain to have a good command of the areas where the laws are different between these sources.

Often with professional responsibility the focus is on the factual analysis. Since many of the professional responsibility topics and rules overlap, any number of professional responsibility rules can provide the basis for a factual discussion and the bar examiners seem satisfied so long as your answer includes a full factual discussion. However, unlike other tested subjects, it is important to reach the correct conclusion on a professional responsibility essay question since the purpose of the question is to ensure that you know and can properly apply the rules.

This question explores some typical and frequently tested topics, including the duty to communicate, duty of care, and duty of loyalty. However, it also tests some less frequently tested topics, including the appropriateness of advancing living expenses in a contingency fee case. In this case, the rules differ depending on whether the ABA or California rule is applied. You are expected to identify both rules and apply the facts to each rule, which could lead you to reach a different conclusion for advancing living expenses depending on whether the ABA or California rules apply. Another unusual rule tested with this essay question is the rule regarding a lawyer having consensual sexual relations with his client. Again, the rules differ depending on whether the ABA or California rule is applied. While the ABA prohibits consensual sexual relations with a client unless the relationship predated the representation, in holding with the state of California's general reputation, the California rule is more permissive.

Note the areas highlighted in **bold** on the corresponding grid. The bold areas highlight the issues, analysis, and conclusions that are likely **required** to receive a passing score on this question. In general, the essay grids are provided to assist you in analyzing the essays, and are much more detailed than what a student should create during the exam to organize their response to a question.

Issue	Rule	Fact Application	Conclusion
Fee agreement	Contingency fees must be in writing, clearly state the method for calculating the fee, and identify if litigation expenses are to be deducted before or after the calculation of the contingency fee. **Advances: L may advance litigation expenses to an indigent client and recover the expenses from the contingency fee.** **ABA: Does not allow advances for living expenses.** **Cal. rule: Does allow advances for living expenses, so long as the advance is a loan and not a gift, and the agreement is in writing.**	Here, there is a valid contingency fee agreement. **Since there is a valid contingency fee agreement, the advancement of litigation expenses is proper under both the ABA and Cal. rules.** The problem is that the advancement agreement was made orally but it must be in writing since contingency fee agreements must be in writing and clearly state the method of calculation. **The advancement agreement should have been in writing in the contingency fee agreement and should have clearly stated the terms under which the advanced expenses would be repaid.** **L has also advanced living expenses of $1,000 a month. Under the ABA, the advancement of living expenses is prohibited in every circumstance, and doing so would subject L to discipline.** **Here, it is unclear if the repayment is made before or after L receives his 1/3 recovery, or is pre- or post-expenses, the timing of which is necessary under the Cal. rules. Again, the problem is that the agreement is oral, which is not permitted under the Cal. rule, and thus, L is subject to discipline.**	**Fee agreement subjects L to discipline**

Continued >

Issue	Rule	Fact Application	Conclusion
Letter to physician	**Duty to communicate: L has a duty to reasonably communicate with a client and keep him informed of the status of the case so the client can make informed decisions.** Duty of loyalty: L has a duty of loyalty to his client.	**L must regularly communicate with his client and relate information about the case's progression so the client has the appropriate information from which to make an informed decision.** L sent a letter on the side to Client's doctor without Client's knowledge, assuring Physician full payment of fees from the case recovery. **This agreement directly affects the amount Client will receive for her injuries since now a fee to Physician will be taken "off the top." Therefore, L violated his duty to communicate because he should have communicated this important information to Client.** L likely did not act in Client's best interest when he assured Physician that he would be paid out of Client's case recovery. L overstepped his bounds when he unilaterally decided that this expense would be taken out of Client's recovery.	**L violated duty to communicate**
Case valuation	Duty of care/competence: L shall represent the client with the legal knowledge, skill, thoroughness, and preparation reasonably necessary.	It appears that L seriously misjudged the value of Client's case in his initial forecast because Driver had "strong legal defenses." It is unclear if the inaccurate forecast is the result of lack of care or competence. If these defenses are something L should have discovered and L did not use the appropriate level of care or skill to discover the defenses, L may have violated the duty of care.	L may have violated duty of care
Consensual sex	**ABA: Prohibits sexual contact between Ls and clients unless a preexisting relationship.**	There is no indication L and Client had a preexiting sexual relationship. Further, they engaged in sex after consuming two bottles of wine. **Under the ABA this is clearly a violation.** It may also be a violation in Cal. since it appears that L was using sex as a means of having undue influence over Client's decision to accept the settlement offer.	L subject to discipline

Continued >

Issue	Rule	Fact Application	Conclusion
	Cal. rule: Allows sexual relationships between Ls and clients unless L • Demands sex a condition of representation; or • Uses coercion or undue influence; or • Represents the client incompetently because of the sexual relationship.		L subject to discipline
Pressure to accept offer	**Duty of loyalty: L has a duty of loyalty to his client.** **L has a duty of loyalty to his client and may never place his own interests above that of his client.** Duty of fair dealing to the public and third parties.	**L pressured client into accepting a settlement offer** when Client expressed reluctance to accept the offer. Client had already incurred $10,000 in expenses and the offer was only for $15,000. L did not want the case to drag on, so he took Client to an expensive dinner where **they shared two bottles of wine,** and finished the evening with consensual sex. **L then renegotiated the contingency fee agreement so Physician would not get paid** to make the agreement more palatable to Client. L counseled client not to pay Physician, exposing Client to further liability, which is not in her best interests. Further, this violates L's own duty of fairness to the public and third parties since L knows Physician has a legitimate claim. L seemed to be self-motivated and encouraged the settlement so he could recoup his expenses. L violated his duty of loyalty to Client by using undue and improper influence to encourage her to settle.	**L is subject to discipline**
Settlement offer	L may take actions to represent the client, but L must abide by the client's decision to settle, plea, or waive jury trial after L has consulted with the client on the matter.	**The decision to accept the settlement offer, or not, was solely Client's decision to make. While it is not clear if L is giving Client bad advice, at the least L is in violation of his ethical duties for using undue influence over Client.**	**L is subject to discipline**

Professional Responsibility Question 1 Sample Answer

July 2006, Question 5

Fee Agreement

Contingency Fee

Contingency fees must be in writing, clearly state the method for calculating the fee, and identify if litigation expenses are to be deducted before or after the calculation of the contingency fee.

Here, according to the facts there is a valid contingency fee agreement.

Advancement

A lawyer may advance litigation expenses to an indigent client and recover the expenses from the contingency fee. However, the ABA does not allow a lawyer to advance living expenses to a client. California is more permissive and does allow a lawyer to advance living expenses to a client, so long as the advance is truly a loan and not a gift, and the agreement is in writing.

Under both the ABA and California rules a lawyer is allowed to advance litigation expenses to an indigent client and then may recoup the expenses from the contingency fee. Since there is a valid contingency fee agreement, the advancement of litigation expenses is proper. However, the problem is that the advancement agreement was made orally and it must be in writing since contingency fee agreements always must be in writing and clearly state both the method of calculation and identify whether litigation expenses are to be deducted before or after the calculation of the contingency fee. The advancement agreement here should have been identified in writing in the contingency fee agreement and should have clearly stated the terms under which the advanced expenses would be repaid, including whether the contingency fee calculation would occur before or after the expenses were deducted.

The lawyer has also advanced living expenses of $1,000 a month to client. Under the ABA the advancement of living expenses is prohibited in every circumstance and doing so would subject the lawyer to discipline.

However, under the California rule a lawyer is permitted to advance living expenses. Such an agreement must be in writing and clearly identify the terms, such as when the loan will be repaid. Here, it is unclear if the repayment of living expenses would be made before or after Lawyer receives his 1/3 contingency fee recovery, or is before or after the expenses advanced, as noted above. Again, the problem is that the agreement is oral and an oral agreement is not permitted under the California rule, thus Lawyer is subject to discipline.

Letter to Physician

Duty of Communication

A lawyer has a duty to reasonably communicate with a client and keep him informed of the status and progression of the case so the client has appropriate information from which to make an informed decision.

Lawyer sent a letter on the side to Client's doctor without Client's knowledge, assuring Physician that he would receive full payment of his medical fees from Client's case recovery. This agreement directly affects the amount Client will receive for her injuries from the accident since now a fee to Physician will be taken "off the top" of any monetary recovery. Therefore, Lawyer violated his duty to communicate because he should have communicated this important information to Client so Client would have appropriate information from which to make decisions about the case.

Duty of Loyalty

A lawyer has a duty of loyalty to his client.

Lawyer likely did not act in Client's best interest when he assured Physician that he would be paid out of Client's case recovery. The lawyer overstepped his bounds when he unilaterally decided that Physician's expense for medical bills would be taken out of Client's recovery. Lawyer violated the duty of loyalty.

Case Valuation

Duty of Care/Competence

A lawyer has a duty of care and competence such that the lawyer shall represent the client with the legal knowledge, skill, thoroughness, and preparation reasonably necessary.

It appears that Lawyer seriously misjudged the value of Client's case in his initial forecast because he did not anticipate that Driver had "strong legal defenses." It is unclear if the inaccurate forecast was the result of Lawyer's lack of care or competence. If these defenses are something Lawyer should have discovered and Lawyer did not use the appropriate level of care or skill to discover the defenses, Lawyer may have violated the duty of care.

Consensual Sex

The ABA rules prohibit sexual contact between lawyers and clients unless they had a preexisting sexual relationship that predates the lawyer's representation of the client. The California rule allows sexual relationships between lawyers and clients unless the lawyer (1) demands sex a condition of representation, or (2) uses coercion or undue influence, or (3) represents the client incompetently because of the sexual relationship.

The ABA Code and Model rules prohibit lawyers from engaging in sexual relationships with their clients. In contrast, California is more permissive and allows such relationships subject to some guidelines that exist to protect the client's interest. There is no indication that Lawyer and Client had a preexisting sexual relationship. Further, they engaged in sex after consuming two bottles of wine at an expensive dinner orchestrated by Lawyer as a ploy to get Client to settle her case. Under the ABA, this is clearly an ethical violation. This may also be a violation under the California rule since it appears that Lawyer's excessive use of wine would have been undue influence on the client to engage in a sexual relationship. Further, Lawyer was using sex as a means of coercion and undue influence over Client's decision to accept the proposed settlement offer, which seems improper. Lawyer is subject to discipline.

Pressure to Accept Offer

Duty of Loyalty

A lawyer has a duty of loyalty to his client and may never place his own interests above the interest of the client.

Here, Lawyer pressured client into accepting a settlement offer when Client expressed reluctance to accept the offer. Client had already incurred $10,000 in expenses and the offer was only for $15,000, so it does not seem like a good offer. Lawyer did not want the case to drag on, so he took Client to an expensive dinner where they shared two bottles of wine, and finished the evening with consensual sex. Lawyer seemed to be self-motivated and encouraged the settlement so he could recoup his expenses from the settlement. Lawyer violated his duty of loyalty to Client by using undue and improper influence to encourage her to settle. Lawyer seems more interested in his own interest than in Client's, and that is a violation of the duty of loyalty.

Duty of Fair Dealing

A lawyer has a duty of fair dealing to the public and third parties.

In an attempt to get Client to accept the settlement offer, Lawyer then renegotiated the contingency fee agreement so Physician would not get paid to make the agreement more palatable to Client. Lawyer counseled client not to pay Physician, exposing Client to further liability, which is not in her best interests since Physician seems to have a legitimate claim to payment for medical treatment. Further, this behavior violates Lawyer's own duty of fairness to the public and third parties since Lawyer knows Physician has a legitimate claim, and now Lawyer is scheming to prevent Physician from receiving payment. Lawyer is subject to discipline.

Settlement Offer

A lawyer may take actions to represent the client, but the lawyer must abide by the client's decision to settle, plea, or waive jury trial after the lawyer has consulted with the client on the matter.

Client has the right to make the substantive decisions regarding her case, including settlement, and the lawyer is responsible for employing the appropriate legal strategy. Lawyer may give recommendations that are in the client's best interest. The lawyer must act in good faith. The decision to accept the settlement offer, or not, was solely Client's decision to make. While it is not clear if Lawyer is giving Client bad advice, at the least Lawyer is in violation of his ethical duties for using undue influence over Client. Lawyer is subject to discipline.

Professional Responsibility Question 2

July 2011, Question 4

Austin had been a practicing physician before he became a lawyer. Although he no longer practices medicine, he serves on a local medical association committee that works to further the rights of physicians to be compensated fairly by health insurance providers. The committee develops recommendations, but its members do not personally engage in public advocacy. Austin is a close friend of several of the other physicians on the committee, though as a lawyer he has never represented any of them.

In his law practice, Austin represents BHC Company, a health insurance provider. BHC has been sued in a class action by hundreds of physicians, including some of Austin's friends, for unreasonable delay, and denial and reduction of reimbursements for medical services. Austin initially advised BHC that he was not confident it had a defense to the lawsuit. After further research, however, Austin discovered that a stated policy of the health care law is the containment of health care costs. He advised BHC that he could plausibly argue that reimbursements to physicians may legally be limited to avoid a dramatic increase in the health insurance premiums of patients. He explained that he would argue for a modification of existing decisional law to allow such a result based on public policy.

When Bertha, counsel for the class of physicians, heard the defense Austin planned to assert in the lawsuit, she wrote him a letter stating that if he presented that defense she would report him to the state bar for engaging in a conflict of interest.

1. What, if any, ethical violations has Austin committed as an attorney? Discuss.
2. What, if any, ethical violations has Bertha committed? Discuss.

Answer according to California law and ABA authorities.

Professional Responsibility Question 2 Assessment

July 2011, Question 4

This professional responsibility essay question covers the frequently tested topics of the duty of loyalty, conflict of interest, and the duty of confidentiality. It also covers the less frequently tested topic of an attorney's duty to report the ethical violations of other attorneys. As is the current pattern of testing, the ABA rule and the California rule are different so the application of the two rules to the facts of this case leads to two opposite results.

This professional responsibility essay question also calls for a very thorough analysis of the frequently tested topic of conflict of interests. The question is somewhat atypical in that the attorney himself has a conflict with the interest of his client, rather than the conflict involving the attorney's representation of some other party. The attorney has a conflict as a result of his service on a committee that has a professed goal that is diametrically opposed to the goals of the attorney's client. Attorney has a further conflict in that the attorney is a personal friend with some of the plaintiffs involved in class action litigation against his client.

Another interesting topic covered by this question is the duty of a lawyer to not bring or defend frivolous proceedings, since the facts here indicate the strategy being employed by the attorney is a long shot and he originally did not think there was any appropriate defense to the class action lawsuit. Since a lawyer may make a good faith argument for the extension or modification of existing law based on public policy, the attorney's conduct is ultimately acceptable and there is no ethical violation. Remember, in the essay it is your job to prove or disprove, and even though there is no ethical violation in this case, there still must be a full factual discussion and application before you reach that conclusion.

Note the areas highlighted in **bold** on the corresponding grid. The bold areas highlight the issues, analysis, and conclusions that are likely **required** to receive a passing score on this question.

Issue	Rule	Fact Application	Conclusion
Call #1: Austin			
Duty of loyalty	**Duty of loyalty: L has a duty of loyalty to his client and may not place his own interests, or those of a third party above the interests of his client.**	**Austin's client is BHC, and thus Austin owes a duty of loyalty to BHC. As a health insurance provider, BHC is interested in minimizing payments to physicians in pursuit of making a profit. The less BHC pays doctors, the more competitive they are in the market and the more money they can make. Further, BHC has an interest in winning the class action lawsuit.**	Austin has a potential violation; see below
Conflict of interest	**Conflict of interest: L may not have a conflicting interest himself to his client.** A concurrent conflict of interest exists if there is a significant risk that the representation of one or more clients will be materially limited by L's responsibilities to another client, a former client, or a third person or by a personal interest of L. ABA rule: **Where there is a conflict, L may represent the clients only if L reasonably believes there will not be an adverse effect, and the client consents in writing after consultation.** Cal. rule: Only requires written disclosure of the conflict where the conflict arises from L's relationship (legal, personal, etc.) with a party or witness in the same matter as the client's that would substantially affect L's representation.	Austin is a former physician, though he no longer practices medicine. **He also serves on a local medical association committee that works to further the rights of physicians to be compensated fairly by health insurance providers, though he does not engage in public advocacy. BHC's interests are directly in opposition to the goals of the committee on which Austin serves.** **If Austin reasonably believes the conflict presented by his service to the committee would not have an adverse effect on BHC, he may continue to represent BHC as long as BHC is fully informed of the conflict and consents.** It may not be reasonable to believe that Austin's conflict would not be adverse to BHC since this issue seems to be one he feels very strongly about. Austin will likely argue that he can compartmentalize his life and that advocating for fairness in health insurance compensation to doctors is not opposed to the work he does for his client, ensuring compliance with existing law but paying no more than required under the law. Even if the laws are changed, it will change for all health care providers and won't put BHC at a competitive disadvantage. **But, it is difficult to believe Austin could put aside his strong personal beliefs on the topic.**	**If reasonable, full disclosure and written consent are required**

Continued >

Issue	Rule	Fact Application	Conclusion
		Assuming it is reasonable and BHC would consent to the Austin's conflict, Austin must make a full disclosure and get written consent. California only requires written disclosure. It does not appear Austin did either of these things, and Austin is subject to discipline. **Austin also counts many physicians among his friends, including several plaintiffs of the class action suit in which he is representing BHC.** Friendship is a personal interest to L and though it should not have an effect on his representation of BHC, Austin may find his enthusiasm to diligently and zealously represent BHC wane. Austin may have to depose or cross examine a friend, which would make adequate representation of BHC very difficult. In light of the conflicts of interest, it would be best if Austin withdrew from representing BHC.	**If reasonable, full disclosure and written consent are required**
Duty of confidentiality	**Duty of confidentiality: L shall not reveal information relating to the representation of a client.**	It would be difficult for Austin to participate in his board duties without discussing his representation of BHC. Should Austin do so, he would be in violation of the duty of confidentiality. On the facts, he does not appear to be in violation.	No violation
Duty of candor to the court	**Duty of candor: L shall not bring or defend a proceeding unless there is a basis in law and fact for doing so that is not frivolous.**	At first Austin thought he had no defense to BHC's case. But, after further research he believed he could make a good argument based on public policy. **However, L is permitted to make a good faith argument for the extension or modification of existing law based on public policy. It appears that Austin's legal strategy is arguing for the extension of law based in good faith, which is permitted,** even if the argument is a "long shot." **Austin may ethically go forward with his argument, even if he is not sure of success.**	**No basis for ethical violation**

Continued >

Issue	Rule	Fact Application	Conclusion
Call #2: Bertha			
Duty to report ethical violations	**ABA: L has an ongoing duty to report ethical violations of another L.** Cal. rule: Permits, but does not require, the reporting of ethical violations.	**Since Austin does have an irreconcilable conflict of interest, Bertha should have immediately reported him to the ABA. Her failure to do so results in an ethical violation for Bertha. In Cal. reporting ethical misconduct is only permissive, not required, so Bertha has no Cal. violation.**	**ABA: ethical violation Cal.: no ethical violation**
Threats	L has a duty of fairness to opposing counsel and the court. ABA: Does not have a rule on point. Cal. rule: Prohibits a lawyer from threatening to present criminal, administrative, or disciplinary charges to obtain an unfair advantage in a civil dispute. **[This concept may have been called a number of things and been acceptable. Both published passing student answers had the ABA rule wrong. The key was the analysis.]**	Under the Cal. rule, **Bertha is threatening Austin with reporting an ethical violation as a means of preventing him from presenting a valid defense. This type of blackmail is not permitted and violates the duty of good faith and fairness owed to opposing counsel and the court.**	**Ethical violation subject to discipline**

Professional Responsibility Question 2 Sample Answer

July 2011, Question 4

1. Austin

Duty of Loyalty

A lawyer has a duty of loyalty to his client.

A lawyer has a duty of loyalty to his client and may not place his own interests, or those of a third party above the interests of his client. Austin's client is BHC, and thus Austin owes a duty of loyalty to BHC. As a health insurance provider, BHC is interested in minimizing payments to physicians in pursuit of making a profit, remaining competitive in the marketplace, and maintaining a viable business. The less BHC is able to pay the doctors that provide the medical services to BHC's insureds, the more competitive they are in the market and the more money they can make. Further, since BHC has been sued by hundreds of doctors for unreasonable delay and improper payments, BHC has an interest in winning the class action lawsuit. Austin has a potential conflict of interest violation (see below), which may prevent him from maintaining his duty of loyalty to BHC.

Conflict of Interest

A lawyer may not have a conflicting interest to his client. A concurrent conflict of interest exists if there is a significant risk that the representation of one or more clients will be materially limited by the lawyer's responsibilities to another client, a former client, or a third person, or by a personal interest of the lawyer.

Austin is a former physician, though he no longer practices medicine. Austin also serves on a local medical association committee that works to further the rights of physicians to be compensated fairly by health insurance providers, though he does not actually engage in public advocacy. BHC's interest in keeping their payments to doctors low is in direct opposition to the goals of the committee on which Austin serves.

Where there is a conflict, the lawyer may represent the client only if the lawyer reasonably believes there will not be an adverse effect, and the client consents in writing after consultation. California only requires written disclosure of the conflict where the conflict arises from the lawyer's relationship (legal, personal, etc.) with a party or witness in the same matter as the client's that would substantially affect the lawyer's representation.

If Austin reasonably believes that the conflict presented by his service to the committee would not have an adverse effect on BHC, he may continue to represent BHC as long as BHC is fully informed of the conflict and consents to Austin's representation in writing. It may not be reasonable to believe that Austin's conflict would not be adverse to BHC since the issue of payment to doctors seems to be one about which he feels very strongly since he is a former doctor and voluntarily serves on the committee. Austin will likely argue that he can compartmentalize his life and that advocating for fairness in health insurance compensation to doctors is not opposed to the work he does for his client BHC, in which he ensures compliance with existing law but that BHC pay no more than required under the law. If the laws regarding payments to doctors are changed, it will change for all health care providers and won't put BHC at a competitive disadvantage, so in that way it would not harm BHC's interest. However, it is still difficult to believe Austin could put aside his strong personal beliefs on the topic.

Assuming it is reasonable that Austin's conflict would not have an adverse effect on BHC and that BHC would consent to the conflict, Austin must make a full disclosure and get written consent from BHC. California only requires written disclosure of the conflict. It does not appear that Austin got informed written consent, and thus Austin is subject to discipline.

Austin also counts many physicians among his friends, including several plaintiffs of the class action suit in which he is representing BHC. Friendship is a personal interest to a lawyer and, though it should not have an effect on his representation of BHC, Austin may find his enthusiasm to diligently and zealously represent BHC wane in the face of opposition from his friends. Austin may have to depose or cross examine a friend, which would make adequate representation of BHC very difficult.

In light of the conflicts of interest noted above, it would be best if Austin withdrew from representing BHC.

Duty of Confidentiality

A lawyer shall not reveal information relating to the representation of a client.

A lawyer must keep confidential any client communications. It would be difficult for Austin to participate in his board committee duties without discussing his representation of BHC. Should Austin do so, he would be in violation of the duty of confidentiality.

Duty of Candor to the Court

A lawyer shall not bring or defend a proceeding unless there is a basis in law and fact for doing so and the claim is not frivolous. A lawyer may not bring an unwarranted claim.

At first Austin thought he had no defense to BHC's case. But, after further research he believed he could make a good argument based on public policy interests. A lawyer is permitted to make a good faith argument for the extension or modification of existing law based on public policy considerations. It appears that Austin's legal strategy is to argue for the extension of law based in good faith, which is permitted, even if the argument is a "long shot." Austin may ethically go forward with his argument, even if he is not sure of success. There is no basis for an ethical violation on these grounds.

2. Bertha

Duty to Report

Under the ABA a lawyer has an ongoing duty to report ethical violations of another lawyer. The California rule permits, but does not require, the reporting of ethical violations.

Under the ABA, a violation of ethical rules must be reported immediately. Since Austin does have an irreconcilable conflict of interest pursuant to his representation of BHC, Bertha should have immediately reported him to the ABA. Her failure to do so results in an ethical violation for Bertha. In California, reporting ethical misconduct is only permissive, and not required, so Bertha has no violation under application of the California rule.

Threats

A lawyer has a duty of fairness to opposing counsel and the court. In California a lawyer is prohibited from threatening to present criminal, administrative, or disciplinary charges in order to obtain an unfair advantage in a civil dispute. The ABA does not have a companion rule.

Under application of the California rule, Bertha is threatening Austin with reporting an ethical violation as a means of preventing him from presenting a valid defense on BHC's class action lawsuit. This type of blackmail is not permitted and violates the duty of good faith and fairness owed to opposing counsel and the court. Bertha is subject to discipline.

Professional Responsibility Question 3

July 1993, Question 4

Attorney represented Wife in an action for divorce by Wife against Husband. During the course of representation, Attorney submitted bills totaling $11,000 for his legal services to Wife. After credit for payments by Wife, the amount due on Wife's obligation was $5,000. Attorney wrote Wife a letter informing her that he would perform no further services in connection with her case until she paid the outstanding balance of her account.

In response to Attorney's letter, Wife called Attorney and informed him that because of financial problems she could not then pay past due or additional legal fees. She asked Attorney if there was any arrangement under which he would be willing to continue to represent her. Attorney stated that he would continue to represent her if she would agree to pay him for his services, in addition to the $5,000, 25 percent of any property award she would receive in the divorce proceedings. Wife told Attorney she would think about it and call him back.

Several days later, Wife called Attorney and informed him that she had decided to retain another lawyer. She asked Attorney to give her the file in her case. Attorney informed Wife that it was her right to obtain another lawyer, but that if she wanted her case file, it would be necessary for her to pay the outstanding balance of her account and sign a general release of liability. Wife said she would try to raise the money and would call Attorney back in a few days.

The next day, Husband's lawyer called Attorney to ask Attorney to withdraw from his representation of Wife. Husband's lawyer reminded Attorney that several years ago Attorney represented a now-dissolved partnership, of which Husband was a limited partner, in an unsuccessful effort by the partnership to acquire an apartment building for investment purposes. Attorney refused to withdraw.

Discuss all ethical considerations raised by Attorney's conduct.

Professional Responsibility Question 3 Assessment

July 1993, Question 4

The call of the question does not provide any guidance on the issues to discuss on this professional responsibility question. The best approach is to go through the question sentence by sentence and address the issues in chronological order. The question is full of potential ethical violations and is fairly straightforward.

The attorney's refusal to continue performing services for the client because of her inability to pay for fees raises the obvious issue of the attorney's duty of care owed to the client, and requires a discussion of the permissive withdrawal rules.

This question calls for a full analysis of the rules pertaining to the appropriateness of payment by means of a contingency fee, and the requirements of a contingency fee agreement. This question also highlights a difference between the ABA rule and the California rule since a contingency fee is permitted for a domestic case in California, so long as the fee agreement does not contribute to the demise of the marriage. However, contingency fee agreements are not permitted under the ABA rules, and are rarely permitted under the ABA code.

Another obvious issue is the attorney's refusal to return the client file to the client until he is paid the fees Client owes for representing her in her divorce. This is a clear ethical violation and should be identified as such in your answer. When there is a cut-and-dried ethical violation, such as the one here, definitively state your determination that the attorney is subject to discipline for the violation.

The final issue is conflict of interest. Conflict of interest is the most frequently tested topic in professional responsibility so be certain to know those rules very well.

Note the areas highlighted in **bold** on the corresponding grid. The bold areas highlight the issues, analysis, and conclusions that are likely **required** to receive a passing score on this question.

Issue	Rule	Fact Application	Conclusion
Attorney's refusal to perform	**Duty of care: L shall represent the client with the legal knowledge, skill, thoroughness and preparation reasonably necessary.** **L may not withhold work for nonpayment of fees.** **Permissive withdrawal: L may request withdrawal from representation where there is no material adverse effect to the client. L must give reasonable notice** (ABA rule).	Attorney has threatened to stop providing legal services to Wife if she does not pay her outstanding bill for the work he has provided for her on her divorce case. **Here, since Wife has failed to pay fees, attorney may request withdrawal from the court, provided such withdrawal does not materially harm wife's case.** Attorney has already performed $11,000 in legal services, **but it is unclear what stage of litigation the proceedings are at.** If the case is in an early stage, withdrawal may be less harmful than if the case is close to trial. **Wife's financial problems may also prevent her from hiring another attorney, which could materially harm her case.** However, she told Attorney she had decided to retain another lawyer so perhaps not. Attorney's threat not to perform puts Wife at unfair disadvantage, which is contrary to her interests. **The proper steps to withdraw would have been for Attorney to give her notice and request withdrawal from the court, which Attorney did not do here so he is subject to discipline.**	**Subject to discipline**
Attorney's request for 25% additional payment	**Generally, L may not have a proprietary interest, or stake, in a cause of action.** However, contingency fess may be allowed subject to the following limitations. **Contingency fees in domestic cases:** • **ABA rule prohibits.** • ABA Code rarely allows. • **Cal. rule only prohibits if it causes marriage to break up. Such an agreement must be in writing** with the percentage clearly identified. Attorney fees must be reasonable. Unconscionable fees are prohibited.	**Attorney seeks 25% of Wife's property settlement, which is essentially a contingency fee in a divorce case since Attorney is representing Wife in divorce proceedings.** **Under the ABA rule this is not allowed in any circumstances.**	**As to the contingency fee: ABA: subject to discipline Cal.: acceptable** As to the unreasonable fee: Subject to discipline

Continued >

Issue	Rule	Fact Application	Conclusion
		However, under Cal. rules, a contingency fee is acceptable so long as it does not cause a salvageable marriage to break up. Since, the couple was already engaged in a divorce proceeding and Wife had already incurred $11,000 in legal bills before the idea of a contingency fee payment scheme was proposed, this fee structure would likely be acceptable since it would likely not be contributing to the marriage's demise. However, such an agreement is required to be in writing and, here, Attorney "stated" his proposal so the writing requirement is not satisfied, assuming this proposal becomes their fee agreement. Wife still owes Attorney $5,000 in fees, and Attorney wants payment of the $5,000 and an additional 25% of any property settlement Wife receives in the divorce. While the size of the estate is unclear, Attorney has refused to perform further services for Wife without receiving a substantial part of the property settlement. This creates an overall compensation package that is unreasonable and unconscionable and subjects Attorney to discipline.	**As to the contingency fee:** **ABA: subject to discipline** **Cal.: acceptable** As to the unreasonable fee: Subject to discipline
Retention of files	**L who withdraws must return all of client's papers and property, even if owed money.**	**Attorney must return Wife's client file so she can continue her case. Attorney may not refuse to do so until he is paid. Attorney improperly informed Wife he would not return her file without the payment of fees, which is a clear ethical violation, and Attorney is subject to discipline.**	**Subject to discipline**

Continued >

Issue	Rule	Fact Application	Conclusion
Malpractice	ABA rule: **L may not agree to limit L's liability to the client without advising the client in writing to seek independent legal counsel regarding settlement.** ABA Code and Cal. rules do not allow L to prospectively limit liability to a client.	**Attorney's attempt to have Wife sign a general release of liability is an ethical violation since L may not attempt to limit malpractice liability unless the client is advised in writing to seek independent legal counsel.** Attorney failed to advise Wife in writing to seek outside legal counsel before obtaining a release of liability, as is required, and Attorney is subject to discipline.	**Subject to discipline**
Conflict of interest	**Duty of confidentiality: L has a duty to preserve the confidentiality of a former client.** **If L reasonably believes he can represent the new client without adversely affecting the old client, he may do so only with informed consent.** **Cal. rule only requires informed written consent.**	**Attorney represented a partnership in which Husband was a limited partner,** which is a completely unrelated matter to this divorce case. Attorney may not disclose any information obtained during that representation or use that information. Attorney likely received confidential financial information during representation of Husband since the partnership was trying to acquire real estate. **If Attorney obtained confidential information during that representation that is relevant to this divorce, Attorney may not represent Wife unless Husband consents after consultation. In Cal. the consent must also be in writing**. However, Husband clearly does not consent since his L is demanding withdrawal of Attorney. **Attorney must withdraw because of the ethical violation created by the conflict of interest; his refusal to do so subjects him to discipline.**	**Subject to discipline**

Professional Responsibility Question 4

February 1990, Question 3

Officer is the treasurer of Bank. Officer called the Bank's regular outside counsel, Lawyer, and asked that they meet immediately. Lawyer offered to come to Bank, but Officer insisted that they meet elsewhere for "confidentiality reasons."

When Officer arrived, he was visibly upset. He began by telling Lawyer that Bank was experiencing financial difficulties which, if not corrected, would lead "to more serious problems." The problem began several years ago when Officer's superior, Boss, the president of Bank, began making loans to fictitious corporations for Boss' benefit. The loans were initially for small amounts, but the amounts increased and now totaled over $1,000,000. Neither Boss nor any of the fictitious corporations is able currently to repay the loans, and interest on the loans has not been paid for some time.

Officer learned of the loans a year ago but agreed with Boss to keep quiet. In return, Boss arranged to have a $25,000 loan made to XYZ, a newly created corporation, for Officer's personal benefit. Officer reminded Lawyer that Lawyer's firm prepared the incorporating documents for XYZ Corporation.

Officer believes that all loans for both his and Boss' benefit could be repaid over time, but because Bank's auditors are scheduled to review Bank's financial statements the following week, the problem loans are likely to be revealed.

Officer asked Lawyer to agree to advise him how to protect himself, Boss, and Bank from liability. Officer requested that the information he had disclosed and Lawyer's advice be kept confidential. Lawyer has not responded to Officer's requests.

Under the ABA Model Rules and ABA Code of Professional Responsibility:

1. Can Lawyer ethically agree to assist Officer, Bank, or Boss? Discuss.
2. Can Lawyer ethically disclose the information she has learned:
   a. To Boss? Discuss.
   b. To other officials of Bank? Discuss.
3. What individuals or entities will be able to waive Bank's attorney-client privilege relating to Lawyer's discussion with Officer? Discuss.
4. What are Lawyer's ethical obligations to Bank given her law firm's preparation of the incorporating documents for XYZ Corporation? Discuss.

Professional Responsibility Question 4 Assessment

February 1990, Question 3

Professional responsibility is a subject that lends itself to a robust factual discussion. Typically, it is perfectly acceptable to discuss the gist of the rule in more general terms compared to the specificity needed for other subjects. However, what is important is a full discussion of the lawyer's conduct and why it is or is not a violation of the professional responsibility rules and standards. A good factual discussion that focuses on the concepts of fairness and the duty to protect client confidences is often sufficient. This question is a good example of this type of more general discussion question.

However, be aware that the type of discussion you are supposed to include in your answer is completely dependent on what the facts of the question are and the issues raised by the question. In recent years the bar examiners have seemed to focus their questions on the particular areas of law where the rules differ between the ABA Model Rules and/or the ABA Code and the California rules. That type of a question will necessarily require a full recitation of each rule, including the identification of whether the rule is ABA or California, and a full discussion of the facts as applied to each of the differing rules. Where the rules are substantially similar, it is not necessary to identify the separate rules in the answer. However, it is key to make the distinction where the rules differ.

Note the areas highlighted in **bold** on the corresponding grid. The bold areas highlight the issues, analysis, and conclusions that are likely **required** to receive a passing score on this question.

Issue	Rule	Fact Application	Conclusion
1. Can Lawyer assist Officer, Bank or Boss?	**Duty of loyalty: L owes a duty of loyalty to the client, which requires L to put the interest of his client above all other interests and to avoid any conflicts of interest.** Corporate client: When L represents a corporation, the corporation itself is the client and all duties are owed to the corporation itself, not to the officers or directors. **Conflict of interest: L may not represent clients with conflicting interests.** L may represent officers of a corporation individually, unless there is a conflict of interest. Where there is a conflict, L may represent both clients only if L reasonably believes there will not be an adverse effect, the clients are not asserting claims against each other, and each client gives informed written consent after consultation.	**Lawyer is Bank's regular outside counsel. Consequently, Bank is Lawyer's client and Lawyer owes a duty of loyalty to Bank.** Out of necessity, Lawyer must communicate with bank officers and employees, but they are not individually owed a duty of loyalty. **Officer or Boss:** Lawyer met with Officer away from the bank for "confidential" reasons, and Officer asked that the information disclosed be kept confidential. Officer disclosed that he and Boss have perpetrated a fraud on Bank. **Officer and Boss's interests are so adverse to Bank's interests that it would not be possible for a disinterested lawyer to conclude that any client should agree to Lawyer representing both parties.** Under the ABA Model Rules this means Lawyer should not even request that the parties agree to such a scheme since it is so patently adverse to their best interests. **Consequently, Lawyer should not assist Officer or Boss. Lawyer should advise them immediately to seek independent counsel.** **Bank:** Lawyer met Officer off-site from the Bank and allowed Officer to share "confidential" information. Since Bank was already Lawyer's current client, Lawyer should not have met Officer "confidentially" off-site or allowed Officer to share this information. However, since Lawyer did so, **it is probably most appropriate for Lawyer to withdraw because Lawyer now possesses Officer's confidential information, which may prevent Lawyer from representing Bank in a matter involving Officer or Boss.**	**Officer or Boss: Lawyer may not assist** Bank: Could conclude either way

Continued >

Issue	Rule	Fact Application	Conclusion
2. Can Lawyer disclose information to Boss, or other bank officials?	**Duty of confidentiality: L shall not reveal information relating to the representation of a client.**	***Boss:* Lawyer has a duty of confidentiality, and all other duties imposed on a lawyer, to his client, which is Bank. Under normal circumstances Bank would be considered a representative of Bank, and confidential communication could be shared with him. However, in light of the information Lawyer received from Officer about Boss's potential fraud perpetrated on Bank, it would not be prudent to discuss any of this confidential information with Boss.** Boss has an interest adverse to Bank and, as such, Lawyer should not disclose this information to Boss. ***Other Bank Officials:* Lawyer does need to communicate with his client, Bank. Most likely, Lawyer should communicate with the Board of Directors since they ultimately are in charge of Bank.** Any discussions should not include Boss or Officer and should remain confidential. **If Lawyer is determined to have an attorney-client relationship with Officer because of the "confidential" nature of the communications here and Lawyer's firm's prior representation of Officer when he incorporated XYZ, then Lawyer may not disclose the confidential communications he received from Officer to Bank.** However, since Officer knew Lawyer represented Bank and had a fiduciary relationship to Bank, it may be found that Lawyer and Officer did not develop an attorney-client relationship, and then Lawyer can disclose the confidential information to Bank.	Boss: no Other bank officials: probably no

Continued >

Issue	Rule	Fact Application	Conclusion
3. Who can waive attorney-client privilege?	**A client has a right not to disclose any confidential communication between L and client relating to the professional relationship.** Client is the holder of the privilege.	Since Officer is a high-ranking officer of Bank, Bank's attorney-client privilege would extend to communications made by Officer. **Since Bank is a corporation, a party with the authority to represent Bank would be the one entitled to waive the attorney-client privilege on Bank's behalf. Normally, this would be Boss. However, since Boss's interests are adverse to Bank, it would need to be another representative. Ultimately, it would be the responsibility of the Board of Directors to waive the privilege.** If Officer was found to have an attorney-client relationship with Bank, Officer would hold the privilege as to his own confidential communications.	Bank may waive the privilege
4. Ethical obligations?	**Duty of confidentiality: L shall not reveal information relating to the representation of a client.** **Duty of loyalty: L owes a duty of loyalty to the client.** **Conflict of interest:** Where there is a conflict, L may represent both clients only if L reasonably believes there will not be an adverse effect on the client, and each client consents after consultation. California only requires written consent.	Where a lawyer represented a client in the past and now represents a client where those matters are in dispute, the lawyer is disqualified. Here, the issue does not involve the incorporation of XYZ, which was the subject of the prior representation, so Lawyer is not disqualified outright.	**Lawyer must withdraw**

Continued >

Issue	Rule	Fact Application	Conclusion
		Lawyer's firm's representation of XYZ, for purposes of the incorporation, seems to be a simple matter of preparing incorporation documents separate and distinct from the current matter faced by Bank. However, that may not be so since XYZ was actually incorporated as a means to commit a fraud on Layer's client, Bank. **There will almost certainly be a conflict of interest in future litigation regarding Bank and XYZ, thus it is improper for Lawyer to believe otherwise and continue to represent Bank. Lawyer also has a further conflict, as she may be a material witness in any fraud action due to her participation in preparation of fraudulent documents. It is also likely Lawyer may have received confidential communications as a result of that representation. Consequently, Lawyer should not represent Bank and should withdraw.**	**Lawyer must withdraw**

Professional Responsibility Question 5

February 2005, Question 4

Ann represents Officer Patty in an employment discrimination case against City Police Department ("Department") in which Patty alleges that Department refused to promote her and other female police officers to positions that supervise male police officers. Bob represents Department.

At Patty's request, Ann privately interviewed a male police captain, Carl, who had heard the Chief of Police (Chief) make disparaging comments about women in Department. Carl told Ann that Chief has repeatedly said that he disapproves of women becoming police officers, routinely assigns them clerical work, and would personally see to it that no female officer would ever supervise any male officer. Carl met with Ann voluntarily during his non-work hours at home. Ann did not seek Bob's consent to meet with Carl or invite Bob to be present at Carl's interview.

When Bob saw Carl's name as a trial witness on the pretrial statement, he asked Chief to prepare a memo to him summarizing Carl's personnel history and any information that could be used to discredit him. Chief produced a lengthy memo containing details of Carl's youthful indiscretions. In the memo, however, were several damaging statements by Chief reflecting his negative views about female police officers. In the course of discovery, Bob's paralegal inadvertently delivered a copy of Chief's memo to Ann. Immediately upon opening the envelope in which the memo was delivered, Ann realized that it had been sent by mistake. At the same time, Bob's paralegal discovered and advised Bob what had happened. Bob promptly demanded the memo's return, but Ann refused, intending to use it at trial.

1. Did Ann commit any ethical violation by interviewing Carl? Discuss.
2. What are Ann's ethical obligations with respect to Chief's memo? Discuss.
3. At trial, how should the court rule on objections by Bob to the admission of Chief's memo on the grounds of attorney-client privilege and hearsay? Discuss.

Professional Responsibility Question 5 Assessment

February 2005, Question 4

This essay question covers some crossover evidence issues, in addition to the professional responsibility issues. The first two calls of the question concern how zealously a lawyer may represent his client when doing so conflicts with other ethical duties that are imposed on the lawyer.

The first call addresses the issue of the limitations imposed on a lawyer to have communications with a party represented by counsel. In this case, it is arguable that the party was in fact represented by counsel, which leads to some protracted factual analysis of that issue. Since in ethics you want to err on the side of caution, it was best to conclude that counsel did represent the party and that it was inappropriate for the attorney to communicate with him. A related issue that stems from the attorney's actions of communicating with a represented party is the attorney's duty of fairness to third parties since this action will have a negative effect on opposing counsel.

This essay also raises the interesting issue of what a lawyer's duties are if opposing counsel accidentally sends confidential communications to the lawyer. Again, keeping and using the document is a clear ethical violation and it is best to clearly identify it as such in your conclusion.

The last call of the question pertains to the potential admissibility of evidence when privileged attorney-client communications are accidentally disclosed to opposing counsel. Professional responsibility is the most frequently tested subject on the essay exam and is the most frequent subject of crossover questions. The evidence issues concern the attorney-client privilege rules and the related rule of the duty of confidentiality. The third call also specifically asks about the admissibility of evidence based on hearsay grounds. The hearsay exception of party admission is also a required part of the discussion, but it is not required to discuss other hearsay exceptions in order to pass this question.

Note the areas highlighted in **bold** on the corresponding grid. The bold areas highlight the issues, analysis, and conclusions that are likely **required** to receive a passing score on this question.

Issue	Rule	Fact Application	Conclusion
Call #1			
Communications with party represented by counsel	**L shall not communicate with parties L knows to be represented by another L unless L has the consent of the other L or is authorized by law or court order to do so.** If the person represented by counsel is an organization, the organization's counsel must grant permission before opposing counsel can 1) Supervise or consult with Ls 2) Communicate with **persons with authority** 3) Communicate with those whose conduct may be imputed to the organization	Carl is a police captain for Dept.; and Patty is suing Dept. for gender discrimination. **By interviewing Carl about potential gender discrimination and hostility by Chief, Ann has directly communicated with an employee of Dept., which she knows is represented by Bob in the pending gender discrimination case, regarding the subject matter of the litigation. A captain of the police Dept. is likely in a position of authority, such that he may obligate and bind the organization on this matter. Since Carl likely can represent the organization Ann may not have ex parte communication with him.** As a captain, his conduct would likely be imputed to Dept., at the very least. Though Ann did interview Carl privately during nonwork hours at home, that does not make the interview permissible. **Ann should not have interviewed Carl without getting the permission of Dept.'s counsel, Bob.**	**Yes, ethical violation**
Duty of fairness to third parties	**L has a duty of fairness to third parties**, including opposing counsel and the court. **[Note: This could have also been called duty of diligence, or duty of competence. The key to passing this issue is the analysis.]**	As the client, Patty asked her attorney Ann to interview Carl. Carl has valuable information relating to Chief's gender bias and employment discrimination that would assist Patty in her lawsuit. However, **Ann may not follow the directions of her client if doing so causes a violation of the ethical rules. While Ann has a duty to diligently and zealously represent Patty, she may not do so in violation of her duty of fairness that is owed to third parties,** opposing counsel, and the court. Ann should have, at the least, advised Carl to seek counsel to represent his interest.	**Ethical violation**

Continued >

Issue	Rule	Fact Application	Conclusion
Call #2			
Duty of fairness to opposing party	**L owes a duty of fairness to the opposing party and his counsel.**	**Bob's paralegal accidentally mailed the memo Chief prepared in anticipation of litigation, which is attorney work-product, to opposing counsel Ann.** In addition, the memo contained Chief's negative views about women police officers, which is the subject of the pending lawsuit. **Ann immediately realized the memo had been sent to her inadvertently and was actually privileged attorney work-product and contained confidential attorney communications.** Not only did Ann recognize the confidential nature of the communications, but also, Bob promptly notified Ann and asked for the memo's return. **An attorney may not ethically keep a document she knows was mistakenly sent. Ann knew this was a mistake and should have notified opposing counsel and returned the memo to Bob or the court.**	**Ethical violation**
Duty to diligently **represent client**	L shall act with reasonable diligence and promptness in representing a client. **[Note: This could have also been called duty to zealously represent a client, or duty of competence, or something similar. The key to passing this issue is the analysis.]**	**While a lawyer has a duty to diligently and zealously represent her client, this duty is constrained since a lawyer may only do so within the confines of the ethical duties imposed on a lawyer. Even though the memo contained information that was very helpful to Patty's case, Ann may not violate any ethical rules to further her client's interest.**	**May not violate ethical rules for client**

Continued >

Issue	Rule	Fact Application	Conclusion
Call #3			
Attorney-client privilege: waiver	**A client has a right not to disclose any confidential communication between L and client relating to the professional relationship.** However, **disclosure of confidential communications to third persons will constitute a waiver of the privilege.**	The memo drafted by Chief and sent to his attorney Bob was created at Bob's request to provide potential information to discredit the witness Carl at trial. As such, this **memo was prepared in anticipation of litigation and is attorney work-product.** Further, the information contained in the memo was **intended to be a confidential communication between the client and his attorney and, as such, is privileged** and not admissible as evidence. There was a disclosure to a third person when the memo was accidentally sent to Ann by Bob's paralegal. However, the disclosure to Ann was not done intentionally and so there was no intentional waiver of the privilege.	**Attorney-client privilege applies** No waiver
Hearsay	**Hearsay is an out-of-court statement offered for the truth of the matter asserted** and is inadmissible unless it is subject to an exception.	**The memo is an out-of-court statement since it is a document, and it is offered for its truth, which is that Chief and the police dept. he runs discriminates against female police officers.**	**Hearsay**
Party admission	**A party admission is any statement made by a party and may be offered against him. The statement need not be against declarant's interest.** **[Note: There are a variety of potential hearsay exceptions in addition to party admission that could have been properly addressed. Both state-released passing student answers briefly addressed several.]**	The Chief would be the highest ranking authority at the police dept. and as such any statement he made would be vicarious admission of the police department. **Therefore, Chief's statement would be admissible against police dept. as the admission of a party opponent,** except it is protected by the attorney-client privilege.	**Party admission**

Continued >

Issue	Rule	Fact Application	Conclusion
Declaration against interest	A declaration against interest is admissible if, at the time it was made, it was against the declarant's financial or penal interest. However, the declarant must be unavailable.	While the statements made by Chief in the memo are certainly against his, or at least the police dept.'s, financial interest since he displayed in the memo the very discriminatory practices of which the department is being accused, Chief seems to be available to testify, so this hearsay exception will not apply.	Not applicable
State of mind	A statement that is being admitted not to prove the truth of the matter asserted, but to prove the declarant's state of mind are exempted from hearsay.	Ann will argue that the statement in the memo is not being offered for its truth that there are negative things about female police officers. Rather, the evidence would prove the Chief's state of mind regarding his thoughts about female police officers.	Hearsay exception may apply

Professional Responsibility 6

February 2001, Question 5

Jones & Smith is a law firm concentrating on plaintiffs' personal injury litigation. The firm has decided to take several steps to increase its business volume.

First, the firm plans to run television advertisements stating that the firm offers to handle cases for discount contingency fees. The advertisements will state that, while most firms normally charge a 33% contingency fee for handling a personal injury case, Jones & Smith will undertake representation for a fee of 25%. In addition, the advertisements will state that the firm offers interest-free advances against prospective judgments in cases of clear liability of up to 50% of the firm's estimated value of the case.

Second, the firm plans to acquire from the police department lists of individuals who have been involved in automobile accidents, and to mail letters to those persons informing them that the firm is available for consultation about their legal rights arising out of the accident. Individuals who have been hospitalized as a result of an accident will receive a flower arrangement, delivered "compliments of Jones & Smith, Attorneys at Law."

Finally, the firm plans to make use of nonlawyers in order to reduce costs. The firm will employ several paralegals and investigators who will be responsible for working up personal injury cases. Their activities will include fact investigation, witness interviews, negotiation with insurance adjusters, meetings with clients to discuss proposed settlements, and settlement conferences with clients to explain releases and to execute other documents necessary to conclude a case.

Do the proposed actions violate any rules of professional conduct? Discuss.

Professional Responsibility 6 Assessment

February 2001, Question 5

This question focuses in detail on an attorney's ability to ethically solicit clients and advertise to increase client volume. It requires you to know the various rules in relation to advancing costs for clients and the use of non-lawyers to assist in cases. Thus, although the question focuses on soliciting and advertising, you need to see what additional possible ethical violations the facts raise in relation to those issues. For that reason, it is crucial to write out your entire issues checklist to avoid missing issues, despite seeing that the entire question focuses on solicitation and advertising to increase the firm's business volume.

It is also important to organize the issues around the facts that give rise to each issue. For example, the issue of solicitation arises under multiple facts. Therefore, it is best to address this issue using headings for the facts to distinguish the two separate IRACs, despite the different facts raising the same issue. This is because although the issue and rule are the same, the analysis will be different because it involves analyzing different facts with the same rule. Thus, you need to analyze the facts involving the mailings in regard to solicitation separately from the flowers in regard to solicitation. This type of factual distinction often arises in professional responsibility questions, requiring you to use issue headings as well as factual headings to properly identify the issues.

Although this question does not specify the source of law the examiners want you to analyze, the grid analyzes both the ABA and the California rules since most current questions require you to analyze both; both state-released answers did analyze both since the call was not specific. Where the rule is specific to the ABA it will begin with "ABA"; where the rule is specific to California, it will begin with "Cal." Where the rules are same for both, there will be no distinction.

Finally, make note of the areas highlighted in **bold** on the corresponding grid. The bold areas highlight the issues, analysis, and conclusions that are likely **required** to receive a passing score on this question.

Issue	Rule	Fact Application	Conclusion
Television ads	**L shall not make false or misleading communications about L or the L's services.** L may advertise services through written, recorded, or electronic communication unless the prospective client made known to L their desire to not be solicited. **All advertisements must** • **Contain the name the office address** of at least one lawyer • **Be labeled as advertising material** • ABA: envelope needs to state "Advertising Material" • Cal.: need to label as communication or solicitation but must not use any particular words so long as in 12-point type on first page Cal.: L must retain a correct copy of the communications for two years. Cal.: Presumes a violation of ethical rules for communications that contain a dramatization, without a disclaimer that it is a dramatization.	**Here, Jones & Smith is allowed to advertise their rates of 25% fees for contingency cases so long as that rate is truthful and not misleading. However, it will need to be verified that other firms do normally charge a fee of 33%. If they do not, then the advertisement is misleading.** **The television advertisements will also need to contain the name and office address** of one lawyer in order to be ethical, as well as be labeled as an advertisement. Further, if there is a dramatization in the television ad, then there must be a disclaimer as well.	**It is possible that the ad could be misleading and in violation of advertisement requirements**
Fees	**Contingency fee agreements must** • **Be in writing** • ABA: signed by the client • Cal.: signed by both the lawyer and client • **State the method by which the fee is to be determined, including percentages**	**Here, it is not clear what the terms of the actual agreements include as the ads do not depict that information, but this information would be necessary in all contingency agreements made.**	**Fee likely fine if all requirements are met**

Continued >

Issue	Rule	Fact Application	Conclusion
	• **State which expenses are to be deducted from recovery and whether this is to be done before or after the fee is calculated** (Cal. looks at whether client will have to pay related matters not covered by agreement) • Cal.: fee must state the fee is negotiable. ABA: All fees must be reasonable. Cal.: All fees must not be illegal or unconscionable.	However, given that it is a contingency fee matter, the 25% fee is likely reasonable and not unconscionable if other firms charge 33%.	**Fee likely fine if all requirements are met**
Proprietary interest	L shall not acquire a proprietary interest in the cause of action or subject matter of litigation unless it is to acquire a lien to secure L's fees or to contract with a client for a reasonable contingency fee in a civil case.	Here, the cases will be based on personal injury contingency cases, which are exceptions to the "no proprietary interest" rule, so long as all contingency fee agreement requirements are met.	No violation
Advances	**ABA: L shall not provide financial assistance to client in connection with litigation except for contingency cases and indigent clients, in which the lawyer can advance court costs and litigation expenses.** **Cal.: L may lend money to the client after employment if the client promises in writing to repay the loan.** **Cal.: Presumes any guarantees, warranties, or predictions to be a violation of the rules.**	**Here, under the ABA, the lawyer cannot advance costs up to 50% of the case value as these costs may not be exclusively for court costs and litigation expenses. Under Cal., the lawyer would need a signed promise to repay by the client and can only lend money after employment, but here they are promising it to future clients.** **Further, by indicating they would offer interest-free advances in cases of "clear liability" indicates that the firm may be guaranteeing a case will win or some warranty thereof or prediction, which is presumed a violation in Cal.**	**Offer for interest-free advances violates rules**

Continued >

Issue	Rule	Fact Application	Conclusion
Solicitation: mailings	**See above (television ads)**	**The envelope would need to be labeled as advertising.** In particular, the words "Advertising Material" are required on the outside of the envelope under the ABA and similar words in 12-point type in Cal. **So long as they obtained the accident list lawfully, which is likely public records, then they could send out mail to individuals if properly labeled.**	**Mailings likely not in violation**
Solicitation: flowers	**L may not conduct in-person or live telephone or real-time electronic contact.** Cal. presumes the following communications to be in violation of the rules: • Transmissions at the scene of an accident or en route to or at a care facility • Delivery to a potential client that the lawyer knows or should reasonably know is in such a fragile physical, emotional, or mental state that he could not exercise reasonable judgment	**Here, the flowers would be a direct, in-person contact that would not be permissible.** Further, the flowers would be presumed in violation of the rules in Cal. because they are being sent to hospitalized patients and patients that as a result of their accident are likely to be physically and emotionally fragile, making them less likely to exercise reasonable judgment.	**Flowers in violation of the rules**
Unauthorized practice of law	**L shall not practice with or form a partnership or association authorized to practice law with a non-L.**	**Here, paralegals and investigators are allowed to gather facts, as investigators often do, and paralegals help to type up such reports.** **The witness interviews may be appropriate if the lawyer has provided the investigators and paralegals with information they want addressed and specific reports are made or they are just doing fact gathering.**	**Some tasks violate the rules**

Continued >

Issue	Rule	Fact Application	Conclusion
		The negotiations and meetings to discuss settlements should be performed only by the lawyers since they best understand what is in their client's interest, and these types of tasks require specific legal knowledge and judgments that should be made by lawyers, and lawyers have a duty to communicate with their clients. Non-lawyers should only execute documents that the lawyer instructs them to prepare, and the lawyer should review them prior to concluding any case.	**Some tasks violate the rules**

PART 9 REAL PROPERTY

REAL PROPERTY TABLE OF CONTENTS

INTRODUCTION TO REAL PROPERTY

Real property questions are often dependent on the sequence of events, similar to a contracts question. It is usually helpful to sketch a brief timeline of the important events and dates in the fact pattern to keep the events straight. Sometimes it is also helpful to draw a diagram of the facts to help get a visual image of the facts. This is particularly true with easements.

Many students feel like real property is a struggle, and the average scores on real property questions on the bar exam tend to bear this out. This is unfortunate because the questions that logically can be posed on the bar exam regarding real property are actually straightforward, the issues are fairly easy to spot, and the analysis is usually not particularly complex. So, why do students struggle with real property? Mostly, because the language is difficult to work with, which makes the concepts more difficult to understand and remember. The language is archaic and the words don't often sound like they mean what they actually do mean. For example, look at the similar concepts of *easements, real covenants,* and *equitable servitudes*. The concepts are similar because they all pertain to the use of land, but the concepts are distinct. Many, but not all, of the elements are the same, however there is nothing about the words themselves to give away the differences between the concepts. To make the situation worse, equitable servitudes are interchangeably called *restrictive covenants*; though a restrictive covenant is not exactly the same thing as a real covenant, which is also called just a *covenant*. The only thing that can be done to tame the tangle is to actually memorize the concepts. A general understanding of the principles will absolutely not foster success on a real property essay because it is much too easy to get the concepts confused and merged together when they aren't properly memorized and understood with specificity.

Estates in land is another area that causes a lot of confusion or anxiety for bar examinees. The good news is that estates in land are infrequently tested on the essay portion of the bar exam, and when they are tested it is usually in a brief way. This makes sense because estates in land do not actually lend themselves to the sort of robust factual analysis that the bar examiners are looking to assess in the essay portion of the exam. You do need to have an understanding of the different estates in land for the essay portion of the exam, and you must understand the details of estates in land for the MBE portion of the exam.

For the real property portion of the essay exam, focus on the frequently tested topics of land acquisition, joint property ownership, landlord-tenant issues, and limitations on land use. The vast majority of real property questions cover issues in those categories in some combination. Issue spotting a real property exam is easy if you focus on the three main areas of inquiry:

(1) Has property been acquired, and are there any issues related to that acquisition? This query covers the issues of adverse possession, land sale contracts, mortgages, deeds, wills, and recording acts.
(2) Who has an interest in the property in question? This query covers the issue of estates in land, joint ownership issues, and landlord tenant issues.
(3) Are there any limits on the way the property can be used? This query covers the issues of easements, covenants, and equitable servitudes.

ISSUES CHECKLIST

HAS PROPERTY BEEN ACQUIRED?

Adverse possession
Land sales contracts
Mortgages
Deeds
Wills
Recording acts

WHO HAS AN INTEREST IN THE PROPERTY?

Estates in land
- Freehold estates
- Future interests

Joint ownership (concurrent estates)
- Joint tenants
- Tenants in common
- Tenancy by the entirety

Landlord/tenant
- Types of tenancies
- Rent disputes
- Condition of premises
- Waste
- Fixtures
- Assignment and sublease

Are There Limits on Land Use?
- Easements
- Real covenants
- Equitable servitudes

MEMORIZATION ATTACK SHEET

LAND ACQUISITION ISSUES

- **Adverse possession**
  - Actual possession
  - Open and notorious
  - Hostile (no consent)
  - Continuous
  - Statutory period
- **Land sale contract**
  - Contract law reqmt.: SOF
    - Writing
    - Parties identified
    - Signed by one to be bound
    - Describes land
    - States consideration
  - Marketable title
  - Equitable conversion
  - Remedy for breach
    - Damages
    - Specific performance
      - Contract is valid
      - Conditions satisfied
      - Inadequate legal remedy
      - Mutuality of perform
      - Feasibility of enforce
      - No defenses
- **Mortgage**
  - Writing required
  - Foreclosure
    - Judicial foreclosure
    - Priority of loans
      - Purchase money mortgage
    - Deficiency
  - Redemption
- **Deeds**
  - Requires
    - Parties
    - Signed by grantor
    - Describe land
    - No consideration required
- **Three Types of Deeds**
  - Quitclaim
  - Warranty—general
    - Seisin
    - Right to convey
    - Encumbrances
    - Title
    - Quiet enjoyment
    - Further assurances
  - Statutory special
- **Deed delivery**
  - Physical transfer
  - Intent to make present transfer
  - Acceptance
- **Merger**—contract merges into deed & deed controls
- **Will**
  - Ademption
  - Exoneration
  - Lapse & antilapse
- **Recording acts**
  - **Three types of acts**
    - Pure race
    - Pure notice
    - Race-notice
  - **Protect bona fide purchasers**
    - Take for value
    - No notice
  - **Three types of notice**
    - Actual
    - Record (constructive)
    - Inquiry
- **Chain of title issues**
    - Estoppel by deed
    - Shelter doctrine

ESTATES IN LAND

- **Freehold estates**
  - Fee simple absolute
  - Fee tail
  - Fee simple defeasible
    - FS determinable
    - FS subject to condition subsequent
    - FS subject to executory limitation
  - Life estate

- Future interests
  - Possibility of reverter
  - Right of reentry
  - Reversion
  - Remainder
    - Vested
    - Contingent
    - Alternative contingent
  - Executory interest
    - Shifting
    - Springing
- **Technical rules**
  - No absolute restraints on alienation
  - Destructibility of contingent remainders
  - RAP—Rule Against Perpetuities: interest must vest not later than 21 years after life in being at creation of the interest. Applies to:
    - Contingent remainders
    - Possibility of reverter
    - Options in gross

JOINT OWNERSHIP

- **Joint tenancy**
  - Automatic right of survivorship
  - Equal right to occupy whole
  - Equal shares
  - **Creation of joint tenancy**
    - Time
    - Title
    - Interest
    - Possession
    - Express right of survivorship
  - **Severance of joint tenancy**
    - Conveyance
    - Mortgage
      - Lien theory: does not sever
      - Title theory: does sever to that JT's share
    - Not severed by will, any attempt is void
    - Lease: jurisdictions are split
- **Tenancy in common**
  - Equal right to occupy
  - Nonequal shares okay
  - Can sell, will, or gift
  - No right of survivorship
- **Tenancy by entirety**
  - Husband and wife only
  - Right to survivorship
  - Severed by death, divorce, or agreement
- **Co-tenancy rules**
  - Right to possession
  - Accounting
    - Tax/mortgage: proportionate share & may seek reimbursement
    - Improvements: no right to reimbursement
  - Partition action

LANDLORD-TENANT

- **Types of tenancies**
  - Term for years
  - Periodic tenancy
  - Tenancy at will
  - Tenancy at sufferance
- **LL-T issues**
  - Duty to pay rent
  - Possession of premises
    - Holdover tenant
    - Eviction
    - Abandonment
  - Condition of premises
    - Constructive eviction
      - Virtually uninhabitable
      - Substantial interference with use
      - Notice
      - LL doesn't respond
      - T actually moves out
    - Actual partial eviction
      - Can't occupy some portion
      - Can withhold entire rent
    - Quiet enjoyment
    - Warranty of habitability
      - Terminate & move; or
      - Repair & deduct; or
      - Pay reduced rent & sue
    - No retaliatory eviction
    - Tort liability—LL must

- Maintain common areas
- Fix latent defects
- Repair nonnegligently
- Duty to inspect areas open to public

- ♦ **Waste** (life tenant & tenants)
  - Voluntary (decreases value)
  - Permissive (neglect)
  - Ameliorative (alterations)
- ♦ **Fixtures stay**
  - Firmly imbedded
  - Peculiarly adapted
  - Destroy chattel or cause damage to remove
  - Trade fixtures are removable
- ♦ **Assignment and sublease**
  - Assignment: entire interest
  - Sublease: less than entire interest

LAND USE

- ♦ **Easements**—right to use land
  - Affirmative or negative
  - Appurtenant (adjoining land)
    - Dominant—receives benefit
    - Servient—burdened to give benefit
  - In gross (to a person)
  - **Creation of easement**
    - **Express**
    - **By implication**
      - Originally one parcel
      - Severed
      - Use existed prior to severance
      - Reasonably necessary
    - **By necessity**
      - Common ownership
      - Strictly necessary
      - No prior use required
    - **By prescription**
      - Actual use
      - Open and notorious
      - Hostile (no consent)
      - Continuous
      - Statutory period
    - **Estoppel (reliance)**
  - **Scope of easement**
  - **Maintain/repair easements**
  - **Transfer of easement**
  - **Termination of easement**
    - Estoppel (reliance)
    - Necessity ends
    - Destruction
    - Condemnation of property
    - Release
    - Abandonment with action
    - Merger of parcels
    - Prescription (in reverse)
- ♦ **Covenants** (promises)
  - **Burden runs with land**
    - Writing
    - Intent
    - Touches & concerns land
    - Horizontal & vertical privity
    - Notice
  - **Benefit runs with land**
    - Writing
    - Intent
    - Touches & concerns land
    - Vertical privity only
    - No notice required
- ♦ **Equitable servitudes** (restrictions on land use)
  - **Runs with land if:**
    - Writing
    - Intent
    - Touches & concerns land
    - No privity required
    - Notice required
  - **Implied reciprocal servitude**
    - Common plan or scheme
    - Notice
    - Writing not required
- ♦ **Termination of covenants & equitable servitudes**
  - Agreement
  - Abandonment with action
  - Changed conditions
- ♦ **Profit** (take from land)
- ♦ **License** (permission to use land)
- ♦ **Water rights**
  - Drain surface water
  - Riparian rights
  - Ground water
- ♦ **Lateral & subjacent support**

REAL PROPERTY RULE OUTLINE

I. **LAND ACQUISITION ISSUES:** Many issues in real property center around the acquisition of real property or an interest in real property. Typically property is acquired by adverse possession or by an inter vivos transfer, such as through a land sale contract or by granting a deed, or by a devise in a will.

   A. **Adverse possession** allows one who has **wrongfully entered a property to obtain possession** of that property when there has been **actual possession, which is open and notorious, and the possession is hostile continuously for the statutory period.**

      1. **Requirements**

         a. **Actual possession:** The claimant must actually have exclusive use of the property; which means he must physically occupy the premises.

            1. **Exclusive use:** The true owner must be excluded from the premises and the property may not be open to the public.

            2. **Partial possession:** A reasonable percentage of the property must be actually used. A claimant may only claim possession of the portion of the property actually used. (E.g.: If a claimant occupies 1 acre of 200-acre parcel, he may only claim adverse possession of the 1 acre.)

            3. **Tenant possession:** The claimant may lease the premises to a tenant to satisfy the actual possession element.

         b. **Open and notorious and visible possession:** The claimant must possess and use the property in a way that a **typical owner** of similar property would use the property. The use must be sufficiently open to **put the true owner on notice** of the trespass by the adverse possessor. (E.g.: If a typical owner would only use the land in the summer months, the adverse possessor may only use the land seasonally also.)

         c. **Hostile possession:** Possession of the land must be **without the owner's consent.**

            1. **Hostile possession is simply not permissive**; it does not mean that the possession must be done in a hostile manner.

            2. **Boundary disputes:** Where one property owner occupies land, mistakenly thinking it is his own but it actually belongs to the adjacent property owner, this possession will be deemed hostile (e.g., building built over property line).

            3. **Ouster of a co-tenant** is required to find a hostile possession with concurrent property owners since all co-tenants have equal right to possession of the property.

               a. **Ouster** occurs when a co-tenant claims an exclusive right to possession and refuses occupancy to his co-tenant.

         d. **Continuous use for the given statutory period**

            1. **Statutory period:** At common law it is 20 years; it varies among the states but is typically at least 15 years.

2. **Continuous possession** means that the owner may not reenter to regain possession during the statutory time. If he does, the adverse possessor's time for possession starts over.
3. **Seasonal use** of a property may still satisfy the continuous possession element if this is the way a typical owner of similar property would use the land. The intermittent activities must be of the sort only done by true owners. (E.g.: Erecting a small cabin to use during hunting season may be typical seasonal use, but simply using the property to hunt would not be since nonowners would do the same.)
4. **Tacking: One adverse possessor may tack his time with the time of another adverse possessor** to meet the required statutory period for adverse possession if the two adverse possessors are in **privity** (e.g., adverse possessor leases the premises to another and acts as landlord).

2. **Effect of adverse possession:** Adverse possession **does not convey marketable title.** However, the title can be perfected and made marketable by means of a judicial action to quiet title.

Adverse possession fact triggers:
- Attempted transfer of property that is ineffective and the purported new owner acts like an owner (contract fails to meet SOF, deed not properly delivered, etc.)
- Fact pattern includes events occurring 15 to 20 years in the past
- Seasonal use of a property, such as a vacation home or hunting cabin
- Building is placed over the property line and onto neighbor's land

B. **Land sale contract:** The contract for a conveyance of an interest in real estate typically governs the agreement until the time of closing, at which time the deed becomes the operative document governing the land transfer.
1. **Contract law governs** a contract for the sale of an interest in land.
   a. **Statute of Frauds (SOF) applies.**
      1. **SOF requirements:**
         a. The contract must be **in writing;**
         b. Name the **parties;**
         c. **Signed by the party to be bound;**
         d. Sufficiently **describe the land;** and
         e. State some **consideration** (purchase price).
      2. **Part performance exceptions to the SOF**
         a. **Possession plus payment:** Buyer has possession of the land and paid all or part of the purchase price.
         b. **Substantial improvements** are made to the premises.
         c. **Conveyance** made by the seller.

2. **Marketable title:** There is an implied promise in every land sale contract that the seller covenants to transfer marketable title at the time of closing. **Marketable title is title free from reasonable doubt** about the seller's ability to convey what he purports to convey.

> Marketable title fact triggers:
> - **Encumbrances,** such as an outstanding mortgage or lien (but the seller has until escrow closes to pay it off)
> - **Record chain of title** indicating the seller does not have a full interest in the property to convey
> - An **easement** that reduces "full enjoyment" of the premises
> - **Use restrictions,** such as real covenants

3. The **doctrine of equitable conversion** provides that once the contract is signed, the **buyer is deemed the owner** of real property, even though closing has not yet occurred. If the property is destroyed prior to closing, the risk of that loss is imposed on the buyer of the property. Some states have statutes that provide for the opposite result.
4. **Remedy for breach of land sale contract:** The nonbreaching party to a land sale contract can sue for damages or specific performance. Specific performance is usually the preferred remedy because land is unique.
   a. **Damages:** Typically, damages are calculated as the difference between the market price and the contract price.
   b. **Specific performance** is a permanent injunction in contract where the court orders the defendant to perform on the contract as promised. The following requirements must be met:
      1. **Contract is valid.**
      2. **Contract conditions** imposed on the plaintiff are satisfied.
      3. **Inadequate legal remedy:** Damages can be inadequate because they are too speculative to calculate with certainty, the defendant is insolvent, there is potential for a multiplicity of suits, or because **property is unique** so money damages are inadequate to compensate for the loss of that property. (**Real property is always unique.**)
      4. **Mutuality of performance:** Both parties to the contract must be eligible to have their performance under the contract ordered by the court.
      5. **Feasibility of enforcement:** The injunction cannot be too difficult for the court to enforce.
      6. **No defenses,** such as laches, unclean hands, or any defenses to the underlying contract (e.g., lack of consideration, SOF, sale to a bona fide purchaser, etc.).

> Exam tip: Use the mnemonic **Chocolate Cheesecake Is My Favorite Dessert** to memorize the six essential elements of specific performance: valid **C**ontract, contact **C**onditions satisfied, **I**nadequate legal remedy, **M**utuality of performance, **F**easibility of enforcement, and no **D**efenses.

C. **Security interests in land:** Real property is often encumbered by a mortgage.
   1. **Mortgage:** A mortgage is a financing arrangement that **conveys a security interest in land** where the parties intend the land to be collateral for the repayment of a monetary obligation. The buyer and/or borrower is the **mortgagor**. The lender is the **mortgagee**.
      a. **Writing required**
         1. **Statute of Frauds:** A mortgage must typically be in writing and satisfy the SOF.
         2. **Exception to SOF:** An equitable mortgage can occur. (E.g.: A buyer delivers a deed to the mortgagee rather than signing a note or mortgage deed. Parol evidence is allowable to show intent of the parties.)
      b. **Rights of the parties:** Until a foreclosure occurs, if ever, the buyer-mortgagor has right to possession of the property and title; the creditor-mortgagee has a lien, which grants the right to look to the land in the event of default. Mortgages are transferable.
      c. **Foreclosure** is a process by which the mortgagee may reach the land in satisfaction of the debt if the mortgagor is in default.
         1. **Judicial foreclosure:** A mortgagee must foreclose by proper judicial proceeding.
         2. **Priority of loans:** The land is sold and proceeds go to satisfy the debt(s) secured by the property. Any debts secured by the property are paid in descending order of priority (usually chronologically). Each mortgagee/lien holder is entitled to payment in full before a lower-ranking creditor receives any payment.
            a. **Purchase money mortgage (PMM)** is a mortgage given to secure a loan that enables the debtor to originally purchase the property. A PMM receives priority over non-PMM mortgages, but a PMM may not get a deficiency judgment against the debtor.
         3. **Antideficiency statutes** limit a lender to receiving no more than the value of the loan. Any excess remaining is returned to the buyer from the proceeds of a foreclosure sale after paying off all debts.
         4. **Deficiency judgment** occurs when the property is worth less than the amount owed on the outstanding loan(s). A lender can only sue the debtor personally for the difference if
            a. There was a judicial foreclosure; and
            b. The loan was not a "purchase money mortgage."
      d. **Redemption:** When a mortgage is paid off, the property is "redeemed" from the mortgage.
   2. **Deed of trust** is similar to a mortgage, except the debtor is the trustor and the deed of trust is given to a third-party trustee.
   3. **Installment contract:** A buyer makes a down payment and pays off the balance in installments. The difference between this and a mortgage is that the buyer does not receive a deed until the land is paid

off, and the foreclosure process is simplified. Typically, if the buyer is in default, the seller gets back the property and gets to keep the installment payments.

D. **Conveyance by deed:** A deed is a document that **serves to pass legal title** from the grantor to the grantee when it is lawfully executed and properly delivered.
   1. **Deed requirements:** Much like a land sale contract, a deed must meet the following formalities in order to be lawfully executed (with the big difference being that consideration is not required for a deed):
      a. **Identification of the parties.**
      b. **Signature of the grantor**, which is witnessed or notarized.
      c. Adequate **description of the property.**
      d. **No consideration is required** (it may be an inter vivos gift).
   2. **Three types of deeds**
      a. **Quitclaim deed:** A quitclaim deed conveys whatever interest the grantor actually has in the property but contains no covenants of title.
      b. **General warranty deed:** Warrants against all defects in title and contains **six covenants for title.** Three of the covenants are present and three are future covenants.
         1. **Present covenants** are breached at the time of the sale (when deed is delivered), if breached at all.
            a. **Seisin:** Grantor warrants he owns what he purports to own.
            b. **Right to convey:** Grantor warrants he has the power to make the conveyance.
            c. **Against encumbrances:** Grantor warrants there are no mortgages, liens, easements, or use restrictions on the land.
         2. **Future covenants** run with the land, are continuous, and are breached, if ever, at the time the grantee is disturbed in possession.
            a. **Warranty of title:** Grantor promises to **defend** should there be any **lawful claims of title** asserted by others.
            b. **Quiet enjoyment:** Grantor promises grantee will not be disturbed in possession by any third parties' lawful claims of title.
            c. **Further assurances:** Grantor will do whatever future acts are reasonably necessary to perfect title.

> **Issue-spotting tip:** Look for a warranty deed issue where there is an undisclosed easement.

      c. **Statutory special warranty deed:** Some states enforce promises by statute where the grantor promises (on behalf of himself only) that he hasn't conveyed the property to others and that the estate is free from encumbrances.
   3. **Delivery of deed:** A deed must be properly delivered and accepted to have effect.
      a. **Delivery requirements**

1. There must be a **physical transfer** of the deed by the grantor to the grantee or a third party; and
2. Words or conduct indicating the grantor's **intent to make a present transfer** of the deed. The following create a strong presumption of present intent to transfer:
   a. Recording the deed.
   b. Grantor giving the deed to the grantee.
3. **Acceptance** of the deed by the grantee must also occur. Rejection of the deed by the grantee defeats delivery.

b. **Title passes immediately** to the grantee upon proper delivery, thus it is not revocable.

> <u>Deed delivery fact triggers:</u>
> - Handing the deed to a third party with instructions
> - Placing the deed somewhere, such as a locked box

4. **Merger doctrine:** Once the property closes, the deed, rather than the underlying land sale contract, becomes the operative document governing the transaction. Any obligation imposed in the contract is deemed discharged at closing unless the obligation is repeated in the deed.

E. **Devise by will:** Property may be conveyed by will. Several issues can arise.
   1. **Ademption** occurs where a testator has devised a **specific property to a specific party** under his will, but that specific property is **no longer a part of the estate** at the time of testator's death. The general rule is that the gift is "adeemed," in other words **fails**, and the legatee gets nothing.
   2. **Exoneration** is the general rule that when a person receives a bequest of specific property, and that **property is subject to a lien** or mortgage, the **encumbrance will be paid off** with the estate's personal property, and the recipient receives the property "free and clear" of the mortgage, unless the testator indicated a contrary intent.
   3. **Lapse and antilapse:** The common law doctrine of **lapse** provides that if a beneficiary named in a will **predeceases the testator, the bequest fails.** Most states have antilapse statutes that allow the predeceased beneficiary's heirs to take, especially if they are kin to the testator.

> <u>Issue-spotting tip:</u> The intersection of wills and real property can provide the basis for a crossover question.

F. **Recording acts** function to provide a purchaser of land with a mechanism to determine whether there is an earlier transaction regarding the property that is inconsistent with his own transaction. The recording acts provide a buyer with a way to ensure he is getting good title.

1. **Common law rule:** Without a recording act in place, the common law rule of "first in time, first in right" applies.
2. **Three types of recording acts**
   a. **Pure race statutes:** The first to record wins. This statute rewards the winner of the race to the recorder's office. (Not commonly used either on the bar exam or in real life.)
   b. **Pure notice statutes:** A subsequent bona fide purchaser (BFP) prevails over a grantee that didn't record.
      1. Language example: "No conveyance or mortgage of real property shall be good against subsequent purchasers **for value** and without notice unless the same be recorded according to law."
   c. **Race-notice statutes:** A subsequent BFP that records first prevails over a grantee that didn't record first.
      1. Language example: "No conveyance or mortgage of real property shall be good against subsequent purchasers **for value** and without notice, who shall **first record.**"
3. **Recording acts protect bona fide purchasers (BFPs)** and mortgagors.
   a. **Bona fide purchaser (BFP):** A BFP is one who **takes for value** ***and*** **is without notice** of the prior interest.
      1. **Recording acts don't protect donees** because a donee doesn't take "for value." However, the court won't look into the adequacy of the consideration; so long as it is more than nominal, it will be deemed "for value."
      2. **Notice can be provided three ways:** Notice can occur by actual, record (constructive), or even inquiry notice. (See I.F.5 below.)
   b. **The recording acts only protect subsequent grantees**, never the first grantee. This is because the common law rule of "first in time, first in right" will apply, unless a recording act functions to allow the second grantee to take over the first grantee.
4. **Recording acts apply to** every instrument by which an interest in land can be created or modified or can be recorded, including conveyances, mortgages, life estates, restrictive covenants, easements, etc.

> <u>Exam tip:</u> The examiners may not tell you which type of recording act statute governs. Rather, they may provide statute language and expect you to determine which type of statute it is. Analyze the language and look for key words: "records first" likely means a race statute; "good faith" and "for value" likely means a notice statute; and if both "records first" and "good faith" and/or "for value" are included in the statute, then it is likely a race-notice statute.

5. There are **three types of notice.**
   a. **Actual notice** occurs when, prior to the time of closing, the buyer has actual subjective knowledge of a prior, unrecorded interest.
   b. **Record (constructive) notice** occurs when the prior interest was **properly recorded within the chain of title**. Where

the prior interest is properly recorded in the grantor-grantee indexes, such that one searching the indexes would find it, notice is imputed.

1. **Exception—"wild deeds":** A wild deed is one that is recorded, but not in such a way that a reasonable search of the grantor-grantee index would disclose it. Wild deeds do not provide constructive notice.

c. **Inquiry notice** occurs where the purchaser of a property is in possession of facts that would lead a **reasonable person to make further inquiry** (e.g., possession of the premises by one who is not the record owner, or visible evidence of the existence of an easement such as a well-worn path).

> <u>Notice issue-spotting tip:</u> The issue of "notice" can arise in several ways:
> - Recording acts
> - Sale to a BFP as a defense to an easement (especially inquiry notice)
> - Equitable servitudes (including implied reciprocal servitudes)
> - Real covenants (for burden to run with the land)

6. **Chain of title issues**
   a. **Estoppel by deed:** If one purports to convey an interest in realty that he does not own, but he subsequently obtains an interest in that realty, he cannot deny the validity of that conveyance and the estate will automatically transfer to the grantee. Estoppel by deed does not apply to a transfer by quitclaim deed.
   b. **Shelter doctrine:** One who takes from a BFP will "stand in the shoes" of the BFP and prevail against any entity against which the transferor-BFP would have prevailed in his own action.

II. ESTATES IN LAND

A. **Freehold estates** offer a present possessory interest in the estate.

1. **Fee simple absolute** conveys absolute ownership of potentially infinite duration. It is the most unrestricted and longest estate.
2. **Fee tail** allows an owner of land to ensure that the property remains within the family. It lasts only as long as there are lineal blood descendants of the grantee. Modernly, it is virtually abolished.
3. **Fee simple defeasible** allows a property to be held or conveyed to another; however, the property is subject to a stated limitation. There are three types:
   a. **Fee simple determinable** automatically terminates at the occurrence of a specified event. If the specified event occurs, the property automatically reverts back to grantor.
      1. **Possibility of reverter** is the future interest the grantor retains.
      2. **Created by words of duration** such as "so long as," "during," "while," "until," or "unless."

b. **Fee simple subject to condition subsequent** has the potential to terminate an estate at the occurrence of a stated event, but the termination is not automatic.
   1. **Right of reentry** is the future interest the grantor retains, but it is not automatic and must be exercised to have effect.
   2. **Created by words that carve out a right of reentry** in the grantor and includes conditional language such as "but it," "provided that," or "upon the condition that" to identify the conditional event.
c. **Fee simple subject to an executory limitation** automatically terminates a preceding estate at the occurrence of a stated event, but the estate then passes to a third person rather than reverting to the grantor.
   1. **Executory interest** is the future interest the third party holds.

4. **Life estate** is an interest that lasts for the lifetime of a person.
   a. A **life estate per autre vie** is similar to a life estate but lasts for the lifetime of an identified third party.
   b. **Defeasible:** A life estate may be defeasible like a fee simple.
   c. **Conveyable:** A life estate holder may convey his interest, but not an estate greater than what is held.
   d. **Waste:** A life tenant has a duty not to commit waste on the property. (See IV.C below.)

B. **Future interests** offer the potential for a future interest in an estate.
   1. **Possibility of reverter** follows a fee simple determinable.
   2. **Right of reentry** follows a fee simple subject to a condition subsequent.
   3. **Reversion** is created when the holder of an estate transfers to another something less than the entire estate.
   4. **Remainder** is a future interest that can only become possessory upon the expiration of a prior possessory estate created by the same instrument. A remainder never follows a defeasible fee.
      a. **Vested remainder** is one created in an ascertained person and that is not subject to a condition precedent.
      b. **Contingent remainder** is one created in an unascertained person, or one that is subject to a condition precedent, or both.
      c. **Alternative contingent remainder** occurs where both contingent parties have the capacity to take over and it pivots on the same condition (e.g., to A for life, then to B and his heirs if B marries C, otherwise to D).
   5. **Executory interest** follows a fee simple subject to an executory limitation. There are two types:
      a. **Shifting executory interest** always follows a defeasible fee and cuts short the prior interest.
      b. **Springing executory interest** becomes possessory at some point in the future, without cutting short a prior interest.

Estate	Language	Future Interest
Fee simple absolute	"To A" "To A and his heirs"	None
Fee tail	"To A and the heirs of his body"	Reversion in grantor, or remainder in third party
Fee simple determinable	"To A so long as..." "To A during..." "To A while..."	Possibility of reverter
Fee simple subject to a condition subsequent	"To A upon condition that..." "To A provided that..." "To A, but if..." **Plus right to reentry language must be included	Right of reentry
Fee simple subject to an executory limitation	"To A, but if X occurs, to B"	Executory interest
Life estate; life estate per autre vie	"To A for life" "To A for the life of B"	Reversion in grantor, or remainder in third party

C. **Technical rules**
   1. **Absolute restraints on alienation are void**, such as a condition that a property may never be sold. However, reasonable restraints on alienation will be upheld, such as a condition that a property only be used for a certain purpose.
   2. **Rule of destructibility of contingent remainders**
      a. **At common law**, a contingent remainder was destroyed if it was still contingent at the time the preceding estate ended.
      b. **Modernly,** the rule is mostly abolished, so the remainderman's interest would be converted to a springing executory interest.
   3. **Rule Against Perpetuities (RAP)** provides that no interest is good unless it must vest, if at all, not later than 21 years after some life in being at the creation of the interest. RAP is easier to work with once the interests to which it can be applied are identified.
      a. **RAP applies to**
         1. Contingent remainders
         2. Executory interests
         3. Options "in gross" or right of first refusal to purchase land
      b. **RAP does not apply to** certain types of interests because it is not possible for them to violate RAP.
         1. Vested remainders (vest at creation)
         2. Reversion (vests at creation)
         3. Possibility of reverter (vests at creation)
         4. Right of reentry (vests at creation)
      c. **Five-step technique to assess RAP issues**
         1. Classify the future interests to determine if RAP applies
         2. Identify the measuring life

3. Identify the triggering event (when an interest must vest or fail)
4. Analyze the possibilities of what could possibly happen (postpone the triggering event 21 years after the lives in being are dead)
5. Reclassify the interest

> Exam tip: Estates in land are very infrequently tested on the essay portion of the bar exam, though they are tested in detail on the MBE. We have included a brief overview of estates in land issues because they are eligible for testing (though unlikely to be tested), and it would seem remiss to eliminate estates in land rules entirely. Though the review here is brief, it is likely much more than what is necessary to properly prepare for the essay exam.

III. **JOINT OWNERSHIP (CONCURRENT ESTATES)**

A. **There are three types of joint property ownership:**
   1. **Joint tenancy**
   2. **Tenancy in common**
   3. **Tenancy by the entirety**

B. **Joint tenancy is when two or more people hold a single, unified interest in a property with a right to survivorship.**
   1. **Attributes**
      a. **Automatic right to survivorship:** At the death of one joint tenant, the remaining joint tenant automatically becomes the owner of the deceased joint tenant's interest.
      b. **Equal right to occupy:** Each joint tenant has an equal right to occupy the entire premises.
      c. **Equal shares:** Each joint tenant must own the property in equal shares with the other joint tenants (e.g., two parties each with 1/2 interest, or three parties each with 1/3 interest).
      d. At common law, a joint tenancy was presumed, but today a tenancy in common is presumed unless the right of survivorship is clearly expressed.
   2. **Creation of a joint tenancy:** A joint tenancy requires the four unities.
      a. **Time:** Interest created at the same time.
      b. **Title:** Parties take in the same title.
      c. **Interest:** Identical equal interests.
      d. **Possession:** Same right to possession of the premises.
      e. And the **express right of surviorship.**
   3. **Severance of a joint tenancy:** Unilateral action by one joint tenant may sever the joint tenancy.
      a. **Conveyance:** A conveyance (sale or inter vivos transfer) made by one joint tenant will serve to sever a joint tenancy.
         1. **Severence with two joint tenants:** The remaining joint tenant will hold the property with the new owner as tenants in common.

   2. **Severence with three or more joint tenants:** The new owner will take his portion as a tenant in common to the remaining joint tenants, but the remaining joint tenants will continue to have a joint tenancy with each other only. (E.g: Three joint tenants—A, B, and C—each have a 1/3 interest. A sells his interest to D. D holds a 1/3 interest as a tenant in common to B and C. B and C continue to have a joint tenancy with each other.)
  - b. **Will:** A joint tenancy **cannot be devised by will.** Any attempt is void because the decedent's interest is extinguished at death since his interest automatically transfers to the surviving joint tenant.
  - c. **Mortgage:** One joint tenant may not encumber the interest of the other joint tenant. The effect of one joint tenant obtaining a mortgage is dependent on whether the jurisdiction adopts the lien theory or title theory approach.
    1. **Lien theory** (majority rule): The execution of a mortgage by one joint tenant does not sever the joint tenancy.
    2. **Title theory** (minority rule): The execution of a mortgage by one joint tenant on his share will sever the joint tenancy as to his share only.
    3. **For both theories:** The joint tenancy is severed if the mortgage is actually foreclosed and the property is sold.
  - d. **Lease:** The courts are split as to whether issuing a lease severs a joint tenancy.

C. **Tenancy in common** is a concurrent estate where two or more own a property with no right of survivorship.
  1. **No right of survivorship.**
  2. **Equal right to occupy:** Each co-tenant has a joint right to possession of the whole property and owns an interest in the property jointly with another.
  3. **Nonequal shares acceptable:** Co-tenants may hold different proportionate interests. (E.g.: A owns 1/3 interest and B owns 2/3 interest.)
  4. Co-tenant **may sell, will, or gift his interest.** The new grantee will step in the shoes of the grantor.
  5. At common law, a joint tenancy was presumed, but modernly a tenancy in common is presumed where there are multiple owners.

D. **Tenancy by the entirety** is similar to a joint tenancy, but only between a husband and wife.
  1. Recognized in 21 states, but not recognized in California.
  2. **Neither tenant can unilaterally convey** their share or encumber the entire property or break the right of survivorship.
  3. **Created only in a husband and wife with the right of survivorship.** In states recognizing tenancy by the entirety, it is presumed in any conveyance to a husband and wife unless otherwise stated.
  4. **Severance:** May only be **severed by divorce, death, mutual agreement,** or execution by a joint creditor of both parties.

E. **Co-tenancy general rules**
  1. **Possession and use of the property by one co-tenant**

a. **Each co-tenant has the right to possess the whole** property, but no co-tenant has the right to exclusively possess any part of the property.
b. **No duty to account for profits and losses:** A co-tenant in possession has no duty to account to another co-tenant for the
   1. **Rental value of his own occupancy** of the premises, or
   2. Any **profits** retained from his own use of the land.
      a. **Except,** any net profits received from exploitations of the land, such as mining, and any rents collected from third parties must be shared. (See section III.E.2.b below.)
   3. A co-tenant is **solely responsible for his own losses** from his use of the property and may not seek contribution.
c. **Ouster:** If a co-tenant has refused occupancy to his co-tenant and claims an exclusive right to possession, this constitutes an ouster.
   1. The co-tenant must account to his ousted co-tenant for the fair rental value of the premises.
   2. An ousted co-tenant may also bring an action to regain possession.

2. **Accounting** of payments made and received on behalf of the jointly owned property
   a. **Payments-made general rule**
      1. **Taxes and mortgage interest:** Co-tenants are responsible for their proportionate share of carrying costs, such as taxes and mortgage interest payments.
      2. **Payments in excess of share:** Where a co-tenant has made payments on behalf of the property for taxes, repairs, or mortgage payments that are in excess of his pro rata share, he may seek contribution, but there is no automatic right to collect the pro rata share from his co-tenant. The co-tenant may deduct these payments from rents received, or seek reimbursement "off the top" if the property is sold.
      3. **Improvements:** Co-tenants have no right to reimbursement for improvements.
   b. **Payments-received general rule:** Co-tenants must share net rents received from third parties, or net profits received from the exploitation of the land itself (e.g., mining).
   c. General **duty of fair dealing** between all co-tenants.
3. **Partition:** This occurs when, through voluntary agreement or judicial action if in best interest of all parties, the property is divided, or ordered sold and the proceeds distributed.
   a. **Accounting:** Each party has a right to have an accounting and be reimbursed for taxes or repairs paid in excess of his proportionate share.
   b. Partition is not available to a tenancy by the entireties, only joint tenant or tenants in common.
4. **Encumbrance:** A co-tenant may encumber his own share of the property with a loan or judgment lien, but may not encumber the share of his co-tenant.

> **Exam tip:** Typical joint ownership issues may include possible severence, such as an inter vivos conveyance of one co-tenant's interest, and/or accounting issues among the co-tenants.

IV. **LANDLORD AND TENANT:** A tenancy is created when an owner of land conveys to another a lesser interest in a property. In addition to the life estate (covered in section II) there are several types of tenancies.

A. **Types of tenancies**
   1. **Tenancy for years** refers to a lease for a fixed period of time. It refers to any fixed time period such as one day, two months, one year, five years, etc.
      a. **SOF writing required** for terms greater than one year.
      b. **Automatic termination:** No notice is required to terminate because a term of years automatically terminates on the end date of the time period.
   2. **Periodic tenancy:** Automatically continues from one period to the next, unless one of the parties terminates the lease by giving notice of termination (e.g., leases running month-to-month, year-to-year, etc.).
      a. Can be **created by implication** if the lease includes a start date, but there is no stated end date.
      b. **Written notice is required to terminate** a periodic tenancy since the tenancy is automatically renewed in the absence of notice of termination. At common law, notice must be in accordance with the length of the time period, except that if the lease is one year or longer, only six months' notice is required.
      c. A **holdover tenant** is one whose lease has terminated, but who remains in the premises and tenders rent, which the landlord accepts. A holdover tenant is considered to have a periodic tenancy with the time period for the tenancy being the time period of the previously expired lease.
   3. **Tenancy at will** is a tenancy for no fixed period of time, which can be terminated at any time.
      a. Can be **created by implication** where the tenant takes possession with permission, but there is no specified start date or time period identified for paying rent.
      b. Can be **terminated at any time** by either party.
   4. **Tenancy at sufferance** is created when a tenant wrongfully holds over past the expiration of a valid lease.
      a. **Landlord election:** When a tenant holds over, the landlord has the option to evict the tenant or hold him over to another term as a tenant with a periodic tenancy.

B. **Common areas of dispute in landlord and tenant**
   1. **Duty to pay rent:** The tenant has the duty to pay rent in the amount agreed to. A tenant may have the following **defenses** available for the nonpayment of rent:
      a. **Failure to deliver possession** of the premises.

b. Breach of the **covenant of quiet enjoyment.** (See section IV.B.3 below.)
c. **Constructive eviction.** (See section IV.B.3 below.)
d. **Destruction of the premises** through no fault of the landlord, or the tenant. At common law the tenant had to continue paying rent, but modernly many states allow the tenant to terminate the lease.
e. **Potential contract defenses**, such as frustration of purpose.
f. **Surrender of the premises** by the tenant, which the landlord accepts.
g. **Re-letting of the property after an abandonment** done on behalf of the tenant. If the new tenant's rent is less, the old tenant will owe the difference, so long as he was properly notified.

2. **Possession of the premises**
   a. **Holdover tenant**
      1. At common law, a landlord could use reasonable force to remove holdover tenant and reclaim the property.
      2. Modernly, a landlord must not engage in self-help, such as manually removing the tenant.
   b. **Eviction:** A landlord may typically terminate a lease for a material breach. A landlord must evict through the courts or continue the rental relationship, give notice, and sue for damages.
   c. **Abandonment:** If a tenant abandons the premises the landlord at his option may:
      1. **Accept the surrender** and terminate the lease; or
      2. **Re-let** on behalf of the tenant (tenant must be **notified**); or
      3. **Leave the premises vacant and sue for rent** as it becomes due.
         a. **Traditionally,** there was **no duty to mitigate.**
         b. **Modernly,** there is a **duty to mitigate** imposed by many courts on the landlord.
3. **Condition of rental premises**
   a. **Common law:** Tenant takes premises "as is" and landlord has no duty to repair or duty to make the premises fit or habitable.
   b. **Modern view:** The landlord must maintain all common areas, fix latent defects of which the landlord has knowledge, and, if the landlord chooses to make repairs, he must do so nonnegligently.
      1. **Constructive eviction** is treated as an eviction.
         a. Applies to **residential and commercial** leases.
         b. **Requires** that
            i. **The premises are virtually uninhabitable** for their intended use because of a **substantial interference** with the property use and enjoyment;
            ii. **Notice** is given to the landlord by the tenant;
            iii. The landlord **fails to meaningfully respond**; and this
            iv. Causes the tenant to **actually move out** within a reasonable time.
      2. **Actual partial eviction**

   a. Landlord makes it physically impossible for the tenant to occupy **some portion** of the premises.
   b. Tenant may **withhold the entire rent** and does not have to move out.
3. **Implied covenant of quiet enjoyment:** Implied in every lease. The landlord warrants that he, or anyone acting for him will not interfere with tenant's use and enjoyment of the premises. (May include acts or other tenants, but won't include the acts of strangers.)
4. **Implied warranty of habitability** applies to **residential leases only** and requires that the premises must be fit for human habitation. Where the premises are not habitable, the tenant has the option to:
   a. **Terminate the lease and move out**; or
   b. **Make repairs and deduct** the cost from the rent; or
   c. **Pay reduced rent**, remain on the premises, and sue for damages.
5. **Retaliatory eviction is barred.** A tenant may not be evicted, have a periodic lease terminated, or have a tenancy for years not renewed because the tenant has asserted that the premises are not habitable.

> Issue-spotting tip: Look for the issues cluster of the condition of the rental premises, implied warranty of habitability, implied covenant of quiet enjoyment, constructive eviction, and possibly retaliatory eviction. Often, if one issue is present they all will be.

6. **Tort liability of landlord and tenant**
   a. **Landlord** must
      i. **Maintain all common areas,**
      ii. **Fix any latent defects** of which the landlord has knowledge, and
      iii. Any **repairs assumed must be made nonnegligently.**
      iv. There is a **duty to inspect** for defects if the premises are held **open to the public**.
   b. **Tenant** is treated like an owner for purposes of tort liability to third parties who come on the property.

C. **Doctrine of waste:** A tenant (applies to a life tenant under a life estate or a regular rental tenant) must prevent waste and cannot damage leased premises without effecting repair. There are three types of waste:
   1. **Voluntary waste** occurs when a tenant engages in conduct, intentionally or negligently, that causes a decrease in the value of the premises.
   2. **Permissive waste** occurs when the tenant neglects the property and it falls into disrepair.

3. **Ameliorative waste** occurs when a tenant makes alterations to the property that actually increase the value of the premises. The tenant must restore the premises to the original condition.

D. **Fixtures**

1. **Fixtures are items that were once moveable chattel** but that have become **so attached to the premises they are deemed fixtures** and considered part of the real estate. The following factors are considered to determine if an item is a fixture:
   a. The item is **firmly imbedded** in the real estate.
   b. The item is **peculiarly adapted** or fitted to the real estate.
   c. Removal of the item would **destroy the chattel or cause damage to the real estate.**
2. **Trade fixtures are those affixed to the real estate by a commercial tenant** for use in business. There is a strong presumption that trade fixtures are removable. The tenant is responsible for repairing any damage resulting from its removal.

> **Issue-spotting tip:** Look for the issues cluster of waste and fixtures since they are usually both present if one is. Note that the issue of waste can also arise in relation to the conduct of a life tenant.

E. **Assignments and subleases**

1. **General rule:** An **interest in a lease is transferable** unless the parties agree otherwise. Prohibitions against assignment and/or subleasing are enforceable.
2. **Assignment is the transfer of the entire interest** remaining on the lease term.
   a. **New tenant is personally liable** to landlord for the rent because there is privity of estate.
   b. **Old tenant is also liable** to the landlord for the rent, unless the landlord specifically releases the old tenant by a novation because there is privity of contract.
3. **Sublease is the transfer of anything less than the entire interest** remaining on the lease term.
   a. **New tenant is not personally liable** to the landlord for the rent because a sublease does not provide privity of estate.
   b. **Old tenant is liable** to the landlord for the rent because there is privity of contract.

V. LAND USE ISSUES

A. **Easements:** An easement is the **right to use the land of another.** Easements are nonpossessory property interests.

1. **Easements can be affirmative or negative.**
   a. **Affirmative** easements entitle the holder to do something on another's land (e.g., use a driveway).

   b. **Negative** easements prevent the landowner from doing something on his own land. These are not common. (E.g: Owner cannot develop land in a way that blocks the neighbor's view.)
2. **Two types of easements**
   a. **Appurtenant easement** is an easement that benefits a particular parcel of land and only occurs when the easement benefit is tied to a particular piece of land. There are **two estates** created by an appurtenant easement:
      1. **Dominant estate is the benefited parcel**—in other words the holder of the easement.
      2. **Servient estate is the burdened parcel**—in other words the parcel providing the benefit to the dominant estate.
   b. **Easement in gross** is an easement whose benefit is provided to an individual and is not tied to a particular piece of land.
3. **Creation of easements:** There are five ways to create an easement.
   a. **Express creation** in writing in a deed or will.
      1. The **SOF writing requirements apply.**
      2. **Reservation in grantor** is a type of express easement where the grantor passes title to the land but reserves for himself the right to continue to use the land for some purpose. Typically this is included in the grant or deed.
   b. **Creation by implication** has the following requirements:
      1. Land was **originally one parcel** with common ownership.
      2. The **land is severed** into more than one parcel.
      3. The **use of the property existed prior to the severance.**
      4. The easement is **reasonably necessary** to the dominant land's use and enjoyment of the property.
   c. **Easement by necessity** has the following requirements:
      1. **Common ownership** of the dominant and servient parcels.
      2. **Easement is strictly necessary**. The necessity must exist at the time of the conveyance (e.g., landlocked parcel).
      3. **Prior use is not required.**
   d. **Easement by prescription** is one obtained using the same principles as adverse possession. Requirements:
      1. **Actual use:** The claimant must have actual use of the property that is adverse to the servient parcel. Unlike adverse possession, it need not be exclusive use.
      2. **Open, notorious, and visible use** of the property.
      3. **Hostile use,** which is without the owner's consent.
      4. **Continuous use** for the given statutory period. Tacking is allowed is satisfy the statutory period.
   e. **Easement by estoppel** can occur where the servient parcel allows use of the property such that it is reasonable that the user will substantially change his position in reliance on the belief that the permission will not be revoked.
4. **Scope of easements**
   a. **Present and future needs:** Courts assume the easement intends to meet both present and future needs of the dominant parcel due to

normal, foreseeable development of the dominant estate. (E.g.: An easement may be widened to accommodate wider cars.)

b. **Excessive use:** Increased use that unreasonably interferes with the use of the servient estate is not permitted.

c. **Remedy** for excessive use or misuse is an injunction and/or damages, but the easement will not be terminated.

5. **Maintenance and repair of easements**
   a. The **servient owner is not required** to repair and maintain the easement.
   b. The **dominant owner has an implied right to repair** and maintain the easement.
6. **Transfer of easements**
   a. **Servient (burdened) estate transfer: An easement runs (passes) with the land** and transfers to the new owner of a servient estate **except** if the purchaser of the servient estate is a BFP who took for value with no notice. [Note: Inquiry notice may be an issue.]
   b. **Dominant (benefited) estate transfer:** Whether the benefit runs with the land depends on whether the easement is appurtenant or in gross.
      1. **Appurtenant easements** normally run (pass) automatically with the transfer of the dominant (benefited) estate.
      2. **In gross easements**
         a. **Common law** rule is that easements in gross are not transferable.
         b. **Modernly, commercial easements in gross are transferable.**
7. **Termination of easements:** Easements may terminate in several ways.
   a. **Estoppel:** The servient owner materially changes position in reasonable reliance on the easement holder's assurances that the easement will no longer be enforced.
   b. **Necessity:** Easement by necessity ends when the necessity ends.
   c. **Destruction** of servient land, so long as it is not willful destruction by the owner.
   d. **Condemnation** of servient estate by eminent domain.
   e. **Release** in writing by easement holder to the servient owner.
   f. **Abandonment action:** The easement holder **demonstrates by physical action the intent** to never use the easement again. Words alone or mere nonuse will not be sufficient to constitute abandonment.
   g. **Merger doctrine:** The easement is extinguished when title to both the dominant and servient parcels become vested in same person.
   h. **Prescription:** An easement can be terminated by employing the principals of prescription where there is an adverse, continuous interruption of the easement for the statutory period.

> **Memorization tip:** Use the mnemonic **END CRAMP** to remember the eight ways an easement can terminate.

> **Easement fact triggers:**
> - Right to use of an adjacent parking lot for a business
> - Right to use specified parking spaces
> - Right to use a driveway, road, or pathway

> **Issue-spotting tip:** Other issues that commonly arise as a cluster with easements are notice (since sale to a BFP would cause an easement not to transfer), particularly inquiry notice (since easements are often visible upon inspection), deed delivery, recording acts, and warranty deeds (since an undisclosed easement would violate many of the warranties).

B. **Real covenants** are **written promises** between two parties that meet certain technical requirements, such that the **promises "run with the land,"** meaning they are binding on future purchasers/holders of the land. The requirements are different depending on whether the benefit or burden of the covenant is running with the land (e.g., build single-family dwellings on the land only). **The remedy for breach of a covenant is money damages.**
   1. **Burden to "run with the land"** requirements:
      a. **Writing** required between original parties/owners.
      b. **Intent** that the promise apply to successors to the property.
      c. Must **"touch and concern"** the land. For the servient parcel, this means the promise **restricts the use of the servient parcel** in some way, thus decreasing the use or enjoyment, or requires the servient parcel to do something.
      d. **Horizontal and vertical privity is required** for the burden to run.
         1. **Horizontal privity** refers to the privity between the original promising parties. They must have shared some interest in the land apart from covenant itself (e.g., developer/purchaser, landlord/tenant).
         2. **Vertical privity** requires that the successor now is the holder of the entire interest that the party making the covenant had (e.g., grantor/grantee, landlord/tenant, buyer/seller, mortgagor/mortgagee, assignor/assignee of lease).

> **Exam tip:** When tested on the bar exam, both vertical and horizontal privity have been present and easy to establish.

      e. **Notice is required** and can be actual, constructive (record), or inquiry notice.

> **Memorization tip:** Use the mnemonic **WITCH VaN** to remember the requirements for a real covenant **burden** to run.
> - **W**riting
> - **I**ntent
> - **T**ouch and **C**oncern
> - **H**orizontal and **V**ertical privity
> - **N**otice
>
> (Picture that the van can carry the burden.)

2. **Benefit to "run with the land"** requirements:
   a. **Writing** required between original parties/owners.
   b. **Intent** that the promise apply to successors to the property.
   c. Must "**touch and concern**" the land. For the dominant parcel, this means the promise **benefits the dominant parcel by increasing the use or enjoyment** of the property.
   d. **Vertical privity** is required, meaning the successor now is the holder of the entire interest that the party making the covenant had (e.g., grantor/grantee, landlord/tenant, or mortgagor/mortgagee).
   e. **No horizontal privity or notice is required.**

> **Memorization tip:** Use the mnemonic **W**hat **I**s **T**he **C**ommon **V**alue to remember the requirements for a real covenant **benefit** to run with the land (identifies the requirements in common with the burden running requirements).
> - **W**riting
> - **I**ntent
> - **T**ouch and **C**oncern
> - **V**ertical privity

3. **Termination or modification of covenants is allowed in the following circumstances:**
   a. **Agreement of all parties** in a sufficient writing.
   b. **Abandonment action:** The covenant holder **demonstrates by physical action the intent** to abandon the covenant. Words alone or mere nonuse will not be sufficient to constitute abandonment.
   c. **Changed conditions:** Conditions have changed so significantly that the purpose of the covenant is impossible to accomplish.

C. **Equitable servitudes** (also called *restrictive covenants*) **are restrictions on how land may be used.** Equitable servitudes are similar to real covenants, but have no privity requirements. (E.g.: Property may be used for residential purposes only, or painted a particular shade of beige.) **The remedy for breach of an equitable servitude is an injunction in equity.**
   1. **Equitable servitudes will "run with the land"** and bind successors if
      a. **Writing** is typically required.
      b. **Intent** that the promise apply to successors to the property.

c. Must "**touch and concern**" the land.
   1. **Dominant parcel:** The promise **benefits the dominant parcel by increasing the use or enjoyment** of the property.
   2. **Servient parcel:** The promise **restricts the use of the servient parcel** in some way thus decreasing the use or enjoyment, or requires the servient parcel to do something.
d. **Notice is required** and can be actual, constructive (record) or inquiry notice.
e. **No horizontal or vertical privity is required.** (E.g.: Neighbors can have an enforceable equitable servitude.)

<u>Memorization tip:</u> Use the mnemonic **W**hen **I**njunction is **T**he **C**ertain **N**eed to remember the requirements for an equitable servitude to run with the land.
- **W**riting
- **I**ntent
- **T**ouch and **C**oncern
- **N**otice

<u>Equitable Servitude fact triggers:</u>
- Prohibition against opening a store or restaurant or competing business within a specified area, such as within five miles
- Prohibition against allowing another similar store to lease space in the same shopping center
- CCR's of a condo prohibiting certain conduct, such as an artist loft community only allowing on-premises sale of art made "in house"
- Covenant in an apartment lease, such as not to disturb other tenants
- Subdivision owners must pay annual fee to one security company

2. **Implied reciprocal servitude** (general or common scheme doctrine): Court can imply a reciprocal equitable servitude if the **original owner intended a "common plan or scheme" and the purchaser has notice** of the scheme. The **remedy for a breach is an injunction** in equity.
   a. The **common plan or scheme** can be evidenced by a recorded plat, or a general pattern of restrictions, or an oral representation to early buyers (e.g., a new housing development where a contract with a company regarding the provision of security services has been recorded).
   b. **Notice is required** and can be actual, constructive (record), or inquiry notice. Inquiry notice can be provided by a visual inspection of the neighborhood that gives the appearance of conforming to certain standards.

   c. **No SOF writing is required.**
3. **Termination or modification of equitable servitudes is allowed in the following circumstances:**
   a. **Agreement of all parties** in a sufficient writing.
   b. **Abandonment action:** The equitable servitude holder **demonstrates by physical action the intent** to abandon the servitude. Words alone or mere nonuse will not be sufficient to constitute abandonment.
   c. **Changed conditions:** Conditions that have changed so significantly that the purpose of the equitable servitude is impossible to accomplish.

> Exam Tip: Real covenants and equitable servitudes are very similar. In an exam it is typically acceptable to analyze one or the other since the elements are mostly similar. However, it's best to note the differences, too, such as the remedy allowed under each.

D. **Profit** (profit a prendre) entitles its holder to the right to enter the servient estate land and **remove soil or a product of the land** itself. A profit is similar to an easement (e.g., mining minerals, drilling for oil, removing timber, hunting, or fishing).
E. **License is the mere right to use the licensor's land** for some specific purpose, and it is revocable at the will of the licensor.
   1. Difference from easement: **A license may be freely revoked.**
   2. **Oral agreements** produce a license, not an easement. However, it is possible the oral license created an easement by estoppel with detrimental reliance.
F. **Water rights**
   1. **Drainage of surface waters**
      a. **Using surface water:** An owner may use all he wants.
      b. **Getting rid of surface water** has three different approaches:
         1. Common enemy: Owner may cast water onto neighbor's land.
         2. Civil law rule: Owner has strict liability for interfering with natural flow.
         3. Reasonable use doctrine allows owner to act reasonably.
   2. **Riparian rights** (waterfront streams and lakes that abut property)
      a. **Common law:** Each riparian owner may use only as much water as he may put to beneficial use.
      b. **Prior appropriation doctrine:** Used by some states, including California. An owner (need not be riparian) must obtain a permit to use the water, and priority of use is determined by permit date.
   3. **Ground water:** An owner may make reasonable use of ground water drawn from his property.
G. **Right to lateral and subjacent support:** Every landowner has a right to receive necessary physical support from adjacent soil (lateral support) and underlying soil (subjacent support).

1. **Lateral support:** The right to lateral support (adjacent property) is absolute. An adjacent property owner using due care will still be liable.
2. **Subjacent support** arises when something is removed from below the surface of the land. The owner of the surface land has a right to not have the surface subside.

> **Exam tip:** Profits, licenses, water rights, and the right to lateral and subjacent support are infrequently tested.

REAL PROPERTY ISSUES TESTED MATRIX

		Crossover Subject	Adverse Possession	Inter Vivos Transfer by Contract or Deed	Mortgage Foreclosure	Warranty Deed	Recording Acts Notice	Future Interests	Joint Ownership Concurrent Estates	LLT Types Rent & Premises Condition	LLT Waste Fixtures	LLT Assignment Sublease	Easements	Real Covenants &/or Equitable Servitudes
July '11 Q5	Andy deeds Blackacre to Beth & Chris jointly		X					X	X					
February '11 Q3	Leo has 3 consecutive lots & lot 3 has Grill restaurant						X					X	X	X
July '08 Q5	Ann, Betty & Celia own a condo as joint tenants			X				X	X					
July '07 Q1	Larry leases 4-room office suite to Tanya	Contracts								X				
February '07 Q1	Builder sells shopping mall, but reserves parking	Torts								X		X	X	
February '06 Q3	Mike has 30-year office lease from Olive	Con Law									X	X		
July '05 Q2	Developer subdivides home sites & security contract w/ASI/MPI	Contracts					X							X
February '05 Q5	Cousins Alice & Bill buy a house as joint tenants								X	X				
February '04 Q4	Lori owns shopping center; leases to Tony, who transfers to Ann									X		X		X
February '03 Q2	Olga wants to give Blackacre to niece Nan	Wills		X										

Continued >

		Crossover Subject	Adverse Possession	Inter Vivos Transfer by Contract or Deed	Mortgage Foreclosure	Warranty Deed	Recording Acts Notice	Future Interests	Joint Ownership Concurrent Estates	LLT Types Rent & Premises Condition	LLT Waste Fixtures	LLT Assignment Sublease	Easements	Real Covenants &/or Equitable Servitudes
July '02 Q2	Able owns Whiteacre, and Baker owns Blackacre				X	X	X						X	
July '01 Q2	Artist leased condo to Weaver who transfers it to Sculptor									X		X		X
July '00 Q2	Sam sells Paul a lakefront parcel, once owned by Owen	Contracts Wills	X	X				X						
July '99 Q5	Artist leases noisy loft w/construction by State Power	Torts Remedies								X			X	
February '98 Q4	Donna's easement on Stan's lot, prepared by lawyer Len	Prof. Resp.											X	
February '97 Q4	Tenant leases apartment w/wiring & noxious slime									X	X			
February '97 Q3	Debbie's oceanfront porch is on Peter's property	Remedies	X											
July '96 Q5	Widower Fred wills Blackacre to his 3 children		X	X					X					
February '95 Q2	Albert owns Blueacre & Clara holds mortgage				X	X	X						X	
February '94 Q3	1950; Al gives Betty an easement, then sells to Cal, then to Dot					X	X						X	
July '93 Q5	Owner owns several apartment buildings w/Lisa and Mary									X		X		X

Continued >

		Crossover Subject	Adverse Possession	Inter Vivos Transfer by Contract or Deed	Mortgage Foreclosure	Warranty Deed	Recording Acts Notice	Future Interests	Joint Ownership Concurrent Estates	LLT Types Rent & Premises Condition	LLT Waste Fixtures	LLT Assignment Sublease	Easements	Real Covenants &/or Equitable Servitudes
February '91 Q4	Orin owns Blackacre, wooded 160 acres on which Arthur camps		X	X			X	X			X			
February '90 Q6	Joe's wealthy brother Steve owns vacant home	Contracts Torts Remedies					X							
July '89 Q5	Nell excavates to build & land subsides under Owen's home									X			X	
February '89 Q2	Arthur owns Whiteacre w/grocery store rented out			X						X	X	X		X
July '87 Q4	Trustee won't fix lot where parking lot has cracks	Trusts Torts												X
February '87 Q3	Owen owns 50 acres of unzoned land	Torts Remedies												X

REAL PROPERTY PRACTICE ESSAYS, ANSWER GRIDS, AND SAMPLE ANSWERS

Real Property Question 1

July 2005, Question 2

Developer acquired a large tract of undeveloped land, subdivided the tract into ten lots, and advertised the lots for sale as "Secure, Gated Luxury Home Sites." Developer then entered into a ten-year, written contract with Ace Security, Inc. ("ASI") to provide security for the subdivision in return for an annual fee of $6,000.

Developer sold the first lot to Cora and quickly sold the remaining nine. Developer had inserted the following clause in each deed:

> Purchaser(s) hereby covenant and agree on their own behalf and on behalf of their heirs, successors, and assigns to pay an annual fee of $600 for 10 years to Ace Security, Inc. for the maintenance of security within the subdivision.

Developer promptly and properly recorded all ten deeds.

One year later, ASI assigned all its rights and obligations under the security contract with Developer to Modern Protection, Inc. ("MPI"), another security service. About the same time, Cora's next-door neighbor, Seller, sold the property to Buyer. Seller's deed to Buyer did not contain the above-quoted clause. Buyer steadfastly refuses to pay any fee to MPI.

MPI threatens to suspend its security services to the entire subdivision unless it receives assurance that it will be paid the full $6,000 each year for the balance of the contract. Cora wants to ensure that she will not be required to pay more than $600 a year.

On what theories might Cora reasonably sue Buyer for his refusal to pay the annual $600 fee to MPI, what defenses might Buyer reasonably assert, and what is the likely outcome on each of Cora's theories and Buyer's defenses? Discuss.

Real Property Question 1 Assessment

July 2005, Question 2

This question is a very typical real property essay question. The major issues are real covenants, equitable servitudes, and an equitable servitude implied from a common scheme. Since the call of the question specifically requests a discussion of Buyer's defenses, some defenses need to be enumerated in the answer (or potential issues must be framed as Buyer's defenses). This question can be technically classified as a contracts crossover, but the contracts issue of the invalid assignment is of comparatively minor weight to the real property issues.

The real covenant discussion should include an accurate recitation of the rule and an application of all pertinent facts. Each element must be analyzed separately. The weightier discussions are regarding whether the security contract "touched and concerned" the land, with an argument on both sides, and a full discussion of the three types of notice. Since the Buyer did not have notice in his own deed, this fact needs to be identified, with the conclusion that the record notice provided by the chain of title was sufficient to provide constructive notice.

The equitable servitude discussion should note the difference between an equitable servitude and a real covenant, which is that equitable servitudes do not require privity and the remedy is injunctive relief. The issue of an equitable servitude implied from a common scheme is less commonly tested and requires a full use of the many available facts in the analysis to demonstrate the existence of the common scheme.

The call of the question specifically asks about defenses, and though none of the defenses will likely be successful, a discussion of defenses is necessary to receive a passing score. The bar examiners are challenging the bar takers to "think like a lawyer" and come up with some creative defenses. The contract defense of the invalidity of the assignment is tricky to spot. However, the fact pattern includes an assignment from ASI to MPI to provide the subdivision security under the contract. There is nothing else that can be done with this unusual fact, except make the unsuccessful invalid assignment argument. A strategy to use when the call of the question calls for one party's defenses is to argue as a "defense" that a required element of an underlying rule was not satisfied, such as the argument here that there was insufficient notice or the covenant did not touch and concern the land. Keep this strategy in mind, as you will likely need it again.

Note the areas highlighted in **bold** on the corresponding grid. The bold areas highlight the issues, analysis, and conclusions that are likely **required** to receive a passing score on this question. The grid is provided to assist you in assessing your own performance. In general, the essay grids are provided to assist you in analyzing the essays, and are much more detailed than what a student should create during the exam to organize their response to a question.

Issue	Rule	Fact Application	Conclusion

Real covenant	**To bind successors there must be:**
	• **Writing (of promise between original parties/owners)**
	• **Intent (to bind future successors)**
	• **Touch and concern the land** (benefit dominant estate by **increased use or enjoyment**; restrict servient estate by decreased use or enjoyment)
	• **Horizontal privity (between originally promising parties)**
	• **Vertical privity: between grantor/ee** or LL/T (new party holds entire durational interest held by the one making the covenant)
	• **Notice**
	  • **Actual (subjective)**
	  • **Record (properly in chain of title)**
	  • **Inquiry (facts put on notice to look into further)**
		There is a written clause that D placed in all 10 deeds regarding the security provided for the tract, and the deeds were properly recorded, so the writing requirement is satisfied.
		The clause itself states that the parties "agree on their own behalf and on behalf of their heirs, successors, and assigns," which indicates that the original contracting parties clearly intended for the security covenant to bind future successors.
		The covenant was to provide security services for the subdivision, and its safety and maintenance has a clear impact on each landowner's use and enjoyment of their property since a safe neighborhood is more enjoyable and will better maintain the property values, and in fact the security probably enticed the original owners to buy.
		However, **B will assert that security services do not touch and concern the land because the personal safety of those on the premises or in the neighborhood is not sufficiently related to the land itself. This argument will likely fail, since the security contract is indeed directed at security provided for the land itself.**
		Horizontal privity exists because the original promising parties were the tract developer and the first 10 buyers, so there is a buyer-seller relationship.
		Vertical privity also exists because S, the party making the covenant, sold his entire interest in his lot to B.
		B will argue he did not have notice of the covenant, and it appears that B did not have actual, subjective notice of the covenant communicated to him by words or in writing.
			The real covenant likely meets the requirements to run with the land and bind successors

Continued >

Issue	Rule	Fact Application	Conclusion
		B will also argue that he was not on record notice of the security covenant because the provision was not recorded in his deed. However, **the deed between D and S was properly recorded in B's chain of title, and a reasonable search of the records would have disclosed the deed, therefore B had constructive notice.** Notice can also occur through inquiry notice, **however it is unlikely there was anything about the appearance of the subdivision that would have put B on notice of his own obligation to pay the security contract, even if there were security signs or personnel present** since there may have been another source of funding for the security.	The real covenant likely meets the requirements to run with the land and bind successors
Equitable servitude	**The rule is the same as it is for real covenants except equitable servitudes are enforced in equity and there is no privity requirement.**	Since the requirements for a real covenant to run with the land are met, the requirements for an equitable servitude will also be met, which will allow **Cora to succeed in obtaining an injunction (equitable relief) enforcing the agreement to pay the $600 annual fee.**	There is an equitable servitude
Implied equitable servitude	**Original owner intended a common plan or scheme** **Purchaser has notice** of the scheme	**There appears to also be a common scheme to create a secure gated community** as evidenced by the advertisements at the time of the original sale of "Secure, gated, luxury home sites." Further, D entered into a 10-year contract with ASI to provide the promised security, **and recording the covenant, so D intended the common plan of a secure development.** **Whether a purchaser had notice of the scheme follows the same analysis as noted above for record** or inquiry notice, **and as such B should be charged with constructive notice of the common plan.**	There is also an implied equitable servitude

Continued >

Issue	Rule	Fact Application	Conclusion
Buyer's Defenses			
Touch & concern not met	See above for rule on touch and concern.	The real covenant is not binding on successors because it does not "touch and concern" the land. As noted above, **the provision of security services to a property are probably sufficient to add value to the use and enjoyment of the property; therefore, this argument will fail.**	**Not a valid defense**
Notice inadequate	**Notice can be actual, constructive, or inquiry.**	As noted above, B may assert that he had inadequate notice of the covenant so it should not bind him, **but the record notice was sufficient so this argument will fail.**	**Not a valid defense**
Invalid assignment	**Services requiring unique skill or expertise are nondelegable.**	**B may assert that ASI was not able to properly assign their rights and duties under the contract to MPI. However, it is unlikely that the provision of residential security services involves a unique skill or expertise such that the duty would not be delegable to another security company.**	**Not a valid defense**

Real Property Question 1 Sample Answer

July 2005, Question 2

Real Covenant

Cora will attempt to force Buyer to pay the $600 security fee by arguing there is a real covenant that runs with the land and binds successors. Real covenants are written promises between two parties that meet certain technical requirements, such that the promises "run with the land," meaning they are binding on successors. The remedy for breach of a covenant is money damages. The technical requirements that must be satisfied for a covenant burden to run with the land are as follows: (1) it must be in writing, (2) the original parties must intend that the covenant will bind successors, (3) it must touch and concern the land, (4) there must be horizontal and vertical privity, and (5) there must be notice.

Writing

The covenant must satisfy the writing requirements of the Statute of Frauds. The Developer placed a written clause in all ten deeds of the subdivision regarding that security provided for the tract by ASI and that the purchaser agreed to pay a $600 annual fee. The deeds likely met all the statute of fraud writing requirements and were properly recorded, so the writing requirement is satisfied.

Intent

The original parties must have intended that the promise would be binding on successors. The clause in the deed described above states that the parties "agree on their own behalf and on behalf of their heirs, successors, and assigns." The use of this language unambiguously indicates the original contracting parties clearly intended for the security covenant to bind future successors to the properties, so this element is satisfied.

Touch and Concern

To run with the land, the promise must "touch and concern" the land. This means the promise increases the use or enjoyment of the benefited parcel. The covenant here was to provide security services for the subdivision. The safety and maintenance of a neighborhood has a direct link to the land itself and a clear impact on each landowner's use and enjoyment of their property since a safe neighborhood is more enjoyable to live in. Further, a more secure neighborhood will also better maintain the property values.

However, Buyer will assert that promising to pay a fee for security services does not touch and concern the land because the promise is more of a personal promise to pay money, and the personal safety of those on the premises in the subdivision is not sufficiently related to the land itself to be found to touch and concern the land. This argument will likely fail, since the security contract is indeed directed at security provided for the land itself, and promises to pay fees that go towards protecting and preserving property do burden the use and enjoyment of the land.

Privity

For a burden to run with the land there must be both horizontal and vertical privity. A benefit only requires vertical privity.

Horizontal privity refers to the privity between the original promising parties. Horizontal privity exists here because the original promising parties were the tract developer and the first ten buyers of land in the subdivision, so there is a buyer-seller relationship between the parties, which satisfies the horizontal privity requirement.

Vertical privity requires that the successor now is the holder of the entire interest that was held by the party making the covenant. Vertical privity also exists here because Seller, the party making the original covenant with Developer, sold his entire interest in his lot to Buyer. Therefore, Seller and Buyer have vertical privity.

Notice

Buyer will argue that he did not have notice of the covenant. For the covenant to run with the land, the successor must have notice of the covenant. Notice can be provided by actual notice, constructive notice, or inquiry notice.

Buyer did not have actual, subjective notice of the covenant. There are no facts to indicate that the existence of the covenant was ever communicated to him in words or in writing, so Buyer did not have actual notice of the covenant.

Bob will also argue that he was not on record notice of the security covenant because the provision was not recorded in his deed to the property. However, the deed that was recorded earlier between Developer and Seller was properly recorded in Buyer's chain of title and a reasonable search of the records would have disclosed the deed, including the existence of the covenant. This proper recordation of the deed is sufficient to provide Buyer with constructive notice.

Notice can also occur through inquiry notice, which is where the purchaser of a property is in possession of facts that would lead a reasonable person to make further inquiry. However, even if there were security signs in the subdivision and security personnel present, it is unlikely this would have put Buyer on notice of his own obligation to pay the security contract had he made a reasonable inquiry. It is just as likely there was an alternate source of the security funding, so Buyer is likely not on inquiry notice.

Equitable Servitude

An equitable servitude is similar to a real covenant and the requirements are the same, except there are no privity requirements and the remedy is in equity, rather than legal damages. Since the requirements for a real covenant running with the land are met, the requirements for an equitable servitude are also met. This allows Cora to obtain an injunction (equitable relief) enforcing the agreement to make Seller pay the $600 annual fee owing under the covenant.

Implied Equitable Servitude

A court can imply a reciprocal equitable servitude if the original owner intended a "common plan or scheme" and the purchaser has notice of the scheme. The remedy for a breach is an injunction in equity. There appears be a common scheme by the Developer to create a community with safety as a focus—as evidenced by the advertisements at the time of the original sale of "secure, gated, luxury home sites." In furtherance of the scheme, the Developer entered into a ten-year contract with ASI to provide the promised security for the subdivision and recorded the covenant. Developer intended the common plan or scheme of a secure and safe subdivision development.

Whether Buyer and a subsequent purchaser had notice of Developer's common scheme follows the same analysis as noted above in the real covenant section for record or inquiry notice. Buyer should be charged with constructive notice of the common plan because of the deed recording.

Buyer's Defenses

"Touch and Concern" Element Not Met

Buyer may argue the "touch and concern" element is not satisfied, which would make neither the restrictive covenant, nor equitable servitude enforceable against him. However, as noted above, the provision of security services to a property development is probably sufficient to "touch and concern" the land since the security adds value to the use and enjoyment of the property. Thus, this argument will fail.

Inadequate Notice

Buyer may also assert that he had inadequate notice of the covenant so it should not bind him. However, as noted above, the record notice was sufficient since the deed was properly recorded, so this argument will fail.

Invalid Assignment

Lastly, Buyer may assert that ASI was not able to properly assign their rights and duties under the covenant to MPI, a different security company, therefore releasing him from the obligation. However, to qualify as a duty that cannot be assigned, the duty would have to relate to the provision of services that require the application of unique skill or expertise. It is very unlikely that the provision of residential security services involves any unique skills or expertise such that the duty would not be delegable to another security company. Having another security company perform the function of the contract does not increase the risk. This defense will not be successful.

Real Property Question 2

February 1994, Question 3

In 1950, Al properly executed and delivered a quitclaim deed granting his neighbor, Betty, an "easement of way, thirty feet wide" along the southern boundary of Al's five-acre residential parcel. Betty never recorded the deed. In 1951, Betty graded and graveled a twenty-foot wide road along the southern boundary of the five-acre parcel. Since then, Betty has used the road daily to reach her house and has maintained the road as needed.

In 1955, Al conveyed his entire parcel to Cal by a properly executed and delivered quitclaim deed. The deed to Cal made no mention of any easement. Cal paid Al $15,000 for the conveyance.

In September 1988, Cal and Dot signed the following contract concerning the five-acre parcel:

> *"Cal agrees to sell and Dot agrees to buy the following land [valid legal description]. Price, $90,000 cash, closing December 15, 1988."*

On December 15, 1988, Dot paid Cal $90,000 cash, and Cal properly executed and delivered a warranty deed conveying the land to Dot. The deed contained no mention of the easement. Dot promptly recorded the deed. Betty has continued to use and maintain the road.

In June 1989, Dot built a fence blocking the road to Betty's house.

1. What right, if any, does Betty have to continue to use the road? Discuss.
2. What rights, if any, does Dot have against Cal based on the contract, the deed, or both? Discuss.

Real Property Question 2 Assessment

February 1994, Question 3

This property question covers some frequently tested real property issues, such as easements, notice, and the recording acts. This question also covers some more obscure issues, such as the rule regarding the transferability of easements, the covenants in a general warranty deed, and the merger doctrine. The challenge for this question is that the facts are vague in areas. The facts indicate that a deed had been recorded, but does not identify the applicable recording act in the jurisdiction. This makes the analysis a bit trickier because it is unclear what the conclusion should be. The best thing to do in this situation is identify for the reader that "if this happens, then this is the result" for each of the possibilities.

The other challenge posed by this question is that if a student does not know the rule regarding the transferability of easements, which is admittedly somewhat obscure, it is difficult to pass the rest of the question. Unless a student can identify that being a bona fide purchaser is a significant part of the rule (and it would be hard to guess at that requirement with confidence), it is likely that all of the issues regarding notice, and possibly the recording acts issues also, will be missed, making it virtually impossible to receive a passing score on this question.

Property questions can be similar to contracts questions in that the sequence of events is very important. It is often helpful to write down a quick timeline of the significant events to keep the events, parties, and dates straight. It may also be helpful to draw a diagram of the property involved, especially on a question such as this where an easement is being described. A sketch of the easement on the property gives a clearer picture of the events that have transpired. For example:

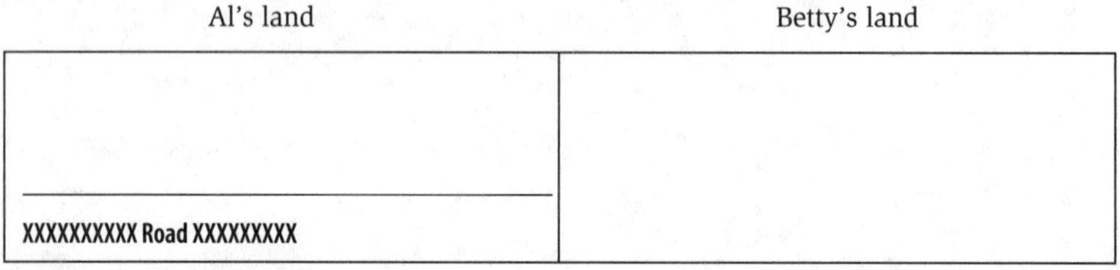

Al's land	Betty's land
XXXXXXXXXX Road XXXXXXXXX	

1955 Al conveys to Cal
1988 Cal conveys to Dot

Looking at the picture makes it a bit more difficult to see whether Cal or Dot would prevail in their argument that the road did not supply inquiry notice of Betty's easement since the road goes directly across the border of Al's land and straight to Betty's property.

Note the areas highlighted in **bold** on the corresponding grid. The bold areas highlight the issues, analysis, and conclusions that are likely **required** to receive a passing score on this question.

Issue	Rule	Fact Application	Conclusion
Betty's Rights			
Easement	**An easement is the right to use the land of another**. Easements are nonpossessory property interests. **An express easement is created in writing.** **Scope of easement:** it is intended to meet both present and future needs of the dominant parcel due to normal, foreseeable development.	Betty has an "easement of way, thirty feet wide" along the southern boundary of her neighbor Al's 5-acre parcel. **This** express **appurtenant easement gives Betty,** the adjacent landowner, **the right to use Al's land and is nonpossessory interest in land. Al's estate is the servient estate, and Betty's is the dominant estate that receives the benefit of the easement.** Easements can be created several ways, including expressly in a writing that satisfies the SOF. Here, Betty's easement is contained in the writing of an executed quitclaim deed, which presumably satisfied the SOF and is **an express easement.** The **scope of an easement** includes the parameters of the writing, and here it is a **30-foot-wide strip of the southern border of Al's parcel.**	**Betty has an express easement**
Easement by prescription	An easement can be created by prescription where there is • Actual use that is adverse to the servient parcel • Open, notorious, and visible use of the property • **Hostile use (without the owner's consent)** • Continuous use for the statutory period	Betty actually used the servient parcel by driving daily on the 20-foot strip of road she graded and graveled on the 30-foot-wide portion noted in the easement. Betty's use was open, notorious, and visible since she graded, graveled, and maintained the road, in addition to her daily use of the road to get to her land. **Betty's use of the easement was with the permission** of Al from 1950 until Al sold to Cal in 1955, so the use wasn't originally hostile, but Betty then used the road every day for 33 years, apparently without consent of the owner Cal, from 1955 to 1988. Assuming the statutory period is less than 33 years Betty has satisfied the statute.	Could conclude either way

Continued >

Issue	Rule	Fact Application	Conclusion
Transferability of easements	An appurtenant easement burden passes automatically with servient land, **unless the new owner is BFP (took for value, no notice)**	Cal in 1955 and Dot in 1988 could claim that the easement should not have transferred with the servient land because each of them were BFPs. Both took for value, Cal paid $15,000 and Dot later paid $90,000 for the parcel. The issue is if they took without notice of the easement.	**Both Cal and Dot took for value,** but without notice is required (see below)
Notice	**Notice** can be provided three ways: • **Actual** (subjective) • **Record** (properly in chain of title) • **Inquiry** (facts put on notice to look into further)	Here, **there are no facts to indicate that either Cal or Dot had actual notice of Betty's easement.** Al's quitclaim deed granting Betty **the easement was never recorded, so there is no record or constructive notice of the easement since a title search would not have revealed the easement.** However, while Dot and Cal would argue otherwise, both Cal and Dot may have been on inquiry notice of the easement. A cursory **inspection of the property would have likely revealed a graveled road on the southern border of the property leading to Betty's land.** Further, Betty used the road daily to reach her home. The existence of the road should have put either Cal or Dot on notice to look into the matter further, thus neither of them will be granted BFP status and the easement will pass with the land. **However, if the road were not sufficiently obvious to provide inquiry notice,** and Cal and Dot wouldn't have known Betty constructed it, **Cal and Dot would be BFPs.**	There was likely inquiry notice, but you could conclude either way

Continued >

Issue	Rule	Fact Application	Conclusion
Recording act	**Common law: first in time, first in right** **Other jurisdictions: notice, race-notice, or race statutes, which offer various measures of protection** Recording acts provide a mechanism to protect a subsequent purchaser from a prior inconsistent transaction. [Note: There were several ways the recording act discussion could have been analyzed. The important factor was that there was some factual analysis addressing the three types of recording acts.]	It is unclear what recording statute, if any, applies in this jurisdiction, but **Dot recorded her deed** with no mention of the easement in 1988, and the easement had never been recorded prior. **If the common law rule applies, Betty keeps the easement since her easement was first in time.** A notice statute would likely not protect Dot since she likely had inquiry notice of the easement. Likewise a race-notice jurisdiction would not protect Dot because of the inquiry notice. **However, if Dot was not found to have inquiry notice, she would prevail as a BFP under both notice and race-notice jurisdictions.** **In a pure race jurisdiction, Dot would prevail because she recorded first.**	**Outcome depends on the recording act jurisdiction**
Obstruction	Servient estate owner can't obstruct the use of the easement.	If Dot is not a BFP, the burden of the easement passes with the servient estate, and Dot can't build fence to obstruct Betty's use of the easement. Betty can sue to get a mandatory injunction ordering Dot to have the fence removed.	Dot can't obstruct easement
Dot v. Cal			
Marketable title	Marketable title is implied in every land sale contract and is title free from reasonable doubt.	An easement reduces the value of a property, therefore an easement would make title unmarketable.	Title was unmarketable
Merger doctrine	In a contract for the sale of land, once the deal has closed, **the contract merges with the deed and the deed controls .**	**The deed will control, so Dot will need to look at the deed for breach.**	**Deed controls**

Continued >

Issue	Rule	Fact Application	Conclusion
Warranty deed	Present covenants: • **Seisen:** grantor owns what he purports to own • **Right to convey** • **Against encumbrances:** grantor warrants there are no mortgages, liens, **easements,** or use restrictions on the land Future covenants: • **Warranty of title:** grantor will defend against lawful claims • **Quiet enjoyment:** not disturbed by any third parties' lawful claims of title • **Further assurances:** do whatever future acts are reasonably necessary to perfect title	**Dot can assert a breach of several warranties since Cal provided a warranty deed** for the sale of the property to Dot and this provides the greatest protection. The covenants of seisen, right to convey and against encumbrances are **present covenants and are breached at the time of conveyance,** if at all. Since Cal was **unable to provide marketable title because of Betty's easement,** Cal is in breach of the warranty of all three present covenants. **Cal did not own a fee simple, was unable to convey one, and there was an easement on the property.** The future covenants run with the land and are breached when a grantee is disturbed in possession. **If Betty asserts her right** to use the easement and have Dot's fence removed, **Cal would also be in breach of the warranty of title, quiet enjoyment, and further assurance, and Cal would need to take reasonable steps to defend the claim.**	Cal may be in breach of the general warranty deeds

Real Property Question 2 Sample Answer

February 1994, Question 3

1. Betty's Right to Continue to Use the Road

Easement

Betty may continue to use the road if she has an easement. An easement is a nonpossessory interest in land that creates a right to use the land of another.

Betty has an "easement of way, thirty feet wide" along the southern boundary of her neighbor Al's five-acre parcel of land. This is an appurtenant easement since Al and Betty have parcels of land that are adjacent to each other. The easement gives Betty the right only to use a portion of Al's land and is thus a nonpossessory interest in land. Al's estate is the servient estate providing the benefit, and Betty has the dominant estate that receives the benefit of the easement.

Easements can be created several ways, including expressly in a writing that satisfies the Statute of Frauds. Here, Betty's easement is contained in the writing of an executed quitclaim deed, which presumably satisfied the Statute of Frauds and is an express easement.

Express Easement

An easement can be created expressly when it is contained in a writing that satisfies the Statute of Frauds. Here, Al properly executed and delivered a quitclaim deed to his neighbor Betty, granting her an "easement of way, thirty feet wide." Therefore, the easement was created by express grant in the quitclaim deed.

Scope of Easement

The scope of an easement includes the use anticipated in the writing and is intended to meet both present and future needs of the dominant parcel due to normal, foreseeable development. Here, the parties specify the scope to be a 30-foot-wide strip of the southern border of Al's parcel.

Upon obtaining the easement deed, Betty graded and graveled a 20-foot-wide road along the southern boundary of Al's parcel. Since the express easement granted Betty a 30-foot-wide section, she is within the scope of the easement in her use.

Easement by Prescription

A prescriptive easement occurs when there is use of the property that is actual and adverse; open and notorious and visible; hostile; and continuous for the statutory period.

Betty may also argue she has a prescriptive easement since she actually used the servient parcel by driving daily on the 20-foot strip of road she graded and graveled, which sat on the 30-foot-wide portion of land identified in the easement. Betty's use of the land was open, notorious, and visible since she graded, graveled, and maintained the road, in addition to her daily use of the road to drive to her land. Betty's use of the easement was with Al's permission from 1950 until Al sold the property to Cal in 1955, so Betty's use wasn't originally hostile. However, after Cal purchased the land, Betty used the road every day for 33 years, apparently without consent of the new owner Cal, from 1955 until 1988. Assuming the statutory period is less than 33 years, Betty has satisfied the statute and likely has obtained an easement by prescription.

Transferability of Easements

The burden of an appurtenant easement passes automatically with the servient land, unless the new owner is a bona fide purchaser, one who took for value, without notice of the interest. Cal (in 1955) and Dot (in 1988) could both claim that the easement should not have transferred with the servient land because each of them were bona fide purchasers. Both took for value, since Cal paid $15,000 and Dot later paid $90,000 for the parcel. The determinative issue is whether they took without notice of the easement, which is discussed below.

Notice

Notice can be provided three ways: by actual notice, constructive (record) notice, or inquiry notice. Here, there are no facts to indicate that either Cal or Dot had actual notice of Betty's easement. Al's quitclaim deed granting Betty's easement was never recorded, so there is no record or constructive notice of the easement since a title search would not have revealed the easement.

The third type of notice is inquiry notice, and this occurs when facts exist that serve to put one on notice to look further into the issue. A cursory inspection of the property would have likely revealed a graveled road on the southern border of the property leading to Betty's land. Further, Betty used the road daily to reach her home. The existence of the road should have put either Cal or Dot on notice to look further into the matter, thus neither of them should be granted bona fide purchaser status and thus the easement will pass with the land. However, in the event the road was not sufficiently obvious to provide them with inquiry notice—especially since Cal and Dot would have no way of knowing Betty constructed the road—Cal and Dot would be bona fide purchasers.

Recording Acts

Recording acts provide a mechanism to protect a subsequent purchaser from a prior inconsistent transaction. It is unclear what recording statute, if any, applies in this jurisdiction. The common law rule is "first in time, first in right." Other jurisdictions have notice, race-notice, or race statutes, which offer various measures of protection to subsequent purchasers.

In 1988 Dot recorded her deed with no mention of the easement, and the easement had never been recorded prior to this time. If the common law rule applies, Betty gets to keep the easement since her easement was first in time. A notice statute would not protect Dot since she likely had inquiry notice of the easement. Likewise, a race-notice jurisdiction would not protect Dot because of the same inquiry notice issue. However, if Dot was not found to have inquiry notice, she would prevail as a bona fide purchaser in both notice and race-notice jurisdictions.

In a pure race jurisdiction, Dot would prevail over Betty because she recorded first.

Obstruction

A servient owner can't obstruct the use of an easement. If Dot is not protected by bona fide purchaser status, the burden of the easement passes with the servient estate and Dot is not permitted to build a fence to obstruct Betty's use of the easement. Betty can sue to get a mandatory injunction to order Dot to have the fence removed.

2. Dot's Rights Against Cal

Marketable Title

Implied in every land sale contract is the warranty that at closing the seller will provide the buyer with marketable title. Marketable title is title reasonably free from doubt.

An easement that reduces the value of the property renders title unmarketable because the property is encumbered. Thus, the title was unmarketable.

Merger Doctrine

The land sale contract merges with the deed at the closing and the deed controls the transaction. A buyer then must look to whether there has been a breach of any warranties made in the deed.

Covenants in Warranty Deed

Cal provided a general warranty deed, which includes six warranties. The general warranty deed provides present covenants including the covenant of seisin, the covenant of right to convey, and the covenant against encumbrances. It also includes the future covenants of quiet enjoyment, warranty, and further assurances.

Dot can assert a breach of several warranties since Cal provided a general warranty deed for the sale of the property to Dot and this provides the greatest protection. The covenants of seisen, right to convey, and against encumbrances are present covenants and are breached at the time of conveyance, if at all. Since Cal was unable to provide marketable title because of Betty's easement, Cal is in breach of the warranty of all three present covenants. Cal did not own a fee simple, was unable to convey one, and there was an easement on the property. The future covenants run with the land and are breached when a grantee is disturbed in possession. If Betty asserts her right to use the easement and have Dot's fence removed, Cal would also be in breach of the warranty of title, quiet enjoyment, and further assurance, and Cal would need to take reasonable steps to defend the claim.

Real Property Question 3

July 2008, Question 5

Ann, Betty, and Celia purchased a 3-bedroom condominium unit in which they resided. Each paid one-third of the purchase price. They took title as "joint tenants, with right of survivorship."

After a dispute, Betty moved out. Ann and Celia then each executed a separate deed by which each conveyed her respective interest in the condominium unit to Ed. Each deed recited that the conveyance was "in fee, reserving a life estate to the grantor." Ann recorded her deed and delivered the original deed to Ed. Celia also recorded her deed and left the original deed with Ann in a sealed envelope with written instructions: "This envelope contains papers that are to be delivered to me on demand or in the event of my death then to be delivered to Ed." Celia recorded the deed solely to protect her life estate interest. Ann, without Celia's knowledge or authorization, mailed a copy of Celia's deed to Ed.

Subsequently, Ann and Celia were killed in a car accident. Betty then moved back into the condominium unit. She rented out one bedroom to a tenant and used the other bedroom to run a computer business. Betty paid all costs of necessary repairs to maintain the unit.

Ed commenced an action against Betty, demanding a share of the rent she has collected. He also demanded that she pay rent for her use of the premises.

Betty cross-complained against Ed, demanding that he contribute for his share of the costs of necessary repairs to maintain the unit.

1. What are the property interests of Betty and Ed, if any, in the condominium unit? Discuss.
2. What relief, if any, may Ed obtain on his claims against Betty for past due rent for her use of the condominium unit and for a share of the rent paid by the tenant? Discuss.
3. What relief, if any, may Betty obtain on her claim against Ed for contribution for the costs of maintaining the condominium unit? Discuss.

Real Property Question 3 Assessment

July 2008, Question 5

This real property question covers some areas that are less commonly essay tested, including the joint ownership of property and the rights and responsibilities among the joint owners to each other, conveyance by deed, and a minor future interest issue.

The possibility of having future interests tested on the essay exam strikes fear into the heart of most students. However, this question provides a good example of how future interests may be raised on an essay question without cause for concern. The content of the future interest rules simply don't lend themselves to essay testing. Bar examiners are looking to assess a bar applicant's analytical skills, and future interests don't create much analytical opportunity. It is more likely that future interests will come up as they are raised in this question: The future interest in question is a life estate, which is a very easy issue to spot and identify. The identification of the life estate provides the setup for the major issue, which is the proper delivery of the deed purporting to grant the life estate. As is typical in essay questions, there are two slightly different fact scenarios pertaining to the deed delivery so that you can demonstrate to the bar graders your nuanced understanding of the delivery rules.

Another typical aspect of this essay question is the ambiguity in the facts pertaining to Celia's delivery of her deed. The facts are purposely ambiguous regarding whether or not Celia intended a present delivery of the deed. Whenever facts are obviously ambiguous, such as they are here, it is a clue to you that you must analyze both sides of the issue. On the bar essays, major points are always allocated for (1) the full analysis of a pivotal issue, (2) the analysis of an issue where there is an abundance of facts available to use in the analysis, and (3) the analysis of any issue where there are facts available to argue both sides of the issue. This doesn't mean that you should create contrary arguments when they really aren't there. But, when the facts are obviously ambiguous, as they are here, you can be certain that identifying both sides of the issue and presenting the competing arguments is essential to receiving a passing score on that essay. The conclusion you reach on an issue where the conclusion could go either way isn't important. However, it is always wise to be mindful that the conclusion you reach may have an effect on other issues. Be careful not to be so firm in the adoption of your conclusion that you fail to spot issues that may be raised if you had reached the opposite conclusion, and write yourself out of the question.

Note the areas highlighted in **bold** on the corresponding grid. The bold areas highlight the issues, analysis, and conclusions that are likely **required** to receive a passing score on this question.

Issue	Rule	Fact Application	Conclusion
Call #1: Property Interests of B & E			
Joint tenancy	2 or more own a single unified interest with the right of survivorship. **Need 4 unities: same time, same title, same interest, and right to possess the whole, and grantor clearly expresses right of survivorship.**	There are 3 of them, which is an acceptable number since it is more than 2, and the right of survivorship is expressly stated since **A, B, and C all purchased the condo and took title as "joint tenants, with right of survivorship."** **They appear to have taken the same title, at the same time, and each have equal interests and in fact even paid in equal amounts (though this is not required), and they each have the right to possess the whole and in fact appeared to initially all live in the condo.**	**Yes, JT created**
Severance of JT	JT is not destroyed by one party moving out since a JT simply needs to have the right to possess the whole; he needn't do so. **An inter vivos transfer will sever the JT and create a tenancy in common with the parties whose interests have been transferred.** Tenants in common have no right of survivorship and own an individual part with the right to possess the whole.	B moving out of the condo does not sever the JT because she still had the right to possess the whole, but chose not to do so. **When A and C transferred their interests to E by executing a separate deed, which gave him a fee simple as a remainderman and A & C each a life estate, they severed the JT, making it a tenancy in common between A, C, and B assuming their conveyances were valid. (See below.)**	**JT became TIC (if conveyances valid; see below)**

Continued >

Issue	Rule	Fact Application	Conclusion
Conveyance by deed	**Need lawful execution and delivery/ acceptance.** Lawful execution: in writing, identifies parties, signed by grantor, and adequate property description **For delivery to be valid, the grantor must demonstrate a present intent to transfer the interest; physical transfer to grantee is not necessary.** The delivery must also be accepted. **A JT must devise their interest during their life and cannot devise it through a will or after death.**	Here, both A and C's deeds appear to be in writing since they are executed deeds, identify A & C & E, and it is likely that both A and C signed the deed and described the land. **A delivered her deed to E and recorded it, indicating that she presently intended for E to have her fee simple remainder interest, and it appears that E did not reject that delivery, so he accepted it** and the deed is properly delivered as to A's interest. **C also recorded her deed, but did so only to protect her life estate interest, indicating her intent may have only been for herself and not for E; however, she knew she was recording E's interest as well as her own since it was in the deed and she chose to record**; also, C would have no reason to protect her life estate if she didn't intend for E to take as a fee simple as a remainder. **Arguably, C may have intended to transfer her interest after her death and not presently since she left the deed with A in a sealed envelope instructing A to deliver it back to C upon her request or to E at C's death, which would not sever the JT or make a present conveyance to E if it wasn't intended to be delivered until after C died**—also, there appears to be the ability for C to revoke since she can ask for it back. **However, C still executed the deed, giving E the fee simple and recorded it knowing this. Further she still intended E to take as a remainder, she simply wanted to ensure her own interest in a life estate. A's delivery of the deed to E against C's wishes would not suffice for delivery if C didn't intend to transfer because it is C's intent that controls.**	**A's deed to E is valid—severing JT as to A** C's deed valid to E—could have concluded either way [each state-released answer concluded differently but both argued both sides]. If conveyance valid, E takes C's 1/3 interest; if not valid, then JT not severed and B still JT with C while tenant in common with A

Continued >

Issue	Rule	Fact Application	Conclusion
Death of A and C	At the death of a life estate holder, the remainder takes the property. In the event of joint tenants, the remaining JT takes the deceased JT portion.	**Here, since A's transfer and delivery were clearly valid, E would take 1/3 of A's share in the condo, making him a tenant in common with B.** As to C, if JT severed, then E will take C's 1/3 interest, giving E a total of 2/3 interest in the condo as a tenant in common, with B having a 1/3 interest. If JT not severed, then B will take C's 1/3 interest as the surviving JT, giving B 2/3 interest and E 1/3 interest as tenants in common.	Answer depends on above E and B are TIC with either E having 2/3 and B 1/3 or vice versa
Call #2: Ed v. Betty			
Tenants in common	2 or more own with no right of survivorship; each owns an individual part and each has a right to possess the whole.	As indicated above, E and B are now tenants in common, indicating they can both possess the whole and must comply with rules among co-tenants. **Due to both being able to possess the whole, B would not have to pay rent for herself to occupy the land and use it as she desires.**	Co-tenant rules apply **B doesn't owe E rent for her use of the premises**
Co-tenant rights	**Co-tenants in possession have the right to retain profits from their own use of the property.** **Co-tenants must share net rents from 3rd parties.**	**As a co-tenant, B is able to use the property for her own use and retain the profits, as she did here by running her own computer business—so all profits from this business would belong to her only.** **As to the rent from the 3rd-party tenant, B would have to share the profits from that rental with E in proportion to their ownership interests (either 1/3 or 2/3, depending on above).**	**E gets nothing for B's business profits, but will get a portion of rent from the 3rd-party tenant**
Call #3: Betty v. Ed			
Co-tenant rights	**Co-tenants must share costs for necessary repairs, but there is no right to reimbursement for improvements.**	**Since the repairs appear to be necessary to maintain the unit, E would have to contribute to the repairs in proportion to his ownership.**	**E owes B for his share of the repairs**

Real Property Question 4

July 2001, Question 2

Artist owns a workshop in a condominium building consisting of the workshops and sales counters of sculptors, painters, potters, weavers, and other craftspeople. The covenants, conditions and regulations (CC&Rs) of the building provide for a board of managers (Board), which has authority to make "necessary and appropriate rules." Board long ago established a rule against the sale within the building of items not created within the sellers' workshops.

Artist accepted a three-year fellowship in Europe and leased the workshop to Weaver for that period. The lease prohibited an assignment of Weaver's rights. Weaver used the workshop to produce custom textiles.

A year into the term, Weaver transferred her right of occupancy to Sculptor for one year. Sculptor moved into the workshop with his cot, electric hotplate, and clothes. He also brought several works of art that he had created during a stay in South America and offered them for sale along with his current works. Sculptor mailed his rent checks every month to Artist, who accepted them. Both Weaver and Sculptor knew the terms of the CC&Rs and Board's rules when they acquired their interests in the workshop.

Three months after Sculptor moved in, Board told Sculptor to stop selling his South American pieces. He refused to do so and thereafter withheld his rent and complained that the regulation was unreasonable and that the building's heating was erratic.

1. What action, if any, may Board take against Artist to enforce the rule against the sale of Sculptor's South American pieces? Discuss.
2. Can Artist recover from Weaver the rent that Sculptor has refused to pay? Discuss.
3. Can Artist evict Sculptor from his occupancy? Discuss.

Real Property Question 4 Assessment

July 2001, Question 2

This real property question is more difficult for most students than the average property question because the issues are raised in an unusual way by using a condominium board as a mechanism to test the concepts of equitable servitudes and/or real covenants, which are contained in the condominium CC&Rs. This question also covered the frequently tested landlord-tenant topics of assignment and subleasing.

As always, the areas highlighted in bold on the corresponding question grid indicate the issues and factual analysis that are required to receive a passing score on this question. You will notice that very little of the grid is highlighted in bold. This happens when a question is so broad that there are a variety of ways students could answer the question to "solve the problem" posed. Consequently, some of the unbolded analysis is required to pass the question, in addition to the bolded areas, but it isn't possible to identify which unbolded areas are strictly necessary because a variety of approaches are acceptable. For example, in call two of the question, it is essential to analyze Sculptor's defense to paying rent, but a discussion of any of the three theories identified are sufficient to pass this section of the question.

For the first call of this question, it is more likely that the question calls for an equitable servitudes discussion since the Board wanted to enforce the provision in equity, but a real covenant discussion is equally acceptable to the bar graders. Where the analysis is similar for two concepts, such as equitable servitudes and real covenants, it's best to fully analyze one and include a brief analysis of the other with the focus on analysis of how the two concepts differ. This approach ensures that you will get all of the allotted points for the discussion.

When you get a broad question like this on the exam, it can be nerve-racking because you are usually not certain about how to best approach answering the question. It may be reassuring to know that everyone else in the room probably feels exactly the same way you do. There is usually at least one question out of the six essay questions administered on each bar exam that leaves everyone stumped. This is when having a memorized checklist of issues can calm your nerves. Methodically go through the subject checklist and identify the topics that are involved. This will help narrow the scope of the question to something manageable. Do your best, don't spend more than an hour on the question, and then move on and don't think about it again.

Note the areas highlighted in **bold** on the corresponding grid. The bold areas highlight the issues, analysis, and conclusions that are likely **required** to receive a passing score on this question.

Issue	Rule	Fact Application	Conclusion
Call #1	Whether the CC&R's are enforceable against Artist depends on whether they can be enforced as a covenant running with the land or as an equitable servitude.		
Equitable servitude	Equitable servitudes are enforced in equity. To bind successors there must be • Writing (of promise between original parties/owners) • **Intent** (to bind future successors) • **Touch and concern the land** (benefit dominant estate by increased use or enjoyment; restrict servient estate by decreased use or enjoyment) • **Notice** (actual, inquiry, or constructive/record) [Or, could also do common plan or scheme analysis since all condos likely had same plan or scheme]	Writing: CC&R's between Condo and Artist likely in writing, giving Board authority to make new rules; also, board meetings and established rules likely put in writing as well to notify condo owners of new rules. **Intent: Board likely intended for the rules to bind successors to maintain consistency among homeowners; also, established long ago, indicating it was intended to continue binding future successors since it has likely been in existence through multiple owners based on time of it being established.** **Touch and concern:** The rule against outside sales would help to protect and promote the identity of the local crafters living within the condos and increase their use and enjoyment of the workshops and sales, as only their works can be sold; it would also restrict the owner's or assignees/subleases/tenants, as they cannot sell imported or other works not created within the condo workshops. On the other hand, it might not benefit the owners since they may want to sell other artworks and paintings and sculptures that they have acquired or made elsewhere, thus not benefiting the owners use or enjoyment of their land. **Notice:** Artist likely had actual notice since owners are often notified of new rules and/or can get Board minutes from meetings in writing; but at minimum, on inquiry notice since Artist could determine that owners only sold items made there, on-site; also, CC&R's are available for owners to view; if CC&R's are recorded in some Board regulations and/or minutes then constructive/record, **notice also met.**	Either way is acceptable

Continued >

Issue	Rule	Fact Application	Conclusion
		[Note: Since all owners had same limitation on sales, you could argue common scheme or plan; A should have been able to see by the fact that they were all selling only their own goods made there.]	Either way is acceptable
Real covenant	Real covenants are remedied with damages Same elements as above but including: • Horizontal privity (between originally promising parties): not required for benefit to run • **Vertical privity**: between grantor/ee or LL/T (new party holds entire durational interest held by the one making the covenant) **[Note: To pass call #1, you only need to do either covenant or equitable servitude, but go through all bolded elements (analysis could vary).]**	Horizontal privity: Artist would have received the CC&R's and new rules from the condo Board when purchasing the condo and rules established thereafter through board minutes or notices. **Vertical privity:** A owns the workshop and appears to be in privity with the original seller (likely the condo builder if he purchased it from the original seller).	Either way is acceptable
Call #2			
Privity of estate/ contract	LL can collect rent from a T with whom he is in privity of estate or contract. A sublease does not destroy the privity of contract. A novation (new contract to substitute a party) releases a party from their contractual obligations.	Since W sublet the condo to S, he is no longer in privity of estate with A because he is not sharing an interest in the land at all. **However, A and W are in privity of contract because they signed a 3-year lease**; also, since lease prohibited assignment, W would remain in privity of contract with A because he cannot assign his rights; the sublease to S would not destroy W/A privity of contract. Although A accepted S's rent checks, there is no indication that the parties signed a new k (here, a lease) replacing W with S.	**Privity of k exists**

Continued >

Issue	Rule	Fact Application	Conclusion
Defenses to paying rent	A T does not need to pay rent if certain defenses are available; W will argue that S does not need to pay rent (and therefore he doesn't either) due to the following defenses: • Constructive eviction • Implied Warranty of Habitability • Breach of quiet enjoyment **[Note: To pass this call, you just need to go through some type of defense, not all 3. The factual analysis could vary depending on the defense.]**	No constructive eviction because T never complained about erratic heat before and continued to live there rather than vacate; also, regulation likely reasonable since it was in place prior to S moving in and is enforced in all condos in the building; as above, notice exists. No warranty of habitability violation because condo is still fit for basic human habitation since S can live there, despite heat being erratic and the regulation; also, this is likely a commercial building and not residential, in which case warranty wouldn't apply because building consists of workshops and sales counters where tenants sell things they make there; also, S had to bring a cot, indicating there was no bed, and a hotplate indicating likely no stove. No quiet enjoyment, despite regulation, because S should have been on notice of regulation and rules prior to moving in and could still sell his works that he makes there.	**No defenses**
Call #3			
Assignment/ sublease	Generally, leases are freely assignable absent a contract to the contrary; **prohibitions against subleasing and/or assignments are enforceable.** An assignment occurs when the entire remainder interest is transferred; a sublease occurs when a portion of the remaining interest is transferred. LL may evict T based on breach of lease agreements or covenants generally if they are in privity of estate or contract. L must evict through the proper channels and not engage in self-help.	**Here, the lease contained a provision prohibiting assignments but not subleasing.** Here, W subleased the condo to S because only a portion of his lease was transferred since he only transferred 1 year to S, when he had 2 years remaining on the lease. **Since S's sublease is valid, A will not be able to evict based on that reason; also, S is not in privity of contract with A, and as a subleasee is also not in privity of estate with A, so A cannot evict S based on any of the CC&R violations.** Since S is not paying rent, LL can seek to evict W and any subtenant, here S, whose rights are derived from W's leasehold, but LL must go through the proper channels by giving notice to W and suing for damages (barring no defenses; see above).	**A can evict W, not S, directly**

Real Property Question 5

July 2007, Question 1

Larry leased in writing to Tanya a four-room office suite at a rent of $500 payable monthly in advance. The lease commenced on July 1, 2006. The lease required Larry to provide essential services to Tanya's suite. The suite was located on the 12th floor of a new 20-story office building.

In November Larry failed to provide essential services to Tanya's suite on several occasions. Elevator service and running water were interrupted once; heating was interrupted twice; and electrical service was interrupted on three occasions. These services were interrupted for periods of time lasting from one day to one week. On December 5, the heat, electrical and running water services were interrupted and not restored until December 12. In each instance Tanya immediately complained to Larry, who told Tanya that he was aware of the problems and was doing all he could to repair them.

On December 12, Tanya orally told Larry that she was terminating her lease on February 28, 2007 because the constant interruptions of services made it impossible for her to conduct her business. She picked the February 28 termination date to give herself ample opportunity to locate alternative office space.

Tanya vacated the suite on February 28 even though between December 12 and February 28 there were no longer any problems with the leased premises.

Larry did not attempt to relet Tanya's vacant suite until April 15. He found a tenant to lease the suite commencing on May 1 at a rent of $500 payable monthly in advance. On May 1, Larry brought suit against Tanya to recover rent for the months of March and April.

On what theory could Larry reasonably assert a claim to recover rent from Tanya for March and April and what defenses could Tanya reasonably assert against Larry's claim for rent? Discuss.

Real Property Question 5 Assessment

July 2007, Question 1

This real property question covers several straightforward landlord-tenant issues and includes a minor breach of contract and contract remedy analysis. This question is a good example of the real-life way a contract issue and a real property issue can be interwoven since underlying all landlord-tenant issues is the lease upon which the tenancy is based, which is nothing more than a contract.

This fact pattern centers on a commercial real estate lease and includes detailed facts regarding several service interruptions that have occurred to the premises, including disruptions to water, electrical, and heating. This question covers several landlord-tenant rules, but the issue spotting is not difficult, and successfully passing this question hinges on detailed and meaningful factual analysis of the issues presented. In particular, there are many facts to work with and include in the discussion and analysis of the various potential bases for a constructive eviction.

It is also worth noting that even though the parties had a commercial lease, and as such the implied warranty of habitability was not applicable, that issue and analysis must be identified in the exam answer. As always, even though the ultimate conclusion is that the rule is inapplicable, since the facts raise the issue it is still worth points on the exam to identify the issue and explain why the rule is not applicable under these facts. As a general rule, an issue should be included in the exam answer if during the time you organized your answer you thought of the issue, and then in your head applied the rule to the facts to reach the conclusion that the rule doesn't apply. If you had to think it through, the issue should be contained in your exam answer, though it is likely not necessary to spend a lot of time on such an issue. As you will note in the attached grid, the implied warranty of habitability issue could be appropriately dispatched in two sentences.

Note the areas highlighted in **bold** on the corresponding grid. The bold areas highlight the issues, analysis, and conclusions that are likely **required** to receive a passing score on this question.

Issue	Rule	Fact Application	Conclusion
Larry v. Tanya			
Type of tenancy	**A tenancy for years is one that has a determined, fixed period of time that ends at the end date with no notice required.** **A periodic tenancy is a lease that continues for successive or continuous intervals; until L or T gives proper notice of termination, there is a specific start date but no end date.**	**Since there is no end date in the lease between L and T, and only a beginning date, the lease would not be a term for years** **L and T signed a lease for monthly intervals to begin on July 1, 2006, with no set end date, making the lease a periodic tenancy since each month is an interval and there is no end date**	**Periodic tenancy**
Termination of lease	**To terminate a periodic tenancy, one party must give notice at the beginning of the interval period (according to the common law) in accordance with the length of the interval, and the termination should end at the end of an interval.** **Generally, the notice of termination must be in writing** and delivered.	**Since the interval is 1 month, the notice should be a 1-month notice as well, at the beginning of a month. Here, T gave L notice on 12/12, which was not in the beginning of an interval; however, her notice was for 2/28, which is still a 2-month notice if her actual notice date would not begin until the next interval, beginning in Jan., which is more than enough of a notice and it does end at the end of the month of Feb. so it ends at the end of an interval.** Here, T's notice was timely and delivered to L, as she informed him of her intent to terminate and the dates; **however, it was oral and not in writing which is required, making her notice ineffective.**	**L will properly assert that T's notice of termination was not valid**
Rent	T has a duty to pay rent, barring any defenses.	Here, since T did not properly terminate the lease, she must continue to pay rent for the months of Apr. and May, barring any valid defenses.	T must pay rent unless defense

Continued >

Issue	Rule	Fact Application	Conclusion
Tanya's Defenses			
Constructive eviction	**Occurs when there is substantial interference with the use and enjoyment of the land, T gives L notice so that L knows about interference, L fails to respond meaningfully, and T vacates in a reasonable period of time.**	Although L may argue that she could have used stairs and didn't need an elevator, **since her office was located on the 12th floor, it would be a substantial interference to walk up 12 flights of stairs**; further, some customers or clients may not be able to walk up stairs. As to the running water, arguably **a commercial office lease** may not need running water like a house, but there are still likely restrooms that **would require running water, making the interference substantial, especially since T was without running water for an entire week at one point and this occurred intermittently during a 2-month period.** **Heat may also be a necessity,** depending on the location of the office and temperatures of the area, without which there could be a substantial interference. **Electricity is certainly needed in a commercial office building suite for printing, faxing, emailing, any computer use, and many other office uses; this too was interrupted intermittently for 2 months and completely off for an entire week, which substantially interferes with any business productivity during those periods.** **T did notify L of these interruptions immediately on each occasion, and L further informed T that he was aware of the problems, indicating L was on notice and had knowledge.**	**Not a valid defense since T did not vacate timely**

Continued >

Issue	Rule	Fact Application	Conclusion
		The fact that L responded by stating he was doing all he could to repair the interruptions would not be meaningful, as required, because he promised in the lease to provide these essential services, and without that, T cannot use the property as she is paying to do so. Although the problems ceased to continue after T's notice to leave on 12/12, T still had a right to vacate since the interferences were substantial and all other elements are met; the problem is that she waited 2-1/2 months to vacate—and since her notice for termination was not written and not proper, **her delay in vacating may not be sufficient for a constructive eviction since it was long after the problems occurred and, at this point, T appears to have remedied the interferences; further, giving herself 2-1/2 months to locate a new office building indicates that it wasn't that substantial of an interference that she could no longer stay there and, in fact, she did continue to stay there.**	**Not a valid defense since T did not vacate timely**
Implied warranty of habitability	**Premises must be fit for basic human habitation; only applies to residential leases**	**Here, this is a commercial lease, not residential, since it is for a 4-room office suite on the 12th floor of a new 20-story office building, so this defense would not work for T.**	**Not an applicable defense**
Covenant of quiet enjoyment	Warranty that T's use and possession will not be interfered with (typically by 3rd parties).	Here, L is interfering with T's use and possession by not allowing her to use her office space as she agreed since he is not provided the services agreed to and she does not regularly have working elevators, running water, heat, or electricity.	Likely a valid defense

Continued >

Issue	Rule	Fact Application	Conclusion
Breach of k	The lease itself indicated that L would provide essential services to T.	Here, as indicated above, L breached the lease agreement by not providing the promised and agreed-to services, which would allow T to sue L for damages resulting from his breach.	Valid defense
Mitigation	L has a duty to mitigate damages.	Here, L did not mitigate the damages properly since he knew that T would be leaving at the end of Feb., yet L did not attempt to re-let the suite until 4/15, at which point it only took him 2 weeks to re-let the suite, indicating that had he attempted to re-let the space during the 2-1/2-month period after T's notice, he likely would have been able to do so, resulting in no downtime between tenants.	L did not mitigate his damages
Conclusion			T likely not liable for rent for Mar. and Apr.

Real Property Question 6

February 2005, Question 5

Alice and Bill were cousins, and they bought a house. Their deed of title provided that they were "joint tenants with rights of survivorship." Ten years ago, when Alice moved to a distant state, she and Bill agreed that he would occupy the house. In the intervening years, Bill paid nothing to Alice for doing so, but paid all house-related bills, including costs of repairs and taxes.

Two years ago, without Alice's knowledge or permission, Bill borrowed $10,000 from Lender and gave Lender a mortgage on the house as security for the loan.

There is a small apartment in the basement of the house. Last year, Bill rented the apartment for $500 per month to Tenant for one year under a valid written lease. Tenant paid Bill rent over the next seven months. During that time, Tenant repeatedly complained to Bill about the malfunctioning of the toilet and drain, but Bill did nothing. Tenant finally withheld $500 to cover the cost of plumbers he hired; the plumbers were not able to make the repair. Tenant then moved out.

Bill ceased making payments to Lender. Last month, Alice died and her estate is represented by Executor.

1. What interests do Bill, Executor, and Lender have in the house? Discuss.
2. What claims do Executor and Bill have against each other? Discuss.
3. Is Tenant obligated to pay any or all of the rent for the remaining term of his lease, including the $500 he withheld? Discuss.

Real Property Question 6 Assessment

February 2005, Question 5

This real property questions also covers some frequently tested landlord-tenant issues. However, the landlord-tenant issues are raised within the context of a fact pattern concerning the potential severance of a joint tenancy, the accounting responsibilities among joint tenants to each other, and the potential defenses for nonpayment of rent centering on the inadequate condition of the premises.

The challenging issue in this question concerns whether one joint tenant's unilateral acquisition of a mortgage operates to sever his joint tenancy. The rules are technical, and there is a jurisdictional split that leads to different results in states adopting the title theory and states adopting the lien theory. To receiving a passing score on this question, it is essential that both theories are identified and discussed. The other issues raised by the question are straightforward, frequently tested landlord-tenant issues.

Note the areas highlighted in **bold** on the corresponding grid. The bold areas highlight the issues, analysis, and conclusions that are likely **required** to receive a passing score on this question.

Issue	Rule	Fact Application	Conclusion
Call #1			
Joint tenancy	**JT: 2 or more own property with the right of survivorship.** **JT requires 4 unities: JTs take interest at the same time, in same title, identical equal interests, right to possess the whole, and clear right of survivorship.**	**Here, A and B took title on the same deed as joint tenants with rights of survivorship, which indicates the title was taken at the same time; in the same title (the deed); in equal interests, since they are identified as joint tenants; and likely both have the right to possess the whole.**	**JT exists**
Severance of JT	**JT can be terminated by severance** through a sale or inter vivos transfer, by partition, or through mortgage. For mortgages, there are two theories: • **Lien theory (majority): execution of the mortgage by one joint tenant does not sever the JT.** • **Title theory (minority): execution of mortgage by one joint tenant on his share will sever the JT as to his share, only making him a tenant in common with the other joint tenants.**	Here, B borrowed $10,000 from L and gave L a mortgage on the house as security; thus, the mortgage may have severed the JT depending on whether the mortgage was in a lien or title theory jurisdiction. **In a lien theory jurisdiction, the JT would not be severed, but rather the mortgage would just create a lien on the house, which would give B all of A's interest in the house when A died. Thus, the Executor would not have any interest in the house since it would not be a part of A's estate once she died; L would still have the mortgage on the house** and could foreclose on the house if B stopped paying on that mortgage. **In a title theory jurisdiction, the JT would be severed as to B's share, and since there are only A and B, they would become tenants in common, resulting in both A and B owning 50% of the house at A's death, but only B's share would be subject to the mortgage since A was not a party to the mortgage because one joint tenant cannot encumber the interest of another joint tenant, as B tried to do here with the mortgage. So the Executor would have the right to A's 50%, not subject to the mortgage, and B would have the other 50%, subject to L's mortgage.**	Depends on jurisdiction

Continued >

Issue	Rule	Fact Application	Conclusion
Call #2: Executor v. Bill			
Rent	**Co-tenants must share net rents from 3rd parties.** Co-tenants have the right to possess the whole; one co-tenant out of possession cannot bring a possessory action unless they are ousted.	**Here, B must share 50% of the rents with A since they are co-tenants, indicating B owes A, or the Executor here, the $250 per month for the 7 months that Tenant paid rent to B.** Since A had the right to possess the whole and chose not to and was not ousted, she is not due any money from B simply because he chose to possess the whole for the 10 years when A did not.	**Executor gets $1,750**
Call #2: Bill v. Executor			
Bills, repairs, taxes	**Co-tenants are responsible for their share of carrying costs, such as taxes and mortgage interest payments.** **Co-tenants must share the cost of necessary repairs, but there is no right to reimbursement for improvements.**	**Bills: B would have the right to reimbursement for the "house-related bills" that were related to necessary repairs and taxes, but not for house-related bills incidental to his use and possession of the property, which he chose to utilize.** **Repairs: B would be entitled to any necessary repairs, but not optional or improvement-type repairs; the Executor would owe B for 50% of any necessary repairs, but not any other repairs.** **Taxes: Here, A and B both have a duty to split and pay the taxes, but only B paid the taxes; thus, B can seek reimbursement from A's Executor for half of the taxes he paid over the past 10 years.** Note: A would not be responsible for the mortgage payments here since B unilaterally and without A's permission created the mortgage 2 years ago, so only B would be liable for that mortgage and could not recover any payments from Executor for it.	See conclusion in analysis.

Continued >

Issue	Rule	Fact Application	Conclusion
Call #3			
Type of LL/T	Tenancy for years: a lease for a fixed period of time.	Here, there is a tenancy for years since the lease is for a fixed period of time—for 1 year.	Tenancy for years (LL/T)
Rent	Tenants have a duty to pay rent, barring any valid defenses.	Here, T must pay the $500 per month rent unless a defense applies since he signed a 1-year, valid written lease, agreeing to do so.	T pays rent unless valid defense
Defenses to rent	Some defenses to rent include: • **Quiet enjoyment/constructive eviction: substantial interference with use and enjoyment; T gives notice to L, L doesn't respond meaningfully, and T must timely vacate** • **Implied warranty of habitability: T may terminate lease and move out, repair and deduct, reduce rent, or remain and sue for damages**	**T may argue that he was constructively evicted since a malfunctioning toilet and drain would substantially interfere with one's use and enjoyment of his rented apartment since those are two necessary items that are used daily and necessarily in an apartment; also, T repeatedly complained to B putting him on notice; B did nothing and T did move out.** **Breach of implied warranty of habitability because the premises—a residential apartment in the basement—would not be fit for basic human habitation if there was not a working toilet and drain and could cause substantial ventilation problems and pose a health hazard in the bathroom area; also, T attempted to repair the problem by hiring a plumber, who was not able to fix the problem, and so he was entitled to withhold that repair cost and deduct it from his rent.**	**T has valid defenses and does not owe B rent money**

PART 10 REMEDIES

REMEDIES TABLE OF CONTENTS

INTRODUCTION TO REMEDIES

A remedies essay question will always arise within the context of a fact pattern involving another substantive area of law. For this reason remedies questions are usually, but not always, crossover questions. A crossover question is one that tests two or more substantive areas of law within one essay fact pattern. Remedies questions typically cross over with contracts, torts, or real property, though any subject on the California bar exam is eligible.

As for the substance of remedies, though they are not identical, there are many overlapping concepts between the remedies available in tort, contract, and property. Consequently, remedies lends itself to several ways of being organized for the purposes of memorization and recall. Remedies is organized here by the underlying subject (torts, contracts, property), but it is equally valid to organize the material by listing all legal remedies and then all equitable remedies, or by the underlying cause of action, or some other way. The best way to organize the material is the way that makes the most sense to you. It is not important how the material is organized, just that it is done in a way that it is easy to recall and is memorable so that issues aren't missed and rules are recalled accurately.

When faced with a remedies essay question, the first step is to identify the underlying substantive area of law and that the defendant in question is responsible. A plaintiff can't obtain a remedy against a random person who didn't do anything actionable to the plaintiff, such as commit a tort or breach a contract or violate some law. Further, there can't be a discussion of remedies without first identifying if there is an underlying cause of action giving rise to the remedy. If there isn't an underlying cause of action that would support a remedy, identify the remedy the plaintiff would seek (if there were an underlying cause of action) and conclude that the relief sought won't be granted.

Pay careful attention to the call of the question and only answer the question asked. The depth of discussion on the underlying cause of action depends entirely on the call of the question. Be sure to determine if the question is asking for a discussion of the underlying cause of action, or if the question is limited to remedies only and respond accordingly. If the question is asking for a discussion of the underlying cause of action be sure to go through your checklist for that subject, in addition to your remedies checklist, to issue spot the exam. As always, carefully read each sentence of the question to determine if the facts contained therein give rise to a legal issue, or can be used to bolster the factual analysis of a rule.

Unless directed otherwise by the call of the question, legal remedies should be discussed first, then equitable remedies. First discuss the legal remedy of all available forms of money damages, using all of the facts and factual inferences available to make calculations. Next, discuss any appropriate legal restitutionary remedies, including money restitution, replevin, or ejectment. Next discuss, any appropriate equitable restitutionary remedies, including constructive trust or equitable lien in tort, and/or rescission or reformation in contract. Lastly, address the equitable remedy of the various types of injunction.

ISSUES CHECKLIST

TORTS REMEDIES

Damages
- Compensatory
- Nominal
- Punitive

Legal restitution
- Money
- Replevin/ejectment

Equitable restitution
- Constructive trust
- Equitable lien

Injunction
- TRO
- Preliminary injunction
- Permanent injunction

CONTRACTS REMEDIES

Damages
- Expectation
- Consequential
- Reliance
- Liquidated
- Nominal

Legal restitution
- Money—quasi-contract
- Replevin/ejectment

Equitable remedies
- Rescission
- Reformation

Injunction
- TRO
- Preliminary injunction
- Specific performance

MEMORIZATION ATTACK SHEET

LEGAL DAMAGES—TORT

- ♦ **Compensatory**
  - General (all P's)
  - Special (this P)
- ♦ **Nominal**
- ♦ **Punitive**
- ♦ **Compensatory limitation**
  - Causation
  - Foreseeable
  - Certainty
  - Unavoidable

LEGAL RESTITUTION—TORT

- ♦ **Money restitution**
- ♦ **Replevin** (chattel)
- ♦ **Ejectment** (real property)

EQUITABLE RESTITUTION—TORT

- ♦ **Constructive trust**
  - Wrongful act
  - Legal title to convey
  - Inadequate legal remedy
    - Damages too speculative
    - Insolvent D
    - Replevin not available
    - Property is unique
  - Property can be traced
    - P gets benefit of value increase
    - Property must be solely traceable
    - Lowest intermediate balance rule
  - Third-party priority
    - BFP over P
    - P over unsecured creditors
- ♦ **Equitable lien**
  - Wrongful act
  - Legal title to convey
  - Inadequate legal remedy
    - Damages too speculative
    - Insolvent D
    - Replevin not available
    - Property is unique
  - Property can be traced
    - Okay if not solely traceable
    - Lowest intermediate balance rule
  - Third-party priority
    - BFP over P
      - P over unsecured creditors

INJUNCTION—TORT

- ♦ **TROs**
  - Irreparable harm
  - Likely success on merits
  - Inadequate legal remedy
    - Damages too speculative
    - Inadequate because health/ safety issue
    - Insolvent D
    - Multiplicity of suits
    - Prospective tort
    - Property is unique
  - Balancing of hardships
- ♦ **Preliminary injunction**
  - Irreparable harm
  - Likely success on merits
  - Inadequate legal remedy
    - Damages too speculative
    - Inadequate because health/ safety issue
    - Insolvent D
    - Multiplicity of suits
    - Prospective tort
    - Property is unique
  - Balancing of hardships
  - No defenses
    - Laches
    - Unclean hands

- **Permanent injunction**
  - Inadequate legal remedy
    - Damages too speculative
    - Inadequate because health/safety issue
    - Insolvent D
    - Multiplicity of suits
    - Prospective tort
    - Property is unique
  - Property interest
  - Feasibility of enforcing
  - Balancing of hardships
  - No defenses
    - Laches
    - Unclean hands

LEGAL DAMAGES—CONTRACT

- **Types of legal damages**
  - Expectation
  - Consequential
  - Incidental
  - Reliance
  - Liquidated damages
    - Difficult to calculate
    - Reasonable relationship
  - Nominal damages
  - No punitives in contract
- **Damage limitations**
  - Causation
  - Foreseeable
  - Certainty
  - Unavoidable
  - Liquidated clause controls

LEGAL RESTITUTION—CONTRACT

- **Quasi-contract** (money restitution)
- **Replevin** (chattel)
- **Ejectment** (real property)

EQUIT. REMEDIES—CONTRACT

- **Rescission** (undo bargain)
- **Reformation** (rewrite the k)
- **Equitable defenses**
  - Laches
  - Unclean hands

INJUNCTION—CONTRACT

- **TROs** (see tort injunction)
- **Preliminary injunction** (see tort injunction)
- **Specific performance**
  - Contract is valid
  - Contract conditions satisfied
  - Inadequate legal remedy
    - Damages too speculative
    - Inadequate because health/safety issue
    - Insolvent D
    - Multiplicity of suits
    - Property is unique
  - Mutuality of performance
  - Feasibility of enforcement
  - No defenses
    - Laches
    - Unclean hands

REMEDIES RULE OUTLINE

I. **TORTS REMEDIES**

A. **Legal damages:** Damages are a legal remedy awarded to make a plaintiff whole. There are various measures of damages available as a remedy for tort.

1. **Compensatory damages** are awarded to compensate the plaintiff for injury or loss.

a. **Potential issues that can limit compensatory damages:**

1. **Causation:** Damages must be caused by the tortious act. This is actual "but-for" causation analysis.

2. **Foreseeable:** Damages must be foreseeable by a reasonable person at the time of the tortious act.

3. **Certainty:** Damages must be capable of being calculated with certainty and not be overly speculative.

4. **Unavoidable:** A plaintiff has a duty to mitigate his losses. The avoidable consequences doctrine limits damages to those that could not reasonably have been avoided.

> Exam tip: The list above is a mini-checklist of issues to consider when analyzing tort damages. These concepts have the **potential to limit an award of damages,** and if any facts in an essay question raise any of these topics as an issue, they should be thoroughly analyzed. However, if no facts are available that raise the issues, they need not be discussed.

b. **Types of damages:** There are two different types of compensatory damages in tort.

1. **General damages** are noneconomic losses directly attributable to the tort that **all plaintiffs** would have because they flow as a natural result of the tort (e.g., pain and suffering, disfigurement, etc.).

2. **Special damages** are economic losses directly attributable to the tort that some plaintiffs may have and are **unique to each specific plaintiff** (e.g., medical bills, lost wages, etc.).

2. **Pure economic loss** is not recoverable for most torts, absent a showing of property loss or personal injury.

a. **Exception: Intentional interference with business relations** does allow for pure economic loss recovery.

3. **Nominal damages** are awarded where the plaintiff's rights have been violated but the plaintiff sustained no loss.

4. **Punitive damages** will be found where the defendant has displayed willful and wanton tortious misconduct. Punitive damages are only awarded if:

a. **Damage award** (compensatory damages, nominal damages, or restitutionary damages); and

b. **Culpability** of defendant is greater than "negligence"; and
c. **Relative proportionality** to actual damages. (Typically, a multiplier of actual damages—e.g., a maximum of ten times actual damages.)

> <u>Exam tip:</u> When issue-spotting the exam, be sure to look for facts that may raise the **four potential limitations** on compensatory damages: causation, foreseeability, certainty, and duty to mitigate. In addition, there are **different measures of damages** that can be suffered by a plaintiff, so consider whether the plaintiff is entitled to compensatory damages—either general or special—nominal damages, or punitive damages. Lastly, use the facts available to **make damages calculations,** if possible.

B. **Legal restitution** is appropriate where the **defendant has derived a benefit**, or been unjustly enriched, and it would be unfair to allow the defendant to keep that benefit without compensating the plaintiff, or where the plaintiff wants his property back. The goal of restitution is to **prevent unjust enrichment.**
   1. **Money restitution** is a legal remedy where the plaintiff is awarded the **monetary value of the benefit received** by the defendant.
   2. **Replevin** allows the recovery, before trial, of a specific **chattel** wrongfully taken.
   3. **Ejectment** is used to recover specific **real property** from which the plaintiff was wrongfully excluded.

> <u>Exam tip:</u> A fact pattern indicating the **defendant has benefited from plaintiff's loss** will often trigger a discussion of restitution. A plaintiff can recover either compensatory damages or money restitution, but not both. However, on an essay answer both should be discussed, if appropriate, to demonstrate the difference between to the two concepts since the rules and calculations will be slightly different.

C. **Equitable restitution** is only available when the **remedy at law,** money damages, is **inadequate.** The goal of any equitable remedy is to prevent unjust enrichment.
   1. **Constructive trust** restores property to the plaintiff that has been wrongfully acquired by the defendant. A constructive trust, fictitiously imposed by the court, **compels the defendant to transfer title to unjustly retained property.** The sole obligation of the constructive trustee defendant is to transfer the property back to the plaintiff.
      a. A **wrongful act** has led to the detention of property from its rightful owner.

b. **Legal title to convey:** Since the court will order the defendant to **reconvey title** to the plaintiff, the defendant must have wrongfully obtained legal title to the property; mere possession is not enough.
c. **Inadequate legal remedy:** The remedy at law, typically money damages, must be inadequate. There are several reasons the legal remedy can be inadequate:
   1. **Money damages are too speculative** to calculate with certainty.
   2. **Insolvent defendant** such that any damages award is worthless.
   3. **Replevin is unavailable** because the property has been sold and thus can't be ordered returned to plaintiff.
   4. **Property is unique** so money damages are inadequate to compensate for the loss of that property.
      a. **Real property is always unique.**
      b. **Personal property is not unique, except** if it is one-of-a-kind or very rare, or if the item has special personal significance to the plaintiff.
d. **Property can be traced:** A constructive trust can apply to specific property acquired by a wrongdoer that is traceable to the wrongful behavior. If the improperly retained property is sold or exchanged for new property, the rightful owner can "trace" and obtain a constructive trust for the new property. (E.g.: Embezzled funds could go in a bank account or be used to purchase real property.)
   1. **Plaintiff receives the benefit of any increase in property value** accrued by the passage of time or the change in property form because it would be unfair to allow the wrongdoer to receive the benefit of any gain.
   2. **Property must be solely traceable to current form** and not commingled with other property because title to the property will be given to the plaintiff. (E.g.: Embezzled funds used to remodel an existing home aren't solely traceable.)
   3. **Lowest intermediate balance rule applies to commingled funds** (where the wrongdoer commingles wrongfully obtained funds with his own funds in a single account). This rule includes application of the "investor fiction," which presumes a defendant invests his own money first, and the **"spender fiction,"** which presumes a defendant spends his own money first.
e. **Priority of plaintiff over third parties** with an interest
   1. **Bona fide purchaser with legal title prevails over plaintiff.** (A BFP took for **value without notice** of the facts giving rise to the potential constructive trust.)
   2. **Plaintiff prevails over unsecured creditors.**

2. **Equitable lien** creates a security interest in property held by the defendant. This is a legal fiction implied by the court where the **property acts as collateral for the money owed to the plaintiff.** An

equitable lien is similar to a constructive trust, except property can be traced to commingled funds with an equitable lien.

a. A **wrongful act** has led to the detention of property from its rightful owner.
b. **Legal title:** Since the court will order a **security interest** in the property itself, the defendant must have wrongfully obtained legal title to the property; mere possession is not enough.
c. **Inadequate legal remedy:** The remedy at law, typically money damages, must be inadequate. There are several reasons the legal remedy can be inadequate:
   1. **Money damages are too speculative** to calculate with certainty.
   2. **Insolvent defendant,** such that any damages award is worthless.
   3. **Replevin is unavailable** because the property has been sold and thus can't be ordered returned to plaintiff.
   4. **Property is unique** so money damages are inadequate to compensate for the loss of that property.
      a. **Real property is always unique.**
      b. **Personal property is not unique, except** if it is one-of-a-kind or very rare, or if the item has special personal significance to the plaintiff.
d. **Property can be traced:** An equitable lien can apply to specific property acquired by a wrongdoer that is traceable to the wrongful behavior. If the improperly retained property is sold or exchanged for new property, the rightful owner can "trace" and obtain an equitable lien on the new property.
   1. **Property *need not be solely traceable* to current form:** *Unlike a constructive trust,* with an equitable lien it is acceptable to trace the plaintiff's property to a different piece of property even if the two are commingled and the plaintiff's property (or money traced from that property) was used to improve another piece of property properly owned by the defendant. The plaintiff can obtain an equitable lien on the commingled property in the amount of the debt.
   2. **Lowest intermediate balance rule applies to commingled funds** (where the wrongdoer commingles wrongfully obtained funds with his own funds in a single account). This rule includes application of the "investor fiction," which presumes a defendant invests his own money first, and the **"spender fiction,"** which presumes a defendant spends his own money first.
e. **Priority of the plaintiff over third parties** with an interest
   1. **Bona fide purchaser with legal title prevails over plaintiff.** (A BFP took for **value without notice** of the facts giving rise to the potential equitable lien.)
   2. **Plaintiff prevails over unsecured creditors.**

> **Exam tip:** Unless instructed otherwise, on an essay **analyze both** constructive trust and an equitable lien and use the facts to explain which of the two is the better remedy to use under the circumstances and why. **Constructive trust is better** when the value of the wrongfully acquired property goes up (because plaintiff will receive the benefit of the increase in value to prevent defendant's unjust enrichment). **Equitable lien is better** when the value of the wrongfully acquired property goes down (because plaintiff can still get a deficiency judgment for the difference), or when property can't be solely traced to its current form.

D. **Injunction** is an equitable remedy where the court **orders one to perform an act** (affirmative or mandatory injunction) or stop performing an act (negative injunction). There are three types, with many similar requirements:
   1. **Temporary restraining orders (TROs)** are designed to **preserve the status quo** for a **short time** pending further litigation regarding a preliminary injunction. TROs are granted for only a short time, typically ten days, and can sometimes be obtained ex parte. A TRO requires:
      a. **Irreparable harm** during waiting time if not granted.
      b. **Likely success on the merits.**
      c. **Inadequate legal remedy:**
         1. **Money damages are too speculative** to calculate with certainty.
         2. **Money damages may be inadequate** to compensate for the potential loss. This is especially true where there is a health or safety concern.
         3. **Insolvent defendant,** such that any damages award is worthless.
         4. **Multiplicity of suits:** An ongoing wrong—for example, an ongoing nuisance for toxic waste dumping—would lead to a multiplicity of suits by the same litigants over the same issue if not resolved by an injunction.
         5. **Prospective tort** where the tort has not occurred yet but is expected to occur (e.g., imminent pollution).
         6. **Property is unique** so money damages are inadequate to compensate for the loss of that property.
            a. **Real property is always unique.**
            b. **Personal property is not unique, except** if it is one-of-a-kind or very rare, or if the item has special personal significance to the plaintiff.
      d. **Balancing of hardships** must favor plaintiff. The court will weigh the **hardship to plaintiff if the injunction is denied** against the **hardship to defendant if the injunction is granted**. The court will also consider the following factors:
         1. A **large disparity in hardships** weighs in favor of the more severely impacted party.

2. **Willful misconduct** weighs heavily against the wrongdoer.
3. **Public interest:** The hardship to the public and/or any public benefit can also be factored into the analysis.

> Exam tip: There is a lot of factual analysis when **balancing the hardships.** It is important to use **all of the facts** and factual inferences, present **both sides**, come to a conclusion, and **explain why** the hardships balance in the favor of the party you conclude should prevail.

2. **Preliminary injunctions** are designed to **preserve the status quo pending a full trial** on the merits. A preliminary injunction is a bit harder to obtain than a TRO, but it is easier to obtain than a permanent injunction. Some of the elements to satisfy are the same as a TRO and include:
   a. **Irreparable harm** during waiting time if not granted.
   b. **Likely success on the merits.**
   c. **Inadequate legal remedy:**
      1. **Money damages are too speculative** to calculate with certainty.
      2. **Money damages may be inadequate** to compensate for the potential loss. This is especially true where there is a health or safety concern.
      3. **Insolvent defendant,** such that any damages award is worthless.
      4. **Multiplicity of suits:** An ongoing wrong—for example, an ongoing nuisance for toxic waste dumping—would lead to a multiplicity of suits by the same litigants over the same issue if not resolved by an injunction.
      5. **Prospective tort** where the tort has not occurred yet but is expected to occur (e.g., imminent pollution).
      6. **Property is unique** so money damages are inadequate to compensate for the loss of that property.
         a. **Real property is always unique.**
         b. **Personal property is not unique, except** if it is one-of-a-kind or very rare, or if the item has special personal significance to the plaintiff.
   d. **Balancing of hardships** must favor plaintiff. The court will weigh the **hardship to plaintiff if the injunction is denied** against the **hardship to defendant if the injunction is granted.** The court will also consider the following factors:
      1. A **large disparity in hardships** weighs in favor of the more severely impacted party.
      2. **Willful misconduct** weighs heavily against the wrongdoer.
      3. **Public interest:** The hardship to the public and/or any public benefit can also be factored into the analysis.
   e. **No defenses** are available.

1. **Laches** applies when the plaintiff has unreasonably delayed, resulting in prejudice to the defendant.
2. **Unclean hands** applies when a plaintiff has conducted herself unfairly in the transaction in dispute.
3. **Ineffective defenses** that may be raised:
   a. **Coming to the nuisance:** Modernly, this is one of several elements used to determine if there is a nuisance at all and does not provide an effective defense to a nuisance action.
   b. **Sale to a bona fide purchaser** is not an effective defense to the tort of conversion (where one is trying to get their personal property returned by a permanent injunction). However, sale to a BFP is a valid defense in a contract action.

> Exam tip: **Injunction defenses** are frequently tested. Analyze laches whenever a time delay is stated. Analyze unclean hands whenever one party expressed any idea/wish/desire to the other party that was later ignored. Often, after analyzing, the conclusion is that the defense is ineffective.

3. **Permanent injunction** is where a court orders one to perform an act or stop performing an act. A permanent injunction requires the following:
   a. **Inadequate legal remedy:**
      1. **Money damages are too speculative** to calculate with certainty.
      2. **Money damages may be inadequate** to compensate for the potential loss. This is especially true where there is a health or safety concern.
      3. **Insolvent defendant,** such that any damages award is worthless.
      4. **Multiplicity of suits:** An ongoing wrong—for example, an ongoing nuisance for toxic waste dumping—would lead to a multiplicity of suits by the same litigants over the same issue if not resolved by an injunction.
      5. **Prospective tort** where the tort has not occurred yet but is expected to occur (e.g., imminent pollution).
      6. **Property is unique** so money damages are inadequate to compensate for the loss of that property.
         a. **Real property is always unique.**
         b. **Personal property is not unique, except** if it is one-of-a-kind or very rare, or if the item has special personal significance to the plaintiff.
   b. **Property interest:** The requirement of a protectable property interest is a historical one and traditionally meant an injunction would only apply to property. California does not require a property

right, and modernly, invasions of personal rights can support an injunction.

c. **Feasibility of enforcement:** The injunction cannot be too difficult for the court to enforce.
   1. **Negative injunctions** are easier to enforce because of the court's power to order contempt for noncompliance.
   2. **Affirmative injunctions** are more difficult to enforce.
      a. **Series of acts** over a period of time can be more difficult to enforce than one required act.
      b. **Act requiring taste, judgment, or skill** is difficult to enforce because of the difficulty in determining if the act has been properly performed.
   3. **Jurisdictional issues** cause enforcement problems where the court would have to supervise events out of their jurisdiction or assert control over nonparties to the litigation.

d. **Balancing of hardships** must favor plaintiff. The court will weigh the **hardship to plaintiff if the injunction is denied** against the **hardship to defendant if the injunction is granted**. The court will also consider the following factors:
   1. A **large disparity in hardships** weighs in favor of the more severely impacted party.
   2. **Willful misconduct** weighs heavily against the wrongdoer.
   3. **Public interest:** The hardship to the public and/or any public benefit can also be factored into the analysis.

e. **No defenses**
   1. **Laches** applies when the plaintiff has unreasonably delayed, resulting in prejudice to the defendant.
   2. **Unclean hands** applies when a plaintiff has conducted herself unfairly in the transaction in dispute.
   3. **Ineffective defenses** that may be raised:
      a. **Coming to the nuisance:** Modernly, this is one of several elements used to determine if there is a nuisance at all and does not provide an effective defense to a nuisance action.
      b. **Sale to a bona fide purchaser** is not an effective defense to the tort of conversion (where one is trying to get their personal property returned by a permanent injunction). However, sale to a BFP is a valid defense in a contract action.

> Memorization tip: Use the mnemonic **I Pray For Big Desserts** to memorize the five essential elements of a permanent injunction: Inadequate legal remedy, Property interest, Feasibility of enforcement, Balancing of hardships, and no Defenses.

II. CONTRACTS REMEDIES

A. **Legal damages** are applicable where the parties have a contract, the defendant is in breach, and the plaintiff has been injured by the breach and wants money to compensate for the loss.

1. **Types of damages**
   a. **Expectation damages** (compensatory damages) in contract compensate plaintiff for the **value of the benefit plaintiff expected to receive** from the contract.
   b. **Consequential damages** seek to compensate for damages that are a **direct and foreseeable consequence** of the contract not being performed and are found in addition to expectation damages.
   c. **Incidental damages** include those **reasonably incurred** by a buyer in rejecting nonconforming goods, or by a seller in reselling goods resulting from a buyer's breach (e.g., storage, transportation costs).
   d. **Reliance damages** seek to put the **plaintiff in the same position** he would have been in had the contract never been made. The measure is the cost to plaintiff of his performance.
   e. **Liquidated damages** are stipulated to in a clause in the contract. A liquidated damages clause is proper when:
      1. Damages are **difficult to calculate**; and
      2. The stipulated amount in the liquidated damages clause bears a **reasonable relationship to the anticipated loss.**
   f. **Nominal damages** serve as a declaration that the contract has been breached, but plaintiff has not suffered a loss.
   g. **Punitive damages are *not* awarded in contract**, unless the misconduct rises to the level of an independent tort.

> <u>Exam tip:</u> When calculating contract damages take the **plaintiff's point of view** and determine the value of the contract to the plaintiff had the contract been properly performed. If the fact pattern provides numbers, use them to **calculate the damages**. If the fact pattern does not provide numbers, use descriptors, such as "lost wages" to explain the potential damages available. **Include all possible damages** in your calculations.

2. **Potential limitations on contract damages**
   a. **Causation:** Damages must be caused by the contract breach.
   b. **Foreseeable:** Damages must be foreseeable to a **reasonable person** at the time of **contract formation.**
   c. **Certainty:** Damages must be capable of being **calculated with certainty** and not be overly speculative. (It is often difficult to calculate with certainty future losses, particularly for a new business.)
   d. **Unavoidable:** A plaintiff has a **duty to mitigate** his losses, and the avoidable consequences doctrine limits damages to those that could not reasonably have been avoided.
   e. **Liquidated damages** clause that is valid will control and be the **only measure of damages allowed** for breach of the underlying contract.

> **Exam tip:** The list above is a mini-checklist of issues to consider when analyzing contract damages. These concepts have the **potential to limit an award of damages,** and if any facts in an essay question raise any of these topics as an issue, they should be thoroughly analyzed before calculating damages. However, these issues need not be analyzed if not raised by the facts.

B. **Legal restitution** is appropriate where the **defendant has derived a benefit**, or been unjustly enriched, and it would be unfair to allow the defendant to keep that benefit without compensating the plaintiff, or where the plaintiff wants his property back. The **goal of restitution is to prevent unjust enrichment.**
   1. **Quasi-contract** (money restitution) applies where there is no legally binding contract, but the **defendant has derived a benefit** and **fairness requires payment** to plaintiff. Quasi-contract can arise three ways:
      a. **No attempt to contract:** The plaintiff can recover the value of the benefit unjustly retained by defendant (e.g., emergency services).
      b. **Unenforceable contract:** The plaintiff can recover the value of the benefit unjustly retained by defendant (e.g., contract is illegal, SOF failure, etc.).
      c. **Breached contract:** Recovery depends on status.
         1. **Plaintiff is nonbreacher:** Plaintiff can recover the value of benefit conferred, or the plaintiff can get his property back.
         2. **Plaintiff is in breach:** The traditional majority rule provides for no recovery. The modern trend allows for recovery.
   2. **Replevin** allows the recovery, before trial, of a specific **chattel** wrongfully taken.
   3. **Ejectment** is used to recover specific **real property** from which the plaintiff was wrongfully excluded.

C. **Equitable remedies** are only available when the **remedy at law,** money damages, is **inadequate.** The goal of any equitable remedy is to prevent unjust enrichment. There are two equitable remedies that are specific to contracts.
   1. **Rescission** permits a party to **undo a bargain** and restores the parties to the position each would have been in if the bargain had not been entered into.
      a. **No meeting of the minds:** There must be a contract formation problem resulting from fraud, duress, mistake, or a material misrepresentation.
      b. **Defenses** of laches and unclean hands are applicable.
   2. **Reformation rewrites the contract** to reflect the parties' true agreement where the written document does not accurately reflect the agreement. There must have been a valid contract in the first place.
      a. **Proper grounds** for reformation include fraud, material misrepresentation, or mistake (e.g., scrivener's error).
      b. **Defenses** of laches and unclean hands are applicable.

D. **Injunction**
   1. **TROs** are the same as in tort. (See I.D.1 above.)
   2. **Preliminary injunctions** are the same as in tort. (See I.D.2 above.)
   3. **Specific performance** is a permanent injunction in contract where the **court orders the defendant to perform on the contract** as promised. The following requirements must be met:
      a. **Contract is valid:** The contract must be valid and the terms sufficiently definite and certain.
      b. **Contract conditions** imposed on the plaintiff are satisfied.
      c. **Inadequate legal remedy:**
         1. **Money damages are too speculative** to calculate with certainty.
         2. **Money damages may be inadequate** to compensate for the potential loss. This is especially true where there is a health or safety concern.
         3. **Insolvent defendant,** such that any damages award is worthless.
         4. **Multiplicity of suits:** An ongoing wrong—for example, an ongoing nuisance for toxic waste dumping—would lead to a multiplicity of suits by the same litigants over the same issue if not resolved by an injunction.
         5. **Property is unique** so money damages are inadequate to compensate for the loss of that property.
            a. **Real property is always unique.**
            b. **Personal property is not unique, except** if it is one-of-a-kind or very rare, or if the item has special personal significance to the plaintiff.
      d. **Mutuality of performance:** Both parties to the contract must be **eligible** to have their performance under the contract **ordered by the court**. This is only at issue where one party could not be ordered to perform. (E.g.: Contract for the sale of illegal goods, the contracting party is a minor, etc.)
      e. **Feasibility of enforcement:** The injunction cannot be too difficult for the court to enforce.
         1. **Negative injunctions** are easier to enforce because of the court's power to order contempt for noncompliance.
         2. **Affirmative injunctions** are more difficult to enforce. Specific performance is an affirmative injunction.
            a. **Series of acts** over a period of time can be more difficult to enforce than one required act.
            b. **Act requiring taste, judgment, or skill** is difficult to enforce because of the difficulty in determining if the act has been properly performed.
            c. **Personal services contract** will likely not be ordered because the court will not order a person to personally perform work for another.
         3. **Jurisdictional issues** cause enforcement problems where the court would have to supervise events out of their jurisdiction or assert control over nonparties to the litigation.

f. **No defenses**
   1. **Laches** applies when the plaintiff has unreasonably delayed, resulting in prejudice to the defendant.
   2. **Unclean hands** applies when a plaintiff has conducted herself unfairly in the transaction in dispute.
   3. **Defenses to the underlying contract:** Any failure of the underlying contract can operate as a defense since a valid contract is a requirement for an injunction (e.g., lack of consideration, SOF, sale to a bona fide purchaser, etc.).

> Memorization tip: Use the mnemonic **"Chocolate Cheesecake Is My Favorite Dessert"** to memorize the six essential elements of specific performance: valid **C**ontract, contract **C**onditions satisfied, **I**nadequate legal remedy, **M**utuality of performance, **F**easibility of enforcement, and no **D**efenses.

III. **REAL PROPERTY REMEDIES ISSUES:** Remedies issues can arise in a real property context. The typical remedies are damages, an ejectment, or an injunction, and they operate the same in a property context as they do in a contract or tort context.

A. **Encroachments** are trespasses where a defendant's structure invades the plaintiff's property. This could also be seen as an adverse possession action. With an encroachment, a plaintiff is entitled to damages, ejectment, and injunction.

B. **Waste** occurs where there is an "injury" to real property by one with a present interest against a future interest holder.
   1. **Voluntary waste** is a deliberate, destructive act. The remedy is damages for the diminution of value or the cost of repair, and/or an injunction.
   2. **Permissive waste** occurs when the property is poorly maintained. The remedy is damages for the cost of repair. Injunction is not usually available because supervision problems make enforcement infeasible.
   3. **Ameliorative waste** is where a present interest holder makes impermissible improvements to the property that actually enhance the property's value. Though a present interest holder is not permitted to do this, there are no damages because there is no loss in value. However, an injunction may be granted.

REMEDIES ISSUES TESTED MATRIX

		Crossover Subject (Other Substantive Issues)	Tort Damages	Restitution in Tort $	Injunction Tort	Constructive Trust/ Equitable Lien	Replevin	Contract Damages	Quasi-contract/ Restitution	Specific Performance	Injunction Contract	Defenses: Unclean Hands/Laches
February '11 Q6	Green's Grocery & lottery ticket w/wrong numbers	Evidence (hearsay, hearsay exceptions, parol evidence)							X			
February '10 Q4	Pat, partner of law firm & Chris the paralegal	Contracts (formation, defenses, gift, condition, waiver)						X	X	X		X
July '09 Q5	Diane builds dam for camp for disadvantaged kids	Civ. Pro. (res judicata); Prof. Resp. (confidentiality)			X							X
July '08 Q4	Barry & Sally; rare Phaeton car	Contracts (anticipatory repudiation)					X	X		X	X	
July '07 Q5	Paula the art dealer & Monay painting	Contracts (SOF, mistake, misrepresentation)								X		X
July '06 Q3	Resi-Clean housecleaning advertises with coupons	Contracts (formation, defenses, modification, breach, performance)						X				
February '06 Q5	Marla, Larry & widget buyer	Contracts (formation, defenses); Prof. Resp. (conflict, honesty)							X			
July '05 Q5	Stan & Barb; land sale/water rights	Contracts (PER, condition, price abatement, anticipatory repudiation)						X		X		X
July '04 Q6	Jack's "Star" uncut diamond & Chip the master diamond cutter	Torts (negligence, wrongful death, legal malpractice)	X					X				
July '03 Q2	Polly & Donald buy a house, but Donald uses embezzled funds	Wills & Trusts (purchase money resulting trust)				X						X

Continued >

		Crossover Subject (Other Substantive Issues)	Tort Damages	Restitution in Tort $	Injunction Tort	Constructive Trust/ Equitable Lien	Replevin	Contract Damages	Quasi-contract/ Restitution	Specific Performance	Injunction Contract	Defenses: Unclean Hands/Laches
February '02 Q2	Berelli & the specialty Tabor tomatoes	Contracts (formation, anticipatory repudiation)					X	X		X	X	X
February '01 Q4	Diane's office bldg & Peter's restaurant and garden	Torts (trespass to land, conversion, ejectment)	X	X	X							X
February '00 Q2	Chemco processing plant discharges waste into river	Torts (nuisance, trespass to land)	X		X							X
July '00 Q6	Don makes pottery & causes an electrical surge	Torts (strict liability, nuisance, negligence)	X									
July '99 Q5	Artist leases a loft & machinist is loud & State Power blocks path to park	Torts (nuisance); Real Prop. (warranties, easements)	X		X							
February '98 Q5	Halfway rehabs former convicts & neighbors form NASS to protest	Torts (nuisance)			X							
February '98 Q1	Carrier k's for all of Maker's transportation needs	Contracts (formation, anticipatory repudiation); Torts (tortious bus. interference)	X	X	X			X	X	X	X	
February '97 Q3	Debbie has oceanfront lot & her porch encroaches on Peter's property	Real Prop. (injunct., adv. poss.); Civ. Pro. (contempt, collateral bar rule)										X
July '95 Q4	Smith brings stolen car to CARS for repairs		X		X	X	X	X	X	X	X	
February '95 Q1	Neptune k's for 250 lbs. of salmon per week from SUP	Contracts (anticipatory repudiation, discharge)						X		X		
February '94 Q4	Fidelity & defective building built by Bildco	Torts (negligence, vicarious liability); Contracts (breach, 3rd PB)	X					X		X		

Continued >

		Crossover Subject (Other Substantive Issues)	Tort Damages	Restitution in Tort $	Injunction Tort	Constructive Trust/ Equitable Lien	Replevin	Contract Damages	Quasi-contract/ Restitution	Specific Performance	Injunction Contract	Defenses: Unclean Hands/Laches
July '92 Q6	Peter & sporting goods store location in ABC's new mall									X	X	
July '91 Q3	Henry, agent for Insco, embezzles funds	Torts (conversion)	X	X		X						
February '91 Q3	Refin operates a smelter & hauls toxic chemicals	Torts (nuisance)	X		X							
February '90 Q6	Joe & wealthy brother, Steve	Contracts (offer, acceptance, consideration, SOF)						X	X	X		
July '89 Q2	Dan interferes with Paul's new restaurant, chef; home purchase	Torts (interference w/bus. relations, IIED)	X	X	X	X						
July '88 Q3	Cobb remodels Owen's house & stops building	Contracts (breach, performance)						X			X	
July '87 Q3	Sam owns Blackacre & Whiteacre	Contracts (SOF, assignment, performance, breach, abatement, reformation)						X	X	X		
February '87 Q3	Owen owns 50 acres unzoned land	Real Prop. (equit. servitudes); Torts (nuisance)	X		X							
July '86 Q5	Alice's stolen $14,000 diamond ring	Torts (negligence, trespass to chattels, conversion)	X			X						

REMEDIES PRACTICE ESSAYS, ANSWER GRIDS, AND SAMPLE ANSWERS

Remedies Question 1

July 2008, Question 4

Barry is the publisher of *Auto Designer's Digest,* a magazine that appeals to classic car enthusiasts. For years, Barry has been trying to win a first place award in the annual Columbia Concours d'Elegance ("Concours"), one of the most prestigious auto shows in the country. He was sure that winning such an award would vastly increase the circulation of his magazine and attract lucrative advertising revenues. This year's Concours was scheduled to begin on June 1, with applications for entry to be submitted by May 1.

Sally owned a 1932 Phaeton, one of only two surviving cars of that make and model. The car was in such pristine condition that it stood a very good chance of winning the first place prize.

On April 1, Barry and Sally entered into a valid written contract by which Barry agreed to buy, and Sally agreed to sell, the Phaeton for $200,000 for delivery on May 25. In anticipation of acquiring the Phaeton, Barry completed the application and paid the nonrefundable $5,000 entry fee for the Concours.

On May 10, Sally told Barry that she had just accepted $300,000 in cash for the Phaeton from a wealthy Italian car collector, stating "That's what it's really worth," and added that she would deliver the car to a shipping company for transport to Italy within a week.

1. Can Barry sue Sally before May 25? Discuss.
2. What provisional remedies might Barry seek to prevent Sally from delivering the Phaeton to the shipping company pending resolution of his dispute with Sally, and would the court be likely to grant them? Discuss.
3. Can Barry obtain the Phaeton by specific performance or replevin? Discuss.
4. If Barry decides instead to seek damages for breach of contract, can he recover damages for: (a) the nondelivery of the Phaeton; (b) the loss of the expected increase in circulation and advertising revenues; and (c) the loss of the $5,000 nonrefundable entry fee? Discuss.

Remedies Question 1 Assessment

July 2008, Question 4

Most remedies essay questions are crossover questions testing both the underlying substantive area of law giving rise to the need for a remedy and the potential remedies, and this question is no exception. For this question, the underlying claim is for breach of contract on the sale of a rare car, though it primarily tests remedies. There is one call of the question devoted to the contracts issue and three calls addressing various specific remedies. This is a good example of what current essay questions look like, with very specific calls of the question. The good thing about this type of a question is that the issue spotting is easier since the specificity of the question limits the possible issues. The bad thing about this type of a question is that if you can't recall the specific rule that corresponds to the call of the question, there is nowhere to hide and it's hard not to panic and mess up the whole question. This is why it is essential to memorize all of the rules in order to succeed on the essay portion of the exam.

Below is a review of the essential points contained in the state-released passing student answers:

1. *Can Barry sue Sally before May 25?* A full discussion of the anticipatory repudiation issue and the result is necessary. Since the question itself states that the contract was written and valid, analysis of the underlying contract is unnecessary and a waste of valuable time.
2. *Are any provisional remedies available, and would the court grant them?* This section is challenging to organize and may be done in several ways. The order of presentation is not as important as making it easy for the grader to find the key analysis by using issue headings for each legal concept. That way, even if you've chosen to organize in an atypical way, issue headings allow the grader to easily find the issues and key analyses. While an injunction has five elements (inadequate legal remedy, property right, feasibility of enforcement, balancing of hardships, and no defenses), a passing answer could focus analysis only on the elements at issue in this fact pattern—here, a full analysis of the inadequate legal remedy and balancing of hardships elements is required. Because the call of the question specifically asks about provisional remedies, a full discussion of a temporary restraining order and preliminary injunction is also necessary. The provisional remedies of TRO and preliminary injunction are being tested with increasing frequency.
3. *Can B obtain the Phaeton (car) by specific performance or replevein?* Analysis of this call is a very straightforward application of facts to the rules.
4. *Can B recover breach of contract damages for the nondelivery of the car, the loss of anticipated revenues, and the $5,000 entry fee?* The damages analysis on the nondelivery of the car is straightforward, but be sure to analyze separately each category of damages asked about. Damages relating from the loss of magazine revenues and the loss of entry fee should focus on analysis of the uncertainty and unforeseeability of damages of this type.

Note the areas highlighted in **bold** on the corresponding grid. The bold areas highlight the issues, analysis, and conclusions that are likely **required** to receive a passing score on this question. In general, the essay grids are provided to assist you in analyzing the essays, and are much more detailed than what a student should create during the exam to organize their response to a question.

Issue	Rule	Fact Application	Conclusion
1. Can Barry Sue Before 5/25?			
Contract	K requires mutual assent: offer, acceptance, consid. K defenses?	• Valid written contract per the facts. Sally sells rare Phaeton car to Barry for $200k, delivery on May 25. • S may claim hardship/unconscionabilty (as to price) or unilateral mistake, but none will work here since it appears to be a bargained-for exchange.	**Valid contract**
Anticipatory repudiation	• **Promisor indicates she won't perform prior to the time performance is due.** • **Buyer may treat as immediate breach and sue.**	• On April 1, S and B have a **valid written k** w/delivery of car on May 25. On May 10, **S told B she sold the same car** to wealthy Italian car collector for $300k, delivery w/in 1 week, which is **clear indication S does not intend to perform.** • Since S has indicated she sold car to another, **B may treat the repudiation as final and sue for breach immediately.**	**There is an anticipatory repudiation** and **B may sue immediately for breach of k**
2. Provisional Remedies?			
Injunction (I Pray for Big Desserts)	Equity to prevent injustice Negative or mandatory: • **TRO** • Irreparable harm • **Likelihood of success** • **Inadequate legal remedy** **Prelim. injunction**, as above, plus • **Nec. for "status quo"** • **Balance of hardships** • Defenses Perm. Injunction, as above plus • Property right • Feasibility	B will seek negative injunction to stop S from delivering the car, and a mandatory injunction to require S to deliver car to B. • 10 days only & okay ex parte. • **Irreparable harm b/c car gone in 1 week w/out TRO.** • **S willfully breached valid k, so B likely to win.** • **Cars not usually "unique,"** but here only 2 in world so $ **can't compensate b/c very rare/irreplaceable,** unable to replace **in time** for Concours auto show Put in place awaiting trial on merits, requires: • **Car will ship to another buyer w/out injunction** • Great hardship on **B b/c may be deprived of only opportunity to buy a Phaeton**. **Hardship to S is slight** b/c even though lost opportunity to sell for $300k ($100k more) she still has car and can sell later if she wins • None (supra) • Right to purchase a car is a property right • Court can use contempt power to enforce injunctions	**B should receive a TRO** to prevent S from delivering the car to the shipper **B should also receive preliminary injunction**

Continued >

Issue	Rule	Fact Application	Conclusion
3. Can B Obtain the Phaeton?			
Specific performance (Chocolate cheesecake is my favorite dessert)	Equitable remedy: orders a party to perform under k if • **Contract valid** • **C**ondition of P satisfied • **Inadequate legal remedy** • **Mutuality** • **Feasibility** • No **D**efenses	• **K is valid** ($200k for Phaeton) • P can perform by paying the $200k (can put in escrow) • Discussion **supra** • Modernly, only reqmt. mutuality **of performance, okay here** • **No supervision problems w/court order that S tender car and B pay $200k** (supra) • None (supra)	**B should be granted specific performance**
Replevin	**Allows P to recover specific property** before trial w/hearing.	**Car** is specifically identified and sheriff could seize the Phaeton, but it may be hard to find so this is not a superior remedy to specific performance or an injunction.	**Allowed**, but not the best remedy
4.a. Recover Damages—Nondelivery of Car?			
Expectation **damages**	In k, puts P in same position as if D performed on k Damages must be causal, foreseeable, unavoidable, and certain.	B would get benefit of the bargain, market price less k price. **S would have to pay $100k difference b/t k price ($200k) and market price ($300k)**, which is causal, foreseeable, certain, and unavoidable. **If B can cover** by buying the other Phaeton, B can recover **the difference in price plus incidental costs.**	B will likely get **$100k in damages**
4.b. Recover Damages—Loss of Revenues?			
Consequential **damages**	Damages for any losses resulting from breach, which are **foreseeable** at time k entered into; damages must be causal, foreseeable, unavoidable, and certain.	B wants to recover for his loss of anticipated revenues from magazine circulation increases and advertising revenues from his expected first-place win at the Concours auto show. However, **a win is uncertain** (he's tried for years) and **future increases in revenues are speculative**. Further, **if S did not know B's purpose** of the car purchase, these damages are **not foreseeable at time k was entered into.**	**B will not recover**

Continued >

Issue	Rule	Fact Application	Conclusion
4.c. Recover Damages—Loss of $5k Entry Fee?			
Consequential **damages**	See rule above [Note: Called *reliance damages* in state-released passing answers.]	**If S did not know B's purpose** of the car purchase, and that he entered the auto show contest, these damages are **not foreseeable at the time k was entered into.**	B will not recover

Remedies Question 1 Sample Answer

July 2008, Question 4

1. Barry—Sue Before May 25

Contract

A binding contract requires mutual assent, which includes an offer and acceptance, and consideration. There is a valid written contract here. Sally is selling a rare Phaeton car to Barry for $200,000 with delivery on May 25. Sally may try to ineffectively argue some defenses to enforcement of the contract, such as unconscionability as to price or unilateral mistake, but there does appear to be a bargained-for exchange and a valid contract.

Anticipatory Repudiation

An anticipatory repudiation happens when a promisor indicates he will not perform under the contract prior to the time performance is due. Sally and Barry entered into a valid contract on April 1 with a delivery date of May 25. On May 10, prior to the time Sally was due to perform, Sally informed Barry she had sold the car to a wealthy Italian car collector for $300,000 instead, and is going to deliver the car to the new buyer in one week. Selling the rare car to another buyer is a clear and unequivocal indication that Sally does not intend to perform under her contract with Barry since the subject matter of the contract will be sold to another. Barry may treat this repudiation as a final and immediate breach and sue immediately to enforce the contract even though the time for performance is not yet due.

2. Provisional Remedies

Injunction

An injunction is a remedy in equity designed to prevent injustice. Barry will seek two types of injunctions here: a negative injunction to prevent Sally from delivering the car to the Italian, and a mandatory injunction requiring Sally to deliver the car to Barry.

Barry will attempt to get a temporary restraining order to prevent Sally from delivering the car to the Italian buyer in one week. A TRO is available for a short period pending a full hearing where irreparable harm will occur in its absence, the plaintiff has a likelihood of success on the merits, and the remedy at law is inadequate. Here, Barry will suffer irreparable harm without the TRO because the car will be shipped out of the country in one week. Barry will likely succeed on the merits of the underlying breach of contract claim because Sally is willfully breaching because she made a more lucrative deal to sell the car to another buyer. Lastly, while cars are usually not unique and therefore the remedy at law would be adequate, the Phaeton car here is very unique since there are only two in the world. Money will not adequately compensate for the loss of buying this particular rare car, especially since Barry plans to enter it in the prestigious Concours auto show. Barry should obtain a TRO.

Barry may also attempt to obtain a preliminary injunction. These are put in place pending a trial on the merits and require a showing of the same elements as a TRO (supra), and that the injunction is necessary to maintain the status quo and that the hardships balance in favor of the plaintiff. The preliminary injunction is necessary to maintain the status quo since if one is not granted, the Phaeton will be shipped to the Italian buyer and unavailable. Here, the hardships balance in Barry's favor because there is a great hardship on Barry since he will be deprived of his only opportunity to buy the rare Phaeton, and the hardship on Sally is slight since though she may have lost the opportunity to make this $300,000 deal, she can still sell the car at a later time if she wins. Since there are no applicable defenses, Barry should receive a preliminary injunction.

To obtain a permanent injunction Barry would have to establish all of the above (TRO and preliminary injunction) and establish that he has a property right and that such an order is feasible for the court to enforce. Barry's right to purchase the car is a personal property right and such an order is feasible to enforce through the court's power to enforce injunctions.

3. Barry—Get the Phaeton Itself

Specific Performance

Specific performance is an equitable remedy where the court orders a party to perform under a contract. To obtain specific performance, a party must establish a valid contract, all conditions imposed are satisfied, there must be an inadequate legal remedy, there is mutuality, the order is feasible to enforce, and no defenses apply. As discussed supra there is a valid contract. Barry can perform by tendering the $200,000 owing on the contract, so conditions imposed on him are satisfied. The remedy at law is inadequate (discussed supra). Modernly, courts only require the mutuality of performance, which is satisfied here since both parties can perform under the contract. There are no court supervision problems since the court can order Sally to tender the car and Barry to tender the $200,000, so the order is feasible to enforce. There are no valid defenses, so Barry can get specific performance and this is his best remedy since it gives him the car itself.

Replevin

Replevin is an equitable remedy, which allows a party to recover specific personal property before a trial. Since the Phaeton car is specifically identified, the sheriff could seize it for replevin, but it may be difficult to find so specific performance is a superior remedy.

4. Damages

Nondelivery of Car

Expectation damages for breach of contract put a plaintiff in the same position he would have been in had the contract been fully performed. Barry can receive the benefit of the bargain, so Sally would have to pay the market price ($300,000) less contract price ($200,000). If Barry could cover by buying the other Phaeton, he can recover the difference in price plus any incidental costs incurred.

Loss of Revenue

Consequential damages compensate for any losses resulting from the breach that are foreseeable at the time the contract is entered into. Barry wants to recover for his loss of anticipated revenues from increased magazine circulation and advertising revenues based on his expected first-place finish at the Concours auto show.

However, a win at the auto show is uncertain since he's tried unsuccessfully for years. Further, future revenue increases from circulation and advertising are speculative and are not certain to occur. Lastly, if Sally did not know of Barry's purpose in purchasing the Phaeton, these damages would also not have been foreseeable at the time of contracting. Barry will not be able to recover his anticipated loss revenue.

Loss of Entry Fee

The loss of the Concours auto show entry fee would also be consequential damages. Again, if Sally did not know Barry's purpose for buying the car was to enter the auto show, the entry fee would not have been foreseeable at the time of contracting and thus would not be recoverable by Barry.

Remedies Question 2

February 2000, Question 2

Chemco built a chemical processing plant in a rural area. As part of its operations, Chemco discharges waste into a local river at levels that are low, but constant. Chemco carefully monitors discharge levels on a regular basis.

About six months after Chemco began operations, Pat, a rancher, purchased a tract of grazing land traversed by the same river approximately one-half mile downstream of Chemco's location and stocked the tract with several thousand head of cattle. Within several months, some of Pat's cattle began to get sick and several died. Pat initially attributed the loss of his cattle to a variety of causes, including a recent change he had made in their feed. After another year following the onset of sickness among his cattle, with continuing loss of animals, Pat decided to test the water in the river. He discovered that the level of toxic substances in the local river is sufficient to cause sickness and death to his animals. During the preceding year, Pat's cattle loss totaled about $100,000, and he projects that his losses will increase every successive year unless Chemco stops discharging waste into the river.

Chemco employs more than 1,000 persons in the rural community, by far the largest employer in the county. As a result of Pat's complaints, Chemco hired an engineering firm to investigate the wastes being emitted at its plant and learned that installation of a new filtration system could substantially reduce, if not eliminate, the emission. The filtration system would cost almost $1,000,000, a sum that Chemco could pay only if it were financed over a ten-year term. Relocation of the plant would cost many millions of dollars and would cause Chemco to cease operations. Hauling, storing and distributing water for Pat's cattle from alternative sources would cost approximately $100,000 per year.

Pat sued Chemco requesting an injunction either to enjoin all operations of Chemco or to require that Chemco cease or remedy the discharge or to require Chemco to furnish Pat with clean water from alternative sources. Pat also claimed that he should be awarded substantial damages to compensate him for his past and prospective losses. Chemco opposed the prayer for an injunction on the ground that its operations in the area preceded Pat's activities, and asserted that either an injunction requiring any of the remedies sought by Pat or an award of damages of the magnitude sought by Pat would put Chemco out of business.

1. What arguments might be made for and against an injunction incorporating each of the forms of injunctive relief being sought by Pat, and what would be the likely result of each? Discuss.
2. How should the court rule on Pat's claims for past and prospective damages? Discuss.

Do not discuss state or federal environmental laws.

Remedies Question 2 Assessment

February 2000, Question 2

For this remedies essay question, the underlying claim is for nuisance in tort based on river pollution, though it is primarily a remedies question. A careful reading of the calls of the question show that although the underlying basis for the remedies was a nuisance tort, it is not necessary to address the nuisance issue at all in order to receive a passing score on the exam. Both calls of the question pertain specifically to remedies, with one call devoted to the injunction issues and one call devoted to potential damages.

The challenge posed by this question is an organizational one. There are always a variety of ways that an injunction discussion can be organized, but the key to success on this essay is understanding that the plaintiff was actually asking for four separate types of injunctive relief: (1) enjoin all operations, (2) cease *or* remedy the waste discharged into the river, and (3) furnish clean water from an alternative source. Although each type of relief is not listed separately, you must pay attention to the use of the word "or" when being asked about the type of relief the plaintiff can seek. This necessitates that each of the four types of injunctive relief being sought be analyzed separately on at least the key elements of feasibility of enforcement and balancing of hardships because the analysis on those elements would be different depending on each type of injunctive relief being sought. This was a little tricky to see at first because the question doesn't provide a visual clue (such as a numbered list) to help you see that the different forms of injunctive relief being sought should be handled separately.

Notice that the discussion pertaining to past damages is fairly straightforward; however, the prospective damages discussion requires analysis of the uncertainty of estimating such damages into the future. The potential limitations on damages relating to causation, foreseeability, uncertainty, and unavoidability are frequently tested, and you should specifically consider whether any of those factors are in issue any time you are doing a damages analysis.

Make note of the areas highlighted in **bold** on the corresponding grid. The bold areas highlight the issues, analysis, and conclusions that are likely **required** to receive a passing score on this question.

Issue	Rule	Fact Application	Conclusion
Nuisance			
Private nuisance	The substantial (anncying to avg. person) and unreasonable (gravity of harm outweighs utility of conduct) interference w/use and enjoyment of land.	Unknown if water is used for other purposes besides cattle, but area is rural so there may be other ranchers. Here, harm to Ps cattle is severe, but there is high benefit of Ds business to the community b/c large employer. Inability to use water from river is interference.	Yes, substantial Yes, unreasonable Private nuisance
Trespass to land	Intentional, physical invasion of the property of another.	There is intent by D to discharge water, and this polluted water runs through Ps property, thus invading it.	Trespass to land
Injunction	**Think:** "I pray for big desserts" **Inadequate legal remedy** (unique or irreparable injury/multiplicity of suits) **Property right** (hist. reqmt.) **Feasible to enforce** **[Note: Since Pat is asking for 4 types of injunctive relief, it is important they be discussed separately where the factual analysis differs.]** **Balancing of hardships** (balance the hardship to P if denied to hardship to D if granted) Conclusion	**Injury to land, which is unique and damage is ongoing b/c cattle will continue to die from toxic water. Damages can't fully compensate for ongoing prospective harm.** Here, Pat does have a **property right in the ranch.** *Enjoin all Chemco's operations:* **No continuing supervision required, so feasible.** *Chemco to cease the discharge:* **No continuing supervision required, so feasible.** *Remedy the discharge:* **This is a mandatory order that would require court supervision of affirmative acts, which is less feasible**, though periodic water testing isn't too difficult for court. *Supply Pat with clean water:* **This is a mandatory order that would require court supervision of affirmative acts, which is less feasible.** *Enjoin all Chemco's operations:* **Cost to Chemco is millions of $ and loss of local jobs; harm to society outweighs harm to Pat to relocate.**	Yes, inadequate Yes, property rt. The prohibitory inj. of enjoining all operations and ceasing the discharge are feasible, while the mandatory orders to remedy the discharge or supply clean water are not feasible. Costs to enjoin operations or cease discharge are significantly higher than P's gain, so inj. should be denied.

Continued >

Issue	Rule	Fact Application	Conclusion
		Chemco to cease the discharge: **Cost to Chemco is millions of $, causing plant to shut down and loss of jobs.** *Remedy the discharge:* **Cost to Chemco is financed at $100k per year w/filtering device, which is the same as cost of Pat's cattle ($100k).** *Supply Pat with clean water:* **Cost to Chemco is $100k per year to provide clean water, which is the same as cost of Pat's cattle ($100k).** Pat can get an injunction to remedy the discharge, or have clean water, provided he can establish these are feasible for the court to supervise.	But, cost to remedy discharge, or provide clean water is approx. same as P's cost, so on balance, the injunction should be granted.
Defenses			
Coming to the nuisance	The nuisance existed before the P moved to the land.	Here, Chemco was only in operation for 6 months. This may be considered in reducing damages.	May reduce damages; not full defense
Laches	Unreasonable delay by P, which prejudices D.	Pat waited over a year from his first injury, but **Pat didn't have an easy way to determine the cause** of the problem, so not unreasonable and no prejudice to Chemco b/c any costs associated w/the injury would be the same.	No defense
Damages			
Past damages	Compensatory damages in tort to compensate P for past damages that are causal, foreseeable, certain, and unavoidable.	**The polluted water caused the loss to cattle and it's foreseeable that could harm livestock in a rural area. The loss calculates w/certainty by FMV × # of cattle lost. The loss was unavoidable b/c Pat didn't know the water was harming the cattle.**	$100,000
Prospective damages	Compensatory damages in tort to compensate P for future damages that are causal, foreseeable, certain, and unavoidable.	**Future damages won't exist if injunction is granted b/c that will solve the problem. If injunction is not granted, it may be difficult to calculate with certainty how many cattle will die over an indefinite time period and what the FMV would be.**	Denied

Remedies Question 2 Sample Answer

February 2000, Question 2

1. Injunctive Relief

Nuisance

A private nuisance is the substantial and unreasonable interference with one's use and enjoyment of their land. It is unclear here whether the river water is used for any purpose other than for drinking by Pat's cattle, but the Chemco plant is in a rural area so there probably are other ranches also unable to use the river water for their own livestock or farms, so the interference is likely substantial. To be an unreasonable nuisance, the gravity of the harm must outweigh the utility of the conduct. Here, the harm to Pat's cattle is extremely severe since they are sick and dying and will continue to do so, which outweighs even the highly beneficial nature of Chemco's conduct as a business, as it is a large employer in the community. There is a private nuisance.

Trespass to Land

Trespass to land is the intentional physical invasion of the property of another. Trespass is established here since Chemco intentionally discharged chemical waste, which is a physical invasion, into the river, which also runs through and invades Pat's property.

Injunction

Pat is seeking four different types of injunctive relief. To obtain an injunction Pat must establish the remedy at law is inadequate, he has a property right, it would be feasible to enforce such an order, the hardships must balance in his favor, and there can be no applicable defenses.

Inadequate Legal Remedy

The remedy at law is inadequate here because Chemco has caused an injury to Pat's land and all land is unique. Since land is unique, money cannot adequately compensate Pat for his inability to use his own land to graze his cattle, or for the requirement that he move his operation to a difference piece of land. Further, the damage will be ongoing since the cattle will continue to get sick and die from ingesting the toxic river water unless the chemical dumping is stopped. Damages are unable to adequately compensate Pat, so the remedy at law is inadequate.

Property Interest

Pat has a property interest in the ranch since it is real property.

Feasibility

The order must also be feasible for the court to enforce. An injunction ordering Chemco to enjoin all operations, or an order to cease discharging waste, poses no supervision problems for the court and is thus feasible to enforce. These are negative injunctions and the court can simply order either of those actions and enforce the order with their contempt power. An injunction ordering Chemco to remedy the discharge or to supply Pat with clean water poses more of a feasibility issue since both are mandatory orders that would require ongoing court supervision of Chemco's performance of either of those affirmative acts. Mandatory affirmative injunctions always pose more of a feasibility issue; however, here, periodic water testing or ensuring that clean water is supplied is not particularly burdensome for the court to supervise, so these orders are feasible.

Balancing of Hardships

The hardships must also balance in favor of the plaintiff. Pat's hardship is clear in that his cattle are becoming sick and dying by ingesting polluted river water caused by Chemco's waste discharge. This has cost $100,000 in lost cattle so far, and this amount is projected to increase every year. The hardship to Chemco if ordered to enjoin all operations is a loss of millions of dollars in revenues, as well as great harm to the greater community in the loss of 1,000 jobs. Because the hardship to Chemco and the greater community is so great, the hardships balance in Chemco's favor and they will not be ordered to enjoin all operations. The cost to Chemco to cease the discharge is similar to the analysis above since Chemco would essentially have to shut the plant down, costing millions of dollars and thousands of jobs to the local community. Relocating the plant to prevent the discharge would also cost millions and cause societal harm in the loss of many jobs. Again, the cost to Chemco and the greater society outweigh Pat's right to have his cattle ranch in this location, so the court will not order Chemco to cease the discharge because the hardships balance in favor of Chemco and the greater community. The cost to Chemco to remedy discharging the waste is the cost of a $1,000,000 new filtration system, which would have to be financed over 10 years at a cost of $100,000 per year. This is the same financial loss that Pat suffers by losing his cattle to illness from the discharged waste in the river water ($100,000 per year). The cost to Chemco to supply Pat with clean water for the cattle is $100,000 per year, which is the same amount Pat is suffering in loss of cattle each year ($100,000). Since the hardship is approximately the same financial cost to each party if the court orders Chemco to remedy the discharge or supply Pat with clean water, on balance the injunction should be granted on either, but not both, of these grounds, provided they are feasible for the court to enforce.

Defense—Coming to the Nuisance

This is a historical defense where the nuisance existed before the plaintiff moved to the land. Here, Chemco was only in operation for six months when Pat moved onto his ranch. This is not an effective defense, but may be used to reduce damages.

Defense—Laches

Laches provides a defense where an unreasonable delay by the plaintiff prejudices the defendant. While Pat did wait over a year from the time the injury began occurring, this was not unreasonable since Pat had no easy way to determine the cause of the cattle's illness. Further, the delay, which occurred while Pat investigated other possible causes such as new cattle feed, did not in any way prejudice the defendant because the costs associated with Pat's injuries are the same either way.

2. Damages

Past Damages

Compensatory damages in tort compensate a plaintiff for past damages that are causal, foreseeable, certain, and unavoidable. The polluted water caused the loss to the cattle and it is foreseeable that waste water dumped in a river in a rural area could harm livestock. The loss can be calculated with certainty by figuring the fair market value of cattle times the number of cattle lost, which is calculated at $100,000. The loss was unavoidable because Pat did not know the cause of the harm to the cattle, and once he did it was not easy or inexpensive to find an alternative water source. Pat is due $100,000 in past damages.

Future Damages

Compensatory damages also can compensate for future damages in accordance with the rule above. If an injunction is granted, future damages won't exist and there will be no order for future damages because the problem will be solved by the injunction. If the injunction is not granted, it may be difficult to calculate with certainty how many cattle will die over an indefinite period of time and what the fair market value of the cattle will be, projecting indefinitely into the future. For this reason, an injunction is the preferred method of addressing the need to remedy the ongoing wrong of toxic river water.

Remedies Question 3

February 2002, Question 2

Berelli Co., the largest single buyer of tomatoes in the area, manufactures several varieties of tomato-based pasta sauces. Berelli entered into a written contract with Grower to supply Berelli its requirements of the Tabor, the only type of tomato Berelli uses in its pasta sauces. The Tabor tomato is known for its distinctive flavor and color, and it is particularly desirable for making sauces. The parties agreed to a price of $100 per ton.

The contract, which was on Berelli's standard form, specified that Grower was to deliver to Berelli at the end of the growing season in August all Tabor tomatoes that Berelli might require. The contract also prohibited Grower from selling any excess Tabor tomatoes to a third party without Berelli's consent. At the time the contract was executed, Grower objected to that provision. A Berelli representative assured him that although the provision was standard in Berelli's contracts with its growers, Berelli had never attempted to enforce the provision. In fact, however, Berelli routinely sought to prevent growers from selling their surplus crop to third parties. The contract also stated that Berelli could reject Grower's tomatoes for any reason, even if they conformed to the contract.

On August 1, Berelli told Grower that it would need 40 tons of Tabor tomatoes at the end of August. Grower anticipated that he would harvest 65 tons of Tabor tomatoes commencing on August 30. Because of the generally poor growing season, Tabor tomatoes were in short supply. Another manufacturer, Tosca Co., offered Grower $250 per ton for his entire crop of Tabor tomatoes. On August 15, Grower accepted the Tosca offer and informed Berelli that he was repudiating the Berelli/Grower contract.

After Grower's repudiation, Berelli was able to contract for only 10 tons of Tabor tomatoes on the spot market at $200 per ton, but has been unable to procure any more. Other varieties of tomatoes are readily available at prices of $100 per ton or less on the open market, but Berelli is reluctant to switch to these other varieties. Berelli believes that Tabor tomatoes give its sauces a unique color, texture, and flavor. It is now August 20. Berelli demands that Grower fulfill their contract in all respects.

1. What remedies are available to Berelli to enforce the terms of its contract with Grower, what defenses might Grower reasonably assert, and what is the likely outcome on each remedy sought by Berelli? Discuss.
2. If Berelli elects to forgo enforcement of the contract and elects instead to sue for damages, what defenses might Grower reasonably assert, and what damages, if any, is Berelli likely to recover? Discuss.

Remedies Question 3 Assessment

February 2002, Question 2

For this essay question, the underlying claim pertains to a requirements contract for specialty "Tabor" tomatoes and, as such, the underlying contract is subject to the UCC.

The call of the question asks specifically about available remedies and defenses. Consequently, the answer needs to be framed to respond to the calls of the question, rather than organized in a typical order based on the lifecycle of a contract where the validity of the contract is analyzed first, then any defenses, and ending with a final discussion of remedies. Instead, here, the key is to frame any potential issues pertaining to the contract's validity as potential defenses to the enforcement of the contract. The same material is covered as with a traditional contract analysis, but the answer is structured in a slightly different way. The way this question is posed causes many students to struggle with how to organize their answer. Keep in mind that any problem with an underlying contract can result in any element of contract formation serving as a possible defense to the contract's enforcement.

This question covers many issues, and there are many facts available to use in the analysis. Good time management is essential to succeeding on this question. It is particularly important to organize your answer before you start writing your answer so you can identify how many issues are covered and how much factual analysis is available for each issue. The analysis related to the second call of the question is much shorter than the first, but still requires a full discussion of expectation damages and consequential damages, as there were many facts available to use in the analysis. It is especially important to use all of the facts to thoroughly analyze the potential limitations on future damages.

It is always important to use an issue heading for each legal concept covered on your essay, but this is especially true when you are unsure about how to organize your answer. Don't waste time worrying about how to organize when you're confused; just make a decision and move forward. Use lots of issue headings and make it easy for the exam grader to find the issues on your essay so you will earn the corresponding points. If the exam grader can't find your great discussion of promissory estoppel, you will not receive credit for it, so don't bury the discussion at the end of your consideration paragraph; instead, put the discussion in its own paragraph set off with "Promissory Estoppel" as the issue heading so it isn't overlooked.

Make note of the areas highlighted in **bold** on the corresponding grid. The bold areas highlight the issues, analysis, and conclusions that are likely **required** to receive a passing score on this question.

Issue	Rule	Fact Application	Conclusion
Call #1: Remedies for Berelli			
Applicable law	• UCC: k's for sale of goods • Merchants: deal w/goods of the kind	• Here, **agreement to buy/sell tomatoes—moveable goods, so UCC applies.** • Also, both parties are merchants because they each regularly deal with tomatoes.	UCC applies, as does provision with merchants
Valid contract	• Offer, acceptance, and consideration • Requirements k: to buy all products needed from other party	• Here, **Berelli entered into a "written contract" with Grower** • **K in writing, terms of price ($100/ton), subject matter (Tabor tomatoes), and reqmts. k, as B agrees to buy all Tabor tomatoes needed from Grower, taking delivery in August.**	Yes, valid k, barring any defenses below
PER	• No evidence of agreements prior to or contemporaneous with k.	• Oral statement by B that it never enforces provision preventing Grower from selling to others not admissible b/c made at same time Ps entered k	PER bars evidence of oral assurance by B
Anticipatory repudiation	• Unequivocal expression by a party that they won't perform. • **Nonrepudiating party may sue immediately, suspend performance, or urge performance.**	• **Grower informed B on Aug. 15, prior to date performance was due that he was repudiating k** and accepted offer for more $ from Tosca • Thus, **B can sue immediately or urge performance,** as B did here on Aug. 20 and then sue, or treat k as discharged	Yes, anticipatory repudiation
Preliminary injunction	Maintains status quo until trial • **Irrep. harm if not granted** • **Likely success on merits** • **Inadequate legal remedy** (unique good) • **Balancing of hardships** • **Defenses** (**unclean hands or misrepresentation or** unconscionable)	• Specialty tomatoes will be sold to another and can't be obtained elsewhere and are perishable, so can't wait for trial • Grower may not succeed at trial b/c of consideration, but court could still enforce via detrimental reliance/promissory estoppel theory • **Likely because Tabor tomatoes are in short supply; B can only use this type of tomato b/c it gives sauce unique color, texture, and flavor, and B is unable to procure from other vendors**	Likely will not be granted due to lack of valid k defenses (see Grower's defenses below)

Continued >

Issue	Rule	Fact Application	Conclusion
		• **B would not have tomatoes to make its sauce and won't be able to get from other vendors, could even possibly go out of business if no sauce to sell; Grower would make less money, but still make money, and likely enough or they wouldn't have contracted at such rate** • **Possibly unclean hands, as B acted in bad faith when it misrep. to Grower it never enforces the provision preventing selling to 3rd parties, when it does so often**, esp. since Grower initially objected	Likely will not be granted due to lack of valid k defenses (see Grower's defenses below)
Specific performance	• Contract is valid • Conditions met • Inadequate legal remedy • Mutuality of performance • Feasibility • Defenses Think: **C**hocolate **C**heesecake **I**s **M**y **F**avorite **D**essert	• K maybe not valid b/c defenses no consideration & unconsc. (below) • Conditions met • See above • Grower can perform by giving B all of its tomatoes and B can pay • Court can easily require both sides perform through contempt power See above	Likely will not be granted due to lack of valid K/defenses (see Grower's defenses below)
Replevin	P can reclaim a chattel wrongfully taken or detained.	B contracted to have all Tabor tomatoes, so B can claim possession of all Tabor tomatoes detained by Grower.	Yes, replevin but limited by defenses below
Call #1: Defenses for Grower			
Consideration/ promissory estoppel	• **K needs consideration** (bargained-for exchange); illusory if only one party bound. • Promissory estoppel: **party estopped by detrimental reliance.**	• **K may lack consideration because B had the right to reject all tomatoes, even if conforming; thus, the promise to buy was illusory**; typically, requirements k's are fine, but not with provision w/unilateral right to reject conforming goods. • But, **B detrimentally relied on Grower's promise to sell all Tabors** since it did not k with any other vendor and no longer can	No consideration, but likely detrimental reliance and promissory estopppel

Continued >

Issue	Rule	Fact Application	Conclusion
Fraud/ misrepresentation	Fraud in inducement or material misrepresentation	B's standard form prohibited Grower from selling Tabors to another w/out B's consent and, despite Grower's objection, **B misrepresented itself by lying and stating they don't enforce the provision when in fact they routinely do**, but arguably that term was not material.	Material misrep. [could have concluded either way]
Unconscionability	Unfairness arose at time of k formation.	**K at time of formation was unfair as B could refuse to buy all tomatoes by rejecting conforming goods, yet Grower could not sell to anyone else without B's consent, so B had all power to do anything it wanted and Grower's power was limited.** But court may just choose to eliminate this provision only and hold rest of k to be valid under UCC.	Yes, k unconscionable
Discharge	Impracticability or frustration of purpose	Neither apply here as Grower could still sell all tomatoes to B, even though in short supply and market price fluctuation is foreseeable.	No discharge
Unclean hands	One party acts in bad faith.	See above in defenses to specific performance.	Maybe unclean hands
Call #2: Damages			
Expectation **damages**	Put nonbreaching party in position it would be in had k been performed (for UCC cover price or market price).	**Had k been performed, B would have its tomatoes and made its sauces, but money cannot help it to buy more tomatoes to make sauces; B may seek difference in k price ($100/ton) and cover price ($200/ton); for 30 tons yet to receive, B may seek difference in k price ($100) and market rate ($250).**	B could get damages

Continued >

Issue	Rule	Fact Application	Conclusion
Consequential **damages/** limitations on damages	Lost profits damages due to breach • Certainty • Causal • **Foreseeable at time of k** formation • **Unavoidable**	• **No certainty as to what profit B would have made on these tomatoes unless B can show expected and certain profit based on past years** • B damages caused by Grower not giving it tomatoes as promised • **Damages foreseeable at time of k because Grower knew B uses these tomatoes in its sauces and only these tomatoes and that without them, they cannot make their sauce**, but damages on reputation may not be foreseeable • **Damages unavoidable as Grower could only get some tomatoes on market at higher price and unable to get any more due to short supply**	B may get lost profit damages if it can prove certainty

Remedies Question 4

July 1986, Question 5

Alice took her diamond ring worth $14,000 to Bob, a jeweler, to have the stone reset. After Bob had agreed to reset the stone and Alice had left the shop, Bob placed the ring on a counter for a few minutes while he helped another customer. Carl, also a customer, took Alice's ring and left the shop.

Carl later sold the ring for $15,000. He deposited $2,000 of the proceeds in a savings account that already contained $5,000 of his own funds and bought Blackacre with the remaining $13,000.

When Alice returned for her ring, Bob told her that it had been stolen, that he thought he knew the identity of the thief, that he had hired a private investigator, and that he hoped to recover the ring. The investigator's activities prompted Carl to admit his theft.

Blackacre is now worth $26,000. The balance in Carl's savings account, which had dropped to a low of $600 after he had deposited the $2,000, is now $3,000.

Carl has revealed that he sold the ring to Dan, who knew nothing about Carl's theft.

What are Alice's rights and to what relief, if any, is she entitled? Discuss.

Remedies Question 4 Assessment

July 1986, Question 5

This question contains an example of what we call a "deal breaker" issue. This is when there is one very important issue to notice, and if a student fails to notice this issue it is impossible to receive a passing score on the question. The key to passing this question is recognizing that Alice has a claim against each of the other three parties involved: Bob, Carl, and Dan. If a student fails to realize that Alice had a valid claim against each party, the student will miss so many issues it will be impossible to recover and earn a sufficient score to pass the question.

The best way to ensure you don't miss a deal breaker issue is to not rush and to methodically organize your answer. Give yourself 15 to 20 minutes to organize your answer before you begin writing. If there is a thought scratching at the back of your head, take a moment to think it through. Often these deal breaker issues are tricky to see and you need to allow yourself some time to think. They may hinge on a subtle fact, or an obscure rule. Where there is a tricky issue like this, often the answer and analysis can be on the thin side and the student will still pass the question by virtue of having spotted the deal breaker. Conversely, an answer with brilliant analysis that doesn't address the deal breaker issue won't receive a passing score. We're not suggesting you can always do a skimpy analysis, or that every question has a tricky issue hidden in it, because that isn't true, but it does happen and you need to be aware of the possibility.

Most students can spot Bob's negligence liability as the careless jeweler, and all students can spot Carl's culpability here as the thief (which necessitates a rather detailed factual analysis of constructive trust/equitable lien and how tracing works under the facts provided). The trickier issues here are Dan's potential liability for converting the ring, even though he is otherwise a bona fide purchaser, and the remedies available to Alice. It is also important to note that even though Alice can potentially recover against three different parties, she may only recover for a single loss once; however, she can choose which remedy to pursue of the options available.

Make note of the areas highlighted in **bold** on the corresponding grid. The bold areas highlight the issues, analysis, and conclusions that are likely **required** to receive a passing score on this question.

Issue	Rule	Fact Application	Conclusion
Alice v. Bob			
Negligence	**Duty** **Breach** Actual cause **Proximate cause** Damages	Bob, as a **bailee, owed a duty of care** to customer Alice. Bob failed to use reasonable care by **leaving ring unattended** on the counter. But for the ring being left on the counter, it wouldn't have been stolen. **Bob may argue that theft is a superceding cause,** since criminal conduct of others can be, but it's **foreseeable here since Bob created the opportunity by careless behavior and, as a jeweler, should have knowledge of thievery.** See below	Negligent
Compensatory damages	To compensate for loss	Alice can recover the **market value** of the ring, either $14k or sales price of $15k.	Market value
Alice v. Carl			
Trespass to chattels	Intentional interference with P's right to possession of chattel	By **stealing ring from counter and taking it, Carl intentionally interfered** with Alice's right to possession of her ring (chattel).	Trespass to chattel
Conversion	Same as TTC but **interference is substantial**	Interference with the chattel is **so substantial (theft and sale to another and ring can't be returned)** that it has been converted.	Conversion
Compensatory damages	To compensate for loss	Alice can recover the **market value** of the ring, either $14k or sales price of $15k.	Market value
Punitive damages	D's conduct is willful and wanton	Since Carl's conduct is criminal, Alice may be awarded punitive damages.	Punitive damages

Continued >

Issue	Rule	Fact Application	Conclusion
Constructive trust	**Conveys title to property** where: • Inadequate legal remedy • D has wrongfully acquired (title) • Of P's property • **Tracing is allowed**	Restitutionary remedy to **prevent unjust enrichment,** so must have inadequate legal remedy (ring's been sold so replevin is unavailable; Carl has spent proceeds) Carl has sold Alice's ring and used proceeds to buy Blackacre for $13k, and $2k added to savings account with $5k balance Alice can obtain **title to Blackacre since it was purchased solely w/proceeds from the ring and thus receives the benefit of the increase in value ($26k). $3k was in the account before adding the $2k from the ring, but then the balance dropped to $600, and is now at $3k. Presume D spent his own $ first, so the $600 was from the ring, but the other $2,400 was added later and can't be traced to the ring.**	**Title to Blackacre; $600 in bank account** **Constructive trust is best option since P gets the benefit of property increase**
Equitable lien	Same as constructive trust above, except **conveys security interest**	Alice could get a **lien against Blackacre in the amount of the value of the wrongfully obtained property**. This provides less recovery than a constructive trust and is **not the best method of recovery.**	**Equitable lien allowed** but constructive trust is better
Alice v. Dan			
Trespass to chattels	Intentional interference with P's right to possession of chattel	**Dan only needs to have intended to perform the act causing the tort (taking possession of the ring). It is irrelevant that he didn't know the ring was stolen and that Carl didn't have title to convey since Alice still has legal title. Carl didn't have lawful title to convey, and Dan didn't obtain lawful title; and even though he's a bona fide purchaser, Dan is still liable for trespass to chattel and conversion.**	Trespass to chattel
Conversion	Same as TTC but interference is substantial	Same analysis as above. Also, the interference was substantial because Alice was deprived of her ring entirely.	Conversion

Continued >

Issue	Rule	Fact Application	Conclusion
Compensatory damages	To compensate for loss	Alice can recover the **market value** of the ring, either $14k or sales price of $15k.	Market value
Punitive damages	D's conduct is willful and wanton	Since Dan unknowingly deprived Alice of her ring, punitive damages are not appropriate.	No punitive damages
Replevin	Allows the recovery of wrongfully taken chattel	Alice **may seek to have the actual ring returned,** and would be entitled to **damages for the time period she was deprived of her ring.**	Replevin
Election of remedies	A plaintiff may **only recover one remedy in satisfaction of one loss**	Alice's **best remedy would be to obtain a constructive trust for Blackacre since it has risen in value** and she would be entitled to the increase in value to prevent Carl's unjust enrichment. **At her option, she could also choose to recover either from Bob or Dan, and if the ring had sentimental value, she may elect replevin from Dan to get the ring back.**	Can only recover once

Remedies Question 5

July 2007, Question 5

Paula, a recent art-school graduate, was trying to establish a reputation as an art acquisition agent, i.e., one who finds works of art for collectors interested in buying particular works. It is a business where reliability and confidentiality are critical.

Paula's first commission was to find for City Museum ("Museum") any one of the three originals in a series of paintings by Monay, titled "The Pond." Museum agreed to pay as much as $300,000 for it and to pay Paula $15,000 upon acquisition. The works of Monay are rare and held by private collectors, and none had been on the market in recent years.

Paula eventually tracked down Sally, a private collector who owned the three originals of Monay's "The Pond." After some negotiations, in which Sally expressed offhandedly how proud she was that she only sold to private collectors, Sally orally agreed to sell to Paula for $200,000 whichever of the three paintings she selected. Paula agreed that, as soon as she could make the selection, she would transfer the purchase money into Sally's bank account. Paula immediately called the curator at Museum, who told her to select the first of the three in the series, and the curator immediately caused Museum's bank to wire-transfer $200,000 into Sally's account to cover the purchase.

The next day, when Paula went to tell Sally which painting she had selected and to pick it up, Sally declined to go through with the sale. Sally accused Paula of deceit, saying it was only when she learned that the money for the purchase had come from Museum, that she realized that the painting would no longer be held privately. Sally tendered to Paula a certified check, which she had signed and drawn from her bank account, refunding the $200,000. In the notation line of the check, Sally had written, "Refund on 1st of Monay Pond series."

Paula refused to accept the check and insisted on getting the painting. She explained that she had not disclosed her principal's identity because she was bound by confidentiality and that, unless she could deliver the painting to Museum, her budding career as an art acquisition agent was over. Sally told Paula, "That's too bad. Our contract wasn't in writing, so you can't force me to sell the painting. Besides, you deceived me about why you wanted to buy it."

Can Paula obtain specific performance of Sally's agreement to sell Paula the painting?

Discuss.

Remedies Question 5 Assessment

July 2007, Question 5

This essay is a good example of a question with a very specific call of the question. The call asks if Paula can obtain specific performance against Sally for a breach of contract, which strictly limits the breadth of the analysis. However, you can be certain that when the breadth of a question is limited, there will be a great depth of factual analysis.

The key to success on this question is noticing that one of the elements of specific performance is that the underlying contract is valid. This means that not only should any applicable defenses be discussed, but once again the opposing party can use any potential problem with the validity of the underlying contract as a defense to the contract's enforcement.

It is important to carefully read the fact pattern to ensure that every available fact is used within the analysis where appropriate. Challenge yourself to think of a way to use every fact available to either bolster your arguments or raise another issue. "Think like a lawyer" and consider all potential defenses that Sally could raise and include those in your answer. Remember, a defense does not ultimately have to be a successful defense to merit analysis in your answer. The key to scoring well is discussing all issues raised by the facts, whether the facts *prove* **or** *disprove* the issues' existence.

Make note of the areas highlighted in **bold** on the corresponding grid. The bold areas highlight the issues, analysis, and conclusions that are likely **required** to receive a passing score on this question.

Issue	Rule	Fact Application	Conclusion
Applicable law	• **UCC: k's for sale of goods** • Merchants: regularly deal w/goods of the kind	Here, contract was for sale of painting. **Painting is a good** (moveable at time of identification to the k). Paula regularly deals in goods of the kind (painting) as an art agent, but as a private collector, Sally does not and so it is not a "merchant."	**UCC applies** Paula is a merchant, Sally is not
Specific performance	Think: **C**hocolate **C**heesecake **I**s **M**y **F**avorite **D**essert • **Contract valid;** needs **offer, acceptance, consid.,** • **definite and certain terms** • Condition of P satisfied • **Inadequate legal remedy** • **Mutuality** • **Feasibility** • No Defenses	• **Sally orally agrees to sell 1 of 3 paintings to Paula for $200,000. Paula agrees to select painting and transfer $ to Sally's bank account.** Terms are: quantity of 1 painting, time is immediately, parties are identified, price $200k, subject matter is the choice of 1 of 3 paintings. **Sally may argue terms are not definite** b/c the painting hadn't been selected, but okay under UCC b/c sufficiently specific to pick 1 of 3 in a series where of equal value. • Though she expressed her desire, Sally did not make the sale to a private collector a condition of sale. • Painting is **unique property because** it's an **original work of art that is "rare . . . held by private collectors,** and none had been on the market in years," so it can't be replaced by money damages. Also, **money can't compensate for harm to Paula's reputation** and credibility and would be difficult to calculate since her **business is new.** • Paula has to pay and select painting; Sally has to provide painting. • Court can order that painting be turned over to Paula and Paula to make payment, so easy to enforce. • See below.	Contract valid & terms sufficiently definite and certain Conditions satisfied Remedy at law inadequate Mutuality satisfied Feasible to enforce

Continued >

Issue	Rule	Fact Application	Conclusion
Defense SOF	**Sale of goods over $500 requires writing.**	**SOF requires a writing because painting was over $500 (at $200k). Writing must be signed by Sally, the party to be charged,** but there is no writing by Sally.	K not enforceable because of SOF, unless exception
SOF exception: full performance	**Goods accepted or paid for** are an exception to the SOF.	Paula transfers **payment in full, but Sally did not accept the payment and tendered check back noting "refund,"** so payment not accepted, despite attempt.	No SOF exception for full performance
SOF exception: promissory estoppel	**Rely to detriment, and** **Reliance reasonable and foreseeable**	**Paula relied on Sally's promise and told museum she got the painting, so her reputation as an honest/reliable art acquisition agent will suffer** if she can't get the Monay. But, reliance not foreseeable b/c Sally didn't know Paula worked for museum and Paula didn't really change position in reliance on promise.	Unlikely promissory estoppel can overcome SOF here
Unclean hands	Plaintiff has conducted herself **unfairly** in the transaction in dispute.	Paula **allowed Sally to believe she was a private collector**, when she actually represented a museum, and **knew Sally only wanted to sell to private collectors**. But, Paula can argue confidentiality is key for art acquisition agents, so probably not unfair.	Can conclude either way
Misrepresentation (fraud)	One party makes a false assertion at the time of contracting, inducing reliance.	Paula **failed to disclose** that she was not a private collector but did not affirmatively say she was, and was **under no duty** to correct Sally's misunderstanding on the point. Sally could have asked if it was that important to her.	No misrepresentation
Unilateral mistake	Mistake made by one party to the deal, and the other party knows or has reason to know of the other's mistake.	Sally was clear that **she only sold to private collectors, so Paula knew Sally was misinformed.** But the mistake isn't to a material term and the risk of the mistake can't be imposed on the party seeking to avoid the contract. Sally bore the risk of selling to a non-private collector without insisting on an express term, so the defense will likely fail.	Likely no unilateral mistake

Remedies Question 6

February 1998, Question 1

In February 1997, Carrier, a trucking company, and Maker, a manufacturer, negotiated an agreement under which Carrier promised to provide for two years all the transportation services required by Maker in exchange for monthly payments based on the number of packages transported. In response to Carrier's concerns over proposed legislation that would restrict its ability to use more efficient "triple-trailer" trucks, the parties agreed that Carrier could terminate the contract if such legislation were enacted. No such law was ever passed.

Carrier drafted a document embodying the agreed terms and, on March 1, 1997, sent two signed copies to Maker with a request that Maker sign and return one copy. Although Maker did not sign the document, the parties immediately began doing business according to its terms. During the next six months, Maker paid all of Carrier's monthly invoices on time. During the same period, Carrier declined two potentially lucrative offers from other manufacturers because performance of the agreement with Maker required most of Carrier's capacity.

In September 1997, Maker began to have concerns about the cost of Carrier's service. Maker sent a letter to Transport, one of Carrier's competitors, describing Maker's needs, Maker's agreement with Carrier, and the amount charged by Carrier. Transport offered to provide comparable transportation services at a lower cost. On September 20, Maker sent a fax to Carrier stating that Maker would no longer use Carrier's services as of November 1. Carrier responded with a fax to Maker which stated that Maker had no right to terminate the contract. On September 21, Maker suspended all business with Carrier and began doing business with Transport. Maker also refused to pay an invoice submitted by Carrier for transportation services rendered in September.

What, if any, rights and remedies does Carrier have against:

1. Maker? Discuss.
2. Transport? Discuss.

Remedies Question 6 Assessment

February 1998, Question 1

As with 95% of remedies questions, this question is a crossover question. It focuses on both contracts and torts rights and the applicable remedies to each right. By a careful reading of the call of the question, you can quickly see that you are required to discuss both substantive "rights" and "remedies." Thus, you should organize your answer first by party, second by right, and third by the remedies particular to that right.

Given that the call does not indicate which subjects are at issue in regard to the "rights," you should read the fact pattern prior to writing out any issues checklist. Also, always be cognizant that more than one subject may be at issue in regard to the rights, especially when multiple parties and their respective actions are involved. After a careful reading of the facts, it is clear that contracts is at issue since there was an agreement made with promises by each party to the agreement. Thus, you should write out your contracts issues checklist and all contracts remedies.

Some students find it useful to list and memorize all remedies with the particular subject to which they correspond. Other students find it useful to memorize all remedies as a separate subject and then divide them into substantive categories. You need to determine which method works best for you by writing out a few crossover substantive rights/remedies questions to see which method enables you to spot all relevant remedies.

When looking at the facts that might give rise to a right that Carrier has against Transport, the only thing that Transport possibly did was to interfere with the agreement between Carrier and Maker. Thus, an entire checklist of torts would not be necessary since the only issue that arises under tort law is interference with contract. However, you should write out all possible torts remedies so as not to miss any, since more than one remedy is likely at issue.

Finally, make note of the areas highlighted in **bold** on the corresponding grid. The bold areas highlight the issues, analysis, and conclusions that are likely **required** to receive a passing score on this question.

Issue	Rule	Fact Application	Conclusion
Carrier v. Maker: Contract Rights	**One right Carrier might have available will be for breach of k against Maker**. Thus, it is necessary to determine whether an enforceable k exists.		
Applicable law	**The UCC governs k's for the sale of goods; the common law governs all other k's.**	**Here, the contract involves the services of transporting packages and not the sale of goods.**	**Common law applies**
Formation	**Need offer, acceptance, and consideration.** Offer: manifestation of willingness to enter into a bargain with definite and certain terms, and communicated to the offeree Acceptance: manifestation of assent to the terms of the offer Consideration: bargained-for exchange of legal detriment **Illusory promise: promise not supported by consideration; requirements k's not considered illusory because of implied obligation of good faith**	Offer: Carrier offered to provide all transportation to Maker that Maker required in exchange for monthly payments by Maker and mailed 2 signed copies to Maker to sign, showing its willingness to enter a bargain with Maker (the offeree). **Although there is no specific quantity of packages that Carrier will transport, this is acceptable for requirements k's in which the seller can agree to supply everything the buyer needs, which is what Carrier agreed to do for Maker here**. Acceptance: Maker arguably accepted by agreeing to make monthly payments to Carrier based on the number of packages transported. **Consideration: Transportation service in exchange for payments, not illusory because both parties obligated by good faith.**	Yes, contract likely exists
Defenses: SOF	**Need writing with essential terms signed by the party to be charged for k's incapable of being performed within 1 yr.**	**Here, k is for 2 yrs., so it can't be performed within 1 yr. and it was not signed by Maker, the party to be charged here.**	**SOF valid defense, unless exception applies**

Continued >

Issue	Rule	Fact Application	Conclusion
Exceptions to SOF	**Performance: k can't be performed in 1 yr., but full performance has occurred.** If court analogizes to UCC, then merchant's confirmatory memo if between merchants, one party receives signed confirmation unless recipient objects within 10 days. **Promissory estoppel: allows plaintiff to recover to the extent necessary to prevent injustice where they detrimentally relied on the agreement.**	**Here, Carrier has only performed for 7 mos. out of the 2 yrs., so there isn't full performance.** Here, both Carrier and Maker appear to deal with packages and their transportation on a regular basis, so both might be considered merchants, and Maker did not object to Carrier's signed document. **Here, Carrier reasonably relied on Maker's promise to use Carrier for 2 yrs. when it declined 2 potentially lucrative offers from other manufacturers because performance with Maker required most of Carrier's capacity.**	Confirmatory memo and promissory estoppel are likely valid exceptions to the SOF
Anticipatory repudiation	**An unequivocal expression by a party that she will not perform under the contract that occurs before the time for performance is due.** **Nonrepudiating party may sue immediately, suspend performance, or urge performance.**	**Here, Maker clearly stated that, as of Nov. 1, 1997, it would not continue under the terms of the k with Carrier by sending Carrier a fax on Sept. 20, 1997, more than a yr. before time for performance was due.** **Thus, Carrier has the right to sue immediately.**	**Maker anticipatorily repudiated the contract**
Carrier v. Maker: Contract Remedies			
Damages	Expectation damages compensate P for the value of the benefit P expected to receive from the k. Expectation damages put P in position he would have been in if the k was performed. **Damages must be foreseeable at the time of contracting, mitigated by the innocent party, and certain.**	Here, to put Carrier in the position they would have been in had Maker continued to use them to transport packages, it is necessary to determine how many packages Carrier would have transported in the remaining months. **It is foreseeable that if you cancel using Carrier, they would suffer the losses of not transporting the packages; Carrier should try to mitigate by finding other companies in need of transportation, and the damages for the unpaid month of Sept. are certain, but the remaining months might be difficult to prove unless it can be ascertained from the amount of transportation Transport is doing for Maker.**	**Carrier likely to receive damages**

Continued >

Issue	Rule	Fact Application	Conclusion
Restitution	D has derived a benefit, or been unjustly enriched, and it would be unfair to allow D to keep that benefit without compensating P, or where the P wants her property back. **The goal of restitution is to prevent unjust enrichment.**	**Here, arguably, Maker derived a benefit of not having Carrier contract with other manufacturers to support Maker, and it would be unfair for Maker to breach contract to go with a cheaper transporter. Also, Carrier already transported Maker's Sept. goods, which benefited Maker and, thus, Carrier should be paid for those services.**	**Carrier able to receive restitution if not damages**
Specific performance	Requires a valid k, k conditions are satisfied, inadequate legal remedy, mutuality of performance, feasibility, and no defenses.	Here, the k is valid, as discussed above, and all conditions have been satisfied, but there may be an adequate legal remedy in the form of damages, also as discussed above; both would be able to perform, and the court could easily oversee that the parties do so.	Specific performance unlikely because damages adequate
Carrier v. Transport: Torts Rights	**One right Carrier might have available against Transport is for interfering with its k with Maker.**		
Interference with contractual relations	**Requires existence of a valid contractual relationship between P and a 3rd party or a valid business expectancy of P, about which D knew or should have known; intentional interference by D, inducing breach or termination of the relationship or expectancy; and damages.**	**Here, there was a valid k between Maker and Carrier, and Transport was aware of the k as Maker described its agreement with Carrier to Transport in a letter, which resulted in Transport offering a lower cost. However, it is unclear if Transport intentionally interfered, but it is likely since Transport should have known that given Maker's letter and Transport's lower offer that Maker could breach its contract with Carrier to go with Transport. Damages are established above.**	Transport possibly liable for interference

Continued >

Issue	Rule	Fact Application	Conclusion
Defense: privilege	D's conduct may be privileged where it is a proper attempt to obtain business for itself or protect its interests (fair competition), particularly if D uses justifiable and fair methods.	Arguably, Transport did offer a comparable service at a lower cost only after being approached by Maker, indicating it was proper to try to compete and obtain business for themselves.	Likely defense for Transport
Carrier v. Transport: Torts Remedies			
Damages	Intentional interference with business relations does allow for pure economic loss recovery. **Damages must be caused by the tort and be foreseeable, certain, and unavoidable.**	**This could include damages due to loss of contract, reputation, unpaid invoice—all if capable of proof. (See above damages discussion for certainty.)**	**Damages possible if Transport liable**
Restitution	See above for rule	Transport has not received any benefit here, but rather Maker did.	No restitution
Injunction	**Need inadequate legal remedy, property interest, feasibility, balancing of hardships, and no defenses.**	**To prevent Maker from contracting with Transport; same problem with specific performance above, in that the legal damages are likely an adequate remedy.**	**No injunction**

PART 11 TORTS

TORTS TABLE OF CONTENTS

INTRODUCTION TO TORTS

Torts essay questions typically involve fewer issues compared to some of the other subjects; however, the factual analysis of each issue has greater depth and many issues can be argued both ways. Consequently, torts essays are very fact-intensive and not only require the use of all applicable facts in the analysis, but also application of logical factual inferences to fully and successfully analyze some of the issues and rule elements. To do this, it is best to approach a torts essay (once you have determined that the subject is torts after reading the question) by quickly writing out your issues checklist for torts, including all defenses. Next, you should read the facts carefully without annotating to get the general idea of what torts issues the fact pattern raises. Then, re-read the fact pattern and cross-reference your issues checklist to spot the issues as you read each sentence. Organize your scratch paper by the call of the question (if there is more than one) and then note the issues chronologically as they arise under each call. If there is only one call of the question, organize the issues sequentially as they arise in the facts.

After you have spotted all of the issues, you should write out the rule elements in shorthand next to each issue. Next, still using shorthand, match the applicable facts or factual inferences that correspond to each element. As you use the facts, you should highlight them or underline them in the fact pattern. This way you can ensure that you have used all of the facts from the question when you are finished organizing your answer. Should you find some "homeless facts" (some facts that are not underlined and, therefore, unused in your answer outline), you should review those facts with your issues checklist to ensure that you haven't missed any issues. Remember: There are rarely "red herrings" in a bar essay question, so all of the facts should be used. Often, the "homeless" facts will correspond to either a missed issue or a missed rule element within an issue, resulting in missed analysis. Given that the analysis portion of torts essays is the most heavily weighted part of your essay, you want to take every precaution to avoid missing these points.

Further, torts essays lend themselves to the use of logical factual inferences to properly analyze the elements of many issues. For example, when discussing duty and breach within a negligence issue, the facts will not tell you what a reasonable manufacturer would do. Rather, you are to logically infer what they would do. To illustrate, in an essay involving a manufacturer failing to include the side effects of a drug, the facts will not tell you that it is common for manufacturers to include such warnings. However, you can logically infer in your negligence analysis (one of the five theories for products liability) that the manufacturer breached its duty to act as a reasonable, prudent manufacturer under the circumstances because a reasonable manufacturer would not only list all side effects on the drugs, but would also likely advertise these side effects and require doctors to review them with patients prior to prescribing the drug. These types of logical, factual inferences are common in torts essays and are often required to receive maximum points in your analysis.

Finally, because torts is such a fact-intensive subject, pay special attention to the various fact patterns that commonly trigger an issue to help you with issue spotting. These fact triggers are included in the torts outline.

ISSUES CHECKLIST

INTENTIONAL TORTS/INTENTIONAL TORT DEFENSES

NEGLIGENCE

STRICT LIABILITY

PRODUCTS LIABILITY

Intent
S/L
Negligence
Warranty
Misrepresentation
Defenses

OTHER TORTS

Defamation
Privacy
Misrepresentation
Misuse of process
Interfere w/business relations
Nuisance

THIRD-PARTY ISSUES

MEMORIZATION ATTACK SHEET

INTENTIONAL TORTS

- ♦ **Battery**
  - Intentional infliction
  - Harmful/offensive contact
- ♦ **Assault**
  - Intentional
  - Causing apprehension of
  - Imminent
  - Harmful/offensive contact
- ♦ **IIED**
  - Intentional/reckless infliction by
  - Extreme & outrageous conduct of
  - Severe emotional distress
  - Third-party liability
- ♦ **False imprisonment**
  - Intentional
  - Confinement/restraint
  - Bounded area
  - No reasonable means of escape
  - P aware or harmed
- ♦ **Trespass to land**
  - Intentional
  - Physical invasion of
  - Real property of another
- ♦ **Trespass to chattels**
  - Intentional
  - Interference with
  - P's right of possession
  - In a chattel
- ♦ **Conversion**
  - Trespass to chattels and
  - Substantial interference
  - P pays full value

INTENTIONAL TORT DEFENSES

- ♦ **Consent**
  - Express
  - Implied
- ♦ **Self-defense**
  - Reasonable belief
  - Reasonable force
- ♦ **Defense of others**
  - Reasonable belief other person could defend
  - Reasonable force
- ♦ **Defense of property**
  - Reasonable force to
  - Prevent property tort
- ♦ **Recapture chattels**
  - Fresh pursuit
  - Reasonable force
  - Wrongful taking
- ♦ **Shopkeeper's privilege**
  - Temporarily detain
  - Reasonable belief stolen
- ♦ **Arrest**
  - D restrains P by
  - Exercising legal rights
- ♦ **Necessity**
  - Reasonably necessary
  - To prevent great harm
  - Public: no damages
  - Private: pay for damage

NEGLIGENCE

- ♦ **Duty of care**
  - General standard—"Reasonable person"
    - Foreseeable Ps (Cardoza)
    - Unforeseeable Ps (Andrews)
  - Special landowner standard
    - Licensee: guest
    - Invitee: business purpose
    - Trespasser
    - Attractive nuisance
  - Statutory—per se
- ♦ **Breach**
  - Failure to meet standard of care
  - Violate statute—per se
  - Res ipsa loquitur
- ♦ **Actual cause**
  - But-for test
  - Alternative causes (only one at fault)
  - Substantial factor (joint causes)

- ♦ **Proximate cause**
  - Direct cause—foreseeability
  - Eggshell-skull P
  - Intervening causes
- ♦ **Damages**
  - General/punitive
  - Duty to mitigate
- ♦ **NIED**
  - P physical injury
  - P zone of danger
- ♦ **Defenses**
  - Contributory negligence
  - Comparative negligence
  - Assumption of risk

STRICT LIABILITY

- ♦ **Animals**
  - Wild
  - Domestic if known
- ♦ **Ultrahazardous Activity**
  - High risk of serious harm
  - Can't eliminate risk with reasonable care
  - Not common in area
  - Danger v. value balance
- ♦ For both, also analyze causation and damages

PRODUCTS LIABILITY—5 THEORIES

- ♦ **Intentional**
  - Substantial certainty
- ♦ **Strict liability**
  - Commercial supplier
  - Places product in stream of commerce
  - Product is defective
    - ◆ Manufacturing
    - ◆ Design
      - Consumer expect. test
      - Risk-utility
    - ◆ Warning
  - Actual cause
  - Proximate cause
  - Damages
- ♦ **Negligence** (see above)
- ♦ **Warranties**
  - Express
  - Implied
    - ◆ Merchantability
    - ◆ Fitness for a particular purpose
- ♦ **Misrepresentation** (see below)

MISREPRESENTATION

- ♦ **Intentional misrepresentation**
  - Misrepresentation
  - Scienter (knowing/reckless)
  - Intent to induce P
  - Justifiable reliance
  - Damages
- ♦ **Negligent misrepresentation**
  - Same as above except only D acted with no reasonable grounds (for scienter)

NUISANCE

- ♦ **Private nuisance**
  - Substantial, unreasonable interference
  - Use/enjoyment of property
- ♦ **Public nuisance**
  - Substantial, unreasonable interference
  - Health, safety, property rights of community
  - Private party can recover w/ different damage only
- ♦ **Defenses**
  - Legislation
  - Coming to nuisance
  - Assumption of risk/contributory negligence

DEFAMATION

- ♦ **Common law**
  - Defamatory statement
  - Referring to P
  - Publication to 3rd party
  - Damages
    - ◆ Libel: presumed
    - ◆ Slander: prove unless per se

- **Constitutional law (addtl.)**
  - Public concern
  - Fault by D
    - Public figure—malice
    - Private figure—negligence
- **Defenses**
  - Consent
  - Truth
  - Privilege—absolute
  - Privilege—qualified

PRIVACY RIGHTS

- **Misappropriation**
  - P's name or picture
  - Unauthorized use for
  - D's financial benefit
- **Intrusion on P's solitude**
  - Intrusion
  - Private place
  - Highly offensive to reasonable person
- **Publicity of private life**
  - Publicized details
  - Private life
  - Highly offensive to reasonable person
- **False light**
  - Public placement
  - In false light
  - Highly offensive to reasonable person

MISUSE OF LEGAL PROCESSES

- **Malicious prosecution**
  - Legal proceedings
  - End in P's favor
  - No probable cause
  - Improper purpose
  - Damages
- **Abuse of process**
  - Wrongful use/process
  - Ulterior purpose
  - Act/threat against P

INTERFERENCE

- **Interference with business relations**
  - Contract or business expectancy
  - D's knowledge of same
  - Intentional interference
  - Damages
- **Defense: Privilege**
  - Fair competition

THIRD-PARTY ISSUES

- **Vicarious liability**
  - Scope of employment
  - Employee v. independent contractor
- **Multiple Ds**
  - Joint & several liability
  - Contribution
  - Indemnity
- **Wrongful death**
  - Next of kin can recover
- **Survival rights**
  - COA survives death
- **Tortious interference family relations**
  - Consortium, or relationship with child

TORTS RULES OUTLINE

I. **INTENTIONAL TORTS**

A. **Prima facie case:** All intentional torts require an **act** by the defendant, **intent** by the defendant to bring about some physical or mental **effect** upon another person, and the effect must have been legally **caused** by defendant's act or something set in motion by the defendant.

1. **Intent** can be achieved by either direct intent when the plaintiff has a **desire or purpose** to bring about the effect, or indirectly when the defendant **knows with substantial certainty** that a particular effect will occur.
2. **Transferred intent** will provide the requisite intent when the defendant held the necessary intent with respect to one person but instead **commits a different tort against** that **person or any other person**, or the **intended tort against a different person**. Transferred intent is not applicable with conversion or IIED.
3. **Causation** is the effect legally caused by the defendant's act or some action that is set in motion by defendant. Causation can also be satisfied if the defendant's act was a substantial factor in bringing about the effect.

> Exam tip: When analyzing intentional torts on an exam, pay attention to the possibility of **transferred intent** when the person harmed is not the one to whom the harm was directed or when the harm is of a different type of tort than that intended.

B. **Battery** is an intentional infliction of a harmful or offensive bodily contact.

1. **Intent:** Intent can be satisfied either by desire and purpose or with knowledge with substantial certainty.
2. **Harmful or offensive**
   a. **Harmful** touching would encompass a touching that causes pain or bodily damage; or
   b. **Offensive** touching is contact that offends a reasonable person's sense of dignity.
3. **Contact:** The contact can be direct or indirect; and includes contact with an object closely identified with plaintiff's body.

C. **Assault** is the intentional causing of an apprehension of an imminent harmful or offensive contact.

1. **Intent:** Intent can be satisfied either by **desire and purpose** or with **knowledge with substantial certainty**. For an assault, the plaintiff can intend to cause apprehension of an imminent touching, or intend to make contact.
2. **Causing apprehension of:** The plaintiff must be put in immediate apprehension of an imminent harmful or offensive touching. Thus, the plaintiff must be aware of the threat.

3. **Imminent:** The defendant must have the **apparent present ability** to carry out the threat.
4. **Harmful or offensive**
   a. **Harmful** touching would encompass a touching that causes pain or bodily damage; or
   b. **Offensive** touching is contact that offends a reasonable person's sense of dignity.

D. **Intentional infliction of emotional distress (IIED)** is the intentional or reckless infliction of severe emotional or mental distress caused by defendant's extreme and outrageous conduct.
   1. **Intent** can be satisfied three ways: 1) By **desire and purpose** to cause emotional distress; or 2) with **knowledge with substantial certainty** that emotional distress will result; or 3) with **reckless disregard** of the high probability emotional distress will occur.
   2. **Severe emotional distress:** The emotional distress suffered by the plaintiff must be severe, though bodily harm is not required.
   3. **Extreme and outrageous** conduct is that beyond all possible bounds of decency.
   4. **Third-person liability** occurs where the defendant intentionally or recklessly directs extreme and outrageous conduct at someone other than the plaintiff (person X). The plaintiff can recover for IIED if:
      a. Plaintiff was physically **present** and **known** by the defendant to be present, and is a **close relative** to X; or
      b. Plaintiff was physically **present** and **known** by the defendant to be present, and the plaintiff **suffers bodily harm** as a result of the severe emotional distress (e.g., heart attack).

E. **False imprisonment** occurs where the defendant intentionally causes the plaintiff to be confined, restrained, or detained to a bounded area with no reasonable means of escape, of which the plaintiff is either aware or harmed.
   1. **Intent:** Intent can be satisfied either by **desire and purpose** or with **knowledge with substantial certainty.** For an assault, the plaintiff can intend to cause apprehension of an imminent touching, or intend to make contact.
   2. **Confined,** restrained, or detained.
   3. **Bounded area:** Confinement must be within a bounded area.
   4. **No reasonable means of escape.**
   5. **Awareness:** Plaintiff must be **aware** of the confinement, or have **suffered harm** as a result of the confinement.

F. **Trespass to land** is the intentionally physical invasion of the land of another.
   1. **Intent:** Intent can be satisfied by the **desire and purpose** to voluntarily invade the land of another. However, the defendant need only intend to invade the land he actually invades, he need not intend to invade the land of another so a mistake as to land ownership will not provide a defense.
   2. **Physical invasion** of the land does not require that the land be harmed by the invasion, and includes:

a. The entry onto another's land without permission;
b. Remaining upon the land without the right to be there; or
c. Placing or projecting an object upon the land without permission.

3. **Real property** of another.

G. **Trespass to chattels** is an intentional interference with a person's use or possession of a chattel.

1. **Intent:** Intent can be satisfied by the **desire and purpose** to interfere with the chattel of another. However, the defendant need only intend to interfere with the chattel in the manner he does, so a mistake as to chattel ownership will not provide a defense.
2. **Interference with use or possession:** The chattel owner is precluded for using or possessing his chattel. Typically, this will be for a temporary time period.
3. **Chattel:** A chattel is personal property.
4. **Damages:** The measure of damages is the chattel's loss of value caused by the loss of use.

H. **Conversion** is an intentional interference with the plaintiff's possession or ownership of property that is so substantial that it warrants requiring the defendant to pay the property's full value.

1. **Intent:** Intent can be satisfied by the **desire and purpose** to interfere with the chattel of another. However, the defendant need only intend to interfere with the chattel in the manner he does, so a mistake as to chattel ownership will not provide a defense.
2. **Substantial interference with use or possession:** The interference with the chattel is so substantial that it warrants the defendant pay the chattel's full value. For example, interference is substantial where one takes possession of a chattel, transfers possession of a chattel to a third person, refuses to return a chattel, or destroys a chattel.
3. **Chattel:** A chattel is personal property.
4. **Damages:** The measure of damages is the chattel's full value.

II. DEFENSES TO INTENTIONAL TORTS

A. **Consent:** Plaintiff consents to defendant's conduct. Consent can be express or implied.

1. **Scope:** Consent may not go beyond the scope of the consent given.
2. **Consent to crimes:** Courts are split as to when the defendant's act against plaintiff is a criminal act. The majority of courts hold that plaintiff's consent is ineffective in this situation.

B. **Self-defense:** A person is entitled to use **reasonable force** to prevent any threatened harmful or offensive bodily contact, and any threatened confinement or imprisonment.

1. **Deadly force:** Use of deadly force is only allowed if the defendant is in danger of death or serious bodily harm.
2. **Degree of force:** Defendant may only use the degree of force necessary to prevent the threatened harm.

C. **Defense of others:** A person may use **reasonable force** to defend another person when he **reasonably believes** that the other person could have used force to defend himself. The same rules regarding use of force apply as in self-defense.

D. **Defense of property:** A person may use **reasonable force** to defend his real or personal property.
   1. **Warning required:** Defendant must first make a verbal demand that the intruder stop, unless it reasonably appears that it would be futile or dangerous.
   2. **Deadly force:** Defendant may only use deadly force **if non-deadly force will not suffice** and the defendant reasonably believes that without deadly force, death or serious bodily harm will result.
      a. **Mechanical devices:** A property owner may only use a mechanical device to protect his property if he would have been privileged to use the same degree of force if present at the time.

E. **Recapture of chattels:** A property owner has the general right to use **reasonable force** to regain possession of chattels taken by someone else.
   1. **Fresh pursuit:** The property owner must be in fresh pursuit.
   2. **Deadly force in not allowed** in the recapture of chattels.

F. **Shopkeeper's privilege:** Shopkeepers have a privilege to temporarily detain individuals whom they reasonably believe to be in possession of shoplifted goods.
   1. **Temporarily detain:** Temporary detention is allowed for a reasonable time to investigate if shoplifting has occurred, typically for 10 to 15 minutes. The police must be called to make an arrest.

G. **Arrest under a legal authority** is allowed when the defendant was exercising his legal rights and duties by restraining the plaintiff.

H. **Necessity:** A person may interfere with the real or personal property of another when it is reasonably and apparently necessary to prevent great harm to third persons or the defendant himself.
   1. **Public necessity** applies when the threatened harm was to the community at large or to many people. Should property be damaged by the public necessity, no compensation is owed.
   2. **Private necessity** applies when a person acts to prevent injury to himself or his property, or the person or property of another. Should damage to property result from the private necessity, the plaintiff must pay for the damage.

> Exam tip: Although intentional torts are not heavily tested on the essays, when they are tested, it is useful to write out a quick **issues checklist** of all intentional torts and their defenses. In addition, it is common for more than one intentional tort to apply to a given fact pattern, so consider all possible intentional torts. Lastly, always look at the potential **applicable defenses,** as these are always issues that should be raised and analyzed even if you ultimately find that they do not apply.

III. NEGLIGENCE

A. **Prima facie case:** Defendant's conduct imposes an unreasonable risk upon another, which results in injury to that other person. Plaintiff must prove the following elements: **duty, breach, cause-in-fact, proximate cause, and actual damage.**

B. **Duty of care:** A person has a duty to act as a reasonable person.
   1. **To whom duty of care is owed**
      a. **Foreseeable plaintiffs:** The **majority** of courts hold that a duty is only owed to foreseeable plaintiffs (Cardozo view).
      b. **Everyone:** A **minority** of courts hold that a duty is owed to **everyone** including unforeseeable plaintiffs (Andrews view).
   2. **Standard of care**
      a. **General: A reasonable person under the circumstances**, unless a special duty applies (see III.B.2.b below).
         1. The circumstances considered generally include the physical characteristics of defendant, but do not include the mental characteristics of defendant.
      b. **Special duty rule categories**
         1. **Affirmative duties to act:** Defendant generally has **no duty to take affirmative action** to help plaintiff, **except**
            a. **Special relationship:** A defendant has an affirmative duty to act where there is a special relationship, such as a business or landowner holding premises open to the public, or landlords and tenants, or other special relationships;
            b. **Causing the danger:** A defendant has an affirmative duty to act when his conduct placed plaintiff in danger; or
            c. **Volunteer assistance:** Where a defendant voluntarily begins to render assistance to plaintiff, he must proceed with reasonable care.
         2. **Professionals** are required to possess the knowledge and skill of a member of their profession or occupation in good standing.
            a. **Fireman's rule** prohibits firefighters (and police officers) who are injured in the line of duty from suing for negligence for injuries sustained that stemmed from the inherent risks they assume with their profession.
         3. **Children** must conform to the conduct of a child of like age, intelligence, and experience.
            a. **Exception—adult activity:** Children engaged in a potentially dangerous activity normally pursued only by adults are held to an adult standard of care.
         4. **Bailment duties**
            a. **Bailor duties:** For a **gratuitous** bailment, the bailor must inform of known, dangerous defects in the chattel. For a bailment for **hire**, the bailor must inform of chattel defects of which he is or should be aware.
            b. **Bailee duties:** Standard of care depends on who benefits from the bailment. Where the sole benefit is to the bailor, the standard of care is low. Where the sole benefit is to the bailee, a higher standard of care is imposed. Where the

bailment is mutually beneficial, an ordinary standard of care is imposed.

5. **Owners and occupiers of land**
    a. **Effect outside the premises**
        i. **Natural conditions:** No duty exists to protect one outside the premises from hazardous natural conditions on the premises.
        ii. **Artificial conditions:** A duty exists to prevent an unreasonable risk of harm for unreasonably dangerous artificial hazards.
    b. **Trespassers:** A landowner generally owes **no duty to make the land safe or warn of dangerous conditions** to undiscovered trespassers or invitees/licensees that go beyond the scope of their invitation.
    c. **Exceptions to general trespasser rule**
        i. **Known or frequent trespassers:** There is a duty to warn known or frequent trespassers of **known dangers and artificial conditions** that pose a risk of death or serious bodily harm.
        ii. **Attractive nuisance doctrine:** A landowner must exercise **ordinary care** to avoid **foreseeable injury to children** if
            (1) The owner **knew or should have known** that the area is one where **children trespass**;
            (2) The condition poses an **unreasonable risk** of serious injury or death;
            (3) The children **do not discover the risk** or realize the danger due to their youth;
            (4) The benefit to the owner and **expense to remedy the condition is slight compared to the risk**; and
            (5) The owner **fails to use reasonable care** to eliminate the danger.

> **Issue-spotting tip:** When there are **children** involved in a tort fact pattern, always consider the **attractive nuisance doctrine** as a possible issue when evaluating negligence. Also, do not think that the children have to actually be attracted to the area or object at issue since that is not part of the rule.

    d. **Licensee** is one who enters the land with the **owner's consent** for his own purpose (i.e., social guests). An owner has a **duty to *warn* of all known dangerous conditions** that create an unreasonable risk of harm that the licensee is unlikely to discover and to **use reasonable care** in conducting its active operations on the property. However, there is no duty to repair or inspect the premises.

e. **Invitee** is one who enters the land in response to an invitation by the owner to do **business** with the owner or as a public invitee for land **open to the public** at large. The owner has a **duty to make a reasonable *inspection* to find hidden dangers** and take affirmative action to remedy a dangerous condition (make necessary repairs).

f. **Lessee of realty:** Lessee (tenant) has a general duty to maintain the premises and must abide by the **same duties owed by landowners** above.

g. **Lessor of realty:** Lessor (landlord) must
   - *i.* **Warn of existing dangers** of which he **knows or should know** that the lessee is not likely to discover.
   - *ii.* **Repair not negligently:** If the lessor **promises to repair,** he must not do so negligently.
   - *iii.* **Maintain common areas:** Lessor must use **reasonable care** to maintain the common areas.

6. **Violation of a statute—negligence per se doctrine**

   a. **Negligence per se:** Defendant is negligent per se if
      - *i.* **Violates a statute** without excuse;
      - *ii.* Plaintiff is **within the class of persons the statute is designed to protect**; and
      - *iii.* The statute is designed to **guard against the type of risk** or accident suffered by plaintiff.

   b. **Violation excused:** Defendant's violation may be excused if
      - *i.* Compliance would create a **greater risk** of harm;
      - *ii.* The defendant was **incapacitated**; or
      - *iii.* The defendant was **unaware** of the factual circumstances that made the statute applicable.

   c. **Establishes duty and breach:** Negligence per se establishes the elements of duty and breach, but plaintiff must still prove **causation and damage**.

   d. **Compliance** with a statute does not itself establish that defendant was not negligent.

> **Exam tip:** When addressing negligence, it is recommended that you start with general negligence duty, analyze that duty first, and then move on to analyze the other possible duties in addition to the general duty. For example, if there is statute in the fact pattern, analyze negligence under both the general duty standard as well as the negligence per se standard. Lastly, do not forget to analyze the remaining elements of negligence.

C. **Breach of duty**

1. **Breach:** Generally, breach occurs when the defendant's conduct **fails to conform to the applicable standard of care.** Courts often use a balancing test to determine if the risk is unreasonable such that the risk outweighs the utility of the act.

2. **Res ipsa loquitur:** Res ipsa loquitur means "the thing speaks for itself" and can be used to establish breach of duty in situations where the event transpiring creates an inference that the defendant was probably negligent because:
    a. The accident is a type that **ordinarily does not occur in the absence of negligence**; and
    b. **Other causes**, including the conduct of the plaintiff and third persons, are sufficiently **eliminated** by the evidence (such as when the defendant had exclusive control).

D. **Causation in fact (actual cause)**
1. **But-for test:** Generally, **but for** the defendant's act, the injury to plaintiff would not have resulted.
2. **Multiple fault**
    a. **Only one at fault:** When there are two acts, **only one** of which could have **caused the injury**, but it is unknown which act caused the injury, the burden of proof shifts to each defendant to show that the other caused the harm.
    b. **Joint tortfeasors (substantial factor test):** Where two or more defendants are at fault and their **conduct combines** to cause the harm to the plaintiff, they will all be jointly and severally liable, as their actions are a substantial factor in causing the injury.

E. **Proximate cause**
1. **Reasonable foreseeability test:** Generally, a defendant is liable for all harmful results that were **reasonably foreseeable**.
2. **Eggshell-skull plaintiff:** The defendant is also liable for any additional unforeseen physical consequences to plaintiff caused by a weakness or susceptibility of the plaintiff because the defendant "takes his plaintiff as he finds him."
3. **Intervening causes**
    a. **Foreseeable:** Defendant is **liable** for **foreseeable intervening causes** (such as subsequent medical malpractice and negligence by rescuers).
    b. **Unforeseeable:** Defendant is generally **not liable** for **superseding intervening causes** that are not a normal response or reasonably foreseeable reaction to the situation created by defendant's conduct; superseding intervening causes often result from an interruption in the chain of causation.

> Exam Tip: When analyzing negligence issues, the majority of the points and analysis are incurred in the breach and proximate cause elements since those elements tend to be the most fact-intensive. Further, since there are no "homeless" facts in the essays, use all of the facts available to analyze these two elements. Finally, it is often necessary to use logical inferences when analyzing these elements. For example, the facts will not tell you what a reasonable person ordinarily does to determine whether the defendant owed a duty and breached a duty, so to properly analyze these elements, you will need to make a logical inference as to what a reasonable person would have done in the given situation.

F. **Damages**
   1. **Actual injury required:** Damages require an actual injury and nominal damages are not available.
   2. **Elements of damages:** Plaintiff may recover damages for direct loss, out-of-pocket economic losses stemming from the injury, pain and suffering, and hedonistic damages (loss of ability to enjoy life).
   3. **Mitigation:** In addition to establishing that the damages/harm are **caused** by defendant's conduct above and that the damages were **foreseeable**, plaintiff must also **mitigate** his damages (i.e., seek treatment).
   4. **Punitive damages** are available if defendant's conduct was wanton and willful.

> Exam tip: Generally, damages are clear since someone is injured. Usually, this element can be established in one line of analysis. Likewise, actual causation can similarly often be analyzed in one sentence using the "but for" rule. So, remember to **wisely allocate your time** when analyzing all of the elements of negligence since each element is not equally weighted in points.

> Negligence fact triggers:
> - Actions or omissions by people
> - Manufacturers, workers, or employees doing a job or task (often incorrectly)
> - Mistakes (failure to file claims timely, put up chemicals, supervise children, leave car running, etc.)

G. **Negligent infliction of emotional distress (NIED):** Defendant is liable for NIED when the defendant engages in negligent conduct that causes the plaintiff to suffer serious emotional distress.
   1. **Actual impact or threat:** Plaintiff may suffer an actual physical impact or the threat of a physical impact that **directly causes emotional distress.**
   2. **Fear for others' safety:** If plaintiff suffers from severe emotional distress without any physical impact to him personally, recovery under NIED depends on the jurisdiction.
      a. **Majority rule:** Most courts require plaintiff to be in the **zone of danger** (physically endangered) to recover for NIED.
      b. **Minority rule (including California)** allows recovery for NIED if plaintiff observes the danger even if he is not within the zone of danger. Some jurisdictions require that plaintiff and the injured person be relatives.

IV. DEFENSES TO NEGLIGENCE

A. **Contributory negligence** is negligence on the part of plaintiff that contributes proximately to his injuries and completely bars his recovery. This is abolished in most jurisdictions.

B. **Comparative negligence** applies when plaintiff's own negligence has contributed to his injuries, but is not a complete bar to recovery. The liability is divided between plaintiff and defendant **in proportion to their relative degrees of fault.**

   1. **Partial comparative negligence** bars plaintiff's recovery if his negligence was more serious than defendant's (in some states, at least as serious). This typically means that if plaintiff's negligence were more than 50% responsible, his recovery would be barred.
   2. **Pure comparative negligence** allows recovery regardless of how negligent plaintiff was but reduces plaintiff's recovery by the percentage he was negligent.

C. **Assumption of the risk:** Plaintiff may be denied recovery if he assumed the risk of any damage caused by defendant's act where he knew of the risk and voluntarily consented despite the risk.

> <u>Exam tip:</u> Always discuss defenses with negligence. It is best to address all three defenses quickly, each with its own heading. Rarely is a full negligence discussion necessary to establish plaintiff's contributory negligence, but the issue should still be raised as a possibility.

V. STRICT LIABILITY APPLIES FOR THE FOLLOWING TWO ACTIVITIES:

A. **Animals:** An owner is strictly liable for:

   1. **Trespass:** Reasonably foreseeable damage done by a trespass of his animals;
   2. **Wild animals:** Nontrespass injuries caused by wild animals that result from a **dangerous propensity that is typical of the species**; and
   3. **Domestic animals known to be dangerous:** Injuries caused by domestic animals only if the owner **knew or had reason to know** of that particular animal's dangerous propensities.

B. **Ultrahazardous/abnormally dangerous activities:** An activity is abnormally dangerous if it is:

   1. An activity that creates a **high degree of risk of serious harm**;
   2. The **risk cannot be eliminated** by the exercise of reasonable care;
   3. The activity is **not common**;
   4. The activity is **not appropriate for the location**; and
   5. The danger outweighs the activity's value to the community.

C. **Defenses**

   1. **Assumption of the risk** is a defense to strict liability.
   2. **Contributory fault is not** a defense to strict liability.

VI. PRODUCTS LIABILITY

A. **Five theories available to establish products liability:** Liability of a seller of a tangible item, which because of a defect, causes injury to its purchaser, user, or bystander, can be based upon any of the following five theories: intent, strict tort liability, negligence, warranty, and misrepresentation.

B. **Intent:** Defendant is liable if defendant intended the consequences or knew they were substantially certain to occur. (Defenses are the same as for intentional torts; punitive damages allowed here.)

C. **Strict liability:** A seller of a product is liable without fault for personal injuries caused by a defective product if the following elements are met:

1. **Commercial supplier:** A commercial supplier is one who places a product in the **stream of commerce** without substantial alteration. A commercial supplier includes retailers and other nonmanufacturers, as well as the product manufacturer.
2. **Breach** of duty is established by proving the **product was defective.** There are three types of product defects:
    a. **Manufacturing defect** exists when a particular instance of the product is different and more dangerous than all of the others because this particular product deviated from its intended design. In other words, the product was not manufactured as intended.
    b. **Design defect** exists when all products of a line are the same and they all bear a feature whose design is itself defective and unreasonably dangerous; courts use the following two tests to establish a design defect:
        1. **Consumer expectation test:** A product's performance must meet the minimum safety expectations of its ordinary users when used in a reasonably foreseeable manner.
        2. **Risk-utility test:** A product is defective if the risk of danger inherent in the design outweighs the benefits of such design and the danger could have been reduced or avoided by the adoption of a **reasonable, cost-effective alternative design.** The court will consider the **cost and utility** of an alternative design compared to the cost and utility of the current design.
    c. **Warning defect** exists when the maker fails to give adequate warnings as to a known (or should have been known) danger in the product or in a particular use of the product that is nonobvious. Some courts use risk-utility analysis when the risk could have been reduced or avoided by reasonable instructions or warnings.
    d. **Compliance with industry standards** is not conclusive evidence that a product is not defective; but lack of compliance can establish that a product is defective.

> <u>Exam tip:</u> In products strict liability questions, there is often more than one defect, so consider all three possibilities. Most of the analysis in products liability questions will involve establishing breach by way of a defect since most facts are applicable to that element.

3. **Actual cause:** Plaintiff must show that **but for** the defect, he would not have been injured and that the defect existed at time it left defendant's control.
4. **Proximate cause:** Same analysis as in negligence cases (foreseeability).
5. **Damages:** Physical injury or property damage must be shown. There is no recovery for purely economic loss.
6. **Defenses**
   a. **Assumption of the risk** is a defense.
   b. **Comparative negligence/contributory negligence** for product misuse is a defense, unless plaintiff's negligence/misuse was foreseeable.
   c. **Disclaimers** are **not effective.**

> Exam tip: Under either strict liability theory, after establishing a strict duty is owed and that it has been breached, plaintiff must still prove actual and proximate cause and damages. Remember to go through all remaining elements.

D. **Negligence:** See Section III above. However, note that **retailers and wholesalers** are rarely liable under a negligence theory for products liability since they only have a duty to inspect or warn of known dangers. A manufacturer would still likely be liable under a negligence theory.

E. **Warranty**
1. **Express warranty:** An express warranty is any statement of fact or promise concerning goods. The plaintiff need only show that the product did not live up to its warranty to establish for breach of express warranty.
2. **Implied warranty of merchantability:** An implied warranty of merchantability is implied in every sale of goods that they are **fit for the ordinary purposes** for which the goods are used.
3. **Fitness for a particular purpose:** A warranty of fitness for a particular purpose is implied in every sale of goods when the **seller knows** or has reason to know that the buyer wants the goods for a **particular purpose** and the **buyer relies on the seller's judgment** to recommend a suitable product.
4. **Defenses**
   a. **Assumption of the risk** is a defense.
   b. **Comparative negligence/contributory negligence** for product misuse (unless plaintiff's negligence/misuse was foreseeable) is a defense.
   c. **Failure to give notice** of breach under the UCC.

F. **Misrepresentation of fact:** Seller will be liable for misrepresentations of fact concerning a product when the statement was a **material fact concerning quality or uses of goods** and the seller **intended to induce reliance** by the buyer and **did in fact induce reliance.** Plaintiff must still prove actual cause, proximate cause, and damages. Contributory negligence is a defense unless defendant's misrepresentation was intentional.

> <u>Exam tip:</u> All questions involving products liability involve more than one theory under which the defendant can be liable, so remember to carefully review all five theories as possibilities rather than simply analyzing the one most obvious theory of strict products liability. Recently, questions have included specific calls about particular elements within the various theories. To answer the call, you sometimes need to fully analyze the products liability issues and defenses and then answer each call after you have completed all of the analysis. (See torts sample question 4 for an example of this type of question and how to answer it).

> <u>Products liability fact triggers:</u>
> - Manufacturers of products
> - Retail sellers
> - Products
> - Injury due to use of product
> - Instructions for product use

VII. MISREPRESENTATION

A. **Intentional misrepresentation** is common law fraud or deceit. One must prove:
   1. **Misrepresentation** (actions or intentional concealment) of a material fact,
   2. **Scienter** (knowledge of statement's falsity or reckless indifference to the truth),
   3. **Intent to induce plaintiff's reliance** on the misrepresentation,
   4. **Causation,**
   5. **Justifiable reliance** by plaintiff, and
   6. **Pecuniary damages** to plaintiff.

B. **Negligent misrepresentation** requires establishing:
   1. **Misrepresentation** by defendant in a **business or professional capacity,**
   2. Defendant acted with **no reasonable grounds for believing the misrepresentation to be true,**
   3. **Intent to induce plaintiff's reliance** on the misrepresentation,
   4. **Causation,**
   5. **Justifiable reliance,** and
   6. **Pecuniary damages** to plaintiff.

VIII. NUISANCE

A. **Private nuisance** is a substantial, unreasonable interference with another private individual's use or enjoyment of his land or land in which he has an interest.

1. **Substantial interference** is that which is offensive, inconvenient, or annoying to the average person in the community.
2. **Unreasonable interference:** The interference is unreasonable if either
    a. The **harm to plaintiff outweighs the utility** of defendant's conduct; or
    b. The **harm caused to plaintiff** is greater than plaintiff should be required to bear **without consideration.**
    c. **Test for both:** Consider the neighborhood, land value, and alternatives for defendant.

B. **Public nuisance** is a substantial, unreasonable interference with the health, morals, welfare, safety, or property rights of the community.
1. **Interference:** Courts consider factors establishing harm to the community including the **location of the nuisance**, the **frequency and duration**, the **degree of damage**, and the **social value** of the activity.
2. **Recovery by a private party** is only available if the private party suffered damage that is **different in kind** and not merely in degree from that suffered by the public.

C. **Remedies for nuisance** include damages and injunctive relief.

D. **Defenses for nuisance**
1. **Legislative authority** is persuasive but not an absolute defense (i.e., zoning ordinance that permits the conduct in the location).
2. **Assumption of the risk** and **contributory negligence** are defenses if the plaintiff's case rests on a negligence theory.
3. **Coming to the nuisance** is a bar only if plaintiff came to the nuisance for the sole purpose of bringing a harassing lawsuit. Otherwise, coming to the nuisance is not a valid defense.

> <u>Exam tip:</u> Many nuisance issues arise where the call of the question asks whether the court should grant an injunction to a plaintiff. To analyze whether the court should grant the injunction, you must analyze the "likelihood of success on the merits" element, which necessitates analysis of the underlying nuisance claim. Go through private and/or public nuisance (as appropriate) and always consider applicable defenses.

> <u>Nuisance fact triggers:</u>
> - Toxic chemicals/pollution
> - Power interruptions
> - Odors
> - Obstruction of views

IX. DEFAMATION

A. **Common law defamation** occurs when a false and **defamatory statement concerning plaintiff** is **published** to a person other than the plaintiff causing **damage to the plaintiff's reputation.**

1. **Pure opinions or true statements** are not defamatory statements.
2. A **publication** can be made intentionally or negligently and must be understood by the other person. Repeaters of the defamatory statement can also be liable.
3. The statement **need not have actually harmed** the plaintiff's reputation, but the plaintiff must show that it would have had it been believed.
4. **Damages** depend on the **type of defamation.**
   a. **Libel** is written or **printed publication** of a defamatory statement. This includes any communication embodied in physical form, including phonograph records, or radio or TV broadcasts.
      1. For libel, the plaintiff does not need to prove special damages and **general damages are presumed.**
   b. **Slander is spoken** or nonscripted defamation.
      1. For slander, the plaintiff must **prove special damages,** unless it is slander per se.
      2. For **slander per se,** damages are presumed. Slander per se is established for language that
         i. Adversely reflects on the plaintiff's fitness to conduct his **business or profession,**
         ii. Alleges one has a **loathsome disease,**
         iii. Imputes morally culpable **criminal** behavior, or
         iv. Imputes serious **sexual misconduct** to the plaintiff.

B. **Constitutional law defamation** must be analyzed if the defamation is a matter of **public concern.** Constitutional defamation requires that the plaintiff prove the elements of common law defamation and establish fault on the part of the defendant. The test to determine fault depends on the **status of the plaintiff.**
   1. **Public figure:** A plaintiff is a public figure when he has achieved pervasive fame or notoriety or voluntarily assumed a role in a public controversy.
      a. **Actual malice standard:** When the defendant is a public figure, actual malice must be proven. Actual malice exists when the defendant made the statement with either (i) **knowledge that it was false,** or (ii) **reckless disregard** as to whether it was true or false.
      b. **Damages are presumed** if actual malice is shown.
   2. **Private person:** A private person is any person not considered a public figure.
      a. **Negligence standard:** When the plaintiff is a private person only negligence regarding the falsity of the statement must be proven if the statement involves a matter of public concern.
      b. **Only actual injury damages** are recoverable (not necessarily pecuniary). But, if malice exists, damages are presumed and punitive damages are allowed.

C. **Defenses to defamation**
   1. **Consent**
   2. **Truth**

3. **Absolute privilege** extends to remarks made during judicial or legislative proceedings, by federal government and most state government officials, and between spouses. This privilege exists even if defendant acted with malice.
4. **Qualified privilege** extends to statements made to protect the publisher's interests if the defamation relates directly to those interests, or for the protection of the recipient or a third party, or to act in the public interest or report on public proceedings. This **privilege can be lost** if the defendant abuses it by acting with actual malice or publishing the statement excessively when it is not reasonably necessary.

Exam tip: For defamation questions, always start by asking whether the issue is a matter of public or private concern. If you can argue both ways as to whether the matter is public or private (as is often the case), include analysis of the constitutional elements and any applicable defenses. Likewise, if you can argue both ways that the defendant is a public and private figure, analyze both rules, since this will affect the damages element. Recently, defamation questions have included very specific calls asking about each element of defamation. (An example is in the Torts Issues Tested Matrix that follows this outline.) Analyze each element as requested to answer the specific calls.

Defamation fact triggers:
- Reporters
- Newspaper articles
- Radio station broadcasts
- Any publication or writing

X. PRIVACY

A. **Misappropriation (of plaintiff's picture or name)** is the **unauthorized use** of the **plaintiff's picture or name** for the defendant's **commercial advantage.**

B. **Intrusion on plaintiff's solitude** is the intrusion into a **private aspect** of the plaintiff's life in a private place that is **highly objectionable to a reasonable person.**

C. **Placing plaintiff in false light** occurs where (1) one **attributes to plaintiff views** he does not hold or actions he does not take; (2) the false light is **objectionable to a reasonable person** under the circumstances; and (3) the publication is **public.**
1. **Public interest:** If the matter is of public interest, **malice** must be proved (First Amendment limitation).
2. **Public figures:** Plaintiff must prove **actual malice** on the part of the defendant.

D. **Publicity of private life is the public disclosure of private facts** that are not a matter of legitimate public concern, the release of which is **objectionable to a reasonable person** where the disclosure is communicated to the public at large, and not just to a single person or small group of persons.

> **Issue-spotting tip:** Privacy issues often arise in combination with defamation questions. So, when you recognize a defamation issue and/or a privacy issue, always write out a brief issues checklist of all possible defamation and privacy issues and defenses. In addition, there are often several privacy issues that will arise in the same fact pattern, so consider all of them when issue spotting.

> **Privacy fact triggers:**
> - Disclosure of information
> - Offensive statements or comments
> - Secret recordings
> - False pretenses to obtain information
> - Facts that give rise to defamation

XI. MISUSE OF LEGAL PROCESSES

A. **Malicious prosecution** occurs when there is an
1. **Institution of criminal proceedings** (and civil proceedings in most jurisdictions) against plaintiff;
    a. Prosecutors are immune from liability.
    b. The defendant can be any person actively involved in bringing about the proceedings.
2. **Termination in plaintiff's favor**;
3. **Absence of probable cause** for the institution of the proceedings;
4. **Improper purpose** of the accuser; and
5. **Damages** suffered by the accused.

B. **Abuse of process** occurs when the defendant **intentionally misuses legal procedure** (i.e., depositions, discovery tools, etc.) for an ulterior purpose and the defendant committed a willful act in a wrongful manner that caused damage to the plaintiff.

XII. INTERFERENCE WITH BUSINESS RELATIONS

A. **Prima facie case** requires establishing:
1. Existence of a **valid contractual relationship** between the plaintiff and a third party or a **valid business expectancy** of the plaintiff,
2. The defendant **knew or should have known of the relationship** or expectancy,
3. **Intentional interference** by the defendant inducing breach or termination of the relationship or expectancy, and
4. **Damages.**

B. **Privileges:** Defendant's conduct may be privileged where it is a proper attempt to obtain business for itself or protect its interests (fair competition), particularly if the defendant uses justifiable and fair methods.

XIII. **THIRD-PARTY ISSUES**

A. **Vicarious liability:** One is vicariously liable to another when he commits a tortious act against a third party and another person is liable to the third party for this act.

1. **Respondeat superior:** If an employee commits a tort during the **course and scope** of his employment, his employer will be jointly liable with the employee.
   a. **Employee:** An employee is one who works subject to the close control of the person who hired him.
   b. **Scope of employment:** The tort is within the scope of employment if the tortfeasor was acting with the **intent to further the employer's business purpose**, even if the act itself was forbidden.
2. **Independent contractor:** One who hires an independent contractor is generally not vicariously liable for the torts of that person unless
   a. The employer is **negligent in hiring** that person, or
   b. The **duty is nondelegable** due to work in a public place or work that involves a peculiar risk of physical harm to others, such as undertaking inherently dangerous activities.

B. **Multiple defendants**

1. **Joint and several liability** exists where two or more negligent acts combine to proximately cause an indivisible harm, making each defendant liable for the entire harm. Plaintiff can recover the entire loss from any defendant, regardless of that defendant's share of the total responsibility.
2. **Contribution** allows a defendant who pays more than his pro rata share of responsibility to obtain reimbursement from another defendant.
3. **Indemnity** is the shifting of responsibility for the entire loss from one defendant to another.

C. **Survival and wrongful death**

1. **Survival actions** allow one's cause of action to survive the death of one or more of the parties.
   a. **Exception:** These actions do not include defamation, right to privacy, or malicious prosecution.
2. **Wrongful death** acts grant recovery for pecuniary injury resulting to the spouse and next of kin and are only allowed to the extent that the deceased could have recovered if he had lived. The decedent's creditors have no interest in the amount recovered under a wrongful death claim.

D. **Tortious interference with family relationships:** A husband or wife may bring an action for interference with consortium and services caused by defendant's intentional or negligent actions against the other spouse. A parent can also recover for the loss of a child's services.

TORTS ISSUES TESTED MATRIX

		Crossover Questions	Intentional Torts	Negligence or NIED	Strict Liability (Abnormally Dangerous Activity)	Products Liability (Any of the 5 theories)	Misrepre-sentation	Nuisance	Defamation	Privacy	Malicious Prosecution/ Abuse of Process	Interference with Business Relations	3rd-Party Liability Issues
February '11 Q4	Gayle, 16, leaves high school and hits officer Paula			X									Vicarious
July '10 Q1	Homeowner kept a handgun; Burglar stole it		Battery, Assault, TTC/ Conversion, IIED	X									
July '09 Q1	Patty transports human organs and David blocks bridge	Civil Proc.			X						X		
February '09 Q4	ConsumerPro lists Paul as ambulance-chaser attorney								X				
February '08 Q1	Peter, pet pigeon, injured on high-voltage wire fence			X	X								
July '07 Q2	Consumer burned by soup using Cold Drink Blender			X		X							Indemnify

Continued >

		Crossover Questions	Intentional Torts	Negligence or NIED	Strict Liability (Abnormally Dangerous Activity)	Products Liability (Any of the 5 theories)	Misrepre-sentation	Nuisance	Defamation	Privacy	Malicious Prosecution/ Abuse of Process	Interference with Business Relations	3rd-Party Liability Issues
February '07 Q1	Builder sold mall to Owner & reserved parking spaces	Real Prop.						X					
July '06 Q1	Paul & Clerk, Delta Gas; candy & carbon monoxide poisoning		False Imprison.	X									Vicarious
February '06 Q1	Oscar v. Autos, Inc. Roadster for injury to child			X		X							
July '04 Q6	Jack's "Star" uncut diamond & Chip the master diamond cutter	Remedies		X									Survival/ Wrongful Death
July '03 Q4	Paula v. KXYZ Radio for broadcasting eavesdropped conversation								X	X			
July '02 Q5	Sally v. Manufacturer of allergy pills for eyesight side effect			X		X							

Continued >

		Crossover Questions	Intentional Torts	Negligence or NIED	Strict Liability (Abnormally Dangerous Activity)	Products Liability (Any of the 5 theories)	Misrepre-sentation	Nuisance	Defamation	Privacy	Malicious Prosecution/ Abuse of Process	Interference with Business Relations	3rd-Party Liability Issues
July '01 Q5	Attorney Ann advises Harry on ugly divorce from Wilma	Prof. Resp.							X		X		
February '01 Q4	Diane's office bldg & Peter's restaurant and garden	Remedies	TTL/ Conversion										
July '00 Q6	Don makes pot-tery & causes an electrical surge	Remedies	TTL/TTC/ Conversion	X	X			X				X	
February '00 Q3	Lee comments about Judge Bright's unfair-ness after trial	Prof. Resp.							X				
February '00 Q2	Chemco pro-cessing plant discharges waste into river	Remedies	TTL					X					
July '99 Q5	Artist leases loft, machinist is loud & St. Power blocks path	Real Prop.; Remedies						X					
July '99 Q3	Susan, Felix, and telephone software	Contracts; Prof. Resp.										X	
July '98 Q4	Transco hauls toxic chemicals by train		IIED	X	X			X					Vicarious

Continued >

		Crossover Questions	Intentional Torts	Negligence or NIED	Strict Liability (Abnormally Dangerous Activity)	Products Liability (Any of the 5 theories)	Misrepre-sentation	Nuisance	Defamation	Privacy	Malicious Prosecution/ Abuse of Process	Interference with Business Relations	3rd-Party Liability Issues
February '98 Q5	Halfway rehabs former convicts & neighbors form NASS to protest	Remedies						X					
February '98 Q1	Carrier k's for all of Maker's trans-portation needs	Contracts; Remedies										X	
February '97 Q1	Peters v. Bladeco, Conco & Homeco for concrete cutter			X		X							Indemnify/ Contribute
February '96 Q3	Dave's gym and injury to Paul	Civil Proc.; Evidence		X									
July '95 Q3	Booker, owner of bookstore, and Walker, the browser		False Imprisonment / IIED						X	X	X		Vicarious
February '94 Q4	Fidelity & defec-tive building built by Bildco	Contracts; Remedies		X									Vicarious/ Joint & Several
July '93 Q1	Dina, age 16, lives at home with mother & stops taking meds		Battery / Assault	X									Vicarious
February '93 Q5	Owen's backyard pool & Petey falls and hits head	Prof. Resp.		X									

Continued >

		Crossover Questions	Intentional Torts	Negligence or NIED	Strict Liability (Abnormally Dangerous Activity)	Products Liability (Any of the 5 theories)	Misrepre-sentation	Nuisance	Defamation	Privacy	Malicious Prosecution/ Abuse of Process	Interference with Business Relations	3rd-Party Liability Issues
July '92 Q2	Dan, student, posted on bulletin board grade A exchanged for sex			X					X	X			Vicarious
February '92 Q4	Amy's restaurant suffers losses because of bad exit	Prof. Resp.		X							X		
July '91 Q3	Henry, agent for Insco, embezzles funds	Remedies	Conversion										
February '91 Q5	Owner hires Plummer & pipe bursts, scalding Carrie			X									Vicarious
February '91 Q3	Refin operates a smelter and hauls toxic chemicals	Remedies	TTL					X					
February '90 Q6	Joe & wealthy brother Steve	Contracts; Real Prop.; Remedies										X	
July '89 Q3	Ed works for Dynorad & exposed to bacteria for germ warfare		IIED						X	X			Vicarious

Continued >

		Crossover Questions	Intentional Torts	Negligence or NIED	Strict Liability (Abnormally Dangerous Activity)	Products Liability (Any of the 5 theories)	Misrepre-sentation	Nuisance	Defamation	Privacy	Malicious Prosecution/ Abuse of Process	Interference with Business Relations	3rd-Party Liability Issues
July '89 Q2	Dan interferes with Paul's new restaurant, chef, and home purchase	Remedies	IIED									X	
February '89 Q3	Dick truck driver for Ace, hits bicyclist Phil			X		X	X				X		Vicarious
July '88 Q6	Jack & David, age 16, racing motor-cycles, causing accident			X									
February '88 Q4	Proff has State College lecture but airline trouble	Contracts; Remedies					X						Vicarious
July '87 Q4	Trustee won't fix lot where parking lot has cracks	Real Prop.; Wills &Trusts		X									
February '87 Q4	Harold uses Rosebrite insecti-cide & neighbor Johnny sprays on self			X	X	X							

Continued >

		Crossover Questions	Intentional Torts	Negligence or NIED	Strict Liability (Abnormally Dangerous Activity)	Products Liability (Any of the 5 theories)	Misrepre-sentation	Nuisance	Defamation	Privacy	Malicious Prosecution/ Abuse of Process	Interference with Business Relations	3rd-Party Liability Issues
February '87 Q3	Owen owns 50 acres of unzoned land	Real Prop.; Remedies						X					
July '86 Q5	Alice's stolen $14,000 diamond ring	Remedies	TTC / Conversion	X									

TORTS PRACTICE ESSAYS, ANSWER GRIDS, AND SAMPLE ANSWERS

Torts Question 1

July 1995, Question 3

Booker is the owner of The Bookstore. Walker, a clerical worker in a nearby office, came into The Bookstore every day at lunchtime to browse. Booker became annoyed because Walker read books and magazines but never bought anything. Finally, Booker told Walker that he would call the police if Walker came into the store again.

Walker returned the next day, and Booker called the police. Booker made a citizen's arrest of Walker for violation of the local vagrancy ordinance that made it a misdemeanor to "loiter in an annoying fashion in any place open to the public." Walker objected loudly to the arrest, yelling, "You can't arrest me, I didn't take anything."

Reporter overheard Walker's remarks. Reporter worked for *The News*, the local newspaper, and recognized Walker because one year earlier Walker had led a movement to remove certain books from the local high school library. Reporter thought that the police were arresting Walker for shoplifting and rushed back to the paper to file a story on the arrest.

The next day, *The News* reported that Walker had been arrested for shoplifting, in a story headlined: "Book Burner Arrested for Book Theft."

Walker was charged with vagrancy. The charge was dismissed on the ground that the vagrancy ordinance had long been construed to require actual disturbance of the peace, and in this case there was no actual disturbance.

1. What claims, if any, does Walker have against Booker? Discuss.
2. What claims, if any, does Walker have against *The News*? Discuss.

Torts Question 1 Assessment

July 1995, Question 3

Among torts questions, this is a "racehorse" question. It tests several issues within torts across the spectrum with limited time. It tests intentional torts, misuse of process, defamation, and privacy issues, as well as many defenses, all of which must be fully analyzed in one hour.

To approach this type of question, you should utilize your issues checklist after reading the call of the question to decide which issues the facts raise. Being cognizant of your fact triggers is also helpful here. Facts such as *The News* and Reporter should make you consider defamation and privacy issues, both of which are at issue here.

This exam also tests issues that lend themselves to arguments on both sides. To pass this question, you should have been able to articulate the arguments for both parties in regard to the various issues raised. As you can see in the following grid, a specific conclusion is not necessary to pass this question. Rather, you merely need to analyze both sides and then explain why one side has the stronger argument and conclude accordingly. In fact, both state-released passing answers came to opposite conclusions on this essay.

Using your issues checklist, you should be able to spot all issues. However, you must know where to focus the majority of your time. As you can see in the grid, there are many more facts that are useful in analyzing defamation and all of its elements compared to the abuse of process issue. Once you organize your answer on scratch paper, you should be able to easily see this and, thus, should focus more of your time on defamation than on abuse of process. If time is running short, be brief on the minor issues and/or save the minor issues to do last in order to maximize your points.

If you miss any of the issues or rules below, you should rewrite your answer or at least those missed issues. Further, you should rewrite any issues where you find that you omit key facts and/or arguments. Writing out essays properly is the best practice you can do to pass the essay portion of the bar exam. For more questions that test these particular issues, or other issues, review the Torts Issues Tested Matrix at the end the torts chapter.

Finally, make note of the areas highlighted in **bold** on the corresponding grid. The bold areas highlight the issues, analysis, and conclusions that are likely **required** to receive a passing score on this question. In general, the essay grids are provided to assist you in analyzing the essays, and are much more detailed than what a student should create during the exam to organize their response to a question.

Issue	Rule	Fact Application	Conclusion
Call #1: Walker v. Booker			
False imprisonment	**• D acts and intends to cause • P to be confined or restrained (physical force, threat of force, failure to release, invalid use of legal authority) • to a bounded area (no reasonable means of escape) • of which P is aware or harmed**	**• Booker acted by doing a citizen arrest on Walker, intending to keep him there until the police arrived. • The citizen arrest caused Walker to remain in store. • Confinement by failure to release and threat because police were called. • Walker is aware he is confined.**	**Yes, false imprisonment, barring any defenses**
Defense: privilege of arrest	Misdemeanor arrest allowed without warrant if breach of peace in front of arresting party.	Here, Walker did not breach peace as he was browsing bookstore in silence and didn't yell until after arrested.	Not a valid defense
Defense: shopkeeper's privilege	Shopkeepers can detain a suspect for a reasonable time if they reasonably believe suspect shoplifted.	Here, Booker knew Walker didn't shoplift, but he wanted him out of the store because he never bought any books.	Not a valid defense
IIED	**• Intentional or reckless act by D • that is extreme and outrageous • which causes • P to suffer severe emotional distress**	**• Booker intended to act by arresting Walker. • Act not E & O because even though people often browse though bookstores, not beyond all notions of common decency to arrest someone after warning them you would do just that; could argue opposite here, too. • No indication Walker suffered severe emotional distress, rather likely embarrassment and humiliation; further publication by the News did cause stress, but not caused by Booker and may not be severe. [Should see both sides here.]**	No IIED [State-released answers came to opposite conclusions, so either conclusion is fine so long as you fully analyze the elements.]

Continued >

Issue	Rule	Fact Application	Conclusion
Malicious prosecution	**• Institution of criminal proceedings against P • termination in P's favor • absence of probable cause • improper purpose, and • damages**	**• Booker instituted criminal proceedings by arresting Walker and calling police. • Charge of vagrancy later dismissed in Walker's favor. • Arguably, no probable cause, as it is common for patrons to browse books in a bookstore and not buy one, but a bookstore owner could find it akin to loitering if the same patron came in every day, read books and magazines, yet never purchased anything since it is not a library. [Argue both ways and decide which is side stronger.] • Improper purpose because Booker wanted Walker out of the store and to never come back simply because he didn't purchase books (but could see as legitimate if Booker reasonably believed Walker's actions were loitering or violating vagrancy statute); likely improper because just angry he never purchased anything. • Damages by humiliation, being arrested itself, further publication by *The News*, likely lost time from work or hired a lawyer.**	**Yes, malicious prosecution**
Abuse of process	• Wrongful use or process for an ulterior purpose, and • A definite act or threat against P to accomplish the ulterior purpose	Booker threatened to call police if Walker came into store again for no reason other than to keep him out because he didn't buy books, not because he was loitering in an annoying fashion.	Yes, abuse of process

Continued >

Issue	Rule	Fact Application	Conclusion
Call #2: Walker v. *The News*			
Defamation	**• Defamatory statement • of and concerning P • published to a 3rd party • causing damage to P's reputation • If P is a public figure, need to prove fault (malice). • If P is a private person, mere negligence is sufficient.**	**• *The News* accused Walker of book theft, which was not true and could damage Walker's reputation. • Statement concerned Walker, as it was about him. • Statement published to several people in *The News*. • Caused Walker to suffer humiliation and embarrassment. • Damages presumed in most jurisdictions because defamatory language in writing (libel). • Here, although Walker led a movement to remove certain school library books and Reporter recognized him, it was a local high school and did not likely lead to Walker achieving fame or notoriety, so likely Walker is a private person. Even if public figure, *The News* arguably acted with malice (reckless disregard as to falsity of statement by not verifying it prior to publishing), but on the other hand, Walker did yell loudly that he didn't take anything, which could lead a reasonable person to believe he was arrested to stealing something. • *The News* acted negligently by not verifying truth of story since they have a duty to report accurate stories, arguably.**	Yes, defamation, barring any defenses (none of which apply here) [State-released answers came to opposite conclusions, so you could have concluded either way, but needed to see both sides in your analysis.]

Continued >

Issue	Rule	Fact Application	Conclusion
IIED	See above	• *The News* intended to publish statement without knowing truth and incorrectly/recklessly assumed due to shoplifting. • News likely did not intend to cause Walker severe emotional distress, rather just publish a story and sell papers. • Failure to further investigate not likely E & O, rather just negligent, especially since reporter heard Walker yelling, "I didn't take anything," indicating that a reasonable person would think he was accused of theft. • Damages—see above	No IIED
Privacy: false light	**• One attributes to P views he does not hold or actions he does not take • False light is objectionable to a reasonable person under the circumstances, and • For publication, need publicity • If matter of public interest, need to prove malice**	**• Publication indicated Walker stole books, which he did not. • A reasonable person would be offended by being accused of theft, when in fact he didn't steal. • Published to public in paper *The News*. • Not likely a matter of public interest, but arguably, the public likes to be informed of shoplifting and crime in their community; even if public interest, *The News* acted with a reckless disregard for the truth possibly, but maybe not under the circumstances based on Walker's comments (see above in defamation).**	Yes, invasion of privacy [State-released answers concluded both ways, but you needed to see both sides in your analysis.]

Torts Question 1 Sample Answer

July 1995, Question 3

1. Walker v. Booker

False Imprisonment

To prevail on a claim of false imprisonment Walker must establish that Booker acted with intent to cause a confinement to a bounded area, of which plaintiff was aware or suffered harm. Booker acted by making a citizen's arrest of Walker and did so with the intent to keep Walker confined in the store until the police arrived. It appears Walker was confined through means of restraint and/or threats to the bounded by the area of the bookstore, and he was aware of the confinement. Walker is entitled to damages for the false imprisonment.

Defense: Privilege of Arrest

While a misdemeanor arrest may be made without a warrant where there is a breach of the peace, Booker's action will not be privileged here because Walker did not commit any crime and was merely browsing quietly in Booker's bookstore.

Defense: Shopkeeper's Privilege

Booker may assert his restraint of Walker is privileged since a shopkeeper may detain a shoplifting suspect for a reasonable time. This will not provide a successful defense because Booker knew Walker did not shoplift anything from the store. Rather, Booker was irritated with him because he never bought anything from the store.

IIED

IIED is an intentional act by a defendant that is extreme and outrageous which causes the plaintiff to suffer severe emotional distress. Booker's citizen's arrest was an intentional act taken by Walker. Walker would assert the conduct was extreme and outrageous because people browse in bookstores all the time without threat of arrest. However, the action probably does not rise to the level of extreme and outrageous conduct because Booker first warned Walker to stay out of the store and that the police would be called if he returned. Since Booker warned Walker first, it was not beyond all notions of common decency to carry out the threat to call police. It shouldn't have taken Walker by surprise, so it is probably not extreme and outrageous, although it is admittedly unusual behavior for a shopkeeper. In addition, there is no indication that Walker actually suffered any severe emotional distress, as required to recover for IIED. Although it is likely the arrest was embarrassing to Walker, this is insufficient to establish the extreme level of distress required for an IIED claim.

Malicious Prosecution

Malicious prosecution requires a showing of 1) the institution of criminal proceedings against a plaintiff, 2) they are terminated in plaintiff's favor, 3) the absence of probable cause, 4) an improper purpose, and 5) damages. Booker instituted criminal proceedings here by making a citizen's arrest, detaining Booker, and calling the police. Booker was charged with vagrancy as a result, but the charge was dismissed because Booker was not actually disturbing the peace, as the vagrancy statute requires since Booker did not cause a ruckus by yelling until after the arrest. It is understandable that Booker would get personally annoyed that Walker came in his store every day at lunchtime to browse and read books and magazines but never buy anything since he is in business to make money, and a bookstore isn't a public library. However, many bookstore patrons browse, and Walker didn't browse in an annoying fashion or disturb the peace, so there was no probable cause for the arrest on vagrancy. Booker's motive was improper because it appears that he knew Walker did not engage in the criminal misconduct of "annoying loitering." Rather, Booker was angry because Walker never bought anything. It is likely Walker suffered damages from the humiliation of being arrested, and suffered actual money damages for any time lost from work and the time and expense incurred in mounting a defense before charges were dropped.

Abuse of Process

Booker threatened to call the police if Walker came into the store again for the ulterior purpose of keeping him out of the store because he didn't buy anything, not because he was loitering in an annoying fashion. Further, Booker accomplished his purpose through means of threats and the action of making a citizen's arrest, which is the abuse of process.

2. Walker v. *The News*

Defamation

A case of defamation requires a defamatory statement be made, that is of and concerning the plaintiff, published to a third party, and causes damage to the plaintiff's reputation. If the plaintiff is a public figure, malice must be established; however, negligence is sufficient for a private person. *The News* reported that Walker had been arrested for shoplifting books using an inflammatory headline identifying him as a "book burner." This was not true and could damage Walker's reputation because he was identified as a potential criminal. The statement concerned Walker and was published to many through means of *The News* publication. Walker likely suffered embarrassment, humiliation, and damage to his reputation as a result of the untrue story. Since the defamation was in writing (libel), damages are presumed in most jurisdictions.

The determinative issue is whether Walker is a public figure or a private person. One year prior to the arrest, Walker led a movement to remove certain books from the high school library, which must have garnered some press since *The News* reporter recognized Walker from that prior situation. However, the book movement was very local in nature and was limited to books in a local high school, which is not an issue of great concern beyond the immediate locale of the high school. This did not likely result in Walker receiving fame or notoriety of the type that would result in his being considered a public figure. As a private figure, *The News* need only be shown to be negligent in their publication, which is easily shown here since they did not check the accuracy of the story and this would have been easy to do since arrests are public record. However, if Walker achieved such notoriety that he is considered a public figure, *The News* may have even reached a malice standard in their publication because of their display of reckless disregard for the truth by failing to verify the accuracy of the story. *The News* will counter that the reporter overheard Walker himself saying that he didn't steal as he was being arrested and therefore it was not reckless to make the inference that Walker was being arrested for shoplifting. Walker is more likely a private figure, and *The News* did act negligently in not verifying the truth of the story before reporting. No defenses are applicable here so *The News* is liable for defamation.

IIED

The News acted with the intent to publish the statement about Walker without knowing the truth and recklessly assumed shoplifting was involved. It is unlikely that *The News* had an intention to harm Walker or cause him any distress (and there is no evidence he suffered severe emotional distress); rather, they were trying to write and sell newspapers. Although they should have investigated further, not doing so is not extreme and outrageous behavior because newspapers do make mistakes and regularly issue retractions, and the reporter did overhear Walker yelling that he didn't take anything, so it wasn't extreme or outrageous to conclude that he was being charged with theft. *The News* is not liable for IIED.

Privacy: False Light

Holding someone in a false light occurs when one attributes to a plaintiff actions he doesn't take, and this false light would be objectionable to a reasonable person under the circumstances, it must be published, and, if it is a matter of public interest, malice must be established. Walker was shown in a false light when *The News* identified him as a shoplifter, when that was untrue. A reasonable person would be highly offended by being referred to as a shoplifter when he did not steal since shoplifting is a criminal activity. This characterization was published for all to read in *The News*. It is not likely that this is a matter of public interest other than a vague interest the public might have in keeping abreast of crime in the community. However, even if it is a matter of public concern *The News* may have acted with a reckless disregard for the truth in not further checking the accuracy of the story, as noted above in Defamation. *The News* is liable for invasion of privacy, false light.

Torts Question 2

February 1987, Question 4

Harold grows roses in his flower garden. To keep the roses in good health, he applies ROSEBRITE, an insecticide solution manufactured by Acme and sold in spray cans. On several occasions Harold has read a warning printed on the spray can which admonishes:

> DO NOT ALLOW THIS SOLUTION TO GET IN EYES OR ON EXPOSED PARTS OF BODY. EXTREMELY TOXIC. DO NOT DRINK. IF CONSUMED, CALL DOCTOR IMMEDIATELY. MANUFACTURER IS NOT LIABLE FOR INJURIES CAUSED BY THIS PRODUCT.

Last week, while Harold was applying ROSEBRITE to the roses, his telephone rang. He left the spray can of ROSEBRITE on the lawn, went inside to answer the phone, and forgot about the ROSEBRITE.

The next day, Johnny, age 5, a neighbor's child who had come over to play with Harold's son, went into the yard, picked up the spray can, and sprayed some ROSEBRITE on his arms. He thought the can was filled with perfume because he noticed a picture of roses on the spray can and he could not read. He became ill almost at once. The children were at the time under the care of a teenaged babysitter, Sarah.

Sarah had been in the house watching television and had not heard Johnny leave the house. Johnny came into the house crying and obviously ill. He pointed to the ROSEBRITE spray can and told Sarah that the "perfume" made him sick. Sarah looked at the spray can and read the warning. Realizing the gravity of the situation, she called an ambulance and got Johnny to the hospital. Johnny suffered cramps, blurred vision, and diarrhea. He was hospitalized for several days.

Though the warning on the spray can did not mention it, washing the exposed area with soap and water would have minimized Johnny's injuries.

What are Johnny's rights against:

1. Acme? Discuss.
2. Harold? Discuss.

Torts Question 2 Assessment

February 1987, Question 4

This is another racehorse question. Not only does it test products liability, but it also tests negligence, aside from the products aspect, as well as other issues. This exam requires you to have a well-organized outline prior to writing to help you determine where the points are so that you know where to focus your time.

As you can see after organizing your answer, the majority of the analysis is in the strict products liability issue. Students often confuse and combine the issues of strict products liability and negligence for products liability. To avoid any confusion or loss of points, it is recommended that you start with the strict products liability issue and then do the negligence for products liability analysis second. This approach requires that you first go through the necessary rules and elements for strict products liability, such as commercial supplier, placing the product into commerce, the three types of defects, and so forth. Once you have completed the strict products liability analysis, move on to negligence with a full discussion of duty and breach (which are different than in strict products liability), and "supra" causation and damages (which are the same).

Also, always consider all five theories of products liability since students often forget about warranty and misrepresentation. If you are not sure whether a theory is or isn't an issue, it is better to err on the side of inclusion. However, if you are not sure whether it is an issue, then it is likely a minor issue, so be brief and concise when analyzing it.

This essay question also raises a minor issue that is not frequently tested: non-products strict liability. One of the state-released answers to this question raised the issue of ultrahazardous activity since the insecticide spray is arguably very dangerous. Although this issue may not have been required to pass the question, it is still worth mentioning. The few times this issue has been raised, it has been with similar facts, such as a gas truck driving down the highway, a high voltage fence, and a chemical spill. These situations are less "dangerous" than the typical blasting fact pattern you likely recall from your torts class. Every time this issue has been raised, it has been minor and many students miss spotting it at all because they do not view the facts as ultrahazardous. If you didn't spot this issue, keep it in mind as a potential minor issue whenever a dangerous activity is in the facts.

This question also requires you to fully use the facts and to see how Sarah, the teenaged babysitter, was a possible intervening cause. It is necessary to analyze whether her television watching was foreseeable (as a teenage babysitter). Again, the facts are there for you to use in your analysis. If you missed any of these key facts or arguments, make a resolution now to underline the facts on your next essay and use all of the facts. This will improve your analysis and your ability to pass this question.

A sample answer is included for this question. The sample answer is not a model or perfect answer, but rather is of passing quality that realistically could be written in one hour. Make note of the areas highlighted in **bold** on the corresponding grid. The bold areas highlight the issues, analysis, and conclusions that are likely **required** to receive a passing score on this question.

Issue	Rule	Fact Application	Conclusion
Call #1: J v. A			
Strict liability for ultra-hazardous activity	One is strictly liable if • an activity creates a foreseeable risk of serious harm, • the activity cannot be done without risk even when reasonable care is exercised, • and the activity is not a matter of common usage in the community.	• Here, spraying insecticide on flowers generally does not create a foreseeable risk of serious harm; although some harm may be foreseeable if it is used for the wrong purpose. • Here, spraying insecticide on flowers can be done without risk when reasonable care is taken, such as wearing gloves and not spraying it on your body or hands as instructed. • Spraying insecticide on flowers is a matter of common usage in neighborhoods with yards and flowers/plants.	No strict liability for ultrahazardous activity
Products liability	5 theories: intent, strict liability, negligence, warranty, and misrepresentation	All applicable theories will be discussed below.	
Strict products liability	• **Commercial supplier/ merchant** • **Places product in the stream of commerce without substantial alteration** • **Defect** **→ Manufacturer** **→ Design (consumer expectation and risk utility tests)** **→ Warning** • **Actual causation (but for)** • **Proximate causation (foreseeability)** • **Damages**	• **Here, Acme manufactured Rosebrite, an insecticide solution.** • Acme placed the product into the stream of commerce by selling it in spray cans; no alteration appears to be present. • Manufacturing defect: There are no facts to indicate that this particular can is different than others. • **Design defect (instructions): A consumer would expect an extremely toxic insecticide to have instructions on it as to what to do in the event of contact,** especially since it states not to contact; the cost to add the instructions to wash the exposed area with soap and water would be minimal compared to the risk of more serious injuries. • **Design defect (picture): It is possible that the can should have had a picture that included a danger symbol,** such as a skull and bones or toxic symbol rather than flowers or, at least, in addition to the flowers; **a consumer would expect for toxic products to have toxic symbols on them for those who cannot read;** further, the cost would be minimal compared to the risk.	Acme strictly liable under products liability

Continued >

Issue	Rule	Fact Application	Conclusion
		• **Design defect (spray nozzle/cap): Arguably Acme should have included a childproof or safety spray nozzle on the spray can since it is extremely toxic; to do so would likely be inexpensive and feasible compared to the risk** since even cough syrups and inexpensive items contain such safety devices. • **Warning defect (both): Although the warning did say to avoid contact and that it was extremely toxic, it did not state what to do if contact was made, such as wash with soap and water; further, it only warned of its toxicity in writing and not in picture form** so it doesn't take into consideration persons who cannot read. • **But for not having instructions on what to do if contact was made, J's injuries could have been minimized since S did read the warning on the can once contact was made; further, but for not having a picture of a toxic symbol rather than flowers, J would not have sprayed the can on himself thinking it was perfume; but for not having a safety spray nozzle, J would not have sprayed the insecticide on him.** • **It is foreseeable that a child (or anyone) may come into contact with a spray can and expose themselves to it; Acme may argue that Harold is an intervening force, but it is also foreseeable that a consumer will leave the product out in the garden and/or that a child may become exposed to it (or anyone for that matter) and need instructions on what to do if contact is made**; as to S, it is also foreseeable that a teenage babysitter may not always watch the kids every second. • **Damages: J suffered cramps, blurred vision, diarrhea, and was hospitalized for several days.**	Acme strictly liable under products liability
Defenses	AOR, comparative negligence, and contributory negligence are not defenses if P's neg./misuse was foreseeable; disclaimers ineffective.	Here, as indicated above, J's misuse, as well as Harold leaving the can out, are all foreseeable; the disclaimer is also ineffective that Manufacturer is not liable for injuries.	No defenses

Continued >

Issue	Rule	Fact Application	Conclusion
Negligence	• **Duty (reasonable person under the circumstances); foreseeable Ps v. everyone** • **Breach (falls below standard of care)** • **Actual cause** • **Proximate cause** • **Damages**	• **A reasonable manufacturer would put all instructions on what to do if contact was made on an extremely toxic product** that specifically advises against contact being made, especially since they advise against contact, they must know of the dangers if contact is made; **also a reasonable manufacturer would look to safety features of a dangerous and toxic product.** • **Here, Acme fell below the standard of care by failing to put instructions on what to do if contact was made, as well as by failing to put a toxic symbol on the can for those who cannot read since most manufacturers include such symbols and instructions; Acme also did not have a safety nozzle** like most manufacturers have for even less toxic and dangerous products, such as cold medicines. • **See above for causation and damages.**	Acme negligent
Defenses	• AOR • **Contributory negligence** • Comparative negligence Possible joint and several liability by H	• Here, J did not know of the risk, so he could not have assumed the risk. • **A 5-year-old child is held to the same standard as another child like him, so here it is not unreasonable for a 5-year-old to think a can with a picture of flowers on it was perfume; so no contributory negligence by J.** • There may be fault by Harold's negligence (joint and several liability), but that will not relieve Acme of its negligence; however, it may offset the damages it owes for negligence.	No AOR; no cont. neg.; possible joint and several liability by H
Warranty	Implied warranties based on merchantability and fit for particular purpose	Here, product was designed to be toxic and needs to be so in order to kill insects; consumers purchase it expecting it to kill bugs/insects, which likely has to include some toxic chemicals (see above for causation and damages).	No warranty liability

Continued >

Issue	Rule	Fact Application	Conclusion
Call #2: J v. H			
Negligence	• **See above** • **In addition, landowner duties—licensee—duty to warn of all dangerous conditions**	• Duty: A reasonable parent would not leave a can of extremely toxic insecticide out in an area where small children play. • **Licensee: Since J came over to play with H's son, he is a licensee, and H owed him a duty to warn of the toxic spray can.** • **Breach: Here, H fell below the standard of care when he left the toxic spray out to go in and answer the phone; a reasonable parent would have brought the can with him, put it away, or simply not answered the phone at that time; this is especially true since H read the warning on the can on several occasions and knew how toxic the spray was.** • **AC: But for H not leaving the insecticide out in the yard, J would not have sprayed himself.** • **PC: It is foreseeable that a child may become exposed to toxic sprays that are left out where they play; H will argue that S was a supervening cause since she was supposed to be watching the kids and did not hear J go outside because she was watching TV; however, it is foreseeable that a teenage babysitter would not keep her eyes on two small children at all times.** • **Damages: See above.**	H negligent
Defenses	**See above**	**See above**	No defenses

Torts Question 2 Sample Answer

February 1987, Question 4

Johnny v. Acme

Strict Liability for Ultrahazardous Activity

One is strictly liable if an activity creates a foreseeable risk of serious harm, the activity cannot be done without risk even when reasonable care is exercised, and the activity is not a matter of common usage in the community.

Here, spraying insecticide spray can create some harm if the toxic chemical is ingested or contacts the skin. However, it is unlikely that it rises to the level of serious harm, as most consumers will not be ingesting or contacting the chemicals with their skin, but rather spraying the flowers. Further, spraying insecticide on flowers can be done without risk if reasonable care is taken, such as wearing gloves or protection while spraying the flowers. Finally, spraying flowers with insecticide is common in areas with yards, gardens, and flowers.

Therefore, Acme is not strictly liable for an ultrahazardous activity by manufacturing and selling Rosebrite.

Products Liability

Plaintiff may pursue a products liability cause of action under five theories including intent, strict liability, negligence, warranty, and misrepresentation.

Strict Products Liability

Strict products liability is established when a commercial supplier places a product into the stream of commerce without substantial alteration, the product is defective, and such defect causes damage.

Commercial Supplier

Here, Acme manufactured and sold Rosebrite insecticide spray, indicating it is a commercial supplier of the product.

Stream of Commerce

Here, Acme placed the Rosebrite insecticide spray into the stream of commerce by selling it to retailers and/or consumers, such as Harold.

Defect

There are three types of defect: manufacturing, design, and warning.

Here, there are no facts to indicate a manufacturing defect as the insecticide spray can at issue does not appear to differ from others from the same line.

Design Defect

A design defect is established when all products of a line are the same but have dangerous propensities. Such a defect can be established under the consumer expectation test, which looks to what a reasonable consumer would expect, or the risk utility test, which looks at whether there are feasible safer alternatives without serious impact on price and utility.

Here, one design defect involves the failure to include a safety nozzle on the spray cap that would prevent a child from accessing the toxic chemicals or an adult from accidentally spraying it. A consumer would likely expect that all extremely toxic chemicals come equipped with such safety features. Further, to add such a safety feature would likely be inexpensive since many other inexpensive products, including cold medicines, do contain such safety opening devices.

Other possible design defects include the picture of flowers without a picture of a toxic symbol for those who cannot read, as well as the failure to include directions to wash with soap and water if exposure occurs. Both of these features can easily be added to each can with minimal additional cost, if any, and a reasonable consumer would expect such directions on a toxic product.

Therefore, there are multiple design defects with Rosebrite.

Warning Defect

A warning defect occurs where the manufacturer fails to give adequate warnings. Here, Acme did not warn of the toxicity of the chemicals in picture form for those who cannot read. The spray should have included a well-known toxic symbol, such as a skull and cross bones, for people to easily see that the spray was toxic. Further, any toxic chemical that is dangerous to consumers and in fact includes directions to avoid contact with skin should include directions about what to do if contact is in fact made, as it is foreseeable that a consumer's skin may come into contact with the spray.

Therefore, there are warning defects with Rosebrite as well as design defects.

Actual Cause

But for the defect that existed at the time the product left manufacturer's control, plaintiff would not have been injured. Here, but for Acme not including a safety spray cap, Johnny would not have been able to spray the solution on his skin. Further, but for the flower picture, as opposed to a toxic symbol picture, Johnny would not have thought the spray was perfume and sprayed the solution on his skin. Finally, but for Acme not placing directions to wash with soap and water, Johnny would not have suffered such severe harm, because Sarah did read the label once she realized Johnny did make contact.

Thus, the defects in Acme's Rosebrite are the actual cause to Johnny's injuries.

Proximate Cause

The harm/damages must be reasonably foreseeable. Here, it is foreseeable that a child, or any consumer, may come into contact with the toxic spray that they are spraying on flowers, as their fingers are near the nozzle where the spray releases. Although, Acme may argue that Harold is a superseding intervening cause because he left the spray can out in the reach of children, and that Sarah, too, is the cause as she did not sufficiently supervise the children, it is foreseeable that a child could access the spray whether the can is left out, they contacted the flowers that were sprayed, or found it in a garage. Further, it is foreseeable that all consumers may not be able to read, indicating that they should have added toxic pictures to the can. Finally, it is also foreseeable that if someone does come into contact with the spray, they will read the can to follow directions about what to do, as Sarah did, and therefore need instructions that tell the consumer to wash with soap and water.

Thus, Acme's defects in Rosebrite did proximately cause Johnny's injuries.

Damages

Here, Johnny suffered cramps, blurred vision, diarrhea, and was hospitalized for several days.

Overall, Acme will be held strictly liable for Johnny's injuries.

Defenses

Assumption of the risk and contributory negligence are generally not valid defenses to strict products liability if plaintiff's negligence or misuse was foreseeable. Further, disclaimers are ineffective. As indicated above, Johnny's misuse, as well as Harold and Sarah's negligence, are all foreseeable and thus there are no valid defenses to strict liability.

Negligence

Negligence occurs when defendant had a duty to conform to a particular standard of conduct, breached that duty, and the breach caused damages.

Duty

A manufacturer has a duty to act as a reasonable prudent manufacturer would act under the circumstances. Under the majority view (Cardozo), such a duty is owed to all foreseeable plaintiffs. The minority view (Andrews) is that a duty is owed to everyone.

Here, a reasonable manufacturer would put all necessary safety instructions on toxic chemicals that they sell. They would also indicate that a product is toxic by using a toxic symbol. Also, reasonable manufacturers use safety nozzles for particularly dangerous chemicals to avoid a child from accessing the product.

Plaintiff here is Johnny, the child of a consumer, who would be a foreseeable plaintiff under both views above.

Thus, Acme owes a duty to its consumers to act reasonably.

Breach

Breach occurs when the defendant's conduct falls short of the applicable standard of care. Here, Acme's failure to include a safety nozzle, appropriate toxic symbols, and washing instructions falls short of the applicable standard because many manufacturers utilize safety spray nozzles and do include such warnings to help protect consumers. Therefore, Acme breached its duty owed to Johnny.

Actual Cause, Proximate Cause, and Damages

See above. Overall, Acme is negligent under products liability.

Defenses

Assumption of the Risk

Assumption of the risk occurs when plaintiff knew of the risk involved and assumed it. Here, Johnny, at the age of 5 did not know of the risks and could not have assumed them.

Contributory Negligence

Contributory negligence occurs when plaintiff's negligence contributes to their injuries. A child is compared to a child of the same age, intelligence, and ability. Here, a 5-year-old child would not likely be able to read warnings about extremely toxic chemicals. Further it is reasonable for a 5-year-old child to think a can with a picture of flowers was perfume and not toxic chemicals. Thus, Johnny is not liable for contributory negligence.

Warranty
There are warranties of merchantability and fitness for a particular purpose that goods are of average quality and are generally fit for the purpose intended. Here, Rosebrite, by its very nature, must be toxic to kill insects and bugs. It is unlikely that it would meet its purpose and kill insects if it was nontoxic. Thus, there is no breach of warranties.

Johnny v. Harold

Negligence
See above for rules.

Duty
Here, a reasonable parent would not leave a toxic chemical out in an area in which small children play, especially if that parent had read the dangerous warning on several occasions.

Further, under landowner duties, a landowner owes special duties to licensees, which are social guests, to warn of all dangerous conditions.

Breach
Here, Harold fell below the standard of care by leaving the toxic spray in an area where his child and other children play. He did not act as a reasonable parent because he did not bring in the can with him, put it away, or wait to answer the phone until he was done spraying the flowers. Further, he did not warn Johnny of the spray causing him to also breach his landowner duties.

Therefore, Harold breached his duty of care to act as a reasonable parent would under the circumstances.

Actual Causation
But for Harold leaving the spray can outside, Johnny would not sprayed in on his skin and suffered injuries. Thus, Harold's breach was the actual cause of Johnny's injuries.

Proximate Causation
It is foreseeable that if a parent leaves a toxic spray out in an area where kids play, that they may come into contact with the spray. Harold may argue that Sarah is a superseding intervening force, as she did not see Johnny leave the house since she was watching TV. However, it is foreseeable that a teenage babysitter may not watch a child every second when they are babysitting. Thus, Harold's breach proximately caused Johnny's injuries.

Damages
See above.

Defenses
See above.

Comparative Fault
Under the doctrine of comparative fault, both Harold and Acme are liable for Johnny's injuries, and both may have to split the damages in proportion to their levels of fault/negligence.

Torts Question 3

July 1993, Question 1

Dina, aged sixteen, lives at home with her mother, Mary, in a state where the age of majority is eighteen. Mary is aware that Dina has recently exhibited a sometimes violent and delusionary nature diagnosed as schizophrenia and has attacked persons in the neighborhood. Medication that can control Dina's behavior has been prescribed, but without Mary's knowledge, Dina has stopped taking it.

A week after Dina stopped taking her medication, she approached a neighbor, Paul, as he walked along the sidewalk fronting Mary's home. When she was face to face with Paul, Dina, without provocation, gestured threateningly and screamed, "I know you're out to get me and I'm going to get you first," and then strode away.

Paul, who had no knowledge of Dina's mental illness, phoned Mary about the incident. Mary told Paul that "Dina has sometimes made threats to others, but I do not think she will try to hurt you and I assure you that this will not happen again." Paul believed Mary's assurances and, for that reason, did not seek to avoid Dina.

Mary questioned Dina about the incident, scolded her, and asked if Dina was taking her medication. When Dina said she was, Mary did not pursue the matter.

Two days after Dina confronted Paul, Dina saw him raking leaves which had fallen into the street fronting their adjoining homes. Dina got on her bicycle and rode it as rapidly as she could directly at Paul. Although Dina swerved away from Paul at the last moment, Paul reacted by diving to one side. He struck his head on the curb and suffered a severe concussion and facial injuries.

Paul has sued Dina and Mary, alleging tortious causes of action.

1. Is Paul entitled to recover against Dina for:
   a. Assault? Discuss.
   b. Battery? Discuss.
2. Is Paul entitled to recover against Mary:
   a. On the ground that Mary was negligent as to Paul? Discuss.
   b. On the ground that Mary is vicariously liable for Dina's conduct? Discuss.

Torts Question 3 Assessment

July 1993, Question 1

This torts question raises the heavily tested issue of negligence, as well as intentional torts and multiple defendant liability. Generally, intentional torts are straightforward and easy to approach when you know the rules. They are more heavily tested on the multiple-choice questions, but do tend to occasionally arise on the essays. Since they aren't frequently tested on the essay, intentional torts are not included on the regular torts issues checklist. Therefore, when intentional torts are at issue on an essay, you should write out a quick mini-issues checklist for all seven intentional torts and their defenses. This is crucial to help you avoid missing any issues and/or defenses. Students will often see either assault or battery, but not both because one of them will clearly stand out. Without a checklist approach, students tend to focus on the obvious one to the exclusion of the other(s). Further, defenses are often overlooked resulting in missed points. Using a mini-issues checklist with all defenses will help avoid this shortfall.

Negligence analysis is often time-consuming and worth many points in an essay. Further, it is heavily tested and has been for years. Many times, negligence will arise several times in one essay from the actions of various parties. This negligence question is comparatively simple because it is only raised once in regard to one defendant. However, the key discussion necessary here is determining foreseeability and proximate cause. There are several facts that go to these issues, as you can see in the grid that follows.

Using all of the facts in the analysis is necessary to pass this question. For this reason, be sure to underline the facts as you use them, so you can identify and address any "homeless" facts. If you are leaving out facts in your analysis, then you are leaving out arguments and losing points. Further, always keep in mind that one fact can correspond to multiple issues. Just because you have used a fact once, does not mean that it cannot go with another issue as well.

Finally, whenever one person commits a wrongful act against another person, yet a third party, one who did not commit the act, is being sued, always consider vicarious liability. Generally, it is a short and minor issue, but it is always worth points that are easy to miss.

With accurate mini-issues checklists and full use of the facts, this type of torts question is one in which you can easily write a passing answer.

Make note of the areas highlighted in **bold** on the corresponding grid. The bold areas highlight the issues, analysis, and conclusions that are likely **required** to receive a passing score on this question.

Issue	Rule	Fact Application	Conclusion
Call #1: P v. D			
Assault (D's verbal threat)	• **Intentional causing of** • **a reasonable apprehension** • **of immediate harmful or offensive contact** • **to another**	• **Here, D acted intentionally by threatening and screaming to P, "I know you're out to get me and I'm going to get you first."** • D acted on her own volition and without provocation, thus acting with intent to threaten P; although D may be suffering from schizophrenia, a person who is legally incompetent may still act volitionally. • Arguably, a reasonable person could be placed in reasonable apprehension of a H/O contact if someone approached them on a sidewalk, and began to gesture threateningly and screamed the above statement, especially since D knew where P lived and could easily carry out the threat; P's apprehension is also shown by his contacting M indicating he perhaps believed D. • However, **D yelled that she was "going" to get him, indicating it would occur at some later time and not immediately, especially since she strode away right after making the statement.**	**No assault (as to threat)**
Assault (D's bicycle attack)	See above	• **Here, D acted with intent by voluntarily riding her bicycle as rapidly as she could directly at P;** although D may be suffering from schizophrenia, a person who is legally incompetent may still act volitionally. • Her intent to cause a H/O contact is furthered by the fact that she just threatened him of such a contact 2 days before and deliberately rode rapidly and swerved at the last minute to cause such apprehension of a H/O contact. • **A reasonable person would be in apprehension of a H/O contact if a person who just threatened them 2 days prior was riding a bicycle toward them rapidly and appeared that they were going to hit them; the fact that he reacted by diving to one side indicates that he was in apprehension of being hit, a H/O contact.**	**Yes, assault (as to bike)**

Continued >

Issue	Rule	Fact Application	Conclusion
Defense: self-defense	Where a person reasonably believes he is about to be attacked, he may use reasonable force to defend himself.	Here, it was not reasonable for D to believe P was going to attack her as he had not done anything to indicate he would; her possible schizophrenic violent delusions are not objectively reasonable since P was simply raking leaves and not doing anything to her.	No self-defense
Battery	• **Intentional causing of** • **a harmful or offensive contact** • **to another** Transferred intent: intent to cause one tort, but actually cause another	• **Here, D acted with intent by voluntarily riding her bicycle as rapidly as she could directly at P;** although D may be suffering from schizophrenia, a person who is legally incompetent may still act volitionally. • Her intent to cause a H/O contact is furthered by the fact that she just threatened him of such a contact 2 days before. • **Although she swerved at the last minute, her riding rapidly toward P and not swerving until the last minute caused P to react by diving to the side, causing his harmful contact resulting in a concussion and facial injuries.** • Under transferred intent, even if D only sought to place P in apprehension and never actually hurt him, her intent to commit an assault will transfer to battery since he suffered a concussion and injuries as a result of her assault.	Yes, battery
Defense: self-defense	**See above**	**See above**	**See above**
Defense: incapacity	Incapacity is not a defense to intentional torts as both children and insane persons can commit intentional torts.	Here, although D is both a child and may be insane/schizophrenic, neither is a defense to assault and battery.	No defense for incapacity

Continued >

Issue	Rule	Fact Application	Conclusion
Call #2: P v. M			
Negligence	• **Duty (reasonable person under the circumstances); Cardozo (all foreseeable Ps)** v. Andrews (everyone) • Generally no duty to act unless special relationship or when one begins to act • **Breach (falls below standard of care)** • **Actual Cause (but for test)** • **Proximate Cause (foreseeability test)** • **Damages**	• **Although there is generally no duty to act, a duty may exist** due the special relationship between D and M and **due to the fact that M knew of D's violence schizophrenic tendencies when she doesn't take her medication as she has attacked persons in the neighborhood before**; further, M was notified of a violent incident by P and acted by assuring P that D's threats/violence would not happen again. • Since M began to act by ensuring P, she has a duty to act as a reasonable person would under the circumstances; arguably, **a reasonable person here would check to ensure that their minor schizophrenic child was actually taking their medication, and a reasonable person would not assure the actions of another.** • **P is a foreseeable P as he is D's neighbor and already had an encounter with D.** • **Although M did ask D if she was taking her medication and D told her yes, a reasonable person/parent here would make sure she was taking her medication** especially since P informed M of D's recent violent threats, which should have alerted M that there is a strong possibility that D was not taking her medication; **further, M should not have assured P that D would or would not act a certain way given that she cannot control her every move and allowed D to act independently.** • **But for M not ensuring that D took her medication, D did not take her medication, and rode her bike toward P, causing him to react and suffer injuries.**	Yes, negligence

Continued >

Issue	Rule	Fact Application	Conclusion
		• **But for M assuring P that D's violence would not happen again, P would have been more proactive and prepared for D's violent tendencies.** • **It is foreseeable that P might be harmed since M knew of D's violent schizophrenic condition if she didn't take her medication, and D had attacked other persons in the neighborhood previously.** • **P suffered damages of a severe concussion and facial injuries.**	Yes, negligence
Defense: contributory negligence	P was also negligent	Here, it was reasonable for P to dive to the side as a reasonable person would dive out of the way if a bike was rapidly heading right toward them, especially since the D previously threatened P 2 days earlier and had attacked other persons in the neighborhood.	No defense
Vicarious liability	**Generally, parents are not vicariously liable for the torts of their children, but they may be financially responsible.**	**Here, M is not liable for the torts committed by her daughter D, but she may be held financially liable for the damages; and, as indicated above, M is liable herself for negligence so she would be liable for the damages anyway.**	M may be financially responsible

Torts Question 4

July 2007, Question 2

Manufacturer designed and manufactured a "Cold Drink Blender," which it sold through retail stores throughout the country. The Cold Drink Blender consists of three components: a base that houses the motor, a glass container for liquids with mixing blades inside on the bottom, and a removable cover for the container to prevent liquids from overflowing during mixing. A manufacturer's brochure that came with the Cold Drink Blender states that it is "perfect for making all of your favorite cold drinks, like mixed fruit drinks and milk shakes, and it even crushes ice to make frozen drinks like daiquiris and piña coladas," and cautioned, "Do not fill beyond 2 inches of the top."

Retailer sold one of the Cold Drink Blenders to Consumer. One day, Consumer was following a recipe for vegetable soup that called for thickening the soup by liquefying the vegetables. After deciding to use her Cold Drink Blender for this purpose, Consumer filled the glass container to the top with hot soup, placed it on the base, put the cover on top, and turned the blender on the highest speed. The high speed rotation of the mixing blades forced the contents to the top of the container, pushed off the cover, and splashed hot soup all over Consumer, who was severely burned by the hot soup.

Consumer filed a lawsuit against Manufacturer and Retailer, pleading claims for strict products liability and negligence. In her complaint, Consumer stated that the Cold Drink Blender was not equipped with a cover that locked onto the top of the container in such a way as to prevent it from coming off during operation and that the failure to equip the blender with this safety feature was a cause of her injuries.

Manufacturer moved to dismiss the complaint against it on the following grounds:

(1) Consumer's injury was caused by her own misuse of the Cold Drink Blender which, as implied by its name, was intended for mixing only cold substances.

(2) Consumer's injury was caused by her own lack of care, as she overfilled the Cold Drink Blender and operated it at high speed.

(3) The design of the Cold Drink Blender was not defective since it complied with design standards set forth in federal regulations promulgated by the federal Consumer Products Safety Commission, which do not require any locking mechanism.

Retailer moved to dismiss the complaint against it on the following ground:

(4) Retailer played no part in the manufacture of the Cold Drink Blender and therefore should not be held responsible for a defect in its design.

How should the court rule on each ground of both motions to dismiss? Discuss.

Torts Question 4 Assessment

July 2007, Question 2

Products liability is another heavily tested set of issues within torts. Since there are five theories under which the plaintiff can sue the defendant, there are many issues that the examiners can test in a products liability question. Generally, these types of questions are easy to spot if you remember your fact triggers. There is often some product (here, a blender), a manufacturer or company that made or sold the product (here, Manufacturer and Retailer), and an injury from use of the product (here, a severe burn from the top of the blender coming off during use).

The first step to this type of question is to write out all five theories and all applicable defenses to products liability. This question is typical of some of the more recent essay questions in that the calls of the question are very specific, and each call is directed at a particular rule element or defense under the various products liability theories. It is best to first determine exactly what each question is asking.

The best approach is to first write out all elements necessary for the applicable theories of products liability. Then, underline or circle the theories/elements to which each question applies. For example, here call 1 focuses on plaintiff's misuse. After writing out your rules for all elements and defenses, you will see that this call goes to the defense of contributory negligence and assumption of the risk, which are not defenses if the misuse was foreseeable. However, before you can even get to the defense, you need to see if the underlying claim is established. For this reason, this question is easiest to answer after a full analysis of all of the products liability and defenses. Then, you can easily answer each call by referring to the appropriate issue above in which you analyzed that element or issue.

This approach is especially useful on a question such as this since call 3 focuses on the defect. You cannot analyze the defenses (covered in call 1) before the actual claim (covered in call 3), so trying to answer the calls as they are asked without first going through a full analysis of the entire underlying issue would be confusing and difficult, likely resulting in many missed issues (and points) along the way.

However, when writing out your answer, always do answer the specific calls of the question. For example, here call 4 asks about whether the court should grant the motion to dismiss. Thus, after fully analyzing the issues, you need to answer the call as to whether the court should or should not grant the motion to dismiss. This requires a little knowledge of civil procedure (to the extent you need to know when a court will and will not grant such a motion and what a motion to dismiss is). Many students do not focus on the question calls enough and end up answering the wrong question or misunderstanding what is being asked of them. Understanding the specific calls and what you are supposed to analyze is crucial to your success.

Finally, make note of the areas highlighted in **bold** on the corresponding grid. The bold areas highlight the issues, analysis, and conclusions that are likely **required** to receive a passing score on this question.

Issue	Rule	Fact Application	Conclusion
Manufacturer Motion to Dismiss			

Products strict liability	• **Commercial supplier/merchant**
	• **Placed product in stream of commerce without substantial alteration** (establishes strict duty)
	• **Defect (establishes breach)**
	→ Manufacture: product emerges from manufacturing different and more dangerous than other products made properly
	→ **Design:** all products of a line have dangerous propensities; two tests—
	  • consumer expectation (not safe for its intended use and doesn't meet a reasonable consumers expectation);
	  • risk utility (D could have made product safe without serious impact on price and utility)
	→ Warning: failure to give adequate warning as to the risks involved when using the product and danger not apparent to users
	Actual causation: but-for test
	Proximate causation: foreseeable
	Damages
		• **Manufacturer designs and manufactures the cold drink blender and supplies it to retailers placing it in the stream of commerce without alteration.**
		• There is no evidence of a manufacturing defect in that Consumer's blender appears to be like all others.
		• **There is a possible design defect because Manufacturer could have placed lock on top of blender to prevent it from coming off during operation.**
		• For consumer expectation test: A consumer would likely expect that the top would not fly off while operating blender, but Consumer wasn't using it for intended use (cold drinks) and filled it to the top past 2-inch recommendation. [Argue both ways here.]
		• For risk utility test, **likely wouldn't cost too much to add such a mechanism, which would establish a design defect.**
		• Warning did recommend not to fill beyond 2 inches of top, but didn't indicate the consequences of doing so, nor did it indicate the consequences of using hot liquids, so arguably there is a warning defect.
		• Compliance with regulations does not indicate that product was not defective.
		• **But for lack of warning of risks and locking top, Consumer would not have suffered burns.**
			Yes, Manufacturer strictly liable

Continued >

Issue	Rule	Fact Application	Conclusion
		• **Arguably, is it not foreseeable that someone would use hot foods in a clearly labeled "Cold Drink Blender" and fill it beyond 2-inch fill directions; however, consumer misuse is often foreseeable as people don't follow directions, and it is foreseeable that a consumer would use hot liquids when no warning indicates the dangers of doing so; likewise, it is foreseeable that a consumer would fill the blender to the top since there is no indication anything will happen if they do so.** • Damages: Consumer suffered burns.	**Yes, Manufacturer strictly liable**
Defenses to products strict liability	Assumption of the risk and contributory negligence are **not defenses if P's negligence or misuse was foreseeable**; disclaimers are ineffective.	**Here, although Consumer did not follow directions to not fill beyond 2 inches of top, there were not warnings not to use hot liquids; thus, it is arguably foreseeable that someone might use hot liquids and fill it to the top, regardless of directions.**	Misuse foreseeable (no defenses applicable)
Negligence	• **Duty (reasonable manufacturer under the circumstances)**; Cardozo (**majority view)—duty owed to foreseeable Ps**; Andrews (minority view) —duty owed to all • **Breach: fell below standard of care** • **Actual causation** • **Proximate causation** • **Damages**	• **A reasonable manufacturer would give adequate warnings about all foreseeable risks and dangers to consumers; any consumer who purchases a product is a foreseeable P as well.** • **Manufacturer fell below the standard of care by not placing all risks of foreseeable misuse on blender (such as what might happen if a consumer were to use hot liquids and/or fill the blender all the way to the top).** • **See above for causation and damages.**	Yes, negligence

Continued >

Issue	Rule	Fact Application	Conclusion
Defenses	• **Contributory negligence (P also negligent)—bars recovery in most jurisdictions** • **Assumption of the risk (P knew the risk and voluntary acted despite risk)** • **Comparative negligence—P's contributory negligence can limit or bar P's recovery** ➔ Majority view—partial comparative: bars recovery by P if P's negligence was more serious than D's ➔ Minority view—pure comparative: allows recovery but reduces by % P negligent	• **P is also negligent because a reasonable person would not place hot foods into a clearly labeled "Cold Drink Blender" and would follow directions as to volume**; failing to follow directions caused her burns and it is foreseeable that if you don't follow directions or use a product for its intended use, you risk injury, especially where blades are involved and high speeds. • Here, **Consumer did not know of risk, as the directions did not indicate what would happen if filled to top or if hot liquids were used.** • Although Consumer misused product, Manufacturer likely held to a higher standard and could have foreseen the risk and didn't warn of risks, so Manufacturer more at fault, so P would recover regardless of jurisdiction.	Yes, contributory negligence; no, assumption of the risk Consumer can recover even if negligent
Motion to dismiss—ground (1)	Goes to possible defenses above	**As indicated above, although Consumer did misuse the product by using hot foods rather than cold drinks, such misuse was foreseeable and is not a defense to strict products liability, even if damages under negligence may be reduced.**	Court should deny motion to dismiss
Motion to dismiss—ground (2)	Goes to possible defenses above	**As indicated above, although Consumer filled blender to the top, this too was foreseeable, and the risks if done were not given to consumers, so this would not be a defense to strict products liability, even if damages under negligence may be reduced.**	Court should deny motion to dismiss
Motion to dismiss—ground (3)	Goes to defect of product above	**As indicated above, there is a design and warning defect for the Cold Drink Blender and compliance with regulations does not negate this defect.**	Court should deny motion to dismiss

Continued >

Issue	Rule	Fact Application	Conclusion
Retailer's Motion to Dismiss			
Strict products liability	See above	**Here, Retailer also sold product to Consumer, so it is also liable under products strict liability theory, but can seek indemnification from Manufacturer.**	Yes, Retailer strictly liable
Indemnification	Shifts loss among tortfeasors	**Here, since Manufacturer designed and manufactured the Cold Drink Blender and sold it to Retailer, Retailer may seek indemnification for damages owed as a result of defective product.**	
Negligence	See above	Here, Retailer acted as an ordinary retailer would by selling products; it is not common for retailers to open and inspect all products it sells looking for possible foreseeable misuse and warnings.	Retailer not negligent
Motion to dismiss—ground (4)	Goes to strict liability and indemnification above	**Since Retailer is still liable to Consumer under a strict products liability theory, the complaint should stand as to this issue, but the court should dismiss the negligence claim against Retailer.**	Court should deny motion to dismiss, but dismiss neg. claim

Torts Question 5

February 2009, Question 4

ConsumerPro, a consumer protection group, published a manual listing the names, addresses, telephone numbers, and specialties of attorneys who represent plaintiffs in tort cases. The manual also included comments rating the attorneys. The manual was distributed by ConsumerPro to its members to aid them in the selection of an attorney should they need one.

Paul was listed in the manual as an attorney who litigates automobile accident cases. In the related comments, the manual stated that "Paul is reputed to be an ambulance chaser and appears to handle only easy cases."

Paul sued ConsumerPro for defamation, alleging injury to reputation and requesting general damages. ConsumerPro moved to dismiss for failure to state a claim on which relief could be granted, on the grounds that (1) the statement was non-actionable opinion, (2) Paul failed to allege malice or negligence under the United States Constitution, (3) Paul failed to allege special damages, and (4) in any event, the statement was privileged under the common law.

How should the court rule on each ground of the motion to dismiss? Discuss.

Torts Question 5 Assessment

February 2009, Question 4

This torts question is another with a set of very specific question calls. The facts state that Paul sued for defamation. With a specific issue stated in the call of the question, there is no need to write out your issues checklist. What is necessary at this point is to write out the specific rule elements and defenses that make up defamation.

After a careful reading of each call of the question, you will see that each call corresponds to one of the elements of defamation. For example, call 1 is about the statement itself and whether it was actionable opinion; this goes directly to the element of defamatory statement. To successfully and completely analyze this call, you need to have a full understanding of what a defamatory statement is. This question illustrates the reason why you need to understand your rules and have fact triggers that help you understand which facts give rise to the various issues, rather than just memorize the rules alone. Rote memorization will enable you to write out a rule statement, but it will not help you to analyze the specific details of that rule as is required here.

A good illustration of this is that many students will memorize the rules for defamation, such as, "defamation is a defamatory statement, of and concerning the plaintiff . . . ." However, if you don't fully understand what exactly a defamatory statement is because you simply memorized the rules alone, then you might find yourself in trouble on exams such as this one. A person who truly understands the rules, and doesn't simply memorize them, knows that a defamatory statement is one that is not mere opinion, but rather a statement that is based on specific facts and adversely affects one's reputation. With this knowledge and a full understanding of the rule, you would be able to properly analyze the first call of this question.

As you can see by the grid below, each of the calls in this question requires a full understanding of the indicated elements and rules of defamation, well beyond a rote memorization of the rules. The best way to fully understand the rules and how they apply is to see the relation between the rules and the fact triggers and to do as many practice essays as you can for each type of issue, especially focusing on those issues where you struggle or perhaps covering subjects you did not cover during law school.

The Issues Tested Matrix at the end of the torts chapter provides further guidance as to which questions cover the various tested issues. Some of the particular torts issues that are not found in this section can be found in the crossover section. Further, for additional practice, the California state bar website has available all questions from 2001 to the present, including two passing student answers. With the rules here, the fact triggers, the practice questions, assessment aids, and other information, you can practice writing out essays until you fully comprehend each issue and are able to articulate and understand how to apply every rule in an essay.

Make note of the areas highlighted in **bold** on the corresponding grid. The bold areas highlight the issues, analysis, and conclusions that are likely **required** to receive a passing score on this question.

Issue	Rule	Fact Application	Conclusion
Motion to Dismiss based on Ground (1)			
Defamation	Statements of opinion can be actionable if they are defamatory. To prove defamation, P must prove • **defamatory statement** (adversely affects one's reputation; **doesn't include opinions unless based on specific facts**) • of or concerning P • **published to a 3rd party** and understood, and • damages (presumed if libel—in writing)	• **Statement at issue here is that Paul is an ambulance chaser and handles only easy cases, which could affect his reputation as an attorney among both his peers and possible clients as being an attorney lacking integrity and taking advantage of people during a state of weakness. Arguably, it is opinion but is based on specific facts that he chases ambulances and takes easy cases only.** [Could have much more detail here.] • Statement specifically refers to P and mentions his name. • Statement was published in a manual and distributed to members of ConsumerPro, and it is likely that someone in a consumer protection group would understand what is meant by "an attorney chasing ambulances in tort practice and handling only easy cases." • Damages: Presumed since the statement was in writing (at least for general damages).	Yes, defamation, so **court should deny motion to dismiss on ground (1)**
Motion to Dismiss based on Ground (2)			
Constitutional limitations for defamation	If a defamatory statement is a matter of public concern, P must prove the above elements as well as falsity of the statement and fault on the part of D. Fault depends on P's status: • **Public figure**—one who has achieved fame or notoriety, or voluntarily assumed a role in public controversy—**P must prove malice (knowledge that the statement was false or a reckless disregard as to whether it was false)**	• **Here, an attorney alone is not necessarily a public figure as not all attorneys achieve fame or notoriety; also, there is no indication that Paul was a well-known, notorious attorney; it is likely Paul was a private person.** • **It is likely that consumers and the public have an interest/concern in lists' of attorneys organized by practice area and their relevant contact information, especially since attorneys exist to provide a unique service to the public; further, the public would likely want to know comments that others who have worked with the attorney may have; however, the particular comments that people have are not likely relevant to the public at large as the majority of the public is not concerned about the comments of various attorneys from different areas of practice.**	P need not prove malice or negligence, so court should deny motion to dismiss on ground (2) Could have concluded either way here based on public concern analysis/negligence analysis

Continued >

Issue	Rule	Fact Application	Conclusion
	• **Private person—only negligence must be proved if the statement involves a matter of public concern**	[Note: The two-state released answers came to opposite conclusions here; the key was arguing both sides.] • If the matter is of public concern, ConsumerPro arguably acted negligently because a reasonable group would verify their comments and allegations prior to publishing them, and there is no indication they did so here, but no indication that Paul alleged negligence; rather, he just plead defamation.	P need not prove malice or negligence, so court should deny motion to dismiss on ground (2) Could have concluded either way here based on public concern analysis/negligence analysis
Motion to Dismiss based on Ground (3)			
Damages for defamation	**For libel (written or printed publication of defamatory language), general damages are presumed and P need not prove special damages.** **For slander (spoken defamation), P must prove special damages unless slander per se** (adversely affects one's conduct in a business or profession, one has a loathsome disease, one if guilty of a crime of moral turpitude, or a woman is unchaste).	**Here, defamatory statement is in writing, thus libel; therefore, P need not prove special damages; rather, general damages are presumed.**	**General damages presumed here, so court should deny motion to dismiss on ground (3)**

Continued >

Issue	Rule	Fact Application	Conclusion
Motion to Dismiss based on Ground (4)			
Defenses to defamation	There are two privilege defenses for defamation: • Absolute privilege—for remarks made during judicial proceedings, by legislators in debate, by federal executives, in compelled broadcasts, and between spouses (this privilege is never lost) • **Qualified privilege**—for reports or official proceedings, statements in the interest of the publisher, statements in the interest of the recipient, statements in the common interest of the publisher and the recipient (this privilege can be lost if abused—beyond scope of privilege or malice) [Note: State-released answers had different rules for qualified privilege, neither of which were completely accurate.]	• Here, the statement was not made during a judicial proceeding, so the absolute privilege defense is not applicable. • Here, the statement about an attorney is in the interest of the publisher since they are a consumer protection group that tries to best inform consumers as to possible attorneys they may hire. • The statement is also in the interest of the recipient, as **a person seeking an attorney would likely want to know if an attorney only wants to take easy cases and chases ambulances, which tends to reflect on the morale and character of that attorney.** • **The qualified privilege may be lost as it is unclear whether ConsumerPro acted with malice in that they arguably printed the statement with a reckless disregard for the truth since it does not appear that they investigated the comment or talked to the attorney or did anything to verify the truth of the statement. On the other hand, they could have published that based on numerous observations by previous clients; the facts are unclear.**	A qualified privilege exists for ConsumerPro, but it may have acted with malice, so the court should deny the motion to dismiss on ground (4) to determine if malice exists by trier of fact

Torts Question 6

July 2003, Question 4

Paula is the president and Stan is the secretary of a labor union that was involved in a bitter and highly-publicized labor dispute with City and Mayor. An unknown person surreptitiously recorded a conversation between Paula and Stan, which took place in the corner booth of a coffee shop during a break in the contract negotiations with City. During the conversation, Paula whispered to Stan, "Mayor is a crook who voted against allowing us to build our new union headquarters because we wouldn't pay him off."

The unknown person anonymously sent the recorded conversation to KXYZ radio station in City. Knowing that the conversation had been surreptitiously recorded, KXYZ broadcast the conversation immediately after it received the tape.

After the broadcast, Paula sued KXYZ for invasion of privacy in publishing her conversation with Stan. Mayor sued Paula and KXYZ for defamation.

1. Is Paula likely to succeed in her suit against KXYZ? Discuss.
2. Is Mayor likely to succeed in his suit against Paula and KXYZ? Discuss.

Torts Question 6 Assessment

July 2003, Question 4

This torts question is a traditional defamation and invasion of privacy question. Many of the same facts give rise to both types of issues. Like the preceding practice essay, knowledge of the fact triggers is extremely helpful in enabling you to spot the issues. Facts such as a broadcast, offensive comments, secret recording, and disclosure of information all lend themselves to defamation and privacy issues.

It is also useful on essay exams to write out all four types of privacy issues since more than one of them often applies to the same set of facts—for instance, here, all four are potentially at issue. When approaching defamation, always start by asking yourself whether the matter is one of public concern. Here, it is rather straightforward that it is, so you would need to analyze both the common law defamation as well as the constitutional limitations in order to pass this question.

After spotting the issues, the most important part of this question is your knowledge and understanding of the rules for constitutional defamation. You have to know the different standards based on the plaintiff's status. Without knowing all parts of the rule for this issue, you will not pass this question because without the rules, you cannot even get to the analysis.

If you are struggling with memorizing rules, you should start by memorizing the issues checklist for each subject. Then, try to state the rule or write it out for each of the issues on the checklist. (Stating it is faster, but if you are struggling with the memorization, writing it out will aid in the memorization.) Check your stated or written rule against the actual rules to see if you were correct. If you were correct, then put a star or a check next to that issue on your checklist and move on to the next issue. If you get a rule wrong, highlight it so you know to review it again in the future.

For rules you do not know, practice writing them out five times, or making flashcards and putting those flashcards on a ring for daily review of each subject. You should be reviewing all of the rules for each subject in this way from the beginning of your bar studies up until the actual exam. The goal is to complete two subjects per day for review, thereby covering all subjects every week. Then, by the time you get to the actual exam, you will know all of the rules and will not miss crucial rules and analysis on an essay question.

Time permitting, as your bar studies progress, you should revisit these sample questions and rewrite them to test your knowledge of the rules and how they apply to a given set of facts. This will also test your timing since you will not spend any time looking up the rules when you write out the essays. Knowledge of the rules is one key to your success on the bar exam.

Make note of the areas highlighted in **bold** on the corresponding grid. The bold areas highlight the issues, analysis, and conclusions that are likely **required** to receive a passing score on this question.

Issue	Rule	Fact Application	Conclusion
Call #1: P v. KXYZ			
False light	• **One attributes to P views he does not hold or actions he does not take,** • The false light must be objectionable to a reasonable person under the circumstances; and • For publication there must be publicity. • **If a matter is of public interest, malice must be proved.**	• **Here, KXYZ's radio broadcast has attributed to P the view that she thinks Mayor is a crook, which she did state to Stan in their recorded conversation indicating this view is not contrary to her view.** • A reasonable person might find the broadcast objectionable as it is possible P did not literally mean that Mayor was a crook and that her statement and conversation were taken out of context; further, a reasonable person might find it objectionable because people tend to say things differently if they know they are being recorded, especially if what they were saying subjected them to tort liability, as it did here. • However, a reasonable person should not find it objectionable if their statement was published verbatim, especially since she was speaking about the issue in a public place, a coffee shop, during a break in contract negotiations with City, in which it is likely someone may have overheard the conversation; the fact that she was whispering indicates there were people around, in which case a reasonable person should know they may be overheard under the circumstances. • Publication occurred, as it was broadcast on radio. • **The matter is one of public interest as it involves the Mayor, a public official, and possible scandal involving a highly publicized labor dispute between City and Mayor.** • P will argue that malice did exist as KXYZ did not ensure that the statement was in proper context and that is was portrayed in the proper light; however, **since KXYZ broadcast the exact conversation, without altering it, there is no indication it is false, as it is exactly what P said to Stan.**	**No false light**

Continued >

Issue	Rule	Fact Application	Conclusion
Public disclosure of private facts	Liability attaches even if a statement is true if there is • **Public disclosure** • **Of a private fact that is** • **Objectionable to a reasonable person of, and** • **Not of legitimate public concern**	• Here, P's statement was publicly disclosed via radio broadcast. • The statement is more public than private in that it involved Mayor, who is a public figure, and it was about a highly publicized labor dispute, in which P is president and Stan is secretary of the labor union and Mayor's voting against them to build new headquarters; however, it could be considered private in context as discussed in objectionable to a reasonable person, discussed above. • **See above for objectionable to a reasonable person analysis. [Needed here to pass, unlike above.]** • **See above as to public interest/concern element.**	No disclosure [could have concluded either way here]
Appropriation	Unauthorized use of P's picture or name for D's commercial advantage, unless newsworthy and in public interest	Here, it is likely that KXYZ used P's name (and statement), as she is the president of a labor union, which is involved in a highly publicized dispute with City and Mayor; further, they likely used it for their commercial advantage to attract listeners and boost their ratings; however, comments about Mayor in regard to a highly publicized labor dispute is newsworthy and in the public interest.	No appropriation
Intrusion upon seclusion	• **Prying or intruding** • **Into a private aspect of P's life that is** • **Objectionable to a reasonable person**	• **Here, KXYZ did not intrude into P's life; rather, the unknown person who gave them the tape did; P may argue they are liable under an agency theory since they knew the tape was surreptitiously recorded and broadcast it anyway.** • Arguably, a statement about Mayor is not a private aspect of P's life as it involves City and a highly publicized labor dispute. • **P does have a right to privacy in regard to her conversations; here, P was speaking to one person in the corner of a coffee shop and whispering to Stan, indicating her conversation was private; this is furthered by the fact that the conversation was surreptitiously recorded.** • **However, a coffee shop is a public place; since they were there for contract negotiations with City and P was whispering, it is likely that others were around and a reasonable person should know that someone might overhear their conversation.**	**No intrusion**

Continued >

Issue	Rule	Fact Application	Conclusion
Call #2: M v. P			
Defamation	**• Defamatory statement (adversely affects one's reputation) • Of or concerning the P • Published to a 3rd party and understood • Damages—presumed if libel or slander per se If it is a matter of public concern, 1st Amend. limitations apply: P need also prove falsity and fault. Fault depends on P's status: • Public figure—need to prove malice (knowledge of falsity or reckless disregard); then damages presumed**	**• Here, P's statement that Mayor was a crook who voted against building new union headquarters because the union wouldn't pay him off would tends to adversely affect one's reputation as it accuses him of criminal activity, which could cause him to lose his job; further, as labor unions are large groups, the entire union would likely view him in a negative light. • The statement refers directly to Mayor and, since the dispute was highly publicized, it is likely that the average person understood which "Mayor" she was referring to. • Published to Stan by making statement, which was later published to public in broadcast. • P's statement was oral, so slander, but slander per se as it affects Mayor in his business/profession, so damages would be presumed.** See above for public concern discussion. **• It is unclear whether P's statement is true or false, but Mayor will need to prove falsity in order to prevail here.** • Public figure: Here, it concerns a public figure since plaintiff is the mayor and a public official involved in a highly publicized labor dispute.	No defamation if statement is true
	• Private figure—need to show negligence if matter of public concern; only actual injury damages recoverable	• Here, **P did not act with reckless disregard for the truth if she was speaking the truth**; further, she was whispering her statement to the secretary of the union in the corner; although she should have anticipated one might overhear her conversation, she likely did not make it with reckless disregard that is would be surreptitiously recorded and broadcast.	

Continued >

Issue	Rule	Fact Application	Conclusion
Defense: truth	Statement is true	Unclear if true of not; burden on Mayor to prove falsity, as discussed above.	
Call #2: M v. KXYZ			
Defamation	**See above**	See above for discussion of defamatory statement, of and concerning P, and published. • **Modernly, radio broadcasts are considered libel, in which case, damages would be presumed; even if slander, it would be slander per se, as indicated above.** • **For malice under public figure, if the statement is found to be false, KXYZ may have acted with malice,** as they did not verify the truth of the matter or attempt to speak with P, S, or Mayor prior to broadcasting the tape.	No defamation if true
Defense: truth	See above	See above	
Defense: qualified privilege	Statements in the interest of the publisher, recipient, or both; can be lost via abuse	KXYZ may argue that it is in the interest of the recipient, the public, to know if their mayor is a crook, as they have the power to vote him out of office if the statement is true.	Yes, qualified privilege

PART 12 WILLS AND TRUSTS

WILLS TABLE OF CONTENTS

TRUSTS TABLE OF CONTENTS

INTRODUCTION TO WILLS AND TRUSTS

Wills and trusts are two distinct subjects, but they are combined here since they are related and often cross over with each other. When tested, approximately one-third of the time the question will cover wills issues only, one-third of the time trusts issues only, and one-third of the time both wills and trusts issues are covered in a crossover question. Crossover questions often arise when there is a will that either contains a trust or refers to a trust outside of the will.

Wills are commonly tested by a fact pattern where a testator has a will detailing provisions for distributing the testator's assets. Unless the facts indicate that a valid will exists, it is first necessary to address the will's validity. Then, organize the question by each asset, and analyze all issues pertaining to each asset in the testator's estate. Another way the subject of wills is commonly tested is with a fact pattern concerning the issues pertaining to the execution of the will itself, rather than what the testator intends to distribute in his will.

Trusts questions often arise in fact patterns concerning the trustee's conduct and the resulting effect on the beneficiaries, which requires analysis of the trustee's duties and liabilities. Trust questions may also involve particular trust types, such as a charitable trust, and then require analysis of the cy pres doctrine and other potential trusts, such as a resulting trust if the trust fails.

The details are important in wills and trusts questions. Pay careful attention to all of the parties since often there are more parties identified in the facts than will benefit from the trust or take under the will. You are expected to discuss how the will or trust will affect all of the parties included in the facts, not just those named in the will or trust. Also, pay close attention to the call of the question and/or parties claiming a share of the estate so that you don't inadvertently omit any parties. Lastly, always consider if there is a two-sided argument. Often, there are competing arguments that result in different possible distributions, all of which must be identified.

Remember that on an essay exam the key is to use the facts to both prove and disprove the rules. This comes up frequently in wills and trusts questions where an element is clearly not met, but there are facts that raise the issue so it must be discussed. For example, the examiners often test the issue of "incorporation by reference," but typically the document referenced was not in existence at the time of the execution of the will and thus is not incorporated. Many students think about the issue and quickly dismiss it because the incorporation fails; as a result, they do not include the issue in their essay and miss easy points. Generally, if an issue crosses your mind, it is worthy of inclusion, even if it is a minor issue or one that is clearly not met. Address it quickly and move on in order to maximize your points.

Finally, wills and trusts questions can be difficult to organize because there are so many parties and assets at issue. It may be helpful to draw a timeline identifying the dates and events, and/or a diagram of the people and how they relate. This helps put the facts into perspective. Then, organize your essay by the call of the question, whether it is by person, asset, duties breached, or any other pertinent issue.

ISSUES CHECKLIST

WILLS

- Validity
  - Execution
  - Capacity
  - Conflict of laws
- Components of a Will
  - Integrated
  - Incorporation by reference
  - Acts of indep. legal significance
  - Codicil
  - Pour-over will
- **Revocation**
  - Physical act
  - Subsequent will
  - Operation of law
  - DRR
- **Revival**
- **Distribution**
  - Classification of gifts
  - Ademption
  - Abatement
  - Exoneration
  - Lapse/antilapse
  - Survivor rights
  - Bars to succession
- **Intestate Distribution**
- **Contracts Relating to Wills**

TRUSTS

- **Creation/Validity**
- **Limitations**
- **Types of Trusts**
  - Express
  - Testamentary
  - Pour over
  - Secret
  - Semi-secret
  - Spendthrift
  - Support
  - Discretionary
  - Charitable
  - Honorary
  - Totten
  - Resulting
  - Constructive
- **Administration**
  - Powers of trustee
  - Duties of trustee
    - Account and inform
    - Not to delegate
    - Impartiality
    - Due care
      - Invest
      - Diversify
    - Segregate
    - Loyalty
    - Invest
    - Defend
    - Enforce
  - Liabilities of Trustee
  - Liabilities of 3rd parties
  - Allocation
- **Modification/Revocation**
- **Termination**
- **Remedies**

MEMORIZATION ATTACK SHEET

WILL VALIDITY/CREATION

- Execution
  - Writing
  - Signed by T, or in his presence & at his direction
  - Signed by 2 witnesses
  - Witnesses know T's will
  - Witnesses see T sign or acknowledge T signature at same time
- Holographic will
  - T's signature
  - Material provisions in T's handwriting
  - Invalid if no date and unclear which will is new
- Capacity
  - 18 years old
  - Sound mind/competent
  - Fraud in the execution (forgery)
  - Fraud in the inducement (misrepresentations)
  - Undue influence
    - Unnatural disposition
    - Opportunity to influence
    - T susceptible to influence
    - Beneficiary active in procuring disposition
  - Presume fraud/undue influence if devise is to
    - Drafter
    - One in fiduciary relationship with T
    - Care custodian w/in 90 days
    - Employee of any of the above
    - Exceptions:
      - Blood relative
      - Less than $5k
      - Attorney consult
- Conflicts of laws
  - Valid if complies w/laws of state of:
    - Execution
    - Place of death
    - Domicile

WILL COMPONENTS

- Integration
  - Present at time of will
  - T's intent
- Incorporation by reference
  - Existed at time of will
  - Will shows T's intent
  - Sufficiently described
- Acts of independent legal significance
  - Separate from effect in will
- Codicil
  - Amendment to will
  - Republishes will as of date of codicil
  - Same formalities of will, or holographic will
- Pour-over will
  - Identifies trust in will
  - Terms set forth in document other than will
  - Trust executed before or at same time as will

WILL REVOCATION

- By physical act
  - Presumed destroyed if will last with T and now gone
- By subsequent will
  - Express or implied
- By operation of law
  - Omitted child/spouse
- DRR
  - T revokes 1st will
  - Mistakenly believes 2nd will valid when it isn't
  - If T knew 2nd will not valid, would not have revoked 1st will
  - 1st will probated anyway

WILL REVIVAL

- 1st will revoked
- 2nd will revoked
- 1st will revived if T intended to revive it
- Extrinsic evidence okay

WILL DISTRIBUTION

- Classification of gifts
  - Specific gift
    - Identifiable property
    - Stock splits follow original stock
    - Stock dividends look to T's intent
  - General gift
  - Demonstrative gift
    - General, but specifies property or fund to take from
  - Residuary—remainder
- Ademption
  - By extinction
    - Gift no longer there
    - Look at T's intent
  - By satisfaction
    - Given to beneficiary during life
- Abatement
  - Gifts reduced to pay all debts
  - Reduced in order:
    - Property not in will
    - Residuary gifts
    - General—nonrelative
    - General—relative
    - Specific—nonrelative
    - Specific—relative
- Exoneration
  - Property doesn't abate to exonerate mortgage, lien, deed of trust, etc.
- Lapse/antilapse
  - Predeceased beneficiary gift lapses to residue
  - If beneficiary kindred, antilapse, so gift to issue
  - Simultaneous death—apply lapse or antilapse
- Survivor's rights
  - Widow elects under will or statutory share
  - Spouse can set aside transfer of CP or QCP
  - Omitted heirs take intestate share
    - Exception
      - Otherwise provided for
      - All of estate to other parent
- Bars to succession
  - No contest—okay to bring
  - if probable cause
    Killers treated as predeceased

INTESTATE DISTRIBUTION

- Intestate succession
  - All CP and QCP to surviving spouse
  - All SP to spouse if no child; 1/2 if 1 child; 1/3 if 1 + children
  - If no spouse/partner, then to
    - Issue
    - Parents
    - Issue of parents
    - Grandparents
    - Issue of predeceased spouse
    - Next of kin
    - Parents of predeceased spouse
    - Issue of parents of predeceased spouse
    - Escheat to state
  - Heir must survive decedent by 120 hours
- Per capita—generation
  - 1st generation with living
  - Each living gets one share
  - Shares of all deceased split equally between next generation living

- ♦ Per capita—representation
  - 1st generation with living
  - Each living gets one share
  - Share of deceased goes to his issue equally
  - If deceased has no issue, goes back to all at that level
- ♦ Strict per stirpes
  - 1st generation with living or deceased with issue
  - Each living or deceased issue gets one share
- ♦ Children
  - Adopted treated as natural
  - Step or foster take only if
    - Relationship during child's minority
    - Continued through life
    - Legal barrier prevented adoption

WILL CONTRACT ISSUES

- ♦ K to make a will, not make a will, revoke a will established by
  - Material provisions of k in will
  - Reference in will to k and extrinsic evidence
  - Writing signed by decedent
  - Clear and convincing evidence
- ♦ Joint or mutual wills do not create presumption of k

TRUST CREATION/VALIDITY

- ♦ Trust created by
  - Declaration by owner
  - Transfer of property during owner's life to trustee
  - Transfer by owner in will
  - Power of appointment
  - Enforceable promise
- ♦ Validity requires
  - Settlor's intention
  - Trust property
  - Legal purpose
  - Ascertainable beneficiary
  - Court can appoint trustee

TRUST LIMITATIONS

- ♦ Real property needs writing
- ♦ Oral trust is by clear and convincing evidence
- ♦ Performed by trustee only
- ♦ Invalidation—see Wills (fraud, undue influence, capacity)

TYPES OF TRUSTS

- ♦ Express—all above validity requirements met
- ♦ Testamentary—in will
- ♦ Pour over—see pour-over will above (in Will Components)
- ♦ Secret—no beneficiary/intent on face of trust
- ♦ Semi-secret—no beneficiary named, but intent there
- ♦ Spendthrift—beneficiary cannot alienate his interest
- ♦ Support—for beneficiary's health, education, maintenance
- ♦ Discretionary—trustee can distribute/withhold from beneficiary
- ♦ Charitable—benefits society
  - Cy pres—if can't be done, court tries to substitute
- ♦ Honorary—no charitable or private beneficiary
- ♦ Totten—beneficiary takes money leftover in bank acct.
- ♦ Resulting—implied in fact; goes back to settlor's estate
  - Arises from
    - Purpose of trust ends
    - Trust fails
    - Illegal trust
    - Excess corpus
    - Semi-secret
- ♦ Constructive—applied to prevent unjust enrichment for fraud, self-dealing, etc.

TRUST ADMINISTRATION

- ♦ Powers of trustee
  - Enumerated and implied

- Duties of trustee
  - Account and inform
  - Not to Delegate unless uses skill and due care
  - Impartiality (treat all beneficiaries fairly)
  - Due care
    - Investigate
    - Diversify
  - Segregate and earmark
  - Loyalty—no self-dealing or conflicts of interest
  - Prudently Invest
    - Statutory lists
    - UPIA—look at portfolio as a whole; reasonable
  - Defend actions and Enforce claims
  - Mnemonic: "**AND I DID SLIDE**"
- Liabilities of trustee
  - Personally liable for violating trustee duties
  - Liable for torts and contracts if within scope
- Duties of 3rd parties
  - Transfer to BFP cuts off beneficiary's interest
  - Transfer to non-BFP can be set aside by beneficiary
  - 3rd party can hold property as constructive trustee
- Allocation
  - Income to beneficiary
  - Principal to remainderman
  - Trustee uses best judgment in allocating

MODIFICATION/REVOCATION

- Majority: Settlor can modify or revoke only if right reserved
- Minority: Settlor can modify or revoke even if right not reserved
- Court can modify to meet settlor's intent or for cy pres

TRUST TERMINATION

- Trustee cannot terminate
- Beneficiaries can terminate if all competent, all consent & doesn't frustrate trust purpose
- Court can terminate if trust purpose frustrated/impossible
- Lapse and antilapse apply

BREACH OF TRUST REMEDIES

- Trustee cannot offset losses
- Damages, constructive trust, tracing, equitable lien, remove trustee, surcharge for resulting loss

WILLS RULE OUTLINE

I. **VALIDITY OF A WILL**
   A. **Execution**
      1. **A valid will must meet the formalities of being in writing, signed and witnessed.**
         a. **Writing:** The will must be in writing.
         b. **Signed:** The will must be:
            1. **Signed by the testator**, or
            2. **Acknowledgement of signature:** Signed by someone in the testator's presence and at his direction.
         c. **Two witnesses:** The will requires the signature of two witnesses who:
            1. **Know the document is a will**; and
            2. **Both are present at the same time to witness** the testator's signing of the will (or acknowledgment of his signature) during the testator's lifetime. However, it is not necessary for the two witnesses to sign attesting to that fact at the same time.

> Exam tip: The two witnesses must witness the testator signature (or acknowledgement of signature) at the same time, but do not necessarily need to sign themselves to attest to that fact at the same time or in each other's presence.

      2. **Witness issues**
         a. **Not properly witnessed:** If witness requirements are not satisfied, the will can still be treated as properly executed if the proponent of the will establishes by **clear and convincing evidence that the testator intended** the document to be his will at the time he signed it.
         b. **Interested witnesses:** Witnesses **should not be "interested witnesses."** An interested witness creates a **rebuttable presumption** that the witness procured the devise by duress, menace, fraud, or undue influence, unless there are two other uninterested witnesses or the devise is made solely in a fiduciary capacity.
      3. **Holographic Will:** A will that does not comply with the formalities required for a valid will can qualify as a valid holographic will if the **signature and material provisions are all in the testator's handwriting.**
         a. **Undated:** If the holographic will does not have a date and there is doubt as to whether it or another will controls, the holographic will is invalid to the extent of any inconsistencies.

> **Witness fact triggers:**
> **Invalid:** Neighbors to act as witnesses—cannot go from one house to the other to sign if they aren't both present at the same time to see testator sign or acknowledge his signature
> **Invalid:** Witness doesn't realize it is testator's will
> **Valid:** Two witnesses that see testator sign with each present, but each sign separately themselves or take will around corner or to another room to sign as a witness

B. **Capacity** is measured at the time of will execution.
   1. **"Of legal age and sound mind":** An individual must be at least **18 years old** and of **sound mind** to make a valid will.
      a. **Mental capacity:** An individual is not mentally competent to make a will if, at the time the will is made, he is unable to:
         1. Understand the **nature of the testamentary act**, or
         2. Understand the nature and **situation of his property**, or
         3. Remember and understand his **relations with family** members that are affected by the will.
      b. **Mental disorder:** An individual is not mentally competent to make a will if he suffers from a mental disorder that results in **hallucinations or delusions** that cause him to devise property in a way that he would not have done but for the disorder.
   2. **No duress, menace, fraud, or undue influence:** The execution or revocation of a will or part of a will is ineffective to the extent that it was procured by duress, menace, fraud, or undue influence.
   3. **Fraud** is the **misrepresentation**, deceit, or concealment of a **material fact**, known to be false by the wrongdoer, with the **intent** to **deprive a person of property or legal rights** or cause injury, and does in fact deprive that person.
   4. **Fraud can occur at three points in the process.**
      a. **Fraud in the execution** occurs when a testator is **unaware he is signing a will** or the will is **forged** by another, resulting in the entire will being invalid.
      b. **Fraud in the inducement** occurs when a wrongdoer influences the testator through **misrepresentations** to include provisions in a will, resulting in only those particular fraudulent provisions being invalid.
      c. **Fraud preventing revocation** occurs when fraud is implemented to prevent a will revocation; a court will still probate the will and the **wrongdoer will take under a constructive trust.** (See Remedies chapter.)
   5. **Undue influence** is found when the testator executes a will
      a. Leaving an **unnatural disposition** of his property, and
      b. The beneficiaries had **opportunity to influence** this disposition, and

c. The testator was **susceptible to their influence**, and
d. The beneficiaries were **active in procuring this disposition.**

6. **Fraud or undue influence is presumed** in an instrument making a donative transfer to
   a. The **person who drafted** it,
   b. A person in a **fiduciary relationship with the transferor who transcribed the instrument** or caused it to be transcribed,
   c. A **care custodian** of the transferor adult during the period services were provided, or within 90 days of provision of services,
   d. A **cohabitant or employee** of any of the above people (in a-c).
   e. **Exceptions to the presumption** include the following:
      1. When the beneficiary is a **blood relative or cohabitant** of the transferor, or
      2. When the property transferred is **valued at $5,000 or less**, or
      3. When an **independent attorney reviews** the instrument and counsels the transferor without the beneficiary being present.
   f. The **presumption can be rebutted** by clear and convincing evidence.

> **Issue-spotting tip:** Whenever a witness takes under the will, even if it is a relative, always think about the undue influence issue. In addition, always consider undue influence when the devise seems unusual, such as the testator giving away part of the estate to his fortune-teller.

> **Fraud fact triggers:**
> - Concealing a letter that one knows would change the testator's will
> - Lying to the testator about the existence or survival of a child or family member
> - Informing testator that he must do something in his will while knowing that it is not true

C. **Conflict of laws:** A written will is validly executed if its execution complies with the law of the place where **testator is domiciled at the time of execution** of the will or **domiciled at the time of death, or** complies with the law of the place where the **will was executed.**

II. COMPONENTS OF A WILL

A. **Integration:** Papers are integrated into the will if they were **present at the time** of the execution of the will and the **testator intended them to be part of his will,** such as several writings connected by a sequence of thought, folded together, stapled, or physically forming one document.

> **<u>Issue-spotting tip:</u>** Integration is at issue anytime there are papers or a reference to papers or notes outside of the will, whether they are found with the will or referenced in the will.

B. **Incorporation by reference:** A writing outside the will may be incorporated by reference into the will if the writing **existed at the time the will was executed** and the will manifests the **intent to incorporate** it and sufficiently **describes the writing** so that it is identifiable.
   1. **Validity not required:** The document referenced need not be valid.
   2. **Special rule for limited tangible personal property:** A writing, even if it cannot be incorporated by reference, may be admitted into probate when it disposes of limited tangible personal property if the writing
      a. Was referred to in the will,
      b. Is dated and either in the testator's handwriting or signed by him unless his intent can be shown,
      c. Describes the items and beneficiaries, and
      d. Each item is worth no more than $5,000 and $25,000 total value.
         1. **Tangible personal property does not include** real property, bank accounts, documents of title, securities, money that is common coin or currency (normal U.S. money, not collectibles), and property used in a trade or business.

> **<u>Issue-spotting tip:</u>** Anytime you issue spot integration, you should also consider incorporation by reference. These two issues often arise together as a cluster and should both be addressed, even if only one of them is met, anytime a document outside the will is referenced in the will.

> **<u>Incorporation by reference fact triggers:</u>**
> - A will that leaves any property to a person named in a document outside the will
> - Any pieces of paper found near the will when the will mentions outside documents (even if it isn't clear that those are the papers incorporated by reference, it still raises the issue)
> - A holographic will or codicil that addresses another will or mentions the other will (attempts to incorporate provisions of one will into the other)

C. **Acts of independent legal significance:** A will may dispose of property by reference to acts and events that have independent legal significance apart from their effect in the will.

> <u>Exam tip:</u> Always consider if an act of independent legal significance will effectively dispose of property that otherwise cannot be disposed of because of the failure to properly integrate or incorporate. **Examples** of references to acts of independent significance include providing income to one for life through a trust (nontestamentary purpose); paying employees based on performance, not just through the will; a reference to newspaper clippings (which provide news and are not just testamentary); collections of articles to devise; etc.

D. **Codicil: A codicil is an amendment to an existing will** made by the testator to change, explain, or republish his will. It **must meet the same formalities** as a will or holographic will.
   1. **Revocation of a codicil** leaves the will remaining valid, but revocation of a will revokes both the will and the codicil.
   2. **Republication: A validly executed codicil** operates as a republication of the will as of the date on the codicil.

E. **Pour-over will:** A pour-over will is a will that identifies a trust created by the testator that he can use to **"pour over" his probate assets into** and thus avoid going through probate if the assets are less than $100,000.
   1. A **pour-over will is valid** if:
      a. The **trust is identified** in the will,
      b. The **terms are set forth in an instrument other than the will,** and
      c. The **trust was executed concurrently or before** the will execution.

III. **REVOCATION OF A WILL**

A. **Revocation by physical act:** A will or part of a will can be revoked by a **physical act** of the testator or another person in the testator's presence and at the testator's direction. The physical act can include the will being burned, torn, canceled, destroyed, or obliterated with the **intent to revoke it.**
   1. **Presumed revoked:** It is **presumed that the testator destroyed the will** with the intent to revoke it if the testator's will was last in the testator's possession and he was competent until death, and if neither the will nor a duplicate can be found after the testator's death.
   2. **Cross out one of two beneficiaries:** Where there is a devise to A and B and B has been crossed out, B's portion goes to the will residue, not to A.

B. **Revocation by subsequent will:** A will or part of a will is revoked by a subsequent will, which either **expressly revokes** the previous will or part of it, or **impliedly revokes** the previous will or part of it **through inconsistencies.**

C. **Revocation by operation of law:** A will is revoked by operation of law to accommodate an **omitted spouse or child or subsequent domestic partner,** or to **remove all devises to a previous spouse** after divorce or annulment.

1. **Omitted child or spouse:** An omitted child or spouse will receive **an intestate share** if they were born or married after the will was made, **unless they were**
   a. **Intentionally omitted** as indicated on the face of will,
   b. **Otherwise provided for outside the will** with an **intent** to do so in lieu of the will, or
   c. The decedent had one or more children and devised substantially all of the estate to the **other parent of the omitted child.**

> **Issue-spotting tip:** Whenever a child or spouse, even if it is an ex-spouse, claims part of the testator's estate, bring up the issue of omitted heir even if you quickly dismiss it because the spouse is an ex-spouse or because an exception applies, such as when the testator left all of the estate to the other parent when there were already other children in existence. Raise the issue and use the facts to establish that the requirements are not met.

> **Omitted child or spouse fact triggers:**
> - Parent mistakenly believes child or spouse is dead
> - Child born after will was executed
> - Parent unaware of child's existence at time will was executed
> - Parent doubts child is his at time will was executed

D. **Dependent relative revocation (DRR):** Courts will apply the doctrine of dependent relative revocation where the testator **revokes his first will** (or part of it) on the **mistaken belief** that a substantially similar **second will or codicil would be effective, but it is not effective** at death (often because the subsequent will or codicil was also revoked), and but for the mistake testator would not have revoked his first will. The court will **disregard the revocation made by the subsequent will** and allow the first will to take effect.

> **DRR fact triggers:**
> - Testator made new will because he mistakenly thought the beneficiary in his old will was dead
> - Testator changes will because he reconciles with persons not in will, but new will is not valid
> - New will is not a valid holographic will, but testator crossed out part of old will thinking new will was valid

1. **Invalid second will:** If the second will is invalid due to fraud, duress, menace, undue influence, or ineffective execution, then the revocation of the first will was never valid so **DRR is not applicable.**

2. **DRR only revives the most recently revoked instrument,** such that if a second will revoked a first will and then a third will revoked the second will, the first will would be still be revoked **unless** it is clear from the third will that the testator intended for the first will to take effect.

> **Exam tip:** About half of the time the issue of DRR arises it applies, and half of the time it does not. Even if DRR doesn't apply—perhaps due to failed witness requirements, or the other will was not actually being revoked as it appeared—still spot the issue, briefly explain why DRR doesn't apply, and move on.

IV. **REVIVAL OF A WILL**

A. **Revival:** When a will is revoked by a physical act or a subsequent will, and then the subsequent will is revoked as well, **the first will is revived if the testator intends for it to be revived.** Extrinsic evidence is permitted when revocation is performed by a physical act.

V. **DISTRIBUTION ISSUES**

A. **Classification of testamentary gifts**

1. **Specific gift:** A specific gift is a gift of **specific, identifiable property.** (E.g.: my diamond earrings, my beach cottage in Malibu, my 2012 Cadillac, my ABC stock portfolio, etc.)
    a. **Special rules for stock**
        1. **Stock splits** follow the original stock and are distributed to the beneficiary of the original stock.
        2. **Stock dividends:** Courts are split on whether or not stock dividends are given to the beneficiary. Generally, the court will look at the testator's **intent** and whether he still owned the stocks at the time of his death, resulting in the dividend often going to the beneficiary.
2. **General gift:** A general gift is a gift from the **general assets** of the estate and does not include specific property.
3. **Demonstrative gift:** A demonstrative gift is a general gift that **specifies** the **property** or a **particular fund** from which the gift should be made.
4. **Residuary gift:** A residuary gift is **what remains** of the estate after all other gifts have been satisfied.

> **Exam tip:** Whenever a gift is devised that consists of a house, car, stocks, etc., but does not contain a specific address or model, argue the facts both ways—that it can be a specific gift or a general gift—and always discuss the testator's intent, even if you must make inferences to do so.

B. **Ademption** applies where the property has changed form from that identified in the will.
   1. **A specific gift adeems by extinction** if the specific item identified in the will is not part of the estate at the time of the testator's death—in other words, the specific gift is void and that purported devisee takes nothing.
      a. Courts will look at the **testator's intent** in determining whether the gift adeems, such that the beneficiary takes nothing.
      b. The beneficiary is **entitled to a general pecuniary gift** of equal value where the specific gift involved securities that changed form, a conservator that sold the property, or eminent domain.
   2. **A gift adeems by satisfaction** if the testator's will provides for deduction of the lifetime gift, the testator or the beneficiary declare in writing that the gift is satisfied, or the same property is given to the beneficiary during his lifetime.

> **Ademption fact triggers:**
> - Testator leaves condo or house to beneficiary but later sells it
> - Testator leaves car to beneficiary but doesn't still own it at time of death
> - Testator leaves specific stocks or shares to beneficiary but sells or transfers them prior to death

C. **Abatement** occurs when gifts are reduced to enable the estate to pay all debts and legacies that it otherwise would be unable to pay.
   1. **Order of gift abatement**
      a. Property not disposed of by the will
      b. Residuary gifts
      c. General gifts to nonrelatives
      d. General gifts to relatives
      e. Specific gifts to nonrelatives
      f. Specific gifts to relatives

D. **Exoneration** applies when a gift of property is made that is subject to an encumbrance, such as a loan, and the will requires the encumbrance to be paid off so that the devisee **takes the property free and clear** of the mortgage.
   1. The general rules of **abatement** apply to enable exoneration.
   2. Where a will requires that a gift of specific property be exonerated from a mortgage (deed or trust, or lien), a **specific gift of other property cannot be abated** for the purpose of exonerating the encumbered property.

E. **Lapse and antilapse rules** apply when the persons taking under a will are no longer alive at the time of the testator's death.
   1. **Lapse:** Traditionally and in some jurisdictions, when a beneficiary predeceased the testator, the gift to the beneficiary lapsed and fell into the residue, or was distributed via intestate succession if there was no residue.

2. **Antilapse:** Modernly and in California, when a beneficiary predeceases the testator, the **issue of the beneficiary** take in his place, thus **avoiding the lapse** of the gift, unless a contrary intention appears in the will.
   a. **Kindred only:** Antilapse only applies if the beneficiary is a person who is kindred to the testator or kindred of a surviving, deceased, or former spouse of the testator.
   b. **Issue will take per capita** if they are the same degree of relation, or per capita with representation if of a more remote degree.
   c. **Class gifts:** Antilapse also applies to **class gifts.**
   d. **Issue includes** all lineal descendants, not just children.
3. **Simultaneous death:** If both the testator and the beneficiary die simultaneously and it cannot be determined by clear and convincing evidence that the beneficiary died first, then the **beneficiary is determined to have predeceased** the testator and the devise lapses, unless antilapse applies.

F. **Survivor rights**
1. **Widow's election:** A widow's election allows a widower or a surviving domestic partner to elect to keep his share **devised** under the decedent spouse's will **or** to take his **statutory share**, which is his half of the community property (CP) and the quasi-community property (QCP), if the decedent spouse attempted to dispose of more than half of the CP or QCP.
2. **Property transfers:** A surviving spouse or domestic partner can **set aside transfers** of property or interests of CP and QCP made by the decedent spouse during marriage, to the extent of half if the transferee has retained the property, or, if the transferee has not retained the property, the surviving spouse can obtain half of the proceeds or value at the time of transfer.
3. **Omitted children** (see section III.C.1 above).

G. **Bars to succession**
1. **No contest clause:** A no contest clause in a will **penalizes a beneficiary if he contests** the instrument and will only be enforced if it is a direct contest brought without probable cause on the grounds of forgery, lack of due execution, lack of capacity, menace, duress, fraud, undue influence, revocation, or disqualification of a beneficiary in a fiduciary relationship to the testator, or if specifically mentioned in the no-contest clause.
2. **Killers:** Intentional and felonious killers do not take under the will or by intestacy, and are treated as having predeceased the testator and antilapse provisions do not apply.

VI. **INTESTATE DISTRIBUTION:** Applies when the decedent died without a will.

A. **Community property (CP):** For all CP and quasi-community property (QCP), the **surviving spouse or domestic partner takes all** of the CP and QCP.

B. **Separate property (SP):** For the decedent's SP, the surviving spouse **takes all** of it **only if the decedent did not leave any surviving issue, parent, siblings, or issue of siblings.**

1. **Decedent dies leaving surviving spouse or domestic partner and**
   a. **One child, or parents, or their issue:** The surviving spouse takes **one-half of the SP.**
   b. **More than one child, or their issue:** The surviving spouse takes **one-third of the SP.**

C. **Intestate succession order:** Applies when decedent dies without leaving a surviving spouse or domestic partner, and/or for the portion of the estate remaining after the surviving spouse receives his share, as noted above.
   1. To issue
   2. To parents, if no issue
   3. Issue of parents, if none of the above
   4. Grandparents, if none of the above
   5. Issue of grandparents, if none of the above
   6. Issue of predeceased spouse/partner, if none of the above
   7. Next of kin, if none of the above
   8. Parents of predeceased spouse/partner, if none of the above
   9. Issue of parents of predeceased spouse/partner, if none of the above
   10. Escheat to state, if none of the above

D. **120-hour rule:** For intestate succession to apply, the **heir must survive the decedent by 120 hours** or he will be deemed to have predeceased the decedent, unless the application of the 120-hour rule would result in escheat to the state.

E. **Advancement:** If a person dies intestate, **property that the decedent gave to an heir during lifetime** is only treated as an advancement against that heir's share of the intestate estate **if the decedent declared and the heir acknowledged such in a writing.**

F. **Per capita—representation distribution**
   1. **Per capita:** When intestate succession applies per capita at each generation (Probate Code § 247) distribution, the first generation with living takers is allocated a share in which all living persons at that generational level take an equal share; next, the shares of all deceased persons at that generational level are combined and then divided equally among the takers at the next generational level in the same way, resulting in persons of the same degree of kinship to the decedent always taking equal shares.
   2. ***Per capita example:*** X has three children, A, B, and C. A has two children, A1 and A2; B has no children; C has one child, C1. A and C are deceased. At X's death, X's estate is divided among three shares at the first generational level with living heirs because there are three children at that level, A, B, and C. Each are attributed 1/3 of the estate. B will take his 1/3 share since he is alive. The remaining 2/3 of the estate will be equally distributed among the next level of heirs alive, which includes A1, A2, and C1. They will each take 2/9 of the estate (each takes equal shares of the remaining 2/3).
   3. **Modern per stirpes, or per capita with representation** (Probate Code **§ 240**) makes an equal distribution at the first level of living heirs. If

any of those heirs are deceased and leave issue still living, their share will be distributed equally between their issue. If any deceased heirs don't leave issue, then their share will be added back to the original distribution and divided among the remaining closest heirs.

4. ***Modern per stirpes, or per capita with representation, example:*** Assume the same family as above. C will take 1/3 as above, but now A's two children will split A's 1/3, such that both A1 and A2 will each take 1/6, and C's child, C1, will take C's entire 1/3. Note that if A, B, and C were all deceased, the first level of distribution would begin at the level of A1, A2, and C1. So, all three of them would each take 1/3.
5. **Strict per stirpes** (Probate Code **§ 246**) makes an equal distribution at the first level in which there are surviving heirs or deceased heirs who left issue; the issue of the deceased heirs share their parents share equally.
6. ***Strict per stirpes example:*** Strict per stirpes operates the same as the modern per stirpes example for the first part, but note that if A, B, and C were all dead, their 1/3 share would be distributed among their heirs if they left issue. So, since B left no issue, B's 1/3 would be distributed equally between A and C, such that A's issue would take 1/2 and C's issue would take 1/2, resulting in A1 and A2 receiving 1/4 and C1 receiving 1/2.

> Exam tip: Whenever distribution is at issue and there are multiple generational levels, draw diagrams for each level and cross out the heirs who are dead or put circles around those who are alive and boxes around those who are dead so you can clearly see which issue go with which parents, and so forth, to determine the proper fractions that each issue will take depending on the type of representation applied. Typically, you need not do the math in your answer; identifying the fraction is satisfactory.

G. **Children**

1. **Parent-child relationship exists** between parents and natural as well as adopted children.
2. **Adoption severs** the relationship of a natural parent and an adopted child unless the spouse of the natural parent adopts the child, and the adopted child and natural parent lived together at any time as parent and child.
3. **Step and foster children:** For the purposes of intestate succession, a relationship exists between a parent and step or foster children **only if** the relationship began during **child's minority**, continued **throughout lifetime** of parties, and a **legal barrier prevented adoption.**

VII. **CONTRACTS RELATING TO WILLS:** These typically arise when two or more testators are coordinating their testamentary efforts.

A. **Proving the contents of a contract to make a will**, to revoke a will or to not revoke it, or to die intestate may be established by **one** of the following:
   1. A provision in the will that states the **material provisions of the contract**;
   2. An **express reference in a will**, or other instrument to a contract, and extrinsic evidence that proves the terms of the contract;
   3. A **writing signed by the decedent** evidencing the contract; or
   4. **Clear and convincing evidence** of an agreement that is enforceable in equity.

B. The existence of **joint or mutual wills** does not create a presumption of a contract to make or revoke a will.

TRUSTS RULE OUTLINE

I. **TRUST CREATION AND VALIDITY**

A. **Methods for creating a trust:** A valid trust may be created by one of the following methods:

1. A **declaration** by a property owner that he holds the property as trustee.
2. A **transfer of property during the owner's lifetime** to another as trustee.
3. A **transfer of property by means of a will** taking effect upon the owner's death (testamentary).
4. An exercise of a **power of appointment** to another person as trustee.
5. An **enforceable promise** to create a trust.

B. **Requirements for a valid trust:** In addition to the method of creation above, a valid trust requires that the following be established:

1. **Intent:** The settlor must manifest an **intent to create the trust.**
   a. **Precatory language**, such as "I wish" or "I hope," **is inadequate.**
2. **Property:** Trust must have **identifiable property.** The property cannot be an expectancy under a will or illusory.
3. **Purpose:** The trust must have a **purpose** that is not illegal or against public policy.
4. **Beneficiary:** There must be an ascertainable **beneficiary**, unless it is a charitable trust or the selection of the beneficiary is left to the discretion of the trustee.

> Exam tip: Sometimes there is an argument on both sides regarding the settlor's intent to create a trust or if the language is too precatory. After arguing both sides, explain why one side has the better argument.

C. **Trustee need not be named:** The court will appoint a trustee if one is not named in the trust.

II. **LIMITATIONS ON TRUSTS**

A. **Real property:** A trust for real property must be in **writing and signed** by either the trustee or the settlor or their authorized agent.

B. **Oral trust:** The existence of an oral trust of **personal property** may be established by **clear and convincing evidence**.

C. **21-year maximum for trustee:** The trustee may perform as trustee for a noncharitable purpose or unincorporated society **for only 21 years** after the settlor's death regardless of the terms of the trust.

D. **Invalidation:** The **execution or revocation** of a trust is ineffective to the extent that it was procured by **duress, menace, fraud, or undue influence.** See Wills Rule Outline, Section I.B since the rules are the same for wills and trusts.

III. **TYPES OF TRUSTS:** There are many types of trusts.

A. **Express:** An express trust is where property is transferred from **one owner to another** and meets the above requirements, such that a **trustee holds legal title** for the **benefit of a beneficiary**, with the settlor having a present manifestation of **intent** to create the trust for a legal purpose.

B. **Testamentary:** A testamentary trust is one **created by a will**, and the will contains the material provisions of the trust, and the trust arises upon the death of the testator.

C. **Pour over:** A pour-over trust is one that is structured to **receive and dispose of assets at the settlor's death**. A pour-over trust is often established through the settlor's will.

D. **Secret:** A secret trust occurs when the settlor leaves a **gift to the beneficiary** on the face of his will without indicating an intent to create a trust in the will, but does so **in reliance on a promise that the beneficiary will hold the property in trust for another**.

E. **Semi-secret:** A semi-secret trust occurs when the settlor leaves a gift in his will to a **person in trust** but **does not identify the beneficiary** of the trust.

1. **Majority rule:** The majority of jurisdictions declare semi-secret trusts as **invalid and apply a resulting trust**.
2. **Minority rule:** A minority of jurisdictions allow **extrinsic evidence** to prove the trust.

F. **Spendthrift:** A spendthrift trust occurs when the **beneficiary cannot voluntarily alienate his interest**, such that his interests are protected from creditors unless for necessaries, alimony and child support, or government creditors.

G. **Support:** A support trust directs the trustee to make **limited distributions to pay for the beneficiary's support**, health, maintenance, or education, and is **not accessible by creditors** to the extent it would interfere with the support.

H. **Discretionary:** A discretionary trust gives the **trustee discretion** to distribute or withhold payments, principal, or income to the beneficiary.

I. **Charitable:** A charitable trust is one that is for **charitable purposes and benefits society.**

1. **Cy pres doctrine:** When a charitable objective becomes impossible or impracticable to fulfill, courts often apply the cy pres doctrine and **substitute another similar charitable object** that is as near as possible to the settlor's intent.
2. **Resulting:** If the cy pres doctrine will not fulfill the settlor's intent, the courts will apply a resulting trust.

> **Issue-spotting tip:** Trusts established to care for animals do not qualify as charitable trusts. Rather, a charitable trust must benefit society, such as a trust to create a library or a public park. Always consider the cy pres doctrine as a possible issue when charitable trusts are at issue.

<u>**Charitable trust fact triggers:**</u>
- Donor dies before gifting stocks, bonds, etc. to build a library, park, etc.
- Trust for a home for the elderly, children, sick, etc. and it goes out of business
- Trust for group of people that do most activities with the settlor (raises issue because it does benefit some members of society, but note that it won't qualify as charitable because it doesn't benefit society)

J. **Honorary:** An honorary trust is one in which there is neither a private beneficiary nor a charitable purpose. Generally, these trusts are **invalid, except** to care for **pets** or maintain **cemetery plots**. However, once the pet dies, a resulting trust is applied.

K. **Totten:** A Totten trust is one where the settlor places money in a **bank account** with instructions that the named **beneficiary takes any amount left at the death** of the settlor.

L. **Resulting:** A resulting trust is an implied-in-fact trust based upon the **presumed intent** of the parties and will **transfer the property back to the settlor or his estate** when:
   1. The **purpose of the trust is satisfied** or ends
   2. An **express trust fails**
   3. A **charitable trust ends** and the cy pres doctrine is inapplicable
   4. The trust is **illegal**
   5. There is **excess corpus** in the trust
   6. A **purchase money resulting trust results** where one party (beneficiary) pays consideration for property but allows title to be taken in the name of another (trustee)
   7. There is a **semi-secret trust**

<u>**Resulting trust fact triggers:**</u>
- Trust to care for someone for life but they predecease the settlor
- Trust to give to someone that engages in a certain activity with the settlor, but then settlor becomes unable to do the activity himself
- Trust to help a business, group, or society that ceases to exist
- Trust that fails due to being invalid

M. **Constructive:** A constructive trust is applied as a **remedy to prevent unjust enrichment** when:
   1. There is **self-dealing**
   2. There is **fraud** in the inducement or **undue influence**
   3. **Secret trusts** are involved
   4. **Oral real estate trusts** are created

IV. **TRUST ADMINISTRATION**

A. **Powers of the trustee:** Trustees have all **enumerated powers** expressed in the trust itself and pursuant to the law. Trustees have the **implied powers** necessary and appropriate to carry out the terms of the trust, such as to sell or lease trust property, incur reasonable expenses, borrow money, or operate a business.

B. **Duties of the trustee:** A trustee has a duty to:

1. **Account** to and inform the beneficiaries with a statement of income and expenses of the trust on a regular basis, even if not requested.
2. **Not Delegate his trustee duties** to others (traditional rule). Modernly, delegation is allowed if the trustee exercises due care and skill when selecting agents.
3. **Be Impartial** when dealing with the **income beneficiaries** and the **remainderman** beneficiaries.
4. **Use Due care** and act as a **reasonable prudent person** dealing with his own affairs, which includes his duty to **Investigate** any investment and a duty to **Diversify** investments.
5. **Segregate** and earmark trust funds and **not commingle** the trust funds with the trustee's own funds, such that all trust funds are clearly labeled as such.
6. **Duty of Loyalty** is owed and the trustee may not participate in self-dealing, must avoid conflicts of interest, and must treat all beneficiaries equally.

<u>Duty of loyalty fact triggers:</u>

- Trustee sells shares/trust property for less than fair market value to benefit himself or his company
- Trustee deals with corporation that he works for in relation to his trustee duties
- Trustee gives money unequally to beneficiaries

7. **Prudently Invest** the trust property to make it productive for the beneficiaries under one of the following methods depending on the jurisdiction:
   a. **Common law utilizes various statutory lists** of good investments, which include federal government bonds, federally insured certificates of deposit, first deeds of trust in real estate, and stock of publicly traded corporations.
   b. **Uniform Prudent Investor Act (UPIA)**, adopted in a majority of jurisdictions, provides that a prudent investor's performance is measured in the context of the entire trust portfolio as a whole and as part of an overall investment strategy having risk and return objectives reasonably suited to the trust.

<u>Issue-spotting tip:</u> This issue arises when the trustee invests in risky or unknown endeavors, or in a new corporation and ends up losing the trust money.

8. **Defend** actions that may result in a loss to the trust and **Enforce** claims that are part of the trust property.

> Memorization tip: Remember the trustee duties with the mnemonic **AND I DID SLIDE** (**A**ccount / **N**ot **D**elegate / **I**mpartial / **D**ue care / **I**nvestigate / **D**iversify **S**egregate / **L**oyalty / **I**nvest / **D**efend / **E**nforce).

C. **Liabilities of the trustee:** A trustee is **personally liable** for
   1. **Violating his trustee duties.**
   2. **Torts** committed by him, and his agents if they were committed within the scope of supervision, against third parties.
   3. **Contracts** made within the **scope of his trust supervision**, unless the contract itself provides otherwise.

D. **Liabilities of third parties**
   1. **Transfer of property to a bona fide purchaser** cuts off a beneficiary's interest, but if the transfer is not to a bona fide purchaser, then the beneficiary can set aside the transaction.
   2. **A third party who knowingly receives trust property** will hold that property as a **constructive trustee** and will be liable for any losses to the trust.

E. **Allocation of trust:** Unless the trust itself states otherwise, trust assets are allocated as follows:
   1. **Beneficiaries** of a trust are entitled to **income** from interest income, cash dividends, and net business income, but must pay interest on any loan debt, taxes, or minor repairs.
   2. **Remaindermen** of a trust are entitled to **principal** from the net proceeds on the sale of an asset, stock dividends, and profits from sale of stock, but must pay the principal part of the loan debt and for major repairs.
   3. **Subject to the trustee's best judgment:** The trustee can utilize his best judgment in carrying out the terms of the trust to follow the settlor's intent even if this requires him to disregard the above rules and provide for a different allocation.

V. **MODIFICATION OR REVOCATION OF THE TRUST**

A. **Majority rule:** A settlor can **modify or revoke** the trust **only if** the power is **expressly reserved** in the trust.

B. **Minority rule, including California: Trusts are revocable** unless stated otherwise.

C. **Modification:** The **court can modify the trust**, such as for cy pres purposes or changed circumstances due to unforeseen circumstances and necessity, in order to meet the settlor's intent.

VI. **TERMINATION**

A. **Trustee:** A trustee has **no power to terminate** the trust except as provided in the trust.

B. **Beneficiary:** Beneficiaries **may compel termination** of the trust if they are all competent, all consent, and termination does not frustrate the purpose of the trust.
C. **Settlor:** A settlor **can terminate** the trust if he **reserved the power** to do so.
D. **Court:** A court **can terminate** the trust if the purpose becomes frustrated or impossible or illegal, or if there are changed circumstances.
E. **Lapse/antilapse rules** also apply to trusts. (See Wills Rules Outline, section V. E.)

VII. **REMEDIES**

A. **Breach of trust** remedy options include damages, a constructive trust (see Remedies chapter), tracing and an equitable lien on the property (see Remedies chapter), ratify transaction and waive breach, sue for resulting loss (surcharge), or remove the trustee.
B. **The trustee cannot offset the losses** where one breach results in a gain and another results in a loss.
C. **Laches:** The trustee can argue laches if the beneficiary waited an unreasonably long period to bring a claim that, as a result, caused prejudice to the trustee or other beneficiaries.

WILLS AND TRUSTS ISSUES TESTED MATRIX

		Crossover	Will Validity	Will Composition	Will Revocation and/or Revival	Will Gift Classification Ademption Abatement	Will Lapse & Antilapse	Will Survivor Rights	Will Intestate Succession	Trust Creation & Validity	Type of Trust	Trustee Duties/and/or Liabilities	Trust Termination Modification Revocation
February '11 Q1	Tess, a widow, left estate to children per stirpes		X		X		X	X					
February '10 Q3	Hank & Wendy had two children, Aaron & Beth					X		X	X		Express	X	
July '08 Q6	Hal & Wilma lived in NY; W's will for XYZ; Carl, Sis	Comm. Prop.		X		X							
February '08 Q4	Wilma, $1 million trust with church as beneficiary		X					X		X	Express/ Charitable	X	X
February '07 Q4	Tom, from CA, executed a will and was married to W	Comm. Prop.		X	X			X	X				
July '06 Q6	Tom, a patient at Happy Home, executes a will		X		X					X	Testamentary/ Charitable/ Result		
February '06 Q2	Tim & Anna divorce, try to reconcile but fail to do so	Comm. Prop.						X	X				

Continued >

		Crossover	Will Validity	Will Composition	Will Revocation and/or Revival	Will Gift Classification Ademption Abatement	Will Lapse & Antilapse	Will Survivor Rights	Will Intestate Succession	Trust Creation & Validity	Type of Trust	Trustee Duties/and/or Liabilities	Trust Termination Modification Revocation
February '05 Q6	Sam executed a valid trust naming Tom as trustee										Testamentary/ Spendthrift	X	X
July '04 Q3	Hank, avid skier, daughter Ann, married W later	Comm. Prop.	X					X	X	X	Resulting/ Express		
July '03 Q6	Tom's will left to Al, Beth, Carl, & State University				X	X	X		X				
July '03 Q2	Polly & Donald bought a house in D's name alone	Remedies								X	Constructive/ Purchase $ Result		
February '03 Q2	Olga, a widow, owned Blackacre; 70th birthday	Real Prop.	X		X								
July '02 Q1	Theresa and Henry, child Craig, second child Molly	Comm. Prop.		X	X			X	X				
February '02 Q4	Richard creates trust at the urging of wife	Prof. Resp.								X	Express	X	
July '01 Q6	Ted, a widower, had a child Deb, and three brothers		X				X	X		X	Testamentary		
July '00 Q3	Hal & Wanda create a trust with Hal's separate property		X	X	X		X	X		X	Express/ Resulting		

Continued >

		Crossover	Will Validity	Will Composition	Will Revocation and/or Revival	Will Gift Classification Ademption Abatement	Will Lapse & Antilapse	Will Survivor Rights	Will Intestate Succession	Trust Creation & Validity	Type of Trust	Trustee Duties/and/or Liabilities	Trust Termination Modification Revocation
February '00 Q4	Tom, a childless bachelor, executed a typed will		X	X	X	X	X						
February '99 Q1	Harry & Wanda execute wills leaving to spouse				X		X			X	Testamentary/ Constructive	X	X
February '98 Q6	Testator, a widow with two adult children, typed will		X		X		X						
July '96 Q6	Tess, a widow with two adult children, Sam & Donna		X		X				X				
February '96 Q4	Connie died in 1989, left a will; son Sam as trustee											X	
February '95 Q6	Gloria, a widow, typed will; Tom, Dora, Max, Seth		X	X		X	X			X	Semi-secret/ Constructive		
July '94 Q6	Tess, a widow and resident of State X	Evidence	X	X				X		X	Testamentary		
July '93 Q6	Ted executed a will, wife Wilma died; Fred, Aunt May	Prof. Resp.	X					X	X	X	Testamentary		
July '92 Q4	Pop's wife died in 1980; Pop executed a will with trust		X		X	X	X		X	X	Testamentary		

Continued >

		Crossover	Will Validity	Will Composition	Will Revocation and/or Revival	Will Gift Classification Ademption Abatement	Will Lapse & Antilapse	Will Survivor Rights	Will Intestate Succession	Trust Creation & Validity	Type of Trust	Trustee Duties/and/or Liabilities	Trust Termination Modification Revocation
February '92 Q1	Tom, trustee of Abe's trust, with stocks, bonds, apt., lot											X	
February '91 Q1	Alfred died in 1989 in State A with will made in State B		X			X	X						
February '90 Q4	Bonnie, Uncle Albert gave parents U.S. Savings Bond									X	Express	X	
July '89 Q4	Bill, a widower, made a will; left stamp collection, Trust			X			X	X		X	Express/ Pour-over		
July '87 Q4	A owned property; had trust; Trustee won't fix parking lot	Real Prop./ Torts									Express	X	
February '87 Q5	Tom's first will created a trust for Lil, then new will		X		X				X	X	Testamentary/ Support		
July '85 Q3	Bill, widower, had one child, a daughter, June; Blackacre									X	Express/ Resulting Testam./ Discret.		

Continued >

		Crossover	Will Validity	Will Composition	Will Revocation and/or Revival	Will Gift Classification Ademption Abatement	Will Lapse & Antilapse	Will Survivor Rights	Will Intestate Succession	Trust Creation & Validity	Type of Trust	Trustee Duties/and/or Liabilities	Trust Termination Modification Revocation
February '84 Q3	Carol, a widow, with son Sam and daughter Dot		X			X		X	X		Constructive		
July '83 Q4	Agatha loaned $300,000 to her brother George										Testamentary/ Spendthrift	X	
July '81 Q4	Troy, a wealthy man, wanted to create a public library									X	Charitable/ Resulting		

WILLS AND TRUSTS PRACTICE ESSAYS, ANSWER GRIDS, AND SAMPLE ANSWERS

Wills and Trusts Question 1

July 2004, Question 3

Hank, an avid skier, lived in State X with his daughter, Ann. Hank's first wife, Ann's mother, had died several years earlier.

In 1996, Hank married Wanda, his second wife. Thereafter, while still domiciled in State X, Hank executed a will that established a trust and left "five percent of my estate to Trustee, to be paid in approximately equal installments over the ten years following my death to the person who went skiing with me most often during the 12 months preceding my death." The will did not name a trustee. The will left all of the rest of Hank's estate to Wanda if she survived him. The will did not mention Ann. Wanda was one of two witnesses to the will. Under the law of State X, a will witnessed by a beneficiary is invalid.

In 1998, Hank and his family moved permanently to California. Hank then legally adopted Carl, Wanda's minor son by a prior marriage.

In 2001, Hank completely gave up skiing because of a serious injury to his leg and took up fishing instead. He went on numerous fishing trips over the next two years with a fellow avid fisherman, Fred.

In 2003, Hank died.

In probate proceedings, Wanda claims Hank's entire estate under the will; Ann and Carl each claim he or she is entitled to an intestate share of the estate; and Fred claims that the court should apply the doctrine of cy pres to make him the beneficiary of the trust.

1. Under California law, how should the court rule on:
    a. Wanda's claim? Discuss.
    b. Ann's claim? Discuss.
    c. Carl's claim? Discuss.
2. How should the court rule on Fred's claim? Discuss.

Wills and Trusts Question 1 Assessment

July 2004, Question 3

This is a typical wills and trusts crossover question. H established a will, which included a trust; thus, both wills and trusts issues will need to be discussed. First, it is necessary to establish the validity or invalidity of the will. To do so, you need to first go through the conflicts of laws provisions since the will was executed in a state other than California. Here, under State X law, the will is invalid because the witness is a beneficiary and, under the laws of State X, the will is deemed invalid. However, if you stopped after that bit of analysis, you wouldn't have any more issues to address and would be done with the question. Since you know that the goal of each exam question is to test more than one issue, you need to review your issues checklist to see what other issues might arise.

The next logical issue is to see if the will is valid under California law since wills are valid if they are valid under the laws of the state in which the testator was domiciled at the time of his death, which in this case was California. Resolving this issue then permits you to discuss all remaining issues since you could overcome the problem of W taking under the will even though she was a witness, since the presumption is rebuttable. When an issue can be argued both ways, always address any issues that arise with either conclusion, since otherwise you may write yourself out of the question and miss analyzing important issues. On a wills or trusts question when there are facts that go to issues other than validity, such as here where there is an omitted child issue, it is important to conclude that the will is valid, or argue both ways and conclude that it is possible the will is valid so that you are able to analyze the remaining issues. Since it is possible the will might be invalid, it is important to go through the rules of intestate distribution to identify the result in the event that the will is found invalid. So, if the facts can be argued both ways, be sure to analyze all issues that arise in regard to the wills and trusts issues as if they were valid as well as the intestate distribution issues in the event the will is invalid.

Wills and trusts are subjects where your conclusions might include "if" scenarios, depending on whether the will or trust is valid. It is always best to address issues related to both possibilities, but also to tell the grader which one you think is the likely result and why. This particular question is unique because in addition to the will, the trust also may be invalid. Identify the result if the trust is valid and analyze the issue of a resulting trust in the event the trust isn't valid. Otherwise, the remaining issues of omitted heir and cy pres are easy to spot since the facts clearly discuss both.

The organization of this question is typical for a wills question. First, analyze the validity issues, and then determine what each party referenced takes in the distribution.

Finally, make note of the areas highlighted in **bold** on the corresponding grid. The bold areas highlight the issues, analysis, and conclusions that are likely **required** to receive a passing score on this question. In general, the essay grids are provided to assist you in analyzing the essays, and are much more detailed than what a student should create during the exam to organize their response to a question.

Issue	Rule	Fact Application	Conclusion
Call #1.a: W's Claim			
Validity of will/conflict of law	**A will is valid if properly executed in the state in which the testator was domiciled at the time of execution, the state in which testator died, or the state in which the will was executed.**	**Here, the will was executed in State X, so Cal. can recognize State X laws for determining the validity of the will; H's will is invalid under State X laws because W, who was a witness, was also a beneficiary.** **Since H was domiciled in Cal. at the time of his death, Cal. laws might allow the will, depending on its validity.**	**Will invalid under State X laws**
Cal. validity	**A will is valid if it is in writing, T signs or acknowledges his signature/will in the presence of 2 attesting witnesses** present at the same time who knew it was a will; **interested witnesses create a rebuttable presumption of undue influence, unless two other uninterested witnesses.**	**Here, W is an interested witness since she is the beneficiary for 95% of H's estate.** W may rebut presumption by showing H wanted her to have the estate since she is the current spouse and would have to take care of two children. **If W can rebut presumption, she will take under the will as it will be valid; if not, she will receive her intestate share.**	**Will likely valid in Cal. or W gets intestate share**
Intestate share	**Spouse gets all CP and QCP and 1/3 of SP if decedent leaves two or more issue.** CP is property acquired during marriage. QCP is property acquired during marriage while domiciled in a non-CP state that would have been CP had the couple been domiciled in Cal.	**W's intestate share would include all CP and QCP of H's as well as 1/3 of H's SP.** All QCP acquired in State X and all CP acquired in Cal. would go to W.	**If will invalid, W gets all CP and QCP and 1/3 of H's SP**

Continued >

Issue	Rule	Fact Application	Conclusion
Call #1.b: A's Claim			
Omitted child	**A child born after a will is executed** or when testator is unaware of their existence will receive their intestate share of the estate unless they have been otherwise provided for or the will expressly states that it is not to include future or unknown children; all other devisees' shares abate to account for this intestate share.	**A will not be an omitted child because she was born prior to H's execution of his will, so A will take nothing if the will is valid.** If the will is invalid, then A will take her intestate share, which would be 1/3.	**A takes nothing if will valid, or 1/3 if will invalid**
Call #1.c: C's Claim			
Omitted child	See above If testator had one or more children and devised substantially all of the estate to the other parent of the omitted child, then the omitted child will not take their intestate share.	**C was adopted in 1998, after the execution of H's will in 1996, so C did not exist as a child at the time H executed the will.** Here, since H left substantially all of his estate (95%) to W, although W is not A's mother, C will likely not take his intestate share because he is a child of H and the will left almost all to his mother, if the will is valid.	C takes nothing if will valid; if invalid, C takes 1/3
Call #2: F's Claim			
Trust	A **trust may be created by** (1) a declaration by the owner of property that the owner holds the property as trustee, (2) a transfer of property during the owner's lifetime to another as trustee, (3) a transfer by the owner in a will taking effect upon the owner's death (testamentary), (4) an exercise of a power of appointment to another person as trustee, or (5) an enforceable promise to create a trust.	• Trust created by H's will including a trust (testamentary trust). • Intent shown by H creating trust. • **Trust property—5% of H's estate.** • Legal purpose—lawful to give beneficiary money over a period of years. • **Beneficiary—person who went skiing with H most often during 12 months preceding his death; but H did not ski in 12 months preceding his death because he stopped skiing in 2001 due to an injury to his leg, and died 2 years later in 2003.**	**Trust likely not valid due to no identifiable beneficiary**

Continued >

Issue	Rule	Fact Application	Conclusion
Validity of trust	• **Intent** • **Trust property** • **Legal purpose** • **Beneficiary** (ascertainable person or group) • **Trustee** (court will appoint if none named) Limitations: **No invalidation (due to fraud, undue influence, capacity, etc.)**	**Court may try to use incorporation by reference to incorporate the person above as beneficiary, but beneficiary not in existence then because not 12 months before death and no document**; same as to integration, nothing in existence then; **as to facts of independent significance—H wasn't skiing anymore, but could argue person he would have skied with (or now fish) would have independent significance**, such as enjoyment of company, separate from will. **Trustee—court can appoint one if none named, so this isn't a problem.**	
Cy pres	**Created to follow settlor's intent—when a charitable trust fails—based on general charitable purposes not specific**	**Arguably, H wanted to leave 5% to the person who skied with him the most in 12 months preceding his death; since his injury, he replaced skiing with fishing and F went on numerous fishing trips with H during the last 2 years; however, the trust purpose was not charitable or beneficial to society, such as benefiting education, so cy pres will not work.**	**No cy pres**
Resulting trust	**If a trust fails due to lack of formalities, a resulting trust is created based upon intent of the parties, which will transfer the property back to the settlor or his estate.**	**Here, it is likely that since the trust fails due to lack of a beneficiary, a resulting trust will arise, so the trust would revert back to H, the settlor, or here, his estate.**	**W would get trust portion if resulting trust**
Conlusion			If will valid, W takes all; if invalid, W, A, and C each take 1/3 of SP and W gets all CP and QCP

Wills and Trusts Question 1 Sample Answer

July 2004, Question 3

1.a: W's Claim

Choice of Law

A will is valid if it is properly executed in the state in which the testator was domiciled at the time of execution, the state in which testator died, or the state in which the will was executed.

Here, the will was executed in State X, so California can recognize State X laws for determining the validity of the will. The problem is that H's will is invalid under State X laws because W, who was a witness, was also a beneficiary, which invalidates the will in State X.

However, since H was domiciled in California at the time of his death, California laws might allow the will to be probated based on California law if it complies with the California will formalities.

Validity of Will in California

A will is valid if it is in writing and T signs or acknowledges his signature or will in the presence of two attesting witnesses who were present at the same time and who knew it was a will. An interested witness creates a rebuttable presumption of undue influence, unless there are two other uninterested witnesses.

Here, W is an interested witness since she is the beneficiary for 95% of H's estate. Thus, although the will is in writing and was witnessed by two witnesses, one of the witnesses was a beneficiary, W. Since this is a rebuttable presumption, W may rebut the presumption by showing that H wanted her to have the estate since they were married with children and, in the event of H's death, H would have wanted her to be able to take care of their two minor children.

If W can rebut this presumption, she will take under the will as it will be valid. If she is unable to rebut this presumption, she will receive her intestate share. Since she was the spouse and parent of his children, it is likely that the presumption will be rebutted. Thus, the will is likely valid in California and W will take under the will. In the event the will applies State X laws, W will receive her intestate share.

Intestate Share

Under intestate distribution, the spouse receives all community property (CP) and quasi-community property (QCP) and 1/3 of the decedent's separate property (SP) if he leaves two or more issue.

CP is property acquired during marriage. QCP is property acquired during marriage while domiciled in a non-CP state that would have been CP had the couple been domiciled in California.

Here, W's intestate share would include all CP and QCP of H's, as well as 1/3 of H's SP since he had two children.

Thus, if the will is valid, W will all of H's estate, aside from the trust if it is found to be valid. If the will is invalid, then she would take all of the CP and QCP and 1/3 of H's SP.

1.b: A's Claim

Omitted Child

A child born after a will is executed or when the testator is unaware of their existence will receive their intestate share of the estate unless they have been otherwise provided for or the will expressly states that it is not to include future or unknown children, or the testator had one or more children and devised substantially all of the estate to the other parent of the omitted child. In this event, all other devisees' shares abate to account for the omitted child's intestate share.

Here, A will not be an omitted child because she was born prior to H's execution of his will, so A will take nothing if the will is valid.

If the will is invalid, then A will take her intestate share, which would be 1/3 of H's SP. If the will is valid, A takes nothing.

1.c: C's Claim

Omitted Child/Adopted Child

See above for rule for an omitted heir. As to adopted children, they are treated as natural children for estate planning purposes.

Here, C was adopted in 1998, after the execution of H's will in 1996, so C did not exist as a child at the time H executed the will. However, since H left substantially all of his estate, 95%, to W, although W is not A's mother, C will likely not take his intestate share because he is a child of H and the will left almost all to his mother, who is caring for A as well since A's mother died years before H married W.

Thus, if the will is valid, C will take nothing. If the will is valid, C will take 1/3, like A, of H's SP.

2: F's Claim

Validity of Trust/Incorporation

A trust may be created by (1) a declaration by the owner of property that the owner holds the property as trustee, (2) a transfer of property during the owner's lifetime to another as trustee, (3) a transfer by the owner in a will taking effect upon the owner's death (testamentary), (4) an exercise of a power of appointment to another person as trustee, or (5) an enforceable promise to create a trust. In addition, a valid trust requires intent, trust property, a legal purpose, and a beneficiary. The court will appoint a trustee if one is not named. Further, the trust must not be invalidated due to fraud, undue influence, or lack of capacity.

Here, H created the trust through his will, which is a testamentary trust. His intent is shown by H creating trust naming a beneficiary as well as a trustee to benefit the person who went skiing with him the most in the 12-month period preceding his death. There was trust property, which was 5% of H's estate. Further, there is a valid legal purpose to give a beneficiary money over a period of years. Finally, the beneficiary is arguably an ascertainable person who went skiing with H most often during 12 months preceding his death, as this is person would be identifiable. The problem is that the beneficiary has not yet been determined and, due to H's accident, never would be since H stopped skiing.

In the event there is confusion on the beneficiary, the court may try to use *incorporation by reference* to incorporate the person above as the beneficiary, but the beneficiary was not in existence then because it was not 12 months before death and there was no document.

A similar result would apply if the court attempted to *integrate* the name of the beneficiary since there was no name or document in existence at that time.

As to *facts of independent significance*, H wasn't skiing anymore, but it could be argued that the person he would have skied with (or now fish) would have independent significance, such as enjoyment of company, separate from will.

Charitable Trust/Cy Pres

A charitable trust is one that benefits society. When a charitable trust fails for any reason, the court may invoke the cy pres doctrine to find a similar substitute to follow the settlor's intent.

Arguably, H wanted to leave 5% to the person who skied with him the most in 12 months preceding his death as a charitable donation. However, it is unlikely that this would constitute a charitable trust, as it would only benefit one person and not society. Thus, the cy pres doctrine would be inapplicable, such that F would not successfully argue that the court should substitute skiing with fishing, since F went fishing with H the most, rather than skiing after H's accident.

Resulting Trust

If a trust fails due to lack of formalities, a resulting trust is created based upon intent of the parties, which will transfer the property back to the settlor or his estate.

Here, it is likely that since the trust fails due to lack of a beneficiary and the purpose being impossible after creation, a resulting trust will arise, so the trust would revert back to H, the settlor, or here, his estate.

Thus, W would get the trust portion if the court imposed a resulting trust, which would result in W taking the trust as well as the CP and QCP and 1/3 of the SP, leaving each child with 1/3 of the SP as well and Frank with nothing.

Wills and Trusts Question 2

July 2000, Question 3

In 1996, Hal, married to Wanda, created a trust that he funded with $200,000 of his separate property. Trustee, Inc., named as trustee, was directed to pay the income to Hal for life and the remainder to Wanda. At the same time, Hal executed a valid will that provided as follows:

Article 1: $20,000 to my friend Frank.
Article 2: $35,000 to the person named on a sheet of pink paper dated December 31, 1989 and located in my top desk drawer.
Article 3: The residue of my estate to my son, Stan.

In 1998, Wanda executed a valid will solely in favor of her son, Stan. Shortly thereafter, Wanda died while giving birth to the couple's second child, Dawn.

Later in 1998, while grieving Wanda's death, Hal regularly consulted a fortune-teller, Florence. In 1999, based on Florence's predictions that Stan would become a criminal, Hal executed a codicil to his 1996 will, changing the residuary beneficiary from Stan to Florence.

In 2000, Hal and Frank, passengers on a commercial plane, were simultaneously killed when the plane exploded on takeoff. The pink sheet of paper referred to in Article 2 of the 1996 will provided: "To my next-born child, if any."

1. To whom should the trust property be distributed? Discuss.
2. To whom should Hal's estate be distributed? Discuss.

Answer according to California law.

Wills and Trusts Question 2 Assessment

July 2000, Question 3

This particular question specifically identifies that there is a valid will. Therefore, you should not discuss the validity of the will. It is not clear, however, whether the trust is valid so you will need to discuss the creation and validity of the trust. Generally, as with the first question, whenever validity of either the will or the trust is at issue, you should address that first since it will affect the remaining issues in the essay.

Further, this is the type of question that provides specific will provisions. Usually, when specific provisions are provided in a will, you will be required to review the composition of the will since there is often one provision that refers to something outside of the will, such as the pink sheet of paper here. In addition, you will often need to discuss gift classifications since many times one of the provisions will be some type of gift where it is unclear whether the gift is specific or general and/or the item isn't in the testator's possession at the time of his death. This requires you to classify the gift in order to determine how ademption might apply.

Wills and trusts are rather linear subjects in that one issue on the issues checklist often leads to another. For example, following the issues checklist here you first have to analyze the creation of the trust. The next issue is analyzing the type of trust. Next, the type of trust created may cease to exist due to some fact, such as here, where W predeceases H and the trust purpose was to care for W after H's death. Thus, in analyzing the type of trust, you will find that it leads to the issue that arises when a trust fails, which is the issue of a resulting trust. Wills and trusts questions often do this such that one issue leads logically to the next.

When analyzing the wills provisions to distribute the estate under call two of the question, you will find the same result, in that one issue leads to the next. For example, when you first start with provision one, you see that the simultaneous death issue arises since both H and F died at the same time. This issue then leads to the issue of lapse and antilapse. Since this type of pattern is often seen in wills and trusts questions, it is best to study and memorize these rules by trying to explain them aloud to a friend or family member so that you can be certain you properly understand how the concepts all relate to one another, rather than just memorizing each rule separately.

To succeed on wills and trusts questions, you must see how one issue relates to another and how the result from one issue can lead to different issues being discussed, depending on the conclusion you reach. Be sure to have a firm understanding of how the principles are interrelated in wills and trusts before trying to write out an essay. When you do try to write out essays, read the facts in a very linear way and start at the top of your issues checklist and look for one issue to lead you to the next.

To see which issues were of greater weight on this essay, make note of the areas highlighted in **bold** on the corresponding grid. The bold areas highlight the issues, analysis, and conclusions that are likely **required** to receive a passing score on this question.

Issue	Rule	Fact Application	Conclusion
Call #1: Distribution of Trust Property			
Creation/ validity of trust	A **trust may be created by** a transfer of property during the owner's lifetime to another as trustee. In addition, validity requires • **Intent** • **Trust property** • **Legal purpose** • **Beneficiary** (any ascertainable person or group) • **Trustee** (court will appoint if none named) • No invalidation (due to fraud, undue influence, capacity, etc.)	• Trust created by T during his life to him for life and W as remainder. • **Intent: H has present (in 1996) manifestation to use his SP funds to pay him during life and remainder to W.** • **Property: $200k** • **Purpose:** Estate planning **is legal.** • **Beneficiary: H during his life; remainder to W.** • **Trustee: Trustee, Inc.** • No reasons for invalidating trust are present.	1996 trust valid
Type of trust	Express: Private trust meeting all above elements. **Resulting: Implied-in-fact trust based upon presumed intent of parties; can arise when a private express trust fails or purpose of trust ends; trust will revert back to settlor or his estate.**	Trust started out as an express trust with Trustee, Inc., holding trust for H and then remainder to W. **If the purpose of the trust was to provide for W upon H's death, then the purpose of the trust ended when W died, which would result in a resulting trust, with the remainder of the trust reverting back to H.**	Express or resulting
Effect of W's death if express trust	**Lapse: When a beneficiary dies prior to receiving his interest, the gift to the beneficiary lapses and falls into the residue.** **Antilapse: Rule of lapse does not apply if the beneficiary is kindred and the beneficiary leaves issue.** Omitted child: An omitted child receives their share and other devisees abate to allow this, unless there is proof of intent to disinherit.	Lapse rules would not apply here because under an express trust, W would have a remainder, rather than a mere expectancy of interest—so W would have acquired her interest as a remainder at the time the trust was created, leaving her interest to her heirs, which would be Stan in her will; **further, antilapse would not apply here because W was not kindred of H, but rather his spouse, so trust would still revert back to H due to lapse.**	

Continued >

Issue	Rule	Fact Application	Conclusion
Effect on W's death if resulting trust	A resulting trust reverts the property back to the settler.	Since W died while giving birth to D and D was not in W's will, D would be an omitted child, and W's remainder would then be split by D and S equally. **The $200k remainder portion would revert back to H and be distributed in accordance with his H's will (discussed in call 2).**	$200k reverts back to H
Call #2: Distribution of H's Estate—Article 1			
Simultaneous death	If both T and devisee die at the same time, and it cannot be determined by clear and convincing evidence that devisee died first, then devisee is determined to have predeceased T and the devise lapses.	Since H and Frank both died simultaneously on a plane crash, Frank did not survive T, and the $20k gift to Frank would lapse and go to the residue.	$20k to residue
Anti-lapse	See above for rule	Antilapse statutes would not apply to Frank since he is not kindred, but rather just a friend.	Frank takes nothing
Call #2: Distribution of H's Estate—Article 2			
Integration	Papers present at the time of the execution of a will that T intended to be part of his will are integrated into the will.	Although H intended for the pink slip to be part of his will, it was not present at the time he executed his will and will not be integrated into his will.	No integration
Incorporation by reference	A document is incorporated by reference when a will refers to a document outside the will if the document is already in existence, the will refers to and shows intent to incorporate, and the document is sufficiently described in the will.	Here, the pink slip was already in existence since it was dated Dec. 31, 1989, which was years before the will (1996); the will specifically refers to H's intent to incorporate the pink slip; and it was described with particular detail in regards to the location being the top desk drawer, the pink color of paper, the date and the person named there, which was H's next born child. Since "next born" indicates one was already born it is likely D; also, S provided for in will, indicating he was already in existence at the time the incorporation was made.	Pink slip incorporated by reference; $35k to D

Continued >

Issue	Rule	Fact Application	Conclusion
Call #2: Distribution of H's Estate—Article 3			
Codicil	A codicil is an amendment to a will that requires the same formalities and capacity as a will. Undue influence: Execution of influence relates to the will, improper purpose; substitutes desires of influencer for testators free will; only that portion of the will or codicil will be invalid. **Undue influence if there is an unnatural disposition, beneficiary has opportunity, T susceptible to influence, and beneficiary actively participates.** **Presumption if fiduciary relationship and they caused it to be transcribed.**	Here, H executed a codicil by amending his 1996 will where he left the residue to his son, S, to leaving the residue to his fortune teller, F. **T was susceptible to influence since he was grieving over his wife's death during childbirth and regularly consulting a fortune-teller; due to his vulnerability, F had the opportunity to influence H since he thought she could tell the future by being a fortune-teller; also, since H regularly consulted her, F actively participated by convincing H that S was going to be a criminal, and leaving the residue of his estate to his fortune-teller rather than to family is unnatural.** **Also, fiduciary relationship since H was consulting F to grieve over his wife's death and likely telling her personal information and receiving advice or future concerns in return.** **Codicil invalid, so original residue to S still valid.**	**Codicil invalid due to undue influence** **Residue to S**
Omitted child/revocation by operation of law	**See above for rule; omitted child will not take intestate share if otherwise provided for.**	**Although the will was executed in 1996, prior to D's birth, D did take under the will in Article 2, indicating she was not omitted and otherwise provided for.**	
Conclusion			Overall, $35k to D and residue to S

Wills and Trusts Question 2 Sample Answer

July 2000, Question 3

1: Distribution of Trust Property

Creation/Validity of Trust

A trust may be created by a transfer of property during the owner settlor's lifetime to another as trustee. In addition, validity requires intent, trust property, legal purpose, and a beneficiary. If there no trustee named, the court will appoint one. Further, the trust must not be invalidated due to fraud, undue influence, or lack of capacity.

Here, T created the trust during his life to him for life and W as remainder. Further, T had the intent to create the trust at the time in 1996 to use his separate property (SP) funds to pay him during life and to have the remainder distributed to W. In addition, there was property of $200,000 and a legal purpose, as estate planning is legal and common. There were two beneficiaries: H during his life and W as a remainderman. Finally, the trust also listed the trustee as Trustee, Inc., so the court will not need to appoint one.

There are no facts to indicate that there are any reasons for invalidating the trust, so the 1996 trust is valid.

Type of Trust

An express trust is a private trust meeting all above elements. A resulting trust is a trust implied in fact based upon the presumed intent of the parties. It can arise when a private express trust fails or the purpose of the trust ends, in which case the trust will revert back to the settlor or his estate.

Here, the trust started out as an express trust with Trustee, Inc., holding trust for H and then remainder to W, meeting all above requirements. However, if the purpose of the trust was to provide for W upon H's death, then the purpose of the trust ended when W died prior to H, which would result in a resulting trust, with the remainder of the trust reverting back to H.

If the court finds that the purpose of the trust was not solely to provide for W after H's death, then the court would look to see who, if anyone, would step into the shoes of W. Although this is unlikely, as the purpose was set up to pay W after H's death, it is more likely that had W predeceased H before he executed the trust, he would have left the remainder to another. However, lapse and antilapse will still be addressed below, as there is a slight chance the court would apply those rather than implementing a resulting trust.

Lapse/Antilapse

When a beneficiary dies prior to receiving their interest, the gift to the beneficiary lapses and falls into the residue. However, the rule of lapse does not apply if the beneficiary is kindred and the beneficiary leaves issue, in which case they step into the shoes of their deceased parents or grandparents or other relatives of lineal relation.

Here, since W predeceased H, lapse would apply, making her gift revert back to H's estate. Further, since W was H's wife and not kindred, antilapse will not apply.

Therefore, the remainder of the trust would revert back to H whether the court implements a resulting trust or applies lapse under the existing trust.

Omitted Child

A child born after a will is executed or when the testator is unaware of their existence will receive their intestate share of the estate unless they have been otherwise provided for or the will expressly states that it is not to include future or unknown children, or the testator had one or more children and devised substantially all of the estate to the other parent of the omitted child. In this event, all other devisees' shares abate to account for the omitted child's intestate share.

Since W died while giving birth to Dawn and Dawn was not in W's will, Dawn would be an omitted child, and W's remainder would then be split by Dawn and Stan equally if antilapse were to apply. However, as indicated above, antilapse will not apply and a resulting trust will revert the property back to the H.

Thus, any amount of the $200,000 remaining after H's death will be distributed in accordance with H's will, which is further discussed below.

2: Distribution of H's Estate—Article 1

Simultaneous Death/Lapse

If both the testator and the devisee die at the same time and it cannot be determined by clear and convincing evidence that devisee died first, then the devisee is determined to have predeceased the testator and the devise lapses.

Since H and Frank both died simultaneously on a plane crash, Frank did not survive H and the $20,000 gift to Frank would lapse and go to the residue unless antilapse applies.

Antilapse

See above for rule.

Here, antilapse would not apply to Frank since he is not kindred, but rather just a friend. Therefore, Frank takes nothing and his devised gift of $20,000 will fall into the residue.

2: Distribution of H's Estate—Article 2

Integration

Papers present at the time of the execution of a will that the testator intended to be part of his will are integrated into the will.

Here, although H intended for the pink slip to be part of his will, it was not present at the time he executed his will and, as a result, will not be integrated into his will.

Incorporation by Reference

A document is incorporated by reference when a will refers to a document outside the will if the document is already in existence, the will refers to and shows intent to incorporate, and the document is sufficiently described in the will.

Here, the pink slip was already in existence since it was dated December 31, 1989, which was years before the 1996 will. Further, the will specifically refers to H's intent to incorporate the pink slip and it was described with particular detail in regards to the location being the top desk drawer, the pink color of paper, and the date and the person named there, which was H's next born child. Since "next born" indicates one was already born, it is likely a reference to Dawn since Stan was already born and provided for separately.

Therefore, the pink slip is incorporated by reference and $35,000 will go to Dawn.

2: Distribution of H's Estate—Article 3

Codicil

A codicil is an amendment to a will that requires the same formalities and capacity as a will.

Undue Influence is the execution of influence that relates to the will for an improper purpose. Only that portion of the will or codicil will be invalid if undue influence is found. Undue influence is found if there is an unnatural disposition, the beneficiary has opportunity to influence the testator, the testator is susceptible to influence, and the beneficiary actively participates in procuring the devise. Further, undue influence is presumed if there is a fiduciary relationship and the fiduciary beneficiary caused it to be transcribed.

Here, H executed a codicil by amending his 1996 will where he originally left the residue to his son, Stan, and changed it to leaving the residue to his fortune-teller, Florence. Thus, the will was amended through a codicil (assuming all formalities were met, which isn't clear from the facts).

As to the undue influence, the testator was susceptible to influence since he was grieving over his wife's death during childbirth and regularly consulting a fortune-teller as result. Further, due to his vulnerability, F had the opportunity to influence H since he thought she could tell the future by being a fortune-teller. Also, since H regularly consulted her, F actively participated by convincing H that Stan was going to be a criminal. Finally, leaving the residue of one's estate to a fortune-teller rather than to family is unnatural and uncommon.

Also, it is possible that a court would find that H and F had a fiduciary relationship since H was consulting F to grieve over his wife's death and likely telling her personal information and receiving advice or future concerns in return, especially since she must have known that he was going to leave his residue to Stan since she advised that Stan might be a criminal, indicating that this residue would not be a good idea.

Thus, the codicil will be invalid due to undue influence and the residue will go to Stan.

Omitted Child/Revocation by Operation of Law

See above for rule.

Although the will was executed in 1996 prior to D's birth, D did take under the will in Article 2, indicating she was not omitted and otherwise provided for. Although the distribution between D and S is unequal, the court will not alter the will to make distributions equal when they are provided for by the will.

Overall Distribution

$35,000 to Dawn and residue to Stan.

Wills and Trusts Question 3

July 2003, Question 6

In 1998, Tom executed a valid will. The dispositive provisions of the will provided:

"1. $100,000 to my friend, Al.
2. My residence on Elm St. to my sister Beth.
3. My OmegaCorp stock to my brother Carl.
4. The residue of my estate to State University (SU)."

In 1999, Tom had a falling out with Al and executed a valid codicil that expressly revoked paragraph 1 of the will but made no other changes.

In 2000, Tom reconciled with Al and told several people, "Al doesn't need to worry; I've provided for him."

In 2001, Beth died intestate, survived only by one child, Norm, and two grandchildren, Deb and Eve, who were children of a predeceased child of Beth. Also in 2001, Tom sold his OmegaCorp stock and reinvested the proceeds by purchasing AlphaCorp stock.

Tom died in 2002. The will and codicil were found in his safe deposit box. The will was unmarred, but the codicil had the words "Null and Void" written across the text of the codicil in Tom's handwriting, followed by Tom's signature.

Tom was survived by Al, Carl, Norm, Deb, and Eve. At the time of Tom's death, his estate consisted of $100,000 in cash, the residence on Elm St., and the AlphaCorp stock.

What rights, if any, do Al, Carl, Norm, Deb, Eve, and SU have in Tom's estate? Discuss.

Answer according to California law.

Wills and Trusts Question 3 Assessment

July 2003, Question 6

This is a straight wills question that focuses on the revocation and revival of a will and codicil. The facts state that there was a "valid will" and a "valid codicil." Thus, for this type of question, you should not spend any time analyzing the creation or the validity of either the will or codicil. Therefore, you need to focus on the other issues on the issues checklist. Generally, when the wills and codicils are valid, the examiners test revocation, revival, and ademption of various provisions of the will. The question can also include a discussion of lapse and antilapse since one of the beneficiaries almost always predeceases the testator in these scenarios. When this occurs, you are also required to show that you understand how to apply per capita with representation distribution rules since that is what California applies.

Also, it is common for the examiners to test more than one form of revocation when they test that issue. So, if it is possible that a will was revoked by more than one permissible type of revocation, be sure to address them all. Even if one form of revocation doesn't work—such as here where the subsequent attempted instrument didn't meet the formalities required—the revocation by physical act did suffice to revoke the will. Nonetheless, you should address both types of revocation in order to receive maximum points on the question.

Another way that the examiners generally test issues is to focus on the gray zone where the result is unclear. On wills essays they do this several ways: with gift classification, similar to the analysis above in the trusts portion where you had to argue how the result would be if the trust failed and a resulting trust applied or if the trust continued, or when you have to go through whether the court would apply cy pres and that result, or not apply it to get the other result. For gifts, it is often arguable whether the gifts are specific, general, or demonstrative. If it is unclear, or if you think the court would want to honor the testator's wishes, analyze all possibilities that are applicable. The key here is to then explain which classification you think is the most applicable and why. However, the results are often irrelevant so long as you clearly state and support your opinion. This is why many state-released passing answers have different outcomes on the issues addressed.

Finally, it is important to answer the call of the question and specifically state what each identified party will receive. It is recommended that you summarize the overall distribution at the end, after going through each party individually.

To determine whether you spotted and analyzed the major issues and properly allocated your time to the various issues, make note of the areas highlighted in **bold** on the corresponding grid. The bold areas highlight the issues, analysis, and conclusions that are likely **required** to receive a passing score on this question.

Issue	Rule	Fact Application	Conclusion
Al's Rights			
Revocation	**A will may be revoked by a subsequent instrument.**	**Here, in 1999, T executed a valid codicil that expressly revoked the gift to A in paragraph 1 of the 1988 will.**	**Al's gift revoked**
Revocation of codicil	**A codicil may be revoked like a will by physical act.**	**Here, T's writing "null and void" on the face of the codicil, followed by his signature, would constitute a revocation by a physical act.**	**1999 codicil revoked**
Revocation of codicil	A codicil may be revoked like a will by a subsequent instrument. Holographic wills and codicils are valid if the material provisions are in the T's handwriting and the T signed it.	Arguably, writing "null and void" and signing the 1999 codicil could constitute the material provisions; however, it is possible that the material provisions are not all in T's handwriting since the gift attempted to be revived and the amount and the devisee are in T's handwriting; even if the revocation by a holographic codicil or will is not valid, the revocation by physical act is still valid.	Codicil revoked
Revival	When a will is revoked by a physical act or a subsequent will, and then the subsequent will is revoked as well, **the 1st will is revived if T intends for it to be revived. Extrinsic evidence is permitted when revocation is performed by a physical act.**	**Here, it is likely that T did intend for the 1st will to be revived because he reconciled with A and, in 2000, he told several people that A need not worry because he provided for him.** These comments to others can also be used as extrinsic evidence because T revoked the 1st will by a physical act of writing null and void on it.	**T's 1998 will revived as to devise 1 to Al**
DRR	**DRR applies where testator revokes the 1st will on the mistaken belief that another 2nd disposition that is substantially the same would be effective and, but for mistake, T would not have revoked 1st will; disregard revocation and probate 1st will.**	**Here, DRR is inapplicable because the 2nd instrument, the 1999 codicil, was valid until T revoked it; since there was no mistaken belief that it was valid when it wasn't, DRR would not apply.**	**DRR inapplicable but will still revived under revival**

Continued >

Issue	Rule	Fact Application	Conclusion
Carl's Rights			
Specific gift	A specific gift is a gift of specifically identifiable property.	**Here, the stock to C is arguably specific because it not only names the OmegaCorp stock but also states "my" OmegaCorp stock.**	Likely specific gift
Demonstrative gift	A demonstrative gift is a general gift that specifies the property or a particular fund from which the gift should be made.	**The court could also classify the stock as a general gift that simply specifies which funds the gift should be paid from, here being the OmegaCorp stock**; it is more likely a specific gift since T used both my language and identified the type of stock.	Not a demonstrative gift
Ademption	**A specific gift adeems by extinction if it is not part of the estate at the time of the testator's death.** **Courts will look at the testator's intent in determining whether the gift adeemed, such that the beneficiary takes nothing.** The beneficiary is entitled to a general pecuniary gift of equal value where the specific gift involved securities that changed form, a conversator that sold the property, or eminent domain.	**Here, the specific gift stock of OmegaCorp is no longer in T's estate, so it is considered to have adeemed by extinction.** **However, T most likely intended to have the stock go to C, as he merely used the proceeds from the one stock to buy the other, indicating he left the stock the same worth and value;** this is commonly done to make better investments on one's money and C is T's brother, so he likely would have wanted the stock to go to C rather than to the residue. **Further, since this is stock, C would likely be entitled to the equal value of the original stock since the stock merely changed forms** even if the court didn't award him the stock.	**AlphaCorp stock is C's**

Continued >

Issue	Rule	Fact Application	Conclusion
Norm, Deb, and Eve's Rights			
Lapse/antilapse	**Lapse: When a beneficiary dies prior to receiving their interest, the gift to the beneficiary lapses and falls into the residue. Antilapse: Rule of lapse does not apply if the beneficiary is kindred and the beneficiary leaves issue.**	**Here, B predeceased T, as she died in 2001 and T died in 2002, so the gift to her will lapse unless she qualifies for application of antilapse. Since B was T's sister, she was kindred to T and since she has issue, antilapse will apply and her issue will take her devise; she left 3 issue, one child and two grandchildren from a predeceased child.**	
Per capita with representation	Issue includes all lineal descendants. **When issues are of a more remote degree, they take by way of per capita with representation,** such that each generation takes their share of their deceased parent.	**N, as B's son, will take 1/2 of B's devise, and then D and E would split B's predeceased child (their parent's) devise.**	**Norm gets 1/2 of house, and Deb and Eve each get 1/4 of house**
SU's Rights			
Residuary gift	A **residuary gift** is a gift that remains after all other gifts have been satisfied.	**Since A's gift is revised and C will get the AlphaCorp stock, and N, E, and D will take the residence, SU will not receive anything, as there is nothing left over from T's estate after that; however, if the court finds that the gift to C was adeemed, then that will go to SU.**	**SU gets nothing unless gift to Carl adeemed (not likely)**

Wills and Trusts Question 4

February 2008, Question 4

In 2001, Wilma, an elderly widow with full mental capacity, put $1,000,000 into a trust (Trust). The Trust instrument named Wilma's church (Church) as the beneficiary. Although the Trust instrument did not name a trustee, its terms recited that the trustee has broad powers of administration for the benefit of the beneficiary.

In 2002, Wilma's sister, Sis, began paying a great deal of attention to Wilma, preventing any other friends or relatives from visiting Wilma. In 2003, Wilma reluctantly executed a properly witnessed will leaving her entire estate to Sis. Following the execution of the will, Wilma and Sis began to develop a genuine fondness for each other, engaging in social events frequently and becoming close friends. In 2005 Wilma wrote a note to herself: "Am glad Sis will benefit from my estate."

In 2007, Wilma named Sis as trustee of the Trust, which was when Sis found out for the first time about the $1,000,000 in the Trust. Without telling Wilma, Sis wrote across the Trust instrument, "This Trust is revoked," signing her name as trustee.

Shortly thereafter, Wilma died, survived by her daughter, Dora, who had not spoken to Wilma for twenty years, and by Sis.

Church claims that the Trust is valid and remains in effect. Sis and Dora each claim that each is entitled to Wilma's entire estate.

1. What arguments should Church make in support of its claim, and what is the likely result? Discuss.
2. What arguments should Sis and Dora make in support of their respective claims, and what is the likely result? Discuss.

Answer question number 2 according to California law.

Wills and Trusts Question 4 Assessment

February 2008, Question 4

First, it is useful to note that this question specified to only answer *call 2* according to California law. On recent exams, the examiners have been specific about this because the California bar exam tests specific provisions from the California probate code for wills, as well as case law that further interprets the code provisions. However, trusts is tested based on general common law for trusts such that your knowledge of trusts doesn't have to be California-specific. The rule outlines provided in this book have been written to reflect this.

This question is similar to many wills and trusts questions in that it crosses over both subjects and tests the validity of both the will and the trust. The one new issue that arises on this question is undue influence. It is imperative to remember to go through the reasons that both a will and a trust might be invalidated after going through the basic requirements of validity. Students often remember the elements that go to the original creation but don't think about the elements regarding actions of those involved with creating the will that could lead to invalidation. You should make your issues checklist as detailed as necessary to avoid missing these issues.

When discussing undue influence, be sure to go through both rules: the general rule and the presumption rule for undue influence. This question also called for a discussion of the omitted heir issue. You may have left out this issue because clearly Dora, who hasn't spoken to Wilma in 20 years, was born before 2001 when Wilma executed her will. However, the issue should have been included because the examiners specifically tell you to address Dora. It is likely that she might argue she was accidentally omitted because it has been so many years since she spoke with her mother. What the examiners want to see is that you know that this is not a winning argument because it doesn't meet the burden required by the rule since Dora was not omitted before her birth, which is key, as opposed to a situation where she may have been forgotten, even after birth.

If you couldn't figure out how Dora fit in or what issues her existence raised, then you should have gone through your issues checklist to see all that might apply to a child, which should have led you to the omitted-heir issue. Since she was omitted, go through the issue of omitted heir, but quickly dismiss it because she was not born after the execution of the will. No matter what, don't just ignore the call as to Dora because you can't think of an issue that corresponds to her. Rather, keep looking at your checklist until you match the fact of a child omitted from a will with the issue of omitted heir, even if you know the rule won't apply under the facts. When facts give rise to an issue, you need to address it regardless of whether the rule is or is not met.

Finally, make note of the areas highlighted in **bold** on the corresponding grid. The bold areas highlight the issues, analysis, and conclusions that are likely **required** to receive a passing score on this question.

Issue	Rule	Fact Application	Conclusion
Call #1: Church			
Validity of trust	• A trust can be created by express declaration by the settlor. • **Intent** • **Legal purpose** • **Trust property** • **Beneficiary** (any ascertainable person or group) • **Trustee** (court will appoint if none named) • **No invalidation (due to fraud, undue influence, capacity, etc.)**	• Trust created by W here expressly. • **Intent: W intended to vest legal title in a trustee with broad powers of administration for the benefit of her church.** • **Legal purpose: To help her Church after her death.** • **Trust property: $1,000,000** • **Beneficiary: Church** • **Trustee: Nt named initially, but named later in 2007 as Sis.**	Valid trust
Type of trust	**Private express: Meets above formalities. Charitable trust: In favor of a large number of unidentifiable beneficiaries for charitable purposes.**	**Here, trust for Church will likely include all members, indicating it could benefit a large number of beneficiaries; whether express or charitable, it is valid.**	**Valid trust**
Revocation	**The settlor can revoke the trust if the power is reserved expressly in trust; minority (includes Cal.) find trust is revocable unless stated otherwise.** **Court can also modify trust to meet settlor's intent.** **The trustee has no power to terminate the trust unless trust provides otherwise.**	**Since Sis is merely the trustee and not the settlor or the court, she does not have the power to revoke the trust.** Further, although the trust gave the trustee broad powers of administration, that was for the benefit of the beneficiary, the Church; canceling the trust would not be beneficial to the Church and thus revocation would not qualify under this broad powers clause.	**Revocation invalid**

Continued >

Issue	Rule	Fact Application	Conclusion
Duties of trustees	Duty of care: Trustee must act as a reasonable prudent person dealing with his own affairs. Duty of loyalty: No self-dealing; conflict of interest.	Since Sis attempted to revoke the trust to benefit herself so that she would take the $1,000,000 as part of W's estate rather than the Church, she didn't act as a reasonable person and engaged in self-dealing; **so Church could ask that she be removed as trustee and that the trust is valid since her revocation was contrary to her trustee duties and against W's intent to benefit Church.**	**Trust remains valid; Church is beneficiary**
Call #2: Sis and Dora			
Sis		Sis will argue that the will is valid and that she will take the entire estate per the will.	
Dora		Dora will argue that she should take the entire estate because the will was a result of undue influence by Sis; even if will valid, she will argue she is an omitted child	
Validity of will	**A will is valid if the testator has capacity** and the formalities of a will are met Formalities include: • Writing • T must sign or acknowledge his signature/ will in the presence of 2 attesting witnesses present at the same time who knew it was a will **Undue influence if T susceptible to influence, wrongdoer has opportunity, actively participates, unnatural result.** Presumption if fiduciary relationship and they caused it to be transcribed.	**Here, W had full mental capacity to execute the trust in 2001, indicating that she likely had mental capacity in 2003 as well to execute the will since there are no facts to indicate she lost mental capacity during that time.** Appears to be in writing since she executed a properly witnessed will. **W not likely susceptible to influence since she was in her full mental capacity** and not suffering from any weakness, and in fact was engaging in frequent social events thereafter indicating she was in adequate mental and physical strength. **Sis did have opportunity to influence W since she was paying a great deal of attention to W, preventing W's other friends or family from visiting.**	**Will valid; no undue influence; Sis takes entire estate (less the $1,000,000 that goes to Church in the trust)**

Continued >

Issue	Rule	Fact Application	Conclusion
		It appears that Sis did actively participate by encouraging W to execute the will since W reluctantly executed the will, indicating that she may have done so at the request of another; further, Sis seems to want W's estate since she attempted to revoke the trust without W's knowledge, which would leave her even more money; **but it's unclear whether Sis asked W to do the will or took part in it at all. Result may appear unnatural due to W giving her entire estate to Sis and not sharing it with any others, but given that Sis had been paying a great deal of attention to W and W was estranged from her only daughter, Dora, and hadn't spoken with her for 20 years, it seems natural to leave her estate to Sis, especially since she had already left $1,000,000 to Church, so Sis would not be taking all of her money.** Since they were sisters and spending a great deal of time together, they likely had a confidential and close relationship, but active participation still not clear and not unnatural result.	**Will valid; no undue influence; Sis takes entire estate (less the $1,000,000 that goes to Church in the trust)**
Omitted child	**A child born after a will is executed is entitled to an intestate share unless provided for otherwise.**	**Here, Dora was born prior to the execution of the will, so she will not qualify as a omitted child.**	**Dora takes nothing**

Wills and Trusts Question 5

February 2010, Question 3

Hank and Wendy married, had two children, Aaron and Beth, and subsequently had their marriage dissolved.

One year after dissolution of the marriage, Hank placed all his assets in a valid revocable trust and appointed Trustee. Under the trust, Trustee was to pay all income from the trust to Hank during Hank's life. Upon Hank's death, the trust was to terminate and Trustee was to distribute the remaining assets as follows: one-half to Hank's mother, Mom, if she was then living, and the remainder to Aaron and Beth, in equal shares.

Trustee invested all assets of the trust in commercial real estate, which yielded very high income, but suffered rapidly decreasing market value.

Hank, who had never remarried, died three years after establishing the trust. At the time of his death, the trust was valued at $300,000. Subsequently, it was proved by DNA testing that Hank had another child, Carl, who had been conceived during Hank's marriage to Wendy, but was born following dissolution of the marriage. Wendy, Carl's mother, had never told Hank about Carl.

Wendy, Mom, Aaron, Beth, and Carl all claim that he or she is entitled to a portion of the trust assets.

1. At Hank's death, what claims, if any, do the trust beneficiaries have against Trustee? Discuss.
2. How should the trust assets be distributed? Discuss.

Answer this question according to California law.

Wills and Trusts Question 5 Assessment

February 2010, Question 3

This is a pure trusts question that gives rise to the heavily tested area of trustee duties. Whenever going through trustee duties, be sure to use the mnemonic "AND I DID SLIDE" to recall all trustee duties. Your checklist may just include the general category of "trustee duties" on it. That is fine so long as you expand on this and write out all of the potential trustee duties using the mnemonic once you realize that trustee duties are at issue.

Make sure that when you are going through the facts and highlighting or underlining the facts you have used, always consider using the same facts again and again for the various trustee duties. Often, the same facts that give rise to one trustee duty will also give rise to other trustee duties. For example, if a trustee engages in a conflict of interest, he is also likely not acting with due care. So, be sure to consider all facts with each type of trustee duty to ensure you don't miss any duties and/or omit analysis by failing to use the pertinent facts.

In regard to call 2, you should approach this call as you would other wills and trusts questions by going through the parties in the order in which they are listed in the question. Then, issue spot and identify each issue that is applicable to each of them. In addition, always sum up the distribution at the end, as to what each party will receive.

This question also shows you how the issues related to omitted heirs, gifts, and abatement apply and operate the same in a trust as they do in a will. If you have a difficult time remembering the issues that apply to both wills and trusts, then you may want to modify your issues checklist accordingly. Otherwise, you risk missing these issues on trusts questions. Take a moment to review which issues apply to both and keep a mental note and/or adjust your issues checklist accordingly.

Finally, be sure to make note of the areas highlighted in **bold** on the corresponding grid. The bold areas highlight the issues, analysis, and conclusions that are likely **required** to receive a passing score on this question.

Issue	Rule	Fact Application	Conclusion
Call #1: Beneficiaries v. Trustee			
Duty of care	**Trustee must act as a reasonable, prudent person dealing with his own affairs; this includes the duty to investigate.**	**Here, investing all assets of the trust in commercial real estate is not reasonable because there is the risk of losing all assets when they are all in one investment; rather, a reasonable investor would diversify his investments.**	**Trustee breached duty of care**
Duty to invest/ diversify	Split in authority: • Statutory lists: Good investments include first deeds of trust in real estate, federally insured certificates of deposit, federal govt. bonds, stock of publicly traded corps. • Uniform Prudent Investor Act (UPIA): Adopted by most states, uses prudent investor test (performance measured in context of entire trust portfolio).	**T should not have invested all assets in commercial real estate**, but under the statutory list authorities, real estate is likely acceptable, but not all assets in commercial real estate; as for the UPIA, the fact that the entire trust portfolio was in one investment is likely not prudent, resulting in low performance for some of the beneficiaries; **T should have diversified the assets among a variety of investments.**	**Trustee breached duty to invest/ diversify**
Duty of loyalty/ fairness	**Duty to treat all beneficiaries equally without favoring any one beneficiary over the others.**	Here, T favored H as a beneficiary by investing in real estate since the investment yielded high income, which under the trust, went to H during his life, but the investments suffered from rapidly decreasing market value, which leaves little value to the other beneficiaries—Mom, Aaron, and Beth—when H dies since they would all take the remaining assets, which wouldn't be worth much due to the decrease in market.	**Trustee breached duty of loyalty/ fairness to all beneficiaries**

Continued >

Issue	Rule	Fact Application	Conclusion
Call #2: Trust Assets			
Wendy	A spouse is entitled to their half of the community property at divorce. Omitted spouse is entitled to intestate share of trust or estate if omitted when trust was made before marriage.	Here, it appears that **H and W were already divorced at the time that H set up the valid revocable trust** so the trust assets would be coming from H's SP; also, since divorced, W is not an omitted spouse.	**W gets nothing**
Mom, Aaron, Beth	A beneficiary will take under the trust, barring any abatement.	**M is entitled to 1/2 of the $300k, and A and B will split the other 1/2,** so M will get $150k, and A and B each get $75k, barring any abatement for C (see below).	**M, A, and B will take subject to C's interest (below)**
Carl	**Omitted child is entitled to intestate share of trust; other beneficiaries abate to allow this; if child born but settlor unaware of child's existence, child still receives intestate share.** **Intestate share: If no spouse, then the issue take all in equal shares.**	**C is H's son, as established by DNA evidence, and he was conceived while married to W but born after dissolution, indicating he may be an accidentally omitted child.** **Here, H set up the trust 1 year after his divorce to W, indicating that C was born prior to the trust being established; however, H did not know of C since W never told H about C, so there is no way H could have included C in his trust at that time, and since he included his other children, he likely would have included C, too.** **C's intestate share would be 1/3 of the trust, since he would be splitting it with his siblings, A and B, so C's intestate share would be $100k, which is 1/3 of the trust's worth.**	**C is treated as an omitted child and is entitled to take his intestate share under the trust, which is $100k**

Continued >

Issue	Rule	Fact Application	Conclusion
Abatement	Gifts will be reduced to satisfy the share of an omitted child by taking pro rata from other beneficiaries.	Since C will get an intestate share of $100k taking pro rata, 1/2 ($50k) of his intestate share will come from M, since she is entitled to 1/2 of the remaining trust, and the other 1/2 ($50k) will come from A and B equally, who are taking the remaining 1/2 of the trust.	Mom will take $100k Carl will take $100k Aaron will take $50k Beth will take $50k Wendy will take $0

Wills and Trusts Question 6

February 2007, Question 4

In 2001 Tom, a resident of California, executed a valid typewritten and witnessed will. At that time, Tom was married to Wynn. Tom also had two nephews, Norm, and Matt, who were the children of his deceased sister, Sue.

Tom's will made the following dispositions:

Article 1: I leave $10,000 to my friend Frank.
Article 2: I leave my shares in Beta Corp stock to my friend Frank.
Article 3: I leave $80,000 to my sister Sue's issue.
Article 4: I leave the residue of my estate to my wife.

The $10,000 figure in Article 1 was crossed out and $12,000 was handwritten in Tom's hand above the $10,000 figure. Next to the $12,000 Tom had handwritten, "Okay. 2/15/02."

In 2003 Tom and Wynn had a child, Cole.

In 2004, Matt died in a car accident. Matt was survived by his children, Lynn and Kim.

Tom died in 2005. Tom was survived by Wynn, Cole, Norm, Frank, and his grandnieces, Lynn and Kim. At the time of his death, Tom owned, as separate property, $500,000 in cash. He also had 100 shares of Beta Corp stock, titled in Tom's name, which he had purchased with his earnings while married to Wynn. The Beta stock was valued at $1.00 per share at the time of Tom's death.

What rights, if any, do Wynn, Cole, Norm, Frank, and his grandnieces Lynn and Kim have in Tom's estate? Discuss.

Answer according to California law.

Wills and Trusts Question 6 Assessment

February 2007, Question 4

This question is predominantly a wills question, but it also requires some brief application of community property law. The two facts that should make you identify the community property issue are that T owned separate property and that he owned shares that were purchased from earnings while married to W. Both of these facts give rise to separate property and community property, which are necessary to properly determine which assets T can give away entirely and which he can only give away to the extent of his one-half. Similarly, you must know the CP laws to know what W is entitled to receive and make sure that any of her shares of the CP are not being devised by T. Sometimes, in this situation it is then necessary to discuss widow's election to determine whether W should take under the will or her statutory share. This question is a prime example of how community property and wills issues overlap.

To properly organize the answer to this question, you need to go through each party one at a time to determine their share of the estate, if any. Overall, this question should be approached like others you have already seen in that you determine which issues are applicable to each individual and then issue spot from there. It is best to do this by writing down the facts about each individual. For example, if you wrote out that Frank was a friend, this fact would raise the issue of lapse/antilapse since a friend is not kindred. Also, pay attention to the facts surrounding the documents, such as when they are revised, marked up, etc., as these facts will give rise to issues such as revocation and DRR.

If you have difficulty spotting issues, be sure to review the fact triggers and exam tips throughout the outlines. Also, the more practice essays you write out, the easier the issue spotting will become. So, keep practicing.

Make note of the areas highlighted in **bold** on the corresponding grid. The bold areas highlight the issues, analysis, and conclusions that are likely **required** to receive a passing score on this question.

Issue	Rule	Fact Application	Conclusion
Presumptions			
CP SP	• CP acquired during marriage • SP acquired before or after marriage or by gift, inheritance, bequest or devise	• Here, Beta stock is presumed CP since it was purchased with earnings during marriage, which are CP. • The $500k is SP, as stated in the facts.	Stock is CP; $500k is H's SP
Distribution of CP and SP	One can only will away their 1/2 of the CP or the other spouse can elect his statutory share of what the will provides them.	Here, arguably, H willed away the Beta stock, but since the facts indicate he willed away "my shares" this could be interpreted to mean his 1/2 since that is all that is technically his.	
Wynn			
	W gets her 1/2 of CP and anything she is provided in the will	**Here, W will get 1/2 of the Beta stock, so 50 shares (worth $50), and the residue of T's estate, which will be determined after all other parties' rights have been determined (see below).**	See below
Cole			
Omitted child	A child born after the execution of the will shall receive their intestate share unless the will shows an intent to disinherit the child, the T otherwise provided for the child, or the T left substantially all of the estate to the other parent if there was more than 1 child.	• **C is omitted because he was born in 2003, and Tom executed his will in 2001, 2 years earlier.** • **T did not show an intent to disinherit C and did not appear to have any other children prior to C, so leaving it to the parent exception wouldn't apply either.** • **C would take his intestate share, which would be 1/2 of T's SP, so 1/2 of $500k**	C gets $250k

Continued >

Issue	Rule	Fact Application	Conclusion
Norm, Lynn, and Kim			
Distribution under will	Issue includes all lineal descendants. When issue are of a more remote degree, they take by way of per capita with representation, such that each generation takes their share of their deceased parent.	• Will states that S's issue receive $80k. • S's issue include N and M, L and K. • N will take 50% and, since M died, his children L and K will split his 50%, so L and K each get 25%.	Norm gets $40k, and Lynn and Kim get $20k each
Frank (Art. 1)			
Revocation	Revocation by physical act includes crossing out a part of the will.	Here, T crossed out the $10k, so this amount will be revoked.	Gift of $10k to F revoked
New will or codicil	**A new will or codicil must meet all the formalities of a will, including witness requirements, signed by T, in writing.**	**Here, there are no witnesses, so F's addition in the amount of $12k does not constitute a new will or codicil unless it qualifies as a holographic will or codicil.**	No defenses
Holographic will or codicil	**A holographic will or codicil requires T's signature and that the material provisions be in T's name.**	**Here, some material terms such as the date and "okay" are in T's handwriting, but the name of the devisee, Frank, which is arguably material, is not in T's handwriting; also, T didn't sign it.**	$12k to F not a valid will or codicil
DRR	DRR applies where testator revokes 1st will on the mistaken belief that another, 2nd disposition that is substantially the same would be effective and, but for mistake, testator would not have revoked 1st will; disregard revocation and probate 1st will.	Here, T revoked Art. 1 of his 1st will under the mistaken belief that his 2nd disposition ($12k to F instead of $10k) would be valid; since holographic codicil not valid, the 2nd disposition is not valid; and it would have been substantially the same—same devisee, property type, but only changed amount slightly; so the court would disregard the revocation and probate the original Art. 1 ($10k to Frank).	$10k to F under DRR

Continued >

Issue	Rule	Fact Application	Conclusion
Frank (Art. 2)			
Devise of CP	See above—can only will away 1/2.	Since H can only will away his 1/2 of the CP of the Beta stock, F will get 1/2 of the Beta stock, which is 50 shares worth $50.	F gets 50 shares of Beta stock
Overall distribution		W will receive 1/2 of the Beta stock and 1/2 of the $250k SP, less the $10k to F and the $80k to Sue's issue, so $160k. C receives $250k (1/2 of the $500k SP). Norm receives $40k. Lynn and Kim receive $20k each. Frank receives 1/2 of the Beta stock and $10k.	

PART 13 CROSSOVER QUESTIONS

INTRODUCTION TO CROSSOVER QUESTIONS

A crossover question is an essay question that tests legal issues from more than one substantive area of law. The bar exam is unpredictable, and while there have been administrations of the California bar exam with no crossover questions, each administration usually includes at least one crossover question, and often times there will be several. Statistically, about one-half of the essay questions are crossovers. A typical crossover question will cover two substantive subjects, and sometimes a question will cover three subjects. Any subject is eligible to be included in a crossover question, and any subject can cross over with any other subject. However, some subjects lend themselves to being crossed over better than other subjects. Further, some subjects naturally cross over together, so there is some predictability to the types of crossover questions you may encounter.

The chart below indicates the frequency with which each subject is tested as a crossover subject when it is tested on the essay exam, and which subjects are typically tested together.

Subject	**Crossover Frequency**	**Frequently Crossed Over With...**	**Also Crossed Over With...**
Business Associations	41%	Professional Responsibility	Contracts
Civil Procedure	25%	Not frequently a subject of crossover questions with any one subject in particular.	Contracts, Professional Responsibility, Remedies, Torts
Community Property	21%	Wills	
Constitutional Law	38%	Crimes	Civil Procedure, Real Property
Contracts	47%	Remedies	Real Property, Torts
Crimes	50%	Constitutional Law, Evidence	Professional Responsibility
Evidence	29%	Crimes	Professional Responsibility, Remedies
Professional Responsibility	50%	Business Associations	Civil Procedure, Contracts, Evidence, Remedies, Torts, Trusts

Subject	Crossover Frequency	Frequently Crossed Over With...	Also Crossed Over With...
Real Property	50%	Not frequently a subject of crossover questions with any one subject in particular.	Contracts, Constitutional Law, Remedies, Torts, Wills
Remedies	95%	Contracts	Business Associations, Civil Procedure, Constitutional Law, Evidence, Professional Responsibility, Real Property, Torts, Trusts
Torts	52%	Remedies	Civil Procedure, Contracts, Real Property, Professional Responsibility
Wills & Trusts	54%*	Wills & Trusts (together) Wills & Community Property	Trusts: Professional Responsibility, Remedies Wills: Real Property

*Wills and trusts are tested with each other 41% of the time. Of the remaining times when one subject is tested without the other, 54% of the time the question will be a crossover question.

Answering crossover questions is a new skill that you will need to practice since most students have never taken a law school exam that covered more than one substantive area of law on the same question. The questions included for practice here are typical of the range of crossover questions you may encounter on an actual bar exam.

CROSSOVER QUESTION ESSAYS, ANSWER GRIDS, AND SAMPLE ANSWERS

Crossover Question 1

July 2007, Question 4

Dan stood on the steps of the state capitol and yelled to a half-dozen people entering the front doors: "Listen citizens. Prayer in the schools means government-endorsed religion. A state church! They can take your constitutional rights away just a fast as I can destroy this copy of the U.S. Constitution."

With that, Dan took a cigarette lighter from his pocket and ignited a parchment document that he held in his left hand. The parchment burst into flame and, when the heat of the fire burned his hand, he involuntarily let it go. A wind blew the burning document into a construction site where it settled in an open drum of flammable material. The drum exploded, killing a nearby pedestrian.

A state statute makes it a misdemeanor to burn or mutilate a copy of the U.S. Constitution.

It turned out that the document that Dan had burned was actually a copy of the Declaration of Independence, not the U.S. Constitution, as he believed.

Dan was arrested and charged with the crimes of murder and attempting to burn a copy of the U.S. Constitution. He has moved to dismiss the charge of attempting to burn a copy of the U.S. Constitution, claiming that (i) what he burned was actually a copy of the Declaration of Independence and (ii) the state statute on which the charge is based violates his rights under the First Amendment to the U.S. Constitution.

1. May Dan properly be found guilty of the crime of murder or any lesser-included offense? Discuss.
2. How should the court rule on each ground of Dan's motion to dismiss the charge of attempting to burn a copy of the U.S. Constitution? Discuss.

Crossover Question 1 Assessment

July 2007, Question 4

This crossover question has an unusual fact pattern where a bystander is killed as the result of another person's exercising his right to free expression.

Like most crossover questions, the calls of the question are very clear and identify the issues that are to be addressed in the answer. The first call of the question addresses the criminal law issues of murder and any lesser-included offenses.

The second call of the question is worth exploring in detail. Note that the second call asks how the court should rule on each ground of Dan's motion to dismiss. Since the question mentions a motion to dismiss, you may think at first that this is a civil procedure crossover question, but it isn't. The examiners will sometimes ask about a motion to dismiss as a mechanism for introducing the underlying issues, which is what they have done here. Call two specifically asks about "each ground" of Dan's motion to dismiss. If you refer back to paragraph five, the question specifically states what the two grounds are for Dan's motion to dismiss and even signposts them for you by numbering them. Organize your answer to call two accordingly, with a separate section for each ground in order.

The first motion to dismiss addresses a more complicated (and less frequently tested) issue of criminal attempt and possible defenses. There were many ways to approach the facts raised in the first motion to dismiss, but it is essential to discuss the nuances of how attempt applies under these facts and to discuss some sort of defense based on mistake or impossibility. The second call of the question addresses the free exercise of speech and expression under the First Amendment, which is not typically found in a crimes question. Further, the facts raise the issue of symbolic speech, which is not commonly tested, compared to regular free speech.

Besides being a crossover question, this question also covers two areas of law that are not commonly tested: the attempt issue and symbolic speech. It is worth noting in the following grid that the bar examiners give wide latitude to students in how they choose to answer on these issues. You can tell because on these issues comparatively little of the rules and/or analysis is bolded and thus was required to pass that portion of the question. There is greater focus on the analysis and the use of the key facts, and more variation is acceptable in passing answers. If you are ever faced with an exam where you are unsure what rule to use to analyze the facts, it's best to think of something that potentially could apply and focus on the factual analysis. Chances are the other examinees are equally stumped and the bar examiners will end up giving wider latitude to acceptable answers and focus on the factual analysis.

Note the areas highlighted in **bold** on the corresponding grid. The bold areas highlight the issues, analysis, and conclusions that are likely **required** to receive a passing score on this exam. In general, the essay grids are provided to assist you in analyzing the essays, and are much more detailed than what a student should create during the exam to organize their response to a question.

Issue	Rule	Fact Application	Conclusion
Call #1: Murder or Lesser-Included Offense			
Murder	**Murder is the unlawful killing of a human being with malice aforethought.** **Malice can be proven by intent to kill, intent to inflict great bodily injury, reckless indifference to an unjustifiably high risk to human life, or intent to commit a felony.**	**Intent to kill: There is no indication that D intended to kill anyone,** as he was not aware of the nearby flammable drum nor of the pedestrian's presence near the drum; also, D involuntarily let the paper go, not intentionally, and did not have a weapon per se, but rather a paper on fire. **Intent to inflict great bodily injury: D's act of burning the document was done to symbolize his political views, and he did not intend to harm anyone**. **Reckless indifference: A reasonable person would not expect burning a document to lead to a death of a person located a distance away from the burning paper.** **Intent to commit a felony: D didn't commit any felony nor did he intend to,** as the state statute only made burning the U.S. Constitution a misdemeanor and not a felony. In addition, he didn't even burn the U.S. Constitution. There is no arson here because D did not intend to burn a dwelling, but rather a piece of paper.	**No murder**
First-degree murder	Premeditated and deliberate murder (need specific intent to kill); or felony murder if one of the enumerated felonies (arson, robbery, burglary, rape, mayhem, kidnapping).	No murder, as discussed above, since D had no intent to kill that could be premeditated and the felony murder rule doesn't apply either.	No first-degree murder

Continued >

Issue	Rule	Fact Application	Conclusion
Voluntary manslaughter	**Need adequate provocation**; sudden and intense passion in the mind of an ordinary person, causing him to lose self-control where D was in fact provoked and lacked sufficient time between provocation and killing to calm down/cool off, and D did not cool off/calm down.	**There was no provocation here to cause D to act with sudden and intense passion**; D did not lose self-control but rather knew what he was doing—burning a document—and involuntarily let it go, not intentionally or voluntarily.	**No voluntary manslaughter**
Involuntary manslaughter	**Unintentional killing that occurs from either criminal negligence or misdemeanor-murder** (which is a lower standard than reckless indifference but higher than general negligence—D aware of risk and acted extremely unreasonably, which caused a death).	Here, arguably, it is foreseeable that a person might be killed when you are burning a paper in front of a half-dozen people in a public place, especially when the document is ignited on a windy day as happened here since the wind blew it away. Further, a reasonable person should know that paper might burn quickly and that he would likely let go of it in the event it started to burn his skin or get close to his hand. **However, a reasonable person would not likely find it so dangerous to burn a piece of paper that it would result in death**; rather, the likely risk is that someone else would be burned or harmed, not killed. It is **not foreseeable that the paper would blow to a nearby drum at a construction site, that the drum would be flammable, and actually explode** at the exact same time that a pedestrian was walking by. The sequence of events is too unusual and unpredictable to make D's actions extremely unreasonable, and he did not commit a misdemeanor, as he did not burn the U.S. Constitution in violation of the statute.	**No involuntary manslaughter**

Continued >

Issue	Rule	Fact Application	Conclusion
Second-degree murder	All other murders—not above determined to be 1st degree, voluntary manslaughter, or involuntary manslaughter—are 2nd-degree murder.	No murder at all, as discussed above.	No second-degree murder
Call #2: Dan's Motion to Dismiss—Ground (i)			
Attempt	An act done with intent to commit a crime when the actual crime is never completed. Mere preparation will not suffice here; need an act beyond mere preparation.	**Here, D did intend to commit a crime, as he intended to burn the U.S. Constitution,** which he indicated by use of the word "destroy," **and this was a misdemeanor under the state statute.** He acted by actually igniting the paper and burning it. **[Note: Only one state-released answer gave a rule for attempt; the other analyzed attempt together with the defenses (though not the best organizational approach).]**	**D is guilty of attempt, barring any defenses below**
Impossibility	Factual impossibility is not a defense; legal impossibility is a defense where a defendant sets out to do things he mistakenly believes constitute a crime.	Here, D's burning would be a claim of factual impossibility, which does not provide a defense, since he did not burn the U.S. Constitution but rather the Declaration of Independence. D could not burn the U.S. Constitution under these facts, although he did intend to, which was a crime. Therefore, since D set out to do an act that was a crime—burning the U.S. Constitution—legal impossibility is not a defense.	No impossibility defense
Defense of mistake	Mistake of fact negates any specific intent crime; it negates malice and general intent crimes if mistake was reasonable. Mistake of law is typically no defense.	Here, the factual mistake was that D actually burned the Declaration of Independence, not the U.S. Constitution, so this could be a defense if D was charged under the actual state statute. However, D was charged with attempt, not violation of the statute. D did intend to burn the U.S. Constitution, even though he wasn't successful, which is why he is still liable for attempt, and mistake of fact will not provide a defense.	No mistake defense

Continued >

Issue	Rule	Fact Application	Conclusion
Mistake or impossibility		**[Note: You MUST have discussed at least one of the defenses above to pass and at least acknowledge the fact that D burned the wrong document and its legal relevance.]**	
Call #2: Dan's Motion to Dismiss—Ground (ii)			
Standing	Injury, causation, redressability	Here, D is injured because he was charged with a crime as a result of the state statute making it a crime to burn the U.S. Constitution. D's injury is redressable because if the statute is unconstitutional, then D's attempt charge based on the same statute would not be a crime.	D has standing
State action	Significant state involvement or traditional public function	Here, state statute is legislation and, thus, state action.	Yes, state action
Freedom of speech (content)	Content-based v. content-neutral Content-based is presumptively unconstitutional and receives strict scrutiny (necessary to achieve a compelling govt. interest and uses least restrictive means; narrowly tailored).	Here, the statute is content-based because it is specific to the U.S. Constitution. [Note: Could argue statute is pure conduct because it is about burning or mutilating. However, since it applies to the U.S. Constitution, it is content-based, not pure conduct, because it is about conduct but only in regard to the U.S. Constitution.] Here, there is no compelling govt. interest because people are free to express their political views and opinions. The govt. may desire that people respect the U.S. Constitution, but it is not a compelling interest nor is the statute narrowly tailored since it is limited to burning or mutilating, which allows for acting disrespectfully in other ways. Further, there are other equally important documents that could be included if that were the govt.'s interest. People have a right under the Constitution to free speech.	Content-based—does not pass strict scrutiny

Continued >

Issue	Rule	Fact Application	Conclusion
Symbolic speech	**Govt. can regulate if** (1) Within constitutional power **(2) Serves an important govt. interest independent of the speech aspects, and** **(3) Prohibits no more speech than necessary.**	Here, the state has the power to regulate laws of activities for persons in their state. **The law does not appear to serve an important govt. interest independent of the speech aspect because the fear of danger due to burning documents isn't aided by limiting the statute to the burning of the U.S. Constitution. If this were the interest, they would ban the burning of all documents, not just the U.S. Constitution. This is also why the burden on speech is greater than necessary. Rather, the statute prevents people from expressing their political views regarding the U.S. Constitution in particular. Unlike the draft cards case, where the govt. interest was to protect and promote the draft and soldiers, here there is no govt. interest independent of its content since there is no crisis involving the U.S. Constitution, such as the draft at that time.** This case is more like the flag burning case since it limits people's right to express their views and is likely unconstitutional.	**Violates the 1st Amend. under symbolic speech**

Crossover Question 1 Sample Answer

July 2007, Question 4

1. Can Dan be found guilty of murder or lesser included offenses?

Murder

Murder is the unlawful killing of a human being with malice aforethought. Malice can be established by showing intent to kill, intent to inflict great bodily injury, reckless indifference to the value of human life, or intent to commit certain dangerous felonies.

Intent to Kill/Intent to Inflict Great Bodily Injury

There is no evidence that Dan intended to kill or inflict great bodily injury on anyone. Rather, Dan was attempting to express his political views. While Dan lit the parchment on fire on purpose, he involuntarily let the burning parchment go when it burned his hand. Dan did not have a weapon, but a piece of burning paper. Nothing indicates that he even knew there were flammable chemicals nearby or that the wind would carry the burning parchment into an adjacent construction site where those materials could cause an explosion and kill a nearby pedestrian.

Reckless Indifference

There is no evidence that Dan had a reckless indifference for the value of human life. While he may have expected some negative consequence could result from lighting a piece of paper on fire outside on a windy day, it would not be foreseeable that such an action would lead to the death of a human being located some distance away from the burning document. Dan did not act with reckless indifference.

Intent to Commit a Felony

There is no evidence Dan either committed or attempted to commit any felony. While arson is a dangerous felony, Dan burned a piece of paper rather than a structure, and thus did not commit arson or any other dangerous felony, so he is not guilty of felony murder. The statute makes burning a copy of the U.S. Constitution a misdemeanor, not a felony, and Dan did not actually burn a copy of the U.S. Constitution.

First-Degree Murder

First-degree murder is a premeditated and deliberate murder, or a felony murder. As indicated above, neither are implicated here.

Voluntary Manslaughter

Voluntary manslaughter is the killing of a human being that occurs in the heat of passion, such that there was adequate provocation that would cause a reasonable person to lose control. There are no facts to suggest Dan acted in the heat of passion or that he lost control or was even aware of the presence of the flammable chemicals or the pedestrian. Dan is not guilty of voluntary manslaughter.

Involuntary Manslaughter

Involuntary manslaughter is the unintentional killing of a human being resulting from grossly negligent behavior or the commission of a misdemeanor. Dan's conduct may rise to the level of gross negligence since he created an unreasonably high risk of harm by purposely lighting a piece of paper on fire while outside on a windy day in the presence of a half-dozen people. It was foreseeable that holding a burning piece of paper in his hand would cause it to burn his hand, thus forcing Dan to let go of the burning paper and that someone could be hurt as a result. However, Dan will assert that the subsequent events leading to the death of the pedestrian were so unusual that it was not foreseeable that burning the paper on the steps could lead to the death of a pedestrian some distance away by means of the burning paper blowing to an adjacent construction site and igniting an open drum of flammable chemicals causing an explosion, which happened just as a pedestrian was walking by. Since the sequence of events that led to the pedestrian's death were so unusual and unforeseeable, Dan will likely not be found guilty of involuntary manslaughter.

Dan could also potentially be found guilty of misdemeanor manslaughter. However, the burning of a copy of the U.S. Constitution is not likely the type of crime that would be included in this rule. Further, since Dan did not actually burn the U.S. Constitution in violation of the statute, he will not be found guilty of misdemeanor manslaughter.

Second-Degree Murder

All murder that is not first-degree murder, voluntary manslaughter, or involuntary manslaughter is second-degree murder. As indicated above, there is no murder under these facts.

2. Dan's Motion to Dismiss

(i) Dan Actually Burned a Copy of the Declaration of Independence

Attempt

An attempt to commit a crime can be a punishable offense even without the commission of the crime where the defendant had the requisite specific intent and has committed some affirmative act in furtherance of the criminal act. Dan had the requisite specific intent to commit a crime since he wanted to burn a copy of the U.S. Constitution, as evidenced by his speech on the capitol steps stating he could "destroy" a copy of the U.S. Constitution. Dan then took an act in furtherance of the criminal act by igniting the parchment with a cigarette lighter. Absent a defense, Dan is guilty of attempt.

Factual Impossibility

Factual impossibility does not provide a defense where the defendant has made a mistake of fact, and if the facts had been as the defendant believed them to be there would have been a crime. Dan argues that he cannot be guilty because he made a mistake of fact since he mistakenly thought the document he burned was a copy of the U.S. Constitution, when in fact the document was a copy of the Declaration of Independence and there is no similar statute prohibiting its burning. However, to be guilty of attempt, Dan need only attempt to do an act that he thought was a crime. Had the facts been as Dan believed them to be, he would have committed the crime of burning the U.S. Constitution and Dan's mistake will not provide a defense to a charge of the attempt of that crime.

Mistake of Fact
Mistake of fact may negate a defendant's ability to form the specific intent required to commit a crime. However, Dan did have the specific intent to burn the U.S. Constitution, which was a crime under the state statute, so his action of mistakenly burning a different document will not provide a defense for the attempt.

(ii) Statute Violates the First Amendment
The First Amendment protects the freedom of expression and includes both speech and symbolic conduct intended to communicate an idea.

Standing
A defendant must have standing to bring suit. Dan was injured since he was charged with a crime as a result of the statute. Dan's injury is redressable since if the statute is unconstitutional any attempt charge based on the statute would not be valid.

State Action
For a statute to be found unconstitutional there must be state action, which is satisfied here since the challenged statute is a state statute.

Content-Based Speech Restrictions
Content-based speech restrictions are presumptively unconstitutional and are subject to strict scrutiny requiring they be necessary to achieve a compelling government interest and use the least restrictive means to do so. The restriction here prohibits the burning or mutilating of a specific document, the U.S. Constitution. Since the rule here prohibiting the burning of a copy of the U.S. Constitution does not apply equally to all documents, it is a content-based restriction. As a content-based restriction it is presumptively unconstitutional. There is no compelling government interest in not allowing the burning or mutilating of a copy of the U.S. Constitution since citizens are free to express their political views and, even if there were a compelling government interest, this regulation would not be the least restrictive means of achieving it and will not pass the strict scrutiny test.

Symbolic Speech
Symbolic speech is the communication of an idea through conduct. Government regulations of symbolic speech are allowable when the regulation is within constitutional power, furthers an important government interest, the interest is unrelated to the suppression of speech, and any incidental burden on speech is no greater than necessary. Where there is some legitimate administrative purpose in the regulation, such as in the draft-card case where the cards were necessary to efficiently administer the draft, a regulation prohibiting the burning of those cards will be allowed. There may be an important governmental safety interest in prohibiting the burning of documents, but since the regulation here is strictly limited to the burning or mutilating of the U.S. Constitution and not all documents, it does not appear to have a purpose other than suppressing the speech of those expressing displeasure with the U.S. Constitution by burning or mutilating it. The regulation here seems similar to that in the flag burning case where the regulation was struck down as being unconstitutionally aimed at limiting the expression of speech. Since

there seems to be no legitimate governmental interest in the regulation other than the suppression of speech, it will be struck down.

Dan's motion to dismiss the charge of attempting to burn a copy of the U.S. Constitution should be upheld because the statute he is charged with violating is unconstitutional.

Crossover Question 2

July 2009, Question 5

Diane owns a large country estate to which she plans to invite economically disadvantaged children for free summer day camp. In order to provide the children with the opportunity to engage in water sports, Diane started construction to dam a stream on the property to create a pond. Neighbors downstream, who rely on the stream to irrigate their crops and to fill their wells, immediately demanded that Diane stop construction. Diane refused. Six months into the construction, when the dam was almost complete, the neighbors filed an application in state court for a permanent injunction ordering Diane to stop construction and to remove the dam. They asserted causes of action for nuisance and for a taking under the United States Constitution.

After a hearing, the state court denied the application on the merits. The neighbors did not appeal the ruling.

Thereafter, Paul, one of the neighbors and a plaintiff in the state court case, separately retained Lawyer and filed an application for a permanent injunction against Diane in federal court asserting the same causes of action and requesting the same relief as in the state court case. Personal jurisdiction, subject matter jurisdiction, and venue were proper. The federal court granted Diane's motion to dismiss Paul's federal court application on the basis of preclusion.

Infuriated with the ruling, Paul told Lawyer, "If the court can't give me the relief I am looking for, I will take care of Diane in my own way and that dam, too." Unable to dissuade Paul and after telling him she would report his threatening comments to criminal authorities, Lawyer called 911 and, without identifying herself, told a dispatcher that "someone is on his way to hurt Diane."

1. Was the state court's denial of Diane's neighbors' application for a permanent injunction correct? Discuss. Do not address substantive property or riparian rights.
2. Was the federal court's denial of Paul's application for a permanent injunction correct? Discuss. Do not address substantive property or riparian rights.
3. Did Lawyer commit any ethical violation when she called 911? Discuss. Answer according to both California and ABA authorities.

Crossover Question 2 Assessment

July 2009, Question 5

This crossover question covers three substantive areas of law; remedies, civil procedure, and professional responsibility. These three subjects do not logically go together, nor is it common for them to be tested together, but expect the unexpected when it comes to crossover questions. The nice feature of this question is that there are three distinct question calls and each call covers a different substantive area.

There is also not much mystery involved in which issues are being tested. The first call of the question specifically asks about a permanent injunction. The third call of the question specifically asks about any ethical violations Lawyer may have committed.

The second call of the question is worth looking at in more detail. The question asks if the court was correct in denying Paul's application for a permanent injunction. A close look at the second paragraph reveals that Paul's federal court application (for a permanent injunction) was denied on the basis of "preclusion." This should have tipped you off that you were dealing with claim preclusion, also known as *res judicata*. Thus, the second call of the question calls for analysis of res judicata.

Aside from discerning the issue in the second call, the question is very straightforward. The rules being tested are clear, and there are many facts and factual inferences available to use in the analysis. There is much opportunity to analyze both sides on many of the issues and/or elements on this question. In fact, failure to do so will result in a not receiving a passing score. Where there are facts to use on both sides of an issue you are expected to argue both sides, such as here on the injunction (particularly on the balancing and laches defense elements) and whether Lawyer's conduct was reasonable in light of the duty of confidentiality.

Note the areas highlighted in **bold** on the corresponding grid. The bold areas highlight the issues, analysis, and conclusions that are likely **required** to receive a passing score on this question.

Issue	Rule	Fact Application	Conclusion
Call #1			
Permanent injunction	**Inadequate legal remedy** • **Money damages are inadequate** • Multiplicity of suit • Difficult to calculate w/ certainty • Land is unique **Property right** • **Protectable interest required** • **Traditional rule: real prop. only** • **Modernly: any prop. interest** **Feasibility: not too difficult for court to enforce** • **Negative: easier to enforce** • **Mandatory/affirmative: harder** **Balancing of hardships Plaintiff if denied vs. to defendant if granted** & consider the public interest **Defense: Laches** **Plaintiff's unreasonable delay prejudices defendant**	Money damages are too inadequate because the damage caused by **crop damage and empty wells** is uncertain, and **money does not solve the problem** since an alternative water source is unclear. The harm is ongoing, which could lead to a multiplicity of suits, and **land is unique and irreparably harmed if without access to water.** Diane may argue that crop loss and loss of well water could be adequately compensated with money for crop loss and the cost of an alternative water source or the diminished land value, but since water is essential, it is likely the **remedy at law is inadequate.** **Downstream neighbors have a protectable property interest in the water since the stream runs through their properties** and they used the water before Diane built the dam. **There is a property interest.** **The "stop building the dam" part of the injunction is a negative injunction and easily enforceable** through the court's contempt power. **The "remove the dam" part of the injunction is affirmative and requires more court supervision,** but probably is feasible to enforce because it is in the court's jurisdiction, no special skills are required, nor is a prolonged time period necessary to achieve the result. **Neighbors: If the injunction is denied, the neighbors lose access to water for their crops and wells, which is a great harm.** **Diane:** If the injunction is granted, Diane is restricted in the use of her own property and can't build the dam for the disadvantaged kids and she loses the money expended. **[Note: It was necessary to make some argument for Diane.]**	The court's denial of the injunction was improper

Continued >

Issue	Rule	Fact Application	Conclusion
		Public: The public has an interest since there is a community benefit from Diane's free camp for disadvantaged kids, but the crops will also help the public since presumably they are a food source for the general public. The interest of the public favors neither side. **On balance, there is a larger hardship to the plaintiffs who would have to go without water.** Further, Diane may be able to provide water sports in another manner, such as a pool, and water sports are not essential like drinking water is. Balancing favors granting the injunction. **The neighbors waited 6 months until the dam was almost complete before filing suit,** which **wasted the defendant's time and money** spent building the dam during this time period. However, the neighbors did immediately ask Diane to stop, putting her on notice. Also, they likely didn't know the extent of the negative effect until the dam was partially constructed. Further, 6 months is not too long of delay, so laches will not provide a defense.	The court's denial of the injunction was improper [Note: Could conclude either way for the defense of laches here.]
Call #2			
Res judicata	**Claim preclusion** **Valid final judgment on the merits** Federal: final when rendered Cal.: final at conclusion of appeals Prior claim was actually litigated (or could have been).	**Judgment was rendered by state court in the prior action** after a hearing "on the merits" and the court denied the neighbors' application for an injunction against Diane. The plaintiffs did not appeal and **it is a final judgment.** The claim for a permanent injunction was based on the nuisance claim and taking grounds, and the claim was denied after a hearing "on the merits," thus these issues were actually litigated and this element is satisfied.	**The court was correct to dismiss Paul's application since res judicata precludes Paul's claim**

Continued >

Issue	Rule	Fact Application	Conclusion
	Same plaintiff/same defendant **Same claim in prior and subsequent case**	**Paul was one of the plaintiffs in the prior state court case and both suits are brought against the same defendant, Diane,** so this element is satisfied. **Paul is asserting the same nuisance and taking claims in the 2nd case that he asserted in the 1st case,** and is requesting the same relief, **so the 2nd case involves the same claim as the 1st. The primary rights theory, which is allowed in Cal., allows for a different cause of action for each primary right invaded, but since both cases involve the same rights, the primary rights theory is inapplicable.**	
Call #3			
Duty of confidentiality	**General rule (ABA & Cal.): Lawyer can't reveal confidential client information** without client consent. **ABA exception:** Permissive, but not required. **Permits to extent reasonably believes necessary to prevent reasonably certain death or serious bodily injury.** **Cal. Rule exception:** Permissive but not required. Permits to prevent criminal act likely to lead to death or serious bodily injury **and requires an attempt to dissuade and inform client of planned disclosure.**	Paul has not given Lawyer consent to reveal any information here. **ABA exception:** Paul has threatened to **"take care of Diane in my own way and that dam, too," which is vague about the type of harm Paul intends to inflict on Diane, and thus it may not have been reasonable for Lawyer to believe death or serious bodily injury was imminent. Paul also made the statement at the time when he was upset from losing so it may have been an idle threat.** But, **Paul was "infuriated" with the ruling** and was unable to calm down even after **Lawyer attempted to dissuade Paul.** In addition, Lawyer seemed to believe harm was imminent since she told the dispatcher that Paul was "on his way" to hurt Diane. It was probably reasonable that Lawyer believed Paul could kill or cause serious bodily harm to Diane and thus the disclosure was permissive. [Note: Could conclude either way here.] **Cal. exception: Lawyer did attempt to dissuade Paul and talk him out of confronting Diane and informed Paul she would report his threatening comments to the criminal authorities,** so Lawyer was likely permitted to disclose the confidential information and is not subject to discipline.	Could conclude either way

Crossover Question 2 Sample Answer

July 2009, Question 5

1. State Court's Denial of Diane's Neighbors' Claim for Permanent Injunction

Permanent Injunction

A permanent injunction occurs when a court orders one to perform an act or stop performing an act. The following requirements must be met for the court to order a permanent injunction: (1) The remedy at law must be inadequate, (2) there must be a property interest to protect, (3) the hardships must balance in favor of the party seeking the injunction, (4) the decree must be feasible for the court to enforce, and (5) there must be no viable defenses.

Inadequate Legal Remedy

The remedy at law, which is typically money damages, must be inadequate to obtain the remedy of a permanent injunction. Money damages can be inadequate because of concerns over a multiplicity of suits, or damages may be too speculative and difficult to calculate with certainty. Where real property is involved money damages are often inadequate because land is unique. Diane has dammed a stream and her downstream neighbors will suffer losses to their land and crops because of a resulting lack of water. These losses are difficult to calculate with certainty since crop yields fluctuate. Further, the downstream neighbors' loss of their source of water for their wells can't be adequately compensated with money since water is required to maintain life, and no amount of money will suffice for the lack of water since the availability of a dependable alternative source of water is unclear. Lastly, the harm to the neighbors is ongoing and a multiplicity of suits will follow if this is not resolved by an injunction. Diane may argue that the crop loss can be compensated with money, as can the cost of an alternative source of water or the resulting diminished land value. However, since water is a necessity of life and this damage is ongoing until the dam is removed, money damages are an inadequate remedy.

Property Right

California does not require a plaintiff to have a property right to obtain an injunction. While at one time a property interest was required to obtain an injunction, modernly, they can be obtained for invasions of personal rights as well. The downstream neighbors have a property interest here since the stream that has been damned by Diane runs through their lands and they had used the water prior to Diane's construction of the dam.

Feasibility

Feasibility of enforcement requires that the injunction sought cannot be too difficult for the court to enforce. Ordering Diane to stop construction on the dam is a negative injunction and is easily enforceable by the court through the court's power of contempt. The neighbors have also asked the court to order Diane to remove the dam, which is an affirmative injunction since it requires Diane to take an action and thus necessitates more court supervision. Though this part of the injunction would require some supervision by the court, it is still feasible to enforce since the land is within the court's jurisdiction, no special skills are required, nor is a prolonged time period necessary to achieve the result. Further, it could easily be verified if Diane complied with the order.

Balancing of Hardships

The court will balance the hardships to determine if the hardships weigh in favor of the plaintiff and injunctive relief is appropriate. The court will weigh the hardship to plaintiff if the injunction is denied against the hardship to defendant if the injunction is granted. Any hardship to the public and/or any public benefit can also be factored into the analysis. If the injunction is denied, it poses a great hardship on the neighbors because they will be deprived on the stream water they use to irrigate their crops and fill their wells, and this could potentially negatively impact the larger community if the public relies on these crops as a food source. If the injunction is granted, Diane will suffer the hardship of being deprived the ability to use her own property as she wishes and the public will be deprived of a free camp with water sports for disadvantaged children. Further, Diane may be able to provide water sports in another manner, such as a pool, and water sports are not essential like drinking water is. The public interest favors neither party. Since water is essential to maintaining life and providing water sports for disadvantaged children is merely a fun recreational pursuit, the hardships balance in favor of the neighbors and the injunction should be granted.

No Defenses

Courts will not order an injunction where there is a valid defense.

Laches

Laches is an equitable defense that applies when the plaintiff has unreasonably delayed resulting in prejudice to the defendant. The neighbors waited six months before filing suit, which had the prejudicial effect of allowing Diane to expend additional time and money on the dam's construction since by then construction was almost complete. However, the neighbors did promptly ask Diane to stop construction, putting her on notice of a potential problem. Further, since it is unlikely the neighbors could have understood the full negative impact of the dam prior to its full construction, it was not unreasonable to delay and laches will not apply.

Conclusion

The court's denial of the injunction was improper.

2. Federal Court's Denial of Paul's Application for Permanent Injunction

Res Judicata (Claim Preclusion)

Res judicata prevents a subsequent suit on the same cause of action where there has been a valid final judgment on the merits in a suit between the same parties over the same claim.

Valid Final Judgment on the Merits

The neighbors, including Paul, first filed an action in state court asking for a permanent injunction ordering Diane to stop construction and remove the dam. After the hearing, the court denied the application "on the merits" of the case so there was a valid final judgment on the merits. The neighbors chose not to appeal the verdict and the ruling is final and the judgment is valid.

Prior Claim Was Actually Litigated

The neighbors had a full and fair opportunity to litigate their nuisance and taking case against Diane and be heard by the court since a hearing was held, which presumably allowed for a presentation of evidence. The court denied the application "on the merits" after hearing evidence, so the prior claim was actually litigated.

Same Parties

Res judicata only bars a subsequent suit where the subsequent cause of action is brought by the same plaintiff and against the same defendant. Paul and the other neighbors were the plaintiffs in the first suit and Diane was the defendant. In the subsequent suit over the same claim Paul was a plaintiff and Diane was the defendant, therefore the subsequent case involves the same parties and this requirement is satisfied.

Same Claim

The subsequent cause of action must involve the same claim for res judicata to preclude the subsequent suit. However, in California, the "primary rights" doctrine allows separate suits relating to the same transaction so long as they assert different primary rights (i.e., personal injury vs. property damage). In the first suit the plaintiffs asserted a cause of action for nuisance and a taking under the U.S. Constitution. Paul's subsequent suit asserted the exact same causes of action of nuisance and taking and requested the same relief as the first suit, so the primary rights doctrine is inapplicable. Consequently, since the suits involve the same claim, this requirement is satisfied.

Conclusion

The court's denial of Paul's application for a permanent injunction was correct.

3. Lawyer's Ethical Violations

Duty of Confidentiality

The general rule under the ABA prohibits a lawyer from revealing information relating to the representation of a client without the client's informed consent. Similarly, California law requires a lawyer to maintain inviolate client confidences. However, this rule is subject to an exception that applies in this situation. Paul's lawyer disclosed Paul's confidences when she called 911 anonymously warning, "someone is on his way to hurt Diane." Even though Lawyer did not identify herself or Paul, she is in violation of the general rule since she disclosed Paul's confidential communications by relating that "someone is on his way to hurt Diane" to the 911 dispatcher, unless an exception applies.

ABA Duty of Confidentiality Exception

A lawyer is permitted, but is not required, to reveal confidential information relating to the representation of a client to the extent the lawyer reasonably believes necessary to prevent reasonably certain death or substantial bodily harm. The question here is if Lawyer reasonably believed the disclosure of Paul's confidential statements were necessary to prevent Diane's certain death or substantial bodily harm. Lawyer may not have been reasonable in believing confidential disclosure was necessary to prevent death or substantial bodily injury to Diane since Paul's threat to "take care of Diane in my own way and that dam, too" was not vague and not specific about the harm he would inflict on Diane. Further, Paul was upset from losing his case at the time and may have just been making idle threats in anger. However, Paul was "infuriated" at the time he made the threat and did not calm down even after Lawyer attempted to dissuade him and talk him out of his threatened retaliation. In addition, Lawyer seemed to believe harm was imminent since she told the dispatcher that Paul was "on his way" to hurt Diane. On balance, it was probably reasonable for Lawyer to fear Paul would cause death or substantial bodily injury to Diane. Thus, the disclosure of confidential information is permissible and Lawyer will not be subject to discipline.

California Duty of Confidentiality Exception

As analyzed above, a lawyer may, but is not required, to reveal confidential information to the extent the lawyer believes reasonably necessary to prevent a criminal act that the lawyer reasonably believes is likely to result in death of, or substantial bodily harm to, an individual. The California exception also requires that before revealing confidential information, the lawyer shall, if reasonable, make a good faith effort to persuade the client not to commit the criminal act, and inform the client of the lawyer's decision to reveal the confidences. Though she was unsuccessful in her efforts, Lawyer did attempt to dissuade Paul from his plan to "take care of" Diane and informed Paul that she would report his threats to the criminal authorities before doing so. Consequently, Lawyer is not subject to discipline for her disclosure.

Crossover Question 3

February 2006, Question 3

Mike had a 30-year master lease on a downtown office building and had sublet to others the individual office suites for five-year terms. At the conclusion of the 30-year term, Olive, the building's owner, did not renew Mike's master lease.

When Olive resumed control of the building, she learned that Mike had failed to comply with the terms in the 30-year lease that required him to renew an easement for weekday parking on a lot between the building and a theatre. The theatre, which, in the past, had always renewed the easement, used the lot for its own customers on evenings and weekends.

Olive also learned that a week before the end of the 30-year lease Mike had renewed for another five years the sublease of one tenant, Toby, at a rate much below market. Toby ran an art gallery, which Mike thought was "classy." Upon signing the renewal, Toby purchased and installed expensive custom lighting and wall treatments to enhance the showing of the art in his gallery.

Because of Mike's failure to renew the parking easement, the theatre granted it to another landowner. As a result, Olive had to request a variance from the town ordinance requiring off-street parking. The Board of Zoning Appeals (BZA) denied the request because a nearby parking lot operator objected. The off-street parking requirement, combined with the loss of the parking easement, meant that several offices in Olive's building would have to be left vacant. The BZA had recently granted a parking variance for a nearby building under very similar circumstances.

Olive commences the following actions:

1. A suit against Mike to recover damages for waste resulting from Mike's failing to renew the parking lot easement.
2. An action for ejectment against Toby and to require him to leave the lighting and wall treatments when he vacates the premises.
3. An appeal of BZA's denial of Olive's variance request.

What is the likelihood that Olive will prevail in each action? Discuss.

Crossover Question 3 Assessment

February 2006, Question 3

This crossover question covers the substantive laws of real property and constitutional law. Real property is the subject of a crossover question a fair amount of the time, but it does not naturally cross over with any particular subject.

The substance of the real property issues involve a commercial lease, which raises some standard landlord-tenant issues, including the doctrine of waste, subleasing, and fixtures. The facts are sufficiently open ended that there is wide latitude in the factual analysis that is acceptable to sufficiently answer this question and receive a passing score.

The constitutional law portion of the question is covered in call three and concerns a zoning regulation, which is a topic that had never before been tested. A zoning regulation is an unusual topic for testing since there wasn't much to say about it or to analyze. It appears that the students who took this exam had a wide variety of approaches to call three, and the bar examiners found this acceptable. There should be analysis of the Taking Clause and an application of the rational basis test, though the rational basis test could be analyzed under Equal Protection, Procedural Due Process, or Substantive Due Process. It is fairly common that when the bar examiners ask a more unusual question, examinees respond by approaching the question in a wide variety of ways. When that happens, the bar examiners seem to be fairly lenient in what is acceptable to pass the question. This is why you should never panic in the exam. When you aren't sure how to answer a question, it's a good bet that all of the other students feel the same way. Answers will vary substantially, and the bar for passing the question will likely be set lower than for a typical question that covers commonly tested principles.

Note the areas highlighted in **bold** on the corresponding grid. The bold areas highlight the issues, analysis, and conclusions that are likely **required** to receive a passing score on this question.

Issue	Rule	Fact Application	Conclusion
Call #1			
Waste	**A tenant must prevent waste, which is harm to the land.** Voluntary **waste occurs when a tenant causes a decrease in premises value.**	**Olive's action is unusual in that it involves financial damage to the leased property rather than physical damage.** Mike's unreasonable failure to renew the parking lot easement with the adjacent theatre has resulted in **diminution in value of Olive's property because several of the office suites must be left vacant since there is now insufficient parking** causing a loss of rental income. **Mike would argue that waste actions typically involve damage to the property itself.** There was no guarantee that the easement would have been renewed by the theatre, and so his failure to renew did not harm the property. However, Olive would respond that the theatre had "always renewed the easement" in the past, and granted the easement to another "because of Mike's failure to renew the easement." Though an action on the doctrine of waste is unusual, Olive would likely prevail because of the diminution in value caused by Mike's failure to renew the easement. In the alternative, **Olive could bring an action for breach of contract under the lease since the easement renewal requirement was a term of the lease.** [Note: Could conclude either way here, but it was essential to analyze the doctrine of waste and argue both sides.]	Could conclude either way

Continued >

Issue	Rule	Fact Application	Conclusion
Call #2			
Sublease	Generally leases are transferable unless the parties agree otherwise. A **sublease is the transfer of anything less than the entire interest** remaining on the lease term.	Mike had a 30-year, term of years lease on Olive's office building, and since leases are freely alienable, Mike was within his rights to sublease office suites to Toby and the other tenants. However, **Mike granted Toby's current lease 1 week before his own 30-year lease on the building ended. Mike cannot transfer an interest greater (or longer) than the interest held, so Mike's final 5-year sublease granted to Toby is invalid. Olive is entitled to possession of the property** at the termination of Mike's 30-year lease period.	**The sublease was invalid**
Ejectment	Ejectment is an action by a property owner **to remove a person in wrongful possession** from the property.	In Cal., ejectment is typically done through an unlawful detainer action. **The lease Mike granted Toby is invalid because it exceeded the time of Mike's own interest in the land.** Olive will prevail in an action to eject Toby from the premises since Toby is in wrongful possession.	**Ejectment is proper**
Fixtures	**Fixtures are items that have become so attached to the premises they are deemed part of the real estate.**	Toby has installed expensive custom lighting and wall treatments to enhance the showing of art in his gallery. The lighting is likely firmly imbedded and/or peculiarly adapted to the space as it was customized. Whether the lighting and wall treatments can be removed without significantly damaging the property depends on how they are affixed and what type of wall treatment was installed. If they can be easily removed without causing significant damage, Toby will not be required to leave the lighting and wall treatments as Olive demanded; if not, he will. **[Note: Some analysis of the fixtures was required, but the factual analysis could vary.]**	Could conclude either way

Continued >

Issue	Rule	Fact Application	Conclusion
Trade fixtures	Trade fixtures are those affixed to the real estate by a commercial tenant for use in business and are presumed removable.	So long as Toby can remove the lighting and wall treatments without damaging the property, he will be permitted to remove the trade fixtures.	Could conclude either way
Call #3			
Zoning	**Zoning regulations are permitted under the general police power** to reasonably control the use of property **so long as they are constitutional.**	The BZA has denied Olive's request for a variance to the town's off-street parking requirement. This action will stand as long as it comports with constitutional requirements.	**Zoning regulation is permissible**
Equal Protection	Prohibits similarly situated persons from being treated differently. If nonsuspect class, do rational basis test: rationally related to legitimate govt. interest.	Olive was treated differently than a similarly situated person because her request for a variance was denied, while it was granted for another nearby building under similar circumstances. However, a parking rule variance is not subject to heightened scrutiny since it is an economic interest and does not involve a fundamental right or suspect class. To prevail under the rational basis test, **Olive has the burden of showing BZA's denial of the variance was not rationally related to any legitimate govt. interest.** Since limiting the amount of on-street parking is rationally related to the legitimate govt. interests of limiting property crime and enhancing public safety, it is unlikely Olive will prevail. **The zoning ordinance passes the rational basis test.** **[Note: The rational basis test could have been raised several ways, however it was important to analyze the rational basis test in some way pursuant to the facts.]**	No Equal Protection violation

Continued >

Issue	Rule	Fact Application	Conclusion
Procedural Due Process	Cannot deprive of life, liberty, or property without due process—typically notice and hearing	Olive may try to argue that she has a property interest in the parking variance; however, there is nothing to suggest she was entitled to such a permit or that proper procedures were not followed if she did have a valid property interest in the variance. Olive will not prevail.	No Procedural Due Process error
Taking Clause	**Private property may not be taken for public use without just compensation.**	**Olive never had a right or property interest in the parking variance, and further, she has not been denied all economic use of her land** since only several of the many offices in the building were left vacant. Olive will not prevail.	**This is not a taking**

Crossover Question 3 Sample Answer

February 2006, Question 3

1. Olive v. Mike

Waste

Waste occurs when a tenant fails to take reasonable steps to protect the premises from damage. A tenant has a duty not to commit waste. Waste can be committed by affirmative conduct or by inaction on the part of the tenant that leads to damage of the property. Typically, waste involves physical damage to the property; however, Olive's action is unusual in that it involves financial damage to the property rather than physical damage. The easement with the theatre was an appurtenant easement that benefited the office building, and its loss led to a diminution in the property's value, which could be considered "waste." As the leaseholder, Mike's unreasonable failure to renew the parking lot easement with the adjacent theatre has resulted in financial damage to Olive's property because several of the office suites must be left vacant since there is now insufficient parking, causing a loss of rental income. The court could find this diminution in the land's value is damage that constitutes waste under the doctrine.

Mike would argue there was no guarantee the easement would have been renewed by the theatre, and thus his failure to renew did not certainly lead to a diminution in value of the property. However, Olive would respond that the theatre had "always renewed the easement" in the past, and granted the easement to another "because of Mike's failure to renew the easement." Though an action on the doctrine of waste is unusual, Olive would likely prevail because of the financial damage caused by Mike's failure to renew the easement. In the alternative, Olive could bring an action for breach of contract under the lease since the easement renewal requirement was a term of the lease.

2. Olive v. Toby

Sublease

A sublease is a transfer of anything less than a tenant's entire interest remaining in a lease to another. A tenant may never transfer an interest greater than the interest held. Mike had a 30-year, term of years lease on Olive's office building and since leases are freely alienable Mike was within his rights to sublease office suites to Toby and the other tenants. However, Mike granted Toby's current lease one week before his own 30-year lease on the building ended. Since Mike cannot transfer an interest greater (or longer) than the interest held, Mike's final five-year sublease granted to Toby is invalid. Olive is entitled to possession of the property at the termination of Mike's 30-year lease period.

Ejectment

Ejectment is an action by a property owner to remove a person in wrongful possession from the property. In California this is typically done through an unlawful detainer action. Since the lease Mike granted Toby is invalid because it exceeded the time of Mike's own interest in the land, Olive will prevail in an action to eject Toby from the premises.

Fixtures

Fixtures are items so attached to the land they are deemed part of the real estate, and they may not be removed by a tenant at the end of a lease. An item is likely a fixture if it is firmly imbedded in the real estate, is peculiarly adapted to the real estate, or if the item's removal would significantly damage the real estate. Toby has installed expensive custom lighting and wall treatments to enhance the showing of art in his gallery. The lighting is likely firmly imbedded and/or peculiarly adapted to the space as it was customized. Whether the lighting and wall treatments can be removed without significantly damaging the property depends on how they are affixed and what type of wall treatment was installed. If they can be easily removed without causing significant damage, Toby will not be required to leave the lighting and wall treatments as Olive demanded.

Trade Fixtures

Trade fixtures are items attached to the real estate by a commercial tenant that are used in a trade or business and are presumed to be removable by the tenant, though the tenant is required to restore the premises to their original condition. Since Toby is operating an art gallery, which is a commercial enterprise, and the lighting and wall treatments were installed to enhance the showing of art, they are likely trade fixtures. As such, Toby will be permitted to remove them so long as he restores the premises to their original condition.

3. Olive v. BZA

Zoning

Zoning regulations imposed by the government are permitted under the general police power to reasonably control the use of a property so long as they are in compliance with constitutional requirements. The BZA has denied Olive's request for a variance to the town's off-street parking requirement. This action will stand as long as it comports with constitutional requirements.

Equal Protection Clause

The Equal Protection Clause requires that the government treat similarly situated people similarly and protects against discrimination. However, unless the discrimination involves a suspect class or fundamental right, the government action must only meet the easy-to-satisfy rational basis test and will stand unless it is an arbitrary and capricious action. Olive was treated differently than a similarly situated person because her request for a variance was denied, while it was granted for another nearby building under similar circumstances. However, a parking rule variance is not subject to heightened scrutiny since it is an economic interest and does not involve a fundamental right or suspect class. To prevail under the rational basis test, Olive would have to show that the BZA's denial of the variance was not rationally related to any legitimate government interest. Since limiting the amount of on-street parking is rationally related to the legitimate government interests of limiting property crime and enhancing public safety, it is unlikely Olive will prevail.

Procedural Due Process

Procedural Due Process requires that the government act with fair procedures when it deprives a person of life, liberty, or property. Olive may try to argue that she has a property interest in the parking variance; however, there is nothing to suggest she was entitled to such a permit or that proper procedures were not followed if she did have a valid property interest in the variance. Olive will not prevail in her appeal on this theory.

Taking

The taking of private property by the government without just compensation is unconstitutional. A government regulation that deprives a property owner of all economically viable use of their land constitutes a taking. Olive never had a right to the parking variance, and further, she has not been denied all economic use of her land since only several of the many offices in the building were left vacant. Olive will not prevail in her appeal under a takings theory.

Crossover Question 4

February 1991, Question 3

For seven years, Refin has been operating a smelter within Zone A of City. A major portion of Refin's operations is the crushing of ores, which produces considerable noise and dust. City's zoning ordinance permits a smelter to operate in Zone A. Last year, several residential subdivisions, the nearest a mile from the smelter but all inside Zone A, were developed and occupied.

Residents of the new subdivisions are concerned because Refin trucks haul granular toxic chemicals in covered drums from a supply depot to the smelter on a regular basis. The only reasonable route to the smelter from the depot is over a street that borders the residential subdivisions. Recently, a cover on one of the drums was blown off by a strong wind; chemicals were scattered and, while causing no personal injuries, badly burned the lawns of four homeowners.

Refin's procedures for disposing of chemical residue also concern the residents. Employees bury the residue in containers, which, because of internal chemical action, will decompose after 10 to 15 years. Chemically active materials could then invade a nearby lake, the source of the subdivisions' main water supply. The residue containers used by Refin are the most durable that are available for sealing the chemical residue.

Residents have urged City to bring suit against Refin, but City has not yet acted. However, Howard, one of those who urged action by City and whose lawn was badly damaged by the chemicals blown by the wind, has sued Refin seeking damages and equitable relief

What are Howard's rights and remedies, if any? Discuss.

Crossover Question 4 Assessment

February 1991, Question 3

This is a very typical torts and remedies crossover question. Remedies is a subject that is almost always a crossover. Remedies is most frequently crossed over with contracts, but it is also crossed over with many of the other subjects, including torts, as is the case in this question. Nuisance in torts, and the remedies associated with nuisance, is a logical intersection of torts and remedies and is predictable as a crossover question.

Both the cause of action for nuisance and the injunction require a balancing of harms analysis. It is perfectly acceptable to do a thorough analysis the first time and then refer to that analysis briefly the next time it arises, as it does here in the analysis for public nuisance, private nuisance, and injunction.

The following grid is organized with the various types of harm associated with the nuisance separated out into separate sections. It is not necessary to separate them out, but it often leads you to create a more thorough answer when the subtopics or subfacts are separated out since the analysis pertinent to each type of harm is slightly different and thus the analysis is different. When you separate the facts out by the type of harm they cause, it is easier to identify the more nuanced analysis associated with each type of harm.

This is an interesting question because there are a lot of detailed facts to use in the analysis. The balancing of the harms analysis requires an assessment of the utility of the defendant's conduct. There aren't any facts given in the fact pattern to work with, but a logical factual inference is that Refin is engaged in a lawful business activity that produces a useful product. Also, whenever balancing the benefit to society of a business, it is a good idea to note their value to the community as an employer since the loss of jobs would always have a negative impact on the community.

Note the areas highlighted in **bold** on the corresponding grid. The bold areas highlight the issues, analysis, and conclusions that are likely **required** to receive a passing score on this question.

Issue	Rule	Fact Application	Conclusion
Public nuisance	**A substantial, unreasonable interference with the health, morals, welfare, safety, or property rights of the community.** **Recovery by a private party is only available if he suffered damage that is different in kind and not merely in degree from that suffered by the public.** **To determine if an activity is a nuisance, courts consider factors of harm to the community,** including the location of the nuisance, the frequency and duration, the degree of damage, **and the social value of the activity.**	Here, the city is not acting and **there is noise, dust, toxic chemicals, property damage, and chemical dumping as a result of Refin's smelter operation.** To prevail for a public nuisance, **Howard must prove he has suffered unique damage, different than the public at large, which he can establish here since his lawn is badly damaged.** Noise and dust: This is probably not a substantial interference with the community's use of the land. Since the subdivisions are 1 mile away, it is unlikely the citizens can hear the noise, or that the dust would interfere with their use and enjoyment of their land by the community. **Toxic chemicals: The chemicals have already caused property damage to four lawns, and chemicals left free to blow in the wind could have a serious negative impact on the health and safety of the community.** This is so even though Refin attempts to use due care by using the most durable containers available, and the cover still blew off in a strong wind, **so this is a likely public nuisance.** **Chemical waste disposal:** Burying toxic waste in containers that will certainly decompose in 10-15 years, **which in turn will likely pollute the nearby lake, which a source of drinking water for the community, is potentially a substantial health interference.** The harm to the community will not be realized until the water pollution actually occurs, but the future threat to the water supply has the potential to be a catastrophic problem that could cause cancer. When considered with the current harm already established, it is also likely a public nuisance.	**Public nuisance**

Continued >

Issue	Rule	Fact Application	Conclusion
		While Refin's smelter operation likely benefits the community by providing local jobs and a socially useful product (crushed ore), there is a serious negative effect on the health and welfare of the community, in particular by the chemicals released into the air and threat to the water supply, which outweighs the benefits of smelting. Alternative measures, such as an alternative route for transporting the toxic chemicals, should be employed.	
Private nuisance	**A substantial, unreasonable interference with another private individual's use or enjoyment of his land.**	**Howard can make the same arguments as were made above in the public nuisance section. Here, he need only establish his own injury and balance that against the utility of the smelting operation. Howard should prevail.**	**Private nuisance**
Coming to the nuisance	Coming to the nuisance is a bar only if plaintiff came to the nuisance for the sole purpose of bringing a harassing lawsuit.	**Refin's smelter operation has been in business for 7 years and the subdivision was developed last year, so the owners in the subdivision knew about the smelter operations** before they purchased their homes. However, modernly, coming to the nuisance is not an effective defense.	**Modernly, not an effective defense**
Legislative authority (zoning)	**Legislative authority (zoning) compliance is persuasive but not an absolute defense.**	**The smelter operations are permitted under the local zoning ordinance. Compliance with zoning ordinances establishes the reasonableness of the defendant's conduct. However, it is not conclusive,** and here substantial harm has been established so the zoning ordinance will not provide a defense.	**Zoning is not an effective defense**

Continued >

Issue	Rule	Fact Application	Conclusion
Trespass to land	Intentional entry of another's land without permission.	Refin's chemicals blew through the wind and entered Howard's land, causing damage to his lawn. While Refin may not have intended this to happen, they had their trucks drive close to the subdivision, and it is likely Howard can establish that Refin was substantially certain such an event would occur. If so, Howard can establish trespass to land.	Trespass to land
Remedies			
Damages	Compensatory damages are awarded to compensate the plaintiff for injury or loss. Damages must be caused by the tortious act, foreseeable, capable of being calculated with certainty, and unavoidable.	**Nuisance: Howard can recover for the damages for the loss of the use and enjoyment of his land caused by the nuisance of the noise and dust and the damage to his lawn, any annoyance caused by the nuisance, and any costs spent in abating the nuisance. If the nuisance persists, he may be entitled to damages for diminished land value.** Trespass: Since trespass is an intentional tort, punitive damages are also available. However, since there is no evidence Refin acted willfully so punitive damages are unlikely.	**Damages are recoverable**

Continued >

Issue	Rule	Fact Application	Conclusion
Injunction	**An injunction is an equitable remedy** **Inadequate legal remedy (unique or irreparable injury/multiplicity of suits)** **Property right** **Feasible to enforce** **Balancing of hardships (balance the hardship to P if denied to hardship to D if granted)** **No defenses**	**Here, the legal remedy is inadequate because there is a continuing nuisance to the land** and residents continue to be subject to exposure to toxic chemicals and/or a polluted water supply. **Land is unique** and, as such, money damages are typically inadequate to compensate for loss. **Further there is a danger of multiple suits from homeowners for the same reason in the future.** **Howard has a property interest in his real property.** **The court can order a negative injunction forcing Refin to cease operations. Negative injunctions are comparatively easy to enforce** through the court's contempt power. **The balancing of hardships analysis is similar to the argument above in the balancing of interest in the public nuisance section, and the hardships balance in Howard's favor.** **There are no applicable defenses that will be effective.**	**An injunction should be ordered**

Crossover Question 5

February 2008, Question 6

Albert, an attorney, and Barry, a librarian, decided to incorporate a business to provide legal services for lawyers. Barry planned to perform legal research and draft legal memoranda. Albert intended to utilize Barry's work after reviewing it to make court appearances and argue motions on behalf of other attorneys. Albert and Barry employed Carla, an attorney, to prepare and file all of the documentation necessary to incorporate the business, Lawco, Inc. ("Lawco").

Carla properly drafted all required documentation to incorporate Lawco under the state's general corporation law. The documentation provided that: Lawco shares are divided equally between Albert and Barry; Lawco profits will be distributed equally to Albert and Barry as annual corporate dividends; Barry is president and Albert is secretary.

Albert and Barry opened their business in January, believing that Lawco was properly incorporated. In February, they purchased computer equipment in Lawco's name from ComputerWorks. The computer equipment was delivered to Lawco's office and used by Barry.

Carla, however, neglected to file the articles of incorporation until late April.

In May, Albert, without consulting anyone, contracted in Lawco's name to purchase office furniture for Lawco from Furniture Mart. On the same day, also without consulting anyone, Barry contracted in Lawco's name to purchase telephones for Lawco from Telco.

1. Is Lawco bound by the contracts with:
   a. ComputerWorks? Discuss.
   b. Furniture Mart? Discuss.
   c. Telco? Discuss.
2. Has Albert committed any ethical violation? Discuss.

Answer question number 2 according to California and ABA authorities.

Crossover Question 5 Assessment

February 2008, Question 6

Business associations is a subject that is frequently crossed over with professional responsibility. This makes sense because it is very easy to draft a question that takes place in a business setting and where one of the corporate actors is a lawyer or discloses information to his lawyer.

The first call of the question asks about the validity of three separate contracts made on behalf of Lawco and if Lawco will be bound to those contracts, but the essay does not concern contract law at all. Rather, it involves the ability of various parties to bind a corporation to a contract and thus requires analysis of the rules pertaining to pre-incorporation contracts and agency principles.

The second call of the question addresses some professional responsibility topics, including the less frequently tested rules regarding the unauthorized practice of law and partnering to provide legal services with a nonlawyer, as well as the more commonly tested rule regarding fee-splitting. The facts in the question are rather vague about how much oversight and supervision the lawyer Albert was planning to exercise over the work performed by Barry the librarian. While it may seem that some of the work Barry was going to perform (legal research and drafting legal memoranda) may seem similar to work performed by a paralegal, there are no facts in the question to suggest Barry was trained as a paralegal, or that Albert was planning on adequately supervising Barry's work product. In the absence of such facts, it is best to err on the side of caution and determine that this planned scheme is in violation of Albert's duty not to assist a nonlawyer in the unauthorized practice of law. Professional responsibility is the one area of law where coming to the wrong conclusion can really be problematic, so it is always best to be cautious in a case such as this one where the facts do not clearly make Albert's planned conduct acceptable.

Note the areas highlighted in **bold** on the corresponding grid. The bold areas highlight the issues, analysis, and conclusions that are likely **required** to receive a passing score on this question.

Issue	Rule	Fact Application	Conclusion
Call #1.a: Computer			
De jure corporation	**A de jure corporation meets all mandatory statutory requirements, including that the incorporators sign and file an articles of incorporation.**	Albert and Barry employed Carla to incorporate Lawco and **Carla failed to file the required articles of incorporation until April, which was after the ComputerWorks contract was entered into.** Therefore, Lawco is not a validly formed de jure corporation at the time of contracting.	**Not a de jure corp.**
De facto corporation	**A de facto corporation exists where there is actual use of corporate power and a good faith, but unsuccessful, attempt to incorporate under a valid incorporation statute.**	A corporation's de facto status can be relied on to enforce a contract that would otherwise not be enforceable. **Both Albert and Barry were operating under the mistaken but good faith belief that Lawco was incorporated at the time of contracting with ComputerWorks since Carla had drafted all required documentation. Lawco was a de facto corporation.**	**De facto corp.**
Corporation by estoppel	**A person who** deals with a business entity believing it is a corporation, or **incorrectly holds an entity out as a corporation, may be estopped from denying corporation status.**	**Lawco purchased computer equipment from ComputerWorks using the Lawco name,** thus **holding Lawco out as a corporation.** Consequently, **Lawco will be estopped from denying that it is a corporation when it entered into the contract since it benefited from claiming it was a corporation and received the benefit of the computer equipment provided by the contract.**	**Corporation by estoppel**

Continued >

Issue	Rule	Fact Application	Conclusion
Adoption of contract	A corporation is not generally liable for, or bound to, pre-incorporation contracts, except **a corporation will be liable where the corporation expressly adopts the contract or accepts the benefits of the contract.**	**The computer equipment was the result of a pre-incorporation contract. The equipment was delivered to Lawco and accepted and used by Barry. Thus, since Barry accepted the benefit of the contract by using the computer equipment, Lawco will be found to have adopted the contract and be bound.**	**Adoption of pre-incorp. contract**
Call #1.b: Furniture			
Agency actual authority	**Actual express authority is specifically granted to the agent by the principal. Actual implied authority occurs when the agent reasonably believes the principal gave him authority** because of necessity (task reasonably necessary to accomplish agency goals), custom, or prior dealings.	**Lawco was properly incorporated at the time of the contract with Furniture Mart. Corporations must act through agents by necessity. Albert entered into a contract with Furniture Mart on behalf of Lawco.** Albert did not have express authority to enter into this contract, unless the articles so provided, but he may have implied authority. Albert is the secretary of the corporation and a 50% shareholder, and **it is likely that he had the implied authority to bind the corporation** to routine contracts, such as this one for the purchase of office furniture.	Could conclude either way
Agency apparent authority	**The agent's actions will bind the principal when the principal has provided the agent with the appearance of authority, on which a third party reasonably relies.**	Furniture Mart will argue they reasonably relied on Albert's apparent authority since Albert held the position of Secretary, and was a 50% shareholder in Lawco (assuming Furniture Mart knew this). Lawco will argue that the role of a corporate secretary is to take notes at meetings, not contract for office supplies. Nonetheless, it was likely reasonable for Furniture Mart to believe Albert had the authority to contract on Lawco's behalf.	Could conclude either way

Continued >

Issue	Rule	Fact Application	Conclusion
Call #1.c: Telephones			
Agency actual authority	See above	**Lawco was properly incorporated at the time of the contract with Telco. Here, Barry entered into the contract with Telco and Barry was the president of Lawco. If he does not have express authority, the president of a corporation has implied authority to contract on behalf of the corporation, and certainly for a routine expense like telephones. A corporation can't act except through an agent and the president is the logical person to contract on behalf of the corporation, so it was reasonable for Telco to believe that Barry had the authority to contract. Telco will be able to enforce the contract.**	**Implied authority is present**
Call #2			
Unauthorized practice of law	**A lawyer may not assist a nonlawyer in the unlicensed practice of law.**	**Barry is a librarian, which is a nonlawyer. His duties involved performing legal research and drafting legal memoranda.** Barry's legal research is probably acceptable, but drafting legal memoranda is more likely the practice of law since it requires the **professional judgment of a lawyer.** There is nothing in the facts to indicate that Albert is properly supervising Barry's work, since the facts indicate Barry is merely "reviewing" it before using it to make court appearances and argue motions on behalf of other attorneys. Albert is subject to discipline. **[Note: Although the facts are vague and an argument could be made that this conduct is acceptable with proper supervision, it is best to err on the side of caution with professional responsibility questions.]**	Albert is subject to discipline

Continued >

Issue	Rule	Fact Application	Conclusion
Partnering with nonlawyers	**A lawyer may not partner with a nonlawyer for the provision of legal services.**	**Albert may not incorporate or form a partnership to provide legal services with a nonlawyer**, and Barry is a librarian. Here, **Lawco is set up as a corporation and Albert and Barry are 50-50 shareholders,** and Barry is in the superior position of president, which is especially suspect since it gives Barry a greater role and influence in their corporation, which is **in the business of providing legal services** for lawyers. **Albert has violated his duty not to partner with nonlawyers.**	**Albert is subject to discipline**
Fee splitting with nonlawyers	**A lawyer may not split fees or share profits with a nonlawyer.**	Lawco's articles of incorporation provide that profits are to be split equally between Albert and Barry as annual corporate dividends. **While Albert may argue this is not fee-splitting, this is a form of profit-sharing** since both Albert and Barry receive 50% of profits, which are derived from fees **and, thus, is not allowed. Albert has violated his duty not to fee split with nonlawyers.**	**Albert is subject to discipline**

Crossover Question 6

July 2008, Question 2

To protect the nation against terrorism, the President proposed the enactment of legislation that would authorize the Secretary of Homeland Security ("the Secretary") to issue "National Security Requests," which would require businesses to produce the personal and financial records of their customers to the Federal Bureau of Investigation ("the FBI") without a warrant. Congress rejected the proposal.

Thereafter, in response, the President issued Executive Order 999 ("the Order"). The Order authorizes the Secretary to issue "National Security Requests," which require businesses to produce the personal and financial records of their customers to the FBI without a warrant. The Order further authorizes the Secretary to require state and local law enforcement agencies to assist the FBI in obtaining the records.

Concerned about acts of terrorism that had recently occurred in State X, the State X Legislature passed the "Terrorism Prevention Act" ("the Act"), requiring businesses in State X served with National Security Requests pursuant to the Order to produce a copy of the records to the State X Department of Justice.

1. Is the Order within the President's authority under the United States Constitution? Discuss.
2. Assuming the Order is within the President's authority, does the Order preempt the Act? Discuss.
3. Assuming the Order is within the President's authority and does not preempt the Act, do the Order and the Act violate the Fourth Amendment to the United States Constitution on their face? Discuss.

Crossover Question 6 Assessment

July 2008, Question 2

This crossover question covers constitutional law and criminal procedure, which is a fairly common subject combination. However it is an unusual question because the constitutional law issues tested are issues pertaining to an executive order, including the power of the president to act against the will of Congress, the war power of a president, and the president's duty to ensure that laws are faithfully executed. This is the only time these rules have been tested on the essay portion of the California bar exam. The fact pattern concerns legislation proposed by the president, but rejected by congress, that was designed to protect the nation against terrorism and that included a provision that the Secretary of Homeland Security could issue "National Security Requests," which require businesses to produce certain business records to the FBI without a warrant. Since Congress rejected the president's proposed legislation, the president issued the same proposed legislation as an executive order. A state then passed an act that was potentially preempted by the executive order. The final call of the question asks if any of this will pass constitutional muster under the Fourth Amendment.

The first call tends to give students the most trouble since it covers issues that had never before been tested on the essay portion of the bar exam. As you will notice by reviewing the following grid, students approach the first call in a variety of ways that are acceptable. The common analysis that the bar graders are looking for in a passing answer is bolded in the grid, and you can see that the rules and analysis that are necessary to pass the first call are not particularly difficult. The second and third calls are much more straightforward and should not be difficult, assuming a student wisely budgets his time and doesn't spend an inordinate amount of time on the first call.

Note the areas highlighted in **bold** on the corresponding grid. The bold areas highlight the issues, analysis, and conclusions that are likely **required** to receive a passing score on this question.

Issue	Rule	Fact Application	Conclusion
Call #1: President's Authority			
Presidential action against the will of Congress	If the president acts contrary to Congress, he must do so within his constitutional powers alone.	Here, the president acted contrary to Congress because he issued the executive order after Congress rejected the very same proposal, indicating that the president must have his own executive constitutional power to enact the executive order. Any possible powers that would allow him to do so will be discussed below. **[Note: Both state-released passing answers discussed this issue differently. The key is that both pointed out that the president acted contrary to Congress.]**	**President acted contrary to Congress**
Vesting Clause	Executive power invested in president	See above	See above
Foreign affairs	President has power over many foreign affairs.	Although terrorism can involve foreign affairs, the order here has to do more with domestic information, not foreign information. Even if foreign information is sought, too, it is not of the type pertaining to foreign policies that the president is typically involved with, such as signing treaties and dealing with foreign presidents and other heads of foreign countries.	Likely no presidential power here
War powers/ War Powers Resolution	**The president is the commander in chief.** The president has the constitutional power not only to retaliate against any person, organization, or state suspected of involvement in terrorist attacks on the United States, but also against foreign states suspected of harboring or supporting such organizations.	**Here, the president has the power to act as commander in chief,** which generally comes into play when there is a war ensuing, not in regard to turning over customer, personal, and financial records from businesses. **However, arguably, if there is a war on terror and the information sought would help stop this war on terror, it is possible that it is within the president's power to request such information, but this typically involves military use and deployment of troops, not customer records**; nor is clear as to how this information will help the president combat terrorism.	**Likely no presidential power here**

Continued >

Issue	Rule	Fact Application	Conclusion
Take care/ execute laws clause	**The president is to make sure the laws are faithfully executed.**	Here, the president's best argument to enforce his order is under the power to make sure the laws are faithfully executed. The law against committing terrorist acts could arguably be one in which the president is trying to ensure faithful execution of the laws and keep the nation safe.	**Possibly valid presidential power here**
10th Amend. commandeering	**Prevents Congress from commandeering the states; powers not delegated to Congress are reserved to the states.**	**Here, Congress cannot require state and local law enforcement agencies to assist the FBI in obtaining the records because Congress does not have the power to commandeer the states.**	**No presidential authority to make Congress act here**
Call #2: Preemption			
Preemption	**Express or implied; state law is invalid if it conflicts with federal law.**	**Here, the state statute does not directly conflict with the Order as it does not have the state acting contrary to the Order; further, there does not appear to be any interference with the state statute and the Order as they both request the same information,** and the state statute may in fact help to execute and comply with the Order and further help combat terrorism and protect the nation, in particular State X.	**No preemption**
Contracts Clause	Cannot interfere with existing contracts.	The state statute could affect existing contracts of confidentiality but that would not affect preemption.	

Continued >

Issue	Rule	Fact Application	Conclusion
Call #3: 4th Amend.			
Search and seizure	**4th Amend. protects against unreasonable searches and seizures.** **Need govt. action and a reasonable expectation of privacy.** **Warrant needed unless search incident to a lawful arrest, automobile exception, plain view exception, consent, hot pursuit, or stop and frisk.**	**Here, the govt. is acting by issuing the Order and requiring the Secretary of State and states to assist the FBI in obtaining these financial records of customers.** **Arguably, customers do not have a reasonable expectation of privacy when they hand their information, such as bank records, over to businesses or third parties.** However, here, the request appears to go beyond bank records and the like in that all of customers' personal and financial records would be available with no limitations apparent in the Order. **Here, the Order requires production of this financial and customer information without a warrant and no warrant exceptions are applicable here since there is no arrest, automobile, hot pursuit, stop and frisk, or consent involved.**	Conclude either way depending on whether you found expectation of privacy in the information sought